## About the Author

Susie Murphy is an Irish historical fiction author. She loves historical fiction so much that she often wishes she had been born two hundred years ago. Still, she remains grateful for many aspects of the modern age, including women's suffrage, electric showers and pizza.

ISBN-13: 979-8729823901

Copyright © Susie Murphy 2021

All rights reserved. No part of these books may be reproduced or transmitted in any form without the express permission of the author, except for the use of brief quotations in book reviews.

This is a work of fiction. Names, characters, places and events are either the products of the author's imagination or are used fictitiously. Any similarity to actual persons, living or dead, or actual events is entirely coincidental.

www.susiemurphywrites.com

Join the Susie Murphy Readers' Club
for updates and free stories:
**https://bit.ly/susie-murphy-readers-club**

# A Matter of Class

Book One: A Class Apart

Book Two: A Class Entwined

Book Three: A Class Forsaken

Susie Murphy

# Also by Susie Murphy

A Class Coveted
A Class Reunited

# A Class Apart

A Matter of Class, Book One

*For Nana and Granda,
who always asked when I would write my story.*

*And for Aoife,
who showed what it was to have tremendous courage.*

# Chapter 1

Bridget twisted in her seat as the horse-drawn carriage reached the top of the avenue and the familiar edifice of warm red brick came into sight.

'There it is!' she exclaimed, heart soaring with emotion.

In the seat opposite, her mother squared her shoulders and gripped her fan tightly, her knuckles straining the material of her glove.

Bridget pressed her nose to the window, striving to take in as much as she could through the dust-streaked glass. All the servants had congregated in the open space before the manor house, waiting to greet their mistress on her return. As the carriage lumbered to a stop, wheels crunching on gravel, Lady Courcey fixed her gaze upon her daughter.

'You shall maintain absolute decorum, as befits a proper lady,' she said in a low, measured tone.

Bridget deflated in an instant but there was no time to respond because a liveried footman had already opened the door of the carriage, letting in a breath of air which alleviated the stifling heat within. He offered his hand to assist Lady Courcey and the lady stepped out. Then he reached for Bridget's hand and she too emerged blinking into the May sunshine.

Oakleigh Manor rose before her. The immense, elegant building remained unchanged, save for the ivy creeping further across its walls. A sea of servants' faces floated in front of it but impeding this view was the form of her massive-bellied uncle, Lord Walcott, three or four small dogs yapping around his ankles. Just behind him stood the butler, Mr Buttimer, who had been in the family's service for several decades. His back and shoulders were as straight as if he were about to receive instructions from a military commander.

Lord Walcott's voice boomed out in welcome. 'My dearest Constance!' He waddled forwards under the weight of his great bulk and stooped to kiss his sister's proffered hand. 'Your journey was comfortable enough, I trust?'

They had spent the past couple of days travelling more than sixty miles south from Dublin but, despite the heat, had dined well at the inns where they had stayed and had suffered no wheel-related misfortunes.

'It was an excruciating necessity,' said Lady Courcey.

Lord Walcott chuckled and turned to bestow a similar kiss upon Bridget. She curtseyed in response. 'How do you do, Uncle Stuart.'

Mr Buttimer stepped up next. He bowed without disturbing the rigidity of his posture and said, 'Your ladyship, you are most welcome back. The estate has not been the same in your absence.' Still bent over, he cast a hasty glance in Lord Walcott's direction. 'That is to say, it has been well managed, but of course we all prefer to see a Courcey in the family seat. Ahem, I don't mean to imply — it goes without saying that his lordship has been a fine substitute — not my intention to demean —'

'Thank you, Buttimer. My daughter and I would like some refreshment after we have settled back into our chambers.'

'Indeed, a luncheon is already being prepared, my lady.'

The butler seemed on the verge of expanding on this subject but Lady Courcey cut him off with a nod and a beckoning gesture of her fan to Bridget. Her mouth was a thin line as she turned towards the red-bricked manor. While for the most part a very happy place, Oakleigh was also the site of some painful memories and plainly those were the ones she was choosing to remember upon their arrival. Bridget felt the poignancy too but it was not enough to quell her joy in coming home at long, long last.

They headed towards the front entrance of the house, making their way through a gap in the neat rows of maids, footmen, stable hands, gardeners, and even some of the local farmers and cottiers. Lord Walcott, who appeared to have taken no offence to Mr Buttimer's babbling, ambled along in their wake, calling his dogs to heel.

Bridget's gaze roamed to either side, recognising familiar faces from her childhood. She was not far from the front steps when she spotted Cormac in the last row, his fair hair standing out among the rest. His presence took her by surprise – she had not thought of him in so long, but when she had it was never to imagine him as a servant. His eyes, like the others, were cast respectfully downwards but as she passed by he glanced up. Startled, she turned her head at once so as not to be caught looking herself.

Somewhat flustered, she climbed the broad, stone steps to the front door and crossed the threshold, the barking of her uncle's dogs shrill in her ears. The enormous entrance hall was pleasantly cool after the sweltering heat outside. Its dominating feature was a sweeping mahogany staircase which rose in splendour to the next floor. At the foot of the stairs stood Mrs Walsh, the housekeeper, a ring of keys hanging at her waist.

'Your ladyship, Miss Muldowney. I am delighted to welcome you both home.'

Lady Courcey sniffed. 'Ryan should be following shortly with the luggage. Send her up to me as soon as she arrives.'

She made for the staircase and Bridget followed, eager to reach her bedchamber, which she entered with a sigh of nostalgia. She had been a girl of only twelve when she had last set foot here but nothing seemed to have altered. The four-poster bed was still decorated with burgundy-coloured curtains, at its foot lay the same sheepskin rug into which she had loved sinking her bare toes, and her old hairbrush rested on the dressing table as though she had just left it there that morning. It even smelled the same, of wood polish and fresh linen and something comforting which she could only label as 'home'.

On the far wall hung a long, silver-framed mirror. A glance into the glass made her pause. Here was the one thing in the room that had wholly changed: her own reflection. She had grown up since the last time she had looked into this mirror and for a moment she did not recognise herself. Her dark brown eyes stared back, struck by the transformation that seven years had wrought upon her, and she looked away, disconcerted.

She turned to the window, which offered a prospect vastly different to the one she could see from her bedchamber in Dublin. Merrion Square, its street busy with passing carriages, had been a sight she had initially hated, then become accustomed to and in the end rather fond of, but it could never replace the view out of any window of Oakleigh Manor, with its endless expanse of nature on every side.

She looked down upon the space in front of the house, where the workers were dispersing back to their duties. The window was open and their voices drifted up to her. Although the rustic Carlow accent was as disparate from the polished intonations of the aristocracy as it was possible to be, the distinctive brogue charmed her now as much as it ever had.

The stable hands remained to see to the carriage and its horses; Bridget saw Cormac grasp a bridle and rub the horse's neck. A donkey and cart laboured into view at the top of the avenue, the back of the cart loaded with large trunks. Ellen Ryan, Lady Courcey's freckled lady's maid, sat beside the driver. She hopped down from the cart and said something to Mr Buttimer who clicked his fingers at his footmen and the stable hands.

Bridget moved away from the window and rang the bell pull. When a breathless maid scuttled into the room, she said, 'Please bring me some water for washing. I would like to freshen up before going down to luncheon.'

The maid curtseyed and scampered out again. Bridget's gaze landed once more on the sheepskin rug and, overcome by an impish urge, she sat on the bed and hitched up her skirts to take off her ankle boots and stockings. She sighed as her feet escaped their sweaty imprisonment, then stood on the rug and buried her toes in the wool. A feeling of contentment settled over her like a blanket.

Footsteps came tapping smartly down the corridor and through the open door she saw two footmen pass by bearing a trunk bound for her mother's room. Close on their heels was another pair who stopped outside her own chamber.

They weren't footmen but stable hands. She let her skirts fall to cover her exposed feet as Cormac and a lanky boy carried the trunk into her room and set it down by the wardrobe with a muted thud.

They both headed back towards the door but some inexplicable impulse made her say, 'Please wait a moment, Cormac.'

After the barest hesitation, he said to the other lad, 'You go on, Liam. I'll be right behind you.'

Liam shot him a quizzical look but left nonetheless. Cormac turned around to face her. At these close quarters, she could see that he had changed too, physically at least. He was much taller now and the skinny frame of his boyhood had developed into the sturdy body of a young man used to hard work. His skin was tanned and his fair hair was longer than it used to be, falling into his eyes, which she perceived were still that astonishing shade of blue.

'I...' She didn't know what to say next. Why had she even called him back?

He saved her by offering a smile. ''Tis good to have you home.'

'It is good to be home,' she said, smiling in return.

'Might you be back for good?' he asked.

'Mother says it is just for the summer, but I am hopeful we shall stay much longer than that.'

He glanced over his shoulder as the two footmen, who had deposited her mother's trunk, passed by again. 'I'd best be going.'

'Yes, of course. Thank you for...' She gestured towards the trunk.

'No trouble,' he said and disappeared out the door.

The maid returned moments later with a pitcher of water and Bridget set about washing the sticky heat from her skin.

# Chapter 2

One particular aspect of living in the countryside which Bridget had forgotten, and very soon remembered, was just how obsessed one could become with the weather. In Dublin, the weather presented a mild inconvenience; a shower of rain might signify a muddy hem on the way to visiting an acquaintance, or a warm day increased the heat inside a ballroom. In the country, the weather conditions entirely dictated the pattern of daily life.

After the sunny day that marked their homecoming to Oakleigh, there followed two solid weeks of rainy, windy misery. Bridget maintained an optimistic outlook to begin with as it gave her an opportunity to explore the house of her childhood through adult eyes. She chose different books from the shelves in the library, admired the paintings on the walls with greater discernment, and relished playing the grand piano in the drawing room with a far more practised touch. She especially loved going down to the kitchens and chatting with the cook, Mrs Kavanagh, something which she had never felt at liberty to do in the Merrion Square townhouse.

However, the more she gazed out of Oakleigh's windows, the more she longed to be outside, and the more it poured. Mrs Kavanagh said it was the wettest month of May she had ever seen.

'And I've seen my fair share of Mays,' she said, her big bosom shaking as she chuckled.

But now June had arrived and with it came the promise of a real summer. The sun had emerged at last, the clouds were feathery white ribbons in the sky, and the green, lush outdoors called to Bridget.

And her mother insisted upon her performing yet another recital in the drawing room.

After the third movement of a Mozart piano sonata, Bridget could bear it no longer. She played the closing chords with an air of finality and, when her mother and uncle's polite clapping had died away, said, 'Mother, it is a fine day to go for a ride, don't you think?'

Lady Courcey folded her hands in her lap. 'If the weather holds, we shall take the opportunity to ride across the estate tomorrow.'

Lord Walcott let out a rumbling laugh. 'That's a mighty big "if" in this country.'

Bridget wholly agreed. She pressed her fingertips to her forehead. 'Do you mind if I retire to my bedchamber for a little while? I feel a headache growing. Perhaps it's from the heat.'

Her mother gave a brusque nod. Bridget shut the lid of the piano and made her escape.

\*\*\*

Cormac slipped through the green-painted door of Oakleigh Manor's walled apple orchard and followed the winding path among the trees, saw dangling languidly at his side. It was shady beneath the canopy and a bird sang somewhere in the branches above his head, its serene melody adding to the peacefulness of the place.

He kept walking until he reached the clearing at the centre where the apple trees subsided and a solitary oak towered over all else. His purpose in coming hung precariously from the oak tree: a branch about four feet long that was close to breaking off. The new under gardener was supposed to have seen to it but the lad was still finding his feet so Cormac had taken it upon himself to complete the job, given that he had the tools to do it.

He pressed his palm to the ancient tree's weathered bark, recalling the first day he had come upon it. At five years old, his thirst for mischief had known no bounds and he had trespassed on the grounds of the big house with no regard for the consequences. More interesting than even the stables or the hay barns had been his discovery of the orchard with this most excellent tree for climbing. He had been perched in its gnarled branches when the sound of singing drifted near and a girl entered the clearing below him. Unable to resist such a prime target, he had plucked an acorn from the tree and dropped it on her head. Even now, he could recall her yelp of surprise and her high voice reverberating around the clearing in indignation.

'I know there's someone up there, I can see your toes!'

Wiggling them had produced a reluctant laugh on her part. He had swung down and greeted her as affably as though the offending acorn was not present between his bare feet and her dainty shoes, and she had found it within her to forgive him. After establishing names (of which hers made no sense to him at the time: 'I'm a Muldowney but I'll be a Courcey when I grow up if Mama and Papa don't have any sons...') and an understanding that acorns must never be tossed onto people's heads, there ensued an education on the topic of climbing trees. She had been a novice but determined not to show fear and the lesson had ended in laughter, two grazed knees and a rip in the hem of her dress.

When they heard her governess calling, she had turned to run, but not before asking hopefully, 'Will you come back tomorrow?'

'I will,' he had promised.

Fourteen years had passed but that chance meeting remained vivid in his memory. Only for this oak tree, they might never have crossed paths at all.

He turned his attention to the broken branch. As thick as a man's leg and still partly attached to the tree, it drooped in the throes of its demise, a few leafy twigs jutting from it like flailing arms. After scrutinising the height of the branch and its angle to the ground, he decided he was better off tackling it from above and climbed nimbly up into the tree. He braced his back against the trunk, secured his grip on his saw, and attacked the branch. It had been nearly ready to fall; the wood snapped and the branch split from the trunk, settling on the leaf litter beneath the tree with a creaking sigh.

'Oh!' said a female voice.

He swivelled in surprise, teetered on his perch, and slung an arm over the branch above his head to catch his balance. Bridget stood in the clearing staring up at him. The irony of their positions did not escape him and he suppressed an impulse to laugh.

Concern filled her face. 'The tree isn't dying, is it?'

'Not at all,' he said. 'Just a weak branch. Otherwise 'tis the finest.'

Her shoulders slumped with relief. 'That's good.' She glanced about, clasped her hands together in front of her, tucked them behind her back, then left them swinging by her sides. 'I came outside for a walk. I had been playing the piano for my mother and uncle but this weather was too lovely to resist.'

'The piano?' he repeated. 'You always used to hate that thing.'

She flushed. 'I know, but I applied myself to proper study of it when I went to Dublin. It is actually an enjoyable pastime.'

He tilted his head but made no further remark on it. He descended from the tree, taking care not to cut himself on the saw's blade, and landed lightly, fallen leaves crackling underfoot. Instead of continuing on with her walk, Bridget lingered where she was.

'It's hard to believe how long it has been since I was home,' she said tentatively.

Fishing a length of string from his pocket, he used it to secure the saw at his waist. 'Seven years,' he said.

'And three months,' she added.

He knelt next to the broken branch and set about stripping twigs from it, glancing at her out of the corner of his eye while he did so.

She looked so...changed. Gone were the wild curls he remembered, the scuffed elbows and knees, the rosy cheeks. In their place stood a docile girl – no, *lady* – whose chestnut brown hair had been tamed into tidy ringlets and whose skin was as pale as porcelain. She radiated such an impression of cleanliness and daintiness that it was difficult to believe she had ever climbed a tree in her life.

She took a few steps closer, her posture a little more relaxed. 'I tried to write, but my mother found me out, even when I attempted to sneak letters to Ellen. Mother burned them all.'

That did sound like Lady Courcey.

'I would've written,' he said, 'but Mrs Walsh wouldn't give me your address. She didn't believe I was able to read.'

'Well, we know better, don't we?' She smiled. 'Do you practise anymore?'

He shrugged, a guilty student. 'Don't have much reason to. Just a few letters from my sister, Mary, but her writing's even worse than mine.'

'Is she still away taking care of your aunt?'

'My aunt passed over a year ago but Mary wrote to tell us she'd found a position in Dublin and she'd send us some money soon.'

He neglected to mention that no money and no more letters had come. Instead, he asked, 'What was Dublin like? Did you hate it there?'

She laughed. 'For several years, yes. I was a demon, steadfastly refusing to do anything or go anywhere. I drove my mother to distraction every single day. But when I eventually came out into society I discovered that attending balls and wearing fancy gowns was not so appalling as I thought and I began to enjoy myself.' She seemed aware of the frivolity of her comment and rushed on, 'And how have you been? You are a stable hand now?'

'I am,' he said, straightening and wiping his hands on his clothes. 'And I do some carpentry as well, whenever 'tis needed.'

'Just like your father! He must be proud of you.'

He hesitated. 'He…was.'

She blinked. 'Was?'

'He died. Three winters ago.'

'Oh, Cormac!' she exclaimed. 'I am so very sorry, I did not know.'

He felt the force of her empathy. She knew what it was like to lose a father.

'I lost my brother too. They died within weeks of each other. Just before Christmas.'

Her hand flew to her mouth. 'How did this happen?'

He looked away into the gloom under the apple trees beyond the clearing. 'D'you remember the bridge we used to cross over the Sruhawn to go to the Tullow horse fair? There was terrible flooding that December. My father was returning from the fair when the stream burst its banks and swept the bridge away, taking him and his horse with it. His body was found downstream two days later.'

Her eyes brimmed with tears. 'What a grievous loss for you and your family.' She shook her head in disbelief. 'And your brother?'

'Patrick died in a fire in the stables. It might've been started by something as stupid as a neglected rushlight, no one knows for sure. Almost the entire structure burned down. We lost two lads and four horses that night.'

She was aghast. 'Your poor mother. How is she coping?'

'As well as can be expected.' Two and a half years had passed but how could his mother ever get over the loss of her husband and her eldest boy?

Without warning, Bridget reached out and clutched one of his hands in both of hers.

'Please pass on my condolences to her,' she murmured, 'and tell her I shall visit her soon.'

When she let go, she could not seem to meet his eyes. She turned and touched the tree trunk, her fingertips tracing the letters they had carved into the bark so many years ago.

'Do you still have that rusty old blade?' she asked. 'You never went anywhere without it.'

'I only keep it for nostalgia's sake. I use my father's tools now he's…gone.'

She gave him a compassionate look, then stared upwards into the branches above her.

'I have not climbed a tree in years,' she said, her tone almost wistful, 'but I spent half my childhood sitting at the top of this one.'

'We had fun, didn't we?' he said. 'Climbing trees, picking apples…'

'Playing hide-and-seek in the quarry,' she contributed. 'Throwing hay in the fields. Wheedling hunks of cheese from Farmer McKinty's wife.'

'D'you miss it? The way it was back then?'

She sighed. 'I miss the simplicity of it all. Life in the city taught me that becoming an adult is a complicated matter. There were so many times when I was obliged to be a prim and proper lady and converse with people I detested, and all I wanted was to be back at Oakleigh with my best friend.'

His skin tingled at the sincerity of her words. 'I wish you hadn't been taken away against your will. Seven years is a long time to be so unhappy.'

She gave him a reassuring smile. 'You have no need to be concerned on my behalf for I did not suffer in perpetual misery. I found much contentment in Dublin. In fact, I have some very happy news to impart.' Her smile widened. 'I am engaged.'

It took a few seconds for her pronouncement to sink in. 'Engaged?'

She bobbed in effervescent affirmation.

He glanced down at her hand. 'But there's no ring on your finger.'

'There isn't,' she acknowledged. 'The proposal was quite spontaneous. He did not have a ring ready at the time.'

She was still beaming. With effort, he schooled his expression into one of pleasure and said, 'My congratulations to you. Who's the lucky fellow?'

'Mr Garrett Lambourne. He is an English gentleman but his father has property in Ireland and they have spent a great deal of time in Dublin over the past couple of years. He is heir to the viscountcy of Wyndham.'

His internal wince matched her visible one, though he had no idea why she would feel reason to react like that. Perhaps the title came with a substantial debt.

'Is he in Dublin now?' he asked without much enthusiasm for the answer.

'No, he was obliged to go back to England for a brief spell as he and his father had business to manage in London. But he is due to return within the month. We are expecting him for a visit here at Oakleigh.'

No doubt Mr Lambourne would be an avid rider and spend half his days at the stables. Cormac felt an urge to hurry the conversation along to its conclusion. 'You must be looking forward to that very much. If you'll excuse me, 'tis past time for me to be going.'

He rolled the broken branch into an easier position for picking up.

'I'm sure I'll see you again soon,' she said.

'Next time you need your horse saddled, I expect.'

Silence fell between them, broken only by the light rustle of leaves overhead. 'What do you mean by that?'

He swallowed. 'I mean we shouldn't be talking like this. It would've been fine when we were children but not now. Not when I'm your servant.'

'I don't think of you that way at all,' she said, and there was absolute sincerity in her dark brown eyes.

'I'm a servant at Oakleigh, you're the heiress to Oakleigh. I'm your servant. More to the point, I'm your *male* servant.'

'Oh, for heaven's sake,' she said, even as her cheeks reddened.

'You're alone with me here in a deserted orchard. I can't say I know much about society rules but I know 'tis enough to ruin a young lady's reputation.'

She caught the tip of her tongue between her teeth, a gesture of anxiety that was so familiar to him from their childhood. 'But we are just old friends, there's nothing else to it.'

'There probably isn't another soul on the estate who'd see it like that. And neither would your future husband.'

Her blush spread all the way down to the neckline of her dress. 'I-I suppose you're right.'

He stooped and hefted the branch onto his shoulders with a grunt.

'I hope you've a happy summer at Oakleigh,' he said and hurried from the clearing.

## Chapter 3

The following morning, Bridget took breakfast with her mother and uncle. As Lord Walcott returned from the sideboard with his third stacked plate of bacon and eggs, he said, 'Another fine day, ladies. How very fortunate. When you go out riding later, you must take note of the design of the stables.' He sat heavily in his chair and puffed out his vast chest. 'I oversaw the reconstruction of them after the fire, an excellent opportunity to indulge my architectural interests.'

Lady Courcey tapped the top of her soft-boiled egg, saying nothing. Bridget remembered Cormac's brother and laid her spoon down, her own egg untouched.

'And if you go as far as the quarry,' Lord Walcott continued after devouring two forkfuls in quick succession, 'you will see that it is prospering since I ordered excavation to begin there again. The limestone is a valuable resource and the workers are very satisfied with progress.' He belched as discreetly as he could behind his napkin.

'I don't believe we shall make it that far today,' Lady Courcey said and added with the faintest hint of derision, 'You set great store by the workers' satisfaction levels, do you?'

Bridget's attention drifted away from the conversation, her confused thoughts returning to her encounter with Cormac in the orchard. Talking with him by the oak tree had brought back so many vivid memories of their friendship that she had actually begun to think they might be friends again. Until he had made some very valid points on the matter.

She could try to convince herself that everyone knew what staunch companions they had been as children and that it was clear their intentions were nothing but innocuous, except for the fact that a world of difference existed between twelve and nineteen. If they had been discovered, there would have been uproar; it was so far from prudent behaviour, particularly when she was meant to be in her bedchamber trying to soothe a headache. Furthermore, she had a strong hunch that her fiancé would not be pleased at the idea of her partaking in any sort of acquaintance with a stable hand beyond the basic requirements.

She felt a surprising sense of loss. Mr Garrett Lambourne was to be her future but Cormac held a link to her past that no one else did. He had been with her at her father's passing and through every other event of her childhood, meaningful or trivial. The one thing that had consoled her during those awful early years in Dublin was that they would return to each other someday. But then over time she had ceased to view her life as a tragedy and hence her longing for Oakleigh and the people there had lessened. Of course, it had helped to be courted by a gentleman who had swept her off her feet with his charm.

She cringed when she recalled her declaration that Garrett was heir to a viscountcy. What had possessed her to say that? It had played no part in her decision to accept his suit – though it had been a substantial source of satisfaction for her mother – and it had sounded shallow of her to mention it. Much as the upper classes praised the virtues of ascending the social ladder, she despised the notion of marrying a man for his title. She was fortunate that theirs was a love match.

'I beg your pardon?'

The tone of her mother's voice drew her attention back to the breakfast table. Though Lady Courcey had used an expression of politeness, it was suffused with a chilliness which indicated she would rather be anything but civil. Lord Walcott was not the kind of man to wilt before a glare but even his massive frame seemed to shrink a little when faced with his sister's hostility.

'Can you repeat that?' the lady said, very quietly.

Lord Walcott cleared his throat. 'Now, Constance, I vow that it was an outstanding decision on my part. The tenants are content with their lot which means the estate is flourishing like never before.'

Lady Courcey dabbed her napkin at the corner of her mouth. 'Indeed. If it has been such a success, then why did you choose not to inform me of it?'

He waved an airy hand. 'You had more pressing issues to occupy you. Marrying off your daughter, for one.' He threw a theatrical wink in Bridget's direction.

'I would consider this issue as pressing as the marriage mart,' said Lady Courcey, 'if not more so, because it pertains to the excessive spending of estate resources.'

Bridget's head swivelled from her mother to her uncle. To what lavish levels could Lord Walcott have overspent that her mother was so displeased? Mrs Kavanagh had mentioned that he had been fond of inviting guests to Oakleigh but no mere party of extravagance would cause Lady Courcey to react like this.

'If you speak to Laurence Enright, he will assure you of the soundness of my claim. He interacts with the tenants on a daily basis and tells me they are deeply grateful for the arrangement. The tithes were an insufferable strain upon them.'

'A strain which you have incurred upon the estate, and my daughter's inheritance, instead.'

'Oakleigh can afford it. And I am confident Bridget will not even notice the expenditure when she is living on a viscount's income.'

'What tithes?' Bridget interjected, exasperated by her ignorance.

Her mother's lip curled. 'If you are so uninformed as to be unaware of their existence, then you are in grave need of an education this summer.'

Exhibiting a greater degree of patience, Lord Walcott said, 'The tithes are taxes paid by the tenants to support the Church of Ireland.'

Bridget frowned. 'But the Church of Ireland is not a Roman Catholic establishment. Why would the tenants be required to fund its upkeep?'

'Seems unfair, doesn't it?' agreed her uncle. 'I elected to absorb the tithes into the outflow of the estate, given that Oakleigh is the only non-Catholic residence for miles around. The tithes are but one of many hardships suffered by the Irish people, hardships which have only multiplied since 1798.' He shook his head. 'Their rebellion lasted no more than a few months but they have endured its ramifications these past thirty years. They have borne the tithes even longer and I deemed this to be a benevolent gesture to encourage goodwill. Your mother's agent helped me facilitate it.'

'A liberty you took without consulting me and which you have purposely kept concealed until now,' said Lady Courcey, the words barely making it past her clenched teeth. 'When I gave you authority over the estate in my absence, I did not expect you to be so wasteful with it. I intend to discuss this further with you and Mr Enright.'

Bridget could tell that 'discuss' meant 'abolish', and in short order. Lord Walcott gave a resigned shrug.

'I counsel you to embrace a philanthropic attitude on this matter,' he said, 'as they will respect you for it and work all the harder. Do take time to deliberate upon it before making a decision. For now, ladies, good morning to you.'

He heaved himself up from the table and gathered the final few scraps of food from the breakfast dishes on the sideboard into a handkerchief: treats for his pets who under no circumstances were permitted to be present at mealtimes while Lady Courcey was mistress of the house.

As he toddled towards the door, Bridget marvelled at the revelation of his generosity. Several years spent in rural Ireland had made a significant impact on him because the uncle she remembered had thought of nothing but his belly and his dogs. She glowed with admiration at his retreating back and resolved that, if her mother chose to eradicate her brother's altruistic deed, she would reinstate it as soon as Oakleigh came into her own possession.

***

Cormac opened the back door into the kitchens and was greeted by a wave of heat as fierce as the June air outside. Steam issued from a huge pot of water boiling over the open hearth. His two sisters, Margaret and Bronagh, stood at a long table in the centre of the kitchen, their faces red as they sliced vegetables. At the far end of the table, Mrs Kavanagh and Mrs Walsh sat on a bench, the cook counting off items on her fingers while the housekeeper made notes on a piece of paper. Mrs Walsh looked up sharply at his appearance.

'What is it, Cormac?' she said, her tone only a touch short of abrupt. She presided over the household with a will of iron as unyielding as the set of keys hanging at her waist.

'I just wanted to check if there are any scraps for the horses?'

Mrs Kavanagh gesticulated towards the two girls chopping vegetables. 'Not yet, you'll have to come back later.' She turned back to Mrs Walsh, pointing at her notes. 'Make that four dozen, better to have too much than too little. Lord Walcott has shown no sign of leaving yet and he's not shy about asking for third helpings.'

Cormac gave the cook a deferential nod. She was a tyrant in the kitchens but she could be softened if one knew how; well-timed offerings of charm had on occasion won him a mouthful of fresh bread or a bite of leftover cake, never mind treats for the horses.

He stepped over to his sisters at the table. Both were younger than him and dark-haired and grey-eyed like their mother, whereas he had inherited his fair hair and blue eyes from their father. Bronagh continued to slice her onion, glancing covertly in Mrs Kavanagh's direction; her eyes were watering so much that, had Cormac not known she was the sort of girl who never cried, he would have been worried that there had been another death in the family. Margaret, the older of the two, laid down her knife and half-chopped carrot and gave him a wide smile.

'Good to see you, Cormac!' she said. 'Is everything well with you?'

He made an effort to grin. 'All's fine. How are you two?'

'Worn out! 'Tis been chaotic for the past two weeks. But 'tis nice to have the family in the house.' Margaret nudged Bronagh, who was wiping her eyes with the corner of her apron. 'Isn't it?'

Bronagh shrugged. 'Way I see it, it just means more work.'

'Don't mind her. She's in a bad mood 'cause she got in trouble with Mrs Kavanagh this morning for burning the servants' porridge. That's why she's stuck with the onions.'

'Don't tell Ma,' Bronagh said to Cormac.

'Cormac McGovern, have you quite finished taking up my maids' time?' came Mrs Kavanagh's voice from the other end of the table. 'Those vegetables won't get chopped by themselves, lad.'

'I'm leaving now,' he said and beat a hasty retreat.

The kitchens were situated at the rear of the big house, facing onto a cobbled courtyard which was bordered by the stables on one side and the orchard on the other. He crossed the cobblestones, entered through the open double doors of the stables and commenced with the task of mucking out one of the stable stalls. Lost in his thoughts, he was startled when he heard his name called and looked up to see the stable master, John Corbett, leaning over the half door of the stall.

The small, wiry man joked, 'Why so down? I know 'tisn't roses you're smelling, but 'tis nothing you haven't smelled a thousand times before.'

Cormac plastered another grin on his face. 'You're right about that,' he said, and started whistling to prevent further questions.

He had no right to be looking glum. After all, he had harboured no expectations of a renewed friendship upon Bridget's homecoming – he had understood very well that the nature of their situation would be infinitely different from that of their youth. But perhaps there had still been the trace of a twelve-year-old boy inside him who had hoped he would get his childhood friend back in some limited fashion. However, their chance meeting in the orchard had established that that kind of familiarity was out of the question.

His whistling faltered. She was *engaged*. The more he thought about it, the more he wondered how he had not seen it coming. She had lived for seven years in the city, maturing to the optimum age of marriage for a young woman and attending balls which would have been frequented by dozens of single men. Looking at it from that viewpoint, he was surprised she was only betrothed and not already married.

He didn't allow himself to speculate about what might have happened had she not been forced to depart from the estate. The appearance of Mr Garrett Lambourne, or some other fellow like him, would always have been the inescapable outcome.

He was once again jolted out of his reflections by a clipped English voice outside the entrance to the stables. 'Fetch the stable master to me and prepare our horses. My daughter and I are going to ride across the estate.'

He heard a murmur of 'Yes, m'lady,' followed by footsteps running to do her bidding. Seconds later, Liam's anxious face appeared above the half door of the stall. 'Will you help me, Cormac?' Though he had started working at the stables a year or so after Cormac and was more than capable, the lad looked daunted by the idea of serving the two ladies of the big house by himself.

'For sure. You go tell John her ladyship wants him and then take care of her horse. I'll look after Bonny.'

Liam nodded and hastened away. Cormac dropped his pitchfork and went into the next stall which housed Bridget's glossy, white mare, a gift from her father on her twelfth birthday. Bonny whinnied at him in greeting.

This encounter presented him with a challenge: how ought he to behave when he saw Bridget? Clandestine meetings were unacceptable but he could envisage no harm in being amicable on accidental occasions such as this.

After grooming and saddling her horse, he grabbed a mounting step and led the mare out of the stables. It was a glorious day, the sky a ceiling of pure blue and a gentle breeze blowing.

John appeared to be praising the design of the new stables to the ladies. The clip-clop of Bonny's hooves made them turn as one but while Bridget's expression lifted, her mother's went sour. The stable master seemed to interpret this as dissatisfaction that her own horse was not yet ready and muttered, 'The lad's thorough but slow,' before hurrying back inside.

Cormac guided the horse up to Bridget, trying to ignore the fact that Lady Courcey walked away with a sniff of distaste. Bridget's uncertainty was plain on her face – she too was unsure how to act.

He decided to take the lead. 'Bonny's happy to see you, Bridget,' he said in a light voice, hoping to convey that friendliness, if not friendship, still existed between them.

He might have said more, only for the exclamation of outrage that intruded upon them.

'Insolent boy,' Lady Courcey snapped, spinning on her heel. 'That is no way for a servant to speak to his superior.'

Bridget looked shocked. 'Mother, please, I took no offence.'

The lady paid her no heed, levelling a ferocious glower at Cormac. 'You shall address my daughter in the appropriate manner, or not at all.'

He could almost feel her disgust burning into his skin. 'Begging your pardon, m'lady,' he said through gritted teeth. 'My apologies, Miss Muldowney,' he added to Bridget, as it was the only thing he could say.

She mumbled something unintelligible, mortification flooding her face.

He set the step on the ground and offered his hand to help her mount. She took it in her own gloved one, climbed onto Bonny and squeezed before letting go. At the same time, Liam scurried from the stables leading Lady Courcey's horse and the lady mounted, her lips pursed.

Cormac stepped back and the two ladies trotted off, their horses' hooves striking the cobbles in rhythm. Humiliation coursed through him, and not a little loathing which he aimed in Lady Courcey's direction. Every line of her figure was rigid, from her straight shoulders to her stiff perch in the sidesaddle. Even her hair, the same chestnut shade as Bridget's, was severely styled under her hat, unlike the softer curls around her daughter's face. She radiated inflexibility and disapproval.

It came as no surprise. She had despised him from the moment they had first met. At the time, he had been just seven years old but he had also been Irish and a stable hand's son and in Bridget's presence, and his bare feet had been standing on a luxurious rug in the big house's library where Bridget was showing him how to read letters. 'I want this vagrant out of my house this very minute!' were the loudest words he had ever heard the lady utter from that day to this. He had been unfamiliar with the term 'vagrant' but its meaning had been unmistakable. Only for Lord Courcey's timely appearance and Bridget's desperate plea for intervention, he would have been driven from the building.

They had taken care to stay out of Lady Courcey's way after that but she could not fail to notice how much time they spent together. It had galled her to be overruled by her husband on such a matter, which had only caused her dislike of Cormac to strengthen. And it transpired that the passage of seven years apart had done nothing to dull the detestation – on both sides, he had to admit, as he gave her turned back a glower as good as the one she had given him.

Just before the ladies rounded the end of the big house, Bridget looked back over her shoulder at him, an apology in her glance. He nodded to show he understood and then they disappeared around the corner.

## Chapter 4

'Bridget, are you paying attention?'

She dragged her gaze from the window, through which she could just make out a young gardener struggling with the weeding of an elaborate flower bed in the manor gardens, and met with three censorious stares.

'Yes,' she said guiltily.

'I feel obliged to remind you,' said Lady Courcey, 'that these proceedings are for *your* benefit.'

The lady was seated behind a large writing desk spread with various papers. Mr Buttimer and Mrs Walsh hovered by her elbow, trying not to look too reproachful – Bridget was a grown woman, after all, and no longer a child to be reprimanded for misbehaviour.

'I understand,' she said, folding her hands in her lap. 'Please continue.'

Since their return to Oakleigh, Lady Courcey had taken to conducting any necessary business in the wood-panelled chamber that used to be Lord Courcey's study and her primary task of the summer now seemed to be extending her daughter's education. Thanks to her ignorance about tithes, Bridget had been forced to endure almost a fortnight of gruelling lectures on a range of subjects relating to the estate and manor household, including how to keep accounts, assess crop yields, evaluate the rates of rent, and hire and discharge servants, as well as learning which domestic issues were pertinent to the butler and which to the housekeeper, the particulars in relation to having guests to stay, and the finer points of hosting social gatherings.

Most of her instruction came from Lady Courcey, but Mr Buttimer and Mrs Walsh also offered their perspectives (long-winded sermons from the former, succinct footnotes from the latter). Even Lord Walcott attempted to contribute advice, but his sister discouraged this based upon recent evidence which indicated, in her opinion, his lack of sound judgement. There had been no further developments on that dispute as of yet but a meeting with the land agent, Mr Enright, had been scheduled. Bridget hoped she would be expected to attend – perhaps three voices would be enough to drown out Lady Courcey's contention.

'Bridget!'

She bit her tongue and sat up straight. 'I was thinking about estate matters, I promise!'

Her mother nodded a dismissal to Mr Buttimer and Mrs Walsh. 'I think we shall finish for today.' After they left the study – with an aggravated cough from the butler implying he was either unhappy with Bridget's attention span or suffering from the onset of a chest cold – she turned back to her daughter. 'It is in your interest to absorb these valuable lessons. In a twelvemonth from November you will reach the age of twenty-one, at which point you will legally inherit Oakleigh. All of this,' she waved a hand at the desk, 'will become your responsibility.'

Bridget gulped. 'I know that,' she said, even though she had never given it much consideration. She recalled some fuss after her father's death relating to the line of inheritance specified in his will because hers was the first in four generations where the baron had fathered no boys. All manner of strangers popped up out of nowhere claiming to be the last surviving son of a distant cousin of a younger brother and wasn't it obvious from the portrait in the drawing room that he had the same colour eyes as the 1st Baron? However, in a rather uncommon proviso, the estate had been entailed by male-preference primogeniture, which meant that, in the absence of any male progeny, the eldest of the female offspring in the family would become the lawful heiress. Thus, Lord Courcey's only daughter would inherit his title, property and assets in her own right, but not until her twenty-first birthday. In the meantime, her mother had been appointed to act as guardian of the estate.

At the age of twelve, nine years had seemed a lifetime. Now her birthright dangled over the not-too-distant horizon.

Lady Courcey sighed. 'Of course, it is unlikely that you will need to put any of this knowledge into practice as you will soon have a husband who will handle the estate for you. But it is wise to prepare for the worst. After all, I intended to live to old age with my husband at my side.'

Bridget gaped at her mother. Her shoulders drooped and her eyes were sad, like they were looking at something that wasn't there. But then she snapped to attention again.

'So do endeavour to focus on what we are telling you. It may prove useful.' She shuffled some of the papers into a neat pile. 'I place no further demand on your time for now. I have letters to write which I wish to do in solitude.'

Bridget made a swift departure from the study. She supposed she could write some letters of her own – no doubt Madeleine and her other friends in Dublin would be eager to hear how she was adjusting back to country life – but that could wait. In truth, she wanted to seek out Cormac which, having been so confined to the house, she had had no opportunity to do since the day her mother had rebuked him in the courtyard. Regardless of their resolution not to meet on familiar terms, he deserved a proper apology for the way he had been treated.

Still, there was something else she had to do which took higher priority. It was time she visited her second mother.

She donned her sturdiest boots before emerging outdoors. While the afternoon had clouded over and the air had turned muggy, it did not look like it was going to rain yet. A circuitous series of lanes presented the long way round to her destination, which most dignified ladies would choose to take, but crossing the fields was the more direct course and today did not strike her as the day to break a lifelong habit.

She couldn't help glancing about for Cormac as she passed the stables and the paddock but she caught no glimpse of him, though there were other stable hands who saluted her. Beyond the paddock lay the boundary to the first field, known locally as the Gorteen. She slipped through the gate and proceeded at a sedate walk to the far end where she entered the next field via a stile in the hedge. Then, when she was certain there was no one around to see, she hoisted her skirts up past her ankles and bounded across the grass, relishing the feel of the solid turf beneath her feet. Granted, it would have been far more liberating to sprint in the riding breeches her father had acquired for her back when she had learned to ride astride, but she was well past the age where such clothing, or such a position on a horse, could be deemed decent. She ran until she became out of breath, halting at last to draw in deep lungfuls of fresh air, a herd of curious cows her only witness to her indiscretion.

After that, she continued along the once well-trodden route at a more comfortable stroll. Most of the landscape triggered cheery memories of childhood jaunts, but she shivered as she crossed one particular field featuring a natural, three-pronged rock formation which jutted up out of the turf like a giant's clawed hand. Cormac had in the past divulged far more of its dreadful history than she had wanted to know. On their braver days, they had played morbid games about rebels and hangmen beneath its shadow, but more often than not they had steered clear of the rocky outcrop. She quickened her pace now and gave it a wide berth.

A few fields further on, she found another stile in the hedgerow, this one leading out into the neighbouring lane, where a round, brick-lined well stood at the opposite side. Someone had been assiduous in trimming back the thick hedge and no brambles tugged at her dress as she clambered over the stile. She followed the lane for a minute or two until a small cottage came into view at the side of the road. It was thatched and whitewashed and a horse shoe hung over the door. Adjoining it was a modest plot of land for growing potatoes, while a patch of woods extended behind it. A column of smoke streamed from the cottage's chimney, a box of wildflowers rested on its one window sill, and two or three hens pecked at the ground in front of it. Everything about the dwelling was familiar and welcoming and she felt a rush of gladness; how blessed she was to have two places in her life which she could call home.

She went up to the door of the cottage, the hens flapping away at her approach. The top half of it was open so she leaned over it and peered into the gloom. 'Is there anyone here?'

An exclamation of astonishment and delight came from the depths of the room within. 'That's never Bridget Muldowney!'

She smiled as a woman appeared at the door. 'Good day, Mrs McGovern.'

'Arrah, none of that now,' said Cormac's mother. 'You always called me Aunt Maggie and I hope that hasn't changed.'

Pulling back the bottom half of the door, she ushered Bridget inside. She had dark hair and light grey eyes but there were more white streaks and wrinkled lines than Bridget remembered. The cottage, on the other hand, was the very same as when she had visited it as a child. Thanks to Jack McGovern's skills as a carpenter, Cormac's home boasted more furniture than the typical cottier's abode. A well-scrubbed table occupied the centre of the single room, with a bench on either side. There was a rocking chair in one corner and a spinning wheel in another. A simple dresser stood against the back wall and next to it a ladder led up to the loft, where the family slept at night.

A fire glowed in the grate despite the heat of the day; she inhaled the smell of the burning turf with satisfaction. Sitting before the hearth was a bare-footed little girl whom she did not recognise. She held a hen in her lap and stared at Bridget with big, round eyes.

'Of course, ye two have never met before,' said Maggie. 'This is Orlaith, my youngest girl. She's only five.' She crossed over to her daughter. 'Orlaith, this is Bridget. She's a good friend of your brother's. She lives in the big house.'

Cormac must not have told his mother about the incident in the courtyard and Bridget was glad of it; she would have been horrified if Maggie had tried to address her as 'Miss Muldowney', given that the same woman had been the one to pacify her at age eleven when she had found blood on her undergarments. That level of intimacy transcended any prospect of formality.

'It is nice to meet you,' Bridget said but Orlaith just gazed back solemnly.

Maggie winked. 'Don't worry, she's like that with everybody, our quiet little one.' She waved her hand at the table. 'Do sit down. 'Tis wonderful to see you! Would you like a cup of milk?'

'That would be lovely,' said Bridget, seating herself on one of the benches.

Maggie bustled over to the dresser, picked up a cup, and went outside. Bridget supposed the pail still stood in its same shady spot behind the cottage. She looked over at Orlaith and tried to catch her eye but the little girl was absorbed in stroking the feathers of her hen and humming softly to it.

When Maggie returned, she set a full cup of milk in front of Bridget and then took a seat opposite her. Bridget sipped from the cup and smiled. 'I feel like I am six years old again.'

Maggie chuckled. 'I remember it so well, the first time you came to visit us. Pouring out of the heavens it was, and that daft boy brought you across all those fields. You were soaked through when you got here, poor craythur. But an hour or two in front of the fire with a blanket and some warm milk and you were fine again.' She gazed at Bridget with affection. 'You've grown up so much since then. Look at your beautiful hair! It must've been some ordeal to get that wild mane under control.'

'Yes, my mother regards it as one of her greatest achievements.' This time they both laughed, recalling the many occasions when Bridget had come blazing to the cottage to recount yet another argument she had had with her mother over her untamed hair.

'I was hoping you might come to visit me once you got settled back,' said Maggie. 'When Cormac told me you'd returned I said to him it was only a matter of time before you showed up here.'

'Of course. How could I not come by? I have always considered this cottage my second home and its inhabitants my extended family.'

In an instant, Bridget's jollity died away.

'Maggie,' she said, reaching across the table and clasping the other woman's hand, which was rough and calloused. 'I want to offer my deepest condolences about Jack and Patrick. I grieved to hear of it. My heart goes out to you.'

Maggie's eyes dimmed. 'Thank you, dearie. That's kind of you to say.'

'It is one thing to lose a parent, but to lose a husband and a child and then be left raising the remaining children by yourself…' Bridget glanced at Orlaith, who would have been only two when her father died. 'I cannot imagine how you have coped.'

'I'd never have managed without Cormac. He's the man of the family now and he's looked after us all without a word of complaint, though he's had to deal with so much himself, poor boy.'

Bridget's forehead creased. 'What do you mean?'

'Didn't he tell you? What made their deaths so hard for him was he was there when they happened. He watched his father and his brother perish and there was nothing he could do.'

Bridget experienced a fresh wave of sympathy for Cormac. 'Oh, how truly awful.'

Maggie cocked her head towards the hearth. 'Orlaith, will you fetch me some water from the well? I'll need it for the supper later.'

'Yes, Ma,' the little girl said and hopped to her feet.

'Don't wander from the lane, and make sure the rope isn't tangled before you lower the bucket,' Maggie cautioned as Orlaith disappeared outside, her hen squawking behind her. A call of assent floated to them over the half door.

Maggie turned back to Bridget. 'Her little ears don't need to hear this.' Her voice became faint as she supplied the details her son had omitted. 'Cormac was accompanying his father home from the horse fair. Jack could see the bridge was weak and said they should cross it one at a time, so Cormac was waiting on the bank when the stream burst. It was a narrow escape. He nearly got swept away himself.' She took a shaky breath. 'And he was sleeping in the stables the night of the fire. The stable hands woke with flames and smoke all 'round them. It was chaos trying to save themselves and the animals. When Cormac realised his brother was still inside he tried to go back in but John Corbett grabbed him just before the loft caved in. Only for John, I might've lost both my boys that night.'

Bridget was horror-struck. Cormac had brushed with death twice and she, in her pretty dresses attending fancy balls, had never known. The very idea of him dying, even though it had not come to pass, filled her with distress. She clutched Maggie's hand all the harder.

'We struggled to survive after that, although Cormac did his best to support us all. I had my spinning and we bartered the eggs, but it wasn't enough. I had to send Margaret and Bronagh out to find employment. Fortunately, your uncle had taken to inviting guests so often that Maura Kavanagh was willing to hire new scullery maids.'

'They must have been very young,' Bridget said, thinking the girls could only be in early adolescence now.

'They started work on Margaret's twelfth birthday. Bronagh was just after turning ten. They're gone over two years now.'

Bridget shook her head. That was too soon to leave a mother's skirts. 'I have seen them on a few occasions when I've gone down to the kitchens. They seem to be reasonably content, especially Margaret.'

'Maura tells me they've shown promise and she sometimes entrusts them with kitchen maid duties, though I gather Bronagh gets demoted more often than promoted.' Her lopsided smile revealed she expected no less from that particular daughter. 'Margaret, at least, hopes to become a proper kitchen maid by next year. They sleep in the servants' quarters at the top of the big house 'cause they rise so early and get to bed so late, which means they don't come home much beyond their afternoons off. I believe they're happy enough but I do wish I could see my girls more.' She sighed. 'Let's speak of more cheerful matters. Tell me about your stay in Dublin.'

'Cheerful? Then I had better leave out the part where I sat on the floor of my bedchamber in my riding breeches and refused to move while my mother and the maids tried to get me to put on a decorative gown.' It was such a trivial thing to say, in light of the McGoverns' hardships, but it made Maggie's eyes crinkle.

'Ah, my dearie. You didn't adjust too well to city life?'

'That is an understatement of the situation.' Bridget folded her arms. 'Once we were out of mourning, my mother wasted no time in announcing she intended to have me presented as a debutante at Dublin Castle as soon as I turned sixteen. I railed against her for as long as I could, and we struggled and quarrelled day after day, until she threatened to take me to the London season instead.'

'London?' Maggie looked mystified by the notion, as though Lady Courcey had suggested taking Bridget to the moon. 'You wouldn't have liked that at all.'

'Precisely,' said Bridget with an emphatic nod. 'So I conceded defeat. And then, after my coming out, I discovered that I had been making a fuss for no reason. I thought it would be nothing but cups of tea and monotonous conversations in drawing rooms and, yes, there was some of that, but I also met the most amiable girls and forged fervent friendships with them. The biggest surprise of all was I learned just how much I love dancing. It transpired that the city was in fact an agreeable place to live once I allowed myself to be happy there.' She twisted her lips. 'It was far from a smooth transition though. I was so tongue-tied in company at first. Mother faced quite a task in teaching me how to dress, speak and behave like a lady. Sophistication is a hard-earned trait, but essential if one wishes to be deemed eligible for marriage.'

She found herself blushing at this. Maggie plucked fondly at her chin.

'You achieved success in that area. Cormac told me about your engagement. My hearty congratulations. A nice gentleman, is he?'

'Oh yes, exceedingly charming. We began courting during last year's season and he has been ever so attentive since then.'

Maggie leaned forwards. 'Do tell me about him.'

Her eagerness spurred Bridget to divulge the full narrative of her courtship with Mr Garrett Lambourne; after all, she was as good as a fifth daughter in this family and heaven knew the unfortunate woman needed some pleasant news to lift her spirits.

'…and in March I was seated in our drawing room when he burst in and said he had been called away to England on urgent business but could not leave without ensuring my hand in marriage first!'

'How romantic,' marvelled Maggie.

'Apart from the fact that it was so impromptu he did not even have a ring,' Bridget said with amusement. 'But he means to bring one when he returns to Ireland. He will be coming to visit Oakleigh soon.'

'I'm sure you'll enjoy showing him 'round your home.'

'If I can find the time. Mother seems to think that every moment of the day should be filled with learning the duties of a lady in charge of her household.'

She went on to describe the regimen Lady Courcey had imposed upon her and the lectures to which she had been subjected; her depiction of Mr Buttimer's pompous pronouncement that he by no means had any responsibility for the chamber pots drew a genuine laugh from Maggie. It was good to hear it.

At length, Bridget swallowed the last of her milk and stood. 'I must go now, but it was lovely to see you again. I am so sorry about Jack and Patrick. I do hope that your grief will ease over time.'

Maggie made a visible effort to look optimistic. ''Tis been difficult but I still have the rest of my family to be grateful for. And we've our horse shoe over the door. It'll bring us good luck, I'm sure of it.'

They hugged warmly. As Bridget left the cottage, Orlaith materialised with a full bucket of water swinging at her knees, its rope wound in neat coils around her arm. Bridget bid her farewell but the little girl edged past with her eyes fixed on her toes.

Head and heart full of her conversation with Maggie McGovern, Bridget set off on her return journey across the fields. The sky looked a good deal more ominous than it had upon her departure and she began to worry that she would not make it back to the manor before a deluge came down.

She reached the Gorteen just as the first, fat drops of rain started to fall.

# Chapter 5

'D'you have potatoes for eyes, boy? Get out of my sight and don't come back to me 'til you've the intelligence to spot a flower from a weed!'

Cormac looked around for the source of the shouting. He was crossing the cobbled courtyard from the kitchens to the stables, bearing a basket of carrot peelings for the horses, and a slender youth was striding from the manor gardens in his direction. Beyond the boy, he distinguished the formidable form of the head gardener, Fintan Kelly, brandishing a rake.

When the lad marched into the courtyard, a black look on his face, Cormac recognised him as Malachy, Fintan's grandson and a new worker at Oakleigh, just shy of two months in his position as under gardener. Cormac had heard from John Corbett that the old man held high hopes he would eventually be succeeded by his grandson in managing the upkeep of his beloved gardens, but the evidence at hand suggested his hope might well be misplaced.

Malachy checked at the sight of Cormac, assumed an air of nonchalance, and grinned.

'Damn grumpy codger,' he said, jerking his thumb towards his grandfather, who had turned away and was stumping back into the gardens, the rake swung over his shoulder.

The lad had to be lacking in wits to defy that redoubtable old man. Once, and once alone, had Cormac trespassed into Oakleigh's gardens as a child and he had received a brutal wallop of a spade on his backside for his efforts. He could not ride a horse for two days after it. Even now, Cormac treated Fintan Kelly with a deep respect tinged with wariness.

'Still got a bit to learn with the gardening?' he said, thinking the boy might be in need of some encouragement. 'You'll soon get the hang of it.'

Malachy, who could be no more than fifteen, laughed. He had shoulder-length, greasy hair which he pushed out of his eyes with a careless flick. 'Ah, I know the difference between a flower and a weed. But I've learned if I pull up too much of the wrong thing, I'll get the rest of the day off!' He looked pleased with himself.

Cormac raised his eyebrows, unimpressed. 'And what d'you plan to do with your free time?'

'Might pop into the kitchens, see if I can pinch some bread from that cook. She's large enough that she must be scoffing it herself all day, but maybe there'll still be some lying about.'

Liking him less and less with every word that came out of his mouth, Cormac said, 'Best not talk like that in front of her,' although part of him hoped Malachy would ignore his advice just so he could hear the whack of the cook's rolling pin on the boy's shins.

Malachy shrugged and sauntered away towards the back door of the kitchens. Shaking his head, Cormac stepped inside the stables just before the skies opened and the rain started to lash down.

He had scarcely deposited some of the carrot peelings in the first occupied stall when a figure came barrelling through the open double doors, desperate to escape the downpour. She gasped upon reaching the shelter of the stables and then again upon spotting Cormac. Her hands flurried as she attempted to smooth the waist of her dress and tuck back wayward chestnut curls, but she couldn't hide her sorry state. His lips twitched because she was embarrassed and yet he thought she looked the finest she had since she'd returned to the estate – a little dishevelled was how he had always known her.

'Out for a walk in this weather, Miss Muldowney?'

The formal address was for the benefit of John Corbett who, currently wedged into the tiny room opposite that served as his personal workspace, was within both sight and earshot through his open door. Cormac could see it bothered Bridget but she couldn't very well object to it in public.

'I didn't anticipate the rain,' she said.

'Most folk could tell 'tis been threatening since morning.'

'Yes, well, perhaps I don't have the same intuition as "most folk".' It was the kind of teasing that might have offended someone else but she took it on the chin; at least her sense of humour hadn't been impaired by her stint in Dublin.

'I recommend the kitchens as the swiftest route indoors,' he said, turning to carry his basket to the second stall.

'Please wait.' He stopped and she took a step nearer to him. 'There's something I wish to say.'

Wary, he glanced around. John appeared engrossed in a sheaf of papers, not seeming to notice there was anyone ten feet beyond his threshold. Down at the further end of the stables' central aisle, Liam sat on a stool, elbows and knees sticking out as he cleaned a saddle. They were in full view but not under scrutiny. 'What is it?'

'I want to express my regret at my mother's behaviour,' she said, her voice low. 'She was downright rude to you that day and, regardless of your position, she had no right to speak to you in that way.'

He was astonished that she still felt the urge to apologise for that, even though it had happened nearly two weeks ago. 'Don't fret about it at all.' He wanted to add that it was no more than he expected from the harridan, but figured that would be a degree past courtesy.

She sighed. 'Mother has such a frightful disposition these days. She was not always like this. I do have vague memories of her laughing once upon a time.'

He would wager they were very vague.

'At any rate, I needed to assure you her perspective was not my own. And I'm sorry I couldn't tell you before now. She has kept me practically incarcerated indoors ever since in order to acquaint me with the never-ending list of duties of an heiress.'

Privately, he speculated that Lady Courcey's demand on her daughter's time had an ulterior purpose beyond the obvious. The more occupied Bridget was in the house, the less opportunity she would have to wander around the grounds and bump into, say, a stable hand.

'Least you got the afternoon off today,' he said.

She nodded. 'I've just been to visit your mother.'

He was touched. 'Thank you,' he said with feeling. 'That'll have meant a great deal to her.'

Bridget's face filled with emotion. 'She told me —'

She broke off as, at the far end of the stables, another stable hand slithered down the ladder from the loft and started making loud conversation with Liam.

'You should go inside and get dry,' said Cormac, thinking it was perilous to allow the conversation to continue, when her dark brown eyes glistened like that. 'I'll find something for you to shelter under as you cross the courtyard.'

Tucking the basket under his arm, he unearthed a saddle blanket from one of the stalls and shook it out.

'It mightn't be the cleanest,' he said awkwardly.

She took it and breathed in. 'It smells good and horsey to me.'

'Just leave it in a corner of the kitchen so and I'll collect it later.'

She dithered for a moment and then, swinging the blanket over her head and shoulders, she ducked out into the rain.

His long working days at the stables meant it was more convenient for him to sleep on a bed of straw in the stable loft than trek home each night to his family's cottage, but he still made the effort to go back two or three times a week for his mother's sake. In view of Bridget's afternoon excursion, he decided that tonight he would head for home.

After he had completed his final tasks that evening, he dropped by the kitchens to retrieve the saddle blanket and see if Margaret and Bronagh had any messages or mending for their mother. The blanket was neatly folded on a stool; he draped it over his forearm and went to look for his sisters in the scullery, where he found them up to their elbows in dishwater. Mrs Kavanagh was giving out to Bronagh as usual.

'If I see another pot come back to me in that state, you'll regret it, girl. I have no qualms about keeping you here until two in the morning if necessary. What do you want, Cormac?'

'I'm just checking if my sisters want me to bring anything home to our mother.'

Mrs Kavanagh's countenance changed at once. 'Dear Maggie, I do wish I could see her more often. Here, I've got something you can take to her, lad.' She led him back into the main kitchen, wrapped a few buns in a cloth, and handed the parcel to him. 'Mind you bring the cloth back to me. I'll be needing it again.' She cast a sharp glance at Margaret and Bronagh, who had followed them. 'Do you have anything for him?'

Bronagh declined but Margaret said, 'I do. May I run up to my room?'

'Fast as you can,' Mrs Kavanagh said in a much kinder tone than Cormac had ever heard her use with his younger sister. Even as Margaret scampered through the door to the servants' staircase, the cook barked at Bronagh, 'See, she has her wits about her. No shoddy work or mooning over boys. You'd do best to follow her example.'

This was peculiar, considering Margaret had always been the romantic sister and Bronagh as tough as nails. Cormac was about to remark upon it – she deserved a fair defence, after all – when the inner door that led to the family quarters above stairs opened and Mr Buttimer appeared in the gap. Mrs Kavanagh bristled; relations became strained between butler and cook whenever the latter believed the former was interfering in her domain.

'How can I help you, Mr Buttimer?' she said with barely disguised antagonism.

For once, he did not retaliate in a similar attitude. His expression was sombre as he held out a note to her.

'This just arrived for you. The messenger was quite urgent about its contents so I thought it ought to be delivered to you without delay.'

It was perhaps the shortest speech he had ever made. The fact that he had chosen to convey the message himself indicated the gravity of what he believed to be inside. Mrs Kavanagh's ruddy face paled and she accepted the note with a trembling hand. Cormac exchanged a glance with Bronagh; neither of them was used to seeing the formidable cook in any state of vulnerability. Bronagh hid her look of vindictive satisfaction poorly. It was not a quality he liked to see in his sister but she did receive an awful lot of abuse from the woman.

Mrs Kavanagh opened the letter. She scanned its contents, crossed herself, and sat heavily on the kitchen bench.

With uncharacteristic compassion, Mr Buttimer said, 'I hope it is not too grim.'

'I-it's from my sister,' she stammered. 'There's been an uprising on the Rathglaney Estate.' She stared at the letter, eyes round with distress. 'A gang of tenants tried to burn down the big house and Lord Fitzwilliam was injured in the attack. M-my sister is unharmed but her son and husband have been captured. Lord bless us and save us, it's likely they will both be hanged.'

This was serious indeed. It wasn't the first rumour of unrest to reach Oakleigh – there had been sporadic disturbances in other counties during recent years, despite the failed rebellion against English rule in 1798 – but to hear of one with such a personal connection made a profound impact. The Rathglaney Estate lay only over the border into Wexford.

Margaret chose that moment to burst back into the kitchens with a bundle under her arm. Cormac tactfully drew her and Bronagh out the back door to give the cook some space to process the terrible news. The earlier rain had diminished to a soft drizzle and it beaded on their hair as he filled Margaret in on what they had just learned.

'Oh, poor Mrs Kavanagh,' she exclaimed. 'How dreadful.'

Bronagh did not look quite so sympathetic but she kept her opinions to herself.

'I'm going to head on now,' said Cormac. 'I'll tell Ma about this. She'll want me to pass on her sympathies. Anything else ye need brought home?' he added, shifting the saddle blanket and buns to take the bundle from Margaret.

They shook their heads and he turned towards the stables to bring the blanket back before setting out across the fields. As his sisters re-entered the kitchens, the sound of quiet sobbing drifted out.

The drizzle was the kind that hardly seemed to be falling and yet soaked into his clothing so thoroughly that he was drenched by the time he reached the cottage. He pushed open the door to find the room lit by the fire in the hearth and a solitary rushlight in a holder on the table. Orlaith had fallen asleep in front of the grate, a hen tucked under one arm; the other hens roosted on a rafter above her head. His mother sat darning a shirt in her rocking chair, pulled close to the table to avail of the rushlight's illumination. She rose at the sight of him, her face full of pleasure.

'*A mhac*, I wasn't expecting you. God above, you picked a dreary night to come home.'

She began speaking in Irish – 'son' – but slid into English out of habit. After the rebellion thirty years ago, Bridget's straitlaced grandfather, the 2nd Baron, had prohibited the use of Irish within the boundaries of the Oakleigh Estate and, while her father had relaxed the ban and Lord Walcott had been lenient with the occasional slip of the tongue, Lady Courcey had made it clear she would not tolerate it. Cormac had learned the language from infancy, when Lord Courcey had been in command of Oakleigh, but had seldom ventured to speak it since gaining employment at the big house.

He shrugged in what he hoped was a casual manner and dropped the sodden bundle he carried on the table.

'Mending from Margaret,' he said before taking off his wet boots and slinging them into a corner of the room.

He accepted the rag his mother offered him and wiped his face and the outer layer of moisture from his clothes, then hung it on a nail by the fireside to dry. As he warmed his hands, he perceived his sister's hazardous position beneath the hens' rumps and gently tugged her to one side, which prompted her companion, indignant at the intrusion, to flutter from the dresser to the rafter to join the others. Orlaith mumbled in her sleep but did not wake.

'Are you hungry?' Maggie asked. 'I can make you some stirabout.'

He would have preferred potatoes to the oatmeal-and-milk mixture but the new crop wouldn't be ready until autumn. 'No need. I've something even better,' he said and produced Mrs Kavanagh's buns from his pocket.

There were three hidden within the folds of the cloth. Maggie's eyes lit up.

'Nothing beats Maura Kavanagh's baking,' she said with appreciation.

They sat beside each other at the table and shared one each, saving the third for Orlaith, who could have it in the morning – it would be a bit hardened by then but still a rare treat. As they ate, he related the dire news which the cook had just received up at the big house. His mother blanched, letting her half-devoured bun fall to the tabletop.

''Tis happening again, isn't it?' she said. 'Oh, how I've feared this. The country's too fragile for the folly of revolutionaries. They need to leave well enough alone. Those *damned men*!'

This burst out of her with such unexpected vehemence that Cormac glanced at the hearth to make sure it hadn't roused Orlaith.

'You don't need to w –' he started to say but Maggie cut in.

'Of course I need to worry. If it can happen in Wexford, it can happen in Carlow. What's to stop the tenants rising up here?'

'Oakleigh's different. That's plain as day when I meet other folk at the horse fair. There isn't the same level of poverty here as on other estates. The land's thriving, and we're not paying the tithes. 'Tis that as much as anything else that gets people so angry.'

'That may be so but they'll find any excuse to revolt. There are still English landowners on our soil. That's what caused the rebellion last time, and look what it did, it decimated both sides of this family. 'Tis why you've no grandparents left alive.'

While he personally believed that fighting English rule was a just cause, he appreciated that his mother only wanted peace after the atrocities of the past. So he said, 'The tenants learned from '98. Oakleigh won't suffer Rathglaney's fate.'

He gave her a reassuring, one-armed hug and she subsided, eating the rest of her bun in silence. When she had finished, she crossed to the dresser and pulled a string of rosary beads from one of its drawers. Draping this around her neck, she returned to the rocking chair and picked up her darning again. She glanced over at him as she moved the needle in and out. 'I had a visit from Bridget Muldowney today.'

He lifted his eyebrows as though this was news to him.

'The craythur, she's pale as a ghost and not a pick on her. Did they not feed her in Dublin?' His mother didn't seem to expect an answer to that, just muttered something about a good appetite not being fashionable in the city.

'What did the two of ye talk about?'

'This and that. She told me about her time away. And her fiancé.'

He frowned at the last bun nestled in Mrs Kavanagh's cloth. He had no particular inclination to discuss Mr Lambourne.

'She sympathised regarding your father and brother too. You hadn't told her your part in all of that. She was terribly shaken to hear of it.'

He tilted his head. Was that what had distressed her so much?

''Tis been seven years but she still cares for you. I could feel it in the way she clutched my hand. Truth be told, I sometimes wondered about you and her. Ye were so close as children that I thought ye might develop a deeper bond when ye got to a certain age.'

He murmured something indistinct, growing warm despite his damp clothes.

'But it wasn't meant to be, once she was taken away. Arrah, it was a fanciful idea in any case, given your backgrounds. Nothing but a silly mother's daydream. Besides, she seems quite smitten with her Mr Lambourne.'

That was more than enough to bring his flight of imagination plummeting back to earth.

Maggie looked pensive. 'She's changed a great deal but I don't think she realises it herself. And I'm not talking about her pretty ringlets, I mean her demeanour. Did you notice? She's so elegant and composed now, a proper lady. The fiery girl we knew is gone.'

'Her mother finally got her claws into her,' he said with a bitter sense of loss for his best friend.

'It was bound to happen. Think about it from Bridget's point of view. 'Til she was twelve, she ran wild 'round the estate and her sole companion was a boy just as wild. When she went to the city, her companions became sophisticated girls who knew more than her about everything. It was only natural she'd feel out of place and turn to her mother to be taught how to fit in. Moving to Dublin must've changed their relationship altogether.'

'It changed her relationship with me too. If she'd stayed…'

Maggie let out a sigh. 'No one can say what would've happened if she'd stayed but it mightn't have been as straightforward as you believe. Her mother would've succeeded in interfering sooner or later. We all know she never approved of your friendship.' She paused. 'There's no place for you in her life anymore. You realise that, don't you?'

He turned his face away. 'I do.' He had already known it, and now both of their mothers had made it plain too.

Maggie got up from her rocking chair again and slid onto the bench next to him, taking his hand in hers. 'Sometimes special people are only meant to be part of our lives for a little while,' she said, and it seemed as though the shadows of her husband and her other son fell over the table. 'You'll get over this disappointment, I know it.'

For her sake, he said, 'I'm sure I will.' He kissed her on the cheek and stood. 'Goodnight, Ma.'

He crossed to the hearth. 'Come on, chicken,' he murmured and, hoisting his sleepy sister over his shoulder, carried her up to bed.

## Chapter 6

Bridget entered her father's study – now her mother's study, she supposed she must allow – to find Lord Walcott pacing before a pair of empty wingback chairs and Lady Courcey standing at the window, lines of tension in her shoulder blades.

'What's happened?' Bridget asked, on the alert at once.

Her mother turned and handed her a letter. 'Rathglaney.'

She skimmed the note with a degree of difficulty; it looked like it had been dashed off without scruples for ink smudges or punctuation. Its author, Lady Fitzwilliam, wrote that the Irish savages had committed the most unspeakable of acts and attacked their property and her husband's own person. Bridget's blood ran cold as the lady's message sank in. An uprising.

She looked up. Her mother's lips were so tight they had all but disappeared; it was a wonder she could still form words as she said, 'Lady Fitzwilliam felt the need to warn as many neighbouring estates as she could. Her advice is unambiguous: get out while we still can. As soon as Lord Fitzwilliam is recovered, they will leave the estate for good. They plan to go to Dublin or even London. Anywhere, so long as it's far away from these delinquents.'

Lord Walcott made a tutting sound. 'Another absentee landlord. It will ruin the Irish countryside.'

Lady Courcey turned an incredulous gaze upon her brother. 'You think *that's* the urgent issue?' She sniffed. 'I feel compelled to remind you that while you reside here you are an absentee landlord at Lockhurst Park in England.'

He inclined his head. '*Touché.*'

'Are you worried, Mother?' asked Bridget.

Lady Courcey deliberated before replying, 'I shall see what Mr Enright has to say on the subject first.'

The land agent was due to arrive any minute, with the ostensible purpose of discussing general estate matters, but everyone knew the topic on Lady Courcey's mind was the paying of the tithes. And now insurgent rebels could be added to the list.

Bridget's role was to make a written record of the proceedings, a dull task which she had offered to take on to ensure her presence at the meeting. She had just assembled her paper, pen and ink on a small table at the end of the large writing desk when a knock came at the door and Mr Laurence Enright was shown in. He gave off an odd air of brawny and bookish, with his muscular build and a pair of spectacles perched on his nose. She was pleased to see him – she fondly recalled how she and Cormac had dogged his heels while they went through a phase of play-acting as land agents, so much so that he had been obliged to shoo them away on more than a few occasions. His manner was serious but, when he acknowledged her, there was a twinkle in his eye that suggested he remembered those times too.

Lady Courcey settled behind the writing desk but Lord Walcott took a more discreet seat in one of the wingback chairs, deferring to the lady's reinstated authority. Bridget dipped her pen and Mr Enright commenced his delivery of a series of reports on the state of the accounts, the collection of rents and arrears, and improvements to estate property, with a meticulous memory for figures and details which could only impress. Even Lady Courcey had no reason to offer a single objection – until the agent asked her if she had any queries.

'Yes, indeed,' she said, her tone dangerously calm. 'I wish to discuss the matter of the tithes.'

Bridget had a suspicion that Lord Walcott had managed to forewarn Mr Enright because he didn't bat an eyelid.

'Which aspect of them do you wish to discuss, my lady?' he said.

'Their irrelevance. They are a church tithe and of no concern to this estate.'

He touched the bridge of his spectacles. 'It is true that the Church of Ireland reaps the benefits of the tithe collections. There is no monetary gain to Oakleigh by covering the tithes on the tenants' behalf.'

'My precise point,' said Lady Courcey, as though her argument had already been won.

'That is not to say there is no other form of gain, however,' he continued. 'This course of action has eased a burden on the tenants. Though they are by no means affluent, they do perceive themselves to be in a better position than their peers in neighbouring estates. I wouldn't go so far as to say they are happy, but their level of satisfaction has been enough to encourage a higher work rate and a deeper allegiance to this estate than might otherwise have been possible.'

Bridget tried to keep up with her note-taking while sneaking furtive glances at her mother. Lady Courcey had been looking smug but, after this last speech, her expression curdled.

'What evidence is there of that?' she bit out.

'I am in regular contact with other land agents who struggle to acquire rents and maintain order because their tenants continue to live under the rule of harsh, and often absentee, English landlords. The rebellion may have been quashed in 1798 but the fire that started it still burns in the people's hearts. However, there is no such disloyalty on the lands of Oakleigh, thanks to the payment of the tithes. Despite their lack of education, the folk comprehend the magnitude of the gesture.'

Lady Courcey had no response for this.

'It is my understanding that the tenants on the Rathglaney Estate were particularly hard done by. The Fitzwilliams supported the procurement of tithes by force if necessary, and in the past twelvemonth also instructed their agent to raise the rates of rent. It was beyond the people's capacity to tolerate such mistreatment. While I do not condone their behaviour, I do appreciate the cause of it.'

At this point, Mr Enright's work was done and it became clear that Lord Walcott and Bridget would have no need to contribute their own voices to the dispute. Lady Courcey was a shrewd woman; she perceived as well as anyone else in the room that the current situation was best, though a faint pink in her cheeks showed how annoyed she was to have been thwarted by unassailable logic.

And so the agent left the study with the instruction that the tithes arrangement should remain unchanged.

Lord Walcott, quietly exultant in victory, departed next to take his dogs for a walk, leaving the two ladies alone. Emboldened by the success of the meeting, Bridget decided it was time to act upon her own campaign of appeal. Following her visit to Maggie McGovern, an idea had taken root in her mind which she now wanted to put forth to her mother. It was difficult to gauge how the lady might react but she had proved once already today that she could be persuaded by rational motivation, if it was in Oakleigh's interest.

Lady Courcey had reached for the notes on Bridget's table and was perusing them with an attentive eye.

'Mother, may I have a word?'

Her mother lowered the pages. 'Yes?'

Bridget cleared her throat. 'I have been speaking with my uncle on matters of labourer appointments, in order to further my knowledge on the subject. While Oakleigh was his responsibility, he had to oversee the hiring of several new workers due to some unfortunate circumstances.' She swallowed. 'There were the two boys who died in the stable fire. A man drowned in the Sruhawn returning from trade at the horse fair in Tullow. And there have been numerous injuries at the quarry since it reopened which, while not life-threatening, have rendered some of the men incapacitated to work. I was wondering about these people and their families. Uncle Stuart said that no compensation was provided to them.'

'What of it?'

She bit the tip of her tongue. 'Don't you think there ought to be? These injuries and deaths happened to Oakleigh workers on Oakleigh land. It seems only fair that the estate recompense the victims or their families in acknowledgement of their sacrifice.'

'Most of those incidents happened a number of years ago. It is too late to offer remuneration now. Not to mention the people already enjoy the privilege of not being required to pay the infernal tithes.'

'Oakleigh's payment of the tithes does not equate to reparation for loss of life, and I don't believe the people would ever feel it was too late to receive what they justly deserve. I imagine their gratitude would spread to the other tenants, spurring them to work even harder for an estate that treats them with such benevolence. Oakleigh can only benefit from this deed.'

She was riding the coattails of Mr Enright's more eloquent reasoning but she didn't care so long as it achieved the result she desired.

Lady Courcey sat back in her chair. 'You advocate quite the resolute standpoint on this.'

Bridget made her voice light. 'You have been teaching me to develop the acumen of an astute landowner. This is the consequence of my education.'

There was a glint in the lady's eye and a rare lift at the corner of her mouth. 'Indeed. I am glad to witness it. I shall look into your proposal.'

'No need to trouble yourself with the details,' Bridget said quickly. 'Uncle Stuart has the records and I am certain I can put together the figures with his help. It should be a simple matter of signing your name to them.'

She only hoped her mother would not notice the name 'McGovern' on the list or her goodwill would evaporate in an instant.

## Chapter 7

June ended with two more days of rain but the first day of July brought a break in the wet weather. Determined not to waste the opportunity, Bridget entered the stables in her riding habit, where she received a warm greeting from John Corbett.

'Going for a ride, miss?'

'Yes,' she said and added, 'A proper one.'

He gave a chuckle of appreciation. Her last mounted excursion had been a sedate trot in the company of her mother, but today she intended to ride to the full extent of her capabilities. John had been her tutor when she had learned the skill as a girl and he had always said she was a natural on horseback.

He himself went to prepare Bonny for her. As she followed him into the stall, she cast a surreptitious glance around for Cormac but he was nowhere in sight. She felt disappointed; their last encounter had left her with an unsettled sensation, like there was more to be said between them.

'And where are you off to this afternoon?' John asked as he groomed her horse.

'I mean to seek out my old haunts,' she said. 'My favourite track will lead me to Ballydarry and then across the fields to the woods. I might even go as far as the quarry if I have enough time.'

'D'you require an escort? I can get young Liam Kirwan to accompany you if needs be.'

'Not at all. I am amply familiar with the terrain.'

'You know the quarry's in use again? Best stay out of the men's way as they'll be working with the rock. 'Tis a more dangerous place than the deserted hole you remember.'

'I shall take due care,' she promised.

His solicitousness was touching and it occurred to her that, had her mother not extracted her from the bosom of Oakleigh, John may well have become a father figure of sorts after her own father's death. Or, perhaps even more likely, that charge may have fallen to Jack McGovern. Moving to Dublin had consigned her to an exclusively female sphere of influence, when a masculine presence would have better suited her tomboyish nature. Still, she had to become a lady sometime.

Even as that thought crossed her mind, she trailed after John into the harness room and threw a longing look at the standard saddles hanging on the rack. However, she made no objection when John lifted up the sidesaddle, though he too seemed to regard it with a faint air of distaste. She hid a smile at their shared unconventional leanings.

After mounting, she bid him farewell and rode out of the courtyard, around the corner of the manor house and down the gravelled avenue. The recent rain had cleared the mugginess, creating the impression that the world had been soaked in a tub of water and left out to dry. Moisture dripped from the trees lining the avenue and the dusty gravel had been rinsed to a clean, dark grey. She gulped in mouthfuls of wholesome air with satisfaction. This experience was unattainable in Dublin, except maybe in the very heart of Phoenix Park.

Negotiating the lanes leading to Oakleigh's local village proved to be a challenge. The ground was muddy beneath Bonny's shoes and flooded in some parts, so they were forced to keep to a slower pace than Bridget had intended. She would have to save the thrill of the canter for the open fields and hope that the grass would not be too slippery.

Rounding a bend in the lane, she spotted two men on foot ahead of her. As she drew nearer, she discerned their uniforms and arms and realised they were members of the constabulary. They turned at the sound of Bonny's hoof beats and stepped to the side of the road at Bridget's approach. One looked old enough to be her father, the other so young as to barely merit the label 'man'.

'Afternoon, Miss Muldowney,' said the older constable. The younger one saluted, then seemed confused over whether he ought to have done so.

It didn't surprise her that they knew who she was; there was no other upper class family living in the immediate vicinity. What did surprise her was their presence. Hadn't Mr Enright only three days ago communicated that Oakleigh was a peaceful estate? Surely these constables would be better off occupying themselves on Rathglaney lands rather than strolling about the serene countryside here. She eyed their rifles and bayonets dubiously as she stopped to greet them.

'Good afternoon...' she said with an enquiring eyebrow.

'Constable Quirke at your service,' supplied the older man. 'And this is Constable Tierney. You appear to be alone, miss. May we have the pleasure of escorting you to your destination?'

'Thank you for your kind concern,' she said, 'but I would be loath to detain you from your duties.'

Whatever little they had to be doing. She offered them a civil nod and rode on.

Just a little way beyond, the road went into a gentle, downhill slope, which gave her a broad view of the village of Ballydarry. It was a small settlement – two streets meeting at a crossroads with a scattering of dwellings and a drinking house – but it was dominated by its pair of churches: St Canice's, the Church of Ireland establishment at the nearer edge of the village, and St Mary's, the Roman Catholic church further down by the crossroads. She had only ever attended Church of Ireland services in the past but Cormac had on a few occasions brought her into St Mary's and taught her some Irish prayers while they sat in the deserted pews.

She and Bonny proceeded into the village at an easygoing pace. All was quiet and she saw no people until she passed through the crossroads and approached the site of the drinking house. Here, a sign depicting a man wielding a pike swung above its door and three of its patrons lounged on a bench by the entrance. When they saw her coming, they nudged each other and straightened up.

'Fine day, miss,' one of them hollered.

'Fair one to be outdoors,' another agreed, jumping to his feet. He was the only one wearing a cap and he swept it off and down to his knees in an elaborate bow.

She smiled and halted. 'Indeed, it is so fresh after all the rain.'

The third man came up and rubbed Bonny's neck. 'She's a top quality beast. I'm quite the horse lover myself.'

'Only 'cause nothing else will lie with you,' the first man said with a throaty laugh.

The man with the cap gave him a whack on the arm. 'Manners, Joseph Hayes.'

Joseph shot Bridget an apologetic grin.

''Tis parched work, all that riding,' the man with the cap said. 'Will you quench your thirst before heading on? I can nip into The Pikeman and ask Bernie to bring you out something refreshing.'

'I'll wager he can find a carrot for this lovely lady too,' said the third man.

She had not been riding long enough to be especially thirsty but they seemed an amiable bunch – bawdy comment notwithstanding – and it would be an opportunity to engender further goodwill between the manor and its tenants.

'That would be very nice,' she said, dismounting and looping the long skirt of her riding habit over her wrist.

The fellow with the cap darted inside the drinking house. 'Bernie!' he bellowed. 'Can the young miss trouble you for a sup of water?'

As she finished tying Bonny to a post in front of the building, he returned with a balding man who was carrying the dirtiest glass she had ever seen, a brown-coloured liquid sloshing inside it. Was that supposed to be water? The Pikeman's proprietor offered it to her with an obsequious flourish and she accepted it without question, not wishing to offend, but resolved to only take the barest sip and then be on her way.

As she brought the glass to her lips, the man who described himself as a horse lover said, 'You going for a ride across all your land?'

She lowered the glass again, grateful to have avoided drinking the putrid-smelling water. 'I am. I do love the countryside.'

''Tis a fine piece of land. Solid, Irish soil, tilled by Irish hands for hundreds of years.'

This made her uncomfortable and she didn't say anything.

'Don't you think so?' he pressed.

'Y-yes, I agree.' She took a drink and it required all her willpower not to spit it back into the glass. It was grainy and sour. She swallowed with difficulty.

They all laughed.

'Can't believe she drank it,' Bernie said to the others. 'I only scooped it from the gutter out the back.'

She set the glass down on the bench; she hoped he was jesting but she wasn't going to touch it again.

Joseph levelled a narrow gaze at her. 'Aren't you going to pay for your drink?'

'I-I didn't bring any coins with me.'

He took a step closer – when had his hands become clenched into fists? 'That's typical of ye English folk. Take what ye want and give nothing for it.'

She stood her ground, though she felt intimidated by his nearness. 'I cannot imagine what you mean.'

His eyes flashed and there was a ripple of muttering from his companions. All three moved to stand next to him and this time she did step back. Fear swept over her; she wanted to flee from the situation right now.

'If you will excuse me –' she began but Joseph cut her off.

'You're not going anywhere just yet,' he said and reached out to grab her arm.

She filled her lungs to scream but, before she could expel the air, there was a bark of warning from the street and the two constables stood there, bayonets glinting.

'Let the young lady pass,' came a youthful voice – which contained only the barest trace of a waver – and the men surrounding her grumbled and fell away.

She hurried to the constables' side, feeling relief mixed with a measure of guilt. Mere minutes before she had believed them to be the objectionable party; now she was deeply thankful for their presence in the village.

Constable Quirke gestured with his bayonet and drove the irate patrons across the threshold of the drinking house, leaving the door ajar as he returned to Bridget.

'We'll deal with them in a moment, Miss Muldowney, and we apologise that they've troubled you,' he said, while Constable Tierney added, 'May one of us accompany you back to the manor house?'

She realised her fingers were trembling and interlaced them.

'Thank you, no,' she said. 'I plan to ride on. I would like to make it to the quarry and back before dinner time.'

The older constable frowned. 'With respect, I don't think that's wise. You've seen what the locals are like. You should return to the safety of the house.'

'I have never felt threatened on this estate,' she said, but a seed of doubt had been sown in her mind.

'Be that as it may, I believe we'll have to insist —'

'I can escort the young lady back, if she doesn't object.'

The three of them swivelled around and Bridget's heart thumped to see Cormac approaching. Where had he sprung from?

The younger constable set his jaw. 'She doesn't need the likes of you.'

'No, this is quite acceptable,' Bridget interjected. 'He is a stable hand at the manor. I am happy to return with him.'

She faced two expressions full of doubt.

'You've just seen how these peasants aren't to be trusted,' Constable Tierney said with an emphatic wave towards the drinking house door.

'I trust him.' They could malign the villagers, but she would brook no slur on Cormac's character. To hammer the point home, she held out her hand to him and he led her to where Bonny stood, boosted her into the saddle with her foot in his cupped hands, and untied the horse from the post.

The constables still looked dubious but made no further protest. As they turned back to the entrance of The Pikeman, she asked, with less success than the youngster at masking the quiver in her voice, 'What do you intend to do with them?'

'It will be a strong warning today,' said Constable Quirke, 'unless you wish to exact a harsher punishment…?'

Cormac gave her a sharp glance but refrained from asking any questions.

'That will not be necessary,' she said. 'My sincere thanks for your assistance.'

She directed Bonny down the street, setting a slow enough pace that Cormac could walk beside her, his hand loose on the reins. They were quiet for the length of time it took to go back through the village and reach the slope of the lane. Then he squinted up at her and said, 'What was that all about?'

She blew out her breath. 'I do believe I've had my first glimpse of just how much the Irish loathe the English.'

His countenance was grave. 'You stopped to talk to the fellows at The Pikeman?' She nodded and he clicked his tongue. 'What possessed you to do that? They're a rough bunch, for crying out loud. And if that was Joseph Hayes I spotted through the door, I can tell you he's the worst of the lot.'

Her hackles rose at his patronising manner. She knew her behaviour had been naïve but she didn't want him of all people to berate her about it. 'I have never had an uncivilised word from any of the locals in my life. How could I have anticipated such treatment?'

'Tell me what happened.'

She did, and watched his grip tighten on the reins until his knuckles grew white. He muttered something she didn't catch but she could guess its meaning.

'You think I was foolish.'

He didn't look at her. 'I do.'

'I don't see how what I did was so very wrong—'

He whipped his head around, eyes blazing. 'D'you have *any idea* what they might've done to you?'

It was the fear in his voice that made her falter. She swallowed. Despite her lack of education on such matters, she had enough imagination to envisage what four men could do to an unprotected woman. Her hands began to shake again and she had to take a few moments to compose herself before she could ask, 'Is this something I ought to have foreseen? The people were always kind to me in the past.'

His outburst over, he said evenly, 'You were a child then.'

'Why should that make a difference?'

''Cause becoming an adult means you're now held accountable.'

She felt injured at the insinuation. 'I have done nothing to hurt them.'

'You rule them, or at least your mother does. What they see is an English aristocrat who's going to inherit the land that's rightfully theirs. They hate you for that.'

She bridled, remembering Joseph's accusation. 'I consider myself as Irish as any of them! I was born on this land. My father was more Irish than English and you know it. He loved this country with every bone in his body. He gave me an Irish name, for heaven's sake!'

What her father had told her – on one of those cosy days when the rain had lashed the library windows and she had nestled in his lap by the fire to listen to him recount the native histories and legends – was that he had wanted to name her 'Brigid' after the Irish saint. Her mother had thought the spelling too ugly and they had compromised with 'Bridget'.

'Your mother's English through and through,' Cormac pointed out.

She tossed her head. 'So I am half and half. But I know which half is truer to me.' She glared down at him. 'Do you regard me as part of this reviled "English folk"?'

'Of course I don't,' he said, his denial so instant and earnest that she felt bad for having questioned him. 'And neither does anyone up at the big house. But I can't speak for every tenant on Oakleigh land, and definitely not for people like Joseph Hayes. You can make your arguments 'til you're hoarse, but they'll never hear what you say.'

She cogitated on that as they continued along the muddy lanes back to the manor. The meeting with Mr Enright had left her with the impression that circumstances at Oakleigh were almost idyllic in comparison to other estates. But unrest still existed and she had unwittingly exposed herself to it. Had the land agent glossed over the fouler details of the situation so as not to alarm her mother, or was he unaware of the extent of it himself? She understood the tenants' dislike of foreign invaders but could they not see that third and fourth generations of Anglo-Irish families, long settled on the land, were much more Irish than English?

The idea that this formed the basis of their resentment still nettled and she felt compelled to plead her case further. 'I can even speak some Irish. I learned bits of it from you when we were young.'

He was facing straight on but the corner of his mouth lifted. 'That's true. D'you recall any of it?'

Without hesitation, she launched into, '*Ár nAthair atá ar neamh, go naofar d'ainm, go dtaga —*'

'Fine, you remember the Our Father,' he broke in with a fleeting laugh. 'Well done to you. Best keep your voice down though. Irish isn't meant to be spoken 'round these parts.'

'It isn't? I thought my father revoked that edict.'

'Your mother restored it.'

That saddened her but her mind had already propelled forwards. 'Faith is another factor to contemplate. I am supposed to be a member of the Church of Ireland congregation, but sometimes I feel more connected to the Roman Catholic teachings. You acquainted me with their principles and I have found them to be a great comfort over the years.'

He looked sombre at this. 'That's a dangerous declaration to make in this country, coming from the people you do. It puts you in an awkward position. What religion will you rear your children in?'

'I-I don't know,' she mumbled.

The silence that descended between them was pregnant with many thoughts unspoken: the notion of having children, the whispers of how such things come about, the impending arrival of her fiancé to whom that future duty would fall…

Her cheeks flamed and, when she worked up the courage to look down at him, she saw that his had too.

She cast about for anything to say to end their discomfort. 'How did you happen to be in Ballydarry?'

His shoulders relaxed and he withdrew a little bottle from his pocket with his free hand. 'Mrs Kavanagh sent me to fetch some holy water from Father Macken. Not one of my usual tasks but John allowed me. We all know how worried she is about her sister.'

'Her sister?'

'She lives on Rathglaney land. Her husband and son were involved in the uprising and arrested afterwards. Mrs Kavanagh's praying their lives will be spared.'

Their conversation had come full circle. She glanced over her shoulder even though the village was now a long way behind them. 'Oh,' she said nervously.

He gave her a look of reassurance. 'Nothing like that'll come to pass at Oakleigh. Fellows like Hayes are all bluster and no action.'

Her teeth nipped the tip of her tongue. 'Didn't you just tell me how much jeopardy I was in at the drinking house?'

'That's 'cause they cornered you on your own. But no large scale revolt's likely to happen. Those men would never get a majority of the tenants behind them.'

'Do you really believe that?'

'Absolutely. I said the same thing to my ma. You've nothing to fear.'

She couldn't tell whether he meant it or was just trying to assuage her misgivings. Either way, his words of conviction appeased her, but she felt a sudden yearning for him to assure her with a tight squeeze of her hand.

His grip remained firm on the reins.

## Chapter 8

On a normal day, the sweet smell of the hay barn brought pleasure to Cormac, but he was so incensed at the present moment that he didn't even notice it as he stamped in to gather a stack of hay for the stables. Twenty-four hours had been insufficient to allay his anger towards Bridget.

Her carelessness and gullibility frightened him. Suppose the constables hadn't come by? Or they had been ten minutes later? He was aghast to think that he himself had been dallying in the church across the road while the men had had her trapped. True, what he knew of Joseph Hayes was enough to admit the man probably didn't have the guts to risk inflicting real harm on the heiress to the Oakleigh Estate – death or transportation would have been the consequence. Still, someday his hatred might push him too far and, had there not been others at hand to intervene, yesterday could have been that day.

As Cormac left the barn, carrying the stack of hay and still grumbling about idiocy and naïveté, Liam came running up to him with the message that Mrs Walsh wanted to see him in the kitchens. He deposited the hay in one of the stable stalls in a hurry; the housekeeper was not a woman to be kept waiting.

Inside the kitchens, the familiar blast of heat was accompanied by Mrs Kavanagh's voice raised in fury. Bronagh stood before her with a mutinous scowl and a burnt pot. The cook seemed ready to explode but all of a sudden her face crumpled and she buried Bronagh in a big-bosomed hug.

'I'm taking my worries out on you, that's all. Bless your heart, you're a good girl. Go and wash that now, won't you?'

Bronagh looked dumbfounded as she scuttled into the scullery.

Mrs Walsh ignored the commotion and crooked a finger at Cormac.

'I have a number of carpentry duties for you to attend to.' She read the items out from a list in her hand. 'Three of the legs have cracked on a chair in Lord Walcott's bedchamber.'

The barest of pauses allowed Cormac to surmise that it was his lordship's substantial weight which had caused the chair legs to fail.

'There are two stools reported broken in the servants' quarters. And a bookshelf has collapsed in the library. The stools and the chair will be sent out to the barns for you to mend but the shelf will have to be repaired where it is. I shall alert you to an appropriate time when you can work in the library and not disturb the family.'

A footman came marching through the inner kitchen door, then stood to attention when he caught sight of the housekeeper. "Scuse me, Mrs Walsh, Mr Buttimer sent me to fetch a stable hand. He needs one to come 'round to the front door right away.'

'Very well, Denis, I have one here.'

Denis looked pleased that his task had been accomplished so expediently when Mrs Walsh nodded at Cormac and said, 'Off you run.'

Cormac left the kitchens and trotted around the side of the house. When he reached the front, he saw Mr Buttimer standing at the bottom of the steps and bowing to a gentleman who had just dismounted from his horse. He did not recognise the tall, black-haired rider, but he guessed instantly from his handsome face and fine clothes who he must be.

Mr Buttimer caught sight of Cormac and beckoned to him. 'Look after the gentleman's horse, quick now.'

Mr Garrett Lambourne handed the reins to Cormac without even glancing at his face.

'My valet will follow shortly with the baggage,' he said to Mr Buttimer. 'Are the ladies home?'

'They are in the drawing room, sir, along with Lord Walcott. I shall announce your presence at once, if you will follow me. And might I be the first to extend you a warm welcome to Oakleigh Manor which, you may not know, has stood on this spot for four generations under the Courcey title and has been served, I am proud to say, by two generations of the Buttimer family...'

Prattling on, the butler led Mr Lambourne up the steps, leaving Cormac behind with the horse's reins in his fist and a boulder's weight in the pit of his stomach.

***

A dreary silence presided over the drawing room. Lady Courcey was perched in a straight-backed chair reading a book, while Lord Walcott had given up all pretence at decorum and lay snoozing on the sofa, his chin drooping on his chest. Bridget would have liked to play the piano, but that was not an option, given the situation of her companions. Instead, she had her latest correspondence gathered in her lap – letters from her friends in Dublin and from Garrett. These ought to have cheered her up but she was too distracted, still thinking of the danger she had narrowly sidestepped. There was no question of her telling her mother about the incident at The Pikeman; they would be in a carriage back to the city before she could insist, 'It's not the same as Rathglaney!' Lady Courcey needed no further encouragement to dislike and distrust the Irish. And on that note...

'Mother,' she said, in a low tone so as not to disturb the sleeping giant, 'is it true that the ban on speaking Irish around the estate has been reinstated?'

Lady Courcey's gaze remained on her page but her mouth tightened. 'It is.'

'May I ask why?'

The lady set her book down with an exasperated sigh. 'You are so like your father.'

A familiar sense of loss tugged at Bridget's heart. 'I don't see how that is such a bad thing.'

'It is only bad when I perceive how you share the same unfathomable blindness for that race.' Bridget expected her to stop there, shutting down as she always did when Lord Courcey was mentioned, but she carried on, 'Angus believed their primitive traditions should be preserved. It was a foolish notion. He refused to recognise that only by relinquishing such customs as that uncouth language could the creatures begin to improve themselves.'

Bridget doubted her mother was motivated by an urge to improve the Irish people; more likely, she didn't appreciate the idea of the tenants talking in a tongue she couldn't understand – after all, they might insult her to her face and she would never know.

It saddened Bridget to see how bitter her mother had become. Though always somewhat reserved in nature, she nonetheless had had a capacity for affection when Bridget was young that she hardly ever revealed now. Of course, it was easy to pinpoint when that change had happened.

In some ways, the memories were a blur to Bridget, and yet a few details stood out in stark definition. Her father's look of surprise as his horse stumbled crossing a brook and lost its footing. The horrifying crack of his head connecting with an unseen rock below the water's surface. The lack of movement in his chest when she laid her ear to it, an action she had performed countless times before to listen to his heartbeat.

She could still remember the overwhelming force of her mother's grief, the way she had crumpled at the sight of her husband's body and clutched at his hands, his face, his clothes, begging him not to abandon her. In a defiant snub to society convention, she had attended both the service and the burial, by which stage all emotion had been wiped from her countenance.

Bridget could not blame her mother for feeling bitter; she too had raged at the injustice of losing her father. But she now had a fiancé with whom she planned to share her life, while her mother still faced the coming decades alone. Had she ever considered remarrying?

Unsure whether she had the courage to voice these thoughts aloud, Bridget deemed it fortunate that Mr Buttimer chose that moment to enter the drawing room.

'My lady, Miss Muldowney, Mr Garrett Lambourne has arrived.'

Her gasp burst from her with such volume that Lord Walcott shot to wakefulness with an indignant, 'What the devil —!'

She twisted around towards the door. 'Really, Buttimer? You are being serious?'

'I pride myself in the assertion that I never joke, miss.'

And there was Garrett, striding in with a broad smile.

'You're here!' She leapt to her feet and, fighting the urge to run to him, clasped her hands together in joy.

Her mother rose with more restraint. 'You are welcome to Oakleigh, Mr Lambourne.'

'Thank you,' he said, bowing with the deepest courtesy. 'I was delighted to accept your invitation to visit.'

He approached Bridget and kissed her hand. When his hazel eyes met hers, she felt her insides dissolve and, not for the first time, marvelled that such an eligible bachelor had chosen her when he could have had his pick of any fashionable lady in London.

Lord Walcott laboured into an upright position with the least alacrity and grace of them all and the necessary introductions were made. After Mr Buttimer departed from the room in response to a summons for tea and biscuits, Garrett took a seat with the others, settling his long frame into a chair with ease.

'We did not expect you for another week at least,' said Bridget. Even though his most recent letter had communicated that he was back in the country, she had been certain a respite in Dublin would have delayed his coming.

'I must apologise for not forewarning of my arrival. I found I had not the patience to wait one moment longer to make the journey and I was in such a hurry to leave the city that I quite forgot to write ahead.'

'No apology is necessary,' said Lady Courcey. 'We judge it to be our good fortune that you have come earlier than anticipated. How was Dublin on your return from England?'

'Quiet. With the social season over, many families have retired to their country estates, in the same manner as yourselves.' He turned to Bridget. 'I happened upon Miss Madeleine Wallace in Merrion Square before I left. She told me in the most spirited language that she positively pines for you. Her family did not remove to the country on account of her mother's infirmity and she is finding the summer interminable without the company of her dearest friend.'

Bridget smiled; she could almost hear Madeleine's animated voice declaring the immensity of her loneliness. 'She disclosed the same to me in her letter. Perhaps I ought to invite her down for a visit.'

'I do believe she would kiss your shoes if you did.'

At this point, Lord Walcott, in an obvious attempt to take the measure of Garrett, asked, 'Do you like dogs?'

'Indeed, I do. I was the proud master of a faithful mastiff in my youth and my father owns the fastest pack of foxhounds in Hertfordshire.'

Lord Walcott gave a rumble of approval. 'Always happy to be acquainted with someone who appreciates animals.' The faintest sniff in his sister's direction might have been construed as an accusation but she elected to ignore it.

Garrett seemed to detect the antagonism but he hid his amusement with a good-natured nod and said, 'Dogs and horses, I've the greatest respect for both. I'm looking forward to some excellent riding on this estate.'

This prompted Bridget to experience an unexpected surge of nerves – how would Cormac react to Oakleigh's new guest?

***

'Oh, he's wonderful,' Margaret breathed. She and Bronagh were standing at the back door of the kitchens, receiving armfuls of kindling from their brother – the remains of Lord Walcott's damaged chair which could not be salvaged and would now serve best as fuel for the kitchen fire. 'He's simply…wonderful.'

'How have ye met him?' Cormac demanded.

'He's come down a couple of times after dinner to compliment Mrs Kavanagh on her cooking. 'Tis cheered her up no end. She's been weak at the knees ever since.'

Margaret pushed the door open wider so Cormac could catch a glimpse of the cook who appeared somewhat dazed as she rolled out dough on the kitchen table.

'And he took the time to thank each of the maids for doing such great work. Even Bronagh melted when he looked at her.'

Bronagh turned bright red and grabbed the firewood in an embarrassed huff.

Cormac thought it was just girls being girls. But John Corbett seemed almost as besotted.

'There's nothing the man doesn't know about horse breeding,' he said in awe. 'His knowledge is near greater than my own.'

If anyone could find fault, it would be Fintan Kelly. Cormac heard that the cantankerous gardener had become involved in a conversation with Mr Lambourne about the quality of the garden shrubs and tried to casually extract from Fintan how the exchange had gone.

Keeping a watchful gaze upon Malachy, who was being forced to trim the privet hedge with the precision of a surgeon, the old man gave an irritable cough at Cormac's enquiry, screwed up his rheumy eyes, and said, 'He's a nice chap.'

It seemed Mr Lambourne could do no wrong.

***

Bridget felt quite satisfied with her situation. She had secured an offer of marriage at the age of nineteen while many of her female companions, some several years older than her, were still unattached. She was marrying for love and not for status or wealth, although it was useful that she would gain both nonetheless. Her fiancé had amply demonstrated his charm and generous spirit by requiring a mere three days to endear himself to the full complement of family and staff at Oakleigh. It was all rather magnificent, she concluded, pushing open the green orchard door and leading Garrett into the shade beneath the apple trees.

Which made it all the more perplexing that she experienced a hiccup of misgiving as she passed under the archway.

Endeavouring to ignore it, she announced, 'This is my favourite place in the whole of Oakleigh, in the whole world,' and waved her arm in an expansive arc. Great quantities of ripening fruit hung from the branches above them; come autumn, they would fill Mrs Kavanagh's delicious apple tarts.

Garrett shook his head in amusement. 'I had no idea you were such a country girl. In Dublin you seemed happy to do nothing more than wear a pretty dress and take to the dance floor.'

That gave her pause. There had never been much occasion during their acquaintance to speak of her love for nature and the outdoors, and now his view of her as a city lady cloaked this entire aspect of herself.

'Do you like the countryside?' she asked. Apart from his early boyhood, he had resided for most of his life in London.

'I do, and I like it all the better because you are in it.' He inhaled deeply. 'I once knew a girl who said she only felt alive in two ways, and one of them was breathing the fresh, country air.'

'What was the other?'

He cleared his throat in a significant manner.

She coloured at the brazen implications of this response. 'Who was the girl?'

'You're not jealous, are you?'

She had had no inkling that he had courted another before her. Considering he was on the brink of his twenty-sixth birthday, it might have been naïve of her to assume she was his first courtship, but it still came as a shock. 'Where is she now?'

A shadow fell across his face but he grasped both of her hands and widened his eyes to convey his sincerity. 'She was nothing to me. A lump of coal compared to your bright star.'

She deliberated over whether to probe the issue further but decided against it. Whatever company he had kept before he met her was no concern of hers; she had no entitlement to that knowledge. She detached herself with a courteous smile and led the way along the path until they reached the clearing with the oak tree. Here, her discomfort increased and, to her consternation, she began to suspect the reason why. She wanted to pass through the clearing with all possible haste but he halted at the sight of the tree.

'My word,' he said, 'what an enormity.'

He stepped closer to the trunk and her heart seized at the thought of him discovering the carved initials. They were not for him to see – they belonged to her and Cormac alone. She tried to guide him on but he stopped her with a gentle tug on her wrist.

'I am glad to finally get you on your own, my darling, and in such an idyllic setting. I have been beyond impatient to give you this.'

He reached into his pocket and produced a small jewellery box. Dismayed that he had chosen this spot for the act, all she could do was utter a soft, 'Oh!' and apply the expected bashful expression to her features.

He went down on one knee with complete disregard for the leaf litter, opened the box and held it out to her, revealing an enormous ruby surrounded by a circle of pearls. It was perhaps a trifle ostentatious for her taste but she felt flattered that he would spend so much on her. She accepted the ring and murmured her admiration, angling her hand to catch the light in the gemstone.

He rose and, pulling her close, bent his head towards hers.

This was their first full kiss since he had come to Oakleigh but his lips felt alien upon hers. Guilt swept over her as she realised she was not overjoyed to receive the attentions of her handsome fiancé.

She ought to be thinking of that unforgettable moment when she glimpsed him across a heaving ballroom, of Madeleine Wallace's observation that he couldn't seem to take his eyes off her, and of the touch of his hand while he led her in the dance.

Instead, her mind insisted upon calling forth a memory wholly unrelated to the man embracing her.

She had not thought there could be anything more wretched than burying her beloved father in the cold earth, but the hours following his funeral had brought the worst news imaginable – her immediate departure from Oakleigh with no prospect of returning. Right below this very oak tree, she had flung herself into Cormac's arms and sobbed, 'How can she be so *cruel*?'

The flow of her tears could not be stemmed until he had assured her they would remain friends forever and suggested they carve their initials into the tree trunk to seal that promise. With a watery smile, she had agreed and he had taken out the rusty pocket knife that was his most treasured possession. He had scratched her initials and she his, and then they had regarded each other with the solemnity of imminent parting.

'I might not see you again before I go,' she had said. 'I screamed at Mama before I ran off. I'm going to be in a lot of trouble when I go back.'

'Stay for another minute,' he had pleaded and, impulsively, he had stepped forwards and kissed her lips.

Shy in his presence for the first time in her life, she had kissed him back before flying away through the orchard.

And, regardless of their positions now, she comprehended that she could kiss no one other than Cormac beneath the branches of this oak.

She broke from the kiss and took a nonchalant step away from Garrett, backing towards the tree trunk to conceal the carved initials from view.

'Shall we return now?' she managed to say calmly, even though her pulse pounded. 'We could go for a walk in the gardens.'

With an amiable nod, he offered her his arm and led her back the way they had come. Her shoulders slumped with relief as they left the clearing.

She would not bring him to the orchard again.

## Chapter 9

Upon receiving another summons from Mrs Walsh, Cormac reported to the kitchens with his father's tool chest.

'You can come up now,' the housekeeper said, motioning him towards the door that led above stairs. 'I have informed the family that they should avoid the library for the afternoon.'

He followed her from the kitchens, up a narrow stairs and out into the massive entrance hall. The splendour of the big house never ceased to fill him with awe, from its high ceilings to the striking paintings on its walls, but what drew his gaze the most was the imposing mahogany staircase which swept up to the floor above them, a stark contrast to the modest ladder in the McGovern home.

When they entered the library, he experienced a brief wave of nostalgia as he remembered all the reading and writing lessons, Bridget looking over his shoulder while he wrote out his name on a slate in large, shaky letters. 'No,' her imperious voice drifted to him from the past, 'you need to do the R again...'

It was easy to see where his skills were needed; one of the shelves in a bookcase by the fireplace had buckled under the weight of its heavy books and collapsed into the shelf below it, which in turn was starting to bend under the extra load. A number of the books had toppled out onto the floor and the original shelf was in two splintered halves.

'I'll need to make at least one new shelf, maybe two,' he said. 'I can do that out in the barns and then bring them in here to fit them.'

'Make sure you're as quick as you can about it. And just set the books to one side. They will need to be put back alphabetically on the shelves once you are done. I can arrange them later.'

'That's fine,' he said, shrugging. 'I can read. I'll sort them.'

She raised her eyebrows and left without comment, her keys jangling.

After measuring the length and width of the shelves, he went out to the barns to unearth any pieces of wood which could serve his purpose. Aside from storage for hay, the barns represented a repository for all kinds of detritus from the stables and the house which had accumulated over time. Enough old furniture had been discarded there that, by the time two hours had passed, he had located, sawed and planed two boards of the right colour into suitable shelves for the bookcase. He hefted them onto his shoulder and carried them back to the house.

Re-entering the kitchens, he discovered Malachy Kelly lounging against the table, chatting rather cosily with a couple of the kitchen maids. The cook was nowhere to be seen.

'Where's Mrs Kavanagh?' Cormac asked the maids.

'Got a letter and ran off,' one said and the other added, 'Bet it was news about her sister's family. She looked fierce upset.'

'They've probably been hanged,' said Malachy in an offhand manner.

Speculating whether he could knock the boards into the back of the lad's head and pass it off as an accident, Cormac chose the path of temperance and settled for a sharp warning about getting back to work; raised in a home where hard graft was a chief principle of life, he couldn't stand to see such idleness. But Malachy merely gave him an impudent grin and returned his attention to the maids. At least Cormac could be thankful that neither was his sister.

Back in the library, he fixed the new bookshelves in place. He was in the process of returning the books to their proper positions, savouring the smell of them as he did so, when he heard the door open. Presuming it was Mrs Walsh coming to tell him to hurry up, he turned to say he was almost done but shut his mouth again when he saw Bridget in the doorway.

'Oh,' she said, 'I wasn't aware there was anyone in here. I came to fetch some of my piano music.' She gestured towards a bookcase against the opposite wall but made no move to approach it.

He nodded and continued with his task. Not all of the long words on the book covers were recognisable to him but he knew his alphabet well enough to arrange the volumes as Mrs Walsh wished.

When Bridget spoke again, she offered an uninspiring, 'It is a very fine day.'

'"Tis,' he said, even though rain had spattered the window panes not ten minutes earlier.

'Have you met Garrett yet?' she asked suddenly.

He cleared his throat. 'I'd the pleasure of seeing to his horse on his arrival.'

'Oh. And not since then?'

He shook his head.

'I believe we are planning a ride across the estate in the coming days so I expect you will encounter him in the stables then.'

'I expect I will.'

After another short silence, she burst out, 'I do hope you will like him.'

He couldn't hide his surprise. 'I don't think I'm meant to have an opinion on him.'

She tugged self-consciously at a chestnut curl dangling at her neck. 'Your opinion matters to me.'

How was he supposed to respond to that? This sort of talk far overstepped the boundary he had established between them that day in the orchard. However, he could not help but see that Bridget's fiancé was a decent man and she was fortunate to be marrying him. Not to mention any servant would be only too delighted to be in his employment, judging by his benevolent conduct to those beneath him.

Taking a quick breath, Cormac stooped to pick up another book and said, 'By all accounts, he sounds like a respectable fellow. I'm happy for you.'

'Are you really?'

'Of course. Couldn't be happier.' He fixed his gaze on the book's spine, which displayed an author's surname beginning with D-I. That would follow D-E then. 'I hope ye'll be happy together.' He needed to stop saying that damned word.

After slotting the book into place, he met her eyes and found them wide and startled. Her lips had parted too but she closed them in a hurry.

'Th-thank you,' she said, 'that is very kind. And I wish you every happiness as well.'

She began to turn back to the door so he reminded her, 'Better fetch your music.'

She reddened and dug out a sheaf of sheet music from the bottom shelf of the opposite bookcase. 'Good day to you, Cormac.'

With that formal farewell, she left him alone in the library, where a faint scent of lilac now floated in the air.

***

Bridget sat in a haze of consternation at the dining table, taking no notice of the discourse passing between her mother, uncle and fiancé. Her thoughts were entrenched in the library, agonising over her encounter with Cormac.

What had induced her to go there? When Mrs Walsh had made it known at luncheon that the library should be avoided while the carpenter worked in it for a few hours, she ought to have accepted the housekeeper's recommendation without question, except that some strange impulse had driven her to fabricate a reason to call by. And then she had spoken to him about Garrett.

It was conceited of her to even entertain the idea. She should not make any assumptions. And yet, his cheeks had coloured, and he had avoided her gaze, and his shoulders had hunched when he had described her fiancé as a respectable fellow…

Heavens above, did he *like* her?

If he did, then her blathering on about meeting Garrett must have been cruel for him to endure. It would also explain why he had been so eager to end familiar contact between them after he learned of her engagement. An interest on his part would have made any acquaintance with her a hundred times more inappropriate.

She didn't know what to think, if she was right. Had she suspected sooner… No, she couldn't permit herself to imagine what alternative scenario might have taken place. Her future was with Garrett and there was no going back from that.

She tried to picture Cormac's future. He would remain as a stable hand on the estate for certain, but it was a good, honest placement and perhaps he might become stable master one day. Conceivably, he'd find a nice girl who would make a good wife for him. At this, she felt a pang which she did her best to overlook. Yes, he would wed and have children, and she would make her own family too, and in the years to come they would meet in passing around the manor grounds and exchange a smile as they recollected the friendship they had once shared.

That would have to be satisfactory for them both.

The removal of the second course dishes drew her attention back to the discussion around the table. Lord Walcott was reminiscing about fox hunting, a pastime which he had enjoyed in his younger and, Bridget presumed, slimmer days.

'There is nothing like the thrill of the hunt,' he declared. 'The chase, the baying of the hounds, the bolt of the fox. There can be no greater pleasure for a man in a rural situation.'

'It's a shame we're not in the season for it,' said Garrett. 'I feel I must seize every opportunity to enjoy these outdoor pursuits while I am in the country. After all, there's no possibility of going hunting in the centre of London!'

'Still, London has its attractions too,' said Lady Courcey.

'Many and varied,' he agreed. 'But it's refreshing to get away from the busy city, even just for a month or two. I do enjoy the peace and quiet here. I'll be sorry to leave when the time comes.'

Bridget attempted to follow the direction of this conversation with difficulty. What was Garrett implying with such comparisons?

'London?' she said, injured that this was the first time she was hearing about this. 'Are you planning to go back again?'

He smiled at her. 'Do not fret. You won't be left behind this time. I promise not to go without my wife.'

At least that meant he would not be leaving until sometime after they were married. Still perplexed, she said, 'Surely you have no wish for me to come along while you conduct your business affairs?'

He chuckled. 'No, indeed, I expect you will be tending to housekeeping matters in our home instead.'

His words struck her like a blow to the chest.

'Do you mean to say that we shall move to London after we marry?' she said in disbelief.

'Of course,' he said, as if it were the most obvious thing in the world.

'You never told me—!' she began but got no further as her mother cut across her.

'Speaking of outdoor pursuits,' the lady said with a touch more volume than normal, 'I wonder whether it will be fine enough for an outing tomorrow. We have been sorely lacking in sunny weather since your arrival, Mr Lambourne, and you are no doubt eager to see more of the estate.'

As Garrett responded with enthusiasm, she threw a quelling look at her daughter and Bridget refrained from saying anything else, though her thoughts had been flung into chaos. He could not have meant what he had said, could he? He had never given her the faintest inkling that he intended for them to live in London after their wedding. Her mind reeled at the prospect.

She volunteered no further contribution to the chat during the meal and maintained her silence when she and her mother retired to the drawing room afterwards. However, once the men came to join them she availed of the first opportunity to snatch a moment with her fiancé, stepping up to him by the mantelpiece where he was enjoying his glass of brandy. Lady Courcey and Lord Walcott were absorbed in their own dialogue on the sofa and would not overhear.

'Garrett, I am a little confused by an allusion you made at dinner,' she said, keeping her words measured. This may all have been a misunderstanding; she did not want to start off in an accusatory fashion.

He looked puzzled. 'An allusion to what?'

'To London. Did you speak in earnest when you said that we shall be going there once we are married?'

'Naturally. What is the matter, my darling? You are very pale.'

'You have never mentioned this before,' she said, her voice tight. 'Why must we go to London?'

He laughed. 'You didn't think we would be staying in this country, did you?'

'What reason had I to think otherwise?'

He was about to laugh again but checked himself when he saw that she was being serious. 'It would not be very practical to live in Ireland when my affairs must be managed in England.'

'But you have some property in Kildare. That is why you and Lord Wyndham came to Ireland and how we became acquainted with each other. Will you not need to be present to oversee it?'

He waved the point away. 'That estate is small and supervised by an agent. The majority of my father's assets and property is in London and thus it is by far the more pertinent place to be.'

'Can you not conduct your business from Dublin?' she appealed, desperation mounting within her. She had envisaged them dwelling here at Oakleigh once it became hers, but she would accept taking up residence in Dublin if London was to be the only alternative. 'We could stay there during the winter and just come back to the countryside for the summer months.'

'My father already relies on me to assist in the running of his estate and my involvement will only continue to increase. Soon I shall be required in London constantly. It would not be realistic to expect me to travel back and forth all the time.'

She said nothing.

'Darling, we have to be sensible. Of course we shall come back to visit, but our primary residence must be where I need to be.'

'And what about where I need to be?'

He frowned. 'What do you mean by that?'

Taking a controlled breath, she said, 'There are two of us in this relationship. Did you consider consulting me in this decision at all?'

He looked taken aback by her frankness. 'It is not a woman's place to dictate such matters.'

'But I am to inherit Oakleigh. As a baroness, my seat will be here and it will be my responsibility to see to my estate and tenants.'

'That Enright fellow will look after all that. Many rural estates in this country no longer have the owner in residence. And if there are matters to attend to, I can correspond with Mr Enright from London, so you don't need to worry about them. Not to mention, your mother will still need a place to live. If she chooses not to remain in Dublin, we couldn't very well eject her from this house.' He phrased this quite delicately but his expression conveyed that he had no desire to share a home with Lady Courcey on a permanent basis.

'Please take my viewpoint into account,' she pleaded. 'Ireland is my home. I would be aggrieved to leave Dublin, of course, but Oakleigh most of all. My seven years in the city, while pleasurable in their own way, have only served to remind me of how attached I am to the fields and the woods and the fresh air. I would be stifled in London.'

'I do not want to hear any more arguments. It will not be possible for us to stay in Ireland after we are married, is that clear?'

She was shocked into silence. Those were the first harsh words he had ever spoken to her.

Sighing, he took her gloved hand. 'I am sorry. I did not mean to be unkind. But you do understand, don't you?'

She nodded numbly.

He pressed a kiss to her knuckles and said, 'We ought to rejoin your mother and uncle now.'

He turned away from her and took a chair opposite Lord Walcott. After a dazed moment, she resumed her own seat, her hand cold inside its glove.

# Chapter 10

As though Lady Courcey had conjured it, the sun nestled in a blanket of blue the next morning, promising a long, hot July day. Bridget and Garrett, confined to the manor grounds for days by unsettled weather, welcomed it with eagerness. They had already formulated a scheme for an opportunity such as this and now put it into effect, sending messages to the kitchens for a picnic basket to be assembled and to the stables for their horses to be prepared.

Bridget meant to show Garrett as many corners of the estate as she could. Her original intention had simply been to display the splendour of Oakleigh but her new motive would be to convince him that such splendour could not be abandoned for stuffy London. She would demonstrate just how content she was in the bosom of the lush countryside; with luck, this form of persuasion would help bring him around to her way of thinking. If he loved her enough, he would wish to do everything in his power to make her happy.

There was no question of them going off for a whole day unaccompanied. They had arranged that Garrett's valet, Brewer, would act as chaperone but it was solely for the sake of etiquette; Garrett was too much of a gentleman to take advantage of her in some isolated copse. Brewer would follow them at an unobtrusive distance and his immediate presence would only be needed to lay out the picnic and see to the horses when they stopped to rest.

After breakfast, Bridget dressed in her riding habit and went out to the courtyard. The horses stood waiting – Bonny, Garrett's own mount, named Commander, and an anonymous third for their chaperone – and a bulging picnic basket sat on the cobbles, appearing to contain enough food for ten people embarking upon a three-day expedition. Garrett, checking over Commander's tackle with a discerning eye, turned at her approach.

'Regrettable news, my darling,' he announced. 'Brewer's unwell. Doubled up in bed with stomach ache and headache and no doubt an ache in his elbow too. Sickly creature, he always falls ill at the most inconvenient times.'

This flippant comment, delivered with a grin, indicated that the valet was not at death's door and she need not be concerned over his continued existence. What did demand concern was the likelihood of their outing.

'Does this mean we cannot go today?' she asked, dismayed at the idea of missing out on such fine weather and the chance to champion Oakleigh at its very best.

'Fear not, I have succeeded in obtaining a substitute. The stable master said he could spare one of his hands for the day.'

'How generous of him,' she said, her dismay by no means allayed. Her luck could not be that bad, could it? Please, anyone but...

Cormac trudged out of the stables.

Her body reacted strangely at the sight of him, her stomach dropping even as her heart pumped in an erratic manner. He gave a polite nod in her direction but didn't quite make eye contact, busying himself with securing the picnic basket to the third horse. All joy at the prospect of a day-long ride leaked out of her. Already, she wanted it to be over. Could she fabricate a plausible reason to delay it to another day? No, her effusion at breakfast over the magnificent sunshine foiled that possibility. And it would cast a shadow upon Cormac's good name if she requested an alternative stable hand without explanation. They were ensnared by the circumstances.

Garrett offered a gallant hand to Bridget to assist her in mounting and then swung up onto his own horse.

'Onwards to freedom and adventure,' he said with a jovial flourish and led the way out of the courtyard, failing to perceive that his zeal met with silence.

As soon as they reached the Gorteen, Cormac allowed his mount to fall behind, giving Bridget and Garrett space and the semblance of privacy. This did little to ease her discomfort, knowing they were still in his line of sight. She hoped Garrett would not attempt to express even the barest sign of affection during the day; there would be no recovery from the mortification.

For a time, she considered feigning an ache of her own, or even boredom, but neither would serve the purpose of endearing her fiancé to the charms of the surrounding land. So, with an effort, she perked up and started pointing out notable landmarks. Perhaps she could impress him with her knowledge of crops and herds and fallow land, making him realise how suited she was to be in charge here. He did not need to know her education had been a recent acquirement.

She fell quiet as they entered the field with the giant's claw; this was one landmark she had no wish to elaborate upon. She tried to accelerate their pace but the rocky outcrop caught his attention.

'What an unusual formation. It looks rather like three curved fingers, don't you think?'

'Mmm,' she said.

'Come now, we passed an unremarkable hedgerow back there and you were able to tell me its entire history from planted seed. Surely you have a story behind this?'

'It is known as the giant's claw,' she said unwillingly. 'The locals named it. I don't know much beyond that.'

'The locals?' He flicked a glance over his shoulder. 'Do you think our companion might know more?'

She flinched. 'Oh, I doubt it. The knowledge of it likely belongs to an older generation.'

'And don't the Irish live by their storytelling? Let's try him.'

They had paused in their progress across the field, which meant Cormac had halted some distance further back. He was not looking at them directly but could not fail to notice when Garrett gesticulated and called, 'You there!'

He trotted up to them, a slight crease between his brows. 'Yes, sir?'

Garrett motioned to the rocky shape towering above them. 'Can you tell us anything of the history of this? I imagine it has a colourful past in the indigenous folklore. Perhaps it marks the site of one of your famed fairy forts?'

Cormac cast a fleeting look at Bridget and she tried to communicate her apology with her eyes. Garrett could not know how inappropriate his curiosity was.

Expression shuttered, Cormac returned his gaze to the other man. 'It has a more recent past than you'd suppose, sir, and one grislier than fairies. It played a part in the rebellion of '98.'

'Did it, indeed?' Garrett said, leaning forward. 'In what way?'

'It was used as a rallying point for the local Carlow rebels. The leaders met here to pass on information and gather arms. Sometimes they buried them in the ground at its base.'

Garrett stared down with interest, as though expecting to see indications of the churned soil disturbed thirty years ago.

'But there was an informant. The men assembled on the eve of one of the battles and were ambushed by English forces. They were hanged the following dawn, every last man. The giant's claw was the gallows.'

Bridget shivered.

'Fascinating,' said Garrett. 'It strikes me as a fitting form of justice that the hanging took place at the location of their plotting.'

Cormac's voice was very even as he replied, 'You'll forgive me if I don't quite see it the same way, sir. Both my grandfathers met their deaths here that dawn.'

'Ah,' said Garrett. He had the grace to look uncomfortable, but also a little wary. Did he wonder whether rebel blood ran through this stable hand's veins? He coughed and turned to Bridget. 'Shall we go on?'

She directed Bonny away without a word, keen to leave the place. She felt terrible that Cormac had been compelled to relive his family's painful history. Once he was old enough, his father had sat him down and related the harrowing events of the rebellion to him – she could still recall his haunted face afterwards and had never pressed him for any details beyond those which he had volunteered to give.

He waited to give them time to move ahead. When she looked back, he sat hunched in his saddle, the claw projecting above him like it would pluck him from his seat.

They rode on through the morning, sometimes at a leisurely pace and every so often cantering across the terrain, Cormac in their wake but always at a respectful distance. Bridget, leading the way, found herself shunning certain parts of the estate. She had no intention of going anywhere near the Sruhawn, which would only act as an unwelcome reminder of Jack McGovern's tragic death. She had no great yearning to venture into Ballydarry after her most recent visit there. And, while she still had not yet made it to the limestone quarry this summer, today was not the occasion for it, entwined as it was with so many childhood memories that had nothing to do with the man at her side and everything to do with the one behind her. She therefore selected a safe route across fields and through woods which, while recognisable, presented no perilous emotional links. She praised Oakleigh and Garrett admired it and both of them pretended they were alone.

When the sun was at its highest in the sky, they stopped at the edge of a large grove of birch trees to take their midday meal. Panting and sweating, they dismounted, eager to quench their thirst. As soon as Cormac caught up to them, Garrett beckoned to him to bring the picnic basket.

Bridget burned with embarrassment. 'Let me do it,' she said, reaching for the basket. She couldn't abide the idea of Cormac in such a role of servitude. Asking him to saddle her horse somehow seemed very different from allowing him to serve her food.

"Tis fine, miss,' he said, his blue eyes direct.

'Leave him be, it's what he's here for,' said Garrett, tugging at his cravat. 'My word, it's hot. I hope the wine is still cool.'

Cormac chose a flat area of grassy ground a little way into the grove, unfolded a blanket and a pair of napkins, and spread out the delicious luncheon Mrs Kavanagh had prepared. There were cold meats, bread and cheese, scones with jam, strawberries, and even two glasses carefully cushioned in cloths, but the splendid array was marked by one conspicuous absence.

'Did she provide nothing to drink?' Garrett asked incredulously.

Cormac displayed the empty basket. 'She must've forgotten to.'

'How does one forget an essential such as wine?'

Cormac's lips tightened. 'I apologise on her behalf, sir. I'm afraid she's a bit distracted at present. There's been a death in her family.'

'Oh, no,' said Bridget, clapping a hand to her mouth. 'She received word from her sister?'

He nodded. 'Her sister's son was executed but they spared her husband. He has generously been permitted to keep his position on the estate.' His inflection conveyed just what he thought of this particular brand of generosity.

She exhaled through her fingers. 'How awful.'

'What are you talking about?' said Garrett, looking from her to Cormac with a frown.

She smoothed the skirt of her riding habit with a sweaty palm. 'Our cook. Her sister lives on Rathglaney land. Do you remember I told you what happened there?'

His expression said he remembered and that he was beginning to think all of Oakleigh's servants had connections to criminals. 'I see. In any case, that does not solve our current predicament. I'm parched.'

Cormac picked up the glasses. 'I'll get ye some water. There's a stream nearby.'

'Will it be clean enough to drink?' Garrett said dubiously.

'I guarantee it'll be the best water you've ever tasted.'

He disappeared between the narrow trunks of the birch trees and returned minutes later with the two glasses brimming. "Tisn't far. I can refill them when necessary.'

Garrett tried a cautious sip, then swallowed the rest of the contents in one gulp. Bridget took a healthy mouthful of her own; it was crisp and very satisfying as it slid down her dry throat.

'While it is no glass of wine, I do believe you are correct about its exceptional quality. It is delicious.' Garrett held out his empty glass, clearly expecting it to be replenished right away.

Bridget seized it before Cormac could even reach for it. 'I will refill them myself. Where is the stream?'

He pointed. 'About sixty yards that way. You'll hear it before you see it. I'm going to bring the horses there next to water them.'

'You should start eating,' she encouraged Garrett. 'I'll be back in a moment.'

She hurried away through the grove. Further in, where the trees grew more thickly, the merry gurgle of water drew her to the location of the stream. Her breath caught as she came upon it and she realised at once how Cormac had already known of its existence. Setting the two glasses on a flat boulder mottled with lichen, she knelt at the water's edge; it spilled over a rock shelf and splashed along a bed of pebbles, glinting in intermittent rays of sunlight. She told herself it was indispensable to wash the perspiration from her hands and neck before luncheon, but she took long enough about it that she was still there when Cormac arrived, leading Bonny between the birches. Betraying no reaction to her lingering presence, he guided the horse to a spot a dozen feet further up from her and the animal's white muzzle dipped gratefully to the running stream.

After a protracted silence, she said in a low voice, 'I have never been so mortified in my life.'

His head jerked towards her. 'What d'you mean?'

She stood, blowing out her cheeks in frustration. 'This! Your role as chaperone, Garrett's inappropriate questions, you laying out the picnic like you're —'

'A servant,' he said firmly. 'Which I am. I've no objection to it.'

'It is beyond absurd when I recall our antics here.'

He glanced at the stream. 'I wasn't sure you'd remember.'

'Of course I remember.'

'Well, it was different then. This is the way 'tis now.' His tone wasn't harsh but he said nothing else and turned back to Bonny, plainly trying to adhere to the assertion he had made that day in the orchard that there could be nothing personal between them.

She, on the other hand, surrendered to the memory. It had been her last summer at Oakleigh and a day as hot as this one, if not hotter. Roaming far across the fields, they had discovered this stream and frolicked in its cool embrace, splashing about in an exuberance of bare limbs and breathless laughter. Then, sitting on the same lichen-covered boulder, they had dangled their feet in the water and, yielding to a rare moment of gravity, talked about the future.

'My da reckons I'll start at the stables next year,' he had revealed. 'And he's going to keep teaching me carpentry. Says I show promise.'

'You really do,' she had said, having witnessed his first attempts at working wood. 'Lucky thing, you'll be outdoors a lot and always with the horses, that will be just marvellous. I, in dismal contrast, shall be stuck indoors reading accounts. Papa wants me to begin learning how the estate works once I turn twelve in November. How dull it will be.'

They had exchanged a look of realisation as they both grasped the significance of her words.

She had straightened her shoulders. 'It's no matter. We shall still find time for each other.'

'Exactly,' he had said, flicking his foot and dousing the front of her trussed-up dress.

She had shrieked and their flash of maturity had evaporated in the face of childish retribution.

What would their eleven-year-old selves have said, had they known just how far apart they would come to be. They doubtless would have scoffed at the suggestion. But then, they would never have predicted that within seven months her father would be dead.

Yesterday, she would not allow herself to envisage what might have happened had she never left the estate. Now, she couldn't resist considering the idea.

With her father's passing, she would have cleaved to Cormac and his family even more; nothing but her mother's curt manner would have awaited her at the manor house. Growing older with him at an age when boys were becoming men and objects for marriage rather than friendship, how would she have viewed him?

She sneaked a sideways glance as he hunkered down by the stream, hair falling into his eyes as he cupped his hands full of water to drink, and felt a quiver of awareness that had not been there before. Her brain ran wild for a moment and she imagined him lifting his gaze to hers, stepping towards her, touching her waist with one hand, tilting her chin up with the other...

She gulped, conscious of Garrett's presence – her *fiancé*, she reminded herself – sixty yards away.

The notion of an heiress kissing a stable hand was preposterous, all of civil society believed so. And yet, when it was her and Cormac it did not seem such an outrageous thought. Perhaps if she had stayed... But no, her mother would never have condoned it. She would have enforced their separation by any means within her power.

A jolt of shock ran through her. Wasn't that precisely what her mother had done?

His attention darted in her direction at her sudden movement. She hastened to pick up the glasses and immerse them in the running water.

When she rose again, she dared to speak her mind. 'Sometimes I wish it could be different,' she said and whisked away from the stream before either of them could say more.

What she had meant was that she wished nothing had changed. But leaving Oakleigh seven years ago had caused everything to change.

She contemplated the prospect of going to London and decided some changes ought to be fought. She refused to be taken away against her will again.

She had formulated her line of reasoning by the time she returned to Garrett.

***

Once he had watered the three horses, Cormac tied them up to graze at the edge of the grove and settled himself at the base of a tree a reasonable distance from the picnic spread. If he turned his head, he could glimpse the pair through the birches but only the faintest hum of voices came to him. It was enough privacy to be going on with. He didn't want to be any nearer, should Mr Lambourne choose to murmur loving endearments to his betrothed.

Mrs Kavanagh had slipped him some bread, cheese and a half-burnt scone when he had collected the picnic basket from the kitchens that morning. After wolfing it all down, he took out his knife and the small block of wood he had been working on over the past week. He whittled away at the shape, bringing wing and beak into clearer form.

He did not know what to make of Bridget's behaviour. Why did she struggle so much with acknowledging him as her servant? He had long since accepted it. Her resistance to the inevitability of their situation was unfathomable.

The knife scraped nimbly at the wood and the shavings drifted down into his lap like snowflakes. It was peaceful for a time, the shade of the trees a welcome relief after the baking heat of the sun. However, he soon became aware that the tone of the nearby voices had changed. They were no longer muted, with the occasional tinkle of laughter. Instead, they had increased in volume and grown sharp and heated.

The tramping of feet on fallen twigs announced that someone had been incensed enough to walk away from the picnic. Mr Lambourne came marching in his direction, shoulders stiff and mouth a disgruntled line. He looked surprised when he saw Cormac.

'Oh, it's you. I didn't know where you had gone to.'

Cormac brushed the wood shavings from his thighs and started to rise but Mr Lambourne waved him back down.

'No need.'

He expected the man to pass on by, seeking solitude to indulge in his strop a little longer, but instead Mr Lambourne folded his arms and leaned against a tree opposite him.

'Sometimes the female mind is impossible to comprehend,' he remarked.

Cormac gave a noncommittal shrug. Mr Lambourne shuffled his feet, then jutted his chin towards Cormac's hands.

'What is that you're doing there?' he asked.

'Nothing much. Just a hobby to pass the time.'

'I'd like to see it.'

After a brief hesitation, Cormac held out the wooden carving. Mr Lambourne took it, admiration growing on his face as he examined it from every angle.

'This is extraordinary. Such attention to detail. Where did you learn the skill?'

'My father taught me what he knew. After that, it was a matter of practice.'

A gleam came into Mr Lambourne's eye. 'Would you be able to replicate it? I have need to make reparation for a silly argument and a peace offering would be ideal. How soon could you make a second?'

'You can have this one, sir.'

'Are you certain? This isn't intended for someone else? Your own sweetheart?'

Cormac swallowed uneasily. 'I'd be pleased for the young lady to have it. I'll just give it a final look-over.'

He took the carving back, adjusted it with a few delicate nicks, and returned it.

Mr Lambourne gave him an approving nod. 'My thanks to you. I believe you have assisted me out of a quandary.'

With a wry twist of his mouth, Cormac watched the gentleman go back the way he had come, his step a good deal lighter.

***

Bridget knelt on the picnic blanket, shredding blades of grass into tiny pieces in her lap. Her fiancé's intransigence had come as an unpleasant discovery; instead of being open to a discussion about London, he had preferred to walk away from the confrontation altogether.

Perhaps it was her own fault. She shouldn't have raised the issue again so soon, not even twenty-four hours since their quarrel in the drawing room. He hadn't had time yet to absorb the reality that she was unhappy with the proposition. She would let him reflect on it for a while before broaching it again.

When the sound of footsteps drew near, her first guilty hope was that it might be Cormac – maybe he had overheard their altercation, seen Garrett storm away, and come out of concern. But it was Garrett weaving his way among the tree trunks. She returned her gaze to the clumps of grass on her skirt, pushing away the irrational disappointment. She ought to be glad he wanted to make peace already.

He didn't say anything. He crouched beside her on the blanket, turned her face towards his, and kissed her lips. It was a tender kiss, full of affection and apology, and she felt a tension ease inside as their ill will faded.

He pressed something into her hand and she broke from the kiss to look down at it. She gasped.

'A gift of conciliation,' he murmured. 'I hope you like it, my darling.'

She did not need to ask him where he had obtained such a treasure. She had spent hours and hours watching Cormac chip at odd bits of wood when they were young, supplying encouragement as he tried to shape them into animals or flowers or people. But the specimen in her grasp was so far beyond any of those attempts. She lifted it close to her eyes, marvelling at the delicacy of the thin legs, the texture of the layered feathers, the half-open beak as if it were about to break into birdsong. It was magnificent.

'What do you think?' Garrett asked, eager for absolution.

He didn't deserve the praise, when he had only procured it and not put the precious time and effort into its creation.

'I think its maker has the finest talent I have ever seen,' she said and then, relenting, added for his benefit, 'Thank you for giving it to me.'

He beamed and lounged back on his elbows, satisfied that all was amicable between them once more.

She stroked the wing of the wooden bird. For whom had Cormac intended it? His mother? One of his sisters? She bit her tongue; maybe he had his eye on one of the maidservants. With such care taken in its making, she felt privileged that she had been the one to receive it.

Presently, Garrett called for Cormac to tidy away the picnic spread. He came at once and set about shaking crumbs from the napkins and packing the leftovers into the basket. As he folded the blanket, he threw a quick glance in Bridget's direction. Clutching the bird so hard that its beak dug into her palm, she offered him a tentative smile and he gave her one in return.

Garrett threw back the last of his water in a long swallow and handed the glass to Cormac. Then he gestured towards the spot where the horses were grazing and said, 'Come, my darling, let us go on.'

She slipped the bird into her pocket and followed him out of the grove.

## Chapter 11

The sun was setting by the time Cormac headed home across the fields, its vivid redness streaking the sky as it sank into the horizon. Exhausted, he hauled himself over the last stile into the lane, making a mental note to trim back the hedgerow again one of these days, and traipsed the final stretch to the cottage.

Despite the late hour, he found his mother at her spinning wheel and Orlaith scraping assiduously at the droppings strewn on the earthen floor beneath the hens' favourite rafter, eking out the last of the daylight with the aid of the glow from the fire. Maggie set a bowl of stirabout in front of him before returning to her work and he dug in as he listened to Orlaith, in an uncommonly talkative mood, describe a brawl that had occurred between two of her hens.

'...and then Chickie squawked and went for Henrietta and I was afraid she'd peck her eyes out!' she said, her own eyes large and round. 'But they calmed down after a lot of flapping about. I *think* they're friends again.'

He felt a swell of fondness for his little sister as she cast a maternal glance at the roosting brood above her.

'Any news from the big house?' his mother asked over the whirring of the wheel.

Knowing that Margaret had made a rare trip home two nights before and enlightened their mother on all the wonderful things Mr Lambourne had done, he just shook his head and scooped up the last of his stirabout.

'There's some water in the rope bucket,' Maggie said with a nod towards the door.

He burped and rose from the table. Orlaith giggled but his mother raised a pointed eyebrow.

''Scuse me,' he mumbled, and carried his bowl outside.

Night had fallen clear and balmy, and the stars were out in droves. He dipped the bowl into the bucket of water by the door of the cottage and rubbed at the food stains with his fingers. Satisfied that it was clean to his mother's standards, he was straightening up to bring it back inside when he caught a sudden movement in his peripheral vision. He whirled around and saw a figure standing in the lane. It looked like the form of a young woman.

'Bridget?' he called falteringly, though there was no logical way it could be her.

The figure stepped into the dim glow of firelight falling through the open cottage door. ''Tis good to see you, Cormac.'

'Mary!'

He was flabbergasted. It had been twelve years since he'd seen his older sister – she had been sent away to live with their aunt, who was poorly and unable to afford hired help. The last they had heard from her was that their aunt had passed away and that she had found employment in Dublin. More than a year had elapsed since that communication. And now here she was, with pale hair and pale skin, emerging like a ghost from the gloom.

She was carrying a bundle, which stirred as she shifted its weight in her arms. He opened his mouth but his mother's voice rang out first.

'Cormac, while you're out there, I need you to get some turf for…' Her words trailed away as she appeared in the doorway and glimpsed her eldest child.

'God above, Mary!' she exclaimed. She ran forwards to embrace her daughter, but hesitated at the sight of the moving bundle. A faint cry from within the rags eradicated all doubt.

'This is Patrick.' Mary held the bundle out to Maggie. 'Take him. He's your grandson.'

Maggie gathered the baby to her chest. 'I see a lot of things have happened since you left us,' she said, looking down at the little face.

'Yes,' Mary murmured. 'A lot of things.'

Maggie kissed her on the cheek. 'Come inside, dearie. You're after coming a long way.'

They went indoors, where they found Orlaith hovering near the doorway, shy of this sister whom she had never met before. Sitting on a bench, Mary gave her a look of reassurance, but Orlaith remained where she was, solemn and silent.

Cormac and Maggie joined Mary at the table, Maggie still cradling the baby. There wasn't a sound for a minute or two; no one seemed to know how to proceed.

Then Mary said, 'I named him after our Patrick. I thought it was the right thing to do.' She had always been closest to Patrick; with only ten months between them in age, they had been as thick as thieves until she left.

Maggie's eyes filled with sadness but she didn't say anything.

Cormac folded his arms. 'Who's the father?' It came out more sharply than he had intended.

Mary's expression became pained and it seemed to take her a lot of effort to gather the words together. 'My husband,' she said.

She placed her left hand on the tabletop so they could all see the plain wedding band on her finger.

'Why didn't you write and tell us you'd married?' said Maggie. 'We haven't heard from you in so long and it would've cheered us to hear the good—'

'He's dead,' Mary interrupted in a cracked voice.

There was a shocked silence.

Maggie covered the ring as she clasped Mary's hand. 'You poor craythur.'

'How did he die?' asked Orlaith, speaking for the first time.

Maggie frowned in admonishment at her youngest daughter. 'You don't have to answer that now, Mary. You should take some time to settle down before you try to talk about such a difficult subject.'

'No, 'tis fine,' said Mary with a brave set to her shoulders. 'I'll have to tell yous at some point, so it may as well be now.'

Her speech had taken on shades of a Dublin accent and it occurred to Cormac that, at twenty-one, his sister had spent more than half of her life away from home. What joys and sorrows had it brought her?

She let out a slow breath. 'When Auntie died, I should've come home. But I'd been away for over ten years and what did I have to show for it? I knew how to care for an invalid and manage a house, but that was it. I wanted to experience the world while I was still out in it 'cause I'd never have another opportunity once I came back.' She raised her gaze to her mother's. 'I realise now it was shameful of me to do what I did. To take myself to the city when yous were trying to cope after Da and Patrick dying... It must've been such a hard time for yous and all I cared about was getting a taste of real life. I was too self-interested to spare a thought for my family. I'm so sorry.'

Cormac had witnessed Maggie's distress at the time – she had been devastated that her first-born had chosen to stay away when her presence and support had been so desperately needed. However, she spoke now without recrimination.

'I don't hold it against you, dearie. It was natural you should want to see the world beyond your aunt's house before being confined to home again. Of course, I would've insisted you return if I thought you were heading to Dublin with no purpose, but the fact that you said your aunt had secured you a position in a household before she passed made me feel much easier.'

Mary's lashes lowered. 'That was a lie. I had no position before I arrived there.'

Maggie stared at her daughter. 'Ah, I see,' she said and stroked the cheek of little Patrick.

It astounded Cormac that their mother could respond so calmly to this appalling news. He himself wanted to shake Mary until her teeth rattled. What had she been thinking when she went to the city with no acquaintances, no guarantee of employment, and no place to live?

She sighed. 'I got what I deserved for lying to my ma. I'd a dreadful time there in the beginning. The only work I could find was helping an old woman sell flowers on the street. I'd nowhere to stay. It was awful. If it'd been winter I think I'd have died. I thought again about coming home, but I didn't want to return a failure. I wanted to make something of myself so yous could be proud of me when I came back.'

Perhaps she had been hoping at this juncture for commendations for her fortitude but neither Maggie nor Cormac offered any. He was too angry at her abysmal lack of judgement. Her actions had been selfish and foolhardy and she did not merit an ounce of praise from her family.

She bit her lip, a tinge of pink appearing in her pale cheeks, and hastened on. 'But that was when my luck turned. I managed to find work in a bakery. It was a family business and so much more than I could've hoped for. They gave me proper wages and a room as well. At first, I just swept out the shop and ran errands for them, but in time they showed me how to make the bread myself and I was really able to earn my keep.' Her head tilted in dreamy reminiscence. 'They'd a son who was to inherit the business when his father died. Oh, he was a gentleman, so courteous, with soft, dark hair and such a charming smile. I don't mind saying I fell for him almost right away.'

Her whole demeanour brightened at the mention of this baker's son; her back straightened, her eyes shone, and her mouth curved in a tender smile.

'He fell in love with me too and we married last September. I would've written to yous but it was such a busy, exciting time, I just didn't have a moment to spare. I gave birth to Patrick a month ago. A strong, healthy boy, oh, his da was so pleased.' Then she lost her sparkle, like a candle snuffed out. 'A few days later, he was working with the ovens. We don't know how it happened but there was a terrible accident and a fire. His burns were... H-he didn't survive.'

The hush in the cottage was broken only by a cluck and a flutter of wings from a restless hen. Orlaith crept on soundless feet to Cormac's side and he laid his arm around her shoulders, wishing they had put her to bed before now.

Tears filled Mary's eyes as she continued, 'His own ma and da would've let me stay with them. Patrick was their grandson too, after all. But I told them I wanted to go home to my own family. They were very kind to me and I do miss them but...I had to come home.'

Patrick whimpered in his grandmother's arms. Mary reached out and Maggie handed him to her.

'Shush, love,' she whispered, and put her wet cheek next to her baby's.

Maggie said, 'I think he's soiled himself...'

Mary wiped her face with the back of her hand. 'I'd better take care of him.'

'No, dearie, I can do it.' Maggie's tone was compassionate. She seemed ready to forgive Mary all of her transgressions; perhaps she felt her daughter had suffered enough without being burdened with accusations from her family as well. 'You're after a long journey. Go up to the loft and get some rest. I'll bring him up to you once I've tended to him.'

Mary gave the baby back to her mother. Maggie cupped her chin.

'You'll feel a bit better in the morning,' she said.

Cormac's gaze followed his sister as she climbed the ladder to the loft. The change that had been wrought upon her during her time away was even greater than that which had come upon Bridget. She had grown into a young woman, but she seemed to have faded in some way. Her manner had lost the bright vivacity he remembered from their childhood and she looked haggard, as though her contact with the wider world had taken its toll on her. Only her fair hair remained the same, retaining the rich colour that just she and he, out of all their siblings, had inherited from their father.

The baby gave another soft cry. He had tufts of dark hair and quite different features from his mother; he must take after his father too. Cormac glanced at Maggie. She already had the glow of a doting grandmother about her as she asked Orlaith to search the dresser for a cloth.

Even though Mary had suffered a tragic misfortune, he hoped her return might bring some long-lost happiness to their mother.

## Chapter 12

Though she was fully dressed and ready to go down to breakfast, Bridget lingered at her dressing table to pore over the wooden bird once again. Still so impressed by the quality of the workmanship, she traced each meticulous contour, picturing the hands and blade that had brought it to life.

A knock at the door startled her and she instinctively hid the bird behind her jewellery box. Why had she done that? It was a gift from her fiancé; she should not feel guilty to be caught looking at it. She placed it out in full view again as she called, 'Come in.'

Her visitor turned out to be Ellen, bearing a glass of an indeterminate brown concoction on a tray. The lady's maid's freckles had bloomed in the summer weather and they splashed across her nose and both cheeks in liberal quantities. Nose wrinkling, she held the tray at some distance from her body as she entered the bedchamber.

Bridget was pleased to see her, dubious burden notwithstanding. Ellen was lady's maid to her mother, not herself, but they retained a personal connection which stemmed from Bridget's early years in Dublin. Ellen had been the only other person in the city who had known Cormac and with whom Bridget could lament his absence, and she had provided solace as much as the limitations of her station had allowed.

Her discretion in such matters was her most admirable trait, given her constant proximity to Bridget's mother. She had travelled with them from Oakleigh as a housemaid but Lady Courcey had set much store by her abilities and groomed her for the higher position of lady's maid, despite her youth, dismissing Ellen's predecessor ('That French *imbécile*...') once she had attained the suitable skill set for the role. When she had been promoted, Bridget had found it difficult to address her by the more correct title of 'Ryan' and both had been happy for her to continue on a first name basis.

Instead of her usual composure, Ellen looked rather embarrassed as she said, 'Her ladyship instructed me to bring this to you, miss.'

She placed the tray gingerly on the dressing table. Bridget squinted at the glass and took a cautious sniff. The stench of vinegar was overwhelming.

'What is it supposed to be?'

'A tonic, miss. To encourage a satisfactory waistline.'
Bridget twisted her lips. 'On my mother's recommendation, you say?'
Ellen gave an apologetic nod. 'She's considering the upcoming wedding.'
'Hmm. Can I not just have my stays tightened?'
'I'm certain she's expecting that as well.'
Bridget made no move to pick it up. 'Maggie McGovern thinks I'm too thin. I saw her eyeing me critically when she thought I wasn't looking.'
With the greatest tact towards her mistress's evident opinion on the subject, Ellen said, 'Maggie McGovern has raised four daughters to fine physical health so I can't fault her general judgement.' She brightened. 'Did you hear her eldest has returned?'
'Mary? She's come home?'
'Just the night before last. It's welcome news. She's been gone from Oakleigh even longer than I, but we were very close as small girls.'
Ellen related how Mary had shown up, so unexpectedly, as a widow and a mother. Bridget pitied Mary for the loss of her husband but was glad for Cormac that, after the deaths of two members of his family, his sister had come back to make them somewhat whole again. She gave the wooden bird a surreptitious caress and then returned her reluctant attention to the mud-coloured liquid before her.
'Could I pour it into the chamber pot?'
'The housemaid who discovered it would think you were dying.'
'And I suppose tipping it into a flowerpot would lead to the plant's actual demise. Perhaps you could ensure its delivery to the scullery? It smells potent enough to be a cleaning agent rather than a refreshing beverage. I believe I shall require you to intercept any future endeavours of this nature.'
Ellen's mouth twitched. 'As you wish, miss.'
Lady Courcey and Garrett were already seated when Bridget went down to breakfast but Lord Walcott had not yet appeared. She went straight to the platters on the sideboard and made a point of stacking her plate a good deal higher than her appetite necessitated.
If her mother noticed, she chose not to comment. Instead, she said, 'I have had a delightful idea, Bridget.'
'Indeed, what is it?' she asked warily as she took her place at the table. She had made up her mind to discourage any more long rides across the estate. Brewer was on the mend but she had no desire to run the risk he might fall ill again.
'As you know, Mr Lambourne's birthday is approaching in August. He was thinking of going back to the city for the occasion but I suggested he stay here and tempt his acquaintances down to Oakleigh for a week or two instead. You could invite some ladies as well. What do you think of that?'
'That sounds lovely,' said Bridget, pleased at the thought of seeing her

friends again.

'There is no need to go to any trouble,' Garrett said modestly. 'I am content for it to be a quiet event.'

'Nonsense.' Lady Courcey waved his protestations away. 'You deserve a birthday celebration and I will be the one to host it for you. It is the least I can do, considering you have given me the greatest gift of all in making my daughter so happy.'

Garrett beamed at Bridget; her returning smile was somewhat less bright.

'It may also prove to be an impetus for my lingering brother to remove himself to his own estate at last,' Lady Courcey added dryly.

\*\*\*

Cormac had located a sunny spot outside the stable doors and was sitting on a stool while he mended some stitching on a bridle when a shadow fell over him and a gruff cough announced the presence of Fintan Kelly.

He jumped to his feet and said, 'Mr Kelly, how can I help you?' but the answer was obvious as the old gardener held out his spade, its wooden handle broken into two jagged pieces. Knowing that Fintan looked after his tools with as much devotion as his gardens, Cormac recognised it as the same weapon which had connected with his rump all those years ago. He accepted it cautiously and examined the splintered shaft, wondering what – or who – had been on the receiving end of it this time.

Fintan seemed to read his mind. 'Years of service has cracked it, is all. I didn't whack it off that boy's head, though I had a mind to. Found him defacing the statue of Venus with clumps of mud.' He didn't go into any further detail but his complexion reddened in rage at the memory. 'I've sent him to Mr Buttimer this time 'cause the goddamn brat won't listen to me. He'll lose his post if he's not careful but he doesn't give a fig for my warning. All he says is he'll make money some other way.'

A look of shame crossed the gardener's lined face. Then he drew himself up and gave a brusque nod towards the broken spade.

'Get that back to me quick, boy,' he said and stalked away.

'Cormac!'

He glanced about and saw Mrs Kavanagh framed in the doorway to the kitchens.

'Leave that, lad, and go around to the front entrance. I've been told they want an extra pair of hands.'

'What for?' he asked, recalling the last time he had been sent in that direction.

'Lord Walcott's leaving. They need some help with his luggage.' Her tone was subdued but she made an effort to bark, 'Hurry on now!' in her old authoritative manner. She could not wallow in her family's misfortunes forever, after all.

She returned to her kitchens while Cormac, abandoning both the spade and the bridle by his stool, made his way around to the front of the big house, where a carriage and a cart stood side by side. Two footmen and a couple of the other stable hands, including Liam, were hoisting some large trunks onto the cart.

'Looks like there's more luggage here than came home with the two ladies,' Cormac said under his breath as he joined them.

Liam, purple in the face from strain, didn't reply as he tried to lift a trunk. Cormac gave him a hand in heaving it onto the cart and then they went back to the steps where several more trunks waited.

Lord Walcott was standing with Lady Courcey at the top of the steps, overseeing the operation. Cormac noted that it was Mrs Walsh, rather than Mr Buttimer, who waited in respectful attendance upon them and presumed that the butler was still giving Malachy Kelly an earful.

'Take care with that,' Lord Walcott called to the two footmen who were struggling with an enormous chest between them. 'It contains the belongings of my precious ones.'

The precious ones in question were worrying his ankles, giving piercing barks of discontentment. Cormac imagined that being shut up in a carriage with those ill-tempered creatures for hours could not be anything but torturous.

Lord Walcott, unmindful of his dogs' yapping, turned to Lady Courcey with an exaggerated expression of melancholy. 'I shall be sorry to say farewell to this place. I have thoroughly enjoyed my time here as lord of the manor.'

'And we shall be most sorry to see you go,' his sister replied, although she seemed to be bearing their imminent separation with a distinct lack of sorrow.

Lord Walcott sighed. 'Nevertheless, we soldier on as pressing needs dictate we must. Affairs at Lockhurst Park demand my immediate attention so I shall travel on to England after only a brief sojourn in Dublin. And from your perspective it is of course advantageous to have more space for future guests.' He looked over his shoulder into the dimness of the hall. 'Is Bridget coming to bid me farewell?'

'I have sent Ryan for her. She should be here in a moment.'

Cormac helped Liam haul the last trunk onto the cart and then he made a quick escape around the side of the house. As he turned the corner, he heard the voices of Bridget and her attentive fiancé floating out the doorway.

***

Following Lord Walcott's departure from Oakleigh, the planning for Garrett's birthday celebrations could begin in earnest. Thanks to her mother's tuition earlier in the summer, Bridget was able to conduct the preparations adeptly and the next two weeks passed in a flurry of activity. She spoke to Mr Buttimer about engaging musicians for a night of entertainment in the ballroom, to Mrs Kavanagh about a menu for the birthday feast, and to Mrs Walsh about accommodations for all the guests. Invitations were issued to ten acquaintances in all, five gentlemen and five ladies. The most important of these to Bridget was Miss Madeleine Wallace, the dearest friend she had made during her time in Dublin. Madeleine's older, married sister would also come, along with Miss Isabel Gardiner – a lively girl of limited means but ample wit – and the twin Hyland sisters who had been presented as debutantes at Dublin Castle on the same evening as Bridget. Some of the company would be travelling from their own country residences but none of these would be superior to Oakleigh and she could not wait to greet them all and show off her grand manor.

Two mornings before the guests were due to arrive, Bridget was seated with Garrett in the drawing room, discussing potential daytime activities which would amuse their visitors during their stay. They were alone and, as a consequence, he had positioned himself quite a bit nearer to her on the sofa than could be deemed proper.

'I do believe everyone would take pleasure in a jaunt across the estate,' she commented.

'Indeed,' he said, shifting even closer, his hazel eyes glowing with ardour.

'We could have picnics and play bowls on the lawn.' Her voice had become rather breathy. She was aware of the whole length of his body a hair's breadth away from her own and, even as she made a half-hearted attempt to retreat to a more respectable distance, thoughts of a particular nature raced through her mind: the vague rumours she had heard of what she might expect on her wedding night. With him in such proximity, her imagination was running amok.

'I hope the weather will be obliging...' Her words trailed off as he reached for her hand and stroked it. When she turned her head, their lips were only inches apart. They met with the lightest of touches. Eyes fluttering closed, she felt his hand move to her torso, resting just below her breast. It was an impertinent gesture and she should not allow it but for the first time since he had come to Oakleigh she was feeling as she had in Dublin, wholly captivated by his charm. She trembled as his fingers skimmed upwards over her bodice...

There was a timid knock on the drawing room door and they jerked away from each other. The door swung open to reveal Cormac's sister,

Bronagh, clutching a tray with a teapot, two cups and a plate of biscuits. The girl could not possibly have seen anything but in a way Bridget felt that being observed by Bronagh was almost the same as having Cormac's gaze on her. She wilted at the very idea of him coming upon a scene such as that.

She waved Bronagh forwards and the girl set the tea tray down on a small table by her knee, eyes averted as she glanced around the room. Bridget supposed she was dazzled by Garrett, just like all the other maids. Only yesterday she had witnessed a housemaid bump into him by accident as she left his bedchamber with his bed sheets bundled in her arms; the girl had expelled a loud squeak, then had started to cry in mortification and fled.

'Thank you, Bronagh,' Bridget said, having come to accept these reactions as normal around her fetching fiancé.

Bronagh gave her a fleeting look and an awkward curtsey and hurried from the room.

'Do you know all the servants by name?' asked Garrett. 'That is quite an accomplishment.'

She pondered the fact that she considered Cormac's sisters to be practically her own. Though she did not like to keep secrets from Garrett, her instinct told her that to declare this sense of affiliation with a lower class family would not be received well.

'No, not all of them,' she said.

He did not seem to much care about her answer; he was already reaching for her hand again. She, however, had recalled her sense of propriety and leaned away to pour the tea.

## Chapter 13

Cormac ducked under the vine-draped arch which marked the entrance to Oakleigh's gardens and followed the path in search of Fintan Kelly. After he had returned Fintan's spade to him with a brand new handle, the gardener, in a rare mood to offer praise, had declared the work of such good quality that he had instructed Cormac to reinforce some of his other implements weakened by long years of heavy use. Thus he now carried a rake and a hoe, each with fresh wooden shafts, over his shoulder as he looked around impatiently for the old man. It was nearing evening time and he still had numerous stable duties to complete before his working day would be done.

The gardens consisted of a broad expanse of lawn in the centre, bordered all around by a walkway lined with flower beds and tall hedges on both sides. Periodic gaps in the hedges allowed access to the central grassy area and every now and then the walkway widened to accommodate a piece of sculpture or a bench. He had almost reached the end of one side of the gardens when he heard voices drifting around the corner ahead of him.

'...so long as you think 'tis safe,' a girl was saying.

'I swear 'tis,' a boy responded. 'It should happen tonight. I'll meet you at the kitchens?'

'I'll be there.'

He rounded the corner and came upon a sculpture on a wide plinth: the statue of Venus, her polished, white body free of mud. On the edge of the plinth sat Malachy Kelly and Bronagh. The boy had one hand on her leg while the other was coiled in a length of her dark hair which had escaped from beneath her maid's cap. She jumped up at the sight of Cormac but Malachy stayed where he was, a lazy grin playing about his mouth.

Cormac glared at them. 'What the hell are ye doing?'

'This isn't what you think—' Bronagh began, her cheeks red with heat, but he cut her off.

'Get yourself back to the kitchens,' he snapped. 'They'll be preparing the dinner already. Mrs Kavanagh will throw a fit if you're not to hand.'

She flung a mulish look at him and a swift glance at Malachy and then she darted away down the garden path. Cormac turned to the boy, allowing the rake and hoe to drop to waist height in a threatening gesture.

'Stay away from my sister,' he said. 'Don't come near her again.'

Malachy gave a careless shrug. 'Whatever you say. I'm not that keen on her anyway.'

He rose from the plinth, thrust his hands in his pockets, and strolled away in the opposite direction to Bronagh.

Cormac watched him go, not trusting him for a second. What had he heard him say? 'It should happen tonight.' It wasn't hard to guess what was on Malachy's mind. His blood boiled – Bronagh was only twelve.

Deciding that he had not given his sister sufficient warning, he strode after her, still clutching Fintan's implements. When he reached the kitchens, he found Mrs Kavanagh in a foul mood and Bronagh nowhere in sight.

'Where is she?' he demanded of Margaret.

'She came in just now and said she'd gotten horribly sick outside.' Margaret's expression was anxious. 'She's so unwell she's had to go straight up to bed. Mrs Kavanagh's furious but it can't be helped.'

'I want to go up and see her,' he said, alarmed that Bronagh could lie so convincingly.

'You'll do no such thing, lad,' Mrs Kavanagh barked from across the kitchen. 'You've your own work to be getting on with. Margaret can look in on her in a while. Out of here now with those tools. We've a dinner to put together and we're down a pair of hands.'

She started shouting orders to the kitchen maids who scurried to do her bidding. Helpless, Cormac retreated from the kitchens, worried that the cook had prevented him from giving his sister the most important cautioning advice she had ever needed.

Later that night, he lay in the stable loft, sleep far beyond his reach. An image of Malachy's insolent face floated before his closed eyelids; he trusted the boy to heed his warning as much as he trusted him to do an honest day's work. Could his and Bronagh's arrangement still be going ahead? Cormac couldn't let such a thing befall his sister.

After dithering a while longer, he rose from the straw. If their rendezvous was happening, it would have to be after all the other kitchen servants had retired for bed, and the blackest part of the night would suit Malachy and his ungallant intentions. Intuition told him that now was the moment to go and investigate. He hoped to God there would be nothing to find.

He slipped down the ladder from the loft without disturbing his fellow stable hands and picked his way carefully across the lower level of the stables in the pitch dark. He knew the dimensions of the building with his eyes shut but there was no telling which careless chap might have left a sack of grain abandoned on the earthen floor. It would do no good to trip and make a noise – if Malachy was skulking about, he wanted to catch the boy, not give him a chance to run away.

Out in the cobbled courtyard, a sliver of moonlight guided him to the door of the kitchens. His stomach sank; a flickering glow glimmered through the gap at the bottom where all should have been darkness at this late hour. He squirmed as he imagined finding Bronagh and the head gardener's grandson locked in an embrace. He could already feel his face flaming with the embarrassment it would cause. But better that than to allow his sister's virtue to be compromised.

Bracing himself, he lifted the latch and pushed the door open. He was relieved to discover Bronagh sitting alone at the bench, a candle beside her on the kitchen table. It seemed she was still waiting for her companion to appear. Maybe he had succeeded in scaring Malachy off after all?

She had been staring miserably down at her lap but looked up in fright at the sound of the door opening. It occurred to him that this was an odd reaction, considering the impending tryst. Her eyes widened upon recognising him and she leapt to her feet.

'What're you doing here?' she hissed.

'I came to stop this,' he said, closing the door behind him. 'I won't allow you to be so thick-headed.'

Her eyes flashed. 'Go away. You don't tell me what to do.'

'Yes, I do,' he said. 'I'm the only man in your family. If Da were here, this is what he'd do to protect his daughter.'

She looked aghast. 'You have to leave now.' With a grunt, she tried to shove him back to the door.

He refused to budge. 'When's Malachy coming?'

She just shook her head and pushed harder, but she was no match for his strength.

He grasped her shoulders. 'Bronagh, think about what you're doing. He'll ruin you.'

Shrugging out of his grip, she said, 'You don't know what you're talking about.'

His laugh was harsh. 'D'you believe he loves you? His intentions aren't honourable. He'll take what he wants and then thrust you aside without a care for what becomes of you. Haven't you thought about the consequences? You'd lose your position here. Your reputation would be destroyed and who'd marry you then? For Christ's sake, *think*!'

She wrapped her arms around herself as if she were cold. 'That'll only happen if he gets caught. And he won't.'

'If *he* gets caught? There are two of ye in this situation. And make no mistake, he'll hang you out to dry if it comes to it, saying you lured him in and suchlike.'

'No, it was his idea!' she protested. 'Him and the others!'

His mouth went dry. 'The others? What d'you mean?'

She tucked her lips in, pressed tight like she would never speak again.

Cormac narrowed his eyes. 'When's Malachy supposed to be getting here?'

She said nothing.

He seized her shoulders again and shook her hard. 'Tell me what's going on! What've you done?'

She gaped at him in shock; he had never been so rough with her before. 'It'll be fine,' she said. 'We'll get away with it.'

'Get away with what? What's happening tonight?' His breath stuck in his throat. 'Is Malachy already here?'

She hesitated and then nodded.

'*Where?*'

After a long silence, she said, 'They were going to start in the drawing room...'

He let go of her as though she were a burning coal and she flopped down on the bench.

'He's stealing from the big house,' Cormac said, stunned. 'And you're helping him?'

All of her bravado leaked away as her chin lowered and wobbled. 'I am,' she whispered.

He sat on the bench and put an arm around her. 'Why on earth would you get mixed up in such a harebrained scheme?' he chided gently.

'Malachy needs the money.' She gulped. 'He says if he makes enough he'll be able to marry me in two years. He wants to leave Carlow and take me to America.'

So beneath the tough exterior she was just another young, infatuated girl with ambitious dreams.

'You've got to tell me everything,' said Cormac. 'What arrangement did the two of ye make for tonight?'

'I was to come downstairs at midnight and unlock the kitchen door to let him in. I've to lock it again after he leaves. Tomorrow some things might be noticed missing but there'll be no telling where they've gone and no proof of who took them.'

Cormac shook his head; only dim-witted Malachy could have come up with a plan of such little finesse.

'How'd you get the key?' he asked. 'Did you steal it from Mrs Walsh's set?'

'No!' She looked affronted; he almost laughed at the irony of it. 'It hangs on a hook by the door.'

'Has Malachy ever set foot in the house before? How'd he know where to go?'

'I told him where all the rooms were. This morning I convinced one of the housemaids she was needed elsewhere and delivered the tea things to the drawing room myself so I could look 'round and see what could be taken.' Shame made her cheeks glow red.

'And he brought others with him?'

'Two.' Her lip curled in distaste. 'I didn't know they were coming.'

'Bronagh,' he said, endeavouring to be patient, though a desperate urgency fired through his veins. 'They're going to get caught.'

She peered up at him fearfully. 'Don't say that.'

''Tis the truth. Malachy's too greedy and won't know when to stop. He'll start with the drawing room and then the library and then he'll see no harm in searching upstairs and he and his friends'll make noise and be discovered. I've got to stop him.'

'No, you can't! He'll be raging!'

'I don't give a damn how he'll feel. I'm not letting him steal from Oakleigh.' Apart from the detrimental effect it would have on his sister's position if the thieves were found out, it was a thundering disrespect to the finest property in the country.

'I won't let you leave this kitchen,' she said, a little of her earlier fire returning.

He stood and strode to the door that led above stairs. She jumped up and dashed past him, trying to block his way.

'Cormac, please!'

'For the love of God, think sensibly!' he exploded. 'If Malachy gets caught, who d'you think he's going to blame for giving him access to the house? And he won't even be lying! You're in serious trouble and the only way to save you is to get him and his cronies out of the house right now.'

A shadow of uncertainty crossed her face and he pressed on, 'If you do have a fancy for him, then this is in his best interests too. You don't want to see him locked up, d'you? Or worse?'

That hit home. After a momentary sagging of her shoulders, she straightened up. 'Then I'm coming with you.'

'No, you're not.'

'He won't listen to you but I might be able to convince him!'

There was no time to debate with her any further; they had delayed long enough.

'Fine. Make sure you're quiet.'

She hopped out of his way and he pulled open the door, hurrying for the kitchen stairs. She had said the thieves were going to start in the drawing room so that was where he would begin his own search, although he didn't think they would still be there if their plan was to make swift work of the place.

He realised he had been giving Malachy too much credit for intelligence when he and Bronagh emerged into the entrance hall, saw the drawing room door ajar, and heard loud whispers coming from within.

Shaking his head in disbelief, he marched across the hall, Bronagh hastening to keep up behind him. Though he was unafraid of Malachy and his boys, he eased the drawing room door open with wariness to survey the room inside.

A grimy lantern rested on the mantelpiece and by its meagre light he could make out the scene before him. He spotted Malachy's greasy hair first, falling across his face as he bent over in front of the fireplace to cram something into a deep sack. Two other youngsters whom he did not recognise were huddled by Bridget's grand piano, laying out their spoils across the long back of the instrument. From what he could see, silver had been their goal, and they were counting out an impressive array of candlesticks, spoons and frames, ready to fill their own sacks.

He pushed the door open as wide as it could go and it produced a faint squeak at its uttermost extension. The thieves looked around in alarm but Malachy visibly relaxed once he saw Cormac standing there.

'Relax, lads,' he said. 'We're not in any danger.'

His companions didn't look convinced. Malachy straightened and flashed a wicked grin when Bronagh appeared by Cormac's side.

'This fellow's the brother of our little accomplice tonight. He's not going to tell on us or he'll get his baby sister into all kinds of trouble.'

Cormac clenched his jaw. Malachy was, of course, right. His only hope was to persuade the boys to see sense and leave before someone else discovered them.

'Put the sacks down and walk away,' he said, his voice even. 'Just get out now, while ye still can.'

Malachy laughed, not even attempting to keep quiet. In a brash gesture, he swept a silver-framed mirror from the wall behind him and placed it in his sack. It made a chinking noise as it settled against the other stolen goods.

'I'm warning you,' said Cormac, 'this won't end well if ye stay. At the very least, you'll be shaming your grandfather who's served the Courceys for decades. At worst, you could be facing a convict ship or a noose.'

'There's nothing you can say to stop me,' Malachy said, unconcerned. 'But you should tell your sister to go back to the kitchens. She's still got a job to do.'

Bronagh stiffened and Cormac clutched her hand to give her support.

'Malachy, please change your mind,' she said, her voice not betraying the quiver he felt in her fingers. 'There must be another way to make money than selling things belonging to Oakleigh.'

'For sure, but this is by far the easiest,' Malachy tossed back and his companions chuckled.

'You tell the hussy,' one said, while the other raised his own sack and began packing it with the silver items on top of the piano.

Cormac was by no means going to stand around and allow his sister to be called a hussy. He darted forwards, seizing the shirt of the first lad while wrenching the sack out of the other's hand.

'Take back what you said,' he growled, 'and then all of ye walk out of here and never set foot on this property again.'

The boy screwed up his face as though waiting for a punch to be delivered. Cormac felt more than happy to oblige but, as he let go of the lad's shirt to pull back his fist, a censorious voice stopped him in his tracks.

'None of you move or I will shoot you dead.'

He whirled to see Mr Buttimer standing in the doorway, clad in a nightshirt and nightcap. The sight of the stodgy butler in such casual attire would have been amusing had it not been for the two grim footmen who flanked him and the pistol he held raised before him. One of the footmen, Denis, had seized Bronagh's arm and she struggled helplessly in his grip.

Cormac watched as Mr Buttimer's face altered upon recognising him. Any hope that the butler might see the situation as it truly was, with Cormac trying to stop the theft instead of being involved in it, disappeared as the man's expression went from disbelief to disgust.

His gaze alighted on Malachy next, who was swearing under his breath. This time Mr Buttimer's surprise was not so great, though his revulsion intensified even further.

'Caught in the most despicable act,' he said through gritted teeth. 'You shall all receive justice for this.'

# Chapter 14

Bridget stirred as a firm hand shook her.

'Miss, you have to get up.'

When she dragged her eyes open, she realised that the shutters were closed and not even a fragment of daylight penetrated the bedchamber. Was it still night then?

'Ellen,' she slurred. 'What time is it?'

Setting a candlestick on the bedside table, Ellen said once again, 'You have to get up, miss.'

This time Bridget caught her urgent tone. She sat up, the bedcovers falling from her shoulders. 'What's wrong? What has happened?'

Shadows playing across her face, Ellen said, 'There's been a burglary in the house. Her ladyship wants you by her side as soon as you're dressed.'

'Oh, my goodness! Has Garrett been wakened too?'

'No, miss, he's still asleep in his chamber. Her ladyship desired this to be a family matter only.'

She would say no more and Bridget understood that she would only get further details from her mother. She hastened out of bed; Ellen assisted her in dressing and then led her to the study.

Despite the very late – or very early – hour, Lady Courcey was in full attire with not a pleat of fabric nor a hair pin out of place. She sat in a wingback chair, hands folded in her lap. Inexplicably, Bridget could read a note of excitement in her mother's countenance.

'Mother, will you tell me what has happened?'

Lady Courcey did not answer, instead indicating that Bridget should take the chair beside her own. With the two ladies facing the room at large, Bridget had the impression of waiting to be attended by royal courtiers.

'Ryan, you may send in Buttimer now,' said Lady Courcey.

The lady's maid departed and the butler entered, his face as grave as though someone had died. He moved to stand in the centre of the room. He too was dressed, though the last two buttons of his vest were improperly fastened.

'Buttimer,' said Lady Courcey, 'you have given me the briefest account of the events which have taken place in this house tonight. I now wish you to provide me and my daughter with a thorough description of the particulars of this most contemptible occurrence.'

'Indeed, my lady,' said Mr Buttimer, bowing. 'As I said to you a short while ago, when I was forced to have your slumber disturbed with this shocking news, by which I myself am so appalled, considering some of the offenders are your ladyship's servants and therefore in principle under my command, a lapse in authority for which I do so humbly beg your pardon, though it must be admitted that the male culprits are outdoor staff and hence not in my direct line of responsibility, and the girl, being a scullery maid, ought in truth to be held to Mrs Kavanagh's account —'

'Yes, yes, go on.'

The butler cleared his throat with a sanctimonious cough. 'To give you a full report, my lady, Mrs Walsh and I had completed our nightly duties as we always do before retiring to bed —' He looked stricken. 'That is to say, before retiring to our *separate* beds for I would never —'

'I understand, Buttimer.'

'Ahem, quite. Our duties upstairs fulfilled, we went upon the assumption that Mrs Kavanagh had done likewise downstairs, as that is her area of dominion, a fact which she has stated to me on several occasions, for she does not wish me to excessively supervise her responsibilities down in the kitchens, though she said it in rather more indelicate terms than that...' At an arched eyebrow from his mistress, he propelled ahead, 'The manor went to sleep, family and servants alike, as usual. But I was roused during the night by' – he reddened – 'a matter of a personal nature, and being thus alert I thought I heard a distant noise in the lower part of the house. Stepping out into the corridor, I heard it again. Voices. I could tell at once that they were not people who had any right to be in the manor at that hour.'

Bridget had been listening to the butler's long-winded and pompous account with amusement but she felt her mirth dissipate at his last words. Intruders inside the house and its inhabitants asleep upstairs? She shuddered at the idea.

'I was swift to wake my footmen, two strong lads with sensible heads on their shoulders. I knew they could be relied upon to act with courage should the situation turn violent. Though I had no intention of using it unless strictly necessary, I brought with me the pistol which his lordship — God rest his soul — bestowed upon me when I gained my position here as butler in order to best protect the household in times of need, which duty I do hope I filled tonight to the best of my —'

'You did. Continue.'

'I led the footmen downstairs, feeling it only right that as head of the staff I ought to lead our advance upon the intruders. I was wary for an ambush from any side but at length I ascertained that the voices were coming from one location, the drawing room. I signalled to the footmen that we should approach with care.'

Not for the first time, Bridget wondered whether Mr Buttimer was a war veteran of some kind – could he have had some involvement in the rebellion thirty years ago, defending the 2nd Baron from angry rebels?

'It sounded like the trespassers were having an argument, which meant we were able to reach the drawing room without detection. Our presence being a surprise, I was able to neutralise a retaliation from them with the threat of a shot from my pistol. They carried no weapons to speak of and desisted with vocal protestations but no physical violence. I ordered my footmen to detain them down in the kitchens and wasted no time in alerting Mrs Walsh who got Miss Ryan to waken your ladyship so the deplorable incident could be brought to your attention.'

He bowed again at the conclusion of his report but Lady Courcey did not deem him finished yet.

'What were they trying to steal?'

'The silver, no doubt with the unpardonable intention of selling it on.'

'Remind me, how many intruders did you count?'

'Five, my lady. Four lads and one girl.'

'And how many did you recognise?'

Bridget saw him shift with discomfort and, strangely, glance in her own direction.

'Three.'

'Thank you. You shall now get your footmen to escort these criminals into my presence to answer for their actions.'

'At once, my lady.'

After the butler had departed from the study, Lady Courcey said, 'This is an unimaginable state of affairs.' Her tone was sombre and yet there was still that animated glint in her eye; she seemed to be quite enjoying herself. 'The perpetrators of this crime must be suitably punished, do you not agree?'

Recalling the vision of strangers rooting through the manor house a floor below them, Bridget did not hesitate to reply, 'Yes, they must.'

Her response appeared to give Lady Courcey immense satisfaction.

Mystified, Bridget said, 'Ought we not to have Mr Enright present though?' Part of the agent's role was to serve as the resident magistrate on behalf of the Courcey title; his attendance seemed pertinent to the proceedings.

'It would take too long to send for him at this hour. He may administer my judgement in an official capacity at a later stage but I wish to dictate it without delay.'

Mr Buttimer soon returned with the information that the offenders were outside the study, ready to be brought in when it pleased her ladyship to receive them. She waved a hand and they filed in, escorted by one of the footmen. Bridget's gaze slid over the boys she did not recognise and instantly latched on to the face of the last person she would ever have expected to see here.

She could not prevent her audible gasp, though her hand flew to her mouth to stifle it. Cormac met her eyes, his expression strained but not ashamed. He straightened his shoulders and took his place in the line next to...was that his *sister*? She was more successful at smothering her shock this time, though she was no less astonished. What justifiable reason could have brought Cormac and Bronagh into contact with this band of burglars?

With the presentation of the criminals, she had no further reason to wonder why Lady Courcey was relishing this incident so much. Of course she would be too impatient to wait for the proper course of justice when here was an opportunity to crush Bridget's longstanding connection with Cormac once and for all. For had Bridget not only just agreed that the thieves had to be punished? That meant imprisonment at the very least, if not... Her heart thudded in her chest. There had to be a rational explanation for this. There *had* to be.

She looked at the rest of the boys in the line. They were lads of maybe fourteen or fifteen, no older. One of them seemed familiar and she thought she might have seen him working in the gardens once or twice, but the others were strangers to her. All three had a disagreeable air about them, with grubby clothes and shifty expressions, and she was positive they were the true instigators of tonight's crime. But convincing her mother of this would be an enormous task.

Mr Buttimer stepped forwards. 'My lady, the identities of the offenders have been established. This boy here is Malachy Kelly, grandson of Fintan Kelly who has tended Oakleigh's gardens these forty years. The pair next to him are his supposed friends, Seamus Sheedy and Billy Maher. Malachy has been working as a gardener on the manor grounds since April of this year but the other two are not known to us on the staff. I would venture to say that Fintan will be outraged by his grandson's actions and have sent for him to come to the house as soon as possible to attest to that.'

Malachy looked unperturbed by his grandfather's imminent arrival.

Mr Buttimer continued, 'The last two are Cormac and Bronagh McGovern, brother and sister, in your employment as a stable hand and a scullery maid. Their father is deceased and they begged for their mother not to be informed of tonight's events. Cormac says he can speak for them both.'

Cormac inclined his head to corroborate the butler's statement. Bridget stared at him, willing him to communicate to her what was really going on but his attention was fixed upon Lady Courcey as she had just risen from her seat. For the first time, Bridget wished she was already the baroness. She had no power here but that of persuasion. And Lady Courcey was out for blood.

Her gaze raked along the line. Seamus and Billy were the most frightened and shrank before her. Malachy looked resentful while Bronagh's chin jutted out in defiance. Cormac seemed the calmest of them all.

She addressed them in cutting tones. 'Do any of you deny that you were in the drawing room of this house tonight?'

They all shook their heads.

'Do any of you deny that an act of theft was taking place in the same drawing room?'

They shook their heads again but Cormac's eyes narrowed and Bridget could see why. Lady Courcey was phrasing her questions so that all five could be condemned together, without individual voices.

'You therefore acknowledge involvement and culpability in this crime. I have already sent for the constabulary to remove you from the premises. For those of you who have been in my employment, I regard this as the most profound betrayal of trust and a terrible reflection upon your positions as servants in my household.'

Cormac's voice rang out. 'Can't we present a defence, your ladyship?'

Bridget admired his nerve and peeked sideways at her mother to gauge her reaction. The lady's mouth tightened but she seemed to still feel she had the upper hand for she indulged him by saying, 'I can see no evidence to the contrary of what I have just pronounced. Do you have facts to offer which can prove otherwise?'

'I do, m'lady.' He paused. 'Though I'm reluctant to tell them as they may be seen to place my sister in a bad light.'

Bridget threw him a sharp look. Did he have a way of absolving himself from this fiasco while implicating his sister still further? That did not sound at all like his nature, and yet if even one of them could get out of this without a sentence of imprisonment, death or transportation, then perhaps that could be considered a success...

'Indeed?' sneered Lady Courcey. 'Proceed.'

Cormac took a breath. When he spoke again, his words were slow and deliberate and it was clear he was making a conscious effort to sound more formal in his manner of speech. 'My sister is only twelve, your ladyship, and impressionable. She is far too young to be having romantic notions but Malachy Kelly turned her head with empty promises. She agreed to meet him tonight because, in her innocent mind, she believed he wanted to talk and get to know her better. This is where I acknowledge my sister's foolishness at not having the sense to recognise the risk she was taking. While I cannot say for certain what would have happened, if anything of a scandalous nature had occurred between them the blame would have had to be laid upon Malachy, him being three years older and taking advantage of a gullible girl with sentimental feelings.'

Bridget was watching Bronagh when the maid's eyes flicked towards her brother and then focused back on the floor. This version of the story was new to her. A quick scan of the room assured Bridget that no one else had noticed the furtive glance. Malachy looked furious but Cormac's words continued without a break, hindering his protestations.

'For my part, I deem it fortunate that this was not what Malachy had intended because I could not stand such a thing befalling my own sister. However, the alternative was no better. He and his friends were waiting in the courtyard when she unlocked the kitchen door. They pushed past her and disappeared into the house, despite her efforts to stop them. I am sure you will forgive a twelve-year-old girl's powerlessness in preventing three lads older and bigger than her from doing exactly what they wanted.'

Lady Courcey did not react to this remark.

'When she saw the sacks in their hands, she could tell they were up to no good. She knew she should inform someone but feared how it would look for her, considering she had unlocked the door through which they had gained access to the house. So she went to a person she could trust.' He shrugged and went on, 'I was asleep in the stable loft. She woke me up and told me what had happened. I too wanted to avoid wrongful blame being placed upon her so I sought to resolve the situation by myself. I followed the boys into the house and was trying to convince them to leave when Mr Buttimer and his footmen found us. I understand how it may have appeared but neither my sister nor I had any involvement in the theft because we bear too great a respect for the rich history of Oakleigh and a deep pride in being able to serve here.'

Malachy seized his opportunity as soon as Cormac stopped speaking. With a snort, he said, 'That's all drivel. The two of them are up to their necks in this too, I swear it.' His face lit up with dawning inspiration. 'In fact, it was the other way 'round. *We* were trying to stop *them* from stealing.'

This assertion lacked so much credibility that Bridget was confident even her mother could not fail to see it. Nevertheless, the lady pursed her lips in deliberation before addressing Cormac again.

'It seems we have one person's word against the other. In the interest of erring on the side of caution, and bearing in mind that your presence in the drawing room cannot be denied, you and your sister will still have to go with the constables.'

'Ask Mr Buttimer,' Cormac said loudly. 'He will tell you who to believe.'

It was a bold thing to prevail upon the butler like that but, to Bridget's surprise, Lady Courcey turned towards Mr Buttimer, seeking his opinion. He too looked taken aback but puffed out his chest.

'My lady, you know I am a man of profound morals and can only ever speak the truth. I am therefore compelled to confess that Malachy Kelly has not proved himself to be the most reliable or honest person in the course of his employment as a gardener at Oakleigh. He has received several warnings about his behaviour, and his grandfather has even been obliged to refer him to me for castigation. Cormac McGovern, on the other hand...' The butler glanced down the line to where Cormac stood. 'I have never been able to fault his hard-working attitude or his loyalty to this estate. John Corbett, the stable master, speaks very highly of him. As for his sister, I cannot claim to know her so we may need to consult Mrs Kavanagh for a true assessment of her character.'

The look on Bronagh's face told Bridget that the cook's testimony would be liable to harm her case instead of help it.

'No need,' she interjected. 'I can vouch for her myself. I have encountered Bronagh on a number of occasions this summer and can say that in all instances she has been a cheerful and charming girl. The idea that she might be involved in this is preposterous.'

Both Cormac and Bronagh maintained bland expressions at this fanciful description. At that moment, there was a discreet knock on the door and the second footman, Denis, entered.

'Fintan Kelly's here, sir,' he told Mr Buttimer.

After a nod from Lady Courcey, the butler said, 'Bring him in.'

The aged gardener stalked into the study, no trace of infirmity in the way he held himself erect. When he laid eyes upon his grandson, his jowls quivered in anger. He swept his cap from his head and faced Lady Courcey.

'M'lady, I can't apologise enough for my grandson's outrageous behaviour.'

This startled her. 'Do you not wish to verify the validity of the accusations against him before accepting them as fact?'

He clicked his tongue. 'I'm not one bit surprised to hear them and can readily believe he's been acting the fool. He's a shame to my family and to Oakleigh and a sound punishment is all he deserves.'

Malachy's jaw dropped upon hearing his grandfather defame him in such a manner. It was plain that up until this point he had expected his connection to the old man to acquit him from any harsh sentence.

'Granda,' he began in indignation, but a glower from Fintan silenced him.

'Do with him what you will, m'lady,' he said. 'And please accept my humblest apologies for the sins of a boy who's no longer a grandson of mine.'

With that, he jammed his cap back on his head and stamped out of the room again.

Confronted with the severity of the old gardener's contempt, everyone perceived that, in a debate of truth between Malachy and Cormac, the odds were overwhelmingly in Cormac's favour. Lady Courcey looked as livid as Fintan Kelly as she realised what she must do.

'The girl and her brother are free to go,' she muttered. 'But,' she said with a vindictive gleam in her eyes, 'they shall each be docked a week's wages for having become embroiled in such an appalling incident. In fact, the girl shall be docked two weeks on account of her loose behaviour, be it innocent or no. I will not have servants engaging in clandestine meetings at midnight on my estate, even if it is just to "talk".' Her tone implied just how much she believed that element of the story.

In light of where they could have been heading when they departed from the room, Cormac and Bronagh seemed disinclined to make any objection to this.

'As for these others…'

Lady Courcey turned her ruthless gaze on the three lads. Billy's chin trembled but Seamus was scowling at Malachy, who appeared to be in a state of utter disbelief.

'Attempted theft of such valuable property is a most serious crime. Had the silver been removed from the premises, a penalty no less than hanging would have been appropriate. Given that the goods are still present and intact, I shall be merciful and consider transportation instead.'

Bronagh swayed as though she might faint at the thought of her would-be sweetheart being banished all the way to Australia.

Bridget hastened to speak up. 'And that would be a just punishment for hardened criminals beyond saving,' she said, nodding vigorously at her mother. 'Although I suppose we must be fair and take into account the young age of these boys and the fact that this is their first offence. A term of imprisonment may well be the more proportionate sentence.'

Lady Courcey gave her a calculating look. After a pause, she said, 'An extremely long term of imprisonment then.'

Some of the tension in the room eased as the threat of transportation receded.

Just then, another knock on the door and a clinking of keys heralded the appearance of an anxious Mrs Walsh. 'My lady, the constables are here.'

To Bridget's consternation, Constables Quirke and Tierney strode into the study. She sent up a silent prayer that they would not allude to their encounter with her at The Pikeman in front of her mother – that revelation was the last thing needed tonight. But they were preoccupied with the matter at hand; Constable Tierney was bouncing with excitement, while Constable Quirke looked like he wished for nothing more than his bed.

'Your ladyship,' he said, 'who do you wish us to take into custody?'

Lady Courcey swept a hand out to indicate the felons, her gesture coming to a reluctant stop just before the McGovern siblings. Bridget read the disappointment on Constable Tierney's features – his judgement of

Cormac that day in Ballydarry was not to be borne out after all.

'Take them away,' the lady commanded. 'I shall ensure my will in this affair is conveyed to my representative in the court proceedings.'

She jerked her head to communicate her dismissal of all present. The constables herded out Malachy and his friends, all three dumbfounded at the way events had unravelled, and Mr Buttimer flapped at the others to follow suit.

Bridget stared at Cormac as he left the study. Just before he passed through the doorway, he cast a glance in her direction. His expression was one of deepest gratitude.

When the door had shut on the last retreating back, Lady Courcey turned to her daughter.

'I hope you will not learn the hard way the consequences of such leniency,' she said with a rather ominous insinuation. Before Bridget could respond, she went on, 'If he has woken, Mr Lambourne will want to know what the commotion was all about. You shall not feel the need to tell him any more than the barest details of what has transpired. And I will tell Buttimer not to let this spread among the servants.'

The lady's message was clear: the fewer people who knew about the incident, the better. On the surface, it did no good to gossip about such grave matters. But furthermore, the attempted theft had exposed a real danger to her property and even her person, had the thieves made it upstairs and been of a more cunning or murderous variety than Malachy and his cohorts. She didn't want anyone else to be made aware of that vulnerability.

'I understand,' said Bridget, and she reached out tentatively to touch her mother's arm.

Lady Courcey gave a cold shrug and turned away.

***

The enormity of the risk Bronagh had taken only seemed to dawn upon her once they left Lady Courcey's forbidding presence. Her knees buckled in the hallway outside the study and Cormac had to support her all the way down to the kitchens.

Although sunrise was near, it was not yet time for the servants to begin their working day so the kitchens were empty. The constables steered their charges towards the back door but Malachy twisted in the older constable's grasp and stretched out a beseeching hand to Bronagh. She fell into his arms and he touched her cheek in a tender gesture quite unlike anything Cormac had ever seen in his behaviour. He wanted to smack the boy's palm away but permitted them this final moment – they would never have another. Malachy leaned in close and whispered something in

Bronagh's ear. Then the constable jerked him away and he, Seamus and Billy lurched out the back door.

When they had disappeared, Bronagh let out an anguished sob and, abandoning the tough exterior she always worked so hard to maintain, wept on Cormac's shoulder with the desolation of a young girl whose world had ended.

'I'm so sorry,' she choked. 'I n-never meant to c-cause such trouble.'

'I know,' he said, stroking her back. 'Don't worry anymore about it. You're out of harm's way now.'

Her tears gradually diminished to intermittent snuffles. After one last hiccup, she wiped her eyes, thrust out her chin, and vanished through the door that led to the servants' stairs. It would be a long climb to her bed at the top of the house, her footsteps heavy with a misery she would bear alone. She would be too proud to divulge this incident to anyone, even Margaret. With a rush of compassion for his stubborn sister, Cormac headed back to the stables, where he would also keep his silence.

Now it was mid-afternoon and he was grooming Bonny in her stall after a bout of exercise in the paddock. He suppressed a jaw-breaking yawn; he was weighed down by fatigue, thanks to lack of sleep and the strain of the previous night's events. At least no one was keeping an eye on him beyond the half door. He didn't envy Bronagh who was enduring an exhausting day under the watchful gaze of Mrs Kavanagh. However, that was a great deal preferable to being escorted by a constable to a sentencing in a courthouse. While her heart was bruised, her reputation and position were secure.

As were his own, but it had been a close call. It had required some quick thinking on his part, not to mention a helpful contribution from Bridget which she had been in no way obligated to provide.

A light rap on the half door made him look up. As though his thoughts had summoned her there, Bridget stood beyond it.

'May I come in?' she said, as if she were at the door of his home.

He waved his arm in a flourish. 'Any visitor's welcome in my grand dwelling.'

She gave a small smile but it was quick to evaporate. She glanced over her shoulder before slipping through the half door and he wondered if Mr Lambourne or Lady Courcey lurked in close proximity. He doubted whether he had the energy to face either of them right now.

'I'm alone,' she said. 'I told them I wished to investigate stable space for our guests' horses.'

He nodded. He knew about the impending birthday celebrations; the whole staff was in a state of frenzy preparing for them.

She approached Bonny and rubbed the mare's forehead affectionately. Then she turned to him and said in a low voice, 'I want to talk to you about last night.'

He picked up a brush and busied himself with Bonny's white coat. 'I can't say enough how sorry I am it happened.'

'You do not need to apologise. I know very well you had no involvement. Your sister though...' Her teeth caught the tip of her tongue. 'Did she have something to do with it?'

Sighing, he said, 'She did, the daft girl.'

Bridget's brow creased. 'Then perhaps I should not have defended her.'

'Please don't regret it. She's been foolish but she knows now what she did was very wrong. The shame'll stay with her a long time, 'specially when our family feels the pinch of the cut wages.'

'I do wish my mother had not resorted to that measure. Still, perhaps there will be compensation some other way.' There was a secretive air about her as she said this but she did not elaborate, instead saying, 'You are sure we can trust her?'

'I'm sure. That Malachy Kelly was a rotten influence. With him gone, she'll never do anything like that again.'

'I hope that is true. I would hate to think I had compromised the security of the manor.'

'You haven't,' he assured her. 'And I'm very grateful for your kind words on her behalf, although calling her a cheerful and charming girl might've been pushing it a bit. She's so sullen sometimes, I want to wring her neck. But she's a good girl at heart. She just has some growing up to do yet.'

'Well, she has a decent older brother to help her out there,' Bridget said, smiling. 'One who exhibits a fine grasp of formal language for a stable hand, I have to say. You acquitted yourself admirably in front of my mother.'

He felt his cheeks go red. 'Arrah, I couldn't have spent so many years 'round you and not pick up a fancy word here or there. But I can't say 'tis a habit that'll catch on. Apart from the fact that my family would be quick to tell me I was having notions about myself, it takes too much effort to pronounce everything right.'

She let out a soft laugh. 'I suppose that is true. Speaking of your family, Ellen told me it has been augmented by the recent return of your sister from Dublin. I am so glad for you that Mary has come home.'

'Thanks. My mother's been in better spirits since she's come back.'

'I am very pleased to hear it,' said Bridget.

He chose not to mention that while his mother seemed happier, his sister did not. In truth, he was worried about her. She flitted about the cottage like a ghost and hardly stirred herself to take care of her own child, save to nurse him. After the first night, she refused to speak of her husband or her time in Dublin. He had urged her to go visit Ellen, since they had been such close friends as young girls, but she had greeted the suggestion with a lethargic shrug. He hoped she would soon settle and become content with her lot in life, altered though it was from what she had expected it to be.

In the silence that followed, the only sound was the brush flicking along Bonny's coat. Bridget's lips parted like she was going to say something else. He looked down, focusing very hard on removing the dirt with short strokes.

When he looked up again, she was shutting the half door behind her.

## Chapter 15

The guests began to arrive the following day. Bridget found that her enthusiasm for the imminent festivities had been tempered by the grave events surrounding the burglary but, when the first carriage rolled up the avenue, she resolved to put all sombre thoughts from her mind. The incident had passed and it was now her duty to be a delightful hostess.

She and Garrett went outside to welcome their visitors, reaching the bottom of the front steps as the carriage drew up and a footman jumped down to open the door. Madeleine Wallace emerged, auburn ringlets bouncing around her face, and gave a squeal of excitement when she saw Bridget.

'Oh, you are a dear angel for inviting us!' she exclaimed. 'I shall be forever indebted to you for brightening the dullest summer of my life!'

Her sister, Catherine, alighted next from the carriage, assisted by her husband, Mr Howard Spencer, a limping gentleman twenty years her senior. Theirs had been a match arranged by her parents and, judging by her grimace as she sidled out of his grasp, it was not an especially happy one. Bridget experienced a dart of gratitude towards her mother that she had refrained from inflicting such a fate upon her.

They had scarcely returned to the house when the next carriage pulled up, this one carrying Garrett's companions, the Ashford brothers and their cousin, Mr Matthew Parnell. A third carriage, bearing Miss Isabel Gardiner and the Misses Hyland, arrived later in the afternoon, by which time there was quite the merry atmosphere all around. A long-time London acquaintance of Garrett's, Lord Newby, happened to be visiting Dublin for the summer and he also travelled down to Oakleigh, though he was the last to make an appearance, not arriving until the next morning.

It had been years since Oakleigh Manor had been so full of life. Every bedchamber was occupied, every stall in the stables contained a whinnying horse, every seat was taken at mealtimes, and every corner of the house overflowed with laughter and chatter from morning to night. For the servants of the household, such a large company signified extra toil in washing, cleaning and cooking, so Bridget had ensured in advance that Mrs Walsh enlisted several local girls to help cope with the enormous workload.

Garrett's twenty-sixth birthday occurred two days after the guests arrived and the entire group celebrated the day with entertaining pursuits. In the morning and afternoon, they held a number of bowls tournaments, starting with individual contenders, then pairs of gentlemen and ladies, and lastly male and female couples. The Hyland twins proved to be an unstoppable force but Garrett and Bridget won the couples tournament to the cheers of all assembled.

In the evening, a sumptuous dinner was to be followed by a night of dancing in the ballroom. Before she went down, Bridget sent for Ellen and asked her to be discreet in bringing Garrett to her bedchamber.

'It is nothing untoward,' she promised upon seeing Ellen's shocked face. 'You may leave the door ajar and listen to reassure yourself.'

Still looking doubtful, Ellen withdrew to obey her instruction and Garrett came in soon after, glancing around in curiosity.

'I don't quite know what to make of such a summons,' he said, winking at her.

She blushed. 'I'm aware this is not quite proper, but I wanted to give you your birthday present in private.'

She held out a small item wrapped in a navy satin cloth. He took it from her and removed the cloth to reveal a striking pocket watch with a gold chain attached. There were some scratches on the casing but the metal shone with long years of assiduous care.

He gaped at it, astounded. 'It is exquisite, my darling. Where on earth did you get it?'

'It belonged to my father. It was the only thing of his that my mother allowed me to keep. I want you to have it.'

He closed his hand over it in reverence. 'This means so much to me. Thank you.'

'I wish you the happiest of birthdays,' she murmured, voice thick with emotion, and they embraced.

As he held her, her feeling of contentment was disturbed by the prospect of London but she pushed it away, determined that the evening would be one of perfect bliss.

They descended the broad mahogany staircase together and led their guests into the dining room for a lavish feast, which was presented with great formality and grandeur. Much later, they continued the party into the ballroom, where a group of musicians struck up a lively waltz as they entered. Garrett guided Bridget onto the floor and then, after waiting for the leading couple to dance a few bars on their own, other pairs began to join in. Mr Spencer declined to partake on account of his limp but his wife accepted Lord Newby's offer to dance with alacrity. Bridget observed that Mr Parnell partnered an enchanted Madeleine three dances in a row and wondered if she was witnessing a match in the making right here in her ballroom. The younger Ashford brother, meanwhile, defied convention and twirled around by himself, waving his arms in the air and calling for more wine. The atmosphere was carefree and festive, and Bridget did her best to convince herself that nothing could make her happier in this moment.

*\*\*\**

Cormac rubbed his eyes as he closed the door of the last stall. The stables had never been so full and his working day had never been so long than since the fine folk from the city had come to stay. It was well after dark and he was looking forward to nothing more than his bed of straw in the stable loft but, just as he started to climb the ladder, he heard his name being called and turned to see Liam's lanky form silhouetted inside the stable doors.

'Don't you want to come to the kitchens? Mrs Kavanagh might be generous with the leftovers tonight, seeing as she put on a spread for about a hundred.'

He considered the suggestion, decided his bed could wait a little longer if a chance to sample Mrs Kavanagh's delicious desserts was in the offing, and jumped back down from the ladder. He and Liam left the stables, crossed the courtyard and entered the kitchens, where he got the immediate sense of the aftermath of a storm. All around the room, red-faced maids slumped in exhaustion on benches, the hearth and even the floor, looking as though they had simply collapsed where they stood. Half-empty dishes lay discarded on the kitchen table, including the remains of some giant fowl in a bed of vegetables which must have been the magnificent centrepiece of the birthday dinner. Most mouth-watering of all, he spied a few leftover slices of two tarts and a cake down at the further end of the table. Mrs Kavanagh herself sat in front of them, arms folded over her enormous bosom as she surveyed the carnage with immense satisfaction.

'All went off without a hitch,' she announced to Cormac and Liam. 'Mr Lambourne sent back a message of his particular appreciation of the raspberry tart.'

'No surprise there. Everyone knows your tarts have no equal,' said Cormac, though he didn't think the cook required much buttering up tonight. He approached the table. 'Raspberry, you said?'

'Help yourselves, lads, help yourselves!' she said, beaming, and they did not hesitate.

Margaret and Bronagh, huddled in the corner by a stack of freshly scoured pots, laughed at their enthusiasm, though Bronagh's laugh was rather shaky. The previous night, she and Cormac had gone home to confess their absent wages to their mother. He had advised Bronagh to invent a story about a breakage in the kitchens while he himself had claimed the necessity to set aside some money to replenish the supply of nails in his father's tool chest; the last thing their mother needed was to learn of the near disgrace that had come upon her two children. Even though Maggie had tried to hide her dismay, Bronagh had perceived it and her remorse had been palpable. She would feel raw about both that and the loss of Malachy for a long while yet, but at least the ache would ease with time and it gladdened Cormac to see her making an effort to be cheerful tonight.

He was on his fourth bite of tart when the inner kitchen door opened and Ellen entered. She too looked fatigued, though not quite as much as the kitchen staff did.

'Lady Courcey has just retired to her bedchamber,' she told Mrs Kavanagh. 'The young people are still dancing but her ladyship says our duties above stairs are finished for tonight.'

'Thank heavens for that.' The cook heaved herself up with a grimace. 'Now I can go and rest my weary bones.'

She departed from the room with a pointed remark about expecting a spotless kitchen the next morning, to which the maids responded with grudging acquiescence. Once she was gone, Ellen sat in her place and helped herself to some of the raspberry tart too. The atmosphere remained relaxed, in spite of her position above the other servants. She displayed none of the airs and graces her French predecessor was rumoured to have had in abundance, nor was she like the supercilious lady's maids who had accompanied their mistresses to Oakleigh for the birthday celebrations but did not deign to socialise in the kitchens. Her approachable manner gave Margaret the courage to slide onto the bench next to her, an eager look on her face.

'Tell us, Miss Ryan, what was it like? I want to know every detail!'

Ellen smiled and began to recount all the things the lowly maids below stairs were not permitted to see, the fashionable gowns and dazzling jewellery and elegant hairstyles. '...and one of the young ladies was wearing a dress the colour of autumn leaves. I heard her tell Miss Muldowney she had purchased it in London.'

'London!' Margaret said, entranced. 'Ah, how I'd love to see it.'

'Miss Muldowney herself had a beautiful comb of pearls in her hair. Everyone commented on how striking she looked.'

'And what about the gentlemen?' Margaret pressed, her eyes starry with romance. She had always been the most fanciful of Cormac's sisters, captivated by stories of chivalrous knights and rescued maidens and everlasting love.

'Needless to say, Mr Lambourne was the handsomest man in the room,' said Ellen. 'I was there attending to her ladyship when he and Miss

Muldowney commenced the first dance together. He danced so well, she was in raptures in his arms!'

Cormac pushed away the last few pieces of tart as he recalled that he could not dance at all.

'And the musicians?' It was plain that Margaret wished to paint a vivid picture in her mind of the whole occasion.

'Oh, they're very talented. In fact, if we go outside we might be able to hear them. Lady Courcey had Denis open the ballroom windows for air before she retired for the night.'

Margaret hopped up at once, all tiredness forgotten. She dragged a half-hearted Bronagh to her feet and then turned to Cormac. 'You coming?'

'Of course he is,' said Ellen, 'and so is Liam.'

Liam, who had gone a little red with all the talk of dresses and dancing gentlemen, now turned the deepest shade of beetroot.

'I don't —' he stuttered.

'You'll come if Cormac comes, won't you?' she said and glanced at Cormac with her eyebrows raised.

He understood her meaning and rose reluctantly. 'Fine, we're coming.'

Margaret clapped her hands and was first out the back door. Bronagh gave a shrug that said she was open to any form of torment to procrastinate the rest of the washing up and went after her. Cormac, Liam, Ellen and some of the other more curious maids followed.

Out in the courtyard, faint strains of music wafted to them, becoming stronger once they went around the side of the house. Moving along until they could see the open ballroom windows but were out of sight themselves, they stood and listened to the swelling music and the buzz of animated conversation of those dancing to it.

Margaret's face lifted towards the stirring sounds. 'I want to dance to it,' she said dreamily.

'Then let's,' said Ellen straight away. 'Cormac will dance with you and I can dance with Liam.'

Cormac had to smother a chuckle at his friend's petrified expression. It might be said that a lady's maid could do a lot better than a stable hand but the greater truth was that Ellen could do a lot worse than quiet, dependable Liam. She took a firm hold of his hands and Cormac followed suit with his sister. The other maids joined in too, giggling.

He stood on Margaret's feet three times and almost tripped her up before she said she might try Bronagh as a partner instead.

'I'm sorry,' he said. 'I've never been able to dance.'

''Tis only that you've never learned.' She patted him on the arm. 'If you practised it, you'd get better.'

He could not envisage any future where he would be required to practise dancing but he just gave her a good-natured kiss on the cheek and allowed

Bronagh to step in. Leaning against the wall of the house, he watched the others dance – Liam looked to be holding his own surprisingly well, judging by Ellen's radiant smiles. Cormac pictured Bridget twirling in her fiancé's sure grasp with the same sparkle in her eyes. The raspberry tart rested like a heavy ball in his gut and he wished he had gone straight up to the stable loft after all.

There was a lull in the music and the servants, laughing and breathless, ended their dance with bows and curtseys.

\*\*\*

The sky outside was beginning to lighten when the revellers in the ballroom chose to retire. Climbing the staircase to bed, everyone congratulated Garrett once more on his birthday and applauded Bridget for hosting a superb party. She beamed at her guests through her exhaustion and made her way to her bedchamber. She had barely eased the pearl comb out of her hair, however, when she heard a knock and opened the door to find Garrett on the threshold. He put his finger to his lips, slid inside, and closed the door behind him.

'What–' she started in surprise, but he cut her off with a tight embrace and a passionate kiss on her mouth. She giggled but pushed him away. 'No, we mustn't.'

'Oh, but we must,' he said and kissed her again.

This time he was rougher, pressing her back against the nearest bedpost. She struggled to break free of his grip and slipped sideways onto the bed, her curls tumbling around her shoulders. He leaned over her and attempted a seductive smile.

'Come to me, my darling,' he slurred.

'No!' She slithered under his reaching arm and darted to the opposite end of the room. 'You are intoxicated. Please leave.'

He staggered on the sheepskin rug. 'But we're going to be married soon. Why not enjoy our wedding night a little earlier than planned?'

Appalled at the suggestion, she spluttered, 'Absolutely not! Leave me this instant.' She pointed to the door to emphasise her order.

He shot her a disgruntled look, swivelled on his heel in a vain attempt at dignity, and stumbled out. She expelled a ragged breath and stared at the door, which he had left ajar. What a way to ruin the end of what ought to have been a perfect evening.

The little sleep she attained was broken and unsatisfactory; every time she began to drift off, she felt the hard wood of the bedpost digging into her back and smelled the alcohol on his breath. She supposed she was at fault for having placed Garrett on such a high pedestal, but this was a disheartening way for him to fall.

When she left her bedchamber later that morning, he stood outside it wearing an expression of utter contrition.

'Darling,' he said as soon as she appeared, 'how can I ever make sufficient apology for my conduct last night? I'm ashamed beyond belief. You must think me a thuggish lout but I swear I did not mean to offend you and I am so very sorry for it. Can you find it in your heart to forgive me?'

She gave him a disapproving glare. 'I shan't pretend that I wasn't shocked at the way you behaved. Please do not ever repeat it.'

'Never,' he vowed, grasping one of her hands. 'Truly, I cannot say what came over me. I don't think I have ever had that much to drink in my life, let alone in one night.' He winced. 'And I have the pain in my head to prove it.'

She smiled against her will. 'It serves you right.'

He grinned and then became serious. 'I promise never to upset you like that again,' he said and brought her hand up to press it to his cheek.

'Very well,' she conceded, and they went down to breakfast reconciled.

## Chapter 16

Over the next week or two, the August weather became punctuated by heavy rainstorms which burst into existence with sudden force and then slunk away as though they had never happened. Bridget, Garrett and their company were obliged to stay indoors and entertain themselves by playing cards and billiards while they waited for the storms to pass. Once the conditions turned fine again, they engaged in outdoor activities, the guests determined to make the most of their sojourn at Oakleigh, which all agreed to be an exceptional country estate.

On one such fair-weather day, the gentlemen seized the opportunity to fish on the banks of the Sruhawn, while the ladies opted to take a stroll down the tree-lined avenue. As they emerged from the front door of the manor, Bridget saw that the blue sky was populated with thick, white clouds which billowed and roiled, never keeping the same shape for long. It reminded her of a game she had played with Cormac when they were children: they used to lie side by side at the very bottom of the abandoned limestone quarry, faces pointed up to the sky, and pick out various shapes in the clouds before they swirled into something unrecognisable. Her greatest triumph had been a cloud which had coiled itself into a letter 'B', although Cormac had disagreed, saying it looked more like a turnip with holes in it.

Nostalgia tugging at her, she followed the other ladies down the front steps and onto the avenue, the fine gravel crunching softly beneath their shoes. A fresh breeze blew about them and she drew her shawl tighter around her shoulders as she listened to her companions lament the changeable conditions.

'It is a shame we have not yet been able to enjoy a picnic,' said Madeleine's sister, Catherine, her expression nonetheless cheerful, as it always was in the absence of her aging, limping husband. 'It would be disgraceful if we came all this way and never had a meal out of doors.'

'Yes, but there is no telling what this weather will do next,' Miss Isabel Gardiner said, squinting skywards. 'Judging by this bright day, I could declare that we ought to go ahead with our picnic right away but, knowing my propensity for misfortune, it would pour down on us before we had the blankets laid out.'

The others laughed.

'What we need,' said Madeleine, 'is a country person. I've heard they have an excellent understanding of weather patterns. I'm sure they could forecast it for us with no difficulty.'

She peered around, ringlets swinging. Just as Bridget was on the verge of making a quip about Madeleine expecting a country person to spring out of the ground at her command, her friend announced, 'There's one, shall we ask him?'

Turning, Bridget saw Cormac making his way around the corner of the manor house. He carried a tool chest in one hand and a few lengths of timber over his shoulder and appeared to be heading for the avenue, just like the ladies. Her insides somersaulted at the sight of him.

'Excuse me,' Madeleine called out.

He approached them, keeping a secure hold on the timber. The breeze lifted his fair hair, tousling it across his forehead.

'Can I help you, miss?' He addressed Madeleine, as she had been the one to hail him.

'Yes, can you tell us if you think it will rain today? We are debating whether to have a picnic but do not want it ruined by the weather.'

He shook his head. 'Today's not the day for a picnic, miss. Looks to me like it'll rain in about ten minutes. D'ye see that blacker cloud over there?'

They swivelled as one to where he pointed and saw that there was indeed a darker cloud blooming among its white companions.

Isabel said, 'Oh, dear.'

'My advice would be to stay near the house today. Save the picnic for a brighter afternoon.'

He started to move on past them. Isabel, however, eyed him up and down in appreciation and, to Bridget's intense annoyance, said coyly, 'But will you not get wet yourself if you keep going? You did say it will rain soon.'

He gave the briefest glance towards Bridget as he turned back to them but she could not tell whether he had picked up on the brazen nature of Isabel's remark. He just said, 'That's a risk I'll have to take, miss. There's a fence down near the entrance needs mending and it's got to be done today, rain or shine.'

Isabel pouted prettily at him but did not say anything else. He made to go again, passing Bridget as he did so. Without warning, he caught her eye, murmured, 'I see a bear,' and winked before striding on down the avenue.

She felt a grin spread across her face. He too had remembered the game. She gazed upwards and glimpsed the bear, its paw raised as though waving, just before the head floated away from the body and the cloud became another misshapen form.

'What did he say to you?' asked Catherine.

'Oh, he wished us a pleasant walk,' said Bridget, the internal parts of her body still pitching about madly.

Meanwhile, Madeleine was saying in a scandalised voice, 'And you, Miss Gardiner! Flirting with a servant, whatever will you do next?'

Isabel tittered, a rather irritating sound to Bridget's ears. 'You could all see he has good looks. It was just some harmless fun!'

Thinking Isabel was a more vacuous girl than she had taken her for, Bridget cut in, 'Let's walk on, shall we?'

Less than a quarter of an hour later, they were hurrying back to the house for shelter as the black cloud opened above them, just as Cormac had predicted.

The following day, however, the afternoon was sunny and warm with seemingly little chance of rain, so the group decided to have their picnic at last in the manor gardens. They sat on blankets laid out on the grass, munched on delicious refreshments prepared for them in the kitchens, and played a rematch of bowls, the men quietly intent on beating the formidable pairing of the Misses Hyland.

Within an hour or two, Bridget found she was developing a bad headache. When the exuberant laughter and heated debates over scoring became too much for her, she took Garrett aside and told him she might go indoors.

'Are you quite well, my darling?' he asked.

'I'll be fine. I just want to lie down for a short time until the headache passes and then I shall come back out.'

'If you are sure—oh, good shot, Newby! Knocked her right out of the way.'

Accepting that his attention would always be divided while sports were at play, she gave him a resigned smile and went into the house. She lay down on her bed, hoping a brief nap might cure the headache, but after a few minutes the pain worsened so she thought perhaps a stroll in the fresh air would do her more good. Not wanting to disturb the kitchen staff, doubtless already in the throes of dinner preparations, she slipped out the front door and walked around the side of the house to get to the cobbled courtyard. She glanced about for Cormac but he was nowhere to be seen. Trying to ignore her disappointment, she passed by the stables and the paddock and opened the gate into the Gorteen.

\*\*\*

Cormac tossed the mouldering rail onto the growing pile at his feet. He was down near the entrance to the avenue again, making further repairs to the boundary fence which divided the manor grounds from the rutted lane beyond. Closer scrutiny yesterday on what had appeared to be a couple of posts fallen into decay had revealed a whole section of fence turned rotten and a bigger task than he had anticipated. He had been obliged to enlist a second pair of hands to help and Liam had joined him to rebuild it. They laboured in companionable silence until he found he was too curious to keep quiet.

'So,' he said casually, as they lifted a new length of timber into place. 'Ellen Ryan?'

He thought Liam would only manage an incoherent stutter but, with no trace of a blush, the lad said, 'Miss Ryan puts the lady into lady's maid.'

Impressed by this unexpected eloquence, Cormac picked up his father's hammer and drove a long nail into the wood. 'D'you think you'll ask for her hand one day?'

'Might not get the chance. Where her ladyship goes, Miss Ryan's got to go too, and Dublin might as well be America for all the good it'll do me.' Liam shrugged. 'Besides, I've a ways to go before I'm worthy of her. I can't offer marriage 'til I've a bit of money saved and a decent home to take her to as well.'

Liam was scarcely a year younger than him but Cormac felt as though the boy had just matured into a man in front of his eyes. As he opened his mouth to wish him heartfelt luck in his endeavour, he realised he could no longer sense the heat of the sun on his back and looked up to see the sky darkening with ominous clouds. A stiff wind plucked at his sweat-dampened shirt and, without so much as a spit of warning, heavy raindrops began to pelt down.

''Tis going to be a monster of a storm,' he called over the instantaneous noise, and they gathered up the implements from his father's tool chest and ran for cover. As they reached the top of the avenue, they spotted the picnickers abandoning their bowls match and hastening indoors.

Their first duty upon returning to the stables was to settle the horses, which had become skittish at the onset of the turbulent weather. Then, in a rare instance of idleness, they stood at the double doors with John Corbett and some of the other men and simply stared out in awe at the torrential downpour. It pounded against the windows of the big house and struck the cobblestones with enough force to drown out the horses' fretful whinnying. Large puddles swelled across the courtyard, spreading like a spilled inkpot on a sheet of paper. Beyond the orchard wall, the tops of the apple trees flailed about and Cormac pictured the fruit making its premature descent to the ground. Even as he watched, the light diminished to the mere visibility of dusk, the storm clouds looming low and black.

All of a sudden, a rectangular glow materialised in the gloom as the back door of the kitchens swung open and none other than Mr Lambourne dashed out into the rain. His valet, Brewer, followed on his heels, hunched against the deluge as though exposure to it would bring about certain death. They splashed across the cobbles and sprinted into the stables, causing the congregated men to jump back from the doorway to make way for them.

'Have you seen Miss Muldowney?' Mr Lambourne exclaimed. 'Is she here?'

Cormac grew alarmed at once. 'Isn't she in the house?' he demanded in return, adding quickly, 'Sir.'

'We've searched all the rooms but cannot find her, and the servants have not seen her for hours. Could it be possible that she has taken refuge in one of the outbuildings?'

'She's not here in the stables,' said John, 'but maybe she's in one of the barns or the orchard.' He signalled to the two stable hands nearest to the double doors. 'Go check them out, chaps, and be quick about it.'

They ducked out into the pouring rain. Cormac itched to follow them.

'Did she take her horse?' John asked the remaining men.

Having only just calmed the mare in her stall, Cormac said, 'No, Bonny's still here.'

'That means she's on foot then, wherever she is.'

Mr Lambourne ran his hands through his damp hair, looking frantic. 'She must have gone out before the storm began. She could be anywhere, and caught in *this*!'

John stayed calm. 'She might yet be discovered on the grounds, sir. And, if not, we'll send out a party to search for her right away. We'll find her, don't you worry.'

Cormac shifted from foot to foot, impatient for the return of the two stable hands. At last, they came running through the doorway, rainwater streaming from their clothes.

'No sign of her, sir!' one of them gasped to Mr Lambourne.

John was swift to take charge, sending Brewer back indoors to seek the aid of every male servant who knew how to ride. Mr Lambourne did not hesitate to authorise the use of any horses belonging to the guests, declaring that they would be only too happy to offer what assistance they could. John nodded his gratitude and turned back to the men.

'Listen up! We'll go out in pairs. Ye two, make for Ballydarry, she may have taken refuge in one of the dwellings there. The rest of ye, spread out in every direction, towards the Sruhawn, the woods, the hayfields. Check any likely place where she could've found shelter. She mightn't see nor hear ye coming so be thorough. And keep alert for thunder and lightning. If it starts, take cover or ye'll be in danger yourselves. Saddle up now, fast as ye can, and let's bring her home safe!'

There was a flurry of movement as the men hastened to the stalls but Cormac ran up to the stable master. 'The quarry, John!'

'The quarry?' he repeated, mystified. 'What reason would she have to go that far, and on foot no less?'

Desperation and conviction rose in Cormac in equal measure. ''Tis a possibility. We shouldn't rule it out!'

Arguing the matter would only cause further delay.

'Fine so, you and Liam head for the quarry. Hurry now!'

By the time he led his horse out of its stall – a fine specimen belonging to Lord Newby – the footmen and guests' valets were flocking into the stables. Mr Lambourne called for Commander to be saddled too but John put out a restraining hand.

''Tis best you stay behind, sir,' he said, 'so you can be here when we get her back to you.'

Mr Lambourne's shoulders drooped and he stood aside to let Cormac tear past, Liam right behind him on his own mount.

The clatter of hooves as they rode out of the courtyard was lost in the din of the storm. Out in the open, the full force of it truly registered and Cormac gasped as the rain battered on his head and back. Thankfully, Lord Newby's horse didn't shy at being plunged into such tempestuous conditions and Cormac pushed forwards across the Gorteen, not checking to see whether Liam kept up with him or not.

The limestone quarry lay beyond a thin belt of woodland to the south of Oakleigh, in the shadow of the Blackstairs Mountains. When it had been deserted during their childhood, it had afforded them an ideal location for a variety of hide-and-seek games. After Bridget had left the estate, he had sometimes visited it by himself and hidden in one of her favourite spots, recalling the echo of her laughter around the stony pit that had always given her away, but once Lord Walcott ordered work to restart there it became a hive of activity again and he was no longer able to extract that little bit of comfort. He hadn't been back in years and there was no reason why she would return there herself. It was a mere bear waving in the sky which drove him towards it now but he cleaved to that hunch with all his might.

A flash of brightness on the horizon made him flinch in his saddle. Several seconds later, a loud crack rumbled all around them. He glanced back at Liam who urged his horse up beside him to shout, 'Shouldn't we –?'

'You can. I'm not.'

It was reckless but he didn't care. He did mind the fact that Liam followed him without further objection, but that couldn't be helped.

They raced across field after field until they reached the shelter of the woods, by which point they were soaked through, their sodden clothes sticking to their skin. Caution compelled them to slow their pace under the trees as the animals could trip over an unseen root if they were not careful.

Impatient, Cormac guided his horse along as fast as he dared.

The canopy of foliage deadened the noise of the storm to an extent, enabling Liam to call from behind him, 'Are you sure about where we're going?'

Cormac only nodded in reply, his whole being concentrated on the way ahead. He cast perfunctory glances to left and right and did not protest when Liam shouted for Miss Muldowney at regular intervals, but his instinct told him she had not taken cover in these trees.

On the other side of the strip of woodland, they were able to increase their pace again. Wind and rain whipped into his face but he disregarded it. He strained to see any sign of the quarry; he knew it was somewhere nearby, though the murk veiled even the lofty mountains from view.

Then a blaze of lightning lit up the way and revealed the boundary of the pit not twenty feet in front of him. Only for the timely flare of light, he would have pitched unseeing over the edge. As it was, he had to halt his horse with a sharp jerk of the reins, skidding on the muddy ground. The animal neighed in fright and he gave it a reassuring pat on its neck before dismounting, his joints stiff with the wet and cold. Liam pulled his horse to a stop next to him and did likewise.

They both scanned the quarry but it was too dark to make out anything other than vague mounds of stone far down in the bottom of the hole. The workers had abandoned the site in their own rush for shelter and it appeared quite as forsaken as when he and Bridget used to play there.

'Can you see her?' he yelled above the raging wind.

Liam chewed his lip as his gaze roved over the pit plunging down before them. Another flash illuminated the scene.

'What's that over there?' he bellowed, pointing.

But Cormac had seen it too. As the light died, he glimpsed something fluttering among the inert boulders. Was it a piece of fabric, the hem of a dress maybe?

He thrust his reins into Liam's hands. 'Keep him steady while I go down there.'

He approached the edge of the quarry and began to pick his way down into it. The rock was slick from the heavy rainfall and he more or less slipped towards the bottom, unmindful of his torn clothes and grazed skin, until he got to the place where he imagined he had seen some movement. Casting around, he thought for a heart-stopping moment that he had been mistaken, that there was nothing here and they were no closer to finding her, but then he distinguished a bare arm stretched out on the ground. He darted forwards. She lay crumpled behind a large boulder, her sleeve ripped and flapping in the wind. Relief flooded through him but it dissipated when he saw her closed eyelids and slack mouth. Was she unconscious? Or worse?

'Bridget!' he cried in panic, dropping to his knees beside her.

She did not respond. He touched the side of her head. His fingers came back dark and sticky before the rain washed them clean again. Terrified, he bent down close to her parted lips. There was a beat of ringing silence, during which he could no longer seem to hear the storm, as though the thunder and wind were suspended by the same dreaded anticipation that filled him, and then he felt the lightest quiver of breath on his skin. She was alive.

The gale resumed in his ears as he lifted her into his arms and turned to make the treacherous ascent back up the wet slope. Struggling up the incline, he was grateful when Liam appeared beside him and together they managed to get her to the top of the pit. Liam had tied the horses to a bush and the two animals stood waiting, eyes rolling. Cormac handed Bridget's limp form to Liam, leapt up onto his horse, and took her back, settling her with care in front of him.

'You go on ahead!' he called down as Liam untied the horses. 'I'll be slower now with two of us. You go on and tell them we're coming.'

Liam nodded, jumped onto his own horse, and swung around to gallop back the way they had come. Cormac followed, trying not to jostle Bridget unduly. She was like a wounded bird in his grasp, frail and motionless. Her hair and clothes were saturated and her skin was freezing to the touch. The blood he had found came from a grim-looking gash at her temple. Petrified for her life, he clung to that delicate, barely perceptible rise and fall of her chest that told him she was still breathing. He held her close to try to pass some of his own body warmth on to her, a somewhat futile gesture for he was almost as cold as she was and wracked by violent shivers.

'Hold on, Bridget,' he whispered, willing her to obey his plea.

She made an effort to rouse herself. 'Cormac?' Her voice was feeble.

'Shush.' He put his lips to her ear. 'Don't worry, we're not far from home.'

His horse picked its way through the narrow strip of woods and then they were riding back across the fields, keeping to the lines of hedges as much as possible to avoid being out in the open. He wasn't sure but he thought the storm might be moving away towards the east. The thunder and lightning had diminished and the wind too had lessened to an extent, though the rain still pelted down. He was just thinking they had to be nearing the big house when the giant's claw loomed out of the gloom. Only a few fields to go. Offering up a prayer of thanks, he pressed his horse forwards on one final spurt.

'Just a bit further, *a ghrá*,' he murmured to Bridget, tightening his arm around her waist.

He rode into the courtyard to find it almost empty of people, the rest of the men still out searching, but Mr Lambourne stood waiting in the rain beside Liam, his arms outstretched to take his fiancée. Exhausted, Cormac surrendered her to him and the gentleman whisked her inside the house at once. He nearly fell as he tried to get down from the horse himself but Liam was there to help.

'There are some spare clothes in the stables,' he told Cormac. 'Mrs Kavanagh said to get changed and come into the kitchens. I met John so he's gone out to spread the word that we've found Miss Muldowney.'

Cormac soon sat on a stool in front of the kitchen hearth in dry clothing, although his hair was still plastered to his head and his hands and feet were numb. He had a blanket wrapped around his shoulders and he huddled towards the fire, urging his chilled bones to heat up. The cook patted him on the back as she handed him a bowl of steaming soup.

'Well done, lad,' she said for the twentieth time. 'Bless you for bringing the young lady home safe.'

Margaret and Bronagh, all work forgotten, clustered near their brother and discussed the state of Bridget, whom they had glimpsed as she was carried through the kitchens upstairs.

'She was pale as death,' Bronagh said in a rather detached manner. 'That wound looked nasty too.'

'Will she recover?' Margaret's tone was hushed.

Bronagh lowered her voice too so that Mrs Kavanagh, who was passing some soup to Liam at the kitchen table, would not hear. 'Depends. I remember when she and Cormac used to go larking about in all weather. Back then, she had the constitution of a horse and no fear of her. But now…'

'What's different now?' asked Margaret, and Cormac grimaced at the many possible answers to that question.

'Haven't you seen her since she's come back? She's a proper lady now, gotten used to easy living. She's so frail a strong wind could blow her over. In fact, it wouldn't surprise me if that's what happened to her today.'

Just then, the back door opened and several more men trooped inside, dripping water. Mrs Kavanagh clicked her fingers at Cormac's sisters and they scuttled away to help her distribute soup, while he slid his stool to the side of the hearth to make room for the others.

He hated to admit it but he had to agree with Bronagh. Seven years of a soft life in the city had transformed a robust, healthy girl into a far more fragile young lady. He feared Bridget would not get through this ordeal without great difficulty.

## Chapter 17

Cormac was right. Tidings spread around the estate the next day that Miss Muldowney was confined to bed, gravely ill with a fever, and her fiancé would not stir from her bedside. Their guests, shocked by the terrible event and loath to intrude, departed from Oakleigh the same afternoon with best wishes for her speedy recovery. The servants, both indoor and outdoor, conversed in whispers about the young lady's poorly state and how there was a strong possibility she might not survive. Cormac felt sick whenever he overheard these covert exchanges and started going home to his family's cottage every night to avoid them, but even there it was an incessant topic of discussion.

'The craythur,' his mother took to saying over and over again. 'How awful. The poor craythur.'

On the third evening, he came home with the news that the physician had bled Bridget with no visible results, and Maggie could not seem to let this go.

'It made no difference? Didn't her fever drop even a little bit? Didn't they notice any change in her temperature at all?'

'I've no idea!' he burst out, weary of the constant questions. 'That was all Ellen Ryan could tell me. I don't know anything except she's still ill and hasn't woken up or said a word.'

He rubbed his forehead in frustration. Bridget's failure to improve was tormenting him. He kept asking himself if there was something more he could have done when he found her to prevent her condition from deteriorating so much. Everyone commended him for having returned her as safely as he did, but he waved away the praise, uncomfortable with the attention and dispirited by the lack of encouraging tidings.

When he dropped his hand, he caught his sister Mary observing him.

'What?' he said, irritated.

'Nothing,' she replied quietly.

After five days he could bear it no longer. He dawdled in the courtyard near the kitchen door after breakfast, knowing that Mrs Walsh came down to the kitchens at the same time every morning to discuss the dinner menu with Mrs Kavanagh, and darted inside as soon as the harassed housekeeper appeared.

'What is it, Cormac?' she snapped.

Dispersing with any preamble, he said, 'I want to see Bridget.'

She looked incredulous. 'That's Miss Muldowney to you. And don't be foolish. You're a servant, her ladyship would never allow it.'

'Then ask Mr Lambourne. He'll allow it.' He supposed he should feel guilty for taking advantage of the man's good nature but in this case he was beyond caring.

She frowned. 'Why do you want to see her? What purpose will it serve?'

'I don't know,' he said honestly. 'I just need to, even if 'tis only for a minute or two.'

She exchanged a glance with Mrs Kavanagh, who muttered, 'It's a brazen request but he did save the girl's life. Remember how close those two were when they were children.'

After considering this, the housekeeper gave a grudging shrug. 'I shall make an enquiry. Come back here at noon and you will find out then.'

'Thank you, Mrs Walsh.' It was as much as he could hope for.

He slipped out of the kitchens. The weather was warm and dry, as it had been every day since the ferocious storm, and the sun winked down in mockery of the dark mood that pervaded the grounds. He glowered up at it before disappearing into the shadows of the stables.

He returned to the kitchens just before noon and helped his sisters peel potatoes until Mrs Walsh arrived. When she swept in, he looked up in anticipation.

'You're to come up now,' she said, her mouth taut with disapproval. 'Her ladyship was against the proposal but the gentleman said he could not refuse. He feels obliged to you on account of you saving his fiancée's life.'

Cormac had counted on this. He nodded, laid down his knife, and followed her to the servants' stairs. She led him up through the bowels of the house to the second floor where they emerged onto a long corridor of closed doors. These were not the usual sleeping quarters for the family; a guest bedchamber must have been set aside for Bridget's sick room.

Mrs Walsh stopped outside one of the doors and knocked softly. A voice answered from within and they entered.

The room was dark; the shutters had been closed over the windows and the only light came from flickering candles on the dresser and a bedside table. By their weak glow, he saw Bridget lying in the bed, a diminutive form on the broad plane of the mattress, shivering in troubled sleep. Her skin was flushed and damp strands of hair clung to the sides of her face. There was one bandage wrapped about her head and another tied around her forearm which lay outside the bedcovers – the first bound the injury she had sustained at the quarry and the second was evidence of the physician's bloodletting.

Mr Lambourne sat beside the bed, clasping her hand. Lady Courcey stood behind him by a shuttered window. She looked displeased – no doubt recalling the last time she and Cormac had come face to face – and made no move to even acknowledge his presence, but Mr Lambourne rose as he came into the room.

'It's Cormac, isn't it?' To his surprise, the gentleman reached out and shook his hand. 'I haven't had the opportunity to thank you for bringing Miss Muldowney back to me. I am very grateful to you. As you can see, she's not well right now but when she is better she will thank you too.'

'You're welcome, sir,' said Cormac, his voice a little hoarse. 'Has there – has there been any improvement in the young lady?'

'None.'

Mr Lambourne waved Cormac forwards. He stepped to the opposite side of the bed from Lady Courcey and stared down at Bridget. Now that he was this near to her, he could see that the rumours around the estate had not been based on falsehoods or even exaggeration. She looked like she was on her death bed. Sweat coated her forehead, she was gaunt from lack of food, and her breathing came shallow and raspy. His heart sank. Could any girl survive an illness like this?

He casually rested his hand on the flower-patterned bedcover, next to where her own lay, clammy and motionless. Gazing at her closed eyelids, he imagined the dark brown eyes beneath and silently begged her to beat the fever. Fight this, he urged her. You have to get better. Please wake up.

She stirred in her delirium and mumbled something incoherent. He grimaced in despair, losing hope that she would ever recover. Was it a matter of days, or even hours, before she lost her weak grip on life? Now he knew why he had wanted to see her – it might be the last time he saw her alive. His chest constricted painfully with regret for all the things that had been left unspoken between them.

After several more long moments, during which he drank in every aspect of her, committing each detail to his memory, he looked up at Mr Lambourne and Lady Courcey.

'I think I should go now,' he said, his voice low.

'Yes, you should,' the lady agreed in clipped tones.

He surreptitiously let his hand touch Bridget's as he removed it from the bedcover. Lady Courcey shifted but passed no remark.

As he followed the housekeeper out of the room, he glanced at Mr Lambourne. The gentleman was wearing a pensive expression and did not acknowledge his departure.

Cormac went home that evening to find Mary wandering in front of the cottage with a preoccupied air. The hens pecked near her feet but she shooed them away crossly. When he approached, she looked up with a nervous glance.

'Come on, let's go for a walk,' she said, eschewing any kind of greeting.

Smothering his perplexity at her strange manner, he followed her around to the patch of woods behind the cottage, an area which had provided the McGovern siblings with excellent opportunities for amusement as they had grown up. She led him in among the trees; it was cool and dusky, and unseen owls hooted as they commenced their nightly forage for mice.

'Any more news on Bridget?' she asked without a great deal of concern.

He hesitated. 'She's still the same. I...I went to visit her today.'

Her eyes widened. 'They let you see her?'

'Her fiancé agreed to it 'cause I was the one who found her and brought her home.'

She pursed her lips as though she did not think much of the fiancé's judgement. 'And how was she?'

'Very sick,' he said, still tormented by the vision of Bridget's wasted form. 'She was delirious, she didn't know I was there. And my being there didn't please her mother.' He sighed. 'Maybe it wasn't the wisest idea to go.'

She snorted as she pushed a protruding branch out of her way. 'Of course it wasn't! I can't believe you did it.'

'I was worried about her, I needed to see how she was. Anyone else would've done the same.'

'Anyone with an ounce of common sense would've stayed away. You're just a servant. You'd no right to be there.'

It was true but he set his jaw, refusing to agree out loud.

After a beat, she said softly, 'Are you in love with her?'

He walked ahead of her without reply.

She gave a short laugh behind him. 'I knew it, I could tell. Listen,' she called, her tone growing urgent, 'don't get involved. Just keep away from her. Trust me, 'tis the best thing you can do.'

He stopped and turned to stare at her. 'What makes you such an expert on the subject?'

Anxiety creased her forehead and then she clenched her fists with resolve. ''Cause I was once in the same position you're in now. I reached beyond my station and received my just punishment for doing so.'

Bewildered, he said, 'What d'you mean?'

'I mean I've never been married. Patrick's an illegitimate child.' And she looked at him with blue eyes as clear as his own.

He was not as shocked as he should have been. The perfect husband, his tragic death – had he suspected all along? 'Why'd you lie to us?'

''Cause I was so ashamed of myself.'

He waited.

She plucked a leaf from a twig above her head and twirled it between her fingers. 'D'you know where Auntie used to live?' she asked cryptically.

'What's that got to do with – I just know her address, from writing to you. Kildare, wasn't it?'

'Yes, in a small village like Ballydarry. It wasn't much to speak of, but the road through it was used by the local gentry.'

She gazed past him with a faraway look in her eyes.

'One day, I was returning from the apothecary's house with Auntie's medicine when I saw him riding up the road. He noticed me too and I swear time stopped. We didn't say anything but kept staring at each other 'til he passed me by. Oh, it was a magical moment! I dallied at Auntie's gate to look back and caught him looking back too. I think I might've fallen in love with him right there.'

She smiled, an expression of joy which made her seem youthful again.

'He started to ride past more often and I always watched for him from the house. In a life dull as mine, it was the only piece of enjoyment I had. Every time he glanced 'round, I wondered was he hoping to spot me. About a week later, I was hanging out the washing in the garden when I heard a voice at the gate. It was him! He said he'd come 'specially to see me, that he couldn't stop thinking about me. I was terrified Auntie would see him through the window — she was a very proper lady, our Auntie — and I told him he had to leave. He asked if I would go for a walk with him that night instead. He was so nice, I couldn't help myself. I said I would, once I'd put Auntie to bed.'

Cormac could not decide if he was more appalled by his sister's lack of inhibition or the blackguard's exploitation of it.

'A walk?' he said, his tone laden with accusation.

Her eyes hardened. 'He was a perfect gentleman in every regard. He took me to a river walk on a remote part of his estate — the most picturesque place I'd ever been, with the moonlight shining on the water — and we talked for hours. Before we left, he kissed me in a way that made me feel like God had put us on this earth for no one but each other. We visited the same spot several more times over the following month or two. He said he felt privileged to share a place of such beauty with a face of such beauty. Oh, he was so gallant and romantic, what girl wouldn't have fallen for him…?'

She trailed away, lost in blissful recollection.

'So what happened?' Cormac prodded.

Her face fell. 'He left to take up residence in Dublin. He didn't want to go but he had to. I was heartbroken. I thought I'd seen his charming smile for the last time.' She dropped the leaf to the ground. 'And then Auntie died. I knew it was my only chance to find him 'cause if I went home, I'd never get away again. So I went to the city to search for him. I stole what little money Auntie had kept hidden under her mattress. It wasn't a lot but it got me to Dublin.'

'And did you find him there?'

'I did, eventually. I was overjoyed! He was so happy to see me too and came to visit me often in my room. You can judge me all you want but our passion had become too great. Patrick was conceived at that time. I didn't tell him at first 'cause I wanted to keep it for the right moment.' She took a long breath. 'And then he stopped coming to see me, without a word of warning. The next I heard of him was he'd gone to England. I couldn't understand it. He said he loved me, that I mattered to him, and yet I didn't matter enough to be told he was leaving the country.'

Cormac shook his head. Had she been so blind that she could not see he had been using her?

'But he came back last month, only a few days after Patrick was born. I hung about near his house, waited 'til he left by himself, and then went up to him and showed him his son.' Her voice had gone husky, but she did not cry. 'He was like a different person. He said he didn't want to see me, didn't want to see either of us again. And he just walked away.'

Cormac's frustration at his sister's short-sightedness was tempered by his compassion for the pain she had endured; she had suffered atrocious treatment from this man. He drew her into a hug and she laid her head on his shoulder.

'That was when I decided to come home. There was nothing left for me in the city. It was rotten there most of the time anyway, smelly and noisy. I *was* working in a baker's but it wasn't like how I described it to yous. They were terribly mean to me. They worked me to the bone and all I got was a dingy room and one meal a day. When they found out I was with child, they kept me on but treated me even worse. I was prepared to suffer it all for him though. I loved him. I still do.'

This time, frustration won out over compassion. 'How can you be so loyal to him? He hurt you, he abandoned you and your son!'

She pulled out of his embrace. 'He made me feel alive.'

In the face of such wilfulness, he stifled any further recriminations; she would never hear them. Instead, he said, 'Why'd you tell me all of this?'

''Cause I don't want you to make the same mistake I did. I believed the son of a rich lord could be happy with a poor girl like me but I was wrong. The upper classes value money and land and social status above everything else.'

He folded his arms. 'Bridget's not like that.'

'Really?' she said with raised eyebrows. 'And who's she engaged to, a stable hand or a wealthy gentleman?'

'She's with him 'cause she loves him,' he mumbled.

'Then forget her right now. If you go on wishing and hoping, you're just going to get hurt like me. Nothing can come of it, only misery and heartbreak.'

'I'm not wishing or hoping for anything except for her to get better.'

'Even that's caring too much. But I won't advise you any further. I've said my piece. And I know you'll keep my secret,' she added, her voice laced with the merest hint of a threat.

She was right, he would. There was no point in burdening their mother with such a tale of compromised morals. Let her hold onto the poignant love story Mary had spun; she would be happier with that.

They returned to the cottage in silence. When they were almost there, a thought occurred to him. 'If you've never been married, where'd you get that ring?'

Her gaze dropped to the wedding band on her left hand. 'I stole it. From a dead woman I found lying in the gutter.' She looked at him. 'You see the desperate things my foolish love made me do? Don't let yourself sink to such a wretched state.'

He hung back as she entered the cottage, her foot swinging out at a hen which came too near. She had warned him against the risks of losing one's heart to the wrong person, but her caution rang hollow.

Because everything in her demeanour had said she would do it all again for one more moonlit walk by the river.

## Chapter 18

As her mind came back to consciousness, she became aware of an acute ache in her temple. Her head felt as heavy as lead; it was fortunate she was lying down because she would not have been able to raise it even an inch. There was a pain in her arm too but that was more remote and easier to ignore.

Where was she? Her eyes seemed glued shut but indistinct sounds came to her – voices murmuring nearby.

'...how long more can she last?'

'...difficult to say, sir...very weak...if she does not wake up soon...'

They were talking about her. She tried to speak but her mouth did not seem capable of forming the words.

A third voice, curt and unforgiving. '...almost a week since she fell ill...your efforts have been entirely ineffective...'

'My sincere apologies, my lady...not easy to treat a fever...'

She was so tired and hot. Sleep tugged at her again but she was just too warm. If only someone would take these suffocating blankets off her. She strove to move them herself but her arms were dead weights.

'Did you see that? I thought her hand twitched.'

'It may have just been a shiver from the fever, sir.'

'No, this was different. More deliberate. Look at her eyes!'

She struggled to open them, to see who was there, to prove she was indeed awake. With a tremendous effort, she cracked her eyelids apart.

And when she saw his face, she knew, even through her exhaustion, that his was not the face she had wanted to see.

At first, she could only stay awake for short periods, just long enough to swallow some gruel. Although the fever had burned itself out, it had left her weakened and disorientated. Still, when she slept it was now a more restful slumber and, as her health improved, her speech became lucid again and she was able to recount what had happened on the day of the rainstorm.

'I had that headache, if you recall,' she told Garrett, after taking a mouthful of water from the glass on the bedside table. Her tongue felt woolly from lack of use. 'Lying down did not relieve it so I thought a walk in the fresh air would do me more good. That did indeed help, which encouraged me to keep going. I had a vague notion that I would like to visit the quarry but I started to turn back when I noticed the weather had changed. I was already too late though. The storm came so quickly.' She rubbed at the bandage on her head as her temple prickled in pain. 'I lost my bearings. The landscape looked so different in the gloom and the rain. I must have circled back towards the quarry and lost my footing at the edge. I remember very little after I fell down the slope. I think I came to once or twice but only for brief moments. The next thing I was aware of was waking up here.'

'What I cannot comprehend is why you would have had any inclination to go to the quarry in the first place,' said Garrett.

'I used to play there as a child, that is all,' she murmured.

But he was not prepared to let it go. 'Who did you play with?'

'Just a friend of mine.'

'Was it that fellow Cormac?' he said, with far more perception than she would have liked. 'The one who found you and brought you back?' When she did not answer, he asked frankly, 'What is your connection with him?'

'We were good friends growing up,' she said, unable to avoid his direct questioning any longer. 'There is no more to it than that.'

'Good friends with a stable hand?'

'He wasn't a stable hand when we were children.'

'And now?' he pushed. 'Are you still friends now?'

'No,' she said, with regret in her heart. 'Not now that he is a worker on the estate.'

He did not look convinced. 'He came to visit you when you were sick.'

Her pulse quickened. 'He did?'

'It was quite unorthodox to allow him in here but I thought I would be generous to him as he had saved your life.' Garrett arched an eyebrow. 'He looked devastated when he saw you. Not quite the reaction of a friend who is no longer a friend.'

She tried to appear indifferent. 'I don't know what you expect me to say. We spent our childhood together. Of course he is going to feel concern for my welfare, even as adults. But there is nothing beyond that. He knows his place.'

With a doubtful shrug, Garrett asked her if she would like some more water, and the conversation moved on to whether she might soon have an appetite for something more than gruel.

When he left her sick room in the evening to dine downstairs with Lady Courcey, she finally had time to reflect on that thorny exchange. Suspicion had been raised in his mind on the nature of her relationship with Cormac. She had made light of its significance but Cormac's coming to visit her was so atypical of a servant's acceptable conduct that it had been bound to provoke scrutiny.

Was it possible that Garrett had grounds to be distrustful? Cormac's actions may have shown he cared more for Bridget than he should, but his feelings were irrelevant so long as Bridget did not reciprocate them. Did she?

At the start of the summer, she had been certain of her love for Garrett – his charming ways had led her to believe no one could make her happier. However, seeing Cormac again had brought that certainty into question. Seven years away had dulled her memory of how special he had been to her, and it was only when she had returned that the strength of that feeling had come flooding back. She had spent much of the summer denying the fact but her recent mishap at the quarry had compelled her to face it at last.

It stemmed from a hazy recollection of her journey back to the manor. She had stirred from unconsciousness to find herself on horseback, encased in Cormac's arms. She had been frozen, drenched and dazed, but she had sensed his sturdy chest at her back, she had felt his lips at her ear, she had heard his words of comfort, and she had been comforted. There ought to have been more fear but she had felt so protected in his grasp.

It had reminded her of their childhood, of his solid presence throughout the distressing experience of losing her father – his swiftness to catch her when she sagged to the ground, too weak to face the reality that her dear papa was dead; his own insistence upon going to the funeral, despite the fact that his class, his religion and her mother forbade it; his expression of such burning compassion that her heart felt too full for words. The sincerity of his friendship had instilled a sheer conviction in her: she would always be safe and well with him because he would do anything for her. How had she allowed herself to forget that?

These thoughts were confusing, not to mention draining. She could feel what little energy she had sapping away even as she lay unmoving in the bed. She began to doze off, her musings scattered and unresolved. In the last moment before oblivion took over, his murmured words drifted to her again. He had probably believed her to be insensible of her surroundings but she had caught what he had said. '*A ghrá*', he had called her.

'My love'.

When she awoke the next morning, she was still alone; her mother and fiancé no longer felt it necessary to keep a constant vigil by her bedside now that it had become clear she would recover. Lady Courcey in particular, after an initial wave of maternal relief, was swift to restore her aloof demeanour, seeming almost self-conscious at having expressed undisciplined emotion. While Bridget felt hurt at this neglect, it provided her with the opportunity to send for the one person whom she was sure could answer her burning questions.

Ellen responded promptly to her summons and entered the chamber with a beaming smile. 'Miss, it cheers my heart to see you awake. You had us all so worried.'

'I am sorry to have been the cause of such distress,' said Bridget, easing herself into a sitting position, 'but thanks be to God the worst is past now. Do come and sit.'

Ellen perched on the edge of Garrett's chair. 'What can I do for you, miss?'

Bridget leaned towards her. 'I have only received vague accounts of the events that took place on the day of the storm. I'm aware that Cormac found me but I know nothing else. Can you enlighten me? Do you know what happened?'

'I do,' Ellen admitted, colouring a little as she added, 'Liam Kirwan, one of the other stable hands, told me afterwards.'

'Then tell me, and do not leave anything out.'

Still rather red, Ellen said, 'Well, when Mr Lambourne raised the alarm after the storm began, Cormac was the one who thought of looking for you at the quarry. Liam said he had a hard time keeping up with him across the fields. Cormac was intent on finding you if he had to go to the ends of the earth to do it.'

Bridget felt something inside her flutter at this. Assuming a calm exterior, she said, 'Go on.'

Ellen became more at ease as she continued her tale. 'It was foolhardy to keep riding once the lightning started, but I suppose if they hadn't it would have been much longer before you were found.' She described their headlong dash to the quarry and Cormac's reckless descent down the rocky slope. 'I saw his shirt afterwards because he brought it to his sister to be mended. It had been so ripped to shreds that Margaret just tore up the rest of it for rags.' She leaned forwards, eyes wide and animated, as she recounted the rest of Bridget's rescue. '...and after Cormac handed you over to Mr Lambourne, he nearly fell trying to get off his horse, he was so cold and exhausted. Mrs Kavanagh gave him hot soup and the best spot in front of the fire. It's hard to please that woman but Cormac could do no wrong in her eyes that day. We were all so grateful to him for bringing you back safe.'

Bridget was speechless. Cormac had gone far beyond the duty of a servant to locate her in the storm – he had risked life and limb in his efforts to do so. It was the most selfless thing anyone had ever done for her.

'I wonder how he guessed you might be at the quarry. That was very lucky.' Ellen attempted to maintain a neutral expression but it was evident that this was not the first time that question had been broached in the household.

Lacking the guile to invent an evasive answer on the spot, Bridget could only speak the truth. 'I suppose he just knows me very well,' she said, feeling she had not comprehended how much so until now. It had been their fleeting reminiscence about cloud formations that had pushed her on towards the quarry that day – she had yearned to revisit that place of youthful joy and innocence and, contrary to the version of events she had given Garrett, had grown determined to get there, even when the storm had begun to brew. She may well have died at the bottom of that hole, had it not been for Cormac's extraordinary intuition.

She did not deem her unguarded remark to be perilous in Ellen's presence but she still hurried on, 'Garrett said that Cormac came to visit me while I was sick, is that true?'

'Yes, I overheard Mrs Walsh telling Mr Buttimer how Cormac as good as demanded to see you. He'd been asking me at every opportunity how you were and I had no news to give him so I suppose he decided to find out for himself. Mrs Walsh said he got quite a shock when he saw how poorly you were. I met him that afternoon and he was miserable. I think he feared the worst was going to happen.'

'But he knows I am recovering now?'

'He does, miss. You should have seen his face when he heard you had woken. He lit up brighter than the sun and moon put together.'

Bridget lay back on her pillows, a warm glow spreading through her whole body. 'Thank you for telling me, Ellen.'

## Chapter 19

Garrett's sigh escaped his lips, unobtrusive but undeniable. He endeavoured to cover it up with a cough as he cast a look of boredom to the sick room's ceiling. Even though Bridget had been disappointed by his increasing absences, she now found his restless company unwelcome. He fidgeted in his chair until her aggravation became too much to suppress.

'Is something the matter?' she snapped. 'Do you need to be elsewhere?'

'No, no, of course not.' He glanced around the dim room. 'I suppose I am a little weary of our surroundings. No doubt you too find it dreary. Never mind, it will not be very long before you are better and can leave this room altogether.'

'If the gloominess bothers you, you can open the shutters.'

'Mr Abbott advised us to keep them shut for now. Your eyes have become unused to the daylight, and we are to expose them only by degrees.'

'My eyes will be fine. Open the shutters, and the windows too. Let some fresh air in.'

With a huff, he stood to pull open the wooden shutters and unfasten the windows. Sunlight streamed into the room, engulfing the meagre light of the candles. The brightness did sting her eyes but she said nothing; more soothing was the refreshing breeze that wafted in. Garrett went to the dresser and the bedside table, blew out all the candles, and then sat back down again. The transformation of the room had a mellowing effect on them both – they smiled at each other, abashed.

'I'm sorry if I have been short with you,' she said, offering her hand in a gesture of peace.

He took it and kissed her knuckles. 'I am sorry too. I should be more supportive. You have been through a terrible ordeal.'

'Let us talk about something else, something positive. Have the apples ripened in the orchard yet?'

'I have no idea,' he said, amused, 'but there cannot be anything more positive to anticipate than our upcoming nuptials. That has to be the most exciting event in any girl's life!'

Her responding smile was tight. 'Of course.'

'Now that the summer is drawing to a close, we shall be returning to Dublin very soon and then you can begin making your preparations for the most wonderful wedding in living memory.' He patted her hand. 'The other girls are going to be so jealous of you, even more so when they see you heading off to the glamorous city of London.'

Her attempt at pleasantry promptly disappeared. 'London again,' she complained. 'Must you keep bringing that up?'

He frowned. 'Yes, I must. We have many arrangements to make with regard to moving your possessions, choosing our servants, and so on. We cannot delay much longer.'

'But I told you I do not want to go to London.'

'And I told you it was not your decision to make.'

'Are you going to force me?' she said, shocked. 'When I become your wife, will my opinion cease to matter?'

He folded his arms. 'This is childish behaviour. Stop pretending that you do not understand how society works. A woman must obey her husband in every respect, you know this very well. Your obstinacy will get you nowhere and I won't tolerate much more of it.'

Eyes smarting, she turned away from him. 'I think I need to sleep now.'

'Yes, perhaps you will wake with a more sensible attitude towards marriage,' he said waspishly, and he left the room without another word.

She stared at the wall, sleep the furthest thing from her mind. Was that really her fiancé who had just left her side? Such nastiness was incongruent with the man she had promised to marry back in March. Did that charismatic, attentive gentleman even exist? Or was it all a facade – had he merely dazzled her the way she had seen him dazzle the maids time and again?

With a sinking heart, she could see that he was unyielding about taking her to London. He had brushed aside her refusal to go with such indifference that it was clear her view on the subject was of no consequence. He saw her as his inferior; her wishes were to take second place to his own. She was only a woman, after all.

Was every woman consigned to this fate when she married, dismissed as easily as a child or a dog? No, she resolved at once. When she was growing up, she had been witness to a happy marriage based on a foundation of mutual support and compromise, not in her own home but in Cormac's. Jack and Maggie McGovern had built a home and raised a family together, sharing the pertaining burdens and joys. Was it therefore a question of social class? If she were poor, would she be treated more equally by her spouse? Such a theory spoke volumes about the shortcomings of the upper classes to which she belonged.

Sighing, she rolled onto her back and gazed up at the decorative cornices that bordered the ceiling. For the first time, she felt stifled at the thought of her future. No decision would be in her control; Garrett would command her in every way. Did she trust him to choose what was best for both of them? Perhaps he believed this move to London would make her content. There was no denying that she would rise higher in society and participate in a far more dynamic social calendar than she had ever known in Dublin. Maybe she would find herself indebted to him for bringing her to such a vibrant city.

Doubtful and disheartened, she fell into an uneasy slumber. When she awoke an hour or two later, an idea that had been hovering in the recesses of her mind came right to the forefront. It was as though she had marshalled her thoughts in her sleep and now she knew just what she needed in the midst of all her confusion.

Her mother came to her with the news that the physician was going to call in the evening to check on her improvement. She was about to leave the room again when Bridget called her back.

'Can you stay for a moment, please?' she said.

Lady Courcey opted to stand at the foot of the bed rather than take a seat beside it. 'What is it?'

Seeing that she was not in the mood for idle chitchat, Bridget mustered her courage and went straight to the point. 'I would like to invite Cormac to visit me here.'

'Certainly not,' said the lady straight away.

This was the reaction Bridget had been expecting and she was already armed with her response. 'I know you think it is inappropriate but you have been kind enough to allow him to come once before. At the time, I was unconscious and unable to express my gratitude for his good deed. I would like the opportunity to thank him in person for saving my life.'

Lady Courcey sniffed. 'It is unnecessary.'

'On the contrary, I feel that it is very necessary. You have raised me from childhood to always conduct myself to the height of good manners. It would be a grave mark of disrespect not to personally convey my thanks to the individual who rescued me from the clutches of death.'

'You are being overdramatic,' said Lady Courcey with the faintest touch of a sneer.

'You nearly lost your only daughter to a terrible fever mere days ago. That is not an exaggeration. I could have perished in the quarry but Cormac delivered me to safety in time. We should both be grateful to him and he should be made aware of it.'

Lady Courcey looked sour. 'Have you mentioned this request to Mr Lambourne?'

'No, but I am confident he will agree with me,' Bridget said with more conviction than she felt.

'We shall go along with what he thinks,' Lady Courcey declared. It was plain that she expected Garrett to side with herself rather than with his fiancée.

To the surprise of both mother and daughter, however, Garrett consented to the meeting. Pleased to have avoided another argument with him, Bridget cast a look of triumph at her mother and, after one last effort on the lady's part to dissuade her, Cormac was summoned.

Before his arrival, Bridget ensured that she was propped up on plump pillows, that her hair was brushed and pinned back from her face, and that a bouquet of flowers had been placed in a vase upon the dresser. The cumbersome bandage around her head had been replaced with a more discreet dressing now that the wound was nearly healed. She did not like to think of the dreadful state she had been in when Cormac had seen her last and meant to make herself fully presentable this time. Lady Courcey and Garrett positioned themselves by her bedside, one taciturn and the other contemplative. Their aloofness detracted from an otherwise pleasant atmosphere.

There was a knock on the door and Mrs Walsh entered, followed by Cormac. Bridget felt her insides flutter as they had done when Ellen had related the story of his bravery in the storm. His fair hair was windswept but he tried to flatten it down as he came into the room. His blue eyes flicked to the corner where Lady Courcey and Garrett stood, registering their cool demeanour. Then his gaze transferred to Bridget and his expression lifted with relief and gladness.

She tried to conceal her own pleasure at the sight of him as she said, 'Good evening, Cormac.'

'Good evening, Miss Muldowney.'

'I appreciate you coming to see me. I hope it was not an inconvenient time to step away from your work.'

'No, miss, I was exercising one of the horses but another fellow is looking after him now.'

'That's good.' She took a breath to steady her nerves. 'You must know why you are here. I want to thank you from the bottom of my heart for saving me on the day of the storm. But for you, I may not have survived to be sitting up in this bed right now.'

'I only brought you home,' he said with humility. 'It was the physician who made you better.'

'If you had not found me, the physician would have had no one to tend to.'

He gave her a respectful nod. 'However it happened, we're all very glad you're on the mend. Everyone in the stables and kitchens told me to give you their best. And my mother sends her regards as well.'

'That is very kind of them all. Please make sure to pass on my thanks for their concern.'

Cormac shifted uncomfortably; glancing to her side, she saw Garrett fixing him with a look of intense interest. His gaze was neither friendly nor unfriendly but he was absorbing every aspect of their exchange. Perhaps his reason for consenting to this meeting had been to get the chance to observe them together.

'Mother? Garrett?' she said. 'Could you leave us for a minute or two?'

'You have thanked him,' said Lady Courcey. 'There can be nothing more to say.'

Bridget turned to her fiancé. 'Please? Just for a few moments.'

His attention switched to her and she kept her expression as innocent as possible as he searched her face.

'Very well,' he said, 'but not for long. Mr Abbott prescribed constant rest. Prolonged visits are not advisable.'

'I shall bear that in mind.'

Garrett, Lady Courcey and Mrs Walsh left the room with several backward glances. As soon as the door was shut, Bridget patted the bedcover.

'Come sit.'

He looked a little shy as he moved forwards and sat on the edge of the bed beside her.

'Thank you again for what you did. The storm was far worse than I expected it to be. I did not realise the danger I was in.'

He gave her a lopsided smile. 'You've never been good at predicting the weather.'

She chuckled. 'True. I am so grateful to you. I shall be forever in your debt.'

'Please forget about it. I'm just glad you're safe and getting well.'

'I'll never forget it.' She hesitated for the merest second before plunging on, her desire to confide in him too great to resist. 'It was an act of gallantry where otherwise I have been exposed to the most uncivil behaviour.'

He was immediately alert. 'What's wrong?'

She dropped her gaze to the bedcover. 'It's Garrett.'

'What about him?' He sounded almost too keen to hear that Garrett had committed a transgression of some kind.

'He is making me move to London.'

There was a beat of silence and she looked up to see that he was as taken aback as she had been when she had first found out.

'*London?*'

She nodded.

'But why? Your home's here.'

'That is what I keep telling him but he does not want to listen. I believed I could convince him at least to remain in Dublin, if not in the countryside, but he is adamant that we shall go to London. The decision has been made.' She sighed. 'I do not want to go. I love Ireland and I love Oakleigh.

I cannot bear the thought of going so far away.'

He swallowed but said nothing. The wall still existed between them as heiress and servant, preventing him from articulating his feelings.

And yet she wanted to hear what he was thinking. She yearned for him to open up to her with the familiarity they had once shared. The flutter inside her insisted upon it.

She grasped one of his hands. It was rough from years of toil on the estate. He stared down at her fingers wrapped around his.

'Do you want me to go?' she whispered.

Liberated, he raised his eyes to meet hers. 'Of course not. I never want you to go.'

It was all she needed to hear. Without further contemplation, she leaned forwards and pressed her mouth upon his. Taken by surprise, he did not react for a second but then all of a sudden he was kissing her back and she could tell that he had been longing for this just as she realised how much she had been longing for it too. They had always had a special connection and now she sensed it flowing between them through their lips and tongues and clasped hands. The kiss should have been clumsy but it wasn't. It felt as though they had been this intimate for years.

When they broke away, they had only a moment to stare breathlessly at each other before they heard the creak of floorboards outside the door. This time, his reaction was instantaneous; he was on his feet and standing at the end of the bed before the door had fully opened. Anyone walking in would believe that he had not moved even a foot closer while he and Bridget had been alone.

It was Garrett. Lady Courcey, Mrs Walsh and a bearded man holding a black case stood in the doorway behind him.

'Darling,' said Garrett, 'Mr Abbott has just arrived to see you. He wishes to assess your condition and advise us on how best to proceed in facilitating your convalescence. He also emphasises that you must not have any more visitors until you are quite recovered,' he added meaningfully.

Bridget nodded at her fiancé and then looked back at Cormac. 'Thank you once again for coming and for your actions on the day of the storm. Do please pass on my thanks to Liam too, seeing as you have just communicated to me that he played no small part in the incident.'

'You're welcome, miss, and I'll be sure to do that. Keep getting better. We all hope to see you up and about the place again soon.'

Then he was gone and the physician was by her side, ready to subject her to his numerous tests.

## Chapter 20

'And that's the last of it,' the farmer's wife announced as Cormac tucked the final parcel into the nearest pannier of the pack horse.

'Thank you, Mrs McKinty,' Margaret said, passing a basket to Bronagh with care.

Mrs Kavanagh had ordered the two sisters to collect an array of produce from McKinty Farm and, as it was too much for them to carry, Cormac had accompanied them with a horse that could bear the bulk of the goods. Now laden with baskets of eggs, blocks of cheese and various cuts of meat, they left the farmyard with an affectionate farewell from Mrs McKinty, who was inclined to reminisce on the numerous times Cormac and Bridget had inveigled titbits from her when they were young.

On a dry day, such a task was a pleasure rather than a chore and the girls were in good spirits as the three of them walked along a leafy lane dappled in autumn sunlight, although a cool wind gusted about them. Cormac let their chatter wash over him without paying much attention, his thoughts deeply occupied elsewhere.

Bridget had kissed him. She had held his hand and kissed him with fervour. He could not say what it might mean in the long run, but it did signify one thing: she was having misgivings about Mr Lambourne. Her act of infidelity and her unwillingness to go to London both showed that she was no longer satisfied with the man she had chosen to marry. All summer, Cormac had stood by and endured her engagement because he believed it was what she wanted. Now he knew differently.

Mrs Walsh's words darted through his head.

'Be careful, lad,' the housekeeper had murmured to him after he had left Bridget's sick room. 'You're treading on dangerous ground.'

At the time, he had dismissed the warning – what did Mrs Walsh know about anything? But now, after the passage of several days, his mind had plummeted back to reality. He had not seen Bridget since their kiss and his initial elation had become tempered by doubt and second-guessing over what she was feeling and what she might do next. If she was still confined to her sick room, she had no means of seeking him out, but the torment of waiting and not knowing was making mere days feel like months.

A woman appeared around a bend in front of them, a thin shawl draped negligently at her elbows. He recognised Mary's distinctive locks of fair hair and waved. It occurred to him that she was precisely the person he could talk to about Bridget. She might not be sympathetic but she comprehended the circumstances and would perhaps offer some female insight.

When she approached, the peevish line of her mouth communicated that she wasn't pleased to see them – she probably deemed them an unwelcome intrusion on her solitude. His mother had confided in him, not without concern, that Mary had taken to going for long walks since she had returned home. She craved her own company over anyone else's, even her son's. She had always been somewhat temperamental in nature but she seemed even moodier now. Still, who could blame her, considering all that she had suffered?

They stopped in the lane, Cormac tugging on the horse's lead rope to bring it to a halt.

'Where are yous coming from?' Mary asked. A flurry of the breeze caused the end of her shawl to trail in the dirt but she didn't seem to notice.

'McKinty Farm,' said Margaret, and Bronagh uncovered her basket to display tidy rows of brown eggs. 'Where are you going?'

Mary shrugged. 'Nowhere in particular.'

Bronagh scowled. She had been only ten when she had been sent to work at the big house – now, two and a half years later, she and Margaret were still toiling away while their older sister had returned to live a life of little responsibility.

'Why aren't you at home helping Ma?' she said, her inflection coloured by more than a trace of bitterness. 'Didn't you learn how to clean house and make bread while you were away? With another pair of hands, she'd get through her work a lot quicker.'

'Ah, I'd only be in Ma's way,' said Mary. She made no mention of the son she had left in her mother's care.

Cormac sensed Bronagh's aggravation and intervened. 'I'm going to come home this evening,' he said to Mary. 'Can I talk to you about something important then?'

She looked indifferent. 'Fine so.'

'We'd best be getting back to the kitchens,' Bronagh said, adding pointedly, 'There's always so much to be done.'

Mary gave another listless shrug, tugged at her shawl, and walked away from them without so much as a farewell. Cormac and the other two girls were about to move on when they heard the clopping of hoof beats and a rider came into sight, trotting up the lane towards Mary. Discerning the figure's black hair and proud bearing, Cormac experienced a lurch of guilt and then anger. He had kissed this man's fiancée but Mr Lambourne wanted to take Bridget away from Oakleigh for good. At last, he had a genuine reason to dislike him.

Mr Lambourne passed Mary first; she started as he rode by, as though shaken from her brooding thoughts. Instead of stopping to hail Cormac and the girls, he nodded curtly and hurried on, vanishing around the next bend in a cloud of dust. Cormac stared after him with an uneasy feeling; did the gentleman suspect that there had been inappropriate conduct between himself and Bridget?

Margaret let out a wistful sigh. 'Isn't Miss Muldowney just the luckiest? Ellen Ryan said she couldn't have made a better match.'

A knot formed in the pit of Cormac's stomach. He glanced behind him, but Mary had already disappeared from view around the turn in the lane. It would have to wait until later.

He encouraged the horse onwards with a click of his tongue, and the three of them resumed their walk back to the big house.

***

Bridget rested in a chair by the window in her sick room with a blanket draped over her knees. September had stolen in while she had been convalescing and she could sense the change of season in the air that came through the small gap in the window. The summer heat was gone and a brisk breeze whispered of cooler days to come.

Her head throbbed with an ache that had nothing to do with her wound. She had kissed Cormac. It had been an impulse she could no longer contain, but what did it mean now she had gone through with it? She could not deny that there was an overwhelming part of her that very much wanted to kiss him again. But another part reminded her emphatically that she was betrothed to a different man. It was appealing to imagine it not being so but absurd to believe it could ever be otherwise.

A sense of foreboding sat heavily upon her. She had the impression that she was balancing a house of cards before her. What would it take for them all to come tumbling down?

A precise rap on the door interrupted her thoughts.

'Come in,' she called and the footman Denis entered, everything from the buttons on his livery to the buckles of his shoes polished to a high shine.

'Are you ready, miss?'

Mr Abbott had, to her relief, granted his consent at last for her to return to her own bedchamber, and so she had enlisted Denis to assist her down the stairs. Lady Courcey was to be occupied until luncheon in another meeting with Mr Enright, Garrett had absconded with Commander for the morning, and she did not have the patience to wait for an occasion more convenient to them.

Putting aside her blanket, she rose to her feet and took Denis's arm. She was very glad to escape this oppressive room that had been the manor's infirmary for over two weeks. Nonetheless, she cast a fleeting glimpse behind her as she left, taking one final look at the spot where she and Cormac had shared their kiss.

Even though she only had to descend a single flight, she could feel her energy depleting step by step; by the time she gained the lower landing, her breath was coming short and her legs trembled.

'Nearly there, miss,' said Denis and she leaned on him gratefully.

As they took the last few steps towards the door of her bedchamber, a man's raised voice came from the entrance hall below.

'…just not acceptable, Brewer!'

The valet's reply was inaudible but proved to be dissatisfying to Garrett, who gave a growl of irritation. 'I expect you to maintain the highest standards at all times. Such slipshod attention to detail is intolerable.'

This was followed by heavy footsteps on the staircase. Denis attempted to urge Bridget on but she stopped him with a light pressure on his arm.

'Just one moment,' she murmured, curiosity winning out over fatigue.

Garrett strode onto the landing, looking like he had taken the stairs two or three at a time. He checked at the sight of her and the strangest expression flashed across his face – was it resentment? He offered her a perfunctory bow, then turned on his heel and marched down the corridor towards his own bedchamber.

By this stage, Brewer had gained the top of the stairs too. He carried a pair of his master's gloves, one of which had a small rip on the cuff. Had something so insignificant provoked Garrett's displeasure?

'Good day, Miss Muldowney,' Brewer muttered and, giving her a polite nod, followed his master.

Frowning, Bridget allowed Denis to lead her on to her room.

*\*\*\**

Cormac entered the cottage at twilight to find his mother and youngest sister in a giggling heap on the hearth. One of the hens squawked from the rafter above, the end of a spool of yarn caught around its legs and the rest of it dangling like a pendulum. Orlaith jumped up to grab it, missed, and started laughing again.

'Silly Henrietta, come down!'

'Hush, you'll wake the baby,' Maggie said, trying to curb her own amusement, but Patrick slumbered in a basket in the corner, oblivious to the commotion. She smiled at Cormac as he kissed her cheek. 'Good to see you, my dearie. How's Bridget these days, do you know?'

'Getting stronger, I hear,' he said evasively, looking around. 'Where's

Mary?'

'Isn't she with you?' She gazed over his shoulder as though she expected Mary to come through the door after him.

'No. Why would you think that?'

'She went for a walk earlier. When she came home, she told me she was hoping to start work at the big house and wanted to get your advice about any available positions. It cheered me no end to hear her talking about her future at last. Didn't she find you?'

'I met her on her walk but never saw her after that. I was working in the stables for the rest of the day though, so she'd have found me if she'd asked anyone where I was.' His brow furrowed. 'And she hasn't been back here since?'

'No,' said Maggie, beginning to look anxious. 'She's never out this late but I assumed she was fine 'cause she was with you. Where d'you think she could be?'

'I don't know. If she's in a better mood, maybe she decided to go see Ellen Ryan? But she'd have to wait 'til Ellen finished attending her ladyship, and that could be any time.'

Maggie relaxed. 'Arrah, that might be it. We'll wait so. But I'll be giving her a talking to when she gets back for worrying her mother. Are you hungry?'

'When am I not?' he said with a grin.

'Well, you can wash that muck off your hands first. I lived with your father long enough to know exactly what you've been shovelling today.'

Orlaith stopped snatching at the swinging spool of yarn. 'I'll go get the bucket,' she said and skipped out the door, returning a moment later with her two arms wrapped around the half-full bucket of water. She offered it to her big brother with an adoring gaze. 'The rope's missing.'

'Thanks, chicken. Is it?' he said, but he was thinking about the conversation he'd planned to have with Mary. Did he dare broach it with his mother instead? He scrubbed his hands together in the water. 'Ma...?'

She was standing beneath Henrietta again, hands on her hips and an appraising gleam in her eye. 'What?' she asked without turning to him.

He lost his nerve. 'Ah, could Mary have gotten lost in the woods?'

Maggie dismissed the suggestion with a flap of her hand. 'She knows those woods better than anyone. Before she went away to live with your aunt, she and Patrick used to run wild in them.' She paused. 'She might've twisted her ankle, or took a tumble. I hadn't thought of that.'

He wiped his hands dry on a rag from the dresser. 'D'you want me to go look for her?'

She bit her lip. 'Maybe you should.'

'I'll go right now so.' He gave her a reassuring smile. 'I bet I'll find her wandering towards home with no notion of how late 'tis.'

But when he headed back outside into the deepening dusk, his own apprehension mounted; not even Mary at her most distracted could fail to notice how dark it had become. He jogged up the lane first, hoping to meet her returning from the big house, cheerful after a nice chat with her old friend.

He stopped dead when he reached the brick-lined well at the side of the lane. 'The rope's missing,' Orlaith had said.

A shiver of dread slithered up his spine.

With a sharp intake of breath, he spun about, retraced his steps to the cottage, and strode into the woods behind it. The very worst idea imaginable bloomed in his mind but he pushed it aside. She had fallen somewhere, that was what had happened. He would stumble upon her huddled at the base of a tree and clutching her injured leg, and she would wipe her cheeks and cover up her fright with an accusatory remark about how long it had taken him to find her.

He picked up his pace until he was sprinting. Please God, he prayed, let her be safe. He shouted her name, calling out to her again and again. He crashed through the undergrowth, casting around for any sign that she had been there. The woods were not very large but she could be anywhere in them. Or she might not even be in them at all. He could hunt for hours and never come across her.

Darkness fell fully but still he ran and yelled, yearning for her to call back. Even though he had been just shy of eight years old when she had left, he had many vivid memories of their childhood together: finding an injured bird and nursing it back to health; waiting for their father to come home from the stables and competing over who would hug him first; playing hide-and-seek among these same trees he was hurtling through now. She had begged not to be sent away to care for their ailing aunt and now he wished with every fibre of his being that she had been able to stay and avoid all the heartache she had experienced since.

His breathing grew laboured and he developed a searing stitch in his side but, though he slowed down, he continued to stumble on, swiping his sweaty hair out of his eyes. After a while, he could not tell whether he was still going forwards or circling back on himself. He too knew these woods well, but somehow the trees looked unfamiliar and ominous, looming from the shadows to scratch his skin and tear his shirt.

At last, long after alarm had turned to blind panic had turned to exhaustion had turned to numbness, he slipped and fell hard on the ground. Ignoring the stab of pain that shot up through his knee, he searched around, his fingers grasping on what had halted his momentum; it felt like a thin piece of cloth. Holding it up in the dark, he could make out the vague shape and thought it might be a shawl. A hand of ice gripped his heart and he leapt to his feet in fear.

He stared about, straining to see through the gloom, and perceived a dark shadow among the trees ahead. He rushed forwards but skidded to a stop as soon as the shape became clear.

It was his beloved Mary, suspended from a tree branch, a rope stretched tight around her bare neck.

His anguished cry reverberated through the silent woods. He ran to his sister, pulled his knife from his pocket, and hacked at the offending rope until it snapped, but he was far too late.

He held her cold body close. As he rocked her and cried out to her vacant, blue-lipped face, something she had said to him rang in his head. 'You see the desperate things my foolish love made me do?'

She had nurtured a tragic view of love – had it played a part in her committing the most desperate act of all?

## Chapter 21

Venturing downstairs for breakfast for the first time in more than a fortnight, Bridget found Garrett brooding alone at the table, an unfinished plate of kippers before him. He jumped to his feet at her appearance.

'Good morning, my darling,' he said with a beaming smile. 'Your presence is a true sign that you are on the mend, and very satisfying to see.'

She mustered a half-hearted smile in return and, when he leaned in for a kiss, hastily offered him her cheek. He stood back, disappointed, but she pretended not to notice as she sat opposite him, relieved to take a rest, although her legs were not quite as shaky as the previous day. At the same time, there was a soft tap on the door and Ellen entered, carrying a tray with a glass of some sort of green-coloured infusion. A sweet, minty scent wafted in with her.

'Another tonic for you, miss,' she said, her voice thick. 'Her ladyship was quite insistent. It is the physician's recipe and supposed to restore your strength.'

She kept her head down as she set the tray on the table but Bridget could see that her eyes were red and puffy.

Her brow creased. 'Ellen? What is the matter?'

'There's nothing the matter, miss.' She dropped into a curtsey, avoiding Bridget's eye. 'Would you like to take your tonic now or after breakfast?'

'Never mind the tonic. I can see you are upset. Tell me what is wrong.'

Garrett folded his arms, evidently bored by her interest in the woes of a lady's maid.

Tears seeped out of Ellen's eyes. 'Oh, it's too terrible to speak of.'

Bridget was now quite alarmed. 'What do you mean? What on earth has happened?'

'I don't know if I should even tell you,' said Ellen, glancing sideways at Garrett. 'But you'll be bound to find out sooner or later.' She gulped back a sob. 'It's shocking news. The poor family. Poor Cormac.'

Bridget's breath caught in her throat. 'Cormac?' Garrett looked at her sharply, but in that uncertain moment she did not care. 'What tragedy?'

'His sister, Mary. She's…dead. She hanged herself.'

Bridget gasped in horror. Garrett made an involuntary movement but said nothing.

'I don't believe it,' she said in a strangled voice. 'What would drive her to do such a thing?'

Ellen was crying freely now. 'I cannot even imagine. When I went down to the kitchens this morning to ask Mrs Kavanagh to prepare the tonic, she told me Margaret and Bronagh had been called home in the middle of the night. A little later, Liam came in with the news that Cormac had found Mary hanging from a tree in the woods.' She faltered. 'H-he brought her home in his arms and their mother fainted when he carried her into the cottage. That unfortunate woman, her husband and now two of her children dead in less than three years. It's dreadful.'

Bridget began to weep too. Her heart went out to Cormac; to discover his own sister dead, how horrifying. What a devastating tragedy for his entire family. Poor, poor Maggie. And little Orlaith, only five years old, she wouldn't even be able to understand what was going on. She would just know that they had lost someone dear to them and could never get her back.

Across the table, Garrett's face was impassive and he displayed no sign of compassion for the luckless family. How could he be so cold? He met her reproachful stare with empty eyes.

'I am sorry, my darling,' he said. 'I do not know who this girl was but it is a tragic loss for her family. Perhaps I should leave you for a while so you can compose yourself.'

And he rose and departed from the room without a backward glance.

\*\*\*

The fire had burned low. Cormac dropped a sod of turf onto it, then leaned his forearm against the hearth wall and stared at the glowing embers. It had to be two or three in the morning but he was wide awake. His vigil would last through to the dawn.

Muted sobs drifted down from the loft above. He was not the only one still wakeful but he had sent his sisters to bed over an hour ago; there was no need for them to stay up with the remains too.

He winced. It was such a detached word. It meant nothing more than bones and flesh. It didn't signify breath or heartbeat, passion or irritability, daughter, mother or sister. Everything that had made her who she was, flawed as she was, had vanished.

He turned and gazed at her body, laid out on the table in preparation for burial. In the subdued firelight, her fair hair shimmered about her face like a halo. A dainty kerchief had been tied around her neck to hide the tell-tale marks of her violent end. A spray of pansies lay entwined in her hands.

Her body rested at peace but what of her soul? Father Macken had refused to come. Mary had committed a mortal sin, precluding any guarantee of salvation for her. Fearing she would writhe in eternal purgatory, Maggie had prayed over her for hours. She continued to do so now in the shadows on the far side of the table, lips moving silently, and would carry on until Mary was removed from the cottage. The immoral nature of her passing stipulated a burial at night but Cormac would not consent to that. He didn't want to hurry her into the ground – she ought to be waked properly, for his mother's sake more than anything.

He stepped up to the table and tenderly tucked a lock of hair behind his sister's ear. Why had she done it? How could she have believed there was no way to go on? He shut his eyes, remembering her confession in the woods. She had been in pain, and only he had known how much. Could he have foreseen this? Could he somehow have prevented it?

He bent to kiss her forehead and murmured, 'Please forgive me.'

The fire crackled as the turf flamed up. On the other side of the table, his mother began to keen.

Needless to say, there was no gathering of mourners; Ellen Ryan had been the only person to come to convey her condolences earlier in the evening. But John, Liam and, somewhat surprisingly, Fintan Kelly turned up the next morning to help Cormac bear his sister to the site of her interment. She had to be buried in unconsecrated ground beyond the walls of the church's graveyard, denying her a resting place next to her father and brother. It was an ignominious departure from this life but she had chosen it for herself.

Fintan declined to come back to the cottage afterwards but Liam hung around awkwardly in one corner while John kept a consoling grip on Maggie's hand by the now-empty hearth. The cottage seemed even more like a tomb when it no longer housed a corpse. Orlaith's hens had been shunted outside and, without their familiar scratching and clucking, the silence was oppressive. All eyes stared at the table, now a bare slab apart from a single pansy which had slipped from its posy. Margaret cradled the baby and rocked him as he stirred in his sleep, unaware that his mother had been buried in the earth.

All Cormac wanted was to get away from the morose faces and dismal atmosphere. He had done his duty as the man of the family; he had held himself together as long as was necessary. Now he sensed the fractures forming in his self-control, felt the despair beginning to smother him as his emotions crowded in.

He could not bear it anymore. He mumbled an excuse to Bronagh, who was standing nearest to him, and ran from the cottage.

It was good to be out in the fresh air – he could breathe again. He strode forwards without any destination in mind; he just wanted to keep moving. His knee still hurt from when he had fallen on it in the woods but he pushed through the pain, inconsequential as it was to all the rest. The lane and fields were quiet except for the merry twittering of birds in the hedgerows. He focused on the cheerful birdsong – anything to forget the thud of soil falling into a freshly dug grave.

The big house came into view on the horizon and he realised that his feet had automatically brought him along the route he followed to get to work. When he saw the imposing building rising in the distance, he knew what it was he yearned for. The only person he wanted to be with on this horrible day.

But it was risky. He had already provoked suspicion by making two visits to her bedside. Mrs Walsh had warned him to be careful so it had become more evident, at least to her, that there was the possibility of some kind of indiscretion. He would have to sneak in and take care that no one saw him.

He passed the paddock, mercifully empty, and reached the stables, where he took cover down the side of the building; he had no inclination to face his fellow stable hands today. Hugging the corner, he peered across the courtyard to the back door of the kitchens. He hesitated. How was he to get to her? The first obstacle was Mrs Kavanagh – she wouldn't be likely to let him pass through the kitchens unimpeded, personal misfortune or no. Then there was Bridget's location. Would she still be in her sick room or had she left it? Moreover, what were the odds that, if he did manage to find her, she would be alone?

Just as he had made the reckless decision to chance his luck and hope for the best, the kitchen door opened and Ellen emerged. Relieved, he gave a low whistle and she looked around in curiosity. When she saw him lurking by the edge of the stables, her eyes widened and she scurried over to him. He pulled her by the elbow into the building's shadow.

'I didn't expect –' she stuttered. 'I came out to look for Liam. I wanted to meet him when he returned from – oh, Cormac, I can only say again how sorry I am about –'

'Thanks,' he interrupted. 'I need to see her. Will you help me?'

She paused. Indecision, sympathy and fear mingled on her face before she said, 'Yes. Wait for a sign from me.'

She went back across the courtyard and re-entered the kitchens. A few minutes later, she reappeared at the doorway and motioned for him to hurry. He darted across the cobbles and was over the threshold in seconds.

'Mrs Kavanagh's in the pantry but she won't be there for long. Miss Muldowney's strength is returning so you'll find her in the drawing room. She's alone. Lady Courcey's in the study writing letters and Mr Lambourne's gone out riding. I don't know how much time you have but I wouldn't stay long if I were you.'

'Thank you, you're an angel,' he said and she coloured.

He crossed to the inner kitchen door and made his way up the narrow stairs into the back of the entrance hall. Stealing over to the drawing room, he eased open the door and crept inside, echoing the steps of the silver thieves that summer.

Bridget lay on a sofa near the piano, propped up by cushions and cocooned in a blanket. A closed book sat on a low table by her elbow; she was staring into space. Her head turned when the door opened and shock registered on her features, instantly followed by sorrow and compassion.

'Cormac,' she breathed.

'Ellen let me in...' He felt he should explain why he had shown up in such an illicit manner, but he supposed that might be obvious, considering the circumstances.

He went over and knelt by the sofa. She touched his cheek. That was all it took for the dam inside him to burst and overflow with anger and regret. She laid his head in her lap and stroked his hair, while he cried for his lost sister.

At length, the outburst of emotion subsided and he grew quiet.

'I wish I could have been there for you,' she whispered. 'I wanted to come but my mother refused to let me out of the house.'

Raising his head, he wiped his face on his sleeve and attempted a weak smile. 'I'm not surprised. I wouldn't have let you come either. You almost died of a fever recently, if you recall.'

She smiled back. 'Since when could something like that ever stop me?'

'Since you grew up and became a lady.'

Her face fell. While her question had been a throwaway remark, his answer had been quite serious. He lifted her palm to his lips and kissed it to show he had not meant to be unkind.

She put her other hand behind his neck and pulled him closer. This was a very different kiss from the last. That one had been spontaneous, urgent, impossible to suppress, but this was tender, delicate, lingering. They drew it out as long as they could, savouring the tastes, the sensations. He breathed in, losing himself in her captivating lilac scent.

The sound of voices out in the hall split them apart.

'Yes, my lady,' they heard Ellen say loudly. 'I'll be sure to do that for you at once.'

'There is no need to shout,' came Lady Courcey's disapproving response. She was almost outside the drawing room door.

Bridget looked at Cormac in panic. His gaze swept the room, taking in the critical lack of hiding places among its decorative pieces of furniture. The door began to open. The only thing he could do was dart behind the sofa and crouch down while Bridget fumbled for her book, just as Lady Courcey entered the room with a very nervous Ellen in her wake.

'Where are you going?' he heard the lady say in annoyance. 'I just asked you to call for the tea.'

'R-right away, my lady.'

The door shut with an ominous snap. Footsteps advanced, changing quality as they passed from floorboard to rug, and then a chair creaked as it took Lady Courcey's weight. Cormac's heart sank.

'How are you feeling?'

'Much better,' Bridget mumbled. 'In fact, I believe I am well enough to go for a walk. Shall we take a turn around the gardens?'

Lady Courcey sniffed. 'Do not be absurd, you are still too weak for that. You cannot venture out of doors until you are fully recovered. Although, if you are feeling that much improved, perhaps we could talk about what we plan to do after your convalescence is over. We ought to remove to the city as soon as possible.'

'Oh. May we not stay here a few months longer?'

'No. Our intention was always to leave at the end of the summer and you know very well that it would be impractical to even attempt to organise the wedding while living in the country. We shall need to make frequent visits to the dressmakers and florists, as well as manage the issuing of invitations and a hundred other things. It would be ludicrous to expect to arrange all of that from here.'

Cormac cringed. This was the last thing he wanted to hear right now. Bridget must have thought the same for she asked, 'Have you heard from Uncle Stuart?' in a patent effort to steer the conversation in a different direction.

'Yes, I was just writing my reply to him. He complains that he is suffering from gout, small wonder. He has postponed his return to England, intending to reside in Dublin until after the wedding. Now, we must consider your appearance. You shall, of course, wear your grandmother's pearls…'

As Lady Courcey went on, Cormac grew more and more uncomfortable. Too fearful to shift his weight and unable to close his ears, he hunched down behind the sofa and listened to her talk about the very event that would separate Bridget from him forever.

Two pairs of steps came into the drawing room the next time the door opened – a tinkle of china indicated a housemaid, while an anxious clearing of the throat communicated Ellen's presence. Over the sound of the tea tray being placed on a table, Ellen said, 'My lady, Mrs Walsh wishes to speak with you on some housekeeping matters.'

'Tell Mrs Walsh I am having tea with my daughter and I shall discuss these matters with her later.'

The two pairs of steps retreated from the room.

Lady Courcey remained for another excruciating hour, the best part of which she spent talking about the upcoming wedding. By the time she rose to leave, Cormac was ready to explode with tension, his body aching and his mind reeling.

'At least this illness has given you a slimmer figure,' was the lady's parting remark. 'You should fit into my wedding dress with very few alterations.'

As soon as the door closed, he let out a low groan and stood clumsily, stretching his stiff legs. Bridget reached out to him.

'I am so sorry —' she began, but he stopped her with a shake of his head and touched her hand to say he understood. Without a word, he headed for the door and, checking first that Lady Courcey was nowhere in sight, made good his escape.

When he entered the kitchens, he found that Mrs Kavanagh had resumed her post, kneading dough on the flour-covered table. An expression of pity filled her face for a brief moment until she realised he had just come from above stairs and her look turned to one of suspicion.

'What have you been doing, lad?' she barked.

He shrugged and did not answer. Ellen was also there, flitting about restlessly; he caught her eye and nodded his thanks. She looked downright relieved as he walked out the door.

## Chapter 22

Cormac returned to work the next day, determined that life should go back to normal as soon as possible. He wanted no more commiseration so he marched into the stables with his jaw set and his chin raised, challenging the men to remind him of the calamity that had befallen his family. John was the first to take the hint and simply ordered him to clean out a particular stall. Liam tossed him a pitchfork and the others turned away to their own tasks. Grateful, he strode into the stall and immersed himself in the physical labour, hoping exhaustion would induce temporary forgetfulness.

However, that night he learned that, while his working life might regain some semblance of normality, his family life was broken beyond repair. He went home across the fields after sundown, bone-weary and longing to be already asleep in the loft above the stables but knowing that to stay there would be an act of selfishness when his mother needed him. Only he had not comprehended how much so until he reached the cottage and heard the wailing from inside.

He flung open the door in panic. The fire had died down to ashes but the moonlight was bright enough to reveal the chaotic scene. Pieces of turf lay scattered on the floor in front of the hearth and what looked like an entire pail of milk had been spilled before his feet; it had soaked into the compacted earth and the room smelled sour. Patrick squirmed in his basket in the corner, his little face screwed up as he screamed at the top of his lungs, while Orlaith was on her knees at the bench by the table, weeping and calling out to her mother.

Maggie sat at the table, silent and unmoving, deaf to her daughter's pleas.

Orlaith's head turned when Cormac entered and she emitted a shriek of relief. Jumping up, she ran over to him and cried, 'Oh, help us, please! Patrick's been bawling for hours, I don't know how to make him stop, and I spilled the milk and I let the fire go out and I tried to start it again but I couldn't and Ma won't get up or say anything at all!' And she burst into sobs.

Alarm coursed through him but he didn't let it show as he lifted her into his arms and hugged her. 'Don't be upset, you've managed fine. Ma's just not feeling well right now. I'll take care of things here, no need to worry.'

He put her sitting on the opposite bench from their mother and set about reviving the fire first. His deft hands were able to coax life where Orlaith's inexpert ones could not, and soon the fire began to crackle. He threw the scattered bits of turf onto it and wiped his hands on his clothes before concerning himself with his screaming nephew. Not having had much experience with babies since his own sisters were small, he took quite some time to calm down Patrick, who needed both cleaning and feeding. Thankfully, some milk still remained in the bottom of the pail. It would do for now, although they would have to try to make arrangements for a wet nurse to come from Ballydarry – with luck, there might be a new mother in the village with some sympathy for their plight. After the baby had sucked every last drop from a rag soaked in the milk, Cormac walked around the room rocking him against his chest until he drifted off to sleep and could be laid back into his basket.

Next, he needed to pacify Orlaith who was still crying in distress. He drew her over to the now-welcoming fireside and wiped at her tear-stained cheeks with his thumbs. 'Have you eaten today, chicken?'

She sniffed and shook her head.

Trying very hard not to feel angry towards his mother, he said, 'There's no milk left for stirabout so I'm going to make you some broth but I need to fetch water for it. Will you stay sitting here while I'm gone? I'll be quick as I can.'

She hiccupped and nodded.

He went outside and felt his heart wrench when his gaze landed on the water bucket, its rope conspicuously missing – he had abandoned it in two hacked-apart pieces in the woods and would never return to that spot to retrieve it. Without the rope, the bucket was useless for collecting water from the well, so he searched the edge of the woods until he found a stream and filled the bucket from that instead. He was not gone for many minutes and he made an effort to stay within earshot of the cottage but, even so, when he came back Orlaith's anxious face told him he had been away too long. He gave her a reassuring squeeze and urged her closer to the fire to warm herself up.

After pouring the bucket of water into a pot, he rooted around the cottage for any vegetables with which he could make the broth. While the absence of potatoes reminded him that he had to set aside time soon to begin harvesting the crop, he did find some carrots and turnips in a cloth bag by the dresser – probably obtained in the village by bartering the hens' eggs – and stood at the table to chop them up, ignoring his mother at his elbow. Then he tossed them into the pot of water which he set over the fire and left to boil.

He eyed the damp patch on the earthen floor with distaste; the odour of the spilled milk would linger for a long time but there was little he could do about it now and he supposed the smell of the hens would eventually overwhelm it. So, while he waited for the broth to cook, he sat down by the hearth next to his sister. She climbed into his lap and he wrapped his arms around her.

'Feeling better?'

Her lower lip jutted out. 'What's wrong with Ma?'

He looked over at Maggie who had not stirred since he came home. Her shoulders were slumped and her blank eyes were cast down to the floor.

'She misses Mary very much,' was all he said.

When the broth was ready, Orlaith gulped it down with the same voracity that Patrick had taken his milk. Afterwards, Cormac put her to bed in the loft, soothing her with gentle strokes down her back and murmuring lullabies until she too fell into slumber.

Now it was time to face his mother. He climbed back down the ladder to the ground floor of the cottage and sat on the bench beside her.

'Ma?' he said tentatively.

She gave no indication that she had heard him.

He took her hands and found them icy cold. Rubbing them briskly, he said, 'Ma, please. Can you hear me? Say something.'

She said nothing, her gaze still vacant of expression.

He got up, poured another bowl of broth, and set it on the table before her. 'Please eat,' he entreated.

No response.

In frustration, he turned for the door. He was going to bang it open in the hope that it would shock his mother into wakefulness, but the more likely outcome was that it would wake Patrick and bring on another bout of wailing, so he eased open the top half of the door and leaned out into the night, inhaling deeply to eradicate the stench of sour milk from his nostrils.

He was in turmoil, despite the calm façade he had portrayed for his sister's sake. What should he do? His mother was falling apart in front of him and it was pitiful to witness. Yes, he too felt the heartache of Mary's death, but Maggie seemed to have given up altogether with the loss of her first-born child. Perhaps it was just too much for her to endure, having already lost a husband and a son. However, this left a burden on Cormac's shoulders which he had no desire to bear; he had been the only man in the family for over two and a half years now but he did not wish to become the only responsible adult as well. He wanted his mother to be strong because otherwise the obligation of caring for her, his three remaining sisters and his nephew would have to take priority over everything else...which would mean he would not be free to pursue Bridget. Guiltily, he knew she was the one he yearned to put first.

Sighing, he ducked his head back inside. He sat down again next to his mother and cleared his throat.

'Ma, you need to accept that Mary's gone. She's gone and we can't get her back. You've got to face up to this.'

There was no reaction at first but then she raised her eyes to his and, at last communicative, they were far too easy to read. Torment and remorse tumbled in their grey depths, a bottomless sea of guilt-ridden despair.

'Jack will never forgive me for losing her,' she whispered.

He gaped. 'You think you're to blame?'

He reached out to embrace her but she tried to push him away, her hands batting him with the strength of a moth's wing.

'I deserve no consolation,' she said in a cracked voice.

Wretched, he said, 'What happened to Mary wasn't your fault.' He wanted to add that if anyone was culpable it was him, but that would mean admitting his awareness of Mary's real grief and divulging the truth of her sordid time in Dublin, which Maggie was in no way ready to hear. 'You couldn't have known what she was going to do. There was nothing you could've done to prevent it.'

'I failed her.' The tears gathered but did not fall. 'Little baby girl, her mother failed her.'

'You did *not* fail Mary,' he said, willing her to believe him. 'You're a wonderful mother. She was just too broken to continue on. You didn't know.'

'I should've known,' she said softly, and her gaze returned to the floor.

Terrified that she would sink back into her frozen state of misery, he grabbed her shoulders and shook her to get her to look at him again.

'D'you know what I blame you for?' he said, allowing some of his anger to finally surface. 'I blame you for neglecting these two children today. When I came home, Patrick was roaring and Orlaith was in hysterics. They were starving. How could you abandon them like that?'

'Wh-wh—' she stammered.

'You've lost a child and that's a terrible thing but there are two more here who still depend on you. Patrick needs a mother now, not just a grandmother, to say nothing of a wet nurse which you should've arranged by now. Are you going to forsake him the way Mary did or are you going to love him and look after him?'

She didn't reply but it was not the desolate silence from before; her eyes were trained on his, steady and focused in spite of their wetness.

'Are you going to love him and look after him?' he demanded again.

Her voice was barely audible. 'I am.'

'Good. Then start with looking after yourself. You've got to eat.'

He pushed the untouched bowl of broth towards her but, doubting the strength of her hand, filled the spoon himself and raised it to her mouth. It had to be cold by this stage but she swallowed it without protestation.

Then she burst into tears and this time she did not resist when he reached out his arms.

## Chapter 23

Bridget stood in her bedchamber, staring into the long, silver-framed mirror. She was steady on her feet, her back was straight, her eyes were bright, and her skin had lost its ghostly pallor. All in all, she gave the impression of being in sound health.

This was not good.

She hunched her shoulders and allowed her eyelids to droop as if she were very tired. Then she grasped the cane which Mr Abbott had provided and leaned on it heavily. There was not much she could do about the hue of her skin but, though she was no longer quite so pale, neither could she claim to be rosy-cheeked.

The overall effect was someone who had recuperated from an illness but still had some way to go to full recovery. Much better.

As she turned to leave the room, her gaze fell upon the wooden bird perched on her dressing table. She picked it up, caressed its wing tenderly and, on impulse, scurried to the bedside and tucked it beneath her pillow. Then she resumed her poorly demeanour and shuffled out of the bedchamber, almost walking into Ellen who was passing by with a dress draped over her arm. The lady's maid looked startled and guilty.

'Good morning, miss,' she mumbled.

'Good morning,' said Bridget, feeling rather discomfited herself. Ellen had enabled Cormac to come to her in the drawing room on the day of Mary's burial. How much had she deduced about what had happened behind the closed door? Did she regret her actions now, considering how close they had come to getting caught?

Bridget did not regret it. To have that opportunity to comfort Cormac in the depths of his anguish meant more than she could say. Ellen ought to know that what she had done had been a good deed.

She put out her free hand to stop Ellen from moving on down the corridor.

'Thank you for your discretion,' she said. 'Your kindness does not go unappreciated.'

Ellen glanced about but there was no one else within sight.

'I shouldn't have done it,' she said, hardly moving her lips. 'But I just felt so sorry for him. I thought he needed…a friend.'

Bridget nodded sadly. 'Yes, he did.'

Ellen opened her mouth to speak again but then shut it as though she had thought better.

'Is there something else?'

The lady's maid shook her head. 'It's not my place to say.'

'You may speak freely. There is nobody else listening.'

'Just…' She hesitated. 'Be careful, miss.'

And she hurried on towards Lady Courcey's bedchamber.

Bridget stood still, staring after her. She was right, it was not her place to say that, even in her senior position on the staff, but she had been given permission to speak her mind. 'Be careful.' It was a reasonable warning, but what did it insinuate? Be careful not to get involved with Cormac? Or be careful not to get trapped in an unhappy marriage?

Leaving the question unanswered, she turned towards the mahogany staircase. At the top, she looked at the steps and then at her cane and then below to the empty entrance hall. It would be tiresome to hobble all the way down when there was no spectator present to make sympathetic note of her frailty.

Lifting the cane, she started down the stairs with assurance but had only descended half a dozen steps when she heard a door opening onto the hall below. She let the tip of the cane drop back to the polished wooden boards just in time; Garrett emerged from the drawing room and gazed up at her.

She resumed her descent in a more tremulous fashion and he climbed the stairs to provide assistance. He offered her his arm and she slid her own through it. His other hand reached over to rest on hers where she had placed it at the crook of his elbow. Whereas once she would have viewed this as a sweet, protective gesture, now she saw it as a display of possession.

When they got to the bottom, she let out a little moan.

'Are you in pain?' he asked, genuine concern on his face.

She gave him a brave smile. 'I'm fine, but I do still find the stairs exhausting.'

He guided her to the drawing room and into a comfortable chair. 'Shall I call for a maidservant? Is there anything you require?'

'No, thank you. I just need to catch my breath.'

He took the seat next to her. 'I thought you had been exhibiting encouraging signs of improvement.'

'I thought so too. It seems we were both mistaken.'

He said nothing else and neither did she. She remembered a time when talking had come so easily to them and they had shared their opinions on every topic, great and small, but now it felt like there was a distance between them which no amount of conversation could surmount. She could not deny that she was distracted by her feelings for Cormac, but he too seemed in a constant state of preoccupation. Perhaps he was beginning to suspect that he was not the sole possessor of her affections anymore.

If he did, he would be right. She had betrayed him twice now with Cormac and an insistent, excited voice inside her promised that that was not the end of it. She was seated next to her fiancé but it was not his lips she imagined kissing again.

She pretended to let her breathing slow. At length, she said in a casual voice, 'I believe I am keeping you too much confined indoors. It is not possible for me to go out riding yet, but please do not feel that this means you cannot go yourself.'

He sat up straighter and she knew she had hit the mark; he longed to get away from the monotony of a household that revolved around a convalescing patient.

'I have already gone out once or twice,' he confessed.

'Yes, I know.' And on the last occasion, she added silently, Cormac came and I kissed him. 'Would you like to go again?'

\*\*\*

Cormac was carrying a bag of oats towards Bonny's stall when he perceived the refined voice of Mr Lambourne outside the stable doors, requesting his horse to be saddled. John Corbett himself entered the stables to carry out the task and the gentleman followed him in, the two conversing about the day's weather and how it might affect riding conditions.

Mr Lambourne was relaxed and affable with John, but his demeanour changed when he caught sight of Cormac; though Cormac was careful to keep his own expression innocent, a subtle coldness clouded the other man's manner. John did not appear to notice anything and continued on to attend to Commander, leaving them alone.

'Fine enough day for riding,' said Cormac.

'Indeed,' said Mr Lambourne coolly. 'The wind is rather fresh but Corbett believes the rain will hold off for the time being.'

'Probably won't come down heavy 'til this evening.'

'I expect to be back before then.'

With a respectful nod, Cormac turned to go on towards Bonny's stall. He had opened the half door when he realised that Mr Lambourne had come up behind him. The gentleman's dark eyebrows rose as he asked, 'Is that Miss Muldowney's mare?'

'It is,' said Cormac, wishing he had chosen a different stall. He could not guess how much Mr Lambourne might read into his personal care of Bridget's horse but he would sooner avoid rousing any further distrust in the gentleman's mind.

Mr Lambourne's mouth puckered in deliberation. 'It is a shame she did not get to enjoy riding her more while we were here. Now that the summer is over and our removal to the city is imminent, the opportunity is all but past.'

Did he expect Cormac to betray his disappointment at this news of Bridget's impending departure? He was better at concealing his feelings than that.

''Tis indeed a shame,' he said politely and stepped into the stall, allowing the half door to swing shut behind him.

John returned presently with Commander and Mr Lambourne disappeared outside. As Cormac fed a handful of oats to Bonny, he reflected that the gentleman was now absent from Bridget's side. Could he seize this chance to go in search of her? But he was reluctant to put Ellen in such a tricky position again. And Bridget might well be in the company of Lady Courcey. It was too great a risk to take, much as he longed to see her.

On this occasion, however, Bridget came to him, not ten minutes after Mr Lambourne had ridden off. He was crossing to another stall with the depleting bag of oats when an irregular tapping sound came to his ears. He glanced out through the stable doors and glimpsed her limping across the courtyard with the aid of a cane, which struck the cobbles each time she took a step.

This was the first time he had seen her outdoors since the storm. Pleased though he was to lay eyes on her, he did not think she ought to be exerting herself so much – she still looked too weak to be walking. John, who had emerged from his workspace to investigate the tapping noise, hastened out into the courtyard to offer his support to her. She took his arm with a grateful dip of her head.

'Miss,' Cormac heard him say, 'while 'tis good to see you're getting better, is it wise to be venturing out so soon after your illness?'

'Thank you for your concern,' came her reply, 'but I believe the benefits of being out in the air far outweigh any subsequent tiredness I might experience. It feels like I have not taken a proper breath in weeks. Although this does lead me to my purpose in coming out here. Is your carpenter in the vicinity?'

Cormac started. Oakleigh only had one carpenter. Was she being too obvious? Would John suspect something? He didn't care. He waited for the stable master to call his name and then emerged from the stables. Her eyes lit up but she was quick to rearrange her expression into one of composure.

'Good day, Cormac,' she greeted him.

'Good day, miss. I'm glad you're back on your feet but would I be right in presuming you don't mean to take Bonny out today?'

She laughed. 'Yes, I am not ready to go riding just yet. However, I do long to be out of doors again. It is so stuffy inside the house.

Unfortunately, my mother insists that I am only permitted to walk for very short periods until my full strength returns.'

'Sounds like sensible advice to me,' he said, and John nodded in agreement.

'But it is difficult to say when that will be,' she said with a pointed look. 'I thought in the meantime I could make a compromise with my mother and find a means of being outside while still dutifully resting.'

'What d'you propose, miss?' asked John.

'I would like a swing seat made for the oak tree. I think the orchard is the ideal location for my recuperation as I shall be sheltered but still able to get fresh air. Do you think you can do it, Cormac?'

He had never made any object quite so big as a swing seat but he said without hesitation, 'Of course. I'd be delighted to do anything to help your recovery.'

She gave him a sweet smile. 'Perhaps, then, you could accompany me into the orchard so I can show you what I would like?'

He had to stop himself grinning in return. 'Happy to, miss.'

John saw nothing untoward about this arrangement and even advised them to take their time so as not to stretch the limits of Bridget's strength. Cormac didn't feel quite daring enough to offer his arm to her while still in the stable master's presence so he just led the way to the orchard door and held it open for her to pass through.

It was peaceful beneath the apple trees, which were laden down with fruit ripe for picking. He made sure to set a slow pace along the path but she seemed to grow sturdier with every step, soon not relying on her cane much at all.

He was about to remark on this when she said quietly, 'How are you?'

He considered the question, thinking about all the events that had happened over the past few weeks, the incredible highs and the despairing lows. 'In all honesty? I'm a bit ragged 'round the edges.'

'I understand what that is like.' She sighed. 'How is your mother?'

'She isn't well,' he admitted. He had not mentioned Maggie's breakdown to anyone at the stables, not John nor even Liam, but Bridget he could tell. 'If I'm ragged, 'tis nothing compared to how she's feeling. She's fallen apart. She blames herself for what happened to Mary.'

'Oh no, does she? But she must know it is not her fault.'

'She refuses to see it that way. The day after we buried Mary, I came home to find her sitting still as a stone with the children and cottage in disarray 'round her. That frightened me. I managed to rouse her but she's only a shadow of a person now. 'Tis a struggle to convince her to eat although she's stirred herself enough to at least take care of Orlaith and Patrick.'

'Poor, dear Maggie,' said Bridget, dismayed. 'How much more can she endure? This is dreadful.'

"Tis like all her energy and happiness has leaked out of her. I've been going home every night to try raise her spirits but I've asked Margaret and Bronagh to go for the next few nights. I'm hoping it'll cheer her up to have all her girls with her for an evening or two. Her remaining girls,' he corrected himself, shoulders sagging.

She slipped her free hand into his; it was only then that he noticed she was not wearing gloves. Her expression was compassionate and her fingers were soft. He looked down at them.

'And this is where the guilt starts,' he said. ''Cause I know my sister's dead and I know my mother's in terrible pain but all I want to think about is kissing you.'

He made himself look back at her. She was biting the tip of her tongue but her eyes were bright with anticipation.

'I do not think you should feel guilty about wanting to be happy,' she said.

He bent to kiss her, releasing her hand so he could wrap both of his arms around her. She dropped her cane and succumbed willingly to his embrace. The kiss became fierce; there was consolation and desire in her lips and he was hungry for both. Her body bowed under the force of his eagerness. They did not stop for air, kissing long and hard and feverishly. When at last they pulled apart, they were both panting.

'Nice not to be interrupted this time,' he said once he had regained his breath.

She stared up at him, stunned. He sensed that she was not fully supporting herself anymore and kept his grip tight around her back.

'You going to faint?' he asked.

'I think I am quite literally weak at the knees.' Her cheeks were pink. 'I have never been kissed like that before.'

That gave him an enormous measure of satisfaction. Mr Garrett Lambourne may have riches aplenty but his kisses had never left her so weak that she could not stand.

'I'm glad you liked it,' he said, colouring too.

'I more than liked it. It was incomparable to any other. I felt as though you had an appetite only I could sate, like you wanted to —' But she cut herself off there, the pink having converted to a flaming red.

He might have pressed her to finish the sentence but he could make a reasonable deduction and he preferred to save her further embarrassment. She was a lady after all and, regardless of his empty pockets, he ought to act like a gentleman.

So he swept her up into his arms and said, 'I don't think you can make it by yourself to the oak tree. Shall I carry you?'

She nodded and turned her mortified face into his neck, her chestnut curls tickling his jaw. Smiling to himself, he followed the winding path to the centre of the orchard, leaving the cane abandoned on the ground behind them. When they reached the clearing, he hoisted her up into the branches of the oak and deposited her safely in a comfortable fork. By this time, she had recovered enough to look at him again. He grinned up at her, his head lower than hers due to her elevated position.

'So where d'you want me to put this swing seat?'

'Oh, yes. That was just an excuse to see you. But it might be a good idea, don't you think?'

They chattered for a while about the proposed swing seat, debating which branch would be most suitable, how far from the ground the seat ought to be, and how wide, and whether it should have arms, and which wood he might use. In the midst of all that, they kissed, she leaning down and he stretching up, their lips meeting tenderly, passionately, and every intensity in between. It was an idyllic interlude of pure contentment.

But it could not last forever. The seconds slid away and too soon it was time to leave. When she said it, his gaze fell to the large ruby on her left hand.

'What're we doing, Bridget?'

She ran her fingers through his fair hair. 'Don't ask that today. Let us enjoy this feeling without any complications. Save the worry for later.'

He accepted this; why ruin the enchantment of the moment? Lifting her down from the tree, he carried her to the spot where the cane still lay on the path, and together they walked back through the orchard, letting go of each other's hand only when they reached the green door.

## Chapter 24

A blustery breeze tugged at Bridget's hair and caused the ends of her shawl to flap about. Garrett tucked the wayward material solicitously around her shoulders, then offered her his arm and gestured towards the vine-draped arch at the gardens' entrance.

Intending to keep up her charade of fragility for as long as possible, she leaned into him for support as they followed the walkway around the gardens. She knew he and her mother both wished to go back to the city now that the summer was at an end, but they would never force her to travel if they feared she would not survive the journey. And right now the very last thing she wanted was to leave the estate.

'Isn't this nice?' said Garrett, motioning to the late-blooming flowers which grew in meticulous patterns on either side of the path.

She murmured her own admiration of the colourful display and they continued on in silence. She supposed she ought to attempt further conversation but she could not stop thinking about Cormac. The kiss they had shared the day before had been a revelation. It had stirred something inside her, a restlessness which could not be alleviated. Every time she summoned the memory of it, she felt a passionate ache deep in her belly. She craved a kiss like that again, and she was deluding herself if she believed the man next to her could ever provide it.

Making an unwelcome intrusion into her thoughts, he announced, 'It is time to return to Dublin.'

She considered carefully before replying, 'We could not expect you to stay for much longer. When you arrived in July, I doubt you had anticipated still being here in September. How soon do you plan to depart?'

He arched an eyebrow at her. 'I meant both of us. The wedding ceremony cannot take place without the bride present.'

'But there is no rush,' she hedged. 'Wouldn't it be splendid to have a spring wedding? Nature would be just coming to life. There would be new growth on the trees and I could use daffodils for my bouquet. It would be so charming.'

'Nature doesn't come into it. We shall be getting married in the city, so it won't matter whether the trees have leaves or not.'

She changed the direction of her argument. 'You know I am still too weak to cope with such a big occasion. Do you want me to faint as I enter the church?'

He made an exasperated noise deep in his throat. 'Of course not. But I do not believe you are as frail as you are making yourself seem. It has been some time since your illness and you ought to be well recovered by now.'

She stopped and glared at him with as much indignation as she could muster. 'Are you saying you think I am pretending?'

He did not flinch under her gaze. 'Yes.'

She attempted a derisive tone. 'Why on earth would I do that?'

'So you can prolong your residence on the estate and continue certain acquaintances,' he answered levelly.

Her lips parted but no words came out. He was more astute than she had given him credit for. Feeling foolish, but unable to think of anything else to say, she whipped her arm out of his grasp and marched away from him.

'You cannot postpone the wedding forever,' he called after her. 'We will be in London by October, I promise you that.'

His assertion echoed in her mind for hours afterwards, to the point where real panic began to take hold, creeping up her throat to suffocate her. How soon before he forced her to leave? A week? A day? Her time at Oakleigh was running out.

So now she gripped her candlestick and opened her bedchamber door with painstaking care. The corridor beyond was dark and silent, the whole household having retired to bed over an hour ago. She abhorred the idea of sneaking through the house at night like a thief but no other option remained to her – Garrett had proved to be disinclined to go out riding during the day and her mother had been desirous of her company in a protracted perusal of the estate's accounts, making it impossible for her to slip away unnoticed. And she was desperate to seek out Cormac; this could not wait.

The hem of her nightdress swished about her ankles as she tiptoed down the mahogany staircase, the candle flame casting her monstrous shadow behind her. She reached the empty kitchens without incident and, taking the key off the hook on the wall, unlocked the back door. It swung on noiseless hinges, smooth from frequent use.

The clear sky was sprinkled with stars and the night-time air was chilly. Gooseflesh rose on her skin as she crossed the courtyard, stubbing the toes of her slippers more than once on the uneven cobbles. The double doors of the stables were shut but, to her relief, not locked.

At the far end of the stables, beyond the stalls, was the ladder which led up to the loft. She climbed it one-handed, careful to avoid catching her foot in her nightdress's hem. She crept up through the hole in the loft floor and peered around. Several stable hands lay in the straw, so fast asleep that the candlelight did not disturb them. At first, she could not see Cormac among them and feared he had gone home for the night, but then she spotted his familiar form sprawled at the other side of the loft.

Leaving the candlestick by the hole, she crawled cautiously past the other men and nudged his arm. He woke in an instant and she put her hand over his mouth to prevent him making a noise. His eyes widened when he perceived her kneeling beside him in her nightdress and slippers. She jerked her head back towards the ladder and he nodded, indicating that he would follow her down.

Once they were below, she whispered, 'I needed to see you. Is there somewhere we can talk?'

After pondering for a moment, he led her out of the stables and over to the furthest hay barn. Inside, she discerned his carpentry workspace in the corner and the progress he had made on her swing seat – several wooden beams lay side by side, sawn with precision to the same length. Yesterday, they had kissed beneath the oak as they discussed the construction of the seat, and she had said they would save the worry for another day. That day had come sooner than she had expected.

He sat on a haystack and she set her candlestick on the barn floor before joining him. The light of the flame flickered over their faces.

'What's the matter?' he said with concern.

'Garrett suspects something,' she said, her voice subdued. 'He thinks I am feigning my weak condition in order to stay longer here with you. Well, he did not specify you in particular, but we both knew who he meant.'

Silence hovered between them.

'And is that what you're doing?'

She swallowed and stared down into her lap. 'Yes, it is. I don't want to leave you.'

There it was, she had said it. Making that declaration filled her with a conviction that was both instantaneous and profound: she loved this man sitting mere inches from her. Her heart beat madly against her ribs at the realisation.

His body trembled in reaction to her words. 'I'm very glad to hear that.'

He cupped her chin and raised it so that they were making eye contact. She could read a mixture of eagerness and nervousness in his gaze.

'So what does this mean?' he asked.

'I don't know,' she confessed. 'I have no wish to leave but I am being given no choice in the matter. I'm Garrett's intended wife and therefore obligated to obey him. What else can I do?'

He took his hand away and his expression became frank. 'What're your feelings for him?'

Now was the time to examine herself and truthfully answer that question. 'I believed that I was happy with him. When we were in Dublin, he always seemed so thoughtful and romantic. But he has shown me his unpleasant side this summer. He has been short-tempered and unkind, and I do not care for his behaviour when he has drink in him. Most of all, I am dismayed by his indifference to my unwillingness to go to London. He has brushed my opinion aside like it does not matter, even though he knows his decision will make me miserable. There can be no joy in a union so unequal. And when I compare him to you…'

She gazed into his eyes, so blue and sincere.

'You,' she repeated. 'I was gone for over seven years and yet you are still here beside me, as constant as ever. I am ashamed that I ever promised myself to another man when you have always been the most important person to me. I was so blind but — oh, Cormac, it is you whom I love!'

She threw her arms around him and they hugged so tightly that she was left quite breathless. He murmured into her ear, 'I think you already know how I feel.'

She drew back to look at him; his face was shining with joyfulness. How long and how much had he yearned for this moment? A flood of giddy delight swept over her but it receded as she remembered Garrett.

'But I am engaged,' she bemoaned. 'I am trapped.'

'You're not trapped. You haven't married him yet. You can still leave him.'

'It is easier to say that than to go through with it. Engaged practically *is* married as far as my mother and society are concerned. It would be an utter scandal if we separated now.'

'Is the scandal really something that'd bother you? Don't you think it'd be better to endure a small amount of gossip in the short term than to suffer for decades in an unhappy marriage?'

She did not answer. What he said made sense but fear of her mother's fury kept her undecided.

'Mother would throw me out of the house,' she said at last.

He could not refute the statement; Lady Courcey was probably capable of much worse.

'But 'tisn't like you'd have nowhere to go. You'd have me. I'd look after you.'

Her smile was dim. 'She would throw you out too and we would both be homeless.'

'We'd be fine,' he said staunchly. 'Don't be so afraid to imagine it. We could be happy together.'

She allowed herself to picture such a future: steady, straightforward Cormac at her side rather than charming, selfish Garrett. It would be a more basic life, with none of the luxuries she was accustomed to, but it would be a truer one. Kind-hearted and devoted, he would always take care of her, and she would do the same for him.

She gave him another smile, this one much brighter. He grinned and took her hand, squeezing it.

'I love you,' he said, 'more than you can ever know. Will you marry me instead of Garrett?'

Thrilled, she flung her arms around him again and cried, 'Yes!' with her voice muffled in his shoulder.

He laughed and held her close, then tilted her back so that his forehead leaned against hers.

'I've never thought of anyone else but you,' he said.

Their lips met. She opened her mouth to him and his tongue slipped inside. She welcomed it with her own, tender at first, but with a growing urgency. This was what she needed, this was how that ache in her belly could be satisfied. She entwined her fingers in his hair and pulled him nearer, kissing him harder.

His hand came to rest on the curve of her breast. Her tongue faltered but swiftly regained confidence. He tugged down the neckline of her nightdress and she pushed herself further into his palm. She might not fully understand what she was consenting to but she knew this was the only man upon whom she could bestow that consent. And even though they were going to be married – as soon as they could manage it, she resolved – the impulses of their bodies declared the impossibility of waiting until that occasion.

He made an attempt to demur nonetheless. Withdrawing from the kiss with a valiant effort, he said, 'Are you sure? 'Tis – 'tis supposed to be painful. For you, I mean.'

A thought struck her and her guts coiled like serpents. 'Do you know – that is, have you –'

'No, I haven't.' He stroked her cheek. 'But the men in the stables talk. I know enough to get us started. And I think maybe instinct might take us the rest of the way.'

Conscious that she should say no, should exercise prudence, should keep him at arm's length, she whispered, 'Lead on.'

He greeted this emancipation with a quivering intake of breath. His intrepid hand trailed down her stomach, over her hip, along her thigh and past her knee until it found the hem of her nightdress. It slid beneath and travelled back the way it had come, the material slithering up with it. Cool air caressed her bare legs but now she didn't feel the cold; rather, her skin burned as he exposed it.

She shifted and he drew the nightdress over her head. Instead of tossing it away, he spread it out on the haystack behind her, while she kicked off her slippers to complete her state of undress. Her nudity ought to have embarrassed her but how could she think that way when he gazed at her with such appreciation? She scrabbled to remove his clothing too, fumbling ineffectually in her haste to uncover him. He stood to hurry the process, providing her with her first full view of a naked man. Every part of her glowed as she pulled him down into an embrace, her breasts thrusting against his chest. He laid her back on the haystack, the soft material of her nightdress protecting her from the spiky ends of the hay.

'God, you're beautiful,' he breathed and pressed his mouth to her skin.

They explored each other thoroughly with hands, lips and tongues, flesh touching flesh in an exquisite collision of sensation. Their inexperience became apparent as they bumped foreheads or scraped teeth but raw passion rendered such knocks comical and inconsequential. They giggled and groaned and gasped and cared for nothing but seeking the satisfaction their bodies craved.

Then, within the bubble of frantic activity, one tiny movement occurred: his hand alighted ever so gently on her knee, a question, an encouragement, a plea. She responded without reservation, easing it away from the other in an action that felt both sinful and exhilarating.

He edged into position and she welcomed him to her. Their gasps mingled together. There was a little pain but not as much as she had expected, and it was superseded by a sense of completion that nearly overwhelmed her. When he moved inside her, her last coherent thought was that no moment in her life had ever been more perfect.

And he was right. Instinct took them the rest of the way.

Overjoyed in their love for one another, they lay in each other's arms until the dawn crept over the horizon and daylight peeked through the cracks in the hay barn's walls. The candle had burned down to nothing but she couldn't recall when it had gone out.

Reluctantly, she sat up. 'I have to go.'

A smudge of blood showed in the folds of her nightdress. He helped her to put it on, every touch and look a tingling reminder of what had passed between them.

'I love you,' he said and kissed her.

'I love you too,' she replied with a happy smile and left the barn.

## Chapter 25

Bridget returned to the house, locked the kitchen door, and replaced the key on its hook. She had got back just in time, judging by the distant sounds of movement on the servants' stairs. She stole through the inner kitchen door and upstairs to her bedchamber, feeling deliciously sore and still able to smell Cormac on her skin. Her plan was to climb into bed and snatch a couple of hours of sleep if possible. After she woke, she would consider what to say when she faced Garrett.

What she did not expect was to find him waiting for her when she opened the bedchamber door.

She took in a sharp breath, too shocked to utter a word. He sat on the edge of her bed, wearing neither coat nor waistcoat, his shirt open at the neck. His face was expressionless and, when he spoke, his voice was just as empty.

'Good morning, Bridget. My behaviour to you in the gardens yesterday was inexcusable so I came to your bedchamber last night to apologise. I'm sorry that I missed you.' He rose and came over to her. 'I'll let you sleep. You must be tired.'

He dropped a weightless kiss on her cheek and left the room.

The breath she had been holding came out in a long shudder. Guilt made her insides squirm. Yes, she had meant to inform Garrett that she wished to put an end to their engagement, but there had been no need for him to know that she had just spent the night away from her bed, undoubtedly in the arms of his rival if he had discerned the incriminating smear of blood on her nightdress. Furthermore, the fact that he had visited her chamber so late at night, and in such a state of undress, implied that he had been intending to make another advance like the drunken one he had attempted on the night of his birthday, perhaps in an effort to seal the bond of their betrothal. She had denied him this experience he so desired and bestowed it upon another instead. He ought to be enraged. So for him to take her betrayal with such composure was unimaginable. She felt far worse than if he had shouted or struck her.

But he had other ways of punishing her. When she went down to breakfast, after spending an hour or two in fruitless pursuit of sleep, she found her mother waiting with a grim expression on her face.

'Where were you last night?' Lady Courcey demanded before she even had time to sit down.

She hesitated. 'Nowhere. In my bedchamber.'

'You are lying to me. I have spoken with Mr Lambourne.' Her mother seethed with anger as she crossed the room to her. 'Were you with that McGovern boy?'

She didn't reply.

Lady Courcey gave her a slap which made her eyes water. She gasped and her hand flew to her smarting cheek.

'So I have a whore for a daughter, do I?' the lady said viciously. 'One who is willing to demean herself with the absolute dregs of society?' She regarded Bridget with narrowed eyes. 'I thought seven years would be enough to rid you of your loathsome fixation but when you gave me that list for compensation I knew that it was not. Did you really think I would not notice his family's name? Are you witless? They got nothing. I would never do a thing to encourage that boy. His association with you was already too dangerous. And it disgusts me to learn how right I was.'

The bottom fell out of Bridget's stomach. Her good deed had failed, and Lady Courcey had shown herself to be far more perceptive than she had realised. Had the lady seen that her daughter still held a deep regard for Cormac ever before she had known it herself?

'I am ashamed to call you mine but consider yourself lucky, girl, for your fool of a fiancé is still willing to marry you.'

She raised her chin in defiance. 'I do not want to marry him,' she declared, and received a harder slap than before. She reeled backwards and reached out to the wall behind her for support.

'You *shall* marry him. Do you think I am going to allow you to bring disgrace upon this family's name? We have a reputation to uphold.'

'I don't care about the family name,' she retorted. 'I do not love him so I will not marry him.'

'And what do you suppose will become of you if you do not? Mr Lambourne's fortune and social status will be lost to you forever. You will lose a mother, for I will most certainly disown a daughter who invites such disrepute upon herself. All you'll have left will be a worthless existence with a penniless, homeless boy who can offer you nothing.'

'He's not homeless,' Bridget said, despite the sickening feeling growing in her belly. She knew what was coming.

But the blow was more terrible than she had anticipated.

'My dear girl, use your head,' her mother snapped. 'Do you think for one second I would keep that boy on my land? He and his whole family would be thrown out of their home faster than you could pack your bags. It would be the end of them, for I am certain they would have nowhere else to go.'

'His whole family?' A wave of horror engulfed her. 'You would not do that.'

'I would, and without a moment's compassion for any of them. It is highly improbable that they would be able to find employment elsewhere to support them all, so they would doubtless starve within months. In effect, you would be condemning them to death. You think about that before you go running to that good-for-nothing boy.'

What made Lady Courcey's behaviour so revolting was that she meant every word she said. She would have no compunction about evicting a whole family out of pure malice. The magnitude of her cruelty was despicable.

Bridget thought of Cormac and the exultation they had shared when they had professed their love for each other last night. She could not give that up; it was so much more genuine than the farce her relationship with Garrett had become.

Then she thought of Cormac's mother. Her husband and two of her children dead, and now the possibility that she would be turned out of her home with her remaining four children and her tiny grandson. She would never survive the emotional turmoil. It was too much for one person to bear.

It seemed to come down to whether Bridget would be selfish and choose her own happiness at the expense of an entire family's wellbeing, or be selfless and relinquish her chance of a future with Cormac for the sake of a family who did not deserve a death sentence.

She began to weep hopelessly.

Lady Courcey ignored her distress. 'Here are your options,' she said with the coldness of a mistress delivering instructions to a recalcitrant servant. 'If you choose the boy, you, he and his family will be consigned to a short life of destitution before you all die in a ditch. If you elect to stay with Mr Lambourne, the family may keep their home and positions. However, either way that boy must go. I want him off the estate by nightfall, do you understand me?'

Still crying, Bridget managed a miserable nod of comprehension. Her mother brushed past her and stalked from the room. After a few frozen moments, she leaned against the wall and slid to the floor in despair.

***

When Bridget left him at dawn, Cormac returned unnoticed to the stable loft. Exhaustion made him drop asleep immediately but too soon he awakened to the sound of the other stable hands stirring. He rose from the straw, yawning and feigning the satisfaction of a good night's sleep.

Despite his fatigue, a current of euphoria streamed through his veins. His beloved Bridget had promised to marry him. She had held him in the most intimate embrace and loved him with a brave and innocent joy that had caused him to adore her all the more. There could be no one in the world as elated as he was right now.

But a lot of things were about to change. Sad though he would be to leave, they could not stay at Oakleigh; Lady Courcey would never abide it. It was going to be hard enough for her to swallow Bridget's cancelled engagement and her choice of a lower class man – and an Irishman, no less – as her husband. It would be best to remove themselves from the animosity that would arise from all that.

They ought to take steps to depart as soon as possible. The most challenging of these would have to fall to Bridget – she was quite possibly at this moment in the throes of a very difficult conversation with her fiancé and mother. After she had concluded that gruelling task, she could gather what few possessions she wished to take with her; the rest of her life would have to be left behind. He did not have many belongings himself, apart from his father's tool chest. His most essential duty would be to explain to his mother that he and Bridget were going away and that they would send for her, Patrick and his sisters once they were settled in a new place. She wouldn't like to be parted from him but he could assure her it wouldn't be for long. There was no need to tell her precisely what had occurred between him and Bridget the night before; he could write and notify her of their marriage once the union had been made official. He bit his lip – who would read the letter for her? He would have to check with Margaret if she had been learning her letters. If not, Maggie might bring the letter to Mrs Kavanagh.

Also of high priority was obtaining a character reference for himself. He would have to find work quickly to support himself, Bridget and, in time, his family, and, while her genteel background might bolster his chances, a character would be the surest course.

To that end, he approached John Corbett at the earliest opportunity that morning, locating him in Bonny's stall where he was examining one of the mare's hooves.

'I think this lady's ready for a visit to the farrier's,' he said, with a glance around at Cormac. 'Might get you to take her tomorrow.'

He cleared his throat. 'John, can I have a word?'

The stable master set the hoof back down and straightened up. 'Fire away.'

'I was wondering if you'd give me a character.'

John looked dumbfounded. 'You're not leaving us, lad?'

'I am, actually. I've decided to move on.'

'Move on? Where?'

'I'm not quite sure yet. But I'll be needing a good recommendation if I'm to find a position elsewhere. Would you be willing to give me one?'

'Of course I would, I can't fault your work in all the years I've known you. So much so,' he added, voice tinged with regret, 'that I'd hoped you'd take over from me here one day.'

Cormac smiled. 'My da would've liked to hear that. And if circumstances were different... But Oakleigh's not the place for me anymore.'

John squinted at him. 'Why? What's happened?'

He tried very hard not to let his smile widen too much. 'I can't really say but 'tis a good reason so don't be troubled.'

John blew out his breath with puffed cheeks. 'Well, I'll be mighty sorry to see you go but my parting gift will be a character that'll knock the boots off any stable master in the country. Come back to me later and I'll have it for you.'

And he left the stall, shaking his head in woe.

In the afternoon, Cormac returned to the hay barn to persevere in his construction of the swing seat, even though in all likelihood Bridget would never have need of it. He kept grinning to himself as he worked, wondering at his own good luck. Behind him was their haystack, an innocuous mound with scattered blades of hay about it. He relived the details of that glorious experience, anticipating the impending bliss of waking next to her every morning and being able to call her his wife.

Liam entered the barn to gather some hay for the horses. He glanced over at Cormac as he dug his fork deep into a haystack beyond the lovers' nest. 'Why are you in such a good mood?'

'No reason,' said Cormac, still grinning.

Liam was silent for a minute or two, teasing out the hay into a smaller stack which he could carry to the stables.

Then he said calmly, 'I know she came to you last night.'

Cormac's head snapped up in surprise. 'What? How?'

'She was quiet, but not quiet enough. I woke when she crawled across the loft.'

Cormac shrugged and continued to saw at a length of wood.

'Be careful, Cormac.'

He heard the warning tone and screwed up his mouth in exasperation. 'Why do people keep saying that to me?'

''Cause you need to hear it, and it doesn't seem to be sinking in,' Liam said frankly.

Cormac stopped sawing and rested the blade on the floor of the barn. 'Enlighten me. Just what do I need to be careful about?'

Liam frowned. 'You've got to realise what you're doing. You groom horses and mend stools. She's a lady engaged to the heir of a huge fortune. She's a respected member of society. And she's the daughter of the meanest woman I know. How can it end any way other than badly?'

'That's one point of view,' Cormac acknowledged. 'But now try this one. I'm not rich and she won't be part of high society anymore, but she doesn't care about either of those things. And what harm can her mother cause us once we're gone? We'll start a new life somewhere else and she won't be able to do anything about it.'

'I wouldn't put it past her to find ways of hurting ye both. And what about your family? Are you going to leave them behind?'

He replied without missing a beat. 'Once I've found work and we've made a home for ourselves, we'll send for my family to come live with us. I've thought it all through.'

'I don't know about that,' said Liam, his doubt clear on his face. 'But I hope it turns out the way you think it will.'

'Thanks,' Cormac said, picking up his saw again. 'We're going to be fine.'

*** 

Bridget sat at her piano, her blank gaze fixed on the closed lid. She felt like she had aged ten years since the morning. The weight of the decision she still had to make rested heavily on her shoulders.

She heard the drawing room door open and shut. After a long time, she mustered the energy to look up. It was Garrett.

He did not seem angry or upset. In fact, the only expression she could discern on his face was something nearing apologetic. He took a seat by the fireplace and they stared at each other across the room.

Eventually, he pointed at her red cheek and said, 'You should put a salve on that. It will alleviate the stinging.'

She was bewildered. He ought to be furious with her, and yet Lady Courcey was the one who directed the finger of blame while he sat there with absurd equanimity.

'Why do you still want to marry me?' she asked, her voice husky from the many tears she had shed.

He pondered her question for a moment. 'Why do you think I wouldn't?'

She shot an incredulous look at him. 'Because I was unfaithful to you. I gave myself to another man while you and I were engaged. I told my mother I did not want to marry you and that I no longer love you. I am amazed you are not already on your way back to Dublin.'

Again, he cogitated before responding. 'I still love you. And I am certain that if you search hard enough inside yourself you could find a little love left for me too. That is my first reason.' He paused. 'The next is a shallow one but it still matters. Appearances are important and we are viewed as a model couple of society. You are not the only person in this relationship with a parent who values social status and reputation. It is too late to back out of the engagement now.'

He picked up a porcelain figurine from a low table beside him and twisted it in his hands, avoiding her eyes. 'And finally, you have not been honest with me but I have not been honest with you either. There have been other women, even while I courted you. I thought it might ease your guilt to learn that neither of us has been faithful.'

She had no right to reproach him but his confession left a bad taste in her mouth.

'I daresay we deserve each other,' he concluded, a noticeable slump in his customarily proud posture.

She grimaced, feeling like the worst kind of human being.

He replaced the figurine on the table. 'Have you decided what you are going to do?' he asked, assuming a more matter-of-fact manner now that he had unburdened his conscience. When she slowly shook her head, he said, 'May I offer some advice?'

She lifted her shoulders in an expression of weary acquiescence.

He leaned forwards, his gaze intent. 'I know the terms your mother has laid out before you. And I know you, better than you realise. You do not have it within you to inflict such pain on that family. Can you in all honesty tell me you would be able to sacrifice their home and livelihoods for the benefit of your own happiness? Such self-serving behaviour is beyond your capacity to allow.'

He spoke further but she stopped listening. She had been churning her tormenting thoughts over and over since Lady Courcey had delivered her ultimatum, trying to find a solution to her horrifying dilemma. She felt like she was drowning in a fathomless sea of anguish and uncertainty but, much as she yearned for aid, she would have to reach terra firma by herself; it would be cruelly unfair to ask Cormac to choose between his lover and his mother.

That, in effect, was what she had to do herself, for Lady Courcey's contemptible conduct had negated any obligation in Bridget's mind of calling *her* 'mother'. Dearest Maggie was the woman who stirred feelings of daughterhood within her, and it seemed like the greatest betrayal imaginable that she would repay her kindness by causing her to be ejected from the home where she and her husband had raised six children – and this on top of the losses she had already suffered. Recalling Cormac's heartbreaking description of Maggie's distressed state the day after Mary had been buried, Bridget knew that such a blow would terminate any hope of her attaining even a modicum of happiness on this earth again.

But ensuring that Maggie and her family remained in their cottage meant losing Cormac irrevocably. Bridget did not fool herself that she might be able to send him away in the short term and afterwards locate him by clandestine means. Lady Courcey intended for that bond to be severed and would do all in her power to guarantee that it could never be reconnected. And the lady's authority was absolute. It would be another year before Bridget came of age to inherit. She was as powerless as an infant in the nursery.

So if Cormac was banished he would disappear from her life forever. This was as inconceivable as choosing not to breathe. She had managed to bear their parting when she was taken to Dublin because she had known she would return to Oakleigh someday. But to be divided from him permanently, with no prospect of ever reuniting? Impossible. Furthermore, their previous separation had been as friends. Now, having joined with lovers' words and touches, the severance would be a thousand times worse. And, reinforcing that shattering loss, she would be required to marry Garrett. Her skin crawled at the thought of sharing that special, private experience with him. Her body had been claimed by Cormac and none but he could have it.

In desperation, she wondered *could* they possibly survive? If she, Cormac, Maggie, the three girls and the baby fled from Oakleigh, what would happen? At the outset, they would have to sleep rough until they found means to support themselves. To her chagrin, she had little to offer in that regard – she boasted no skills useful for gaining viable employment and, if any money lay hidden in the manor house, she had no knowledge of its whereabouts and no notion how to appropriate it. While Margaret and Bronagh might be able to find maids' work, their wages would be a pittance, and in reality the family's hopes would lie in Cormac securing a good position. On his own, he would get by, but how far could the earnings of a stable hand or even a carpenter stretch when there were seven mouths to feed? They would be consigned to a level of poverty hitherto unknown to any of them.

She would do it in an instant if it were just she who would suffer. But to bring that misery upon innocent people whom she loved… An image swam into her mind of the family huddled together on a dirty roadside, cold and sick, begging for help from passersby. The little baby Patrick too weak even to cry. Though it was no more than her imagination, the distress of it was too much to stand.

She longed to feel Cormac's arms around her and hear him say that everything would be fine. But it was not within his control to salvage them from such a dire situation. And, if someone had to be wounded in this tragedy, it could only be the two of them and no one else.

Garrett was right. God help her, he was right.

Heart ripping from its mooring in quiet agony, she raised her eyes to meet his. After a moment or two of respectful silence, he said, 'Can Cormac read?'

She gaped at the unexpected question. 'Y-yes. Why?'

He drew a sealed note from his pocket. 'I am acquainted with a family in the city who recently had to dismiss a manservant. They discovered that he was stealing from them, a dreadful affair. But this means they have an opening and I have no doubt they would be pleased to appoint someone as hard-working as Cormac. They are a decent family and would treat him well. I have written their address on this paper. Perhaps you could pass it on to him, if you think he would consider the offer.'

She was stunned. He crossed the room and she accepted the slip of paper wordlessly.

'I shall write to the family with my highest recommendation that they take him into their employ. I am sure it will be a comfort to you to know he has somewhere to go when he leaves the estate.'

He kissed her on the forehead and left her alone.

She stared at the folded note, its plain wax seal a dull red. It astounded her that he could be so noble but she was very grateful to him for it. A measure of relief filled the cavity in her chest to know that Cormac would not have to be homeless or penniless after he was sent away from Oakleigh.

She contemplated breaking the seal and reading the address but resolved against it. She could not bear to know where he was going when he would be forever out of her reach.

It would only make it harder to forget him.

## Chapter 26

Bridget left her cane behind when she went out to the stables. She saw no point in keeping up the pretence anymore; it was for nobody's benefit now that her motive for doing so had been so starkly laid bare.

John Corbett saluted her at the stable doors. Feigning cheerfulness, she returned the greeting and said, 'Could you tell me where I might find Cormac? I would like to see how the swing seat is coming along.'

Even that lie seemed redundant. The purpose of it was to prevent suspicion being raised, but soon Cormac would be gone and any question over their association would no longer exist.

'He's in the last hay barn, working on it as we speak. Shall I escort you there?'

'No, thank you. I know where it is.'

She certainly did. It was the place where mere hours ago she had experienced the most profound event of her life. But she needed to bury that memory and those feelings.

When she entered the barn, she found Cormac kneeling over the partly constructed wooden seat. His face lit up at the sight of her and she felt her insides shrivel with dread at what she was about to do to him. He laid his tools on the sawdust-coated floor and stood up, but she did not go any closer. If she allowed him to touch her, her resolve would disintegrate.

'There is something I need to tell you,' she began. Her teeth clamped down on the tip of her tongue. Did she have the strength to say it?

But he wasn't paying attention. 'What happened to your cheek?' he asked, concern changing to mounting anger. 'Did he strike you?'

She shook her head. 'My mother.'

His hands folded into fists. ''Cause of me?'

She took a breath, though it felt like the air did not reach her lungs. 'Yes.'

'Goddamn it,' he muttered, almost to himself. 'The sooner we get away from that woman, the better.' He let his fists unfurl with a conscious effort. 'So what happens now?'

It pained her to read the expectancy on his face. She had to force the words out of her clogged throat. 'I am going to stay with Garrett.'

He stared. 'What?'

'I cannot be with you, I'm sorry,' she said, and it tore at her heart to witness the crushing impact of that declaration.

'But last night —'

'I know,' she interrupted, keen to end the exchange as soon as she could. 'I know what we vowed to each other, but we were not thinking straight. It was just a silly fancy in our heads. It could never happen in reality.'

He was dazed but at this he lifted his chin boldly. 'Why not?'

'Because we come from different backgrounds. And because I am already engaged to someone else. And because we would have no money and nowhere to go. There are a hundred reasons.'

'I thought we'd decided none of those reasons mattered,' he countered.

'But they do. Of course they do. It was ridiculous of us to believe otherwise. Homelessness is not a minor inconvenience. We were being naïve.'

'We'd manage somehow,' he said with desperation in his voice. 'I promised I'd look after you.'

'And what about your mother and your three sisters and little Patrick?' she demanded. 'Would you be able to look after them too? Tell me, how do you provide for seven people when you have no income?'

He looked taken aback by her caustic tone. 'They wouldn't come with us straight away. They could stay here 'til we got settled somewhere ourselves.'

'My mother will throw them off the land if I go with you. She told me so herself.'

Realisation dawned on him. 'Is that why you're doing this? 'Cause she threatened to evict my family? Don't let her bully you. You're a grown woman, able to make your own choices. If you give in to her, you'll never forgive yourself.'

He stepped towards her and she backed out of his reach.

'Please don't,' she said.

His jaw clenched. 'She intimidated you. Well, I'm not afraid of her, or of him. I'll go to them right now —'

'No!' she exclaimed. If Lady Courcey or Garrett set eyes on him inside the manor house, they would send for the constabulary, a threat they had mercifully not made so far. 'That will only make this worse.' She hesitated. 'You won't do it if I do not want you to. If — if I do not want you.'

His bafflement was evident as he tried to reconcile the girl who had loved him so ardently with the fortress of resistance before him. 'Last night —' he tried again.

'Last night you bedded me on a stack of hay,' she said ruthlessly. 'That is not my idea of everlasting bliss.' She hated herself but could think of nothing else to say to persuade him they had no future together.

Her message had the desired brutal effect at last. The blood drained from his features and his body sagged as though the breath had been knocked out of him. She got the impression that she had just destroyed the happiest memory of his life. She felt wretched.

'I won't force you into an inferior situation,' he murmured, 'if you truly don't wish it.'

He searched her face and she pretended with all her might that the luxuries of her class were enough to surpass the desires of her heart. His air of abject resignation informed her that she had missed her calling on the stage.

'You have to leave the estate,' she said, her throat thick with emotion. 'Your family may stay but you must go. And you can never come back.' She produced the note from Garrett. 'Please take this. It is the address of a family in Dublin with a vacant position for a manservant. If you go to them, they will give you work.'

She decided not to tell him who the note was from in case he refused to accept the offer out of pride. He took it from her dumbly.

'You must be gone by nightfall,' she croaked, cast one last glance at his desolate blue eyes, and turned away.

As she left the barn, her whole body screamed at her to go back, to beg for forgiveness, but she kept walking. She felt a strange mixture of revulsion at the duty she had just performed, relief that it was over, and some consolation in the fact that at least he would have somewhere to go when he departed from Oakleigh for good.

*\*\**

Cormac was still standing immobile some minutes later when Liam came into the barn carrying a long length of rope wound in circles.

'I just found this in the stable loft. D'you think it'd be suitable for the swing—?' He stopped when he registered Cormac's frozen state. 'Something wrong?'

Cormac shook himself as though he were waking from a dream.

'I'm fine,' he said tonelessly.

He looked down at the note in his hand, paying no heed to Liam's curious expression. With sluggish fingers, he broke the seal and unfolded the paper.

There was no address but a short message written in a smooth script:

Cormac,

If you are reading this, then you know that Miss Muldowney has chosen to remain with me. I hope you will realise in time that this was the best decision for all concerned, most of all for the lady in question. I am sure you can appreciate how much she will benefit from the comfort and security which I can, and which you regrettably cannot, offer her.

I do not mean to gloat. I take no pleasure in your current misfortune, and this coming so hard upon the recent, tragic death of your sister. I extend my commiserations that this lamentable situation did not transpire as you would have wished and also my gratitude for allowing my fiancée to be returned to me.

Do not try to contact her again. Good luck wherever you go next.

Regards,
Garrett J. Lambourne

He read the note twice. Then he put it into his pocket, placed his saw and other implements in his father's tool chest, picked up the chest, and turned his back on the half-made swing seat which would now never be finished.

'Best of luck to you, Liam.' He held out his hand.

His friend shook it, mystified. 'What's going on?'

'You were right,' he said simply.

He left the barn and made for the stables where he found John Corbett closeted in his workspace, the tiny room barely able to accommodate the man, a stool and a narrow table covered with untidy stacks of papers.

'John,' he said and his tongue stuck.

The stable master stared at him. 'Are you not well, lad? You look like a ghost passed through you.'

He swallowed. 'I'm just looking for that character, if you have it.'

John came to the threshold and laid a hand on his shoulder. 'You were all smiles when you asked for it this morning. What's changed?'

'I need it for a different reason now.'

He watched John make the connections in his mind. Maybe he had glimpsed Bridget passing by a short while earlier. Or maybe he was shrewd enough to piece together all the little clues over the past few weeks. Either way, his eyes widened with sudden clarity.

'I think I see,' he said.

Cormac could only nod, again struggling for words. John didn't rebuke him and he was grateful for it.

'By rights, the order will come down to me not to give you a character. If your offence is serious enough' – one look at Cormac's face confirmed that it was – 'then you'll be expected to leave empty-handed.'

He squeezed his eyes shut and then opened them again. 'I understand.'

He tried to step away but John's grip on his shoulder held him back.

"Tisn't fair,' the stable master muttered. 'Whatever you might've done, you're a hard-working lad and deserve a decent position somewhere, if not at Oakleigh.'

He reached for a page lying on the messy table behind him.

'I already have it written. Take it. I can tell them I'd given it to you before…before anything was discovered.'

A lump obstructed Cormac's throat and for a moment he was afraid he would cry in front of the man. John clapped him on the back.

'Hurry on now,' he said gently, handing him the page, and Cormac turned away, his words of thanks unspoken but received.

He left the stables and headed for the kitchens, setting down the tool chest by the doorstep as he went inside. He located his two sisters in the scullery, where they were toiling over a mound of dirty dishes at the sink. They looked surprised to see him, even more so when he gave each of them a tight hug and a kiss on the cheek, disregarding their wet arms and flushed faces.

'What's the matter?' said Margaret, her brow furrowing.

'I have to go,' he replied. 'Look after our ma.'

They followed him back into the main kitchen where he took Mr Lambourne's note out of his pocket. Mrs Kavanagh grumbled something about idleness but the three of them ignored her.

'What's that?' Bronagh asked.

'Nothing.' He threw the paper into the cooking fire and watched it burn. Then, with a sad smile towards his sisters, he walked out the kitchen door.

He dragged his feet all the way across the fields, tool chest thumping heavily against his thigh, because he did not want to reach the cottage, did not want to face his mother in his disgrace. But the daylight would not last forever and his time was running short. He took a deep breath and pushed open the half door.

She was sitting at her spinning wheel, something which she had not done since Mary had died. This sign of progress cut through him like the blade of a knife; he suspected that what he was about to tell her would eradicate all her endeavours to revive herself. Patrick was sound asleep in his basket and Orlaith was nowhere to be seen.

Maggie twisted around at the sound of his arrival and her expression lifted.

'*A mhac*,' she said with just the slightest waver. 'I didn't know you were coming home this evening.'

He set the tool chest down. 'It was supposed to be Margaret and Bronagh but I expect they'll still be along later.'

She brightened even further. 'It'll be a rare pleasure to have ye all home together.'

His chest constricted. 'Where's Orlaith?'

'I let her go playing in the woods when the wet nurse visited a short while ago, but she promised to stay close to the cottage. Shall I call her?'

'No, don't.' This would be easier without the little girl present. His mother started to rise but he said, 'Please stay sitting. I've got to tell you something.'

She sat back down, looking puzzled. Feeling sick, he crossed the small room and knelt on the floor by her. He took her two hands in his own, just like the night after Mary's burial.

'Ma, I need you to listen and to be strong. This'll be hard for you to hear but I — I've got to leave you.'

Her eyes clouded over and he could tell she had not absorbed the meaning of his words.

He said distinctly, 'I have been ordered off Oakleigh land and I may never come back.'

'I-I don't understand. Wh-what's happened?'

Shame scalded his insides. Could he really tell his mother this? 'I've done — I've behaved — improperly...' And then he added, with an awful heaviness in his heart as he said her name, '...with Bridget.'

'Bridget?' she repeated, and her eyes cleared. She comprehended what he meant. She stared down at him. 'But she's engaged.'

'I know,' he said bitterly. 'We disregarded that fact.'

'Please tell me 'tisn't true. Such a dishonourable thing... She belongs to another man.'

'I *know*,' he said again. ''Tis too late for accusations now. We can't change what we did. The important detail is that Lady Courcey found out and she's commanded me to leave the estate before sundown tonight.'

A frightened look filled her face as the message sank in. 'No, you can't leave. Cormac, you cannot leave.'

'I have to. I've been dismissed from my position. And if I stay, the rest of ye will be thrown out too. I can't let that happen. 'Tis got to be this way.'

He stood and it was that action which caused his mother, so fragile now, to burst into terrified sobs.

'No!' she cried and clung to his hands. '*No!*'

Her weeping woke her grandson and he began to howl as well. Cormac tried to disengage himself from his mother's grip.

'I've got no choice. Please, you have to let me go.'

She just sobbed all the harder.

'Cormac?' came a small voice from the doorway. He spun about; Orlaith stood there, a posy of wildflowers clutched in one little fist. 'Why's Ma crying?'

Without waiting for an answer, she started to cry too.

He looked around at them all in desperation. How could he leave them

when they needed him so badly?
How could he stay when to do so would hurt them even more?

## Chapter 27

That evening, after dining in an atmosphere of glacial silence, Bridget, Garrett and Lady Courcey retired to the drawing room, which welcomed them with the comfortable glow of candlelight and a merry blaze from the fireplace. The room had a mellowing effect on the others and they took their seats in a more relaxed manner, but Bridget could not settle. She paced restlessly to the windows and twitched aside the curtains to peer outside. Night was descending, the sky tarnished a deep purple with only the last vestiges of daylight lingering on the western horizon. Shadows thrashed in the gloom: the trees on the edge of the avenue, whipped about by a strong wind which had begun to stir in the late afternoon. Now it blew around the manor in gusts, whistling through minute gaps in the windows and down the chimney.

An indefinable awfulness suffused every part of her, from her bones to her skin. However worthy her intentions, her decision today had inflicted the most grievous pain upon the man she loved. She pictured him preparing to leave his home, saying farewell to his mother, taking one last look at familiar surroundings, and felt a remorse beyond anything she had ever experienced. To save his family, she had ripped them from him. It was unpardonable but she had to believe she had made the right choice, or else succumb to an irreversible despair.

She had condemned herself too in the process, though she could not summon the energy to dread the rest of her life just yet, still too consumed by what she had lost to contemplate what she must face in the future. How could she come to terms with the heart-rending fact that she would never see Cormac again? It was as though he had died, and with him a significant portion of her. A sob threatened to erupt from her throat and she suppressed it with a desperate gulp. She had to continue to exist, one excruciating second at a time.

Turning back to the room, she found that Lady Courcey had become more loquacious since her taciturn performance at dinner and was now conversing with Garrett about the forthcoming wedding, all plans in that direction having been reinstated without opposition.

'If you obtain a licence and bring the date forwards to the beginning of October,' she was saying, 'I think you could indeed be in London by the end of that month. With such little time to prepare for it, it will need to be a much lesser affair, but that is all well and good considering recent events. We can say that Bridget was severely weakened by her illness this summer and that she would only be able for a small occasion. We shall just invite the most eminent guests. Everyone else will have to read about it in the paper.'

'That sounds acceptable to me,' said Garrett, with the blasé air of one who has got his own way on the most important matter and is not too bothered with the details.

Her spirits seeming to improve with every passing minute, Lady Courcey swivelled to her daughter and said in a positively chirpy voice, 'I think I should like some music. Why don't you play for us, Bridget?'

She obeyed because anything was preferable to joining that odious conversation. She seated herself at the piano, her fingers automatically seeking the keys, as her mother returned her attention to Garrett.

'While we are organising the wedding, you can be coordinating the travel arrangements for London. No doubt you are looking forward to going home.'

'I am, indeed. When we get there, I shall assume a larger role in the managing of my father's estate, so there will be many matters to attend to. Of course, I am also partial to the city itself. As you know, there is never a dull moment in London.'

'Quite true, it is a vibrant place. I thoroughly enjoyed the two seasons I spent there in my youth. I have a mind to take up residence at Oakleigh again after the wedding, but I hope to come and visit you and Bridget once you are settled.'

'For certain, you will always be welcome in our home.'

Bridget struck a discord on the piano but carried on.

'That is very kind, Mr Lambourne. I can see that family is important to you, which is as it should be. Family should always be the most imperative consideration in everything we do.' A deliberate pause. 'And I must say, I get a great deal of satisfaction from knowing that one particular family will be homeless by tomorrow morning.'

Both Bridget's heart and playing came to a standstill.

'What?' she exclaimed.

Her mother gave her a look of innocent enquiry. 'Why have you stopped? I do so enjoy Beethoven.'

'You promised they could stay! You said if Cormac left, then his family would not be evicted!'

Lady Courcey frowned. 'Yes, I did, didn't I?' She thought for a moment. 'Oh, well.'

Bridget wasted no more time. Eyes blazing, she slammed down the lid of the piano and dashed from the room. Neither her mother nor her fiancé made any move to stop her.

Out in the entrance hall, she took no notice of Mr Buttimer's appearance and sheer astonishment as she wrenched open the manor's front door. She raced around the side of the house, tearing through the courtyard, past the paddock, into the Gorteen and across the fields, the shortest way to Cormac's home. She ran as fast as she could, though her dainty shoes were no match for such a flight. The wind buffeted her, blowing her hair into her face, and she leaned forwards into it, struggling to make headway against its brute force. The giant's claw materialised out of the shadows, beckoning to her in menacing greeting as she passed, but for once she paid it no mind.

If homelessness was to be that family's fate no matter her decision, then of course she was going to go with Cormac, despite the hardships they would have to endure. There was no advantage to remaining with Garrett – she would not be saving any lives and she would be committing herself to a lifetime of restraint under his and her mother's command. She did not know how she and the McGoverns might survive the coming months of poverty, but at least she and Cormac would be together.

She glanced up at the dark sky. Night had fallen fully which meant that Cormac ought to have left the estate by now. But maybe he had lingered a little longer, perhaps in defiance of the order he had been given, or because he found it difficult to part from his family. She clung to these hopes, urging her body on even though her legs protested and her lungs burned. The wind whistled in her ears and her heart beat uncontrollably in her chest.

At last, she reached the McGoverns' little cottage, gasping for breath. She spared a fleeting look for the horse shoe above the door – what sort of luck had it brought the family within tonight? The door was closed but a faint light glowed through the crack underneath it. She burst in without knocking.

'Cormac!' she cried.

A pitiful sight met her eyes by a sputtering rushlight on the table. Cormac's mother sat on the bench, her face buried in her hands, her rosary beads twined between her fingers, her body shaking with sobs. Orlaith stood beside her, arms around her shoulders, trying to comfort her. The baby lay crying in his basket in the corner. There was no one else in the room.

Bridget's heart leapt into her mouth. Cormac was gone from the cottage but he might not be gone long. She ran back outside and screamed his name. The wind whisked her voice away as if she had never spoken. She darted down the lane, calling out to him again and again, but even if he had been just around the corner he would not have been able to hear her. And she had little expectation of catching up to him in the darkness; she could not even be sure which way he had taken.

But she did not give up yet.

She tore back the way she had come, forcing herself to breathe in short, painful wheezes. Twice she tripped over in the fields but she picked herself up and kept going, paying no heed to her filthy dress. All she cared about was undoing the tremendous mistake she had made.

She barrelled into the drawing room where Garrett and Lady Courcey still sat in an environment of tranquillity. Her mother tutted at her dishevelled state but Bridget ignored her and went straight to Garrett, who got to his feet at her approach.

'What is the address?' She clutched at his lapels. 'The address you gave to Cormac. Please tell me!'

He looked blank but then he understood what she meant and chuckled.

'Oh, my darling,' he said, patting her hands. 'Your naïveté is truly charming.'

'What do you mean?' she demanded, throat strangling with fear.

'There was no address. Did you really believe I would help him after he nearly broke up our engagement?' He snorted. 'I have learned that he did manage to depart the estate in possession of a character reference—John Corbett swears he was unaware of the situation until too late—but it will not stand to him in the long run. Be assured, I will take every action within my power to counteract its worth and guarantee his downfall.'

She was still for all of five seconds. Then her shock was overcome by rage and she shrieked at him and pounded his chest with her fists. She dimly registered her mother's sharp reprimand at her conduct but flouted the warning, shedding the ladylike exterior she had cultivated for so long and invoking the spirited nature repressed inside her as she attempted to take out all her fury on the man who had misled her into making the greatest error of her life. When he grabbed her wrists and held her at arm's length, she started kicking out at him. He forced her back with a little push and she lost her balance and fell over in front of the hearth. All at once, the fight drained out of her and she collapsed on the rug in floods of tears.

She had no means of locating Cormac. He had been sent away from the estate with nowhere to go and with a gentleman's revenge on his heels. What would he do? Wander around the countryside until he died of starvation? Make his way to Dublin where his prospects might be better? But, in his destitute circumstances, how could he gain honest employment anywhere? She allowed herself to imagine what might happen to him and recoiled from the devastating vision, weeping all the harder.

And his family were to be subjected to a similar fate. Whatever hope Cormac had of finding a way to support himself, they had none at all, for now they would be facing poverty without a man to provide for them. It was coming into the winter season, the worst time of year to be without shelter. Could they even survive until Christmas?

The hatred she felt for her mother in that moment was overpowering in its intensity. Lady Courcey had brought about the suffering of every person involved in this sickening power play. They were nothing but pawns in her quest to control and further her family's fortunes. And Bridget had played her part to perfection. If only she had gone with her heart instead of being ruled by her mother, everything could have turned out differently.

Utter desolation engulfed her and she whimpered in physical and emotional pain. Her whole existence was reduced to this crushing sphere of anguish; the voices beyond it signified nothing. It was not until a pair of tender arms encircled her that she returned to reality, believing for one irrational moment that Cormac had come back to her. Then she realised that the arms belonged to Garrett.

'Hush,' he murmured. 'Please do not cry. This is not the end of the world.'

She tried to push him away from her, though she felt as weak as if the fever were upon her again.

'Take care of her,' he commanded to someone over his shoulder, and then Ellen was crouching beside her, tugging at her hands.

'Please, miss, come upstairs.'

Still crying, she stumbled to her feet and allowed herself to be guided up the staircase to her bedchamber. Ellen changed her into a clean nightdress, washed her hands and feet, and helped her into bed, tucking the bedcovers around her. At last, the tears stopped.

'Oh, dear God,' she said, her voice hollow. 'What have I done?'

Ellen's freckled face was fearful. She didn't know what had happened yet but she soon would. By tomorrow, everyone at Oakleigh would learn that the McGoverns had lost their positions and their home. How quickly would they ascertain the reason why? Bridget and Cormac, however innocent of these terrible ramifications, were responsible for the sequence of events that had brought them about. The shame was nearly unendurable.

'Can I do anything else for you, miss?'

She shook her head and Ellen slipped out of the room. At once, her hand slithered under her pillow and withdrew the little wooden bird, fingers curling around the one thing she had left of Cormac. She pressed it to her breast, mourning its creator with a speechless grief.

Ellen had left a candle lighting on the bedside table; Bridget turned onto her side and stared at it, calling to mind the heartbreaking scene lit by rushlight at the cottage. Her eyes became wet again as she recalled the depth of Maggie's distress. That poor woman did not deserve this. She had never been anything but kind to Bridget in all the years she had known her, embodying the role of mother much more than Lady Courcey had ever tried to. Apart from her beloved father, Bridget's real family had always been the McGoverns.

She gulped. Yes, that was so true. Then why would she stay here? She may have lost Cormac – and the agony of it choked her – but she still had a surrogate mother and three almost-sisters and there was a sweet baby too. She would leave Oakleigh with them and they would find a way to survive together. That would be a far better alternative to remaining with her own evil mother and manipulative fiancé.

For the second night in a row, she decided to sneak out of the house after dark. She flung back the covers and climbed out of bed, then pulled the burgundy curtains around it to deter anyone who might check on her from probing further. She groped in the drawer of her dressing table for a pocket to tie around her waist – into this she placed the precious bird and a few trinkets from her jewellery box, judging the value of these latter items to be sufficient enough that they might be pawned for the purpose of the family's subsistence. In her haste, she did not give thought to dressing properly; she just hauled on her boots and a cloak over her nightdress and headed to the bedchamber door.

She could not risk descending the mahogany staircase and passing the drawing room where Garrett and Lady Courcey were likely congratulating each other on a task well accomplished. It would be wiser to take the servants' stairs down to the kitchens. She stuck her head out of her bedchamber, looked up and down the deserted corridor, and then darted for the inconspicuous door across the way. Beyond it was the narrow servants' staircase which snaked through the belly of the house, with an access on each upper floor to allow the servants to come and go. She had explored these hidden stairs as a child but otherwise had never had any need of them.

Though there was nobody on the stairs, she still made her way down on tiptoe. Would the kitchens at the bottom be empty, the clean-up after dinner already finished? With any luck, that would be the case.

She reached the last step and pushed open the door into the kitchens.

She caught a glimpse of Mrs Kavanagh first, her face confused.

Then she saw her fiancé sitting on the bench by the kitchen table, his hazel eyes sad.

And there was her mother standing in the centre of the room, her arms folded.

'Foolish girl,' the lady said.

Bridget threw away all caution and ran for the outer door. She tried to wrench it open but it was locked. She twisted to grab the key from its hook but it wasn't there.

'No!' she screamed. 'Let me out!'

She had to get to Maggie, she wanted to be with the McGoverns. She banged on the door in desperation. Two strong hands grabbed her from behind.

'I have no wish to manhandle you,' came Garrett's voice, 'but I will use force if you do not come with me now.'

He wanted her to go quietly but she would not. She made it as difficult for him as she could, jerking away from him and digging her heels into the floor. He swept her up into his arms, as far from the romantic gesture Cormac had made in the orchard – had that only been the day before yesterday? – as it was possible to be. He carried her struggling back up the servants' staircase to her bedchamber, thrust aside the curtains, and deposited her on top of the bed with rather more gentleness than she had anticipated. For one terrified moment, she wondered whether he would choose to exert his rights as her future husband right there and then, but he spun around and strode from the room without looking at her.

A faint jangling signified the presence of Mrs Walsh, and it was followed by the sound of a key turning in the lock.

It did not turn again until the next morning when she was immediately bundled from her bedchamber into a carriage waiting at the front of the house. She saw nobody on the way, not a single soul to whom she could appeal for help. The door of the carriage slammed shut, the coachman whipped the horses, and the warm red bricks of Oakleigh receded rapidly from view.

Garrett and Lady Courcey shared the carriage with her, both on edge as though they expected her to launch herself out the door while they were moving. But she made no more effort to resist.

She had not slept at all and fatigue threatened to consume her. However, her thoughts were clear and in the nadir of her sorrow she knew that she had been defeated. The McGoverns were beyond her reach. It was no use vowing that she would overturn her mother's eviction notice as soon as she came into her inheritance; that was still over a year from now, by which stage all trace of them would have disappeared. They were as lost to her as Cormac was.

She felt like her passionate outburst of the night before had caused every drop of energy and enthusiasm to seep out of her, leaving a void inside. She was now a husk, submissive and primed for marriage. The appalling realisation had finally come to her that she had been very naïve to believe she had any real say in the choices she made. She understood now that she had no free will and that Garrett and her mother would direct her life in every respect from now on.

And she resigned herself to her lot. What else could she do?

The wedding in Dublin the following month was a quiet affair. Miss Madeleine Wallace and Lord Newby performed the honour of attending the bride and groom. Madeleine was Bridget's closest friend in the city but

Bridget did not breathe a word to her of what had happened at Oakleigh that autumn. It was an unspoken agreement that those events would never be mentioned again within the Muldowney or Lambourne families.

Bridget and Garrett informed their guests that they would be postponing their official honeymoon until a later period, as Garrett had urgent business to attend to which expedited his return to England. But both of them knew there would never be a honeymoon.

However, their wedding night was an inevitability. She was unsure what to expect but in the end he came to her without spite. Still, there could be no pleasure for her in it. She merely performed her duty as a good wife should.

They were in London by the end of October.

## Chapter 28

On a bright morning in late May, there was a knock on Bridget's bedchamber door and the midwife opened it to admit Garrett.

'Come in, sir. You have a beautiful, healthy baby girl.'

He approached the bed and stared at the sturdy bundle in Bridget's arms. Such bright, blue eyes. And a head of soft, golden curls, so fair they were nearly white. Bridget's gaze met his. They both fully comprehended.

He leaned over and placed a cold kiss on his wife's forehead. 'Congratulations, my darling,' he said and left the room, shutting the door behind him.

In the midst of her exhaustion, Bridget held her baby close. The midwife fussed around, plumping the pillows and chattering about Bridget's good fortune.

'You're blessed that the child is healthy. Born a whole month too soon! I feared for you both, that's the God's honest truth. There can be so many complications with early birth. Naturally, I didn't say any of that to you before, but all is well now so it's fine. Who do you think she favours more, her mother or her father?'

Bridget started and a tear squeezed out of the corner of her eye.

'Now, now,' said the midwife, patting her shoulder. 'Don't you worry, he'll be back. He's just disappointed that it's a girl. The men always are. Wait until he gets to know her.' She laughed. 'And remember to bring him a son next time.'

She packed her various intimidating-looking implements into a leather case and cast a kindly look at Bridget. 'Shall I send your maid up to you now?'

'Please wait a few minutes before you do. I would like to be alone with my baby for a little while.'

Nodding understandingly, the midwife left the bedchamber.

Bridget stared down at the bundle she cradled and her daughter stared back, wide-eyed. The midwife had wrapped her in a blanket so only her head was visible above its folds. Bridget absorbed every minute detail: the delicate curve of her ears, the plump cheeks, the dainty mouth, the button nose. She had no eyelashes yet but her eyes... According to the midwife, a baby's eye colour could change, but Bridget somehow knew that that familiar shade of blue was here to stay.

She inhaled the sweet fragrance of clean newborn skin. Touching the top of her daughter's head, she felt the swelling on the scalp. Although the midwife said it had been caused during the delivery and would fade in a few days, Bridget couldn't help feeling anxious; she wanted no harm to befall this tiny, perfect person. She kissed the bruised spot. The fine, fair hair was like silk against her lips.

The emotion inside her became too much to contain and tears of joy spilled over. She held a part of Cormac in her arms. He was not completely lost to her after all. A tear splashed onto her daughter's cheek and the little girl blinked in surprise. Bridget pressed her to her chest in the fiercest hug she could manage while not crushing the small body. God, how she cherished every single bit of her. How she wished Cormac could too. How she wished the girl could cherish him.

Her crying halted in a short, stuttering sob. She hiccupped and looked over at the dressing table. A distance of ten feet. Her legs felt like water and she was in a good deal of pain after the birth, but she could make it.

She pushed back the bedcovers and, reinforcing her tight grasp on her daughter, eased herself out of the bed. Letting out a low moan, she stumbled over to the dressing table and lowered herself onto the stool before it. With her baby nestled in one elbow, she used her other hand to grope in one of the drawers of the dressing table.

She withdrew the wooden bird from the back of the drawer. Every morning and every night, she took it out and pressed a kiss to its carved beak. Now she loosened the blanket wrapped around her baby, freed one of her arms, and touched the wooden bird to her daughter's miniature fist. The fingers wouldn't unfurl but a tiny thumbnail scraped the bird's wing.

'You *shall* know your father,' Bridget whispered fiercely. 'I will tell you about the land where he and I grew up and you shall learn his tongue and speak his prayers.'

She made the sign of the cross over the baby's forehead.

'*Emily is ainm duit*,' she said. 'I have named you and I promise, my precious Emily, that you shall know your father.' A fountain of unfounded yet unshakeable hope surged up inside her. 'And I pray with all my heart that you shall meet him someday.'

# A Class Entwined

A Matter of Class, Book Two

*To my husband, Bob,
for being my rock in wild storms,
and for always waiting patiently while I took 'two more
minutes' to finish up what I was writing before dinner.
(Sorry for all the times dinner went cold.)*

# Chapter 1

'Oh, help me, help, I'm going to fall!'

'No, you're not,' Cormac said, doing his best not to wince; the girl's shrill voice was piercing enough to cause earache. 'Just be calm. He won't throw you.'

He tugged gently on the lead rope and continued to guide the horse around the paddock, while Cecily clung to the pommel of her sidesaddle like she expected her mount to buck at any moment. A more mild-mannered horse Cormac had never encountered, so he harboured no concern in that respect, but convincing his student of the same was proving impossible.

'What if a hare runs out in front of us? Or Papa goes shooting pheasants nearby? Or a bee stings him? Oh, oh, I'm so frightened! Please, Cormac, let me down.'

He reiterated his reassurances but refused to give in to her plea. She would never learn if she did not keep trying. And it was past time she did learn. At sixteen, she was woefully uneducated in the art of riding a horse, despite having grown up on an estate which boasted one of the finest studs in the country. But then, she was only a daughter and hence of no great consequence to Lord Strathroy, who had three sons – more than enough offspring to secure the future of Willowmere Estate and Stud.

It was no surprise that Cecily existed so far beneath her father's notice for, aside from being a girl, she was also the most timid creature Cormac had ever encountered. One of the kitchen maids had told him that the young lady seldom ventured out of doors for fear of catching a cold, was afraid of sewing in case she pricked herself, and never once expressed a moment's interest in getting on a horse. That was, the maid had added slyly, until the stable master had hired a new stable hand.

Within a week of gaining his position at Willowmere, Cormac had been informed that the daughter of the house finally wished to learn how to ride and that the task must fall to him to teach her. He had embraced the challenge at first but soon came to loathe the time of day when she arrived at the stables with a simpering smile. The sessions invariably contained much squealing and cowering on her part and sorely tested the limits of his patience. It was repugnant to him who had once known the most fiery female spirit on horseback.

He tightened his grip around the rope until his nails dug into his palm. It was the eleventh time he had thought of Bridget since Cecily's lesson had begun. He tried his hardest to block her out but she always found ways to slip through his defences.

Oakleigh and the events that had transpired there were in the past, he had to remind himself. Now he was a stable hand on a new estate with a new family to serve and a different path to tread, however much he might wish it be otherwise.

Following his banishment from Oakleigh and a period of deep melancholy which he would rather not recall, he had crossed Carlow's south-western border into Kilkenny and reached Willowmere Estate, where, upon his enquiry into any vacant posts in the stables, John Corbett's character reference had played a vital role. His former stable master's glowing account of his diligence and reliability had been sufficient to earn him a trial which had converted to a full position after just two days. He had swiftly gained a reputation for being an adept carpenter as well, and he and his father's tool chest had been put to work on more than one occasion already. He had even met Lord Strathroy when the gentleman had visited the stables to appraise his livestock and believed he had left his employer with a strong impression of his competence.

While he did not suppose he would ever be happy again, he could at least tolerate his new life at Willowmere.

If only Cecily would stop her yammering.

He was about to coax the horse from a walk to a slow trot when, above Cecily's bleats of panic, he heard someone shouting. He turned and saw Lord Strathroy himself striding across the field towards the paddock, waving his arms and bellowing something unintelligible. His noisy approach merely startled Cormac but it gave Cecily a severe shock. With a whimper, she lost her balance and started to slide out of her sidesaddle. He saw it happening and was there in time to catch her. He eased her feet to the ground, which was muddy with recent rain, and she beamed up at him within the circle of his arms.

'Oh, thank you,' she said breathily.

He tried to release her but she kept a tight grip on his shoulders, as though she did not quite trust herself to stand without support.

By this point, Lord Strathroy had reached the paddock's fence. 'Get your hands off her,' he growled.

'Let go, miss,' Cormac said sternly and she loosened her hold with obvious reluctance.

'Cecily,' Lord Strathroy said in chilling tones, 'go back up to the house at once.'

'But Papa, we are not finished —'

His forbidding look quelled her. She gave a frightened squeak and, after a bashful glance up at Cormac, disappeared through the gate in the paddock fence, her boot squelching as it got stuck in a puddle of mud. She peeked one more time over her shoulder and then ran back across the field towards the big house, the long skirts of her riding habit bunched in her fist.

Lord Strathroy stalked into the paddock. Cormac patted the horse's neck and waited for the gentleman to speak. He clutched a piece of paper that had been scrunched into a ball and his features were twisted into an ugly snarl.

'How long did you think you would last?'

Cormac stared. 'M'lord?'

'I am disgusted that one so vile as you has lived three weeks under my protection. Well, no more. You are gone, blackguard, and immediately so.'

Cormac had no response to this incredible defamation. What on earth was he talking about?

'You have nothing to say to defend yourself. That all but confirms that the charges against you are true.'

'M'lord, I haven't said anything 'cause I don't understand you. What charges d'you mean?'

Lord Strathroy brandished the crumpled page at him. 'Deceit. Disloyalty. Dishonour. You are a scoundrel of the highest order.'

'I don't —'

'Does the name *Garrett Lambourne* signify anything to you?'

Cormac's blood ran cold.

'I discern that it does. Further proof, though I had no need of it. How you managed to procure a character, I cannot imagine. Its author must have been coerced into writing it. You shall leave my property at once and never show your face here again. I have Stafford on his way to run you off if necessary.'

'Whatever that letter says, I swear 'tisn't —'

'Do not even attempt to refute its contents,' Lord Strathroy retorted. 'I wholly believe Mr Lambourne's words and count them far higher than those of an ignorant stable hand.'

Cormac reached out. 'May I see what crimes I'm supposed to have committed?'

Lord Strathroy laughed without any trace of humour. 'And now you pretend you can read! It would be comical if it was not so repulsive.'

Cormac dropped his hand to his side. 'What does he say?'

Lord Strathroy smoothed out the letter with a flourish. 'That he feels it is his obligation to contact landowners both within the county of Carlow and beyond. It is possible a fellow named Cormac McGovern may come seeking work in the stables but he is not to be trusted for he took advantage of an heiress during his previous employment and had to be expelled from the estate. No young lady is safe in his presence.'

Cormac felt heat rise in his cheeks. 'That's outrageous!'

'Do you deny there was inappropriate conduct between you and the heiress?'

He tried to school his features into bland denial but the lord was not fooled. He went purple with rage.

'To think you have been in Cecily's company these past weeks! What have you done to her? Have you ruined her prospects?' He advanced towards Cormac, eyes bulging at the idea that his daughter's only value as marriage fodder might have been spoiled.

Cormac took a step back. 'I didn't touch her! I'd never —'

'I don't believe you. You had her in your arms just there, and I saw the way she looked at you. Did you defile her?'

Without waiting for an answer, he swung his fist out. Cormac ducked and instinct made him push at his attacker. Lord Strathroy stumbled and regained his balance by grabbing onto the paddock fence.

'And now an assault on my own person,' he said in vindictive triumph. 'Get out of my sight, you miscreant, and never set foot on Strathroy property again.'

Cormac realised that any further effort to argue his case would be useless. There was no convincing the gentleman that he was no danger to his daughter. Apart from the fact that he only viewed Cecily as a source of annoyance, the truth was that there could never be anyone for him but Bridget. However, he had no way of explaining that and, what was more, he could see Lord Strathroy's agent, Mr Stafford, sprinting towards them from the big house and carrying a long, rifle-shaped object against his chest.

'I'll get my things,' he said, resigned to the loss of his employment.

'You shall not. Turn around and be gone this instant.'

'You can't —'

'I damn well can. We shall burn your belongings and hope that your brief spell here will soon be forgotten.'

Mr Stafford came up to the paddock gate, panting. It was indeed a rifle he held. 'My lord?' he said, looking like he was itching to level it at the criminal before him.

Cormac thought of the precious possessions they expected him to leave behind: his father's tool chest, John Corbett's character reference. Where could he go without those? 'Please, if I could just have one minute to get —'

'Stafford,' said Lord Strathroy and the agent handed him the rifle over the fence.

Cormac spun and fled, his humiliation superseded by his fear. Not fully acquainted yet with the terrain around Willowmere, he just opted for the nearest route that would take him far away from Lord Strathroy and his rifle – a copse at the end of the field behind the stables – and hurtled towards it, a warning shot ringing in his ears.

He had nothing but the clothes on his back. He was done for.

## Chapter 2

Cormac made for the distant tree line, dashing over the field as fast as he could, and crashed into the undergrowth with his heart pounding and his breath coming in shuddering gasps. Though he didn't think they would follow him, he kept pushing forwards, slapping wayward branches out of his way and imagining that each one bore the face of the fiend known as Garrett Lambourne.

The lengths that gentleman had gone to in order to ruin him were unfathomable. Not content with ensuring Cormac's separation from Bridget and his permanent exile from his home, now he had taken steps to prevent Cormac from making any kind of new life for himself. Garrett was a person of far-reaching influence; no doubt a copy of that wretched letter had been sent to every establishment with a stables within a hundred miles of Oakleigh. Anyone who received it would be on high alert for a stranger seeking work. Cormac could lie about his name but the letter would raise enough suspicion to deter any employer from taking the chance. Garrett had obliterated Cormac's entire livelihood as a stable hand with a ruthless stroke of his pen.

A carpenter without tools was no temptation either. Cormac blazed with rage and distress that the last things belonging to his father were also to be destroyed. In the three years since Jack McGovern's death, Cormac had cherished that tool chest and preserved every implement in its best condition, keeping handles polished, metal clean and blades sharp. He could still recall in perfect detail his father's agile hands, wielding the hammer or the chisel or the saw and showing him how to use each one. Now he pictured them being tossed into a fire, the wood of the chest blackening and disintegrating, and let out an inarticulate scream of grief. Somewhere above him, a startled bird emitted an answering shriek and flapped away through the branches.

When he broke out of the other side of the trees, he found a small lake before him, gentle swells lapping against a reedy shoreline. He knew he should not linger but he stopped to slake his thirst; his throat and lungs burned after the mad sprint for cover. He squatted among the reeds at the water's verge and gulped greedy handfuls of the cold, clear water. Wiping his mouth on his sleeve, he tried to take his bearings but the sky was still overcast following the earlier rain, the unending bank of cloud hanging low and oppressive.

In any case, at that moment he was less concerned with the compass points than with the feeling of despair that was building inside him. It grew and grew, like a colossal wave racing for the seashore, then reared up and crashed over him with enormous force. The weight of it bore him down and he hunched at the edge of the lake, his head heavy in his hands. Mere weeks ago, he had had a mother, three sisters, a nephew, and a girl who loved him. He had had a position of employment, a social standing in his own small way, and a home. Since then, the whole lot had been stripped away, leaving him naked and lost in the world. The desolation he felt was unlike anything he had ever experienced. It was devastation with the complete absence of hope.

When he dragged himself to his feet again, it was not by an impetus to go in any specific direction but by the dim recollection that he didn't have permission to remain where he was. He meandered along the periphery of the lake and up a gorse-covered incline beyond it, without any of the drive that had propelled him forwards through the copse. He had no way of telling precisely when he would pass over Willowmere's borders but he supposed that if the big house was behind him then he could not go far wrong. The rain returned, a light drizzle which spat into his face, and prompted the vague thought that Cecily would be relieved she had gone indoors before the inclement weather could induce an attack of pneumonia.

The rest of the day, and the night which followed, passed by in a haze. He fell into a dreamlike state where nothing was real except for the notion of keeping his body moving. He crossed fields, streams, lanes and woods but took no notice of the landscape around him; so long as the ground supported him, he did not care whether it was wet or dry, soft or hard. Exhaustion threatened to take him over but he kept going mechanically, one painful step after another. It wasn't until the morning of the next day, when he tripped over a tree root and fell sprawling to the ground, that he considered taking a rest. Then the tiredness washed over him so powerfully that he just lay where he had fallen and allowed sleep to pull him into oblivion.

When he awoke, it was nearing dusk, the sun a low, orange orb in a sky clear of cloud. He sat up stiffly. He was in a large meadow where a scattering of cows grazed in the distance. The wide-spreading canopy of a horse chestnut towered above him; several sore spots along his back informed him that he had been lying on a bed of fallen conkers. Though the rain had stopped, his clothes felt damp and chilly against his skin.

A ravenous growl alerted him to his empty, aching stomach; it had been almost two days since he had eaten. Hopelessness may have dulled his spirit but it had not abated the demands of his body. He regarded the cows with closer attention. Cows meant a farm, and a farm meant people, and people meant food.

He struggled to his feet and, to gain a more elevated view of the landscape, clambered awkwardly into the branches of the tree, many of them bare as their leaves had begun to drop for the winter. Sure enough, a thin plume of smoke coiled skywards on the horizon beyond the grazing animals. His gnawing insides clenched with relief. He jumped back down to the ground, numb limbs quivering upon impact, and set off across the meadow. The cows turned their heads lazily as he passed. He tried to ignore his frozen extremities and chattering teeth – if he was cold now in October, he did not care to imagine what December might feel like.

After crossing two more fields, he distinguished a cluster of farm buildings through the twilight. It was not a large homestead – just the main house, from which the chimney smoke issued, and a number of sheds nearby – but its swept yard and clean windows spoke of a proud proprietor. As he approached, a broad-shouldered woman emerged from the front door of the farmhouse. She strode over to one of the sheds, opened it, and shooed a brood of flapping hens inside. Shutting the shed door against the gathering night, she turned to go back to the house.

Taking a deep breath for courage, Cormac called, "Scuse me,' and stepped forwards into the yard.

She started and squinted into the gloom. Suspicion and distaste coloured her features. Did he look that much like a beggar already?

'Go away,' she said. 'We don't want any trouble here.'

He did not know what he should say. Though he came from a humble background, his family had never been so poor that he had been forced to beg. This was a new and altogether degrading experience for him.

'Please,' he said. 'I need something to eat, that's all.'

'We don't feed tramps.' She started hurrying towards the house.

'Then just give me some directions,' he said loudly.

She stopped and looked back, curiosity getting the better of her. 'Where to?'

'Dublin,' he replied without hesitation.

There was nothing for him in the countryside. If he stayed here, he would starve. He might have had a better chance of surviving if it were summer and the bushes and trees were laden with fruit. But the end of autumn was drawing near and whatever fruit had not already been taken by the birds was falling to the ground to rot. He needed to make his way to a place of civilisation which could offer the prospect of obtaining some kind of labour. Failing that, at least he could scrounge through rubbish for food or – he desperately hoped it would not come to it – steal.

The woman snorted and folded her brawny arms. 'Don't be foolish. 'Tis several days' walk and you've got no food.'

'I'm going to try,' he said, wondering how far he had wandered in his dazed state. Just his luck to have strayed further from the city instead of nearer. 'Please can you tell me which way I should take?'

She stared at him, assessing his scruffy appearance, his polite manners, and the determined set of his jaw. Then she tutted in irritation and, without a word, stalked back to the house and disappeared inside. He dithered – should he wait, or give up and leave?

His patience was rewarded when her stout form reappeared at the front door, silhouetted by candlelight. She carried a small sack in one hand and a folded blanket in the other, both of which she held out to him. He stumbled up to the doorstep and accepted them, feeling a mixture of shame and deepest gratitude.

'You guilted me into it,' she said with a frown. 'I'd never have peace of mind if I let you attempt a journey like that without giving you some kind of help. You'll find apples and some bread and cheese in the sack. The blanket isn't very thick but 'tis better than no blanket at all. You'll need it, 'tis going to freeze over the next night or two.'

Gaping at her generosity, he managed to stutter, 'Th-thank you.'

She nodded, still looking annoyed at herself. 'As for directions, 'tisn't complicated. Go across the land north-east from here. After about a mile, you'll come to an untilled field of weeds which belongs to the farmer next to us. He's too elderly to till it himself and too miserly to sell it to anyone else. Next to the field, you'll find a crossroads. The main road will start you along the route towards Dublin. Now, go before my husband comes home and sees what I've done.'

He stammered his thanks once more and hastened from the farmyard. Using the emerging stars to guide him in a north-easterly direction, he passed a pond, its surface like black glass, and climbed over a stile into another field. He wanted to keep going but, now that he had food in his grasp, his hunger overwhelmed him. Crouching in the shelter of a hedge, he wolfed down two wizened apples (looking like the last of the autumn crop) and some of the bread (fresh enough that it might have been baked that morning) before he remembered that he should ration his provisions to make them last as long as possible. Resolutely, he tied up the sack, though his stomach ached for more nourishment, and stood again.

The woman's forecast about the weather had been correct – the air was growing even colder as night fell fully. He wrapped the blanket around his shoulders, loose strands of material scratching the skin at the nape of his neck. Marching across the field at a quick pace, leg muscles straining after two extended spells of motion and inertia outdoors, he headed for the crossroads.

## Chapter 3

The tea tray rested on a low table by her knee, tea cup full and biscuits untouched. A fire blazed in the hearth and a soft blanket covered her lap but still she felt the November chill seep into her bones. With the passage of every second, the ticking of the pendulum clock on the wall beat loud and relentless in her ears, drowning out the sounds of the bustling Berkeley Square beyond the windows.

The drawing room door opened. Bridget did not turn her head but a figure stepped into her peripheral vision and stood there waiting until she dragged her gaze away from the fireplace. It was her new housemaid, Lizzie. The girl had bad skin, her forehead, nose and cheeks marred by a haphazard sprawl of pockmarks and pimples, but it was self-consciousness which made her face so red.

'Begging your pardon, mistress,' she said with an awkward curtsey. 'I can't help noticing you ain't had nuffin to eat nor drink.'

Bridget didn't speak for a while, counting the clock beats until the maid would fade from view.

'I was not hungry or thirsty,' she said at last when it became clear Lizzie was staying put.

'But you ain't had nuffin for breakfast neither. And hardly a scrap at dinner yesterday evening. You need to eat something.'

Although she tried to appreciate the maid's concern, she could only muster a sense of mild irritation. 'I shall eat when I feel like it.'

She waved languidly in dismissal but Lizzie stood her ground, clutching at the folds of her apron.

'The tea'll be cold by now. I'll fetch you a fresh cup. And if you ain't liking these biscuits, Muss-yoor Lévêque can make you something else. A bowl of broth? Anything you fancy, mistress, I can get it for you.'

'I am fine. I do not desire anything.' Though a lie in general terms, it was true for the purposes of this conversation. She genuinely had no appetite. Whenever she tried to force down even a morsel, it roiled in her stomach until it came back up again.

'But you must look after yourself, mistress.' Lizzie gulped, gathering her courage. 'You're wasting away.'

Bridget supposed that a proper mistress would remonstrate her servant for the effrontery of such a comment. However, she glanced down at her thin arms and knew the girl was right – and yet she could not stir herself to care. She no longer paid heed to any part of her existence. Her lady's maid dressed her and her butler announced dinner and her housemaid reminded her to retire to her bedchamber, and that was all. She had stopped weeping every night in the confines of her lonely bed because the effort of it had become too much. Now she just did nothing and thought of nothing. To think would be to face the grief and the guilt, and that would finish her.

'I do not want —' she said faintly, but Lizzie's nerve held out.

'I'm going to refill the tray,' she said, voice firm. 'Would you like anything in particular?'

Bridget had no energy to heave a sigh, but a tiny breath of exasperation escaped her. 'Some broth would be nice, thank you.'

She remained motionless after Lizzie departed from the room. Her correspondence also lay on the low table but she disregarded the two letters arrayed neatly side by side. By the writing styles of the addresses, she recognised one author as Miss Madeleine Wallace, her closest friend during the seven years she had spent in Dublin, and the other as her mother, now residing full time at Oakleigh. However, neither held any appeal, when she could only presume the former to contain a dramatic string of trivialities and the latter to be as cold as her bones.

She did not react when Lizzie scurried back into the room and set down the replenished tray, now bearing a bowl of steaming beef broth, but she blinked when the girl knelt beside her and lifted the spoon to her lips.

Lizzie gave her a lopsided smile. 'I'm determined to get you to eat, mistress, even if I have to feed you myself.'

Had Bridget not felt so numb, she would have cried at the despair and the shame of it all. But she just opened her mouth to accept the spoonful of broth and swallowed, like a child.

She made it through half the bowl before she refused to take any more. Still, Lizzie looked quite satisfied.

'The master'll be pleased,' she said, dropping the spoon back onto the tray.

Bridget's fingers twitched. 'He spoke to you about me?'

'He's worried about you, mistress. We all are.'

She shrugged. If Garrett was worried, it was probably about what society would think were his wife to be found starving in their own house. London would get weeks out of that bit of gossip.

Lizzie stood and picked up the tray with a hopeful expression. 'Now you've eaten something, would you feel equal to going for a stroll in the gardens across the way?'

Bridget looked away. 'Did *he* suggest that?'

'No, mistress, I did. I open the windows in here every morning but it ain't no match for the proper outdoors. It'd do you a world of good.'

'Perhaps another day.'

And she was left in solitude to stare at the fire, listen to the clock, and sense neither heat nor time.

The door opened again.

'I'm not hungry, Lizzie.'

'It's not Lizzie.'

Garrett came around into her line of sight and took the chair at the other side of the fireplace.

'Is this some sort of protest?'

She didn't reply.

'If it is, you will achieve nothing by it. You need to stop this absurd behaviour.'

Her stomach churned. She imagined the broth sloshing around inside it, masticated meat tossing in bile-coloured juices, and closed her eyes against the sickening image.

'Forget him, damn you!'

Her eyelids flew open. Garrett was sitting forward, hands clenched and jaw line rigid.

'He's *gone*. You cannot get him back, so wake up from this trance and let us move on with our lives. I am weary of living with a ghost.'

It was the first time he had alluded to Cormac since they had left Oakleigh, preferring on the whole to act as though the events of the summer had not occurred. His capacity to ignore reality's more disagreeable aspects was remarkable, given that he had married her, even though she was not a virgin, and then brought her from Dublin to London, despite the fact that the move was blatantly against her will. But it seemed there was a limit to his talent, and the skeleton in his drawing room was it.

'What would you have me do?'

'Your duty. Be my wife.'

She had fulfilled her wifely obligations a number of times after their wedding but not since their arrival in London, where they kept separate bedchambers. Was that all he sought?

'Very well. Tonight, if you wish it.'

His gaze hardened further. He detested this, having to ask for her cooperation in the matter. With his silky, jet-black hair and captivating hazel eyes, he had never had to solicit such attention in his life.

He folded his arms. 'If we must negotiate it thus, then so be it. I shall come to you.'

He stalked out of the room and she sank back into her chair, relieved to be alone again.

The relief did not last long. The broth still bothered her stomach and a surge of queasiness sent waves of heat over her, making her skin clammy and her head dizzy. She would need to lie down until it passed. She pushed the blanket off her lap, rose shakily to her feet, and went out into the hallway. Praying no one would come upon her in this state, she took the stairs one slow step at a time. Her legs wobbled and her insides pitched about, reminding her of the unpleasant sea crossing from Ireland.

She entered her bedchamber but, instead of dropping down onto the bed, she fell to her knees, dragged the chamber pot out from under it, and expelled the contents of her stomach. It came out in sour, watery spurts and she gasped in misery and disgust. The smell was horrible. She crawled away towards the bell pull on the wall. Lacking the strength to stand, she moaned and stretched up to tug on its tasselled end.

Lizzie came running. 'Oh, mistress!' she exclaimed. 'I'll remove it at once.'

She returned with a clean pot and a damp cloth which she pressed to Bridget's forehead. Bridget did not protest; it felt cool and soothing.

Lizzie coughed discreetly. 'Mistress?'

'Mmm?'

'Do you think you might be with child?'

Bridget gaped at her.

Lizzie coloured, the pimples on her face turning redder too. 'I remember what it was like for my mother when she was carrying my youngest brother. She was sick for months. You ain't as bad as her, but it might be a possibility, if...'

If Bridget had had relations with a man. She had.

Her breath hitched in her throat.

Two men, in fact.

Her heart raced. 'How can I tell how long it's been?'

'It's hard to know. Do you remember when you last had your courses?' Lizzie's blush deepened even more. This was far beyond her remit as a housemaid.

Bridget tried to recall the last time she had noticed the blood. Never in London, that was certain. They had spent a month in Dublin around the wedding but she had no recollection of seeing it then either. Could it be as far back as Oakleigh? If that was the case...

'Thank you for bringing this to my attention,' she said and took the maid's arm to struggle upright. 'Please keep it to yourself for now. I shall inform my husband once I am very sure.'

Lizzie nodded. 'Can I do anything else for you, mistress?'

She looked ready for the usual dismissal but Bridget said, 'Yes, I would like hot water for a bath. I feel grimy after sitting idle for so long. Lay out a fresh gown for me and have Monsieur Lévêque prepare something that will easier for my stomach to tolerate. Some dry toast, perhaps, and a cup of very weak tea. Can you do that?'

'Of course!' The girl looked ecstatic as she bounded out of the bedchamber.

Bridget stumbled over to the bed and sat on the edge, cradling her still-flat belly. 'I'm sorry. I didn't know you were there and I neglected you. But I will get healthy again for your sake. I promise.'

She had thought her life was empty, that *she* was empty. Far from it. Hope flickered within her; perhaps all was not lost as she had believed. She could make enquiries, send out letters in an attempt to locate Cormac. Maybe, by a miracle as great as the one growing inside her, she would find him.

She had been standing on a precipice but now she scrambled back from the plunging darkness beyond. This baby would keep her alive.

## Chapter 4

'Get off my property!'

Cormac struggled into consciousness as something hard dug into his side. He looked around with blurry eyes and discerned a burly figure standing over him, brandishing a shovel.

'You heard me.' The man's voice was rough. 'Get out of here!'

Cormac clambered clumsily to his feet, his thin blanket slipping from his shoulders to the ground. He had been curled up on the man's doorstep, taking what little shelter he could from the freezing night. Now he gathered up the blanket and staggered away with the man's words ringing in his ears.

'Don't you come back here again!'

Out on the open street, the bitter wind cut into him. He would need to find another refuge or suffer through the remainder of the night exposed to the cold. He felt so exhausted at this late, dark hour that even the cobblestones looked inviting, but he wrapped his blanket around himself and lurched onwards.

Two streets over, he passed by a church with a welcoming porch but did not stop; he had learned the hard way that the porch was the territory of a belligerent crone with a crutch and a viciously-accurate swing. As he blew on his hands to warm them, he walked through a pool of light cast by a gas lamp. Upon his arrival to Dublin, he had stared in awe at the extraordinary spectacle of street lighting – now he plodded beneath without an upwards glance.

Further on, he came upon a greengrocer's shop, silent and shuttered on the corner of the street. Though it was his first winter in the city, he had learned quickly that the alleys behind such establishments, where rubbish tended to accumulate, were popular scavenging grounds for the homeless. The competition for scraps was fierce but he deemed it unlikely that anyone would be there at this time of night; the rest of the city's impoverished denizens would have enough sense to be holed up somewhere out of the cold.

His mouth watered as he imagined what pickings he might find behind the shop if he was lucky, and he decided to put aside his search for shelter in the hope of abating his ever-present hunger. He crept around to the back of the building and entered the alleyway. With one disappointed glance, he saw that he was not the first to come here tonight – the waste from the shop was strewn all over the filthy alley, as though it had been flung about during a very thorough search.

Not to be deterred, he dropped to his knees and began his own hunt for food, rummaging through the piles of refuse with shaky hands. He yelped when his thumb scraped something sharp. Groping more carefully, he uncovered a broken length of wood, several nails jutting out of it at bent angles. It looked like part of a crate that had once held fruit or vegetable produce. Had any of its contents been thrown out with it?

He continued to fumble around, and his dubious reward for his patience was the discovery of three shrunken potatoes which had been trampled into the dirt, evidently dismissed by the previous forager as inedible. He had no such dignity left to him. He pried the potatoes from the grimy ground, gave them a cursory wipe with his fingers, and choked them down. It was better fare than nothing at all and he cast his gaze upwards with a mumbled prayer of thanks.

He gave the alley another appraising look. Here was as good a place to sleep as any, he supposed. Gathering mounds of the rubbish together, he fashioned a sort of nest against the back wall of the shop and huddled down into it with his blanket over him.

He had never felt less like a human being.

It was either December or January; he could not be certain because he had lost track of the days, each one dissolving miserably into the next. Had he heard the church bells ringing in the new year? He could not recall. He only knew that mere months had passed since he had left the Oakleigh Estate, and yet it seemed like it had happened a hundred years ago to somebody else.

He often called to mind his brief encounter with the woman on the farm for that had been the last occasion when he had witnessed any act of compassion. Dublin had proved to be an unforgiving place. Arriving on the cusp of winter, he had found the city inhospitable and bleak with not a soul willing to lend a helping hand.

It was laughable to expect that he might gain employment anywhere. His trek from the countryside had taken its toll; the weather had been harsh, his rations had depleted too quickly, and he had reached Dublin in a dreadful state, unkempt, dirty and malnourished. His desperate enquiries at mews behind grand townhouses had been fruitless – no stable master would consider him for an instant. Acquiring labour at the docklands was even less likely; though he was young and opportunities were available, the local men were always given precedence and an interloper like himself didn't stand a chance. So he endured destitution on the streets, scrounging for scraps and skulking on doorsteps, and strove to convince himself that remaining in the countryside would have been worse.

He tried not to think too much about his past life or the people he had known then. The loss of human companionship cut him bone deep now that not another sinner ever spoke to him, except to tell him to clear off. He sorely missed his friend Liam, and the stable master John Corbett, who had once confessed his hope of seeing Cormac become stable master himself at Oakleigh one day. What a fine future that would have been.

Even harder to bear were memories of his dear mother and his sisters. His older sister Mary entered his mind more often than any of the others, because he was now walking the streets she had previously walked herself. She, too, had come to Dublin with no position and no place to stay; she, too, had experienced the brunt of the pitiless city. But she had eventually obtained employment and lodgings at a baker's and, regardless of how badly they had treated her, that was still a stroke of luck he had yet to receive himself. She had also found brief happiness in the arms of an upper class gentleman, although he had turned out to be a blackguard who had subsequently abandoned her and Patrick, their newborn son. Recalling how the despair of that had ultimately brought about the sad end to her life, Cormac revised his earlier assessment; Mary's luck had been no better than his own. He tucked her back into the recesses of his mind, unwilling to remember any more.

Of Bridget he blocked out all thoughts.

The pale light of dawn came, accompanied by yet another voice telling him to beat it or the dog would be set on him. He pushed the rubbish aside and shuffled away.

His breath puffed out in clouds as he trudged along the quays, the stink of the River Liffey pungent in his nostrils. It was no better than himself, which shamed him, but there was no way to get clean, not in this city. He peered over the quay wall into the river's murky depths – a dip in there would leave him grimier than before. Mercifully, he did not have to rely on the Liffey for drinking water; fountains dotted around the city meant that at least his thirst, if not his hunger, could be alleviated with little trouble.

The wind gusted up the river, stinging his cheeks with the promise of snow. During his childhood at Oakleigh, a snowfall had always been a tremendous surprise and delight. Now he regarded the prospect with trepidation, given that he could not skip home to a solid roof and a warm fire.

As he wandered into the maze of cobbled streets beside the quays, he became aware of the cramps burgeoning in his stomach: the price of eating soiled, uncooked potatoes. With a groan, he slumped onto a step in front of a boarded-up doorway to wait for the pains to pass.

An intermittent squeak drew his attention to an old man in tattered garb traipsing up the street and towing a small wagon. He had a long beard matted with dirt, and a grubby sheet of canvas was stretched across the hidden contents in the wagon bed. Cormac's carpenter instincts compelled him to assess the condition of the wagon; one of the wheels wobbled perilously on its axle, and the front section of the wagon had a large crack down the middle – a violent jolt on the cobblestones could split it apart. Despite the man's evident homelessness, he had somehow acquired a variety of mysterious items to fill his laden wagon, making him an object of acute envy to those who had nothing. Two or three barefoot children shadowed him, their covetous eyes on the covered mound, but he was wise to them and shouted abuse over his shoulder to scare them off.

He steered the wagon carelessly past Cormac and the wheels ran over Cormac's toes.

'Ow!' he protested.

The old man turned back and waggled thick eyebrows at him. 'You got something to say to me, boy?'

His self-assurance gave Cormac the impression that this was a king of the Dublin streets and not someone to be crossed. In any case, he had no inclination to assault an elderly fellow, even if he looked like he could fight back tooth and nail.

'No,' he muttered.

The man scratched his nose. He wore frayed, fingerless gloves and his nails were black.

'You new?'

'New enough.'

'Seems maybe you could do with a bit of help.'

'You offering?'

The man hawked and spat a gobbet of phlegm on the ground. 'I don't give nothing without getting something back. What can you offer me?'

Cormac was about to slouch back against the doorway – he had nothing, after all – until his gaze landed on the wagon. The wheel was beyond his skill to repair but a flash of inspiration made him point at the front section.

'That's soon going to break apart. You've got too much weight on it. I can fix it for you.'

The old man's eyes lit up. 'Can you indeed?'

'Depends. If there's something under that canvas I can use as a hammer, then maybe I can.'

'A hammer's no good without nails,' the man scoffed.

'You worry about the hammer, I'll worry about the nails.'

The man considered him for a moment, then crouched down beside his wagon. He lifted up the edge of the canvas, squinted at Cormac to make sure he wasn't sneaking a look, and poked around inside. At length, he produced a rusted chunk of scrap iron with a flourish.

'How's this?'

Cormac recalled his father's polished, balanced hammer with a pang of longing. 'I'll manage.'

'So what about the nails? Going to produce them from your backside?'

'I'm going to get them now. Can I borrow the, uh, hammer?'

The old man looked outraged. 'You trying to steal from me, boy?'

Cormac shrugged. 'No, but you can come with me if you don't trust me.'

He tied his blanket around his waist and set off without looking back. After a short pause, he heard a sporadic squeak trailing after him. He was glad; it might prove worthwhile to be owed a favour from someone with clout on the merciless streets of Dublin. At the very least, the venture would distract him from his stomach cramps.

He found his way back to the greengrocer's, now busy with its first shoppers of the morning. Sidling into the alleyway, he discovered that no one had troubled to clear it up yet and he stooped to search through the scattered waste. He located the broken piece of crate with a triumphant grunt and unearthed another beside it, which he hadn't noticed in the dark. Half a dozen battered nails protruded from the two lengths of wood.

'You here again? I told you to beat it!'

The greengrocer's incensed exclamation was followed by his shout for his dog. Cormac snatched the wood and ran.

The old man had waited at the head of the alleyway, too cautious to bring his wagon into the tight space. Cormac jerked his head up the street and they put some distance between themselves and the angry greengrocer, halting on the next corner where a fishwife was yelling lustily to passersby, thrusting her hand out to the wares on display in her wheelbarrow. Cormac breathed in the salty smell of fresh fish greedily but she took one look at him and his companion and pushed her barrow away, nose wrinkling.

Shoving thoughts of a nourishing meal and a sated appetite out of his mind, he turned to the old man and said, 'Let me have that hammer now.'

Seeing that he was in earnest, the man handed over his precious lump of iron, albeit with a glare that warned against any contemplation of theft. Cormac knelt and first tackled the task of removing the nails from the wood. Most had been pulled halfway loose whenever the crate had been forced open but it still took a good deal of persuasion, a few whacks from the makeshift hammer and some skinned fingers before he could prise them all out. He hissed and cursed when his thumb scraped the rough, wooden surface and acquired two splinters. The man let out a callous chuckle but Cormac ignored him, determined to finish now that he had started.

He used the piece of iron to straighten out what nails he could, discarding one that was too crooked to be salvaged. Then he squatted in front of the wagon, got the man to hold one of the boards across the split section and banged a nail into place. It was a shoddy job, with none of the finesse he could have achieved with the right materials and tools, but, by the time he had finished, the two lengths of wood were attached to the wagon and the nails, though awry, were in no danger of falling out.

He stepped back from his handiwork and the old man pushed the wagon backwards and forwards, testing its mobility. He cast Cormac a pleased glance.

'Nice work, boy.' He pointed at the chunk of iron. 'Now give me that.'

Cormac handed it over and the man secreted it beneath the canvas again. When he straightened up, spine cracking in several places, his expression was pensive.

'You hungry?'

'D'you have any reason to believe I'm standing here with a full stomach?'

The man barked a laugh, hoarse and humourless. 'That I don't. But I been 'round long enough to know the best places to get food, don't you reckon?'

'I suppose you have.' Cormac leaned against the wall and folded his arms. His intuition told him that the more eager he appeared, the less forthcoming his companion would be.

The man sniffed. 'Seeing as you did me a good turn, I'll do you one. I know a place where they'll give you hot, tasty soup for free.'

'Sounds like a tall tale to me.'

The man rubbed his beard and a few crumbs of dirt drifted down onto his shabby coat. 'It's no tale. You head up past the castle and you'll find them. A nice-looking building with big double doors and a shiny plaque. No idea what it says, mind, but they're very generous to folks like us. You want to pay them a visit?'

'I might do, sometime.' Cormac itched to make for the place at once but strove to maintain his air of nonchalance. 'Thanks for the advice.'

'Thanks for fixing my wagon.' As the old man trudged away, accompanied by the ever-present squeak, he muttered, 'And we'll see if you're desperate enough to take the soup.'

Once he was gone from sight, Cormac turned and hastened in the other direction. He knew where Dublin Castle was, of course – he could not wander the city streets and fail to notice that impressive edifice, which managed to dwarf even Oakleigh in stature and grandeur. He searched the warren of lanes beyond it with an attentiveness to his surroundings which he lacked in his usual, aimless ramblings. It took some time to locate the place and he began to suspect the old man had deceived him, but eventually he found it tucked down a narrow street; it had a welcoming facade of scrubbed steps and a gleaming, bronze plaque which proclaimed it as the site for the 'Grace of God Mission Society'. Seeing this undeniable proof that the old man had been telling the truth, he had to restrain himself from running up the steps.

Despite the cold weather, the double doors were wide open in invitation. He edged inside and met a woman wearing a spotless apron.

'Do come in,' she greeted him warmly, betraying no acknowledgement of the smell that wafted in with him. 'You're hungry, no doubt. Would you like something to eat?'

'Yes, please,' he said, feeling his lips stretch into something like a smile.

'What lovely manners you have. Come along and I'll show you where you can get some soup.'

She guided him down a hall and into a large room filled with long tables and benches. A vast fireplace dominated one wall and threw out so much heat that it made him momentarily dizzy. Several ragged individuals sat at the benches, eating soup from big bowls; there were a couple of adults but most were children and youths. Two clergymen sat among them, reading to them from Bibles. The woman in the apron beckoned to one and he desisted from his preaching to come over to her.

'We have a new boy, Deacon,' she said. 'I'll go and fetch him a bowl of soup now.'

She bustled away as the deacon turned to Cormac.

'I'm Deacon Haybury,' he said and shook Cormac's hand, showing no distaste at the grime. 'You are very welcome here. Come sit.'

He led the way to a bench near the fireplace and Cormac dropped onto it gratefully, untying the blanket from his waist and relishing the thawing effects of the fire on his back. He couldn't understand why the place wasn't teeming with people – it was a paradise compared to the desolate streets outside.

The woman came back and set a spoon and a bowl of mouth-watering soup, thick with vegetables, in front of him.

'You eat your fill and there's more if you want it,' she said with a kindly touch of his arm and she departed again, presumably to resume her post at the front door.

Cormac seized the spoon, wondering how long Deacon Haybury would stay beside him. He wanted to guzzle the soup in a most indecorous way but really couldn't in the presence of a man of the cloth.

Unfortunately, the deacon settled himself on the bench beside him. 'What is your name?'

'Cormac,' he replied, resigned to taking a more reserved approach to his first proper meal in over two months.

'Just before you start to eat, Cormac, I wish to say first of all that the Grace of God Mission Society is delighted to accept you, and we are committed to looking after both your physical and spiritual health. But you must answer one question for me. Are you of the Catholic faith?'

Cormac dipped the spoon in the soup, loading it with hunks of carrot and turnip. 'I am.'

'To be very clear, we are more than willing to feed you, but we cannot allow you to remain here as a Catholic. However, if you convert to our beliefs then we shall welcome you into the fold as one of our own and you will never again have to worry about where your next meal will come from.'

Cormac's gaze snapped from his spoon to the deacon. 'What?'

The deacon looked both patient and regretful, as though this scene was not unfamiliar to him. 'Yes, we espouse the Protestant doctrine here and can only assist members of our own congregation. But converting is a straightforward process and your body and soul will be the better for it.'

The hunger pangs in Cormac's belly warred with his conscience but it was a short battle. The deacon might as well have asked him to relinquish one of his limbs.

With a longing glance, he let the spoon drop back into the soup with a splash.

'Don't make any hasty decisions,' Deacon Haybury advised. 'The streets are a frozen and barren wasteland. This institution can be your saving grace.'

'I can't,' Cormac said simply and grabbed his blanket.

He stalked from the room, marched past the woman in the apron without even looking at her, and emerged onto the steps to realise that the first few snowflakes had begun to fall. The icy air slapped his face, excruciating after the blazing fire he had left behind. He pulled his blanket tight around his shoulders and stamped away.

Rage burned inside him. The old man knew. He had to have known. A fine trick to play on the young, green, unsuspecting fool who had the naïveté to do him a kindness and expect some in return. Well, he had learned his lesson, and he would be giving the bastard a piece of his mind if he ever saw him again.

That happened only three or four days later. He was passing the fishwife's corner when he stumbled upon the old man, sprawled on the ground, eyes staring up to the sky. Whether it was as a result of age, cold or ill health, Cormac could not tell. However it had come about, the king was dead. He was now no more than food for the crows and pickings for the homeless whom he had lorded over.

His wagon lay on its side next to him, ransacked and abandoned. The canvas had been ripped away, revealing that he had been hoarding nothing but the most worthless detritus scavenged from the streets – the chunk of iron had probably been his most valuable possession and it was gone. Someone had swiped his coat but they had left the tattered, fingerless gloves. Cormac debated the morals behind thieving from a corpse, decided the man still owed him a good deed, and peeled the gloves off his rigid hands. He pulled them on and then patted him on the shoulder, his cruelty forgiven. There was no sense in harbouring animosity towards the dead.

At least he had the questionable luck to still be alive.

## Chapter 5

Bridget cast a nervous glance around the assemblage of ladies. They were gathered in small groups at round tables and their incessant chatter filled the air like an invisible swarm of bees. Footmen hovered about, ready to refill a glass or pick up a dropped handkerchief. Fragrant flowers decorated the tables and the weak, early spring sunshine fell in through long windows down one side of the room. She felt as discomfited as she had on the day of the debutantes ball at Dublin Castle, when she had been sixteen and bereft of any trace of sophistication or social ease. But she had promised herself she would make an effort to live again. And living in London meant going out in society.

She searched the crowd for the one face she would recognise and was relieved to espy that distinctive nose, a good deal larger than the average but borne by its owner with admirable aplomb. Lady Newby was the wife of a close acquaintance of Garrett's; he had orchestrated the introduction once Bridget had shown she was endeavouring to lift the fog of gloom that shrouded her. Her new friend had vowed to facilitate her immersion into the most privileged London circles, and this included securing her an invitation to a charity event organised by the Ladies of Compassion Association.

Lady Newby was sitting near the long windows with two other companions. She spotted Bridget and gave an enthusiastic wave. Plucking up her courage, Bridget weaved her way among the tables to join them.

'Mrs Lambourne, I am so glad you could come! Do sit down. This is Lady Radcliffe and Miss Caulfield.'

Bridget took the empty chair between the two ladies she did not know. Lady Radcliffe, dressed in the height of fashion, was a beauty and comported herself with the confidence of one who knew it. Miss Caulfield, on the other hand, had mousy features and her clothes, while by no means shabby, were decidedly less fashionable. She cast Bridget a timid smile and then dropped her gaze as Lady Radcliffe leaned forward, intent on interrogating the new addition to their group. She had soon elicited the salient information needed to establish Bridget's credentials, including her childhood at Oakleigh (a rustic upbringing but not unsalvageable), her coming out in Dublin (a crucial step up in the world), and her recent marriage to the heir to the viscountcy of Wyndham (an estimable match which merited a high level of respect).

'And you are not long in London, Lucy has told us. How do you like it? You doubtless find it a marked improvement from the quaintness of Irish society!' Lady Radcliffe's laugh tinkled like the chime of a bell.

Aware of Ireland's inferior status in the eyes of the English aristocracy, Bridget had prepared herself to encounter such blatant denigration of her country.

'We arrived in October,' she said with extreme civility, 'but I have not had much opportunity yet to enjoy the delights of the city. I have been rather poorly these past months and am only lately back to good health.'

Although the curve of her belly was still neat enough to be concealed beneath her full skirts, the ladies added the necessary facts together – a new bride, a sea crossing, a prolonged illness – to make the correct assumption that she must be with child, and they required no further explanation.

'Do not fret, you have not missed a great deal.' Lady Radcliffe spoke with the earnestness of one assuring another that the death of a beloved relative had not occurred. 'Many of us are just returning to the city after having spent the winter on our country estates. But the season will begin soon and I declare I will do my utmost as always to make it a memorable one.'

Lady Newby grinned at Bridget. 'An invitation to a party at the Radcliffe residence is considered the most coveted prize in the social calendar.'

Lady Radcliffe affected a modest expression. 'I merely endeavour to promote the entertainment of my guests. And, of course, to secure a husband for Alice.'

Miss Caulfield went pink at this. 'Oh, I — no, Cassandra — that is —'

'Come now, dearest,' said Lady Radcliffe, pressing a quelling hand over her friend's. 'You are out three seasons already. You cannot hide in the corner of the ballroom forever. For a suitor to offer for you, he must be able to *see* you.'

Miss Caulfield looked around in desperation. 'I wonder when the speaker is going to come?'

Her deliverance appeared in the form of the leader of the association – 'Lady Ainsley,' murmured Lady Newby to Bridget – a rigid-shouldered lady who entered the room accompanied by a woman in drab clothing with a mannish sort of face. They walked to a dais beyond the top cluster of tables and Lady Ainsley compressed her lips primly together until silence fell.

'Ladies, thank you all for coming. I applaud your eagerness to support the efforts of this association in alleviating the deplorable plight of the poor in London. Allow me to introduce Miss Blythe. She has petitioned to speak to us today as a representative from St Swithun's Workhouse and

Soup Kitchen.'

Lady Ainsley stepped back to make way for the speaker. Miss Blythe stumbled as she climbed onto the dais and Lady Radcliffe tittered behind her napkin. Undeterred by her clumsiness, Miss Blythe cleared her throat.

'I am here to talk about a very important matter,' she said in a deep voice, 'that of poverty relief in this city. St Swithun's is only one of many institutions and it distresses me to describe the appalling things I see there each day. The people who come to our soup kitchen are in rags, barefoot, emaciated from hunger. In the workhouse itself, diseases of every kind run rampant and we cannot keep vermin out of the building.'

Bridget saw several of the ladies shudder in revulsion. They had not bargained on such a vivid account of the poor people's troubles; it was incongruous with this sunlit room filled with pretty hats and dainty china cups.

Miss Blythe carried on relentlessly. 'The accommodation situation is outrageous. They sleep four, five, six to a bed, the healthy sharing with the sick. We feed them as best we can but the quality of the food is unacceptable and the quantity is insufficient to satisfy so many hungry mouths. I come before you today to implore you to aid us. We need more funds to improve the services we provide. With your generous contributions, we could acquire more beds, better food, clothes, medicines, to help these poor souls. I beg you to pledge as much as you can spare.'

As she listened to the speaker, Bridget felt a vague sense of awfulness descend upon her, a dismay that clung to her skin like a thin layer of slime. It was guilt again, but of a different kind.

Miss Blythe persevered to her beseeching conclusion. 'The true horrors of St Swithun's must be witnessed to be believed. I entreat you to come visit to see for yourselves. Your presence would be welcomed and your eyes would be opened. My sincere thanks for your time.'

The ladies did their best to hide their distaste behind sympathetic murmurs and there was a smattering of polite applause as Miss Blythe stepped down. They occupied the next few minutes signing pledges for what they believed to be the adequate amount for donation; their husbands would later write the appropriate cheques. The footmen were on hand to convey the pledges to Lady Ainsley, but Bridget felt compelled to deliver her own herself.

'Excuse me one moment,' she said to Lady Newby and the others, and she negotiated her way between the round tables to the top of the room. She approached Miss Blythe, who was hovering beside the dais, eclipsed by Lady Ainsley's more imposing presence.

'Miss Blythe, I am Mrs Lambourne,' she said. 'You spoke well, I commend you.'

Miss Blythe rubbed her wide jaw self-consciously. 'That is kind of you. I practised it a hundred times before going up.'

'The state of affairs at St Swithun's sounds very serious. Is the institution sufficiently staffed?'

'Far from it. We are too few to cope with the volumes of people that come through our doors. We are always in need of more hands. And provisions, of course.'

Bridget handed her the pledge. 'I do hope this will be of some use.'

Miss Blythe's eyes widened when she looked at it. 'Good gracious, this is most generous.'

'It is for a worthy cause.' She would deal with Garrett's indignation later. 'Tell me, when may I come visit?'

The woman's gaze snapped back up to hers. 'You truly wish to come? Begging your pardon, but I didn't think that anyone in this room would actually respond to that particular plea.'

'Having listened to your speech, I would not be satisfied with simply writing a figure on a piece of paper. I want to contribute in a more tangible way, if you believe I might be of some help.'

Miss Blythe smiled in astonishment, adding a touch of femininity to her masculine features. 'We would be ever so grateful for your assistance.'

They arranged for her to visit the very next day. When she returned to her table and proposed the scheme to her new companions, only Miss Caulfield expressed an interest and she was unavailable. Lady Newby and Lady Radcliffe both demurred and endeavoured to dissuade Bridget from the enterprise too, but she paid no heed to them. She was determined to keep this appointment.

The following afternoon, she instructed her coachman, Sawyer, to take her to St Swithun's Workhouse and Soup Kitchen, but she regretted the action when she emerged onto the street and was beleaguered by a gaggle of barefoot ragamuffins begging for coins; a carriage announced her status in society as loudly as a town crier with a bell. She distributed what she could and then hurried to the entrance of St Swithun's, a narrow door with rotting wood, peeling paint and rusted hinges.

As soon as she stepped through it, she felt bile rise in her throat. The air was full of the stench of unclean bodies. She swallowed and breathed shallowly through her mouth. She was in a long, low-ceilinged room which contained a scattering of mismatched benches and stools, vastly inadequate for the multitude of bedraggled people crowded inside, most of whom were forced to stand or sit on the grimy floor. A cacophony of coughs, groans and children's crying emanated from the teeming mass.

For the first time, the dangers of being exposed to such a situation occurred to her and she began to worry, not for herself but for her unborn baby. Her feet were taking a hesitant step back towards the door when Miss Blythe detached herself from the throng and came over to her. She strode with a confidence lacking in her demeanour yesterday; she looked far more comfortable in this environment where she was the unequivocal person of authority and not subordinate to a bunch of frivolous ladies to whom she had to grovel for financial support.

'Mrs Lambourne, thank you so much for coming.'

'I-I'm pleased to be here, Miss Blythe.'

'In this place I am just Frances,' Miss Blythe said with a wink.

'Then I shall be just Bridget,' Bridget replied, taking courage from the other woman's self-assurance.

Frances proceeded to show her around the soup kitchen. It was atrocious. The long room represented the entire extent of the institution's ability to provide outdoor relief – this 'kitchen' consisted of nothing more than boiling pots over a hearth tended by a couple of harried-looking women, and a few dirty bowls which had to be shared among the countless starving wretches who came to the door each day. The vegetables for the soup were already mouldering and there was nowhere near enough to feed all the clamouring mouths both inside and outside the ramshackle building. Bridget declined to enter the workhouse looming forbiddingly beside the kitchen, recalling Frances's allusion to rampant diseases, but understood that the conditions within were just as dreadful for those who were desperate enough to seek the dubious refuge which the indoor relief was supposed to offer.

'You are gravely underfunded,' she said, appalled by all she saw. 'I trust the revenue from yesterday's event will go some way towards rectifying the situation.'

'Not everyone was quite as generous as you. But it will still be an enormous help.'

'I shall speak to the association on your behalf and try to arrange regular donations from them. With more substantial resources, we could significantly improve the quality of the services provided at St Swithun's.'

Frances blinked. 'We?'

'Yes,' Bridget said with resolve. 'I would like to take a more active role here, if I can be of use. However, I must disclose that I am with child and fear I ought not return until after the birth. Until then, I shall campaign at more charity events and ensure the delivery of whatever supplies you require.'

Frances's sizeable jaw dropped. 'Good gracious, I don't know what to say.'

Bridget glanced over her shoulder at the miserable individuals slumped around the kitchen. 'Say you will agree.'

It shamed her to recollect her weeks of apathy in the drawing room when there was such work to be done. There would be no more idleness on her part.

## Chapter 6

As she perused a list of financial contributions obtained at the most recent meeting of the Ladies of Compassion Association, Bridget shifted her chair closer to the open drawing room window, seeking a puff of air to cool her flushed face. Everyone said it was the nicest May they had seen in years, and the gardens of Berkeley Square were swarming with gentlefolk enjoying sunny strolls, but she found the heat suffocating. At this advanced stage of her pregnancy, she just could not find a way to get comfortable.

After dabbing at her sweaty neck with a handkerchief, she picked up her pen, dipped it and wrote the total amount donated at the bottom of the page. She sat back, pleased; she intended this money to go towards new beds and blankets for the workhouse. She had already negotiated an agreement with the local greengrocers to supply the soup kitchen with produce at a reduced price, which Frances and the other women working there had received with deepest gratitude. Lady Ainsley seemed a trifle irked that the newest recruit to the association appeared to be supplanting her in terms of efficacy, but she could not deny that the association's goals were being achieved like never before.

The shout of a coachman drew Bridget's attention back to the window; a carriage had come to a stop on the street directly below her. Her mood darkened when she saw her mother emerge, the lady's appraising gaze sweeping up and down the grand facade of Wyndham House. The location spoke of status and money and met with her obvious approval.

Bridget grasped the little bell which had been placed near her for her convenience, the bell pull on the far wall presenting too much of a challenge in her expectant state. She rang it and Lizzie appeared.

'My mother has arrived and will be in need of refreshment. Please bring us some tea and biscuits.'

'Yes, mistress, at once,' Lizzie said with a curtsey and vanished.

Bridget looked out the window again. Wyndham House's imperturbable butler, Thrussell, and handsome footman, Peter, had come out onto the steps to greet the new arrival and see to her luggage. Lady Courcey superciliously accepted their welcome as though she were an exalted duchess instead of a mere baroness, then twisted around to bark an order at the two maidservants who accompanied her. It gladdened Bridget to perceive the freckled face of Ellen Ryan, her mother's lady's maid, but she did not recognise the other girl and could not imagine why the lady would have brought a second maid – Ellen was more than capable of tending to all her needs.

Peter lifted a trunk from the carriage and started to struggle up the steps with it. When Bridget heard Lady Courcey's sharp tongue turn in his direction, she frowned. She hoped her mother would remember that she was a guest now rather than the mistress of her own house.

The figures disappeared from view and their voices echoed in the hall below before footsteps sounded on the stairs. Thrussell showed Lady Courcey into the drawing room and then withdrew at a nod from Bridget. She rose unsteadily to her feet; her large belly made her feel off balance and she gripped the arm of her chair for support.

'Welcome, Mother,' she said in a clipped voice.

Lady Courcey came over and embraced her with care, the enormous bump protruding between them. Then she stood back and surveyed her.

'You have put on a good deal of weight,' she said, clearly not referring to Bridget's stomach area. 'The sooner that baby is out of you, the better. You cannot be a fat lady of society. People will talk about you.' She looked around the room. 'What a horrendous choice of colour for the curtains. Did they have nothing better?'

Bridget bit the tip of her tongue to prevent her retort, regretting for the hundredth time that her sense of duty as a daughter had triumphed over her detestation of her mother. She had felt obliged by society's expectations to invite Lady Courcey to London and be present when her first grandchild arrived into the world, even though she had no wish for the woman to be there, not after the irreparable harm she had caused the previous summer on the Oakleigh Estate.

Her chest tightened unbearably at the memory. Breathe, she reminded herself. You must continue to breathe.

Lizzie entered at that moment with a tray. She set the tea things on a low table and Bridget smiled at her in thanks. Lady Courcey squinted critically at Lizzie's departing back.

'Well, that maid will have to go,' she said as she and Bridget sat down. 'I cannot fathom why you have not got rid of her already.'

'Pardon me?' said Bridget, stunned.

Her mother's tone was matter-of-fact. 'You cannot keep such an ugly servant. Her skin is quite appalling. It is offensive to any guests who may see her.'

A blaze of fury rose up inside Bridget. 'I will not hear of it,' she said, keeping her voice controlled as she poured tea for them both. Her hand shook a little but she did not spill it. 'Lizzie is a girl of absolute reliability and irreproachable character. I quite depend upon her.' To prevent her mother from arguing the point further, she hastened on, 'Speaking of servants, I noticed that you brought two maids with you. I did not recognise the younger girl. Who is she?'

A sly look crept onto Lady Courcey's face as she picked up her cup. 'That is Cathy, one of the new maids at Oakleigh. It was necessary for me to fill a couple of vacated positions following certain events last summer.'

Bridget felt like her mother had just dealt a devastating blow to her abdomen. Lady Courcey was referring to her unfair dismissal of Cormac's two sisters, which had coincided with her eviction of his entire family from Oakleigh land after Bridget's love affair with him had come to light. The lady had gone to the exorbitant expense of bringing a superfluous maid, from the scullery no less, across the sea to England for the sole purpose of delivering this smug jibe.

Sickened, Bridget reached for her bell. 'You must be tired. Lizzie will show you to your bedchamber,' she said, disregarding the fact that neither of them had even touched the biscuits.

She sipped her tea and kept her eyes averted until Lizzie had escorted Lady Courcey from the drawing room.

Alone, her tears began to fall. Her stupor last winter had been excruciating but, now that she allowed herself to feel again, her remorse was equally crushing. She knew that if she lived to ninety years of age she could never make any mistake larger than the one that had destroyed the McGovern family.

She started when the door opened again and Garrett entered the drawing room. His timing was perfect if he had wanted to avoid greeting his mother-in-law. While courting Bridget, he had remained on the best of terms with Lady Courcey, drawing on the depths of his patience and charm. Now that his position within the family was utterly secure, he seemed more adjusted to the idea of risking the lady's displeasure. Bridget suspected that he had even forewarned his father, whose house this still was after all, of Lady Courcey's acerbic nature because Lord Wyndham had conveniently been called away to Swifton Hall, the title's country seat, just before her impending arrival.

Garrett took one look at his weeping wife and his mouth narrowed into a thin line. 'Ten minutes in the house,' he said, 'and the woman is already eliciting tears.'

He approached as though to put his arms around her but she wiped her cheeks and looked away. 'I am fine.'

They were at a sensitive point in their relationship. While she still could not forgive him for the cruel part he had played in Cormac's banishment and for his subsequent unsympathetic conduct, his own manner had wholly transformed when she had revealed to him that she was with child. Full of anticipation of the birth of his heir, he was now trying to be as tender towards her as he had been at the beginning of their courtship. But she was uneasy. If the coming baby was the result of a union that had taken place after she was married, then the due date was almost a month away. On the other hand, if it was the product of illicit relations before her marriage, then the birth would be quite a bit sooner. She did not dare to speculate how he might react should the event not transpire as he expected.

With a wounded shrug, he stepped back. 'I hope it was not an error in judgement to invite her. I don't wish for anything to disturb your comfort at such a delicate time.'

She refrained from pointing out that a state of comfort was entirely unattainable at this stage, or that she had always known Lady Courcey's presence would add stress to an already stressful event. Instead, she mumbled something about obligation and resigned herself to her fate.

They got a reprieve, however, when Lady Courcey sent word that she was suffering from a headache and would remain in her bedchamber until dinner. Welcoming this news with relief, Bridget set aside her figures for the Ladies of Compassion Association and took the opportunity to retire to bed herself. She ached all over her body and the baby was kicking so mercilessly that sleep would be out of her reach, but at least she could rest in preparation for the trials to come.

Lizzie – whose role had come to extend beyond that of housemaid as Bridget relied upon her more and more – had hardly helped her under the covers when an idea occurred to her.

'Lizzie,' she said, 'will you enquire after the lady's maid, Miss Ryan? Find out if she is currently attending to my mother and, if she is not, please ask her if she would come to my chamber.'

Lizzie scurried off and Bridget lay back on her pillows to wait. In the coming weeks, there might never be a suitable moment when she and Ellen could be alone, so she ought to seize this chance to speak with her in private while Lady Courcey was not nearby to overhear.

When Lizzie returned with Ellen, the lady's maid did not seem surprised to have been summoned like this – perhaps she had been expecting or even hoping for it. She took a seat next to the bed and Lizzie left them in solitude.

Bridget smiled. 'How are you, dearest Ellen? I have missed you.'

'And I have missed you,' Ellen replied with feeling. 'I am well and glad to see you in good health.'

Something relaxed inside Bridget, a coil of imprisonment and secrecy loosening ever so slightly. Ellen had always been an ally and knew more about Bridget's past than most. Last summer, she had helped Cormac sneak into the manor to be consoled by Bridget after his older sister, Mary, had ended her own life. Once Ellen had become aware of the blossoming attachment between them, she had cautioned Bridget to be careful but she had also been discreet with the secret she kept – an uncommon trait in a lady's maid, a position notorious for gossiping to the mistress. Bridget wished she could have taken Ellen to London with her but she was Lady Courcey's servant and obliged to remain in her employ. Now, Bridget felt the burden of memory diminish, if only temporarily, at having her confidante beside her once more.

'How is everything at Oakleigh?' she asked, conjuring an uplifting image in her mind of her childhood home, the elegant building of warm red brick surrounded by stables, orchard, gardens, and green fields unfolding to the horizon.

'Very busy, since her ladyship chose to take up permanent residence there again. She entertained a number of guests over the winter. The land is flourishing too and Mr Enright told her ladyship that the limestone quarry is proving exceedingly lucrative for your inheritance.' Ellen paused. 'Do you think you will ever return?'

Homesickness pricked the back of Bridget's eyelids. 'It is impossible to say. I long to go back and yet sometimes believe it would be unbearable to set foot there after – after what happened.'

She could not even imagine the pain of standing beneath the oak tree in the orchard and recalling the man who had kissed her there, the lover she had lost and failed to find. So far, the enquiries she had sent to Ireland – to stables of manor houses in counties neighbouring Carlow, to townhouse mews in the cities of Dublin and Cork, to shelters, soup kitchens, workhouses – had yielded no positive responses. A needle in a haystack would have been easier to unearth. She swallowed the emotion that welled in her throat.

'Of course,' she said, 'it is out of the question altogether until the baby is old enough to travel.'

Ellen glanced at the large bump under the bedcovers. 'And how do you feel in anticipation of that particular arrival?'

'Scared,' she admitted. Garrett's father had secured the services of one of the most respected midwives in the city for the coming of his first grandchild, but childbirth was a perilous affair and neither a viscount's money nor a midwife's experience was any guarantee of a safe delivery. 'Although I am in such discomfort that I just want it to happen already.'

Ellen's expression was full of sympathy. 'When do you expect the birth to take place?'

Bridget hesitated. Should she speak the accepted truth or divulge what she suspected to be the very possible alternative?

'It might be as much as three or four weeks,' she said, then went on in a small voice, 'or as little as three or four days.'

Ellen's gaze connected with hers.

'Oh, my,' she murmured.

She made no recriminations and Bridget was grateful, though she still felt the inescapable shame which accompanied the thought of producing an illegitimate child. It had never been her intention – she and Cormac had promised to wed each other but had simply found it impossible to delay their reckless night of passion until after their vows, which Lady Courcey and Garrett had then thwarted. Still, she need not worry about society's perception of the situation. Should the baby come sooner than expected, it would nonetheless be born within the confines of a lawful marriage, if not that of its natural parents.

The main concern was whether Garrett would be able to tell if the child was his or not.

Ellen's own reflections had led her down a different track. 'So Maggie McGovern may yet have another grandchild. She would be happy to know it, if...' Her sentence trailed away into dismal silence, unfinished.

But Bridget could finish it.

If Maggie still lived on Oakleigh land.

If she and her family had not been evicted, forced to leave the only home they had ever known.

If they were still alive.

Bridget stared down at her hands resting on her pregnant mound and felt her heart twist as though an invisible fist had reached inside and wrenched at the fragile organ, tearing at the names imprinted on it. Maggie, who was Cormac's mother but had been as good as a mother to Bridget too. Cormac's three surviving sisters, Margaret, Bronagh and Orlaith, all still girls and unacquainted with the wider world. And little Patrick, the son Mary had left behind when she committed that terrible act – he had been mere months old when the family had been thrown out of their cottage. They had been condemned to a wretched existence of homelessness and poverty, and Bridget was to blame.

'Did you hear what became of them all?' she asked, her words barely audible.

'No,' Ellen said with a regretful shake of her head. 'None of them could write so there was no hope of expecting a letter, and any travellers who came through from nearby villages had no news of them. They just disappeared.'

Bridget gripped the bedcovers fiercely. 'Perhaps they made their way to the city, thinking that Dublin would offer them better employment prospects. Do you know if they had any destination in mind? Did you speak to them before they left?'

Ellen grimaced, the freckles on her nose and cheeks scrunching together. 'I was there when they left, and it is a scene I shall never be able to forget.' She sighed. 'The morning you were taken back to Dublin, while you were still locked in your bedchamber, Liam Kirwan and I ran down to the cottage. Mr Enright was present too, looking like he'd rather be anywhere else, but as the estate's agent he had to supervise the eviction. Poor Maggie didn't seem to understand what was happening at all. Bronagh nearly had to push her out the door. It was dreadful to see her so dazed and broken. Margaret was trying to calm the two young ones, Orlaith and the baby, and I could tell it would be herself and Bronagh taking care of the family from then on, no doubt about it. I saw Liam press a few coins into Margaret's hand. It was all he had to spare from his stable hand's wages but she wept with gratitude. And after that they just wandered away with no notion where to go next.'

Her voice cracked. Bridget found she could not speak. She clutched Ellen's hand and they clung to each other, grieving for the unlucky McGoverns and the hardships they had been made to endure.

They drew apart when a knock sounded at the door. Lizzie peered around it, looking shocked to see their pale, tearful faces.

'M-mistress,' she faltered. 'Her ladyship's awake and calling quite insistently for Miss Ryan. She said—she said Cathy don't have brains enough to tend a beetle.'

Bridget sniffed and nodded. 'You had better go to her, Ellen. Thank you for coming to see me. That family is in my prayers.'

'And in mine. We can only hope and pray that good fortune finds them.'

Wiping a tear from her eye, Ellen rose, curtseyed and departed with Lizzie.

## Chapter 7

'I blame the poor quality of the city air,' Lady Courcey declared. 'The smoke is not conducive to my health.'

She, Bridget and Garrett were seated at the dinner table and Garrett had unwisely enquired after their guest's welfare, following her earlier retreat to her bedchamber.

'It is for the same reason that I have chosen to reside at Oakleigh on a more permanent basis,' the lady carried on. 'I am weary of Dublin's noxious environment. The country is far more wholesome to one's wellbeing.'

Bridget noted that her mother had kept her adoration of the countryside conveniently concealed throughout the seven years they had spent in Dublin, a good deal of which Bridget had spent pleading with her to take her home to Oakleigh.

Lady Courcey gave a delicate cough, then smiled angelically. 'I am for the most part recovered now though.'

'We are very glad to hear it,' Garrett said with the enthusiasm of one hoping to close down the current line of conversation.

In any case, she had turned her attention to the venison dish that was the centrepiece of that evening's dinner.

'Too tough,' she announced, pushing her plate away. 'Mrs Kavanagh knows how to cook it to perfection.'

'It is most regrettable that you feel that way,' said Garrett, cutting into his own portion of venison with more vigour than necessary. 'I am quite enjoying it myself.'

Bridget cast her gaze over the lavish range of dishes crowding the table, far too much for three people to consume, and compared it to the basic provisions she had scraped together for St Swithun's.

Pursing her lips, she said, 'We ought to appreciate what we have. There are many unfortunate souls who would be grateful for even a crumb from this table.'

Lady Courcey squinted at her. 'I suppose you are referring to that soup kitchen you mentioned in your letter. What possessed you to get involved in such ludicrous nonsense?' She swivelled towards Garrett. 'I'm surprised you are permitting her to indulge in it.'

'It is a commendable cause,' Garrett said mildly, neglecting to mention his and Bridget's heated argument about it. When she had first told him of her commitment to the Ladies of Compassion Association, he had objected to the notion of his wife demeaning herself among the common folk and had forbidden her involvement at such a practical level. He had only relented when she insisted that it was in fact fashionable for ladies to occupy themselves in charity work and promised she would not visit the soup kitchen or workhouse until after the baby was born. She supposed her passionate plea had made him realise that having such a purpose in her life played a significant part in preventing her from reverting to the dejected shell he had beheld in the drawing room.

'Hmm,' was Lady Courcey's doubtful response. She took a sip of her wine. 'This is not quite balanced,' she said with regret. 'I have a very sensitive palate. Buttimer knows my tastes well. His discernment ensures that Oakleigh's wine cellar is incomparable.'

Thrussell, standing behind Garrett's chair, stiffened at this and Bridget marvelled at Lady Courcey's talent to offend – she had managed to get under the skin of even the unflappable butler.

However, then her commentary shifted to a reflection on the most superb wine she had ever sampled (a mature bottle opened in celebration of Bridget's birth twenty years ago) and from there to the subject of children and the art of being a mother.

'You are going to love motherhood,' she said to Bridget. 'And if I may say so, I think you are going to make a fine mother.'

Bridget blinked. Was her mother making a statement that contained not one negative aspect to it? She looked at Garrett – the same incredulity was obvious on his face. Shrugging, he raised his glass.

'I could not agree more,' he said and drained the red liquid.

'Naturally, I shall assist you in every way I can,' Lady Courcey went on. 'I have had two decades of experience in the area so you could not ask for better guidance.'

Bridget gritted her teeth and stabbed at her own venison with her fork. It was delicious – whatever Lady Courcey had to say about the quality of the food, Bridget was more than satisfied with Monsieur Lévêque's abilities.

'There is no better person to whom a girl can turn for advice than her own mother,' said Lady Courcey sagely. 'Of course, you know that already. I have always been there to steer you along the right path. Without my help, you would have made quite a shocking blunder last summer, that is the undeniable truth. But I chose the right husband for you, didn't I?'

The lady leaned back in her chair and looked very pleased with her own success as a mother.

Right then, the baby gave an almighty kick inside Bridget and she imagined that it was as enraged as she was by Lady Courcey's arrogant words. This was beyond endurance.

She stood up so fast that she felt dizzy. She threw her fork on the table and it clattered off her plate and fell to the floor.

'I cannot tolerate this anymore!' she exploded.

Both Garrett and Lady Courcey stared at her in astonishment.

'What on earth—?' her mother began.

'You!' Bridget flung at her. 'I cannot tolerate *you* anymore!'

Lady Courcey looked indignant. 'That is no way to speak to your mother!'

Bridget glared at her. 'I have decided that I no longer have a mother. You haven't behaved like one in years so I shall not feel like I am missing anything.'

'You need to watch your tongue,' her mother warned, 'or it will get you into trouble.'

'What trouble?' Bridget crossed her arms over her protruding belly. 'There is nothing with which you can threaten me. You have already taken away all that I held dear. What would you do now, cut off my inheritance? Even if you could, I have no need of it. Spread ugly rumours about me? You never would, because that would besmirch your own name by association. You cannot touch me, my family or my status now.'

Lady Courcey, highly affronted, appealed to Garrett for support. 'Are you going to let her talk to me like this? Control your wife, for heaven's sake.'

Garrett raised his hands in a gesture that said he was taking no responsibility for this. 'I would never presume to interfere in the complicated relationship between a mother and daughter.'

Bridget continued to rant. 'You are a mean, bitter woman who finds fault with everything and loves no one. You have inflicted misery upon innocent people and *relished* it. You think you have been a good mother to me? You have brought about more heartache in my life than I ever deserved to suffer, flawed though I am. I am determined to be the exact opposite of you when my baby is born.'

'You ungrateful girl.' Lady Courcey's voice was low but the colour had risen in her cheeks. 'I have done everything in my power to provide for you, to secure your happiness. And this is the thanks I get?'

'You said the right word,' said Bridget with growing fury. 'Power. And you do not have it anymore. I want you to get out of my house this instant.'

'Don't be absurd,' said her mother, reaching for her glass of wine.

'I am being deadly serious!' Bridget shrieked and her mother's hand froze in mid-air. 'I never want to see you again! And you shall never set eyes on your grandchild. I do not want you to poison its life the way you have poisoned mine and the lives of so many others. Get out of my sight and do not ever try to come here again or I will throw you out into the gutter myself!'

Beginning to realise that Bridget truly meant what she was saying, Lady Courcey again implored Garrett to intervene. 'You must talk some sense into her. It is almost nine o'clock at night. Where could I go at this hour?'

He thought for a moment. 'A distant cousin of mine resides on Brook Street. She is an elderly widow and lives on her own. I could send a message to her. I am sure she would take you in, even at this short notice.'

Lady Courcey looked horrified that Garrett was choosing to take the part of his wife. She swung back to Bridget, aghast. 'You cannot mean to do this. Are you really going to drive me away? Your own mother?'

'Yes, I am,' Bridget said and beckoned to the butler, who had observed the entire scene without intrusion. 'Thrussell, please ask Miss Ryan to pack some of my mother's things, any essentials she will need for the next day or two. Then get Sawyer to bring around the carriage. You,' she added, addressing her mother again, 'can send Ellen and Cathy back for the rest of your possessions whenever it is convenient for them.'

Thrussell bowed and departed from the dining room. Bridget felt a wave of heat pass through her and leaned over the table, resting on her palms and breathing heavily. Out of her peripheral vision, she saw her mother reaching towards her and snatched her hand away before the lady could touch it.

'Bridget, p-please,' said Lady Courcey, stammering a little.

Bridget gave her a derisive look. 'A strange word to hear coming from you. You are not used to begging, are you?'

'Please,' Lady Courcey repeated. 'Do not do this.'

'Go and wait outside in the hall,' said Bridget. 'Your very presence makes me sick to my stomach.'

'Pl—' Lady Courcey started again but Bridget interrupted by slapping her hand on the table.

'Didn't you understand me? Don't you respect anybody's feelings but your own? I said *get out!*'

Her voice had risen so high in pitch that Garrett jumped to his feet, ready to step between them if they came to blows. Bridget felt a pain low down and fancied that the baby itself was eager for a fight. But, with a rueful glance at her daughter, Lady Courcey stood and turned towards the door.

Suddenly, Bridget gasped. She had felt the pain again but it was ten times worse than before. She clutched at her belly and staggered; Garrett darted to her side and kept her upright. Lady Courcey whipped around and came forwards, arms outstretched to help.

'No!' Bridget snapped, clenching her jaw against the awful ache that was intensifying deep within her. 'Leave me alone!'

'But the child,' her mother said in anguish. 'It is coming too soon. You need me here.'

'I...do not want...you here for this,' Bridget managed to say and then sank to the floor. Garrett knelt beside her, supporting her against his chest. He looked up at Lady Courcey.

'You had better leave,' he said. 'Seek out Lizzie and tell her to send for the midwife as swiftly as possible.'

Lady Courcey had probably never been asked to deliver a message in her life but she nodded and hastened from the room. Bridget moaned and Garrett rubbed her back in reassurance.

'Do not fret, the midwife will be here before long,' he murmured. 'Our baby will be fine. You have no need to worry.'

And the baby was fine. After a short, difficult labour, the little girl came into the world in the early hours of the following morning. Bridget, through a haze of tears and emotions, knew with a single glance at her daughter's golden head and blue eyes that, though everybody else might accept the child had been born premature, neither she nor Garrett could be in any doubt of the truth.

His disappointment was achingly palpable. He had desired an heir, of course, but she suspected he had also hoped this birth would mend the rift between them, bringing them closer together in the way a child sometimes could. With the reality so blatant in her features, the baby could only serve to widen that distance.

At first, Bridget feared his wrath would be so great that he would turn them out of the house. On reflection, however, she realised he would not be that imprudent – in society's eyes, his loving wife had just provided him with his firstborn child. Even so, he made no effort to return to her chamber after the birth. Society, after all, could not see beyond closed doors. There would be no cause for suspicion within the household; the servants would probably attribute his disinterest to the baby's inferior sex.

Bridget cared not one jot. She kissed her daughter's fingers, each one perfect in miniature detail. The little girl would have no grandmother and an indifferent father figure but Bridget had more than enough love to compensate for them both. Whatever had happened to Cormac, wherever he was, at least one piece of him – a tiny, beautiful, wondrous piece – was right here in her arms.

'I will cherish her for you,' she whispered. 'Our sweet, beloved Emily.'

## Chapter 8

Cormac was plodding along the street, minding his own business, when a rapid patter of footsteps came up behind him and he felt his blanket being ripped from his shoulders.

He swore, whirled around and grabbed for the end of the tattered blanket as it whipped away in the thief's grasp. He got a secure hold and yanked it back towards himself. The thief didn't let go but lost his balance and fell on the cobbles with a thump that foretold of imminent bruises on his backside.

Cormac halted in momentary shock when he realised his opponent was a youth with skin as dark as soot and one milky eye, which stood out starkly against the black around it. His astonishment at such a foreign vision dissipated as a tussle for control over the blanket ensued between them. They were as malnourished as each other but Cormac was taller and had the advantage of a standing position. He pulled with all his strength and the blanket jerked out of the would-be thief's hands. The youth fell onto his elbows, then scrambled backwards and hopped up. Before he could run, Cormac seized him by his ragged shirtfront and cuffed him about the ear.

'Try that again and I'll make your other eye milky too,' he growled.

The youth wrenched out of his grip and darted away, hollering obscenities in his wake. Cormac shouted a few of his own in return and stamped off in the opposite direction, swinging the blanket back over his shoulders.

After a year on the streets, every inch of it was stained with filth, it reeked even worse than himself, and it had become so threadbare that its protection from the elements was minimal. But it was the only possession he had and he was damned if he was going to relinquish it without a fight, especially with autumn coming to an end and winter's cold fingers beckoning once more.

He strode on, keeping his eyes trained on his feet. He made no apology when he bumped into a chimney sweep, causing him to drop his brushes, and disregarded the angry bellow of a coachman when he crossed the street in front of a carriage. The idea of good manners was laughable, and perhaps a very tiny part of him hoped to be mown down by the wheels of a carriage. It wasn't like he had anything to live for.

He paid no heed to where he was going until he registered the sound of a polished accent that could not belong to any of the lower class folk he customarily encountered. He raised his head and realised that he had meandered into a more affluent area of the city. The streets were clear of waste, the doorsteps were scrubbed clean, and people of elegance populated the footpaths. The voice he had heard originated from a dapper-looking gentleman smugly telling his companion about a property he had just sold for a handsome price.

'On Mountjoy Square, you know. The fool was so eager to buy. He didn't seem to grasp that the city's south side is the prime location now.'

The gentleman caught sight of Cormac and levelled a disdainful glare at him. Cormac averted his gaze, turning in towards the wall of a millinery shop as the two men passed by.

In general, he avoided these prosperous parts of Dublin. No one took much notice of him in the areas of extreme poverty, but in this neighbourhood his presence was highly objectionable and he risked being apprehended by a constable. Still, he was here now and a recklessness made him decide to try his luck. Though the shame of it nearly crippled him, he hunkered down next to the door of the millinery shop and cupped his hands into a gesture of supplication. The fingerless gloves had unravelled down to his knuckles and his nails were almost as black as those of the gloves' previous owner. Just as he was wondering whether the old man would have labelled this wisdom or folly, an elderly lady exited the shop accompanied by her maid, who carried a hat box.

Cormac raised his hands towards the lady. 'Begging you for a little help, m'lady,' he said humbly.

She clicked her tongue in repugnance and jerked her head at her maid. The girl vanished back into the shop and reappeared seconds later with the owner of the establishment. She was clutching a broom which she waved towards Cormac in a threatening manner.

'You get out of here right now,' she barked. 'This is a respectable business. I don't want you repelling my customers.'

Imagining he could hear the old man's hoarse chuckle, he slouched away. But he didn't admit defeat just yet. He found another spot, this one by the locked gates of a park in the centre of a fine square, where it soon became apparent that the gates could only be opened by residents of the square who possessed a private key. Though a chilly wind made the branches of the park's trees whip about, the weather was dry and several of the local inhabitants seemed disposed to go for their daily constitutional. Every time footsteps neared, he peered up meekly and muttered an entreaty for a morsel of assistance. The gentlefolk either ignored him or gave him the briefest look of disgusted accusation for daring to mar their view before continuing on into the park.

Until the two young ladies came along.

He heard the heels of their ankle boots clipping smartly on the path, their voices chirping about a new shawl which one of them had purchased and the other was admiring. He cast his beseeching glance upwards, started to mumble his plea, and froze.

He recognised them. At first, he could not recollect where and all he could see was Bridget's face floating before him. Then he realised why he connected her with them – they were two of the guests who had visited Oakleigh for Garrett Lambourne's birthday celebrations. He fished about in his memory for their names. Miss Wallace and Miss…Gardiner, maybe?

The details began to filter back to him with more clarity. The group of ladies had chosen to go for a stroll down the avenue, even though it had been a squally day. Miss Wallace had asked him about the weather and he had warned them of a shower due to come down very soon, at which point Miss Gardiner had flirted with him, making some coy remark about him getting wet. It had been an inconsequential exchange but he couldn't help feeling flattered that he had attracted her interest and that this had perhaps provoked a whisper of jealousy on Bridget's part.

His insides ached to recall a time when he had held some small value as a human being, when he had been more than mud under someone's shoe. He drew his cupped hands back, tucking them under his arms. He had no desire to invite these ladies' attention.

They had noticed him nonetheless. Miss Gardiner's gaze slid over him with a wrinkle of her nose but Miss Wallace's eyes glanced away and then snapped back to him in disbelief. He did not linger a second longer. He clambered to his feet and stalked away, shoulders bent and blanket pulled tight around his ears. He didn't look back and she certainly did not call after him.

She couldn't have recognised him, not looking the way he did. His hair fell to his shoulders now, unkempt and so grubby that its fair colour was obscured to a dirty shade of ash. He was unshaven, a bedraggled beard covering his jaw, and his clothes were shabby and soiled. He bore no resemblance to the clean, groomed stable hand with whom Miss Gardiner had flirted.

But his appearance had struck a chord of familiarity with Miss Wallace. Still, she wouldn't be able to place where she had seen him. At least, he sincerely hoped she wouldn't. The idea that she might remember the man he had once been made him want to scream with humiliation.

He pounded the Dublin streets back to more familiar territory, having learned his lesson that only trouble came from straying into the city's wealthier districts. He decided to make for the docklands, even though this was a somewhat perilous venture, given that on his last visit a week ago he had stolen a bottle of French wine out of an unattended crate that had just been unloaded from one of the docked boats. He had traded it at the back door of an inn for a cold, greasy chicken leg and half a loaf of bread – the innkeeper would offer him no more than that, deducing that he had obtained the wine by dishonest means. He hadn't cared; the food had been glorious and for once he had gone to sleep on a doorstep without the usual ache of hunger gnawing at his belly.

But that was a week past and he had been famished many times over since then, with only rancid scraps from alleyways to satisfy him. The potential at the docklands was worth the danger – he would just have to trust that no one would identify him as the pilferer of the wine. Tying his blanket around his waist to liberate his hands, he skulked around the quays and warehouses, keeping a keen eye out for sentries or cargo ripe for filching.

Several hours of patience yielded nothing but an encounter with some startled rats scurrying behind a row of barrels. Dusk arrived and the dockworkers departed, all goods safely stored or dispatched. Dispirited, he wandered along by the waterside, hands and feet frozen and stomach empty. He would have given anything for the warmth of a glowing fire in the hearth and a bowl of stirabout on the table.

Suddenly, he heard the crackle of a real fire close by. Peering down an alley between two warehouses, he discerned a group of three or four men clustered around a brazier which blazed with light and warmth. The men were holding their hands over the fire and passing around a bottle of whiskey, each one knocking back a mouthful before handing it on to his neighbour. Cormac could tell that they were not homeless; they wore good winter clothing, looked well-fed and had clean-shaven faces.

He knew he ought to move on. His experiences over the past year had established that the majority of Dublin's populace were not inclined to be friendly to strangers and he did not expect these men to be the exception. But the fire looked so inviting and his extremities felt so icy that he found his feet moving forwards almost of their own volition. He crept down the alley, his eyes transfixed on the leaping flames. At first, the men did not notice him, occupied as they were in their drinking and loud conversation.

'–made up some story about having a sick child,' one of them was saying. He was thickset and bull-necked with enormous hands that could easily wrap all the way around the whiskey bottle. 'Needed the money for medicine. I told him his priority was paying back Cunningham what he owed and after that he could buy all the medicine he wanted.'

'Too right,' a thin-lipped man agreed, accepting the bottle and drinking, then passing it on around the circle. 'It's his own fault if one of them brats gets sick. Shouldn't have had so many in the first place. Don't know how they all fit in that poky house.'

Cormac edged nearer, not taking care to keep concealed. If the men looked in his direction, they would see him at once. But just a few more steps would bring him into the circle of heat from the fire. His whole body quivered with anticipation.

'I said I'd be back tomorrow to collect the rest,' the first man continued, receiving the bottle once more and taking a large swig. 'And I'm telling yous, more fool him if he doesn't have it by then.'

He was raising the bottle for a second draught when he caught sight of Cormac lurking nearby.

'Oi! Get out of here,' he said with a careless wave.

Cormac didn't move.

'Didn't you hear me?' the man snapped. 'I said clear off!'

The others turned to see what nuisance was bothering their comrade. With a nasty grin, the thin-lipped one picked up a heavy stick, probably intended for firewood, and threw it at Cormac. It glanced off his shoulder and clattered to the ground. The blow didn't hurt much but it incensed him nonetheless; he was tired of being treated like a dog, like a piece of rubbish, like a nobody. He was still a person and he wanted to be recognised as one.

Anger erupting inside him, he lurched forwards and swung at the man who had thrown the stick. Surprised, the man did not duck out of the way in time and Cormac's fist connected solidly with his mouth. The man fell backwards against the brazier and the elbow of his coat caught fire. He yelled and batted at his arm to quench the sizzling material. The other men were stunned at the unexpected attack and, in the time it took for them to register what had happened, Cormac seized his chance to assail another fellow, pummelling him in the chest and stomach. He had lost all reason, he didn't know why he was doing this; he just knew that he was filled with rage and that he had to take it out on somebody.

But now the men were beginning to react. One of them grabbed him around the waist and tried to pull him off his companion. The thickset man who had first noticed him was still holding the whiskey bottle and he swung it at Cormac's head. He felt the impact of it on the back of his skull and saw stars. He let go of the man he had been punching and staggered. In the next moment, he was dragged to the ground and pinned there. His vision swam and then he saw the man with the bottle standing over him.

'You're going to regret doing that,' he hissed.

However, before anyone could act, they heard a smooth voice coming from the entrance to the alley.

'Now, now, Munroe. Do not make any rash decisions.'

The man with the bottle, Munroe, looked up quickly at a person beyond Cormac's field of sight. 'Mr Cunningham, sir. I didn't see you, sir.'

'That is evident,' came the voice again. 'Do explain to me what you are doing.'

'It was self-defence,' said Munroe, swift to make his case. 'He just came at us fists flying. Nearly knocked out Lawlor's teeth.'

'I see. And I suppose the stick just hit him of its own accord?'

Munroe looked mutinous at the patronising tone of the unseen person. 'What's it matter? He's homeless. No one's going to care if he gets battered.'

'*I* shall care,' the voice corrected him and, at Munroe's incredulous expression, said, 'One does not pass up an opportunity when it walks so freely into our midst. We have a need to replace O'Connor after recent unfortunate events. A homeless man is a desperate man, and a desperate man can be a useful man. Let him get up.'

The man pinning Cormac to the ground released him and hauled him to his feet. He shook his matted hair out of his eyes and got his first look at the owner of the smooth voice. Cunningham displayed an impeccable sense of fashion, dressed in a tall hat, tailored coat and elegant gloves. He had a slender moustache and, for a man who seemed to command so much power, was rather short. As he strolled down the alley towards the group, it became plain that he was at least a head shorter than anyone else present. Nonetheless, the other men shuffled backwards respectfully at his approach.

He came to a stop in front of Cormac and gazed up at him.

'What is your name?' he asked in the same silky tone.

'McGovern,' said Cormac, taking his cue from how the other men were addressed.

'When did you last have a hot meal?'

'I can't remember.'

'Where do you sleep?'

'Anywhere.'

'What would you be willing to do to improve your fortune?'

Cormac eyed him. What kind of underhand dealings was this man involved in?

'I don't know,' he said honestly.

Cunningham seemed pleased with his answer. 'If you will agree to work for me, I shall pay you in food and board. You will have a roof over your head, clean clothes and three meals a day. Do you accept?'

'That depends,' Cormac said, with more bravery than he felt. He did not want to anger this powerful man but he also did not want to enter into the agreement blindly. 'What d'you do for a living?'

'I am a money lender,' Cunningham replied.

A number of things became clear to Cormac then. He now understood the conversation that Munroe had been having with his fellows before they spotted him. He fully comprehended how Cunningham was able to exude the authority that he did. He had a fair idea of what his own role would entail. And he knew that he was too weak, cold and hungry to refuse.

He nodded and Cunningham clapped his hands together once. 'Excellent. Munroe, take him back to the lodgings and get him cleaned up. He can start as soon as he has had a decent meal and a rest.'

Munroe, who was still fuming that his quarry had been snatched away from him, seized Cormac by the upper arm and marched him back up the alley. The rest of the men followed except for Cunningham. As Cormac exited the alley, he glimpsed the man staring down thoughtfully into the brazier, the light of the flames dancing across his face.

## Chapter 9

Cormac questioned the wisdom of his decision until a full plate of food was placed in front of him, and then he was too busy devouring it to ponder over right and wrong. He didn't even notice what he was eating, he just knew that it was hot and that it tasted better than anything he had ever eaten in his life. When he had satisfied his appetite, he was shown to a starkly-furnished room – no more than a narrow bed, a chair and a stained mirror on the wall – where he was able to bathe and shave, relieve himself in a chamber pot, and dress in a set of fresh clothes. After months and months of grime, it was overwhelming to feel so clean.

Among his discarded, ragged garments, he espied the threadbare blanket which he had guarded so fiercely for the past year. He fingered its frayed edges, the coarse material familiar and unpleasant to the touch. With a grunt, he tossed it into a corner of the room, intending to throw it on the fire as soon as the opportunity presented itself. Then, once he had brushed through his tangled hair, he collapsed on the bed, whose hard mattress felt like a carpet of clouds, and fell asleep without the dread that he might freeze to death before the morning.

But he was aware that this salvation came at a price and the next day he discovered just what he was willing to do to 'improve his fortune'.

He had hardly dressed when Munroe banged on the door of his room and stalked in.

'Take this,' he said, shoving a long, slim object into his hands.

He found himself holding a leather scabbard, from which he withdrew a dagger, plain apart from its sharp and gleaming blade. He stared down at it.

'Hide it inside your coat,' Munroe instructed. 'You might be needing it later.'

He fumbled as he slid the sheathed dagger into a pocket sewn into the lining of his coat, feeling very uncomfortable at the thought of carrying such a weapon. Why did Munroe believe he might need it? He tried to put it out of his mind as they left the lodgings but it was hard to forget when he could feel its constant pressure against his chest.

Munroe led him through a labyrinth of cobbled streets, many of which he recognised. He marvelled at the fact that, having previously stumbled along them in deep despair, he was now able to stride down them with some sense of purpose.

They turned onto a narrow street lined with cramped houses on both sides and came to a stop halfway down in front of a particularly grubby building. The brickwork was discoloured and the filthy windows had numerous broken or missing panes of glass. A scruffy child dawdled on the doorstep; when he saw Munroe and Cormac, he squeaked and vanished into the house.

'Just follow my lead,' Munroe said and approached the door, where another figure had appeared, presumably the boy's father. He wasn't a small man but fear hunched him over and he looked insignificant next to the strapping build of Munroe. He tried to block their way but Munroe pushed him aside and marched indoors. Cormac trailed after him with deep misgivings.

Munroe settled himself at a cluttered table in the kitchen and began rummaging through assorted bits of crockery, sewing, rags, and other domestic articles as though they were his own possessions. Cormac lingered awkwardly just inside the kitchen door. The man came in after them; he glared at Munroe but his hands were clutched together in profound anxiety. The child from the doorstep crept in too but the man pushed him out again.

'Go upstairs,' he hissed. 'And keep the others away too.'

The boy remained in the gap of the doorway, seeming like he was going to disobey his father, but the man reached out to smack him and he ran away down the hall. Cormac heard his feet thumping up the stairs, muffled voices in a room above, and then silence.

Munroe looked up at the man with an expression of severe disappointment. 'My eyesight must be getting worse, Doyle. For the life of me, I can't see any money set aside here for Mr Cunningham at all. Unless you have it hiding in a safe place somewhere else in the house? Do we need to search for it?'

Doyle shook his head.

'I remember saying I'd be back for it today,' said Munroe in a placid tone. 'D'you remember me saying that?'

The man nodded.

'Then where is it?'

Doyle's answer came out in barely more than a whisper. 'You might also remember the other part of that conversation where I told you I didn't have it.'

Munroe's eyes glittered with anger. 'Don't get mouthy with me,' he said, all pretence at civility disappearing in a second. 'You owe Mr Cunningham and we're not leaving 'til your debt's been paid.'

'I told you already, my daughter's ill. We need all our money to pay for her medicine. Without it, she might—'

'I don't give a damn about your daughter,' Munroe retorted, knocking over his chair as he shot to his feet. 'Makes no difference to me if she lives or dies. What I care about is ensuring Mr Cunningham's happy, and what'd make him happiest right now is to see the money you borrowed two months ago in his hand again. With the interest, of course.'

He moved closer to Doyle until they were only inches apart.

'Give me one more week,' said Doyle, his voice shaking.

Munroe's massive hands darted out and closed around Doyle's throat.

'Mr Cunningham gave you a second chance,' he snarled, 'and he never gives a third. If you can't give us money, we'll have to take something else that's worth the same value. What about your pretty wife? How much d'you think we'd get for her if we sold her to a brothel?'

Doyle's eyes bulged and he tried to speak but he could only make a choking sound with Munroe blocking his windpipe.

Throughout this exchange, Cormac had stood tensely by the door, feeling more and more unsure about his decision to accept Cunningham's offer. Munroe's behaviour was despicable. He supposed that threats were the only way a money lender could guarantee a return on his loans but was he, Cormac, capable of stooping to that level? Could he do this for a living?

He heard a muted whimper and looked down. A small, curly-haired boy, no more than two years old, had appeared in the doorway. His thumb was in his mouth and he gazed up at Cormac with wide, frightened eyes. He could not see Munroe and Doyle behind the door but the sounds his father was making were enough for him to know that he should be terrified of these strangers in his home.

Cormac had two choices. He could turn away from this scene, walk out the door and never return to Cunningham's lodgings, or he could assist Munroe in the task he had been assigned to do. In the first scenario, he would maintain his integrity but be back on the streets for his troubles. In the second, he would be able to hold on to the basic comforts of food and quarters which he had only just acquired, but he would run the risk of compromising his moral values in the process. Would he survive if he ended up homeless again, facing into another winter? Would he still be himself if he followed through this current situation to its resolution? What should he do?

An icy blast of wind through a broken window pane in the kitchen resolved his dilemma. He pulled his hidden dagger from its scabbard, dragged the small boy into view, and placed the blade at the boy's neck. Munroe and Doyle swivelled around and Doyle nearly fainted at the sight of his son being held at knife point. He shook his head frantically.

'All he needs is a little incentive, Munroe,' Cormac said in a low voice. 'Let him go so he can speak.'

Munroe relaxed his grip on Doyle's neck and the man took in deep, ragged breaths.

'Please,' he croaked. 'Please don't hurt him.'

'Tell us where the money is and I won't.'

Doyle put out a pleading hand. 'I'm begging you, don't do this.'

'Give us what you owe,' said Munroe, 'and he won't have to.'

Cormac contemplated the desperate man and then moved the dagger so that the tip of it was pressing into the boy's skin. The child began to wail. Anxious talking broke out above them before someone came running down the stairs. A young woman burst into the kitchen, wild-eyed at the sight before her.

'No!' she shrieked and stretched her arms out for the child, but Cormac jerked him out of her reach.

'Ye can have him back,' he shouted over the boy's cries, 'soon as we get what we came for.'

'Just give it to them!' the woman screamed at Doyle.

He scrabbled in the drawer of a dresser behind him, withdrew a teapot and fished out some money from inside it. He handed it over to Munroe and Cormac let go of the boy immediately. The woman snatched him up and buried her face in his curls.

Doyle stared at Cormac with bitterness. 'You didn't murder my son but you've probably killed my daughter. That was all the money we had left.'

'Mr Cunningham doesn't run a charity,' Munroe said and strode out of the kitchen.

Cormac followed, resisting the urge to look back at the devastation he had caused. Before today, he would never have believed himself capable of doing such a thing. But, faced once more with the prospect of destitution, he had committed a merciless, unscrupulous act that left him unrecognisable to himself. Disgust flooded through him and it was all he could do not to be sick on Doyle's doorstep.

'Nice work, McGovern,' Munroe said as they reached the top of the street. 'Cunningham'll be pleased with you. Looks like you're going to fit right in.'

Back at the lodgings, Cormac escaped to his room as soon as he could. Once the door was shut behind him, he dashed to the basin he had used yesterday for shaving and vomited into it. Crawling to his bed, he found he did not have the energy to pull himself up onto it so he just sat on the floor and leaned against the bed frame, legs weak and hands shaking.

He had just killed someone. If the daughter's condition truly was life-threatening, and should Doyle prove unable to procure the money from somewhere else to pay for her medicine, then Cormac's actions would be the major contributing factor to her death. He would be no less culpable had he gone upstairs and driven the dagger into her heart.

He pressed his fists into his temples. He was the lowest of human beings – he had inflicted pain upon others in order to deflect it from himself. If there was any humanity left in him, he would take that money and return it to the people who so badly needed it. Cunningham could manage without it. He should not have insisted that the loan be repaid at a time when the Doyle family could least afford it.

But Cormac quailed at the thought of defying Cunningham. At the very least, he would be thrown back onto the streets to starve and freeze again. If Cunningham was in a murderous mood – and Cormac was in no doubt that the money lender was capable of murder – then he might even lose his own life. What had happened to O'Connor, the man he had replaced? What 'unfortunate events' had Cunningham alluded to? An accident? Or an execution?

Part of him could not fathom how he had allowed himself to become embroiled in such sordid company. But another part remembered the alternative: the constant pain of an empty stomach…the agony of a cold so deep it went right through to his bones…the intense loneliness…the fear that he might die in a gutter and no one would bother to notice. He glanced at the tattered blanket, still puddled in the corner of the room. He could not return to that existence. He just could not.

Self-loathing surged within him. He knew he was being a coward, but his instinct for survival was even stronger than his compassion for others in distress. He did not attempt to justify it to himself. There was no point saying that almost any other person in this situation would have done the same. No point hoping that the Doyles had a friendly neighbour who might be able to help them. He had done a terrible deed and he could not deny it.

With a tremendous effort, he struggled to his knees and then to his feet. He looked into the mirror opposite him, his image visible despite the blemishes and cracks on the glass. His vivid blue eyes stared back, haunted by his appalling conduct. His shoulder-length fair hair, now that it had been washed, revealed once more that distinctive shade that only he and his sister Mary, out of all the McGovern children, had inherited from their father. What would Jack McGovern say if he stood before his son right now?

Cormac recalled the Grace of God Mission Society and their precondition for offering aid to the poor. He may as well have taken their soup when he had had the chance. He had lost himself anyway.

He stepped up to the mirror and drove his fist into the centre of it. Shards of glass scattered all over the floor.

## Chapter 10

The baby's wailing pervaded the nursery, high-pitched and hysterical.

'Oh, Emily,' Bridget crooned, swaying her daughter in her arms. 'Shush, don't fret, shush, shush.'

Her muscles ached; at six months, Emily was a plump, solid mass of flailing limbs. Bridget transferred the writhing body to her other hip and continued to murmur pacifying reassurances.

'You can entrust her to me, mistress,' the nurse said, hands outstretched, and there was more than a hint of 'I know better what to do with babies' in her tone.

Bridget remained polite. Mrs Crewe was only trying to fulfil the duties of her position, though it was one to which she had been appointed on Garrett's instruction and without Bridget's approval. 'Thank you, but no. I want to be able to calm her myself.'

Mrs Crewe's mouth compressed into a straight line. She could not seem to comprehend why a gently-bred lady would wish to concern herself with the messier side of raising children. Far better to surrender the child to a person of experience and only take her back once she had become quiet again.

But Bridget had promised herself from the start that she would not be one of those mothers. *She* would be the woman to raise her daughter, not a hired stranger, and she would cherish every aspect of that bond, from the gurgling laughter to the ear-splitting screams. Furthermore – Mrs Crewe's face had transformed into a picture of horror when she had been made aware of it – Bridget would require no wet nurse to feed her child. Some would consider it positively vulgar, but the sensation of her daughter's mouth suckling her breast was a marvellous wonder to her and not for one moment would she entertain the notion of giving it up for the sake of society's conventions.

However, she did rely otherwise on Mrs Crewe for her extensive knowledge and advice, for she had to concede that she knew very little about negotiating the intricacies of motherhood. She could remember when Maggie McGovern had given birth to Bronagh but she had been only seven at the time and had paid no attention to how Maggie had carried out critical tasks such as changing her soiled clothing or putting her to sleep.

On that point, even Mrs Crewe was struggling today. Emily shrieked and bawled with no sign of stopping, leaving Bridget with the desperate wish that her baby could speak and tell her what was the matter. She had been cleaned and fed and her temperature had seemed normal when Mrs Crewe had checked her forehead for fever. There appeared to be nothing wrong except that her small, red face was screwed up in unexplained distress.

When Bridget shifted Emily's weight again, Mrs Crewe's fingers convulsed.

'Would you mind very much leaving us alone?' Bridget asked her, striving for forbearance. 'I should like to accomplish this unaided, if you understand me.'

Clearly, Mrs Crewe did not understand at all, but she could not contradict her employer.

'As you say, mistress,' she said with forced composure and withdrew from the nursery looking aggrieved.

As soon as she was gone, Bridget let out a moan at the pain in her arms.

'Oh, Emily, Emily,' she said. 'Tell your mama what's amiss, my little gooseberry.'

She walked around the room while Emily continued to cry. With a glance at the closed nursery door, she bent her lips close to her daughter's ear. She started by speaking the prayers but switched to singing them, attaching an invented melody to give them a soothing quality and rocking Emily to the rhythm of the words. Over and over she recited the Our Father and the Hail Mary in the guttural lyricism of the Irish language. She was able to recall all of the Our Father but, to her chagrin, her memory could not summon up the full text of the Hail Mary. Every time she reached '*Tá an Tiarna leat*', she reluctantly had to skip the next two lines and go on to '*A Naomh Mhuire, a Mháthair Dé*'. Of course, there was no one in this country from whom she could seek illumination. For good measure, she crooned it all the way through in English as well.

Whether the prayers worked or Emily had simply tired herself out, she gradually grew quiet and nodded off, a slumbering boulder in Bridget's embrace. Thankful, Bridget laid the little girl into her cradle with infinite gentleness. Then she slipped her hand beneath the corner of the mattress and withdrew the wooden bird. It was an exceptional example of workmanship, a skilled carving of a bird about to break into song. She opened Emily's small fist and tucked the bird into it, letting the tiny fingers stretch across the bird's wing.

'Your papa wishes you a pleasant sleep,' she whispered.

She knew she could not get away with the sentiment for very long. Once Emily began to understand words, she would become confused if Bridget continued to make such oblique references to Cormac. But for now Bridget could console herself. And in the future, the bird would merely be a wooden toy of Emily's – she would not need to know where it had come from.

It was for Cormac that Bridget spoke the prayers, not wanting Emily to lose sight of the Irishness in her that came so much from her father. After the birth, Bridget had momentarily considered giving her an Irish name but then had thought better of it. Garrett knew Emily was not his, and knew it more each day as her eyes remained that astonishing blue and her golden curls grew in abundance. Bestowing an Irish name upon her as well would have rubbed salt in his wounds, which might have been no more than he deserved, but every single person of her acquaintance would have found it peculiar. Besides, Emily was a beautiful name.

Bridget stared down at the little girl. Where was her papa now? How Bridget yearned to know. Hope had risen in her a mere week before when a letter had arrived from Ireland, the address written in an unfamiliar hand. She had opened it with trembling fingers – would it contain information concerning Cormac's whereabouts? Was she moments from learning how to find him? Would she be able to get a message to him?

She had scanned the page swiftly, eager for good news. It had been penned by a Deacon Haybury who led the Grace of God Mission Society in Dublin. He could confirm that a young man called Cormac who fitted the description in Bridget's letter of enquiry had entered their building almost a year ago. Deacon Haybury himself had offered Cormac the chance to save his soul, but he had refused. The deacon could not say where the young man had gone next. He wished he could have been of more help, both to herself and to Cormac.

Bridget had pressed the letter to her breast and shed tears of relief and despair. To learn even this much – that Cormac had still been alive less than twelve months ago, that he had made it to Dublin – felt like a blessing, and yet the knowledge left her no better off than before. It had brought her to a dead end, just like all the other letters. Cormac was no nearer to her, no more tangible than the wooden bird carving.

The baby's fingers squeezed reflexively around the body of the bird. After leaving it there for a few minutes longer, Bridget eased it out of her grasp and slid it back under the mattress, hiding it from view. She kissed Emily's forehead and stole out of the nursery.

The nurse had lingered in the hallway and looked startled at her appearance, as if she had been caught listening at the keyhole.

'I just wanted to stay within earshot, mistress,' she said quickly. 'In case you called for my assistance.'

'Thank you, Mrs Crewe. She is sleeping now but I would be grateful if you would watch over her while I go speak with my husband on another matter.'

Mrs Crewe dipped her head in compliance and sidled back into the nursery.

Bridget walked down the long, cold corridor, shivering as a draught from a nearby window slithered across the nape of her neck. They were at Swifton Hall, the country seat of the Wyndham title and the home where Garrett had grown up. This was her first visit but she suspected there would not be many. As they had drawn near to the estate, she had sensed his whole body tautening like a length of rope stretched to its outermost limit. His mother had died here when he was a boy but she knew no more than that; he rarely spoke of Swifton Hall and never of his mother. The only reason they were here now was that Lord Wyndham had asked them to stay for the hunting and Christmas seasons and Garrett felt he could not refuse, given that Lord Wyndham had never voiced any objection to his son and daughter-in-law occupying the London townhouse on a full-time basis. The lord was out riding with his hounds at present but Garrett had remained behind today, informing Bridget that he wished to speak with her after luncheon. As though they were conducting a meeting of business, she had agreed to see him at three o'clock.

She found him sitting at a desk in the library, the fire in the hearth unable to penetrate the room beyond its meagre circle of warmth. She took up a position with her back to it and watched him peruse a document, the line of a frown creasing his brow.

'You desired to speak with me,' she eventually prompted when he made no effort to acknowledge her presence.

He waited a few seconds more before raising his gaze to hers, a childish attempt to assert his authority. 'I did,' he said and, unexpectedly, went on, 'I wanted to wish you a happy birthday.'

She had not forgotten the day but she had been certain he had.

'Oh,' she said. 'Thank you.'

'I have something for you.'

A birthday gift? Another surprise. She felt awkward about accepting it, considering the strained atmosphere that had burgeoned between them since Emily's birth, until he held out the document he had been reading. She approached the desk, puzzled, and took it from him. A quick glance at it explained all.

'Oh,' she said again, her voice harder.

He leaned back in his chair. 'It cannot have escaped your notice that twenty-one is a significant birthday for you.'

With all her thoughts absorbed in caring for Emily, it had, but she wasn't prepared to admit that. She shrugged.

'You now legally inherit the Oakleigh Estate and the Courcey title. Which means we have some papers to sign.' He gestured at the document.

She looked down at it. 'What exactly does this say?'

'It confers the guardianship of Oakleigh onto your mother in perpetuity.

She will continue to be responsible for supervising the estate on your behalf, along with the assistance of the agent, Mr Enright, and you will have no need to concern yourself with it.'

She turned away from him and went back to the heat of the fire, still clutching the document but disregarding its contents. Her heart fluttered in her chest. Oakleigh was hers. By rights, she could assume the title of Lady Courcey this very day and take charge of the estate.

She felt like an imprisoned bird whose cage door had been unlocked. She was free to fly out through that opening and take wing with Emily to Ireland. Such an action could not be viewed as desertion; she would merely be fulfilling the legal obligation of her position.

Oakleigh was a place of agonising memories, there was no doubt about that. But it had also been where she had spent her childhood, a truly happy time when she had been surrounded by friendly faces and picturesque countryside. It was *home* and it would be a joy to raise Emily there.

Moreover, she was certain she would relish the challenge of managing the estate, of attending to her tenants' affairs and overseeing the productivity of the land. And she could not forget that that was the role her father had intended for her once it had become clear there would be no sons in the family.

The one setback which might clip her wing and knock her out of the sky was that her mother still lived at Oakleigh. Could she contemplate sharing a home with her, after the transgressions she had committed? No, she could not. She would have to send her away, perhaps to occupy the Dublin townhouse in Merrion Square again. Turning her out with nowhere to go would be a sweet serving of poetic justice but Bridget supposed she was not that ruthless. In any case, she would have no need of the townhouse, not when she and Emily would be more than content to spend all their time in the heart of the country. It was an enchanting image and, astoundingly, it was within her reach.

She looked at Garrett where he still sat behind his desk, arms folded as he stared at her. As her husband, he had every power to compel her to do what he wanted because, in marrying him, she had rescinded her privilege to administer her property in her own right. She would need to determine the best way to negotiate her path to freedom.

'May I have some time to think about this?' she said.

'What is there to think about?'

'I must consider the terms carefully. After all, I have a duty to my tenants and to the legacy left to me by my father —'

'Take all the time you need,' he interrupted, his voice smooth. 'But allow me to assist you in your "decision". I am by no means disposed to permit my wife to live apart from me, not only on a different estate but in a different country. If, however, you choose to persist in that intention then be aware that Emily will remain in England with me.'

All of the air leaked out of her lungs. She inhaled to refill them but still struggled for breath. 'Are you…are you capable of callousness of that magnitude?'

'I am.'

'Why would you want her to stay, when you know…'

He narrowed his eyes. 'I want a son, a child of my own. And I cannot very well achieve that goal without my wife, can I? To keep you here, I must keep her here.'

He delivered this with a coldness more severe than the chilly air of the library. She stalked back to the desk and tossed the paper on its surface. He had forced her hand.

'I'll sign it. Of course I will,' she said, with no little frostiness of her own.

A look of grim satisfaction crossed his face. 'No time like the present.'

He passed her a pen. She came around to his side of the desk, dipped the pen in the inkpot, and signed at the bottom of the document. He took the pen from her and signed his own name, her authorisation not being complete without his signature.

'There is one more thing,' he said when she made a move to leave. His satisfied look had disappeared and the contour of his jaw had stiffened. 'Your mother's solicitor sent me all the records relating to Oakleigh and the entailment on the estate.'

'Fascinating reading material, I'm sure.'

'I have examined the stipulations of the entail in detail. You must already be aware, given your own position as heiress, that the inheritance of Oakleigh is governed by male-preference primogeniture.'

She raised her eyebrows.

'It was an extraordinary decision by your ancestors. Quite unorthodox. But it means that in the event of there being no male issue, the birthright will pass to any female progeny of the title holder. Hence…'

'Emily will inherit Oakleigh,' she said, awed.

'If we do not have any sons,' he finished, decidedly unimpressed.

She had an overwhelming urge to laugh. No doubt her great-grandfather had never envisaged a scenario like this when Oakleigh first came into existence. But, as it turned out, the daughter of a stable hand could someday preside over one of the finest properties in Ireland.

She was prevented from saying anything further by the sound of frantic running and the appearance of a servant in the doorway to the library. He looked ashen and dishevelled, quite out of line with the meticulous standards of Swifton Hall's staff.

'Sir, beg pardon!' he gasped. 'I must tell you —'

Garrett got to his feet. 'What is it?' he demanded.

'It's his l-lordship!' The servant gulped. 'We were on the hunt and I s-saw him clutch at his chest afore…afore he fell from his horse. I'm so sorry, m'lord.'

'M'lord'. The only way Garrett could be addressed thus was if his father was dead.

Garrett turned to Bridget. 'I need you,' he said, sounding surprised. Then his knees buckled.

## Chapter 11

Cormac twirled the dagger lazily, weaving it back and forth between his fingers. The wine merchant's eyes followed the blade, mesmerised by the sinuous motion.

'Ten pounds,' said Cormac.

The merchant licked his lips. 'I have five. I can give you the rest next week.'

'Ten,' said Cormac. 'Today.'

They sat on either side of a table in a dingy corner of the merchant's warehouse, stacks of empty crates all around them. Cormac's feet were propped up on the tabletop, casually crossed at the ankles, while the merchant's palms were splayed out on the rough surface.

'I'm due a shipment before the end of May,' he said in a pleading tone. 'It'll bring in money for me. Just one more week, that's all I'm asking for.'

Cormac's gaze was enough to make the merchant shrink back in his chair. He swung his feet to the ground, went around to the other side of the table, and sat on its edge.

'Are you left-handed or right-handed?'

The merchant blinked. 'Wh-what?'

Cormac repeated the question.

'Why?'

'I'm just trying to decide whether to be generous and take your bad hand instead of your good one.'

The merchant jerked his hands behind his back, leaving sweaty marks on the tabletop. 'No!'

'You're not leaving me with much of a choice. Mr Cunningham was very clear. The full amount with interest today or a penalty for the delay. He wasn't specific on the details but I've got an active imagination.'

He wrenched on the man's right arm, twisting it to expose the blue veins on his wrist, and pressed the sharp edge of the dagger to his flesh. The merchant cowered, his body nearly slipping off the chair as he sank further down into it, his arm outstretched in Cormac's iron grip.

'Please, no…' he whimpered.

'D'you have an alternative proposal? Ten pounds perhaps?'

The blade glided over the skin and beads of blood bubbled up and trickled down the sides of the man's wrist.

'I don't have the money! But I will when the shipment comes in, I swear!'

Cormac eyed the tip of the dagger, now shining red. 'Big shipment, is it?'

'Yes!' the merchant said, head bobbing eagerly. 'I'll be able to get the other five pounds for you as soon as it arrives.'

'I think we can do better than that, don't you?'

He wasn't long in making it back to the lodgings after that.

'Smart lad, this one is!' Munroe hollered to the other men who lounged around the dining area of the lodgings, enjoying their drinks and the attentions of the scantily-clad girls draped about them. Cormac sat on a bench wolfing down his meal and did not react when Munroe clapped him on the shoulder.

'Got the five pounds today and half of the shipment's profits next week. Far better outcome than the original ten. I'm telling yous, no one gets past this fellow!'

The men cheered and raised glasses to Cormac. He shrugged and said nothing.

'Cunningham was well pleased to hear it. Here you go.' Munroe placed a tumbler of first-rate whiskey on the table in front of Cormac with a flourish. 'Compliments of the chief himself.'

Cormac didn't reach out to take it. 'What'd he say when you told him?'

'That it was a lucky day when Lawlor threw that stick at you.' Munroe grinned. 'You've really made a name for yourself now. Might be someday soon you'll advance to the upper ranks.'

After a year and a half, Cormac was still a lower henchman, doing the grunt work. But Cunningham had a small ring of men around him, including Munroe, who handled mysterious dealings the underlings knew nothing about. Cormac suspected it involved giving loans to more respectable members of society, which required a level of intellect and discretion not found in your average lackey. A promotion to that level would indeed be a sign of faith in his abilities.

Munroe thrust the glass towards him. 'Take your time and enjoy. You've earned it.'

Cormac swallowed the drink in one, ignoring the burning sensation in his throat, and pushed himself up from the bench. 'Thanks. See you tomorrow.'

In his room, he lined up the plank against the back of the door and started practising. Every thunk of the blade into the wood was satisfying to his ears. He stood further back and aimed again. The dagger sailed through the air and lodged halfway up the plank. It wasn't quite where he had intended it to land, but he could feel the effects of the whiskey dulling his dexterity as the alcohol spread through his body.

A raucous roar drifted up from the dining area below. The men were settling in for the evening, boisterous after the news of his success with the wine merchant – no doubt a crate from the shipment's profits would end up in the lodgings for their consumption. Such bounty would go a long way towards easing their resentment of his unsociable behaviour. Not that he cared much for popularity anyway. He had their respect and that was enough.

He yanked the dagger out of the plank, remembering the similar force he had used on the merchant's arm. It was likely he had sprained the man's elbow, an injury more damaging than the shallow cut on his wrist. But the fool had resisted longer than Cormac had expected. He must not have been acquainted with the reputation that preceded Cunningham's man McGovern – most people he threatened were already aware that he was capable of terrorising a small child. They were the ones who succumbed to his demands most quickly. Then again, the merchant had probably found the devil he met today difficult to reconcile with the affable fellow full of pleasantries he had encountered when he came to Cunningham looking for help. Who would have believed that such a friendly chap would be willing to draw a blade on a man in dire trouble?

It was a poor way to repay him, Cormac supposed. Although he could not be certain, he was reasonably confident that the warehouse had been the same one from which he had stolen a bottle of wine a year and a half ago. The trade for that wine had staved off his hunger for a night – in token of that, a person of compassion might have viewed the confrontation with the merchant as an occasion to be lenient. But that was not how the world of money lending worked. If he had shown one sign of weakness, Cunningham's response would have been a ruthless punishment instead of a tumbler of whiskey.

Just as he threw the dagger again, a knock on the door disturbed his concentration. The shot went wild and the flat side of the dagger struck the wall before clattering to the floor. He cursed and bent to retrieve it, then removed the plank and opened the door. One of the half-clothed girls from the dining area stood there, one hand on her hip, the other resting on the door jamb. She had long, black hair and full lips which were quirked into a suggestive smile. Her breasts bulged above the low neckline of her bodice, bursting to escape it.

'What d'you want?' he said roughly.

'I'm a gift,' she said. 'From the men below. They thought you deserved a reward for your hard work today.'

'Not interested.'

'Ah, now, don't go hurting a girl's feelings. Come on, you'll enjoy it.'

He started to close the door but she said quickly, 'Wait!'

He paused, levelling her with a gaze of absolute indifference.

'If I go down right away, they'll take the money back. Can I just come inside for a few minutes? I promise I'll leave after that. We can say you couldn't wait to finish.' She grinned.

He gave an irritated nod, let her in, and shut the door.

She sidled over to the bed and sat on the edge of it. He made a point of taking the chair by the window and laid the dagger on the windowsill.

'I'm Thomasina.'

He didn't offer his own name.

She looked at the scars on the plank. 'You've got good aim.'

'I'm working on it.'

She leaned back on her hands. Her open-fronted skirt was designed to show off pretty petticoats but, as she suffered from a deficiency of these, it revealed her stockings and a substantial amount of bare thigh instead. The end of a short shift was a negligible attempt to protect her modesty.

'Sounds like you're a man to be feared, according to the stories downstairs.'

He didn't bother to reply.

'How come you never hang about down below? Good-looking fellow such as yourself, all us girls have been eyeing you for months. I'd to fight the others off to get this job.'

'I like my solitude.'

She squinted at him. 'Is that really it? Or would you prefer if my name was Thomas?'

He frowned. 'No.'

'Just checking.'

She stood and wandered over to the window. One of her shift's diaphanous sleeves slipped down, baring the curve of her white shoulder.

'I like this time of year, when it's so late but there's still a bit of brightness in the sky. Look at that, past nine o'clock and I can still see down into the alleyway.' She turned to him. 'You ever been with a girl?'

'Why d'you ask?'

'I thought maybe you're afraid. But I'm good with the virgins. I can show you what to do.'

She was being persistent, he had to give her credit for that. 'No need to worry yourself.'

'So you have. Who was she? Not anyone in this building, that's for sure. Those hussies would be boasting about it if they had.'

He was silent.

'Go on, tell me. Have there been many? Or just one? Ah, I think just the one.'

She was reading his face too well and he didn't like it.

'Did you love her?'

'Can we change the subject?'

'That's a yes anyway. Did she love you or did you take advantage?'

That riled him up. 'I'd never—!'

'I hear you, calm down. Where's she now?'

He looked away. 'Not here.'

'That's good to know. I was thinking of checking under the bed. D'you still love her?'

'I'd like you to leave now.'

'Just a little longer. I don't want them to doubt whether it happened. Even if you were very quick, there'd usually be a bit of time afterwards to catch our breath.' She touched his arm. 'So you do still love her. How'd you come to be apart?'

'I'm not answering any more questions. You talk too much.'

'Well, you know the easiest way to get me to stop talking, don't you?'

She slid into his lap and he surprised himself by not protesting. Maybe it was the whiskey. Or maybe he was just goddamned lonely.

She ran her fingers through his hair. She smelled of smoke and sweat but there was something sweet there too, her natural female scent. She leaned in closer so that her round lips brushed his earlobe.

'They paid the full amount. You can do whatever you want. If you want to.' She wriggled in his lap and giggled as his body responded. 'And I think you do.'

To hell with it.

He pulled her to him and covered her mouth with his. She was quick to react, straddling him and rising up so that her hair fell like a curtain around his face. Their tongues stroked together and he savoured the feeling of connecting with another human being in a way other than threats and violence; it had no foundation in sincerity or sentiment but he told himself that didn't matter. He squeezed the fleshy mounds of her breasts while her own hands delved downwards, expertly negotiating buttons and fall to gain access. Her explorations were thorough, eliciting a ragged intake of breath from him as sensation overcame reason.

He stood and she wrapped her legs around his hips. He carried her over to the bed and laid her down on it.

'D'you have any preferences?' she asked.

She rolled onto her stomach, tossed back her skirt to expose shapely buttocks, and peeked over her shoulder with a coquettish wink. He caught hold of her hip and flipped her onto her back again.

'A traditionalist,' she said and for an instant seemed rather shy, as though she was not used to performing the act face to face. She opened her legs to entice him in and he accepted her invitation.

He just wanted to forget about everything in his life and focus on this one instant of reckless abandon. But the memories tugged at him, buzzing in his mind like insistent flies. Instead of a bed, a haystack. Instead of black hair, chestnut curls. Instead of lust, love. God, this was wrong. He was using the girl. And betraying Bridget in the process. But he was never going to see her again. And he was certain her bed was not empty.

It was anger which powered him through to the end. He groaned and fell to the side. She stretched like a cat.

'There now, don't you feel better?'

She could not be further from the truth. He closed his eyes. 'Get out.'

'Y'know, I thought you'd be rougher.' Her hands crept across his chest. 'It's half price if you want a second go.'

He opened his eyes and slapped her hands away. She stared at him, goggling.

'I said get out,' he growled.

'Fine, I can tell when I'm not wanted,' she said, even though that had patently not been the case for most of their encounter.

She started to slither off the bed but he seized her ankle to hold her back.

'Ow, that hurts!' she protested.

He pinched harder, making her squeak in pain.

'Nothing that's been said or done goes outside this room, d'you understand me? There'll be no sniggering with your companions later. And I don't want to see you or any of them darken my door again, d'you hear?'

He glanced over at the dagger which rested on the windowsill. For the first time, she looked fearful. She nodded and he released his grip. She straightened her clothes and darted from the room like she couldn't leave his presence fast enough.

He slid off the bed and went over to the window. He gazed at the blade for a moment. Then he picked it up, turned, and hurled it at the closed door. It landed exactly at the height of Thomasina's head.

## Chapter 12

Emily tottered towards Bridget, crying, 'Birdie! Birdie!' and waving her wooden bird gaily above her head. Bridget laughed and swept her up and around in the air.

'You can fly like the birdie too!' she exclaimed.

Emily shrieked with delight. 'Again!'

Bridget swung her around once more and then they collapsed together on the floor of the nursery in Wyndham House, her skirts billowing about them. She panted for breath; having just celebrated her second birthday, Emily was a ball of energy and every single day was an inquisitive, exhausting adventure of discovery.

Without warning, the door opened and Garrett appeared on the threshold. Bridget's heart lurched and she threw the hem of her gown over Emily's hand, concealing the object she grasped. Emily deemed this to be an entertaining lark and proceeded to crawl entirely beneath her mother's skirts.

Bridget glanced back at Garrett. Had he seen the bird? She thought not; he expressed no sign of recognition or anger. He advanced into the room while his valet, Brewer, hovered in the hallway beyond.

'I am going to the club,' he said, 'and I expect to be detained until late into the evening. It is best I stay there tonight instead of disturbing the house at all hours.'

'Very well,' she replied. She couldn't stand without revealing the bird so she remained on the floor, pretending that it was Emily's antics which prevented her from rising.

He stooped and dropped a kiss on her forehead. The tender gesture would have felt out of place only for what had occurred between them a month ago.

Upon the sad circumstance of his father's passing eighteen months previously, he had displayed a vulnerability which she had not seen in him before. To lose one parent at Swifton Hall had been bad enough; to lose the second there was intolerable and in his grief he had sworn they would never go back. To her surprise, the weight of the viscountcy had settled on his shoulders as an unwelcome burden.

'What man could ever desire to come into his inheritance when it necessitates the death of his own father?' he had burst out to her.

It had taken quite a while before he was able to accept his new place in the world, his ascent to the peerage and the obligations that came with such a status. During this adjustment period, he had relied upon Bridget to provide a sense of stability in their household. The servants had known to go to Lady Wyndham on matters that did not require their master's urgent attention. She had deflected many visits from acquaintances who wanted to sympathise or wish him well on attaining his birthright, conscious that he had no inclination to make civil discourse. She had liaised with Brewer to ensure that he was attended to whenever he called for it and left in peace whenever he did not.

She didn't think he had perceived her role of support and she hadn't looked for any acknowledgement of it. She was his wife and now a viscountess; it was no more than her duty demanded. Over time, he had emerged from his miasma of mourning, taking his seat in the House of Lords and socialising more regularly at his club again, and their lives had returned to a semblance of normality.

And then last month he had come to her. He had avoided her bed for so long that she hadn't expected his appearance and she had found herself wordless when he had entered her chamber and slipped under the covers beside her. But he had made no move to possess her. Leaning on his elbow, he had gazed at her with an expression free of any false emotion.

'I want to thank you,' he had said. 'You may believe I didn't notice, but I did.'

He had held her and kissed her and, when they had engaged in that intimate act, he had thought of more than his own pleasure, giving her a measure of satisfaction for the first time in their marriage.

Afterwards, she had been plagued by guilt, worried that the experience of such sensations by Garrett's caress was a treachery to the man who had first given them to her. All she could do was remind herself that she had not invited Garrett's attentions and felt no inclination to receive his advances that way again. Still, she could not deny that having a form of amity established between them was more restful. They were by no means a blissfully-married couple, but their relationship had lost some of its antagonism. She comprehended how badly he yearned for a child, a son, and she realised that she was not averse to the idea herself, knowing the joys that motherhood could bring. Perhaps their newfound tentative concord would lead to that happy event and to a lessening of the strife in their lives.

She looked up at him from her position on the nursery floor and offered him a cautious smile. He touched her shoulder and took his leave.

The next day, she paid a visit to St Swithun's, now a customary component of her weekly routine. The servants at Wyndham House had become well-versed in what was expected of them on these occasions. Her lady's maid, Audley, laid out her plainest gown and sturdiest boots and only assisted in lacing up her stays before leaving the bedchamber to let her finish dressing by herself. Neither Thrussell nor Peter stood at the front door to see her out. The carriage was not brought around; she would make her way there and back on foot. She could not avoid these trappings of her upper class position in the general scheme of things, but it seemed hypocritical to benefit from them on days when she would be in the company of people who would never have any hope of attaining such luxuries.

Upon her arrival to the soup kitchen – which now boasted four neatly-dressed women who tended the cooking fires and presided over a plentiful assortment of clean bowls and spoons – she was alarmed to find Frances in a state of some agitation.

'There was an official-looking fellow here this morning,' she told Bridget, even as she chopped up a cabbage to add to a boiling pot of water. 'Poking around and making enquiries.'

Bridget frowned. 'Enquiries about what?'

Frances tossed the cabbage pieces into the pot and wiped her hands on her apron. 'He asked about the poor folk, the numbers in the workhouse, the volume of people coming to the kitchen each day, how many able-bodied individuals are abusing the system, and so on. And he made some comments about the insupportable strain on the state due to the extensive funding it provides. As though it gives us that much.' She scowled. 'I think it's a bad sign. There are rumours of a commission being established to investigate it further. Not just here but all around the country.'

Bridget bit the tip of her tongue. 'Surely they couldn't be thinking of shutting us down? The relief we provide is immeasurable.'

Frances lifted one shoulder in an expression of doubt. 'Who knows what's on their minds? But it's causing concern in mine. Will you pass me another cabbage?'

As Bridget did so, she caught a whiff of the steam emanating from the boiling pot. In her distraction, Frances must have left a previous batch of cabbage cooking for too long; the unpleasant smell made Bridget's stomach turn. Choking back her nausea, she donned her own apron and set to work.

She returned to Wyndham House later that afternoon to learn from Lizzie that Garrett had come back an hour before her. Given how much time he had taken to spending at his club, he was rarely around to witness her dressed-down attire, but she knew it wouldn't please him to see it – especially the large soup stain she had acquired on the skirt – and she hastened to her bedchamber to change. However, a wail drifting down from the next floor sent her running up to the nursery instead.

She found Emily in floods of tears and inconsolable by the nurse.

'What has happened?' she demanded after a swift visual assessment confirmed that no physical harm had befallen her daughter.

Mrs Crewe patted Emily's head. 'Poor thing has lost her toy. I've told her it's likely to be under some piece of furniture but we haven't managed to find it yet.'

A block of ice formed in Bridget's stomach. 'Which toy?'

'That pretty little bird she's always playing with. Where are you going, my lady?'

Bridget was hurrying from the nursery before Mrs Crewe had finished speaking. She pounded down the stairs to Garrett's bedchamber. She almost stormed in without knocking but at the last moment gave a sharp rap on the door instead.

'Enter,' said his smooth voice.

She stalked in. A strong scent of cologne hung in the air and a fire crackled in the hearth; it was a cold day for May. He was standing before the window, his back ramrod straight. When he turned to her, his steely countenance said he knew she would come and he was ready for her fury.

She didn't have to ask if he had taken it. 'Give it back,' she said, low and ominous.

'No,' he replied.

She pointed an accusing finger at him. 'You have no right to keep it from her. Give it back.'

'I cannot.'

'You would choose to leave her in hysterics instead?'

'It is not a question of choice. I cannot return it to her now.'

'What do you —'

She froze. Then she swivelled to the fireplace.

'No!' she gasped.

She dashed to it and fell to her knees on the hearth rug. The blackened chunk of wood was missing its legs and its beautiful beak but the shape of one wing was still recognisable. She grabbed the tongs and endeavoured to clasp the remains in its grip. The wood disintegrated upon contact and the bird was no more.

A wave of anguish rose up in her throat but she pushed it back down. She would not let him see her cry. She dropped the tongs and stood to face him.

'The level of your cruelty is unimaginable.'

His fists clenched at his sides. 'You have no entitlement to speak of cruelty when it is your greatest weapon.'

'I beg your pardon?' she said, stunned.

'Don't act innocent. You are a mistress of cruelty.'

'I don't have the faintest idea what you mean!'

He gesticulated at the charred mess in the grate. 'That! And the Catholic prayers! And the Irish words!'

She baulked.

'Yes, I decided to spend some time with your daughter when I returned today. I may have no comprehension of the language myself, but I can still tell that her own grasp of Irish is near enough to that of English. It is *unacceptable!*'

He roared the last word at her. She took a step back but he strode forward and grabbed her by the shoulders.

'He is a phantom in this house. His presence is everywhere where you and that girl are and I will not tolerate it any longer. This is the last time you and I shall mention him. I tell you now that the prayers will stop, the Irish will stop, and any attempt on your part to pursue them further will result in punishment, not for you but for her. For all intents and purposes, and in all likelihood in reality, he is *dead* and you shall expel him from this house or, so help me God, I will make you regret it.'

He flung her away from him and marched back to the window. When he spun to confront her again, he had eradicated all emotion from his expression. With a detached air, he said, 'You may have already suspected this but, if you have not, let me enlighten you. I have a mistress. I was with her last night. She is not the first since the beginning of our marriage. I'll make no allusions to her or any others again, but know this: as long as you continue to hurt me, I will continue to hurt you.'

Her senses rioted in response to this unforgiving speech. Her vision blurred, her ears hummed, her throat closed to any intake of air. In the midst of her shock, she felt a grain of thankfulness that he had never become aware of the letters of enquiry she had sent to Ireland, fruitless though they may have been. Had he learned of those, she feared he might actually have raised his hand to her now.

When she finally trusted herself to speak, all she could think to say was, 'I understand.'

She stumbled to the door. On the threshold, she turned and looked back at him.

'I did not know when to deliver this news to you. But I shall return your honesty in kind. Though I cannot say it with absolute certainty, I believe I am with child.'

And she walked out without waiting to see his reaction.

## Chapter 13

Cormac strode along the docks, conscious of the dual weights of the dagger against his chest and a bag of coins against his thigh. He had just made his final visit to the wine merchant, who had relinquished the last of the negotiated profits with a poorly-disguised glower. It had taken nearly four weeks for him to amass the full amount from the sale of his cargo but Cunningham had instructed Cormac to be lenient at this juncture, given the substantial revenue to be gleaned from the bargain. Cormac had adopted a courteous and relaxed demeanour as he collected the remainder of the money but the merchant, holding his right arm in a gawky manner, had bid him farewell with a murderous tone to his own civil words.

Dusk was setting in, a blanket of pink-orange sky suspended over the River Liffey. The lingering rays of sun gilded the rigging of a ship moored nearby. Crewmen scurried over its deck and passengers queued on the dock, waiting to board. A lone seagull wheeled overhead and landed on the ship's tallest mast, shrieking softly.

As he went by the open double doors of a warehouse, he heard scuffling within and a girl's tremulous remonstration floated out. 'I s-said no kissing.'

The deep voice of a man responded, 'Come on, love, one little kiss won't hurt.'

'Kissing c-costs extra.'

He forced himself to keep moving. A whore's affairs were no concern of his. However, he had barely passed the end of the warehouse when there was a muffled crash, followed by a scream that was cut short.

He hesitated. It was none of his business; the sensible course of action would be to stay out of it. But the girl's voice had stirred something inside him, something he had not allowed himself to feel for a long time. A brotherly instinct. She sounded very young, as young as Margaret or maybe even Bronagh. Not much more than a child. What had happened to her that she had been reduced to the most disreputable of occupations at such a tender age?

He whirled around and marched back to the entrance of the warehouse. The customer might have paid for the girl's services but he had no right to mistreat her. Cormac stood in the doorway and let his eyes adjust to the gloom. A pile of overturned crates lay strewn on the dusty floor of the warehouse. Next to them, a man in dirty clothes and scuffed boots was kneeling over a ragged, redheaded girl and pressing his mouth hard on hers. She was whimpering and struggling to heave him off herself.

Cormac approached the pair, grabbed the man by the back of his coat, and hauled him off the girl. She scrambled out of the way, gasping.

The man gaped at Cormac in disbelief. 'What the hell d'you think you're doing?'

'She said no kissing.'

The man looked ready to throttle him. 'Get your interfering nose out of my business,' he growled and made to turn back to the girl.

Cormac laid a restraining hand on the man's shoulder and withdrew his dagger. He winced at how swift he was to produce the weapon; the act had become far too natural for him.

'I think you should leave,' he said calmly.

The man's eyes widened as they focused on the razor-sharp blade. 'Who're you?'

'I work for Cunningham. D'you know who that is?'

The man's face filled with foreboding. However, he tried to put on an air of bravado as he said, 'I paid good money for the wench. She's got to do her job.'

Cormac beckoned to the girl, who was cowering next to the fallen crates. 'Give him back his money.'

She fumbled in her shabby bodice and dropped some coins on the floor. Cormac stared at the money in pity; she had been selling herself for next to nothing. The man plucked up every single coin and passed his hand through the dust to make sure he had not missed any. With a last resentful look at Cormac, he lumbered out of the warehouse and into the dusk.

Cormac offered his hand to the girl but she shrank back further against the crates. He realised he was still gripping the dagger and quickly put it away, then held out his hand again.

'I won't hurt you,' he said.

After another faltering moment, she reached out and he helped her to her feet. She touched a cut on her arm, casting a grimace at the upended crates. The wound did not appear to be deep though and it had already stopped bleeding.

She peered up at him from beneath pale eyelashes. 'Why'd you do that?'

'He was a thug. If he doesn't play by the rules, he shouldn't be allowed to play. How old are you?'

'Eighteen.' She had to be lying; she looked a lot younger than that.

'How long have you been doing this?'

She hung her head in shame. 'That was my first time.'

'Might I suggest you make it the last too?'

She continued to look down at the floor. 'I can't. I need the money.'

He didn't say anything else. He just stood there and surveyed the pitiable young thing in front of him. She was the exact opposite of Thomasina. That black-haired seductress had known her talents in the bedchamber and had flaunted them to the best of her ability. This girl huddled in on herself like she was embarrassed by her own body. Her red hair hung in dull, straggly clumps, the bones of her arms stood out starkly, and there was a yellowish tinge to her skin and eyes. She had to be either living on the streets or in the most basic of shelters.

He understood the desperation of her situation and did not try to offer any platitudes. How could he tell her to find a more honourable way to survive when he himself had been unable to take that advice in his own hopeless circumstances?

He imagined what it would feel like if it were one of his sisters who had been reduced to this vulnerable state, forced to sacrifice the purity of her body in order to feed herself. Once again, he experienced a strong, brotherly impulse to protect, followed by an intense wave of homesickness which threatened to overpower him. Ever since he had left Oakleigh, and especially since he had joined Cunningham's crew, he had actively blocked out all thoughts of his family and his past. But this girl, this pathetic, would-be prostitute, had broken through his defences and set loose a thousand memories which all clamoured for recognition inside his head. Mary's temperamental expression, fluctuating from irritable to tender in a heartbeat. Margaret's faraway smile as she daydreamed about true love. Bronagh scowling after receiving yet another reprimand from the cook. Orlaith's diligence and affection in caring for her chickens. And his mother. Darning in her rocking chair, praying over her rosary beads. Scolding him, hugging him, weeping in his arms.

All of a sudden, he felt so emotionally shattered that his legs went weak and he had to sit down on one of the crates. The tremendous effort he had put into barring himself from thinking about any part of his old life was too much to sustain any longer. It had consumed him, made him forget who he was, led him to commit unspeakable acts. Now there was nothing left but a broken shell that even his mother would not recognise. He felt drained, ashamed, conscience-stricken.

It was easy to pinpoint the rotten source of his circumstances. Cunningham was the poison running through his veins. He had twisted his view of the world, made him believe that he had nothing left to lose, that it was acceptable to hurt others, that inflicting harm and unhappiness was a small price to pay for a hot meal and a bed. But the cost of these luxuries had been enormous; he had damaged the lives of countless people, and he had lost his integrity in the process.

The solution to this horrifying revelation came to him in an instant. He had to get away from here. Not just from the warehouse, not just from the city, but from the country. If he ever hoped to find his way back to the person he used to be, he needed to distance himself as much as possible from this place of violence and corruption and from the fiend who cultivated that sordid environment.

Standing again, he groped in his pocket and withdrew the bag of coins he had collected from the wine merchant. Wordlessly, he held it out to the redheaded girl, tugging on its string to reveal its contents. During his internal battle of emotions, she had started to cry, but now her tears stopped as she stared, amazed, at the money.

'What—?' she said in a tone of utter bewilderment.

'Take it,' he urged and thrust the bag into her hands. 'You need it a lot more than that goddamned bastard does.'

She was too flabbergasted to either ask him who he meant or to be offended by his language. After the briefest flash of uncertainty, she crammed the bag deep inside her bodice. She hovered on the balls of her feet, about to run, so he grabbed her wrist to hold her back.

'Use it carefully,' he warned. 'Mind you don't find yourself here again.'

She nodded. He released her and she fled. When he was certain she was gone, he approached the warehouse's entrance. From the doorway, he had a clear view of the ship he had seen earlier. A pair of gangways now stretched from the dock to the deck and the waiting passengers were crossing over them in two groups, the well-heeled separated from those of more modest means. It looked like they were about to embark on a night voyage.

He considered the ship and made his decision. There was no point in delaying and he had no personal belongings to go back for. Regardless of where the vessel was headed, it was perfect for what he needed.

He thought of the money he had just given away and wondered whether he ought to have retained some of it for himself. But he couldn't very well pay for his new life with money stained by his past actions. So he would have to figure out how to get on board without a ticket.

He emerged from the warehouse and strolled back along the docks. Dusk had darkened into night and one of the crewmen on the ship was holding up a lantern to light the way for the boarding passengers. There were more lanterns hanging at sporadic intervals along the ship's deck; by their dim illumination he could make out the full length of the vessel. The gangways seemed to be the only method of boarding it. But that would not do for a stowaway.

Going as close to the edge of the dock as he dared without raising suspicion, he scrutinised the structure of the ship. A portion of the rigging for the sails was attached to the hull, stretching down almost to the waterline; the ropes would make decent footholds for an adept climber. If it was the same on the other side, where there would not be so many watchful eyes, then that would be his access point.

He ambled further up the docks until he was out of sight of the ship. Glancing around for any onlookers and finding none, he swung his legs over the wall of the dock, lowered himself from the edge by his fingertips, and dropped the last few feet into the water. The cold was instantaneous but bearable. He tried very hard to ignore the questionable quality of the reeking River Liffey.

It had been a long time since he had gone swimming, but he and Bridget had spent many carefree days frolicking in the Sruhawn on the Oakleigh Estate in their youth. He struck out in the direction of the ship, slicing through the water as quietly as he could. The weight of his clothes made progress slower but not impossible. When the vessel came into view, he took a deep breath, ducked below the surface, and swam the rest of the way underwater. He did not break the surface again until he had come alongside the flank of the ship facing onto the river.

Sucking in lungfuls of air, he floated in the water as he scanned the hull in search of the rigging. He spotted it, swam over, and grabbed onto the mesh of rope. Water dripped from his heavy clothing as he hauled himself up and he expelled an involuntary grunt with the effort of it. Panicked, he clung to the rigging and waited for an inquisitive head to peer over the side and raise the alarm. No one appeared, but he counted for a hundred seconds before he deemed it safe to climb again.

When he reached the gunwale, he hoisted himself inch by inch above it until he had a view in both directions of the deck, which was lit by another scattering of lanterns. Luck was with him; it was deserted. The crew's attention must still be occupied with the gangways at the far side of the ship, while the passengers were probably ensconcing themselves indoors for the night crossing.

He scrambled over the gunwale and hunted around for an adequate hiding spot. Further down the deck, he noticed a long chest shrouded in a sheet of tarpaulin. He feared the chest might have a locked lid but, upon closer examination, he found that the tarpaulin was its only cover and it was secured by knotted rope. His fingers were numb from the water and it took him several minutes to work through a number of the complicated knots. He stayed on the alert for the sound of footsteps and kept glancing over his shoulder, expecting to be discovered at any moment, but the deck remained empty.

He eventually loosened enough of the tarpaulin to investigate the inside of the chest. It was filled with coils and coils of rope, neatly looped and stacked together, but there was just enough space for a man's body to squeeze in on top of them. He slithered into the gap and flattened himself against the uppermost layer of ropes, bending his knees to fit. Then he did his best to rearrange the tarpaulin so it did not look like it had been disturbed. He knew he had left wet footprints on the deck, as well as puddles of water from his sodden clothes, but that could not be helped; he hoped they would dry out before anyone happened to pass this way.

He let out a long, slow breath as he registered exactly what he had just done. He supposed Cunningham was at this moment wondering why McGovern had not yet returned to the lodgings after visiting the wine merchant. He would be enraged once he realised that neither his lackey nor his money would be coming back. The promise of his retribution alone was enough reason for Cormac to never show his face in Dublin again.

The final spell of waiting was interminable, and he spent it chewing his lip in dread that he would be found and ejected from the ship before it ever departed. But then he felt the vessel stir as though rousing from slumber, and at last it was moving, away from the shore of his home country, away from the mess he had made of his life.

## Chapter 14

The euphoria of his successful escape lasted about as long as it took for the ship to pick up pace, indicating that it had departed from the docks and was out on open water. Then his qualms began to set in.

It was all very well to renounce the contemptible existence he had led in Dublin for over a year and a half – he didn't regret that decision for an instant. However, his impetuous actions now found him holed up in a tight space with no food or water for an indeterminate period heading towards an unknown destination.

'This is no time to lose your nerve,' he muttered, prodding ineffectually at a coil of rope that was poking into his hip.

True, he had no notion which city, or even which country, would be the ship's next port of call. Nevertheless, anywhere had to be better than the godforsaken place it had just left. He pictured the coloured globe Bridget's governess had used in her geography lessons, and which she in turn had shown to him whenever she felt the urge to educate him in more than the rudiments of reading and writing. The ship was not large enough to be undertaking a transatlantic crossing to the Americas. Somewhere up or down the coast of Ireland was a possibility, but the more likely course was across the Irish Sea to Scotland, Wales or England. There was an outside chance it might be making for the northern shores of France but he prayed that wouldn't be the case. Bridget had never taught him a word of French.

Once he arrived there, wherever 'there' would be, his initial challenge would be to alight from the ship undetected but, if it came to it, he could always disembark by the same route he had taken to come aboard. After he got back onto dry land, his main priority would be to find work of some kind, but this time he would ensure that it was honest labour involving no daggers whatsoever. He was an able-bodied young man who knew how to work with wood and horses – these talents had proved inadequate in Dublin but there might be better opportunities for him on foreign soil.

In the short-term, he was more concerned with the inevitable onset of thirst and hunger. At a minimum, several hours stretched ahead of him without any form of sustenance and he hoped once again that the ship was not destined for somewhere as distant as France. Hunger he could manage – heaven knew he had enough experience in that area – but thirst could only be endured for so long. Did he dare venture out of his hiding place if it became too severe? He could attempt to pass for a steerage passenger and obtain a cup of water from the ship's supplies. It was an option, but he would bide his time for now. Perhaps the ship would dock before he needed to court that danger.

The minutes dragged by. A single set of footsteps pounded past the chest in a hurry to get somewhere else, and then all was quiet again.

He shifted restlessly. The ropes dug into his back and his cold, wet clothes stuck to his skin with nauseating clamminess. As they dried, the stench of the river water became more prominent and he tried to take shallower breaths. To distract himself, he imagined how the legitimate passengers were occupying themselves on their voyage. The less well-off had probably located the least uncomfortable parts of steerage to lay their heads, while the more affluent were no doubt well settled into their cabin quarters and availing of hot beverages. He swallowed, disregarding the dryness of his throat.

After a while, it grew even more difficult to breathe. The small space was stifling and he had drawn the tarpaulin so tight against the lip of the chest that there was no chance of any fresh air getting in. Could he risk opening it a little? Deciding that the threat of detection was minimal, he tugged at the tarpaulin from the inside until he had created a narrow gap between it and the edge of the chest. He put his face to the slit and breathed in. A cold breeze stung his nose but it was blessedly fresh. He pulled the tarpaulin to make the opening wider and adjusted the way he was lying to let the air waft across his cheeks.

The sensation was sweet at first but soon he became aware that his new position was causing an ache in the lower half of his left leg. It was turned at an awkward angle and he could feel a cramp building in the muscle. He tried to massage it but he was too restricted under the flat tarpaulin to reach down to it. He cursed fluently under his breath in Irish. It would be agony to suffer through the rest of the journey like this.

The cramp spiked painfully and forced him to act. He would have to get out of the chest and walk around to ease it. Wincing at another excruciating spasm, he listened hard for any sound of people nearby. He could hear nothing except the waves. He would scarcely be on the deck for two minutes before ducking back under the tarpaulin again. It was an acceptable risk to take.

He squeezed out from beneath the heavy tarpaulin and stood gingerly on the deck. The throb in his leg heightened and he hobbled in a circle to alleviate it. Looking out across the water, he could only distinguish an inky expanse spreading in every direction. Above, stars dotted the equally black sky. He shivered in his half-damp clothes and rubbed at his aching calf. At length, the pain dissipated until it was no more than a faint twinge. Relieved, he was just stooping to climb back into his hiding place when…

'Good evening.'

He froze.

Stupid, stupid, stupid. How foolish of him to emerge from his concealment. Now what would happen? Would he be incarcerated in whichever city the ship docked next? Or would he be brought back to Dublin where, imprisoned or not, he would have to confront Cunningham's wrath? Either way, he had wasted his shot at a fresh start, for nothing more significant than a leg cramp. He gritted his teeth and turned around.

Instead of a crew member, he found himself facing one of the passengers. The young man belonged to the wealthier social class on board, judging by his well-fitting coat, high shirt collar and white cravat, although he wore no hat. He was about Cormac's own height and he had neat brown hair and pale blue eyes which looked at Cormac with a quizzical expression.

'Good evening,' he said again.

Because he could not think of anything else to say, Cormac replied, 'Good evening.'

The young man took a step closer. 'You're a stowaway, aren't you?'

Cormac sent a wry glance down at the chest with the tarpaulin folded back. 'What gave it away?'

The man smiled. 'Do not look so worried. I'm not going to report you.'

Cormac felt some measure of relief but did not allow himself to relax. 'Why not?'

'I don't want to draw attention to myself either,' the man said cryptically. He stuck out his hand. 'I'm Oliver.'

Cormac thought it odd that a gentleman would introduce himself by his first name instead of his surname or title but he shook the fellow's hand nonetheless. 'Cormac.'

'It is a pleasure to meet you,' said Oliver, with the amiability of one who believed he had just made a firm friend.

Making an encouraging gesture to follow suit, he strolled over to the edge of the deck and leaned on the gunwale. After a moment's indecision, Cormac joined him. He knew he ought to be concerned that someone else might come along, one who would be less merciful towards stowaways, but something about this young man had sparked his curiosity. Maybe it was the fact that he had chosen not to acknowledge the vast social divide between them, which was an attitude Cormac had only ever witnessed in Bridget and her father. As he rested his forearms on the smooth wood, he felt embarrassed by the smell of the Liffey on his skin and clothing, but Oliver seemed not to notice. He was gazing ahead as if he could see all the way to the horizon, even though the weak light from the ship's lanterns illuminated only a small area of water before melting into the darkness beyond.

The sea breeze stirred his neat hair as he turned to Cormac. 'So I assume you did not elect to hide in a ship's chest for your own amusement. Are you a fugitive from the law? Should I fear for my safety?' He spoke with the serenity of one enquiring about the weather.

Cormac's lips twisted sardonically. 'A few hours ago, perhaps. Not anymore.'

'Turning over a new leaf, are you?'

'You could say that.'

'Who were you a few hours ago?'

'Someone I didn't want to be any longer. Someone I never wanted to be in the first place,' he added, his voice laced with bitterness.

'And you blame another individual for this?'

He shot Oliver a surprised look.

'Or am I mistaken?' the young man said mildly.

'No, you're not.' This stranger had, with disturbing perception, hit it quite right.

'Who was the party at fault? Your parents? Your employer? Your lover?'

He was so nonplussed that he answered with the truth. 'My lover.' He supposed 'my employer' would also have been accurate, but Bridget had been the one to reject him, thrusting him into a desperate set of circumstances. 'Though I guess she wasn't really mine.'

'Ah. Another man's wife?'

'Fiancée.' He sighed. Thinking about her made his chest feel like there was an iron strap tightening around it.

'What happened?'

'We had an affair. Her mother, my employer, banished me from the estate when she found out.' Had he actually summarised the whole complicated disaster in so few words?

Oliver exhibited no condemnation at his confession. 'So that was what induced the unfavourable alteration in yourself?'

Having no inclination to delve into a more detailed account of his misdeeds, Cormac said, 'That's the long and the short of it.' He looked sideways. 'Why are you so interested?'

'When I saw you, I perceived a kindred spirit. I thought it might be nice to empathise.'

'Nice?' He raised his eyebrows. His tale had not been one of uplifting inspiration.

'Helpful,' Oliver amended. 'Tell me, what are your prospects at this current juncture? Are you travelling to someone who can assist you?'

'No.' Cormac watched the waves below them splash against the hull of the ship; a sprinkle of sea spray moistened his cheeks. 'I've just forsaken the last place in the hope that the next one won't be so unforgiving.' He frowned in recollection of Oliver's comment. 'A kindred spirit? So d'you also have a delightful story to tell?'

'I do, indeed. It is about as amusing as your own. Would you care to hear it?'

'Go ahead.' He was now quite intrigued by this enigmatic young man.

'It has the same root as yours. A lover.' Oliver tugged at his cravat and collar to loosen them, exposing his pale throat. 'I was besotted. And my Vic was besotted. Although, as it turned out, not with me. I was cast aside for another man after I discovered them together. Oh, yes, and then my beloved parents died.'

Cormac gaped at the calm delivery of this shocking disclosure.

Oliver smiled without humour. 'It has been the best six months of my life.'

With an uneasy feeling in his gut, Cormac wondered if the fellow was a bit unstable for a wild glint had crept into his eyes. 'I'm very sorry to hear that. D'you have any other family?'

'My uncle and aunt live in England. I am journeying to them now.'

'England?' said Cormac, diverted. 'That's where this ship's heading?'

'Yes.' Oliver did not look pleased at the prospect. 'My uncle and aunt will be waiting for me when we dock. I have never met them but I know they have no children of their own so doubtless they will smother me and expect me to take over their substantial estate when they die.'

'Are they very rich then?'

'Richer than I'd care to admit. My uncle is an earl. But I do not want to inherit, how tedious it would be.'

It was a singular statement to issue from the mouth of a gentleman.

'What would you prefer to do instead?' Cormac asked, mystified.

'I have always wanted to be a poet. However, my parents believed that the literary life was beneath me and encouraged me to study law instead. My Vic was the only truly happy point of my existence. And then…' He trailed off, his Adam's apple bobbing as he swallowed.

Cormac shifted in discomfort. 'Maybe things'll improve once you settle in England. You might meet a new girl and…' His voice too faded away.

Oliver shrugged with a sardonic expression. 'I do not believe so. But I suppose I shall have to make peace with my fate.'

His hands flexed, as though anxious to be occupied. Fishing in his pocket, he withdrew a knife with an ornate handle, flicked it open, and began scratching idly on the gunwale.

'It could be worse, y'know,' said Cormac. 'Least you've somewhere to go once we've crossed the sea. My first challenge is going to be figuring out where my next meal'll come from. I'm not trying to feel sorry for myself,' he hastened to add. 'I'm just attempting to give you some perspective.'

Oliver didn't look up but he seemed to contemplate Cormac's advice seriously. After a long pause, during which there was no sound but the waves and the scrape of metal on wood, he said, 'If you were in my place, what would you do?'

Cormac hesitated. With reluctance, because he knew it was not what Oliver wished to hear, he replied, 'I think you're duty-bound to go to your uncle and aunt, for a time anyway. But after a while, if you explain to them you're not content, they might let you write your poetry instead.'

Betraying his first hint of melancholy, Oliver murmured, 'You and I both know that will never happen.'

He blew at the shavings that had accumulated on the gunwale. The breeze caught them and they whirled away into the night, revealing the single word he had scored into the wood.

'Victor'.

Startled, Cormac glanced from it to Oliver, but the fellow offered no clarification regarding this unforeseen revelation. Pocketing the knife, he drew in a gulp of air and expelled it by jerky degrees. When he spoke again, it was so quietly that Cormac could barely hear him.

'It will be nothing but obligation and obedience, a lifetime of pretence for a withered soul.'

He stared at Cormac with sudden intentness. 'Here are a few details you ought to know. My full name is Oliver Davenport. The date of my birth was the eighth of February, 1809. Twenty-five years ago, my father, Mr Gerard Davenport, came to Ireland where he met my mother, Miss Caroline Prendergast. They married and had three children. Two died in infancy, only I survived to adulthood. In March of this year, my parents drowned in a boating accident on a lough near our home in Meath. Our estate was sold and I am now travelling to Bedfordshire to live with my uncle and aunt, Lord and Lady Bewley. Oh, and my quarters here on the ship are in B5. Here is the key to my cabin.'

He withdrew a key from his pocket but, baffled, Cormac did not take it.

'Why do I need to know all of this?'

'Because I am weary of my life,' said Oliver. 'You may have it if you want. And my thanks to you. It was comforting to have a friend at the end.'

He dropped the key on the boards of the deck and turned swiftly to the gunwale, grasping the top of it to heave himself over the edge. Letting out an exclamation of shock, Cormac darted towards him and seized his shoulders just before he plunged overboard. He hauled him back and they fell onto the deck, Oliver struggling in his grip with a growl of frustration.

'Get off me!'

They tussled back and forth on the wooden boards, Oliver fighting to extricate himself while Cormac refused to relinquish his hold. At last, Oliver gave up and went limp.

'You win,' he said. 'Will you let me go now?'

'Only if you stay well away from the edge,' Cormac warned.

Oliver gave a grudging nod and Cormac released him. The fellow scrambled back and stood, brushing down his fine clothes with fastidious displeasure.

'What were you *thinking*?' Cormac demanded, panting as he got to his own feet.

Defiant, Oliver said, 'I'm done with thinking. And feeling. And existing.'

He thrust his hand into his pocket, pulled out his knife, and dragged the blade across his throat in a deep slash. Blood spurted from the gash, staining the white skin and pristine cravat bright red. Horror-struck, Cormac caught him as he sagged towards the deck. Oliver's pale blue eyes widened in surprise and fear, losing focus as his head lolled to the side. Cormac sank to his knees and yanked the sodden cravat over the wound in a frantic effort to staunch the stream of blood.

'Jesus Christ, don't die! Come on, damn you!'

But the air in Oliver's lungs gurgled pathetically out of his ravaged windpipe and Cormac found himself supporting the weight of a dead body in his arms.

He averted his face and heaved the contents of his stomach onto the boards of the deck. His mind screamed, one endless howl of shock and incomprehension. Had that really just happened? An act so abominable, so inconceivable, that his head swam as he attempted to deny its occurrence. He took a deep breath to steady himself and inhaled the reek of blood and vomit, making all denial impossible. For the next few seconds, he concentrated on not getting sick again. When he was in control of his bodily functions once more, he tried to assess the alarming situation into which he had been plunged.

Oliver Davenport, this stranger whom he had known for little more than ten minutes, had just killed himself. What had compelled him to do such a monstrous thing? Granted, he had suffered the recent death of his parents and the loss of his beloved Victor, and he had faced the prospect of being the unwilling heir to his uncle's estate. But did that merit giving up on life altogether? He had relayed no warning that such desperate thoughts had been preying on his mind. For most of their encounter, his demeanour had been nonchalant. Even towards the end, he had seemed downhearted, but not suicidal by any means. It was unthinkable that the young man who had shaken his hand with such affability was…gone.

Cradling Oliver's lifeless form, he was forcefully reminded of another senseless tragedy. His sister Mary had ended her own existence with a noose around her neck. Both she and Oliver had chosen the most extreme course of action without confiding in anyone else. How could they believe that suicide was the only option, when that sin condemned the soul to perpetual damnation? Oliver may have thought he had lost everyone worth living for, but Mary had still had her family, she had still had her son Patrick. He felt anger rise up in him at their inherent failings, their inability to reach out for help, their refusal to fight on. In the next instant, he berated himself for thinking ill of his sister. She, like Oliver, had been intolerably unhappy and, in both cases, he had been too blind to see what was coming.

He became aware of something hard beneath his knee and looked down to see Oliver's pocket knife on the deck. It had slipped from his hand as life escaped him and now lay there in lethal inertia. Cormac picked it up gingerly, the slick smear of crimson oozing down the handle and onto his fingers. It hadn't been Oliver's planned means for his demise – was it a more ghastly end than drowning? Cormac experienced a queer surge of guilt; his well-meant intervention had doomed Oliver to make that choice.

At that moment, he heard a crewman bark an order towards the front of the ship. He suddenly recollected where he was and a wave of panic swept over him. Should somebody stumble across him right now, they might see a suicide but they could also very well see a murder. Once they coupled their suspicion regarding the incident with the fact that he was not even authorised to be on the vessel in the first place, he could anticipate a punishment no less than death. He needed to act fast.

What should he do with Oliver's body? If he abandoned it, then it would be discovered, alarms would be raised, and stringent security checks would make it almost impossible to leave the ship undetected. He supposed he could hide it, perhaps in the very chest he had used to take cover himself – there was a strong likelihood that the ship would have already docked and the passengers alighted by the time it was found. But concealing the corpse would definitely make it appear as though a murder had taken place and he did not know whether he would be able to get away in sufficient time. If he were caught and connected with the crime, again he could expect to follow Oliver sooner rather than later.

A third course of action would be to get rid of the body entirely. He could dump it over the side of the ship and wipe away the evidence on the deck, and no one would ever know the atrocity had occurred. But when the crew checked the ship's passenger records after docking, they would realise that they were short one passenger and there would be a missing person inquiry. And of course, he remembered with a jolt, Oliver's uncle and aunt would be waiting for him at the docks. Once he did not show up as expected, they would become distraught and instigate an inquiry of their own.

It was only then that he recalled Oliver's words: 'I am weary of my life. You may have it if you want.' He had been so shocked and nauseated by the bewildering turn of events that the young man's extraordinary comments had flown out of his head in the immediate aftermath. Now he tried to analyse what they could mean. The intention was clear enough but the logic behind them was impossible to fathom. Had Oliver really believed that he, Cormac, could step into someone else's shoes just like that? It was a ludicrous notion.

He chewed the inside of his mouth, wincing at the acidic tang of vomit. Could it work? Of course not. How could one man assimilate himself into the life of another without the people around him seeing through the deception at once? Then he remembered that Lord and Lady Bewley had never met their nephew and therefore would not be familiar with either his looks or his personality traits. At the present time, Oliver Davenport was nothing but a name to them; given that Cormac was only four months older than him, he could feasibly slip into the role without their knowledge. There was the issue that Oliver came from an upper class family and Cormac did not, but he had a decent handle on his reading and writing and was familiar enough with the manners of the aristocracy – having served them for so many years – that he thought he could pass for a lord's nephew without an excessive degree of difficulty. So impersonating Oliver Davenport would not be an unachievable task.

But what about not being Cormac McGovern anymore? The man he had been, the life he had led for over two decades, would be eradicated as though it had never existed. Then again, what was so estimable about his life that was worth preserving? He had failed his family by ending up in a position where he could no longer support them and neglecting to uphold the values he had been taught since infancy. Indeed, for the last year and a half he had lived as though he were a different person. Perhaps Cormac McGovern was already gone. Which would make the decision before him quite easy after all.

Feeling like a criminal, he groped around on the deck and found the key to Oliver's cabin. Holding it between his thumb and forefinger as though it were a serpent about to strike, he weighed his options for the future. If he continued on as himself, he could remain hopeful for better luck across the sea but still ran the risk of falling back into a seedy life similar to the one he had led in Dublin, or else returning to the misery of homelessness. If he accepted Oliver's proposal, he had a chance of infinitely improving his quality of life. He would rise to an elevated position in society that would never have been possible for him to reach as Cormac McGovern, lowly stable hand turned beggar turned money lender's lackey. He would also have access to money which he could send home in secret to his family and start to make amends at last for the pain he had brought upon them. He had to admit he was becoming more open to Oliver's idea.

But there was still the question of what to do with the remains. Whatever path Cormac chose, he would be obliged to do something despicable.

Abandoning, hiding or disposing of the body were all hideous acts for the one who had to do the dirty work and undignified ends for the one who had died. With an ironic pang of realisation, the thought struck him: had he let Oliver depart this world in the manner he had wished to, his own situation would now be a lot simpler.

Wavering in indecision, he was almost too preoccupied to heed the voices issuing from around the corner of the deck towards the ship's stern. But they broke into his consciousness as they grew louder and shriller.

'Oh, Millicent! This sea crossing is ghastly, isn't it?'

'Yes, I do not know when I have felt so ill. What a horrid experience.'

'You were right to suggest we come out on deck. The fresh air should do us some good.'

'But it is a touch too breezy here. We ought to try the next side, Gertrude, it might be more sheltered.'

Dismayed, he heard the heels of the two ladies clicking nearer. He was out of time – he had to make his choice now. He stared down at Oliver's slack face, the hideous wound on his neck, his fine clothes ruined by blood. This disillusioned young man's attempt to live his life had been unsuccessful but he had sanctioned the passing of its ownership to another. Cormac viewed this as justification enough to take a shot at it himself.

He thrust the cabin key into his own pocket, struggled to stand with Oliver's body in a macabre embrace, and heaved it over the gunwale. It fell into the sea with a sickening splash. He hoped it would sink before anyone within earshot investigated the source of the noise. Oliver's pocket knife followed him into the water. Next, Cormac whipped off his coat, mopped at the pool of blood and vomit on the deck and, just as the seasick ladies rounded the corner to his side of the deck, threw it overboard as well. A faint discolouration remained on the wooden boards of the deck but he would have to trust that no one would recognise it for what it really was. He realised his dagger was still in the inside pocket of his coat and felt no compunction over its loss. A watery grave was the best end for it.

'May it rust there,' he muttered bitterly.

The two ladies turned their heads in surprise as they registered his presence on the deck. After bowing politely in their direction, he spun on his heel and strode away from them. He needed to get inside fast. Anyone he met would regard it as suspicious to be out-of-doors on a ship without wearing an outer layer of some kind. Furthermore, if they looked more closely, they could not fail to discern the blood stains on his hands.

Ducking through the first door he found leading below decks, he descended a stairwell and hurried down a passageway lined with numbered doors. A steward passed him going the opposite way; Cormac slowed his pace but did not make eye contact. After stalking along two more passageways in mounting agitation, he finally located a small sign proclaiming the quarters for B5. He unlocked the door, entered, and shut it behind him with an exhalation of relief.

He found himself in a small but comfortable cabin containing a bed and a table with a pitcher, basin and towel. There were no windows but a lit lamp hung in an alcove beside the door. A trunk stood beneath it.

He dropped onto the bed, his heart racing. Had he truly just done that? He was both appalled and exhilarated by his actions. It had been a dreadful incident but now he was journeying to a lord and lady who were going to take him in as their own nephew. This guaranteed two vital aspects of his future: he would not have to go back to starving on the streets and he would not be required to threaten poor people for money anymore. Both of these certainties were worth the horror of tossing a dead body overboard.

He knelt by the trunk, unfastened its clasps and rummaged through its contents. There were sets of clothes, pairs of boots, a coat and a hat, as well as a small case holding items for shaving and grooming. Underneath this at the bottom of the trunk lay a slim notebook with a navy cloth cover. He flicked it open and swallowed. Oliver's poetry. The handwritten words rose from the pages, clouding the air with their despair. *The torment of drawing breath, already breathing death.*

Cormac's exhilaration evaporated. With a heaviness in his chest, he closed the notebook. In respect of Oliver's memory, he would keep it in his possession, to preserve the remnants of the anguished spirit who had crafted those hopeless verses.

He needed to start preparing himself for his arrival in England. Crossing to the table, he poured water from the pitcher into the basin. He scooped up a mouthful to rinse the sour taste from his mouth, and another to slake the dryness in his throat, and then set to scrubbing the blood stains from his palms and the odour of the River Liffey from his hair and skin.

Once he had dried himself with the towel, he extracted the grooming case from the trunk. With the aid of a small mirror, he shaved the layer of stubble that covered his jaw. Next, he found a scissors and, recalling Oliver's tidy haircut, chopped at his own long hair until it had amassed in golden piles at his feet. He trimmed it as best he could, though the style was a bit rough and he had no way of telling how it looked from the back.

Last of all, he needed to dress like a gentleman. He stripped out of his garments and crammed them into the trunk, along with the mound of cut hair; he would find a way to dispose of them all at the earliest opportunity. He donned shirt, waistcoat, coat and trousers, admiring the fine quality of the material. By a stroke of fortune, there had been less than an inch in the difference between his and Oliver's heights and the sleeves and trouser legs, while a little short, were not noticeably so. He dubiously picked up a cravat and wondered how to tie it. Following a number of failed attempts, he managed to fashion it into something resembling a neat knot. He completed his ensemble with a pair of leather boots, which were only a touch on the tight side.

After that, all he could do was wait for the vessel to dock and for his new life as an impostor to begin.

## Chapter 15

Bridget entered the nursery to find Garrett bending over the cradle, shaking a silver rattle and making uncharacteristic baby noises.

'You are the best boy, yes, you are,' he chattered, and an answering gurgle came from within the cradle. 'Goo goo ga, that's right, good boy.'

The sounds were incongruous with the man she knew and yet that man did not stand before her.

He had transformed upon the birth of their son. The thing he wanted most on this earth had come to him at last and he had become disposed to be kinder towards everyone, even Emily, rendering him unrecognisable from the devil who had destroyed the wooden bird and roared at Bridget and announced his infidelity with such indifference.

In that last respect, she was reasonably certain those activities had ceased. During the past three months since James had been born, Garrett had spent so much time at home and away from his club that he could have had little opportunity to invite the interest of any mistress. That did not mean he had returned to Bridget's bed, however. She had provided him with a son and he therefore had no further use for her. All of his attention was now focused on giving James a wealth of love which she had never believed to be within his capacity and which she could only assume he had stored away until the advent of this vital individual into his life.

Her own heart overflowed with adoration for James too. Not for one instant would she say that she loved her son more than her daughter – Emily still meant the world to her. But James had two advantages which Emily did not: he was male, and he had the benefit of two loving parents, not one. The atmosphere in Wyndham House was positively festive.

James, who would be the seventh gentleman to hold the title of the Wyndham viscountcy, had been named for his grandfather, the fifth in that line. Blissfully unaware of the great honour that would one day rest upon his shoulders, he babbled from the depths of his blankets. Bridget approached the cradle and gazed lovingly down at him. He had a shock of black hair on the crown of his head but thus far not much growth towards the front. He wriggled and produced a gummy smile at the sight of her, but it disappeared as a fretful cough shook his little body. Garrett leaned over and touched his forehead.

'Still hot,' he said.

The boy had been out of sorts over the previous two or three days with a rather high fever. Garrett, taking on the role of overprotective father, had scarcely left the nursery in all that time. Concerned that the fever had not yet passed, Bridget placed her palm on James's forehead too.

'I think we ought to send for the physician again,' she said.

'I agree. I shall do so directly.'

He started to turn away but hesitated. He cleared his throat and looked at her. 'Before I go,' he said, 'there is something I wish to say.' He cleared his throat once more, as though he found it difficult to get the words out. 'I believe I owe you an apology.'

Startled, she said nothing. Was he bedding a mistress after all? A sense of disappointment settled over her, not for her own sake, but because such an admission would mean that the happy mood in their household had been yet another lie.

But then, to her shock, Garrett said, 'I have treated you badly during our marriage. Neither of us is blameless in the whole affair, but I have come to accept that I made things worse.' He smoothed his thumb over the surface of the rattle; it was wet at the top where James had been sucking on it. 'We should not have wed. You were right, and I see that now. I saw it quite soon after the event but of course by that stage it was too late.'

She gaped. What on earth had prompted this confession? This man had been her husband for three and a half years and yet she still could not become accustomed to his mercurial ways. Recalling the last period of reconciliation they had enjoyed before the onset of his fury over the wooden bird, she resolved not to be deceived by a false sense of peace this time.

The rattle jangled softly as Garrett turned it over in his hands. 'I was blinded at the time by my anger and humiliation. To be jilted by a woman...' He shrugged. 'I wanted to exact revenge, to hurt you the way you hurt me. On top of that, you were my possession. I had no intention of standing by and allowing you to be snatched away from me. I had to win.'

She experienced a spark of anger herself. This did not sound like much of an apology, and all he was doing was dragging up agonising memories which *he* had stipulated must never be alluded to again.

'You don't need —' she began, hoping to forestall any further attempts on his part to 'apologise'.

He held up his hand to cut her off. 'My revenge came with unwelcome repercussions. I had no more wanted to get trapped in a loveless marriage than you had, but that is precisely what happened. I was mistaken in thinking you had been the victim of a mere infatuation, a wild impulse to rut in the hay that would be swiftly overcome once you regained your senses. I knew you had loved me once and I thought you could love me again, despite the events of that summer.'

She tried, and failed, to mask her incredulity. He smiled wryly.

'I was a misguided fool, yes, but you still owe me some thanks. Have you thought about what would have happened had I not married you? You would have been a fallen woman with a bastard child.' He didn't let her argue the point, but pushed on, 'You wouldn't have found him. I would have made sure of that. At least our marriage gave legitimacy to Emily's birth. Her life could have been a great deal more unpleasant, had she not been born in wedlock.'

Bridget's hands curled tightly in the folds of her skirts. 'I'm afraid your understanding of what constitutes an apology is drastically different to my own.'

'True, I'm not doing very well at it,' he admitted. 'Let me backtrack. This is meant to be my acknowledgement of how I was at fault. What I'm trying to say is I ought to have seen that your feelings could not be so easily overcome.' He sighed. 'I recognise now the depth of your regard for him. I once experienced that feeling too, not with you, but with another woman.'

He delivered this so casually that he appeared unaware of its impact, not seeming to realise that she had received it like a punch to her gut. She had known he had dallied with other women, but had he truly loved any one of them as much as she loved Cormac? She didn't think it could be possible – but then she glanced down at James, his small fist inserted in his mouth, and remembered that Garrett did indeed have that ability, even if he had never demonstrated it towards her.

'I did a lot of damage that summer,' he said now. 'And while I don't know if I would have acted any differently where he was concerned, I am sorry for what has transpired between us since.'

He set the rattle down in the cradle, touching the back of his knuckles against their son's cheek.

'But now we can say that some good has come from our union at last. You have my deepest gratitude for that.' He let out another sigh, this one a long breath of joy and devotion. 'I shall send for the physician now.' He made to move away but looked back down at James with a frown.

'What is it?' she asked.

He reached into the cradle and drew back the blankets, exposing more of the boy's skin. His face went ashen.

Bridget peered in and gasped. A red rash had begun to spread from behind James's ear and along his neck. She stared up at Garrett, horrified.

'Measles,' he muttered. 'Dear God, it's measles.'

Her mind raced through all the facts she knew about the disease. *Contagious* came top of the list.

'Have you ever –' she started.

'Yes, you?'

'When I was two. But Emily –!'

Emily, a month shy of three years old, had never contracted the measles. To remain one minute longer in this house would endanger her as well as James.

Without further communication, she and Garrett hastened from the nursery, he to summon the physician and she to seek out Emily.

Within the hour, Emily was bouncing around the seat of the carriage and straining to peep out the window, excited at the unexpected expedition through the teeming London streets. Bridget restrained herself from constantly checking the girl's forehead and skin for signs of fever or rash. She had kept Emily far away from the nursery until they had left the house so the risk of exposure was minuscule – but anxiety still compressed her lungs like a pair of stays pulled too tight.

She had ordered the coachman to take them to the Newby residence. Lucy, who had become such close friends with Bridget that they were firmly on first name terms, accepted Emily into her home without hesitation, verifying that everyone in the household had survived the disease and would not be in any danger.

'What a dreadful misfortune!' she exclaimed, her large nose scrunching in consternation. 'I do hope James will recover quickly.'

'Thank you, dearest, I am so grateful,' said Bridget. 'I shall come back as soon as possible to see Emily but I cannot say exactly when –' The words clogged in her throat.

Lucy clasped her hand in both of her own. 'Take all the time you need. She will be perfectly fine here with Angela and Valerie.'

Emily confirmed this by beaming from ear to ear when Lucy's two young daughters appeared from behind her skirts. Even so, it was agonising for Bridget to leave her little girl behind and she nearly ran for the carriage, feeling torn between her two children. But right now James needed her more.

The next few days passed in a blur. Hazy faces went to and fro around her: Garrett, the physician, and an unfamiliar maid to replace Lizzie, who had to be sent away because she had never suffered the measles before either. Their voices drifted about Bridget, distant and vague, like they were calling to her from the bottom of a deep well. The only thing she was in tune with was her son – his plaintive cries, his wracking coughs, his sore, red eyes, his hot, rash-covered skin. She willed his tiny body to fight the disease. Her own body felt numb. When she spoke, her lips seemed moulded of wax, hardly able to move.

'Save him,' she croaked to the physician. 'Please save him.'

Could God be so cruel, to bestow such happiness upon her family and snatch it away again so quickly? Three months was nothing, the blink of an eye. She did not know yet what sort of person her son was. Would he have a sweet tooth for jellies and cakes? Would he ride a horse well? Would he be the kind of child to run crying to his mother when he got hurt or bear it with a man's silent endurance? How she yearned for the day he would come home from Eton conjugating Latin verbs, reciting Homer's Iliad, and boasting about his school's win over Harrow in their annual cricket match. And when he grew up, she hoped he would be a gentleman in every respect, incomparable in courteousness to ladies and servants alike.

She knew it was all over when she saw Garrett slumped on the floor of the nursery, back against the wall, head in his hands, sobbing so hard that his whole frame shuddered with grief.

She floated over to the cradle in a fog of bewilderment, oblivious to the murmured sympathies of the physician. She looked down. He had been making so much of a commotion with his crying and coughing that the inert, silent form seemed unnatural. She stroked the black tuft of hair. Her eyes misted, becoming sightless, and in that moment her world was reduced to two senses: the touch of that soft, soft hair and the sound of her devastated husband's weeping. One was achingly familiar. The other she had never witnessed before in her life, not even at his father's death.

'White gloves,' she said dazedly.

'Beg pardon, m'lady?' the strange maid mumbled by her side.

'White gloves,' she repeated. 'And a white coffin. That is what is required for a child's funeral.'

Her voice cracked and the tears spilled over.

The following day, she went to Newby House to retrieve her one surviving child. Emily clung to Bridget's knee as the carriage hit a rut in the street on the way back, jostling them about. The little girl fingered the black crape of her mother's dress and looked up with blue eyes full of confusion.

'Baby James not at home?' she asked hesitantly.

'No, gooseberry, I'm afraid he's not.'

'Where he now?'

'He's gone to live with the angels in heaven. Do you remember me telling you that?'

'When he coming back?'

'He won't be coming back. He is going to stay in heaven where God will take such good care of him.'

Bridget gulped and clutched Emily to her breast so the girl would not see the wetness in her eyes. Emily continued to ask questions and she answered them in muffled tones, trying as best she could to express what had happened in a manner the child could understand. An absurd notion, given that she herself could not understand why her precious boy had been taken from her.

Thrussell met them at the door of Wyndham House, his sorrow under control save for an escaped sniffle. As they crossed the threshold into the entrance hall, Garrett came down the stairs. Emily's face lit up and she ran forwards.

'Papa!'

Before James's death, Garrett might have been benevolent enough to give the little girl a swift hug or a pat on the head. Now his livid expression made her falter and shrink back from him.

The reason for his resentment was palpable: the stable hand's child lived, but his own had not. Any scrap of affection that might have existed between them was irrevocably lost.

Bridget put a soothing hand on Emily's small shoulder. 'Let's not trouble Papa right now,' she murmured.

Garrett brushed past them both, anger and anguish radiating from him in equal measure.

'I am going to the club,' he said and vanished out the door.

## Chapter 16

Cormac hunched over a hefty volume in the library, hungrily scanning its pages. Though the subject matter was not part of the education Lord and Lady Bewley had prescribed for him, it was essential reading nonetheless; every member of the aristocracy possessed this knowledge, so he needed to understand it too lest he be caught off guard at some inopportune moment.

The book contained a comprehensive description of the peerage of the United Kingdom, listing the various grades of nobility and the principal families therein. A viscount, it revealed, ranked higher than a baron but lower than an earl. He tried to absorb the information in general terms but could not help applying specifics. Bridget had risen above her station when she married Garrett but Cormac, in his current role, was due to inherit an earldom which would place him above that supercilious gentleman. It was so extraordinary that he laughed softly to himself.

'Amusing material, my boy?' came a voice from behind him.

He shut the book with a snap and spun around. Lord Bewley stood at the library door. He had a head of fine, white hair and he leaned on a beechwood cane with a brass, T-shaped handle. Despite these signs of infirmity, he was hale and hearty for his advanced years and the cane was more of an affectation than a crutch. His eyes crinkled as he smiled.

'I am pleased to see you being so diligent with your studies, Oliver, but the humans in the house would enjoy your company on occasion. What are you reading?'

Cormac gave an embarrassed shrug. His tailored clothes glided comfortably with the movement.

''Tis—I mean, it's nothing important, Uncle,' he said, pronouncing the words with care. 'I apologise for my unsociable behaviour.'

'Never apologise for striving towards an educated mind. It is an admirable quality and I am happy to encourage it. Having said that, I must interrupt your scholarly exploits to request your presence in my study for a brief meeting.'

Concealing his curiosity, Cormac slid the book back onto its shelf before following his 'uncle' out of the library and down the cavernous hallway to the study. Bewley Hall was the ancient seat of the Davenport family and its enormous rooms, luxurious furnishings and extensive grounds spoke volumes of the earldom's noble status and ample fortune. Moreover, Cormac had learned that the assets connected to the Bewley title spread much further than this, encompassing several properties around the country and a fine establishment in London too. He had believed Oakleigh to be an impressive estate but it paled in comparison to what the Earl of Bewley could boast of in his possession.

They entered the study to find Lord Bewley's land agent, Mr Sandler, already waiting with a benign expression on his squashed face, his sizeable forehead and equally substantial chin constraining his other features into the narrow space between them. He handed a thick ledger to his master as Lord Bewley sat behind a broad desk covered with neat stacks of letters, a few books, and an elegant inkstand. The earl indicated that Cormac should occupy the seat opposite him, while Mr Sandler took up a position a discreet distance behind Cormac's chair.

Lord Bewley cast a fleeting glance through the pages of the ledger and then put it aside. 'I shall not prevaricate on the matter, Oliver. I wish to speak to you about the entailment of my estate.'

Cormac hoped he would be able to follow the intricacies of what the earl meant to discuss. Inheritance law was just one small part of the vast education he had acquired over the past twelve months, which also included mathematics, politics and philosophy – not to mention the appropriate etiquette in dressing, dining and conversing, and, entirely unanticipated, the proper steps to all the popular dances of the ballroom. While he managed to muddle through most of it well enough, Latin and Greek had proved to be beyond his capabilities and he had found it necessary to invent a lie about Oliver's parents' aversion to conventional tutoring as an explanation for his inadequate edification. Though Lord and Lady Bewley had not expressed any reproach, they had put forward their recommendation that the discrepancies be remedied and had retained a personal tutor for that purpose. It had been far from a simple undertaking but he had made considerable improvements across the year in his objective of becoming a refined gentleman. Lord Bewley must have thought so too; this was the first time he had summoned his 'nephew' to his study and Cormac sensed it was for an interview of some significance.

'The critical detail I must reveal to you,' said Lord Bewley, 'is that there is, in fact, no entailment.'

Cormac gathered that this was an unusual circumstance and adopted a suitable air of surprise.

'You may well be taken aback. The original entail expired in my grandfather's generation and he neglected to renew it. He was fortunate that my father answered his prayers for an heir and I, in turn, obliged my father. The countess and I, on the other hand…'

He trailed off. Cormac knew that Lord Bewley would never blame his wife for their lack of offspring – having spent a full year in their home, he was in no doubt that theirs was a happy marriage of love and understanding. But the truth remained that, no matter how much they desired it, they had never been blessed with children.

'Without an heir of my own blood,' Lord Bewley continued, 'my deceased brother's son is the next in line, and the noble title must pass that way regardless. However, in the absence of an entailment I am not obligated to bequeath my material estate to you, Oliver. I am free to bestow it upon anyone of my choosing. I could give it to an urchin in the village if I so wished, though naturally I do not wish that. I intend to leave the estate in capable hands upon my death. Mr Sandler, for example, would be an ideal candidate, having occupied the role of land agent here for almost two decades. His extensive knowledge of the Bewley lands and the tenants who live and work upon them is surpassed by none but myself.'

Lord Bewley gestured respectfully towards the agent. Mr Sandler made a noise of humble dissent but Cormac kept his eyes trained upon the earl. He suspected that the real Oliver Davenport had never known of these particulars and wondered what point Lord Bewley was leading to. Instinct told him he need not be concerned that his deception had been discovered; he was positive that Lord and Lady Bewley wholly believed he was their flesh-and-blood nephew.

Confirming this, Lord Bewley said, 'You have resided with your aunt and me for a year now. I confess we found you a little rough around the edges upon your arrival. You had received a somewhat coarser upbringing than we had anticipated, but doubtless we have the less civilised environs of Ireland to thank for that.'

Cormac tried not to bristle. He understood that Lord Bewley harboured no personal ill will towards Ireland or its people but, like all the other English Cormac had encountered, the earl accepted without question the assertion that the Irish were an inferior, unsophisticated race, and therefore no more could be expected of his nephew than to have appeared in the state he had.

'We communicated our hope that you would rise to the standards befitting a gentleman bearing the name of Davenport, for this family is old and revered, both here in Bedfordshire and further afield. And I am delighted to observe that you have acquitted yourself creditably, embracing your improvement in all respects, from erudition to comportment, with aplomb. In short, we are very proud of how much you have progressed.'

Cormac felt gratified by the praise. 'I never cease to be grateful to you and Lady Bewley for affording me these opportunities to better myself. I am glad to hear that you are satisfied with the results.'

'More than satisfied,' said Lord Bewley, steepling his hands on the desk. 'You are a fine young man, unafraid to admit what you do not know and eager to cultivate your advancement. It is plain that, if you continue upon this trajectory, you will indeed be worthy of your inheritance.'

'Thank you, Uncle,' said Cormac. He contemplated how to phrase his next statement in the most eloquent terms. The words were coming to him more easily, the more he spoke the tongue of the upper classes. 'I shall endeavour to meet your expectations to the best of my abilities.'

Lord Bewley gave him a look of unmistakable fondness. 'I know you will.'

## Chapter 17

She stood beneath the branches of the oak, a smile of welcome lighting up her face. He felt his own mouth broaden into a grin as he strode towards her; he could not wait to sink his hands into her luscious, chestnut hair. Just before he came within arm's reach, her smile faltered. The ground shifted under their feet and, glancing about in alarm, he realised they were on the pitching deck of a ship. He grabbed onto the gunwale to keep his balance. Sea spray splashed his cheeks. He looked back at her and saw that her jaw had dropped in horror.

'What did you do?' she gasped.

He had no time to answer her. The hand was already snaking around her throat, gripping a blade with a razor-sharp edge. It drew across her tender flesh and red blood blossomed on pale skin.

'No!' he bellowed. 'Stop!'

But she was already slumping to the deck, her dark brown eyes glassy and empty. Her collapse revealed Oliver, a maniacal sneer stretching his lips. He pointed the bloody blade at Bridget's body.

'That was your fault,' he said. 'And so is this.'

He raised the knife to his own throat.

Cormac roared again for him to stop but the words were choked off. He touched his neck and felt the gash there, the blood welling up and spurting out, the breath leaking from his body...

He woke with a start, shaking from head to foot. He reached up to his throat and found it intact. His hand rose further and discovered that his cheeks were indeed wet, though not with sea spray. He was dashing the tears away when a voice spoke, making him jump with fright again.

'Oliver, dear?'

Lady Bewley hovered in the shadowy doorway of his bedchamber, her plump figure silhouetted by the glow of the candlestick she held. As she came further into the room, the flame illuminated the deep concern in the fleshy creases of her face.

'A-aunt,' he stuttered. 'What are you —'

'You were shouting,' she said, her voice full of sympathy. 'Was it another nightmare?'

He had roused her before with his night-time struggles but she had always waited until the following day to make solicitous enquiries. He must have been shouting violently indeed to draw her to his chamber at this late, dark hour.

'I—yes—I'm so sorry for disturbing you.'

'There is no need to be sorry.' She set the candlestick on the bedside table and sat on the edge of his bed, taking his sweaty hand in her own. 'I only wish I could ease your suffering. You do miss your parents most dreadfully.'

She and Lord Bewley believed that the deaths of Gerard and Caroline Davenport haunted his dreams, and he allowed them to think so. He could not, after all, tell them that it was their true nephew who visited him nightly, along with the lover he yearned for with the despair of eternal separation. But her words served as a wretched reminder that his own parents were lost to him too; his father had passed away a long time ago and his mother might as well be dead, living on Oakleigh land where he was forbidden to ever set foot again. She was as unreachable as the suicidal Oliver, whom he tried to save every night in the nightmarish landscape of his tormented mind.

Quite beyond his own volition, a sob escaped his throat.

'Oh, you poor dear,' Lady Bewley said and pulled him to her.

He found himself unable to resist. He let her wrap her large, comforting arms around him, press his head to her shoulder and stroke his back, and he cried in her embrace like a boy with a grazed knee. He was undeserving of such solace but he accepted it greedily, wanting for just a short time not to feel the loss of all the dearest people in his life.

They said nothing else. Somehow she knew the moment when he was ready to be released and she freed him from her grasp with no more than a gentle kiss on his temple. She picked up the candlestick and left the chamber, gliding away like a guardian angel.

The next morning, he entered the breakfast room with some trepidation, wondering how much she had told Lord Bewley of what had happened during the night. But neither the earl nor the countess acted like anything was amiss and he went to the sideboard, relieved. While he was grateful to Lady Bewley for her consoling presence, he was also acutely embarrassed that he, a grown man, had fallen apart to such a degree. The less said about the undignified affair, the better.

He filled his breakfast plate with the usual twinge of guilt. He still found it hard to tolerate the vast amounts of food at his disposal, and the criminal waste of what was left uneaten, when he was conscious of the awful poverty that existed across the sea in his home country. In the beginning, he had guzzled more than his fair share at every meal, fearful that he would wake from his hallucination to find himself back on the streets of Dublin, emaciated and starving. Unfortunately, his stomach had not been accustomed to such a rich diet and, after a disagreeable period when he did not stray far from the chamber pot, he had learned to control his intake. Now, his body was well-nourished and stronger even than it had been when he had worked as a stable hand.

'Lord Sinclair will be calling today,' Lord Bewley announced as Cormac took his seat at the table. 'He and I mean to resolve the dispute over the boundary line in the forest.'

Lord Sinclair's estate bordered Lord Bewley's along its northern side and some confusion had arisen over where the boundary lay through a section of woodland that Lord Sinclair was having cleared for tillage. All was amicable between the two lords but the neighbour was punctilious to a fault and had insisted that the matter be dealt with promptly.

'Mr Sandler will also be present at the meeting,' said Lord Bewley. 'In the meantime, I should like you to visit two of the farms beyond the village. They are having an issue regarding fallen fences and wandering livestock which I want you to settle. Mr Comerford will accompany you as he is already familiar with the situation.'

It seemed that Lord Bewley, having declared his intention to bestow his estate only upon one worthy of the honour, now expected Cormac to earn that honour by contributing to its management. Both daunted and eager, Cormac accepted his duty with due deference. He was glad to hear that Mr Comerford would be his companion – apart from the fact that Mr Sandler's second-in-command would steer him away from any major blunders, the man actually had some Irish ancestry, a connection which Cormac secretly treasured. Never mind that the fellow was as gruff as an ill-tempered bull.

'Have some coffee, Oliver,' Lady Bewley said, pouring a cup from the copper pot and pushing it over to him. 'It's fresh.'

'Thanks, Ma,' he said without thinking and nearly knocked over the cup. 'I mean, Aunt,' he corrected at once and busied himself with swallowing the scalding liquid almost in one gulp.

When he dared to look up, Lord Bewley was gazing blandly out the window and Lady Bewley was rising to replenish her plate at the sideboard. As she turned from the table, he caught a glimpse of the private smile that lifted the corners of her mouth.

After breakfast, Cormac and Mr Comerford set out together, following a lane that led away from the grounds of Bewley Hall and towards the local village of Gildham. A light haze had burned off and left a glorious summer day in its wake, the sun beaming down on an undulating carpet of verdant fields. Though Cormac regarded England as a foreign country, he could not deny that its landscape resembled the Irish countryside so much that it was almost like riding across Oakleigh land. His heart tugged at the wistful memory of home.

There was silence between them apart from the jangle and creak of harness and saddle and the steady beat of hooves on dusty ground. Mr

Comerford, a bachelor past his prime who sported a remarkable set of mutton chops, was not a man inclined to indulge in casual conversation. Cormac didn't think the fellow was inherently churlish, only that he hadn't quite grasped the nuances of human interaction.

Deciding to take the proverbial bull by the horns, Cormac charged into discourse. 'These surroundings remind me of the area where I grew up. Tell me, what part of Ireland was your grandmother from?'

Mr Comerford made a gravelly noise in his throat as though he had not yet used it that day. 'Kerry.'

They trotted on another hundred yards.

'Do you still have family there now?'

'Some distant cousins.'

This time Cormac waited a mere fifty yards before asking, 'Did you ever visit it?'

'Once, in my early twenties.' Mr Comerford surprised him by adding gruffly, 'A striking place. Have you ever been there?'

'No.' In reality, he had never left Carlow until his banishment and had only spent that brief spell on the Willowmere Estate in Kilkenny before heading to the unforgiving city of Dublin. In the past of the young man he was impersonating, he could make the safe assumption that Oliver had lived the majority of his life in Meath or Dublin and would never have had occasion to visit the most south-westerly county of Ireland. 'I have heard tell of its wild beauty though and it sounds comparable to the rest of the country, a breathtaking panorama of every shade of green that can be found in the moss and the leaves and the clover. It is no wonder Ireland is called the Emerald Isle.'

He experienced another deep pang of homesickness and pushed it away, while Mr Comerford, unmoved by his poetic digression, lapsed back into taciturnity.

They passed through Gildham, a peaceful hamlet with a church and parsonage, numerous cottages with pretty gardens, and the dwellings of several craftsmen, including the skilled lacemakers for which Bedfordshire was known. Some of the inhabitants recognised Cormac as the nephew of the earl and hailed him in their strong accents.

It had taken him a long time to adjust to being among the English. Thirty-four years had elapsed since the failed rebellion of 1798 but the fire of revolution continued to simmer in every Irishman's heart. He hated the way England had such a stranglehold on Ireland, crushing its people and traditions at every opportunity. Still, he had to acknowledge that most of the English people he encountered were not the ones to blame for the hardships put upon his countrymen. Lord Bewley might claim some responsibility, being a peer in the House of Lords, but these locals had probably never travelled far beyond the environs of Gildham. In fact, just

*A Class Entwined*

like the land on which they lived, they were not so dissimilar from the folk he had left behind.

This impression was borne out when they arrived at the first farm and the farmer's wife, Mrs Marsh, insisted they sample some of her freshly-made cheese before going about their morning's business. As she was setting a stacked plate on the table, two small boys, barefoot and giggling, dashed through the kitchen, snatched a couple of squares of cheese, and scampered out the door. Mrs Marsh picked up her skirts and ran after them, scolding at the top of her lungs. Cormac hid a smile; the bustle and racket was so reminiscent of Mrs Kavanagh's kitchens at Oakleigh.

After filling their bellies with the flavoursome cheese, he and Mr Comerford met with the two parties involved in the wandering livestock dispute. Farmer Marsh was accusing his neighbour, Farmer Fletcher, of neglecting to maintain his fences, with the consequence that Fletcher's cattle had strayed into Marsh's fields and trampled a substantial portion of his crops, but Fletcher protested that he had only fortified his fences the previous winter. The four of them went out to inspect the fallen fence in question and, having scrutinised the area, Cormac thought he could identify the problem.

'This patch is very boggy, despite the good weather,' he said, digging his booted heel into the ground with a squelch of confirmation. 'That means it must be even worse in wet conditions. The heavy rainstorms this past spring can't have helped matters. The fence posts are loosening as a result, which then enables the animals to push them down.'

'What choo propose we do about it, sir?' Fletcher said dubiously.

Cormac reflected on the lessons he had received from his tutor on the subjects of estate management and agricultural concerns, as well as his own experience building fences in the past.

'Plant vegetation,' he said. 'Trees, hedges, something with strong roots to hold the soil together. That ought to secure the fence in a more solid position. In the meantime, we can erect a makeshift fence thirty feet that direction,' he pointed towards some higher ground, 'as a temporary measure.'

He shrugged out of his riding coat. Mr Comerford and the two farmers gaped at him.

'What choo doing, sir?' said Marsh.

'An extra pair of hands will get the job done quicker.' He grinned at their astounded faces. 'Let's get to work.'

Much later, he and Mr Comerford returned to Bewley Hall, mucky, sweaty and tired. His companion betrayed no opinion on the day's events but he himself was quietly exultant. It had felt good to stretch his muscles in such physical exertion and he believed he had found a reasonable solution to the farmers' grievances. As they entered the house, the butler,

Sheppard, informed him that Lord Bewley once again required his presence for a meeting. He hurried to wash and change his clothes – assisted by his valet, one of the most extraordinary aspects of his new life – and then made his way to the study. As he went down the corridor, he passed a striking display of lilacs assembled in a patterned bowl. He held his breath and did not let it out until he had gone past the display and could be sure the scent of the flowers could no longer reach him.

A thin woman with a set of keys dangling from her waist hovered outside the study door. She was so skinny that the bones of her elbows and shoulders stuck out, even beneath the layers of her black uniform.

She was the housekeeper of Bewley Hall and also Mr Sandler's wife, though the pair's typical interaction with each other would not make that connection apparent. Professional at all times, they were aloof in their public exchanges, and just once had he glimpsed them behaving in any kind of demonstrative manner. Not long after his arrival to Bedfordshire, he had spent a full afternoon out in the stables – the only place where he felt he could take a breath from his false existence – and afterwards had thought it best to come into the house by a side door so as not to drag mud and straw all over the floor of the entrance hall. He had caught sight of the housekeeper lingering in an inconspicuous alcove along the passageway, Mr Sandler by her side. He seemed to be reassuring her about something and, in a sweet gesture, he had taken her bony hand, kissed her knuckles, and pressed her palm to his cheek. She had looked pacified and gratified by his attention. Then her gaze had slid past him and alighted upon Cormac and she had jumped back at once. Cormac had given them a genial nod to indicate that he had no objection to such familiarity between husband and wife, and he had walked on, envying their intimacy. He was not as lonely as he had been in Dublin, but bearing a secret he couldn't share with even a single soul was its own form of isolation.

That wasn't to say that the intimacy of marriage was beyond him altogether. In fact, it was positively on the cards if he chose to remain at Bewley Hall. Lord and Lady Bewley had made no attempt to disguise their anticipation of the great many grandnephews and grandnieces they looked forward to doting upon and had already suggested he appraise the jewels on offer during the next London season. About a month ago, he and Lord Bewley had been drinking brandy at the dining table after dinner when the earl had brought up the subject with his usual frankness.

'Amorous congress,' he had said, causing Cormac to nearly spit out his brandy.

Coughing and swallowing, he had sputtered, 'P-pardon?'

'I have no wish to appear indelicate, but we are men and there are no ladies here to offend. Did my brother ever speak of such matters with you?'

Cormac had just shaken his head, incapable of words.

'You are at an age where it would be safe to assume you have had some dalliances with the opposite sex. Am I correct?'

He had felt himself go red to the tips of his ears. He wasn't sure how comfortable he would have been engaging in such a conversation with his own father, let alone this elderly gentleman who was no blood relative of his. He had mumbled something unintelligible but the earl had evidently understood.

'I am not here to censure but to counsel. All I ask is that your conduct befits a gentleman and that your discretion befits the lady. Be prudent and, once you marry, be loyal.'

It had been a chivalrous speech and it had made Cormac examine his past entanglements with a perturbed conscience. An heiress and a prostitute – both had been consensual but he could judge neither to be a success when one had discarded him and he had discarded the other. Ashamed, he had promised himself that his next conquest would be undertaken with much greater consideration.

But preferably in the far distant future.

'I appreciate your sound advice, Uncle,' he had said. 'In light of it, I beg to be allowed whatever length of time may be necessary to make myself deserving of that lady to whom I will be unfailingly loyal. May we defer any contemplation of a visit to London until I have accomplished that?'

Lord Bewley had raised his brandy glass in a gesture of approval. 'That is indeed an acceptable request.'

No more had been said on the matter since, but being summoned to the earl's study twice in two days made Cormac worry that Lord Bewley might have begun to view the situation in a more accelerated way.

Mrs Sandler shuffled aside as Cormac approached the door to the study. 'Good day, sir,' she muttered.

As he nodded in greeting to her, the study door opened and both Mr Sandler and Mr Comerford emerged.

'A word with you, Mr Sandler, if you please,' the housekeeper said, and she and her husband walked stiffly away down the hall.

Mr Comerford made a grunting sound that might have been construed as a salutation to Cormac or a gripe about bellyache, and he too disappeared.

Cormac knocked on the door, waited for Lord Bewley's call of invitation, and entered.

'Have a seat, Oliver,' said the earl from behind his desk. He idly stroked the brass handle of his cane, which rested against his knee. 'You must be weary. I hear you have been involved in an inordinate amount of physical exercise.'

Cormac sat, his first misgivings beginning to stir. Was he about to receive a condemnation of his actions?

'Do not look so anxious,' Lord Bewley said with a good-humoured smile. 'I am very pleased. Mr Comerford has given me a glowing account of your efforts today.'

Glowing? Cormac sent a glance of bafflement towards the closed door. Mr Comerford obviously liked to play his cards close to his chest.

'Very well done, my boy.' Lord Bewley tapped his cane on the desk. 'And you will be happy to hear that all has been settled with Lord Sinclair as well. He is the most pedantic fellow I ever met but that is well and good, I suppose, where land boundaries are concerned. Carruthers will handle the documentation with thorough attention to detail. We do not want to cause headaches for future generations.'

Cormac shifted with uneasiness but Lord Bewley didn't notice, absorbed as he was in locating a specific letter from the neat pile in front of him.

'Here, take this.' As Cormac stretched out his hand, he continued, 'It is from your mother's sister.'

Cormac froze in the action of taking the paper. Oliver's aunt? He had not even been aware of the connection. He drew back slowly and unfolded the page but could not make himself read the words. This was it. His duplicity was about to be discovered; he was moments away from being arrested and sent to prison.

'I have never met your mother's side of the family, as you know,' said Lord Bewley. 'I understand she was descended from a line of rather impoverished Irish nobility but, when it came to sanctioning my brother's marriage to her, that was not a material issue for me. He was in love with her and she with him. I could not have opposed the match on grounds of eligibility when they were so suited to each other.'

Even in the midst of his fear, this remark brought a realisation that caused Cormac's gut to twist in sadness: Oliver Davenport had perished needlessly. He had deemed death to be preferable to a life suffocated by obligation, but Lord and Lady Bewley were eminently decent people – they would not have forced their nephew into a situation that would have made him unhappy. And Lord Bewley himself had said he was under no commitment to bequeath his estate to his heir presumptive. They might have been disappointed but they would have allowed Oliver to pursue his dream of a poet's life. With a wave of remorse, Cormac experienced afresh the loss of that anguished young man.

Lord Bewley recalled him to the present with his next disastrous statement. 'Mrs Gibson has intimated that she should like to visit Bewley Hall.'

That was the worst news possible. She would lay eyes upon Cormac and scream the house down that he was not Oliver.

'I surmise, however, that seeing her dear nephew is not her objective, as she alleges, but seeing what her dear nephew is due to inherit. And, I further deduce, claiming that he has a Christian duty to provide aid to his poorer relatives.'

Lord Bewley's lip curled at the notion of such vulgarity and Cormac seized the opportunity to circumvent the impending calamity.

'She ought not come then,' he said and added in wild invention, 'I regret to disclose that this is not the first time she has attempted to inveigle funds from our family. My parents were kind-hearted enough to satisfy her requirements on several occasions but she always coveted more. There was no love lost between her and my mother.' Guilt pricked at him but Gerard and Caroline Davenport could not contradict him. 'I have no great desire to see my aunt when her purpose is so distasteful. Perhaps, if you are amenable to the proposal, I could send a small sum of money to placate her.'

The irony of the circumstances was that this unexpected complication might lead to a solution to a private concern of his. He had been wondering for some time how to surreptitiously send money back to his family in Ireland, now that he was in a position of affluence. Mrs Gibson had opened up the avenue to his accessing the necessary funds.

Lord Bewley set aside his cane and reached for the inkstand. 'Yes, I think that would be the best course of action. I'm certain Mrs Gibson would then find that a journey across the sea would not be so agreeable to her after all.'

Cormac sat back in his chair, affecting a relaxed pose. Although the immediate danger had passed, the tension did not leave his body. He had been growing comfortable in his role but now he realised he must always be watchful; his was a highly precarious position and he could be exposed at any time.

## Chapter 18

'That was most entertaining!' declared Lucy.

'Yes,' Cassandra enthused, 'the sets and costumes were magnificent!'

'I felt the music was not as strong as some of his other compositions, but otherwise I enjoyed it,' said Alice in her soft voice. 'What did you think, Bridget?'

Bridget bobbed her head at her companions. 'I agree with you all, though I believe the portrayal of the plight of the lower classes was vastly underemphasised.'

The four ladies were returning from the theatre in a single carriage, which Lucy's husband, Lord Newby, had put at their disposal for the evening.

'Dearest,' said Lucy, rubbing Bridget's arm with affection, 'you always do advocate so generously on behalf of the common man.'

Cassandra sniffed. 'I cannot imagine why. The creatures have no one to blame for their poverty but themselves.'

Bridget's mouth tightened but she restrained herself from berating her friend; though Cassandra was a wealthy countess, she could not boast of a broad education. 'Perhaps if you accompany me to St Swithun's sometime, you will observe that that is not the case.'

Cassandra looked horrified at the idea of setting foot in the workhouse, but Alice said, 'I do believe I should like to come with you. I have deferred a visit for far too long.'

Lucy's interjection reflected Bridget's own thoughts. 'Sweet Alice, you have too gentle a soul for such a venture. One look at the miserable wretches and you would dissolve into tears.'

Alice seemed near to weeping at the very thought. 'Oh dear, it may be that you are right. How do you bear it, Bridget?'

'And why do you even bother?' said Cassandra.

The halting of the carriage prevented Bridget from answering. The Newbys' footman opened the door and announced, 'Wyndham House.'

She gathered her mantle around her shoulders. 'Goodnight, ladies, and thank you all for an enjoyable evening.'

'Do not forget my party in two days' time!' Cassandra trilled in farewell.

'Indeed, I shall not,' Bridget called back as she stepped down from the carriage.

A blast of chilly January air hit her and she drew her mantle tighter around herself. Breath billowing out in front of her, she climbed the front steps of the townhouse where her own footman greeted her at the door.

'Thank you, Peter,' she said after he had closed the door and shut out the cold. As he took her mantle and bonnet, she said, 'My goodness, it's bitter out there. Tell me, how has your mother been since the stove was installed?'

'Very well, m'lady. I can't thank you enough. That stove's been a godsend. She says the house ain't never been so cosy and her lungs have cleared right up.'

'I am so pleased to hear that. Do let me know if there is anything else we can provide for her comfort.' Bridget moved further into the entrance hall and perceived the stillness within the house. 'Is my husband not here?'

'No, m'lady, he hasn't returned home yet.'

Perhaps Garrett had chosen to remain at his club for the night. In a neutral tone, she said, 'You may go to bed now. Leave the door locked but unbolted. My husband will let himself in if he comes back.'

After Peter had bowed and retreated, she picked up a candlestick from the hall table and ascended the staircase all the way to the third floor. There, she paused outside a door, listened for a moment, and stole into the chamber.

The air was warm from the small, slumbering body sprawled on top of the large bed. Bridget crossed the room and the candlelight flickered over her daughter's face. More than six and a half years had passed since her arrival into the world, but Bridget still found herself captivated by every endearing aspect of her, from her tiny button nose to her slightly chubby cheeks, flushed now with sleep.

But it was her hair that made everyone gasp in admiration. Thick curls, even thicker than her mother's, fell in natural waves down her back. And their extraordinary shade, such a golden hue that they shimmered in even the faintest light. Of course, there were the inevitable comments: how unusual, both parents so dark and the child so fair, that had to be a very uncommon occurrence? Bridget's reply remained consistent – that it was more common than one might expect – but she was certain people talked. No matter. Her conduct in society was exemplary; other than the colour of her daughter's hair, there was no foundation for that one vague rumour.

A single curl had fallen across the little girl's mouth and it fluttered out and back with each gentle breath. Heart full, Bridget bent over to kiss her forehead. Emily made a snuffling noise but didn't wake up. She had kicked off the covers at some stage in her sleep so Bridget pulled them back up over her shoulders to prevent her from catching a chill. Then she left the room without a sound.

She descended the stairs to her own bedchamber on the second floor.

Audley, her lady's maid, assisted her with her nightly regime, placing her jewellery in the box on the dressing table and taking out a fresh nightdress from the chest of drawers. Once Bridget had slipped it on, she dismissed Audley and climbed into bed, humming one of the more memorable tunes from tonight's theatre performance.

That was when she realised with a jolt that it must be past midnight and tomorrow had now become today. The humming died in her throat and she looked back at the chest of drawers. The lowest drawer contained some of her saddest memories, and only once a year did she permit herself to look inside.

She slid back out of bed, stumbled across the room, knelt by the drawer, and pulled it open. A small pillowcase rested at the top; she withdrew it with a sigh. Embroidered on the front was his name: James. She kissed the stitched letters and rubbed the soft fabric against her cheek.

Next there were several baby gowns, tiny and neatly folded. She took them out one by one and stroked them before setting them on the floor. At the bottom of the drawer lay a velvet pouch. She untied it and a lock of soft, dark hair fell out onto her lap. The tears came and she didn't stop them, allowing herself to grieve for her little boy. He would have been four today.

She was not sure how long she sat there crying but at length the tears subsided and she felt better for the release of emotion, despite the pain that had accompanied it. She touched the lock of hair to her lips, tucked it back into its pouch, and returned everything to the drawer.

As she climbed into bed for the second time, she heard the distinct sound of the front door opening and shutting two floors below. A few clumsy bangs and a muffled oath told her that he had been drinking heavily tonight. Footsteps mounted one set of stairs, and the next. She held her breath and listened to their erratic movement across the landing, trying to determine their direction. They faltered and then there was a knock on her door.

She exhaled in resignation. 'Come in.'

Garrett sidled into the room and closed the door behind him, tilting back against the door panels as though his sense of balance was uncertain. She waited for him to speak first.

'It is very cold outside,' he said with the barest hint of a slur. 'I think it might snow.'

She arranged her expression into one of polite interest.

Running a hand through his black hair, he approached her bed and sat on the edge of it. A strong smell of spirits wafted from him.

'I have not forgotten what day it is,' he murmured.

She stared at him, dumbfounded.

He frowned. 'Do not look so surprised. Do you think I am heartless?'

She could not find the words to form a reply.

'He was my son,' he muttered. 'And I loved him.'

That was true but he had no right to be injured by her astonishment when he had for so long suppressed any hint of such emotion. After James's death, he had turned into a statue of ice, shunning her and Emily while simultaneously making it his ambition to frequent every drinking and gaming establishment in London. The loss of their boy had broken him and obliterated any hope of a peaceable marriage between them; all they had left was a fabrication for the eyes of society. During these past long years, they had each carried a burden of sorrow in solitude, the weight of it doubled because he had refused to share it. She didn't think she could ever forgive him for that, but now was not the time for reproach.

'May God look after our boy,' she said, her speech as indistinct as if she had been the one imbibing alcohol.

'Amen,' he said.

He shifted his weight and she thought he was going to leave, but instead he slid closer and leaned over to press his lips to hers. At first, she kissed him back, hoping it was merely a goodnight kiss. However, when the kiss became prolonged and his tongue pushed through, she stopped responding and he pulled back from her.

'What is wrong?' he asked, annoyed.

'I do not think this is appropriate,' she said, 'considering what day it is.'

'On the contrary. Today is James's birthday. I know it is a sad day but it should also be a hopeful one. Why don't we look to the future where there could be another little boy dressed in the clothes you keep tucked away in that bottom drawer?'

'We cannot replace James!' She was aghast at the suggestion.

'Of course not, I did not say that. But he is no longer with us and I think in honour of his memory we should try again. I want a child.'

'You already have a child,' she said and instantly bit her tongue, wishing she could bite back the words too. What a foolish thing to say. It was an unspoken rule within the house that they should never allude to Emily as his daughter if it could be at all avoided.

His eyes flashed. 'I desire a son,' he said, his quiet voice making the assertion no less threatening. 'One I can acknowledge. I want you to give me an heir.'

He put his hand on the bedcovers over her thigh and his head lowered towards hers again. She closed her eyes and submitted to him.

## Chapter 19

Garrett did not choose to remain in her bed so the next morning Bridget woke alone. After Audley had helped her to dress in sombre clothing, she went upstairs to her daughter's bedchamber. Now that Emily was older, Mrs Crewe's services were no longer required and the nurse had been replaced by a governess, Miss Davison. Bridget had been apprehensive about engaging the young lady, aware of the notorious role a governess could play in the carnal proclivities of the master of the household. But it had turned out to be a fortunate appointment for Miss Davison's features had proved too plain to tempt Garrett's interest and she had come to adore her charge. Though it was not within the remit of her educational duties, she revelled in combing through Emily's curls every morning, in which position Bridget found them as she entered the chamber. At her appearance, Emily slithered out of Miss Davison's grasp and ran into her arms.

'Mama, I dreamed last night that you and I grew wings and were able to fly over all the rooftops of London!'

'How wonderful that would be.' Bridget plucked at Emily's small chin. 'We would never have to worry about tripping over the cobblestones. Our poor horses would be left unemployed though. What would they do without a carriage to pull?'

'They could grow wings too and join us up in the clouds,' Emily replied as though this were the most sensible thing in the world. She surrendered again to Miss Davison's clutches and sat patiently on a stool while the governess arranged her hair.

'Not the red bow,' said Bridget. 'Please choose something plainer for today.'

'Why can't I wear my red bow?' Emily asked, disappointed.

'It would not be very fitting, gooseberry. Today is your brother's birthday.'

Emily took in the solemnity of her mother's dark-coloured dress and understood.

'Not the red bow today, Miss Davison,' she said gravely. 'I shall wear my navy one instead.'

The two women exchanged a sad smile over her fair head.

Bridget and Emily went down to breakfast, the little girl still chirping about her dream. When they entered the breakfast room, they found Garrett seated at the table reading a newspaper. Emily ceased her chatter and gazed down at the floor.

'Good morning, Papa,' she mumbled to her toes.

'Good morning, Emily,' he said tersely. He had no pet names for her.

They took their places at the table. As Bridget buttered some toast for Emily, the little girl spoke up, her expression thoughtful.

'Am I still a sister even though baby James isn't here anymore?'

Bridget glanced at Garrett, whose face had hardened.

'You will always be his big sister and he will always be your little brother,' she said. 'That will never change.'

'I wish the measles hadn't made him go to heaven,' said Emily. 'I would have enjoyed showing him how to paint when he was old enough.'

Garrett shoved his chair back and left the room without another word. Bridget was anguished to see how Emily's face fell.

'It's supposed to snow today,' she said. 'Wouldn't that be exciting? If enough falls, you could build a snowman in the gardens.'

Emily brightened at once and dashed to the window to check for falling flakes.

They heard Garrett depart the house soon after, gone to spend the day lounging about his club or whiling away the hours at Parliament or perhaps attending a meeting with his solicitor or his agent – enduring James's birthday anywhere but at home.

After breakfast, Bridget relinquished Emily into Miss Davison's care for her morning lessons and sat at her writing desk to respond to two letters.

She dealt with the easy one first. It was to her friend, Madeleine Wallace, now Mrs Matthew Parnell following her marriage to an acquaintance of Garrett's. She was still living in Ireland and happily married with two children. She related all the gossip about the girls Bridget had known back in Dublin, while Bridget in turn updated her on the latest London fashions. Their correspondence amounted to nothing more than vacuous nonsense but Bridget had to be content with that. Much as she yearned to unburden her long list of heartaches to a sympathetic friend, there was no one who would be able to understand, least of all the frivolous Madeleine.

The other, more troubling, letter was from her mother. She had not seen Lady Courcey since the night of Emily's birth and had not heard from her in nearly all that time. But a month ago, just before Christmas, Lady Courcey had finally written. She had wished the family a happy and peaceful season and expressed the hope that they were all in fine health. She had spoken of the Oakleigh Estate and how well it was prospering. Then, in a startling demonstration of humility, she had begged her daughter to forgive her and allow her to visit them in London. The closing line had intimated that she was not in the best of health and that she was finding the winter cold and lonely.

The tone of the letter was so melancholic that Bridget wondered whether her mother had sunk into a depression. How ill was she? Perhaps that was why she wanted to make amends.

But how could she make amends? Some acts were unforgiveable. Apart from her transgressions against her own daughter, Lady Courcey had been responsible for the appalling fate of the McGovern family, forcing them into destitution and rendering their chances of survival almost nonexistent. And the most unconscionable part was that the lady had known full well the ramifications of her actions and it had not inhibited her in the slightest.

Bridget's hand was heavy as she reached for her pen.

> Mother,
>
> Thank you for your correspondence. I am glad that the estate is thriving under your guardianship.
>
> We are all in good health. Emily is six and a half now and full of chatter. She is very intelligent and loves to paint.
>
> I am sorry to hear that you have been poorly; I trust that Mr Abbott is taking good care of you.
>
> I regret to say that I cannot grant you the forgiveness you desire. You have hurt too many people and the wounds have not yet healed. But I maintain the hope that one day they will be healed and we shall be able to bridge the gap that necessarily came between us.
>
> However, that day is not today. Please do not write again. You will hear from me when I am ready to communicate once more.
>
> Your daughter,
> Bridget

She sealed the letter and set it aside to be sent with the other household messages.

Later that morning, she pulled on her sturdy boots, her plainest bonnet and a weathered cloak, and left the house on foot. A few snowflakes had started to drift down but that did not deter her; this was one commitment she could never neglect.

She arrived at St Swithun's out of breath and flushed from the vigorous walk. There was no clamouring crowd outside the soup kitchen and the building itself was dark and deserted. Despondent as always at the sight, she trudged past it to the entrance of the forbidding workhouse.

It was the new Poor Law which had brought about the grievous state of affairs. Two years previously, Parliament had passed an act banning all outdoor relief – from then on, the poor could only seek succour within the confines of the workhouses, and the conditions inside those were made as unpleasant as possible to discourage all but the most desperate from entering them. Bridget and Frances Blythe had done everything they could to incite the Ladies of Compassion Association into righteous protest against such barbaric measures, but the ladies' complaints had been lacklustre at best – they were only concerned with the appearance of altruism rather than the actual improvement of the lives of the misfortunate souls they purported to aid. Bridget had even petitioned Garrett to speak against the proposed act in the House of Lords but she knew it was futile; he wouldn't entertain the notion for an instant when it would mean aligning himself with the minuscule minority. The whole endeavour felt like trying to break through an iron door with a feather. The soup kitchens around London were shut down, charitable financial assistance to the workhouses was repressed as much as possible, and St Swithun's became as good as a prison for the creatures forced to take refuge there.

Nevertheless, Bridget persevered. She still had two able hands to distribute food and a smile to offer comfort. She would volunteer in whatever manner she could and damn the people who were unwilling to support their fellow man and who were unable to see that their own good fortune was merely by chance of birth.

Frances had been appointed as an assistant matron in the workhouse once the soup kitchen had closed and she never failed to inspire Bridget with her tenacity and kind-heartedness. She was the only member of staff in the place who tried to insert an element of humanity into the proceedings, which made St Swithun's just a little less unbearable than the other workhouses around the city.

Today, she assigned Bridget to the men's dining hall, while she would serve the women and children under the age of six in a separate hall. The dinner bell rang and, under the watchful eye of a warden with a truncheon at his belt, the inmates shuffled in, queuing up in a straggly line to collect their meal of boiled beef, bread and a pint of beer.

Bridget invited the first person, an elderly man with hardly any teeth, to approach her bench. He received his plate and mug with shaky hands and whispered, 'Thank you, m'lady,' in a quavering voice before sitting at a table near the back of the hall to mash the gristly meat and hard bread with his gums.

She handed out the rations to each man and boy. Some took them from her in silence, others with murmured thanks. She smiled at everyone, whether they raised their eyes to her or not, and tried to put a little extra on the plates for the younger boys.

At length, the line began to peter out and the hall filled with a low din of muttering and clunking of dishes. The last man in the queue had a lopsided gait and shambled up to her with a scowl.

'About time,' he grumbled.

She presented him with a smile and his plate and mug.

'What're you smiling at?' he demanded, making no move to take them from her.

She was taken aback. 'I—nothing. Your dinner, sir.' She held them out again.

He closed his hands into fists. '*Sir*? Don't you mock me. You think I don't know where you come from? The kind of people you come from? If they were here, there ain't no chance you'd be calling me *sir*!' He spat on the floor.

'I meant no insult,' she said and placed the dishes on the bench for him to pick up himself.

'Your very presence is an insult,' he said, his words dripping with vitriol. 'Don't you know you're good for nuffin but lying on your back in a rich man's bed and pushing out his brats?'

She gaped at him. What had she done to deserve this kind of abuse?

'That's enough, Joe,' came another voice and she was relieved to see Frances appear by the man's side; she must have already finished dispensing food to the women and children. She grasped his arm but he shook her off and seized Bridget's left wrist. She jerked in surprise and pain.

'You think you're such a saint,' he growled, 'coming down here for a few hours to take pity on us poor folk afore going back to your fine house, thinking you've done your duty. You ain't nuffin but a fraud.'

Frances's attempts to drag him away were ineffectual. He twisted Bridget's wrist so that her palm was facing down, exposing the engagement ring on her finger: a large ruby encircled by pearls.

'Look at that! Why fool yourself? You ain't making a bleeding bit of difference!'

By this stage, the warden had come to intervene. He forced Joe to let go of her with a blow of his truncheon between the shoulder blades. He hauled the belligerent man out of the dining hall but she could still hear him shouting expletives all the way down the corridor. For such an infraction, he would spend up to twenty-four hours in the refractory cell, which the inmates called the 'dark hole'. He must truly have been incensed to risk a punishment so grim.

Her hands were shaking and she felt winded as though the truncheon had landed on her own back. Frances steered her into a back room, away from the staring eyes of the men and boys.

'Don't you fret about him,' she said in bracing tones, rubbing Bridget's upper arms briskly. 'He's just bitter because life dealt him a bad hand and he thinks you're holding a royal flush. He saw you as an easy target for venting his frustration.'

Bridget could not speak. Her wrist hurt abominably.

'Let me get you something to drink,' Frances said and bustled away.

Bridget blinked back the tears that threatened to fall. Joe had misjudged her, but of course she could tell neither him nor Frances the truth. She was not here for self-gratification. The real reason she threw herself into her charity work was because she nurtured the hope that if she was being kind to these poor individuals then maybe, if there was any justice in the world, in some unknown place there were other compassionate people who were aiding Cormac and his unfortunate family. She would do this work for decades if it meant that some sort of balance might be restored.

That was, if any of them was still alive.

## Chapter 20

By the next morning, the pain in her wrist had somewhat receded. It still looked swollen but thankfully not enough for Garrett to notice. If he heard that there had been real danger at the workhouse, she feared he would forbid her to go there again. Therefore, in order to give the impression that all was well, she kept her promise to attend Cassandra's gathering that evening. She would be going without Garrett, of course; he seldom made the effort to socialise with her acquaintances.

She travelled to Radcliffe House with Lucy and her husband. Lord Newby was fifteen years Lucy's senior and usually uncomfortable at this type of assembly, where dancing was a favourite activity, but he bore his discomfiture with stoicism. They ascended the steps to the open front door and a pair of fetching footmen conducted them into the grand entrance hall where their hostess came forwards to meet them. Cassandra was wearing an extravagant, green gown with a waist so narrow it was a wonder she could breathe, while an emerald-encrusted tiara nestled in her hair. She never did anything by halves; when she threw a party, her guests always remembered what she wore.

'You are all most welcome!' she greeted them before casting a look of amused disappointment towards Bridget. 'Lord Wyndham could not make it again? What a pity, your husband has far too many clashing engagements! Alice is already here, do come and join her.'

She led them into the drawing room where they found Alice hovering forlornly in a corner.

Cassandra cried, 'I declare, Alice, we cannot have you alone like this a day longer. We must find you a husband. And I do believe I have just the gentleman, a new fellow from Henry's club who will be in attendance tonight. I shall have to introduce you both. Excuse me, while I go ask Henry about him.' And she fluttered off in pursuit of her husband.

Alice turned pink. She had neither beauty nor fortune and, at the age of twenty-eight, had almost resigned herself to spinsterhood, but the colour in her cheeks indicated a small degree of optimism.

A footman passed by with a tray of champagne flutes and Lord Newby secured glasses for each of the ladies. Bridget took hers with her left hand, winced at the sudden stab of pain in her wrist, and switched the glass to her right hand.

Lucy perceived her grimace and said with concern, 'Good gracious, do you have an ache?'

Bridget glanced at Lord Newby. He attended the same club as Garrett and the two men were in frequent company together; she had no wish for her tale to reach Garrett's ears. Lord Newby seemed to understand, however, that his presence was not desirable and tactfully moved away to converse with a puffy-cheeked gentleman.

Once the three ladies were alone, she gave her companions a brief account of what had happened at St Swithun's. As to be expected, they were both horrified.

Alice exclaimed, 'An attack on your own person, how shocking!'

Lucy added, 'There is no question that you ought to cease your involvement at once.'

Bridget stood her ground. 'One man's desperate act is not enough to frighten me from my duty.'

'You should confine your obligation to making charitable donations,' said Lucy with a shake of her head.

Bridget was saved from defending herself further by Cassandra's reappearance.

'Excellent news, ladies. The gentleman's name is Mr Oliver Davenport and he is the sole heir to a vast estate in Bedfordshire. Now, wouldn't that be a fine match for Alice? He and his aunt and uncle are in London for the season. Here he comes now with Henry.'

Bridget, Lucy and Alice craned their necks towards the doorway, where Lord Radcliffe was just entering the drawing room in the company of…

Bridget's heart stopped and she gasped so loudly that all the people in the room turned to look at her.

'Are you feeling unwell again?' Lucy asked, clutching her elbow.

The room spun around Bridget; she could not breathe. *Cormac*? For a moment she believed she might faint, but Lucy's pinching grip kept her alert and upright.

'I'm fine,' she managed to rasp. 'Just a twinge in my wrist again.'

She sat in a chair that Lord Newby offered her but refused some smelling salts from Alice. The other guests looked away once they could see she was not in any immediate peril and their collective attention returned to the newcomer at the party. Without their gazes upon her, she could try to recover some semblance of composure.

She could not have been more shocked and winded than if somebody had pushed her down a flight of stairs. Cormac, *her* Cormac, a stable hand, was being ushered into the room and introduced to some of the highest people in London society. And he looked like one of them too, resplendent in the stylish evening wear of a wealthy gentleman. But it was not just the clothes that made him look the part; he held himself like a nobleman, tall and proud. His comportment was impeccable and he greeted each guest with incomparable courtesy.

This sophistication was so unlike the Cormac she knew that she had to blink and stare at him again. It was unquestionably him but some things were very different. His skin, which used to be so tanned from the sun, had grown paler and his fair hair had been cut shorter so that it did not fall into his eyes anymore when he bent his head. And he was bending his head an awful lot – every woman in the room seemed to want to make his acquaintance and he bowed respectfully to each one, appearing flattered and humbled by their attention.

She was flabbergasted. Where on earth had this suave Cormac come from? Far more crucially, where had Cormac himself come from? The last she had known of him was that he had refused the help of the Grace of God Mission Society – how did he proceed from that deplorable situation to attending a gathering at one of the most fashionable residences in London? It was astounding. She would have been less surprised if Emily had turned into a rabbit.

She blanched when she saw Cassandra approach Cormac and coax him in their direction. She was not ready for this. She must be in a dream and he was no more than an apparition from her past. This could not actually be happening.

'– and it is my delight to introduce you to Lord and Lady Newby.' Cassandra sounded as distant to Bridget as though she were speaking from the other side of a closed door.

'I am most pleased to make your acquaintance,' said Cormac, bowing to Lucy and her husband.

It was unmistakably his voice but it, too, seemed altered. His accent was more cultured and there wasn't a trace of his former rural twang. Even the language he used was more formal than his old way of speaking.

'And this is Lady Wyndham,' said Cassandra.

Bridget rose from her seat and did the only thing she could do – she offered her hand and murmured, 'My sincere greetings, Mr Davenport.'

'A pleasure, Lady Wyndham,' he said and bent over her gloved hand with the charm of a gracious stranger. This was Cormac but he was far removed from the Cormac she had once known so well.

He let go of her hand very quickly.

'And may I present Miss Caulfield?' Cassandra went on with an ostentatious flourish in Alice's direction.

Alice went as red as beetroot and tripped over her words as she squeezed out her greeting. It was evident that she was quite taken with Cormac, and why not, for he was more dashing than any other gentleman in the room. Bridget had always thought him good-looking, but now, polished up as he was, he had become exceptionally handsome.

After these introductions, Lord Radcliffe commandeered Cormac for the company of a cluster of gentlemen by the fireplace, providing Cassandra, Lucy and Alice with the chance to put their heads together.

'Did I not tell you?' said Cassandra. 'I can think of no better match for a woman seeking a husband.'

'He is very attractive,' Lucy remarked, somewhat breathless. 'What an eligible gentleman. Indeed, Alice, you could not go wrong with this Mr Davenport.'

Alice's eyes widened. 'Oh, but he will never consider me. You saw how the other ladies behaved, they will all want him. And I have no fortune.'

Cassandra waved the argument away. 'Have I not already said he is to inherit a substantial estate? He has more than enough money for you both.'

It was Lucy who noticed that Bridget was not contributing to the conversation. She touched her arm solicitously. 'Is your wrist hurting very much? Do you need to go home?'

'No, not at all,' Bridget replied swiftly. Departing this party was the last thing she wanted to do. She had to observe more of this new Cormac and, if possible, speak with him alone. The initial shock was beginning to wear off and now she was consumed with a blazing desire to find out how he had come to be here. 'I do not need to leave. I did feel unwell for a moment but it has already passed.'

Just then, the bell sounded for dinner and the guests drifted into the dining room, which was filled with several round tables, each laid out with twelve place settings. Bridget went in on the arm of Lord Newby and Lucy was escorted by her husband's puffy-cheeked companion. Bridget and Lucy sat, while the men remained standing until the rest of the guests had arrived to the table. To Bridget's left were two ladies and two gentlemen whom she recognised as Cassandra's distant cousins, and the last four places were claimed by Cassandra, Lord Radcliffe, Alice and…

'Mr Davenport, do come sit here by Miss Caulfield! You must tell her about the beautiful countryside in Bedfordshire for she is very fond of nature.'

Cormac held out a chair for Alice with a smile – the matchmakers were on the road to success already – and, as all the men sat down, he took his own seat which happened to be opposite Bridget, leaving her in a good position to watch him and listen to his conversation during the meal.

He himself turned out to be the main topic of discussion. The female guests in particular were eager to learn more about him and paid rapt attention as he answered questions on everything from his political standpoint to his favourite sport. This kind of treatment was customary for any new addition to their circle but it seemed to be even more intense with Cormac, no doubt because he was unattached and so pleasing to the eye.

'Mr Davenport,' simpered one of the ladies on Bridget's left. 'Some of us find it difficult to believe that there is no Mrs Davenport. Is there any reason why you have not yet married?'

'Miss Norwell, how very forward of you!' Cassandra remonstrated and then turned to Cormac with a gleam in her eye. 'Although I suppose it would be rude not to answer, now that the question has been asked.'

He chuckled. Bridget was amazed at the effortless way he was able to flirt with these brainless women. 'I'm afraid the answer is quite dull. I have simply never sought a Mrs Davenport. My aunt and uncle preferred me to concentrate on learning to manage the estate in Bedfordshire before becoming distracted by such matters. Having said that, I do believe that marriage was one of their motives in our coming to London this year. They are of the opinion that I should consider settling down in the near future and that I may find a potential wife here in the city.'

A flurry of whispers passed between Miss Norwell and the other female cousin and then they both looked up and beamed.

'I am astonished that you have never been to London before,' said Lucy. 'Why is it you are only making your first visit now?'

'There are two reasons for that,' he said, taking a sip from his wine glass. 'First of all, I was born in Ireland and most of my upbringing took place there, so for a long time I never had the opportunity to visit this splendid city. Then, when I did move to England, I persuaded my aunt and uncle to delay my acquaintance with London as long as possible.'

'Why would you do that?' Cassandra asked incredulously.

'I suppose I felt that, having grown up in another country, I was somewhat rough-edged and needed to refine my style and manners before venturing among you fine people.'

He looked embarrassed as he said this and even more so when a chorus of protestations arose vouching that he had the most gentlemanly conduct in the world. Bridget doubted if much of his story was genuine but she suspected this last bit almost certainly was. While always well-mannered, the Cormac she had known wouldn't have had the first idea of when a gentleman should remove his gloves or which cutlery he ought to use when dining. If he had shown up in London with his former rustic manners, he would have been laughed out of the city.

'Why did you grow up in Ireland?' said Alice. 'Were your parents from there?'

'My mother was Irish. When she married my father, he decided to stay in Ireland rather than bring her back to England. She would have been heartbroken if he had forced her to leave her home.'

Bridget experienced a wrench of sorrow as she compared this tale to her own life, while the ladies made hushed comments to each other about how romantic and selfless the elder Mr Davenport had been to make such a personal sacrifice for his wife.

'Are they still there now?' That was Alice again; she must indeed be smitten to overcome her shyness long enough to pose three questions in a row.

'I regret to say that they have both passed away,' he said and sympathetic murmurs rose up on all sides. 'They drowned in a boating accident. Lord and Lady Bewley were the only family I had left so that is when I came to live in England.'

Barely trusting her voice to work, Bridget summoned up the courage to ask, 'And how many years ago was that?' She hoped she might extract a snippet of real information that could help her decipher his true story.

He looked at her across the table with a tilt of his head and she could swear he knew precisely what she was thinking. 'About four and a half years ago.'

Lucy said, 'Do you plan to return to Ireland in the future?'

'I would very much like to go back again sometime,' he replied, and the conversation moved on to the topic of travelling abroad, and choice holidaying destinations, and had Mr Davenport ever visited the continent.

After the dinner had ended, the party transferred to the ballroom so the dancing could commence. Mr Davenport was by far the most popular candidate for a partner and every lady tried to catch his eye, hoping he would write his name into her dance card. Bridget marvelled at the way Cormac moved out on the floor. Even though she had never seen him dance back at Oakleigh, she was positive he could not have been knowledgeable in such steps back then. He must have received lessons in the meantime. Which raised one of many burning questions: what sort of life had he led in the intervening years that he'd had occasion to obtain dancing lessons? Who in God's name were Lord and Lady Bewley? Had he invented them or were they real people? Was he coercing them into pretending to be related to him? Or had he hoodwinked them into believing he was their nephew? Idea after idea, each one more ridiculous than the last, churned through her head until it was sore.

A quiet voice interrupted her thoughts. 'Good evening, Lady Wyndham. Would you do me the honour of taking the next dance with me, if you are not already engaged?'

Her stomach flipped over. 'Oh, I—no—I mean, yes—that is to say, I am not engaged.'

Cormac looked like he was trying to hide an amused smile as he offered her his arm and said, 'Shall we?'

He escorted her out onto the floor and they took their place on one side of a quadrille square. She glanced up into his familiar blue eyes and felt her breath catch in her throat. It was a surreal moment, standing next to someone whom, until tonight, she had feared to be dead. She was bursting to ask him dozens of questions but she would have to choose her words with care in case the pairs of dancers on the other three sides overheard.

'Are you real?' she whispered as the musicians struck up the tune and their hands clasped together. Despite the two layers of gloves, the contact made her heart skip a beat.

'Indisputably so.'

They took a turn within the perimeter of the square, his movements as graceful as if he had been born to be a gentleman.

'Who is Oliver Davenport?'

'I am.'

'But who is he really?' she pressed.

He hesitated. 'Too long an explanation for one dance.'

She swallowed, unsure what to make of that. The dance separated them for several bars, obliging them to partner with the couple opposite them. When they returned to each other, the adjacent pairs took up the pattern, giving her the opportunity to ask, 'How did you come to be here?'

'Here at the party, here in London, or here in England?'

She was taken aback by his casual tone. How could he not see the gravity of the situation? 'Did you come here seeking me?'

He looked disgusted. 'Don't be so self-obsessed. Believe it or not, you aren't the reason for my being in London.' It was their turn again to participate; they circled smoothly around the square. 'I didn't spend the last seven and a half years pining for you. I made a new life for myself and our paths just happened to cross at this moment. You will not even see me again after tonight.'

Crushed by this rejoinder, she endured the rest of the dance in silent turmoil, which he did not seem disposed to disrupt. When they were nearing the end of the quadrille's final figure, she said at last, 'Don't you want to meet another time? When there are not so many people around?'

'What good would that do?'

His bluntness was scalding. Doing her best to conceal her distress, she said, 'So you do not have any wish to become reacquainted?'

'How is Garrett?' he said pointedly in response, just as the music finished and the dancers reformed the square. He gave her a stiff bow, not allowing her time to answer, and all she could do was curtsey and watch him walk away.

What a dreadful encounter. It left her feeling lightheaded again; she had a sudden and desperate need for air. A set of French doors led from the ballroom to a secluded terrace outside; retreating out to it, she found it empty of guests. Grateful for the solitude, she closed the doors behind her, blocking out the clamour of the dancing and chatter.

A light snow had fallen and the terrace and its balustrade were coated in white. It was bitterly cold but she did not feel it – she was smouldering with emotion. Now that she was on her own, she could let her feelings spill out. She began to weep.

The relief was overwhelming. Cormac was alive. For more than seven years she had lived every day in the fear that he was not, and to learn the truth was a release from that imprisonment. How he had become an apparent gentleman of society was unfathomable to her but it mattered less than the realisation that he was alive and very well.

She started in alarm when she heard the French doors open again and whirled to see Cormac emerging onto the terrace. She tried to wipe her tears away but it was too late to hide them. Was that regret on his face? He shut the doors as she had done, though that was not quite proper now that they were a man and a lady alone.

He approached her, withdrew a handkerchief from his pocket, and held it out. 'Am I the cause of these tears?'

There was no need for her to reply. She took the handkerchief and dried her eyes.

'I had better apologise for my discourtesy during the dance,' he said. She noticed that he did not drop the formal language of the upper classes even though there was nobody to hear but her; she supposed it must come to him naturally now after so many years playing the part.

She shook her head. 'You had every right to speak as you did.'

A pregnant silence fell between them. Unable to bear the weight of it, she asked, 'You say you did not seek me out, but did you know I was going to be here tonight?'

'No, though when I came to London I suspected I might happen upon you.'

'I all but fainted when you entered the drawing room.'

'You did look quite appalled. The sight of me must have indeed been a shock to you.'

She said tentatively, 'Did you not feel something similar?'

He paused. 'It took a moment to adjust,' he said, but she was convinced he was underplaying the emotion he must have experienced. No one could share a past like theirs and not have a strong reaction – whether positive or negative – when they saw the other again.

A few stray snowflakes floated onto their hair and clothes but she paid them no mind. 'You received your invitation to the party through Lord Radcliffe?'

'Yes, we became acquainted at our club.'

'You are fortunate it is not the same club as Garrett's. Had he encountered you, he would have exposed your masquerade immediately.'

'I made advance enquiries to avoid such a scenario.' For the first time, he seemed apprehensive. 'Can I trust you not to divulge my secret?'

With all her sincerity, she said, 'I swear I will not do anything to hurt you. But will you tell me how you have managed to rise in society by no legitimate means that I can think of?'

The set of his jaw was enough; she was not entitled to know that information. He cast around for a change of subject. 'Are you well yourself?'

'As well as I can be.'

'Do you have a family?'

Her heart twisted and she turned her face away so that he would not see her pain. 'I have a daughter. Her name is Emily.'

'How old is she?'

'A little over six and a half.'

'Quite the hasty marriage.' His voice was hard.

That grieved her, his assumption that she and Garrett had conceived Emily directly after they had married. But, dear God, how could she find the words to tell him the truth?

They were startled by the sound of the French doors opening once more. This time it was Lucy who appeared, silhouetted by the candlelight from the ballroom. She checked at the sight of Bridget and Cormac on the terrace alone – they were standing rather closer than propriety dictated. Bridget balled up the handkerchief into her fist and Cormac took a respectful step away.

Acting unperturbed, he said, 'Lady Newby, is it not? I have been introduced to many new faces tonight but I believe I have it right.'

'You do, indeed, Mr Davenport,' said Lucy. 'Are you enjoying the evening's entertainment?'

'Most assuredly, yes. Lady Radcliffe knows how to throw a fine party. However, I anticipate my joints will be stiff tomorrow. Perhaps next time I shall not attempt to participate in every single dance.'

Though it took an enormous effort on her part, Bridget added her laughter to Cormac's with the cordiality of two people who had only made their acquaintance a few hours ago. Lucy laughed too before throwing a quizzical glance at Bridget.

'I came to look for you. I cannot imagine what you are doing out here in the freezing cold!'

Bridget could think of no quicker excuse than, 'My wrist was bothering me again. I thought to put some snow on it.'

'You injured your wrist, Lady Wyndham?' Cormac asked.

She reddened. 'It is nothing. I hurt it in an incident yesterday.'

Lucy linked arms with Bridget. 'Lady Wyndham is our heroine of the workhouse.'

Genuine surprise filled his features. 'The workhouse?'

'Oh, yes,' said Lucy. 'She is the most philanthropic person of our acquaintance, devoting herself wholeheartedly to the cause of the poor. Not even a deranged man's assault can discourage her.'

'How very admirable,' said Cormac. 'And please accept my best wishes for a speedy recovery. Ladies, I shall return indoors. I would advise you not to stay out much longer in this weather.'

He bowed to them both and headed back to the ballroom.

Lucy gazed after his retreating back. 'Good gracious, he really is a fine-looking man. He has such beautiful eyes. We must do everything we can to match him with Alice before that Miss Norwell can get her claws into him. He and Alice would make a lovely couple, do you not think?'

'Mmm,' said Bridget noncommittally.

## Chapter 21

'So, Oliver,' said Lady Bewley, executing a precise rap on the top of her soft-boiled egg, 'you sampled the delights of London's season last night. I trust that went well?'

Cormac, whose own thoughts had also been dwelling on the party at Radcliffe House, looked up. 'Yes, it was an enjoyable evening.'

'No doubt you encountered a great many pleasing young ladies,' she said with a twinkle in her eye.

From the top of the table, Lord Bewley winked at Cormac. 'Beware,' he said. 'She is scheming again.'

Cormac withheld the weary sigh that threatened to escape him. 'I believe you are right, Uncle.'

'Well?' Lady Bewley prompted. 'Were they agreeable to you?'

'They were, I suppose, but what is the hurry? Do you need me to find a wife within a month of our arriving in London?'

They both stared at him in surprise.

'Forgive me,' he backtracked. 'I did not mean to be impertinent.'

Lady Bewley reached across the table and patted his hand. 'There is nothing to forgive. We have been putting a good deal of pressure on you about this, more than we should. From now on, we shall step back and let you take your time. It is important that you find the right woman, a proper lady who will make a worthy lifelong companion for you.'

Bridget's face swam into his mind but he banished her at once. 'I promise I shall keep looking. If I search hard enough, I am sure she will appear.'

'Make certain you choose a lady who is willing to have a large family,' said Lord Bewley with a chuckle. 'Your aunt and I are looking forward to spoiling our many grandnephews and grandnieces.'

'I shall take that into account,' Cormac said, laughing along with him, though his gut clenched at the daunting task they had set upon his shoulders.

'I hope the company at the party was stimulating, at any rate,' said Lady Bewley. 'Impartially speaking, did you make any interesting new acquaintances?'

Irresistibly, Bridget surfaced again. 'I met Lady Wyndham, who helps at a workhouse,' he said before he could help himself. That particular detail had stuck with him ever since he had heard it.

Lady Bewley, who was herself involved in charitable works in Bedfordshire, perked up with interest. 'Does she indeed? How intriguing. Did she mention where the workhouse is situated?'

'I did not ask for further information.'

'I would be most eager to hear about the workhouses here in the city, for they must accommodate hundreds of poor souls. Perhaps you could arrange for Lady Wyndham to come visit me? I should very much like to talk with her about her endeavours.'

He nodded, but found he had no appetite anymore and pushed his plate away.

As soon as breakfast was over, he escaped to the gardens of Raynesworth House. Situated on Park Lane, the Earl of Bewley's London residence reflected the affluence of its distinguished address, and its grounds were no exception, comprising an expanse of lawn, well-tended flowerbeds among winding paths, and a walled orchard. Cormac paced along one of the paths, sloshing through the melting remains of the previous day's snowfall, and took deep breaths to calm himself.

These discussions about taking a wife were becoming alarmingly frequent. It had been all very well to agree to the suggestion back in Bedfordshire when the potential wives were in distant London – but now they were right in front of him and he was expected to choose one. Could he make such a long-term commitment to his false persona? There would be no way out if he got married; he would be Oliver Davenport forever and Cormac McGovern would be no more.

And what of his unfortunate bride, whoever she might be? She would have to remain ignorant of his deception, meaning that their marriage would begin upon a bed of dishonesty. Now that he could afford to have scruples again, the very notion of it revolted him.

He approached the walled orchard and pushed at the door, which resisted due to a sheltered snowdrift on the other side. Shoving his way through, he found himself in a small enclosure with fewer than a dozen apple trees and a stone bench in one corner. It was a decent size for a garden in a well-populated city, but paltry in comparison to the sprawling orchard at Oakleigh.

And that, of course, directed his thoughts once more to Bridget.

He would have liked to convince himself that her existence was immaterial to him now, but in reality he had been vigilant for a glimpse of her ever since his arrival to London. He had sought her chestnut curls whenever he passed a lady on the street or at the park or in a ballroom, hoping and fearing it would be her.

And then he had entered the drawing room at Radcliffe House. It had taken every ounce of his willpower to retain his composure, but at least he had had years of practice in maintaining a facade. He had managed to preserve his self-control, while an ignoble part of him had experienced a small amount of vindictive satisfaction in her stunned bewilderment.

She was greatly altered, he had perceived that at once. Though an outsider would deem her an image of perfect loveliness, he discerned the waxen quality of her too-pale cheeks, the drooping lines of sadness around her mouth, the haunted look in those dark brown eyes. This profound change in her had consumed him all night, making sleep impossible. What unhappy things had befallen her since they had last met?

And why should he care so much?

He supposed he was drawn to her because for a decade and a half she had been the brightest point of his life; seeing her again stirred up feelings which had long lain dormant. But what were those feelings now? There was such a great deal unresolved between them that he found them impossible to identify.

He knew he should hate her. She had given him her promise and then rejected him to satisfy her tyrannical mother and manipulative fiancé. Now her husband, he amended resentfully. On top of that, her actions had forced him to forsake his family and sink to the status of a wandering beggar, and there was no joy in recalling *that* agonising time.

Lost in his wretched memories, he did not realise that he was no longer alone in the orchard until he heard Lady Bewley say, 'Oliver, dear? Are you not feeling well?'

He came to himself and found that he was sitting on the stone bench, his elbows on his knees and his hands clenched tight in his hair. Knowing how disturbing this must appear, he jumped up and tried to arrange a smile onto his face.

'Aunt, you startled me.'

Her forehead furrowed into plump folds of anxiety. 'You are as white as a ghost. What is the matter?'

'Nothing at all,' he tried to assure her.

'That is not the truth. You looked like you were attempting to tear your hair out.'

'Did I?' he said with as much innocence as he could muster. 'I was preoccupied with inconsequential thoughts, that is all. There is no need to worry.'

'Please know that you can confide in me whenever you wish to. I am always here to share your burdens.'

'I do know that and I thank you for it.' He took her hand and held it affectionately in both of his own. 'I owe you and my uncle more than I can ever repay you.'

She relaxed, mollified. 'You are such a dear,' she said. 'Come, let us go inside.'

She slipped her arm through his and they walked through the garden back to the house.

***

By the time two days had passed, Bridget had reached a high state of agitation. Having received no word from Cormac after the party, she could only assume he remained resolute in not wishing to meet. She had made some discreet enquiries about the Earl of Bewley but it seemed he was a legitimate peer; there wasn't a whisper of fraudulence in connection with the family, and all reports claimed that his heir was an estimable gentleman in every regard. Baffled and frustrated, she wondered what she ought to do. Did she dare seek Cormac out? It was unseemly for a lady to call upon an unmarried gentleman, but she could not tolerate the idea of encountering him at further social events and pretending to be strangers. There was a history between them which they needed to address, for good or for ill.

She was brooding over her dilemma at the breakfast table, while at the same time trying to persuade Emily to eat the last of her bacon, when Garrett spoke.

'So tell me about this Oliver Davenport.'

She gaped at him, nearly dropping Emily's fork. 'Pardon me?'

'I was talking to Newby at the club yesterday. He mentioned there was a new bachelor on the scene turning all the ladies' heads.'

'Oh, yes, that's right,' she said and gave a false laugh. 'Mr Davenport.'

Garrett sat back in his chair with a smirk. Was he recalling the days when it had been he who had set all the ladies swooning? 'What are his circumstances?'

How she wished she knew. 'There is not much to tell. I believe he is in the city for the season with his aunt and uncle. They have a sizeable estate in Bedfordshire. That is all I know about him.'

'Newby said he was quite the star of the party the other night.'

'I suppose he was. Lucy and Cassandra regard him as a perfect match for Alice.'

She held her breath, fearful that Lord Newby's loose tongue had also divulged her near-fainting episode, but Garrett made no mention of it. He sat forwards to eat again.

'I shall have to meet the fellow sometime. Newby had a fine conversation with him about horse racing.'

'Indeed,' she said placidly, even as her insides shrivelled. Garrett meeting Cormac was the least desirable event imaginable and she would have to do all in her power to prevent it from ever happening.

A few minutes later, the messages arrived, two for Garrett and one for

Bridget. She opened hers and peered at the signature. A small gasp escaped her which she hastily converted into a cough. After glancing at Garrett to make sure he had not noticed her unusual reaction, she swept her gaze down the page.

> Dear Lady Wyndham,
>
> I trust this letter finds you well and that your injury has fully healed. I am writing to invite you to luncheon the day after tomorrow at Raynesworth House, where my uncle and aunt, Lord and Lady Bewley, are residing while in London. I mentioned to my aunt that you are engaged in charitable work in the city and she is most eager to discuss that subject with you as she too is involved in such efforts in Bedfordshire. She also asked me to request that your daughter accompany you for she adores children and has a little gift for her.
>
> I look forward to your response.
>
> Your servant,
> Oliver Davenport

She admired the elegant script, a far cry from the stocky letters he used to scrape onto slate. He had worded it well too; to any eye, this was nothing more than polite correspondence between acquaintances. She supposed he had written it like that in case it happened to fall into the wrong hands.

She reread the message with a measure of apprehension. She was keen to accept on her own behalf but the invitation had also been extended to Emily. How wise would it be to allow Emily into his presence? There was so much she did not yet know about his unexplained past that she wondered whether it would be best to be cautious for now where Emily was concerned. Until she could trust him, perhaps she ought to keep the truth concealed.

In the end, she concluded that it would be discourteous not to bring Emily when Lady Bewley had made a particular request for her attendance but that she need not be so fretful over Cormac and Emily being in each other's company. He had no suspicions of fatherhood so why would he look too closely?

After breakfast, she penned her acceptance and instructed Peter to carry it to the Bewleys' residence. However, the day before the visit to Raynesworth House could come to pass, she came unexpectedly face to face with Cormac again.

She and Alice had decided to go to Regent's Park to enjoy a bout of skating on the ice-covered lake. The snow had retreated, a weak sun had emerged, and a hard frost the night before promised good skating conditions. Neither Lucy nor Cassandra accompanied them; Lucy had a prior arrangement at the milliner's, while Cassandra considered putting on a pair of skates a pursuit as agreeable as visiting the disease-ridden workhouse.

When Bridget and Alice arrived at the park, they found the lake already teeming with skaters. Men and women glided across its smooth surface, chattering and laughing, the ice sparkling beneath their boots. The gentlemen were being attentive in assisting the ladies to stay upright, their helpful hands clutching arms, elbows, and sometimes waists. Here and there, less experienced skaters lost their balance and tumbled to the ice, rising to their feet with embarrassed grins.

Bridget had debated the wisdom of skating so soon after she had injured her wrist, but she resolved to be cautious on the ice and stay well away from other skaters who might wobble into her path. She desired a spell outside in the bracing cold. Though it stung her nose and made her fingertips numb in spite of her gloves, the activity would be a welcome distraction from her chaotic thoughts.

Or so she had believed. She and Alice had been on the ice for scarcely a few minutes when a pair of gentlemen came skating towards them and she distinguished Cormac's familiar face below his fine hat. She teetered on her skates and it took all her effort to maintain her equilibrium, in every sense of the word. How could she ever become used to the idea of Cormac dressed in the best fashions of the day, socialising with the upper classes, and betraying not the barest hint of his lower class beginnings?

With Cormac was Cassandra's athletic husband, Lord Radcliffe. That gentleman was the exact opposite of his wife – he was most likely to be found where there was sport of some kind, preferably out of doors; the extravagant parties were all Cassandra's doing and he was merely obliged to suffer them. His lithe form glided with ease over the frozen lake, and he chuckled as Cormac made some sort of amusing joke alongside him.

There was a moment when Bridget thought they might all just skate by each other without interaction. She could identify the precise instant when Cormac spotted her by the sudden stiffening of his previously relaxed posture, but he made no move to acknowledge her. Flummoxed, she did not dare initiate the greeting herself.

But then, as the men drew nearer, Lord Radcliffe glanced their way. Recognition filled his features and he hailed them, causing all four skaters to skid to a halt.

'Greetings, ladies,' said Lord Radcliffe. 'Are you enjoying the skating?'

'Very much,' said Bridget. She could not rely upon Alice to make conversation; her friend was shrinking further inside her scarf.

'I hope you're being careful on the ice. It can be treacherous to the unwary skater. I saw one young fellow slip not ten minutes ago and achieve a painful twist of the knee in the process.'

'Thank you for your concern,' said Bridget. 'We are taking the utmost care.'

Lord Radcliffe turned his genial expression on Alice, offering her the opportunity to contribute.

The bit of Alice's face that was visible above her scarf went blotchy with self-consciousness. 'I do love to skate,' she said, her voice coming out in a squeak.

'It's an invigorating pastime, is it not?' said Cormac, casting her a kind smile of his own.

'Indeed, Mr Davenport. Do you' – Alice took a breath and plunged on as though she were asking a very personal secret – 'do you get much opportunity to skate during the winter in Bedfordshire?'

'There is a river that runs through my uncle's estate. When it freezes over, the greatest sport is partaking in skating races along it.'

'How exhilarating,' said Alice. Her chin started to emerge from her scarf, like a small animal nosing out of its burrow.

'It is a pity we cannot attempt such a challenge here,' said Lord Radcliffe ruefully, 'but circling around the lake is pleasurable too. Perhaps we may accompany you for a while?'

He held out his arm to Bridget, leaving Cormac to offer his to Alice. Bridget experienced a twinge of paranoia. Cassandra had known about the skating trip – had she persuaded her husband to instigate this encounter in order to further the matchmaking plans she had hatched with Lucy? The crisp air and the glimmering winter sun provided a romantic setting for the encouragement of an attachment.

She could say nothing as Alice shyly accepted Cormac's arm. They turned to skate away closer to the centre of the lake. Lord Radcliffe gestured to Bridget, indicating that they would follow, but she stopped him with a shake of her head.

'Thank you, but I am feeling tired from the exertion. I should like to take a rest, if you do not mind.'

With a courteous bow – all the more impressive for having been executed while wearing a pair of ice skates – he escorted her to the side of the lake and, after her repeated protestations that she would be fine by herself, he returned to the ice. Instead of rejoining Cormac and Alice, however, he sailed off on his own, making Bridget suspect even more that the meeting had been by design rather than by chance.

She sat on the bank of the lake. At first, she spent some time untying and retying the laces of her skating boots but, irresistibly, her gaze was drawn upwards and across the surface of the lake.

Even at a distance, she could tell that they were enjoying each other's company. As they skated along, Alice's gloved hand rested comfortably in the crook of Cormac's elbow and she looked up into his face with a beaming smile. Then she lurched on the ice and lost her footing. She clung to Cormac as she tottered, causing him to stagger too. They hovered on the cusp of falling but managed to regain their balance, his arms around her waist to keep her steady. Their laughter drifted over the lake, warm and genuine.

Bridget hated the black feeling this roused in her. Alice was so sweet and affectionate once she overcame her timidity; she deserved to have a good man fall in love with her. But Cormac…

She imagined how it might play out. They would encounter Cormac at more parties and balls. He would make sure to write his name in Alice's dance card, no doubt for the waltzes where the giddy speed, the close embrace, and the opportunity for uninterrupted eye contact afforded a more sensual, intimate experience. They would go riding along the popular Rotten Row in Hyde Park, and others would begin to comment on how much time the two young people were spending together. And then the announcement would be in the paper: an engagement, a perfect match, a very happy couple.

But the name of the groom-to-be would be Oliver Davenport. Who on earth was Cormac pretending to be? How was any of this even possible? And how would poor Alice feel if she ever learned how she had been deceived?

Bridget had promised Cormac she would keep her silence. But in knowing the truth about his past, she was now complicit in whatever unknown act he had committed to obtain his place of prominence in society. If only he would speak to her, explain how he had come to be here, help her to make sense of it all. She was adrift in ignorance.

At length, he and Alice came skating over to her. Alice was breathless and pink-cheeked, her eyes sparkling. Cormac's cheerful expression transformed into a controlled mask of detached civility as soon as he met Bridget's gaze. He held Alice's hand as she stepped carefully off the ice onto the bank.

'Until our next meeting, ladies,' he said and glided away from them.

## Chapter 22

Though it was no great distance from Berkeley Square to Park Lane, the weather was bitter and Emily's legs were short so she and Bridget travelled by carriage to the door of Raynesworth House, where the butler greeted them and escorted them to the drawing room. Bridget felt her nerves heighten at the prospect of seeing Cormac again but he was not present when she and Emily entered the room. Lady Bewley came forwards to receive them, her rotund body bobbing with pleasure.

'Lady Wyndham, you are most welcome! I am so pleased you could visit. And this adorable cherub must be your daughter! How do you do, little one?'

Once the initial exchanges of introduction were complete, Lady Bewley led them to a round table laid out for luncheon. As they sat, Bridget could not restrain herself from asking, 'Will Mr Davenport be joining us?'

Lady Bewley laughed. 'Oh, no, he has no interest in ladies' conversations. He and my husband have gone out for the afternoon. And now, my pet, what have I got for you?' she added, directing her words towards Emily, who was eyeing a small, wrapped package next to the sugar bowl. Lady Bewley handed it to her and Emily pulled back the layers of material to reveal a delicate, silver-handled hairbrush.

'My goodness, it is beautiful,' said Bridget. 'Emily, what do you say?'

'Thank you!' Emily said with delight, looking like she longed to pull down her neatly-arranged curls to prove the brush's efficacy at once.

Bridget sent her a suppressing glance and turned back to Lady Bewley. 'This is exceedingly generous of you, thank you very much.'

'Do not mention it. I gain the utmost content from witnessing a child's happy face. We were never fortunate enough to have children of our own. In all the years of our marriage, I believed only once that such joy might be within our grasp, but I was mistaken. However, I hope that one day Oliver will find a charming lady who will help him bring some little Davenports into the world. In the meantime, I have this enchanting vision to look upon. What wonderful hair and such blue eyes! She is a treasure to behold.'

Bridget expressed her gratitude again for the gift and for the lady's kind praise, privately wondering how Cormac felt about the lofty ambitions his 'aunt' held for him. Howsoever he had assumed the persona of Oliver

Davenport, he had let himself in for an incalculable amount of strife in the process. The aristocracy retained high expectations of their class; was he going to be able to live up to them?

While they dined on a luncheon of dainty sandwiches, cakes and tea, Bridget and Lady Bewley talked about their involvement in charitable activities, particularly lamenting the egregious effects of the new Poor Law. Emily, having nibbled enough to satisfy her mother, grew bored of sitting still and hopped off her chair to wander around the drawing room. Lady Bewley made no objection when the little girl discovered the connecting door into the music room and encouraged her to thump away vigorously on the piano she found there, despite the fact that Emily knew nothing more of the instrument than where the high and low sounds were. Though the ladies winced at the discordant noises wafting in from the music room, it was better for Emily to be distracted for, in the course of their conversation, Bridget found herself revealing the details of her recent assault at St Swithun's. Lady Bewley sympathised most earnestly and then surprised her by confessing that she too had been a victim of such violence in the past.

'He was starving, the poor wretch,' she said. 'There were more holes than material in his clothing and his ribs protruded in the most appalling way. This was before the soup kitchens were shut down, but that winter was harsh and the demands of the needy outstripped our supplies. I was obliged to go outside and announce that there was no food left, which meant he must endeavour to last another day with an empty stomach. It was too much for him to endure. He became distraught and needed to release his anger, of which he deemed me to be the rightful recipient.'

'What did he do?' asked Bridget, horribly fascinated.

Lady Bewley's cheeks, red from eating and enthusiastic chatter, turned pale. 'He slapped me across the face so hard that I fell to the ground. I tried to crawl away but he grabbed me around the neck and started to strangle me.'

Bridget clasped her own throat in horror. Her twisted wrist now seemed utterly insignificant.

'Was there nobody to assist you?' she breathed.

'My fellow volunteers were inside the kitchen attempting to keep control over the desperate creatures who had already managed to gain entry. Those left outside were others who had also been turned away and, in their despair, they simply jeered and made no move to save me. I believe I would have died had Oliver not come to my rescue.'

'Cor—' Bridget began but caught herself. 'Mr Davenport was there?' she said quickly.

Lady Bewley's expression lifted with pride. 'After our nephew came to live with us, he always insisted on escorting me to and from the soup kitchen. I think he would have preferred for my own sake that I had no involvement at all but, as I remained adamant in that regard, he made every effort to ensure my safety. He was standing at a distance with our horses, waiting for me to finish my work, but he saw what was happening, thank the Lord, and dashed to my aid. He hauled the man off me just in time, for a moment later I would have been wholly out of breath. As it was, I suffered severe bruising around my face and neck, leaving me in acute pain for many days. Oliver tended me throughout my recovery.'

Bridget's eyes widened. 'It sounds like your nephew is a very caring person.'

'Oh, he is. He treats me with such devotion that anyone would think he was my own son. I do believe he misses his own mother dreadfully. But I am glad that I have been able to stand in as a sufficient substitute.'

Bridget felt compassion rise within her. Cormac had been very close to Maggie; it must have been unbearable for him when they had been torn asunder. Perhaps the severance of that maternal bond had driven him to fill the gaping hole left behind. It seemed he harboured a genuine fondness for Lady Bewley; was it possible that not everything about his new life was an act of falsehood?

Lady Bewley carried on, 'After that incident, he tried to convince me to cease all association with the soup kitchen. I comprehended that he pleaded only out of concern for my welfare but I refused. The benefits of this kind of work far outweigh the evils. Perhaps you will view your own regrettable episode in the same light? Even with the restrictions imposed by the new Poor Law, we do more good helping those unfortunate people as much as we can than sitting in our drawing rooms drinking tea.'

Bridget looked down guiltily at her cup.

'Everything in moderation, however,' Lady Bewley said with an understanding smile. 'It is important that we always return to our proper stations. We are gentlewomen, after all, and must adhere to the duties of our class.'

After a maid came to remove the luncheon plates, Bridget rose to take her leave; there was no polite way to wait any longer for Cormac to make an appearance and the cacophony from the music room had increased to a level beyond fortitude. Lady Bewley instructed for the Wyndhams' carriage to be brought around from the mews behind the house, where it had retreated upon arrival, while Emily obeyed her mother's call and skipped back to the table to seize her new hairbrush.

'Would you like to come meet our footman?' she asked Lady Bewley, as though she were offering a gift equal to the one she had received. 'His name is Peter and he sometimes slips me biscuits from the kitchens.'

She sent an alarmed glance in Bridget's direction, plainly suspecting that she had revealed too much, and Lady Bewley hastened to intervene.

'What a lovely suggestion, my pet. It would be a privilege to make his acquaintance.'

Once they were all clad in cloaks, she accompanied them to the door and down the front steps to the street. Peter was flummoxed to be gravely introduced to the countess by the little girl but regained his equanimity, bowing and apologising that he had not thought to bring any biscuits today.

'Perhaps next time,' Lady Bewley said, twinkling down at Emily. Turning to Bridget, she added, 'And I do hope there will be a next time. I would be very interested in making a visit to St Swithun's, if you were amenable to the idea?'

Bridget was just expressing her agreement to that venture when two figures came walking up the street towards them, their breath puffing out in the cold air: Cormac and a white-haired, older gentleman. She hiccupped and stumbled over her last few words to Lady Bewley.

'—shall write to y-you to arrange a d-date.'

'Thank you, my dear. And here are the men now! How fortunate. I know my husband will be charmed to meet Miss Lambourne.'

With a beaming salutation, Lord Bewley proved to be as jovial as his wife and, after Bridget and Emily had been presented to him, he said with frank disappointment, 'Are you leaving already?'

'Yes, they must return home before it gets dark.' Lady Bewley laid an affectionate hand on Emily's head. 'The night comes so early at this time of year.'

'Well, it was an honour to make your brief acquaintance,' he said, lifting his hat to Bridget and winking at Emily.

Cormac concurred with a similarly civil remark, though he did not spare a glance for Emily. Bridget examined him surreptitiously to see if he regretted having missed this opportunity to speak with her but his face was unreadable. She curtseyed to them all and stepped up to the carriage door, her heart heavy.

After she and Emily had settled themselves, Peter hopped onto the footboard at the back of the carriage and, up front, Sawyer clicked his tongue at the horses. As they jolted into movement, Lord and Lady Bewley ascended the steps with Cormac to their front door, Lady Bewley's voice carrying back faintly to Bridget.

'—delightful young lady. And her daughter, what an angel. Those eyes! The only other person I have seen with eyes as blue as hers is you, Oliver.'

She saw Cormac's head whip around after the carriage and then her view was obscured as they continued down the street. She sank back in her seat and let out a shaky breath. He knew. Or, at least, the idea had been put into his head. She put her arm around Emily who was twirling the silver hairbrush around and around.

What was he going to do next?

She did not have to wait long to find out. The evening sky was darkening to a deep navy and the lamps had been lit in Wyndham House when Thrussell entered the drawing room and informed Bridget that a gentleman had left his card.

She had been warming herself in front of the fireplace. With a tremulous hand, she took the card from the butler's silver tray and read the name.

'Shall I tell him you are not at home, my lady?'

She reached out to the mantelpiece to steady herself before replying, 'No, you may send him up.'

Once alone, she pressed her fingers to her lips in distress. What could have possessed Cormac to show up unannounced like this? It was improper on a number of levels. He should have been able to restrain himself until he could speak to her at a more appropriate time and venue.

One look at his face when he entered the room told her he was beyond that kind of self-control. His eyes were wide and frantic and his hair was untidy as though he had run his fingers through it many times. He wore no gloves or hat and he forgot to acknowledge Thrussell for showing him in or bow in greeting to Bridget. He stood rooted to the spot until Thrussell had departed, leaving the door ajar, and then he burst out, 'I'm sorry, I had to come!'

Her pulse thrummed in her ears. 'Why?'

'Why!' he said helplessly. 'I had to—find out...' He trailed off, unable to articulate anything further.

'You need to leave,' she said, her voice low and full of urgency. 'Garrett could arrive home at any time. Did you even consider the possibility that you might have come face to face with him just now?'

Finding his tongue again, he said, 'I asked the butler if his master was here. If he had answered in the affirmative, I would have handed in my card and left.'

'And what do you think Garrett will do if he returns in the meantime and discovers Cormac McGovern in his drawing room? He will be enraged and we shall all pay the price for your rashness.'

She had not meant to place emphasis on 'all' but it came out that way anyway and he picked up on it. They were not the only ones who would suffer the repercussions.

His eyes fixed upon hers. 'I am not going anywhere until you tell me the truth.'

She sagged. He was not going to be dissuaded and, in all honesty, she could not blame him. The truth he was searching for, the truth he suspected, was well-deserving of this kind of reaction.

Conscious of the open door, she sat down on the sofa nonetheless, her heart beating like mad. 'What do you wish to know?'

He crossed the room swiftly and knelt in front of her, clutching her hands with both of his own. His skin was soft and smooth to the touch, nothing like the roughened surface it used to have.

'Tell me,' he entreated, staring at her with such intensity that she found it difficult to hold his gaze. 'Please. Your Emily. Is she' – he swallowed – 'mine?'

'Yes,' she said and squeezed his hands.

He rocked back on his heels, total shock written across his face. It was several moments before he was able to speak again. 'How can you be so sure?'

'She was born just less than eight months after Garrett and I married. If she had been his, she would have been frail and underdeveloped. But she was a fine, healthy baby come to full term. Her birth took place almost exactly nine months after you and I...' She blushed at the memory, recalling the event in vivid detail with his fingers so tightly entwined in hers.

Understanding flickered in the blue irises. 'Does Garrett know?'

She nodded. 'It is obvious that she does not resemble him in her looks. There is some of me in her. And a lot of you.'

He let go of her and stood to pace back and forth. 'This is too much to take in,' he muttered. 'I have a child. A daughter. How does one process this kind of information?' He stopped abruptly. 'Can I meet her?'

Her teeth fastened on the tip of her tongue. 'I do not believe that would be a very good idea.'

'Why not? Why shouldn't a father see his own daughter?' he said, his voice rising.

'Shush, or you will alert the servants! As far as Emily is concerned, she sees her father every day. It would not be prudent to introduce you to her right now, as Mr Davenport or anyone else. She is not familiar with any of my other male acquaintances. It would arouse suspicion.'

'I beg you,' he said and knelt before her again. 'I just want to look at her. She does not have to know I am there.'

She considered his eager, desperate countenance. This revelation had wiped all the aloofness from him; the refined gentleman had vanished and been replaced by a young man ruled once again by his emotions. He was almost the Cormac she remembered from Oakleigh.

'Very well,' she said and his face lit up. 'But you must not let yourself be seen.'

They rose and she led him from the drawing room, up the stairs to the third floor, and along the landing to the nursery. Despite her warning, it was likely that Garrett would remain at his club for several more hours, therefore this action, while ill-advised, did not place them within too great a risk of discovery, so long as they were discreet.

The door to the nursery was open a few inches. Emily was visible painting at a small table and Miss Davison sat nearby reading a book. Both were absorbed in their occupations and did not notice that they were being quietly observed from the doorway. Bridget watched Cormac looking at Emily. He appeared to be drinking in every aspect of her: her hair, the exact same shade as his own; her eyes, as blue as Lady Bewley had described; her mouth, screwed up in concentration; her small hand, directing her paintbrush with precision across the page in front of her. Bridget knew she was biased but she could not imagine that there was a more beautiful child anywhere else in the world.

At length, she tugged on his arm and he reluctantly dragged himself away from his first proper look at his daughter. Neither of them spoke until they were alone in the drawing room once more, having avoided any servants on their way back down through the house.

'How do you feel?' she asked.

Breathless, he said, 'I just cannot fathom how perfect she is. Lady Bewley was right, she is a little angel. Everything about her seems so pure and sweet. And,' he went on, full of wonderment, 'we made her. Can you believe that? Out of all the tragedy of that summer, it amazes me that something so exquisite emerged. She is the one good thing we ever accomplished together, Bridget.'

It was the first time he had spoken her name since he had shown up out of the blue; it sounded so familiar, so right to be coming from his mouth. He smiled at her and she felt her eyes brimming with emotion. Overwhelmed, she had to look away. In the next moment, his arms were around her, enfolding her in a tight embrace, and she sensed a pressure deep inside her ebbing away. She was relieved that he finally knew.

When at last they pulled apart, his expression had become serious. 'We have many things to talk about. Will you meet me tomorrow?'

'Yes,' she said without hesitation.

'The gardens across the street? At noon?'

'I shall be there,' she promised.

## Chapter 23

Cormac did not sleep that night. His mind was racing too fast to even contemplate rest. He sat before the fire in his bedchamber until the embers went dark and then he lay down on his bed, fully clothed and eyes wide open. He felt as though the world had upended itself, or else that the world was the same and he was upside down within it. It was impossible to adjust to the idea that he was a father, that he had been a father for more than six and a half years and had not known it.

Emily. His thoughts fluttered about like fallen leaves in the wind but they kept returning to her. His heart broke with the knowledge that he had missed so much of her childhood. He had not heard her say her first word or seen her take her first step. He had never had the opportunity to take a curl from her golden head in order to always keep her in his pocket with him. And she did not know that he even existed. She believed that smooth, selfish, manipulative Garrett was her true father. It was cruel and unfair.

Then there was the notion of fatherhood. Had he ever contemplated it before? Of course he had; every man desired progeny to strengthen his family tree. But that was a viewpoint he had taken when the prospective children were mere specks in the future, not yet conceived. Emily was real and living in the present and that made an enormous difference. He no longer possessed a vague urge to produce offspring; his awareness of Emily's existence had reduced that indistinct compulsion to a tangible purpose – to protect and cherish his daughter with every fibre of his being.

The most crucial thing now was to communicate this to Bridget.

The next morning dawned foggy and very cold. He suffered the slow passing of the hours in agitation until noon approached and he could head for Berkeley Square. He could not enter the private gardens without a resident to unlock the gate, so he lingered by the entrance, the tension of waiting burning deep into his bones. Barely three or four minutes had passed – though it felt like an hour – before Bridget emerged from Wyndham House and crossed the road towards him. His insides writhed with nerves.

When she reached him, he said, 'Does the weather bother you? If you feel too chilled…'

'No, this is fine,' she said. 'It is easier to breathe out of doors.'

He understood exactly what she meant.

They entered the gardens, which were deserted due to the freezing conditions. They began walking along the path beneath the plane trees but, now that she was beside him, he found himself tongue-tied.

After the silence stretched between them, she prompted, 'You said we had many things to talk about?'

'I did.' Which eloquent words would best convey what he was feeling? When he opened his mouth, the sentence came out in a clumsy rush. 'I want to be a part of her life.'

Her expression was tender. 'Of course you do, and I would not wish to prevent you from seeing your daughter.' He experienced a burst of optimism until she continued, looking torn, 'But at least one of us must think in realistic terms here. There are so many impediments to such a venture. What would happen if Garrett saw you?'

'We could arrange to meet far from wherever he was likely to be,' he said, quick to quash her doubts. 'That could be managed without trouble.'

'What about Emily? Who would you be to her? How would we come up with a plausible explanation for your meetings?'

'I could simply be an acquaintance of her mother's whom she encounters every now and then. Perhaps you could say that I am a benefactor of the workhouse. If she let that slip, Garrett would not get suspicious and would have no reason to wonder why he has never met me.'

'And what if she did not want to see you?'

His chest tightened. 'Then I would leave her be. But I hope it will not come to that.' He shot her a hopeful look. 'Are those all the obstacles you can think of?'

'Not all,' she said cautiously. 'Will you not be returning to Bedfordshire after the season is over?'

He baulked. 'I refuse to consider the future responsibilities entailed to the persona of Oliver Davenport when the consequences of my true self are right before me.'

'That is all very well to say but you *are* Oliver Davenport now. I have conversed with Lady Bewley and know her expectations of you. You do not have the freedom to remain in London, where Emily is. You have promised to marry, to produce children, to inherit Lord Bewley's estate. Who will do that if not you?' She hesitated. 'Where is the real Oliver? Could he be prevailed upon to return to his own life, liberating you from it?'

'No,' Cormac answered. 'He could not.'

Accepting this, she did not press him for further details. He let her step ahead of him along the path and, staring after her, was struck by how affecting it was to be in her presence again. He had never been closer to anyone than this woman; they had shared the innocence of childhood, they had shared the intimacy of a sexual embrace, and now they shared a child.

That relationship required absolute trust. He took several quick strides to catch up to her.

'I will tell you everything,' he said, seizing her gloved hand and forcing her to stop and look into his eyes. Her dark brown ones stared back in surprise. 'I have concealed my past but I open it up to you now.'

She lowered her gaze and then looked up at him again. 'I confess that, when we were young, I prided myself on thinking I knew you better than anybody else. But now you are a mystery to me, a locked door.'

During the silence that followed this statement, Cormac was sure he could hear both of their hearts beating very fast.

'So unlock me,' he said.

He disengaged her hand and they started walking again. Neither of them made any acknowledgement of the sudden heat that had just risen between them despite the coldness of the day.

She was patient and did not push him; she seemed to recognise that this would be a difficult tale to tell, and indeed it was for it meant that she would learn the very worst parts of him. He gazed across the gardens, his view hampered by the encroaching fog, and gathered his memories from the past seven and a half years. When he spoke, his voice was low. He tried not to let the story of his poverty in Dublin become too grim but it was impossible to relate it without making some reference to the hardships he had endured. He chose not to mention his encounter with Thomasina, resolving that such a disclosure was irrelevant to the case. However, he did not hold anything back when he related his dealings with Cunningham and, later, Oliver Davenport – she had the right to know just what kind of man he had allowed himself to become. His recollection of the appalling incident with Oliver on that night-time sea crossing weighed heavily upon him; his voice became even fainter until he stopped speaking altogether.

He was shaken out of his despondency by the sensation of her arm slipping through his own.

'I am so sorry,' she whispered. 'Can you ever forgive me for the horrors I have caused you?'

'You played no part in my decision to work for a dirty money lender.'

'If I had not sent you away, you would never have had to make that decision.' Her eyes were full of tears.

'Please do not cry. We cannot change what happened and we gain nothing by holding on to remorse.' He realised that he meant what he was saying. He did not want to see her suffer, in spite of the fact that at least part of the guilt should rightfully be laid at her feet.

Her tears fell nonetheless. 'The things you have been through.' She gulped. 'The things you have been compelled to do.'

She was horrified, he could tell. He could not make her come to terms with it but he could at least offer some alleviation to her dismay.

'Some things in life are so complicated and have so many varied consequences that we cannot merely label them honourable or wicked deeds. I disposed of Oliver's body in a vile fashion. I took his identity and deceived everyone I became acquainted with over the past four and a half years. But I did it with his permission. And I am alive today because of it, as opposed to the very conceivable alternative. Not to mention the fact that it has also led me back to you. When I left Oakleigh I never dreamed it possible that we would meet again, but the ragged course of my life has served up this opportunity to see you once more and to learn of the existence of our daughter. I am very glad that we have been able to reunite in this way.'

Her cheeks flushed as she said, 'I am glad too.'

They followed the path's wide arc around the edge of the gardens yet another time.

'How did you adapt when you became Oliver?' she said after a while. 'I cannot imagine you slipped into the life of the upper classes entirely without mishap, did you?'

'No,' he confessed. 'It was challenging at first. I thought I had an adequate understanding of a gentleman's proper conduct but I did not know enough. When Lord and Lady Bewley took me into their home, I learned the graces and manners of the aristocracy and studied everything from philosophy to politics. I have quite the educated mind now,' he said with a hint of pride. To him it was one of the most valuable things he had gained from his new life.

'So they did not suspect anything? You were never in danger of exposure?'

'The closest I came to it was when an impoverished aunt of Oliver's expressed a worrying interest in visiting Bewley Hall. I sent money on several occasions to deter her and thankfully she never followed through on her scheme. As for Lord and Lady Bewley, I am certain they believe I am their nephew but I think they sensed there was something unusual about me when I came to them. Apart from my "coarse upbringing" as they called it, I used to get terrible nightmares about Oliver and I often woke them up as a result of shouting in my sleep.'

'Nightmares?' she repeated, her tone sympathetic.

He dipped his head. 'I still get them but not so often now.'

An elderly man emerged from the fog ahead of them, accompanied by an equally ancient dog. Bridget's arm was still linked through Cormac's; they detached inconspicuously and strolled forwards. Cormac nodded to the man and bent to pat the dog, and the old fellow ambled on without a single suspicious glance.

Even so, after he had disappeared behind them, they made their way without comment to the entrance of the gardens.

'We should part here,' she said, stopping outside the gate. 'Thank you for your confidence. I comprehend how hard it must have been for you to tell me all of this.'

'The burden is not so heavy now that someone else knows,' he said, feeling the truth of his words in the way he was able to hold his shoulders a little straighter. 'Can I hope to hear from you regarding Emily?'

'I promise to write to you.'

She locked the gate. Then she curtseyed and walked away from him.

***

Bridget maintained her composure while she crossed the street, entered Wyndham House, and climbed the stairs to her bedchamber. However, once she was behind the door and leaning up against it, she let out a shuddering breath that shook her from head to toe. Her hands trembled and not from the cold. Poor, dear, unfortunate Cormac, the awful existence he had been driven to lead.

His confession in the gardens had been outright shocking. He had carried out monstrous deeds which no principled human being could ever have the capacity to commit. He had threatened harm to deprived and desperate men, women and – her heart constricted in abhorrence – children. He had thrown another man's body into the sea like a common criminal. He was no longer the person he had been in his youth; those unspeakable acts did not belong to that honest, honourable boy.

And yet, look at what life had thrown at him. Starvation and loneliness and misery. Who would not have buckled under the hopelessness of it all? Who in the world would have had the strength to resist the opportunity that had presented itself in the form of Oliver's demise? A chance to live well and be valued by others once more. In many ways, he would have been a fool not to seize it.

There was also the undeniable fact that he would never have ended up in that dreadful position at all had she only stood up to her mother all those years ago and not let him be sent away. Her weakness was very much to blame for the path he had been forced to take following the events of that summer. So how could she censure him when it was by her actions that he had fallen into disgrace? Ought he to be held accountable for her mistakes?

Furthermore, since those murky times he had become a decent man again. She could tell by the way Lady Bewley spoke so fondly of him. Perhaps there was still a salvageable soul inside him, craving forgiveness and trying to make amends through kindness towards others.

And now he knew that he was Emily's true father. His reasonable request was that he be permitted to see his child, his own flesh and blood. It was within Bridget's power to prevent it, but was it her right or her will? Emily deserved the warmth of a father's love and, needless to say, Garrett was not forthcoming in that area. Allowing Cormac and Emily to spend time together would be a positive experience for them both.

But there were dangerous complications. Bridget and Emily were irrevocably tied to Garrett; there was no scenario in their future which did not include him. Where, then, could Cormac fit in?

She was startled by a smart rap on the door. She turned and pulled it open to find Garrett standing beyond the threshold. Her first instinct was to pray that Cormac had departed Berkeley Square at once so that he would not be visible from the windows of the house. Her second was to wonder what Garrett was doing home at this time of the day.

'I came to collect a few personal items,' he said in response to her unspoken question. 'Brewer is packing them now. I intend to stay at the club tonight.'

She raised her eyes to his but he would not meet them, focusing instead on adjusting his cuffs.

'The other fellows and I have planned a lengthy card game, and it will be too late for me to return home afterwards.'

She felt a wry twist of black humour at the blatant lie. What pretty young thing had caught his eye this time? And how long would it last before the poor girl was put aside, her reputation ruined? Bridget did not know which was worse, to be the mistress who pleasured him for a time or the wife who could say not a word against it.

Did he feel any regard at all for the women he bedded, or was it nothing more than satisfaction of the flesh? He may have harboured some superficial attachment towards herself in the past, but she suspected that the only woman he had truly loved was the one to whom he had referred when he had tried to apologise to her by James's cradle. What had happened to that lady? Did he ever yearn for her the way she had yearned so long for Cormac?

As she recalled the heat of clasped hands and fast-beating hearts in the fog-enshrouded gardens, light footsteps came skipping down the stairs and Emily appeared on the landing. She faltered at the sight of Garrett and then stepped forwards shyly, holding out a sheet of paper.

'I brought this down to show Mama but I painted it for you, Papa.'

It was the shape of their house with a yellow circle above it.

Garrett looked impatient. 'Not now, Emily.'

He gave Bridget a curt nod and headed for the staircase.

She was reaching for her pen and notepaper before the front door had snapped shut.

## Chapter 24

'I wish the snow would come back,' said Emily, hopping along on one foot beside her mother.

They were in Berkeley Square's gardens, passing by sodden plane trees which dripped with rain that had fallen the night before. It was not raining at present but grey clouds loomed above and Bridget had an umbrella tucked under her arm.

Emily wobbled and flung out her arms to keep her balance. 'Snow is so much more fun than rain.'

'Indeed? Why do you think so?'

'You can't throw rain,' said the little girl emphatically, as though that ended the argument right there.

'But you can slip in the snow.'

'You can't build snowmen out of rain.'

Bridget chuckled. 'You win. Is your leg getting tired?'

Emily switched feet and continued to hop her way along the path. 'I'm exercising my ankles.'

Bridget smiled and cast a furtive glance towards the entrance of the gardens, where she had left the gate unlocked. She and Cormac had arranged by letter that his first meeting with Emily should take place here, because they could pass it off as a chance encounter. She expected him to appear at any moment.

As if he had read her mind, the gate opened and he came striding into view. At the sight of him, she felt an unusual sensation somewhere in the region of her stomach.

Trying to keep her voice steady, she said, 'That gentleman is a friend of mine. We met him outside Lady Bewley's house, do you remember? Shall we stop to speak to him?'

Emily nodded and placed both feet on the ground just as Cormac reached them, lifting his hat in greeting. He too carried an umbrella.

'Lady Wyndham, it is a pleasure to see you again,' he said, bowing.

'How do you do, Mr Davenport?' In her letter she had urged that they use his false identity, lest the name slip from Emily's mouth afterwards in Garrett's presence. 'Emily, what do you say?'

Emily dropped into a sweet curtsey. 'It is a pleasure to see you again, Mr Davenport.'

He grinned at her endearing manners. 'The pleasure is all mine.'

Emily frowned. 'No, some of it's mine too,' she insisted.

He laughed. 'Agreed,' he said, bowing to her as well. 'And what brings you to the gardens today?'

'I'm exercising my ankles. Mama is just walking the normal way.'

'And how does one exercise one's ankles?'

'Like this,' she answered and started hopping on one foot again. 'Miss Davison says jumping is good for making my bones and muscles strong.'

'Hmm,' he said, surveying her with barely-concealed delight. 'Do you think it would work for my bones or am I too old?'

She considered his question as she danced on the spot. 'I suppose it is never too late to start.'

He began hopping from one foot to the other, his arms waving like the vanes of a windmill. 'Am I doing it right?'

She erupted into peals of laughter. 'You look silly!'

He ceased his madcap antics. 'Perhaps it is not for me then,' he conceded and straightened his coat.

'Perhaps not,' Bridget said, endeavouring to keep a straight face. 'Would you care to walk with us, Mr Davenport?'

'I would be honoured. That is, if Miss Emily is happy to consent to that arrangement?'

'I am,' she said regally.

The three of them set off along the path. Emily chattered away about everything that came into her head, from painting pictures to the shapes of puddles on the ground, and did not seem to find it at all extraordinary that her mother's friend was so engrossed in what she was saying. After all, who wouldn't find it interesting to know what colour was made when blue and yellow were mixed together?

As it had threatened, the moisture-laden clouds opened above and poured down on them for ten minutes straight. They huddled under a plane tree, listening to the heavy drops fall onto their umbrellas. At first, Emily stood with Bridget, holding her hand, but after a minute or two she sidled under Cormac's umbrella, claiming that the drops did not sound so loud there. He glanced over her head at Bridget; his face was full of elation. She wondered if he had been worried that Emily might not warm to him. The small girl's guileless, engaging nature had eradicated the notion.

It was with a great deal of reluctance that he parted from them at the end of their walk. Bridget sensed that he wanted to say something to her in private so she suggested to Emily that she do one last ankle exercise before they left the gardens. The girl hopped off with her arms outstretched.

When Bridget looked back at Cormac, she found him staring at her with such a fervent expression that she felt breathless.

'Thank you,' he said, 'for raising this wonderful child and for allowing me the privilege of knowing her.'

'Oh, I—you're welcome. She seems to like you.'

'I am awestruck by her,' he murmured, his gaze now following Emily as she leapt one-footed over puddles.

Instead of turning to watch her too, Bridget continued to observe him. His blue eyes were bright and his cheeks glowed with exhilaration. There was no mistaking that his first proper contact with Emily had meant very much to him.

He dragged his gaze back to Bridget. 'Can I see her again tomorrow?'

She hesitated. 'It might seem unusual to meet two days in a row,' she said, but her objection was half-hearted. Though she wanted to exercise caution, she too was keen for another meeting.

'The day after tomorrow?' he pressed.

'Very well then,' she said, knowing she was giving in far too easily.

His smile was so brilliant that she found herself matching it with her own.

## Chapter 25

Bridget noted the blood on her undergarments with dispassion. Garrett's latest attempt to produce an heir had failed. Usually, she felt a small stab of regret at the sight of the red smear, for it reminded her that the possibility of having another baby had escaped her yet again, but today she had no room for sorrow. Today, her mind was occupied with only one prospect: she and Emily would be seeing Cormac.

They were to pay another visit to Raynesworth House. She had initially questioned the wisdom of such a visible encounter, but he had rationalised that meeting under circumstances so legitimate would raise no suspicion. She would call upon Lady Bewley to ostensibly continue their discourse on London's workhouses, bringing Emily again for the lady's doting pleasure, and he would just happen to be present this time.

Bridget's insides quavered as the carriage drew to a stop on Park Lane. She realised that she wanted very much to see him again, not just for Emily's sake, but for her own.

He delayed a while before making his appearance to further the impression of accidental meeting. She and Lady Bewley were deep in discussion at the luncheon table and Emily, having received the instruction to be seated and give the suffering piano a rest, was swinging her legs listlessly back and forth when he entered the drawing room and gave a courteous bow. The little girl brightened at once.

After exchanging the necessary pleasantries with the ladies, he shot her a wink and said, 'And how are you today, Miss Emily?'

She glanced towards Bridget and Lady Bewley and then imparted in a carrying whisper, 'I'm a bit bored.'

He looked dismayed. 'Bored? We cannot allow such a lamentable state of affairs to persist. Lady Wyndham, would you permit me to steal your daughter for a time, to remedy this tragic situation?'

'That would be most kind of you, Mr Davenport. But only if she will not be a nuisance to you.'

'I am certain she will not. Miss Emily, are you fond of a game called hide-and-seek?'

She straightened her shoulders with glee. 'Yes! And I am very good at it.'

'I warn you, so am I. Who will be victorious?'

He darted out the drawing room door and she raced after him, her gaze fierce with determination.

Lady Bewley's face glowed. 'How natural he is with her. It is a joy to see him with children. How I do hope he will find a wife soon.'

Bridget's own pleasure at the image of father and daughter together diminished as Lady Bewley's innocent wish brutally reminded her of the transitory nature of the situation. What on earth were they doing? How could they sustain this, for where would it all end but with separation? Cormac had mired himself in obligations which he could not shun and, if Emily became too attached, his return to Bedfordshire would be a distressing blow to her.

And yet, Bridget could not resist granting her daughter this experience of fatherly love. The child deserved to know what it felt like to be cherished in such a way.

Knowing she was being cowardly, she shied away from any further contemplation of the dangerous consequences of their actions, and returned to her conversation with Lady Bewley. They spoke at length about measures they could take regarding the workhouse crisis – a renewed appeal to the Ladies of Compassion Association, a petition to Parliament, the recruitment of more volunteers – and, at the conclusion, established a date for Lady Bewley to visit St Swithun's.

'You do not think Miss Blythe will deem me an interference?'

'Not for one instant. Frances welcomes help from any quarter and is always grateful for it.'

They heard a few thumps and laughter from the floor above, which sounded as though the most recent hider had been found.

'I ought to release your nephew from my daughter's clutches,' Bridget said, eager to witness the merriment. 'I do believe he has been obliged to entertain her for long enough.'

'I doubt he minds but off you go. I shall remain here, if it please you. I try to avoid climbing stairs as much as possible.'

With a reassurance that Lady Bewley should stay behind for her own comfort, Bridget departed the room in search of the playmates. All had become quiet upstairs again. Ascending the staircase, she came upon Cormac at the top, eyes closed as he mouthed a silent countdown.

'Three, two, one,' he said aloud. 'Ready or not, here I come!'

He opened his eyes and grinned when he saw Bridget.

'She's winning,' he said.

'I'm confident that you are both savouring the triumph of the occasion,' she replied.

'Truer words were never spoken.' He marched along the corridor, making no attempt to subdue the noise of his footsteps. 'I will find you,' he called. 'You shall not elude me this time!'

He sidled through a door and she followed him. Aghast, she realised they were in a bedchamber. Her consternation was two-fold: she could not countenance the idea that Emily might be concealing herself in what must be Cormac's own bedchamber – judging by the shaving apparatus on the washstand and the stylish clothing his valet had already laid out for dinner – but she was also astounded by the wave of heat that swept through her body at the spectacle of the neatly-made bed and the sudden, unbidden vision of its covers in disarray.

'Please tell me she is not hiding in here,' she said faintly, thankful that his back was to her, for she didn't think she could control her flushed features in that moment.

'There is only one way to find out,' he said. 'I'll wager she has taken refuge in the wardrobe.'

He flung open the wardrobe door but only a tidy display of shirts and waistcoats greeted him.

'Perhaps she has hidden behind the curtain? Is that a toe I see peeping out?'

He swept back the material but all was empty behind it.

'She cannot be small enough to fit into the pitcher, can she? If I turn it upside down, shall I expose her or shall I just get very wet?'

A muffled giggle, swiftly stifled, came from beneath the bed.

'Ah, Miss Emily,' he said, sounding disappointed. 'How clumsy of you.'

He dropped to the floor and peered under the bed. A burst of hilarity bubbled out.

'I've found you!' he announced.

Emily wriggled into view, her dress and shoes dusty and her hair falling down in bedraggled coils. Bridget thought to berate her but stopped before the reprimand left her lips. She remembered when a young boy had taught her to climb a tree and she had descended from it in a similarly dishevelled shape. She would not detract from Emily's enjoyment now.

'I believe you have lost, *a stór*,' Cormac informed his daughter.

'Only because I laughed,' she said. 'Next time I will be so quiet you will never find me.'

'I accept your challenge,' he said gravely. 'Do your best.'

She ran for the door.

'Downstairs!' Bridget called after her. 'No more hiding in bedchambers!'

When she looked back at Cormac, he was leaning against the bed post, his face alight with jubilance.

'What was that you called her?' she asked.

His expression softened. '*A stór*. It means "my treasure".'

'Did she not wonder what you were saying?'

'When we went upstairs, I suggested that it could be a secret code of friendship between us. She doesn't know its translation.'

She bit her tongue. 'Don't you think it was risky to do such a thing?'

'It's too late to take it back now,' he said without repentance.

She understood his impulse; he desired a special connection with Emily, something that no one else – especially not Garrett – could have with her.

Moved, she said, 'I did speak Irish to her when she was very young. I wanted her to have some awareness of that part of her parentage, if obliquely. But Garrett put a stop to it.' Her heart squeezed at the memory of the burned wooden bird and how great that loss had been, and she marvelled yet again that its maker now stood before her. 'I whispered the prayers to her, over and over and over. Except I could not remember a section of the Hail Mary. What comes after *Sé do bheatha, a Mhuire, atá lán de ghrásta, tá an Tiarna leat*?'

He picked up the next line. '*Is beannaithe thú idir mná, agus is beannaithe toradh do bhroinne, Íosa.*'

As he carried on with the rest of the prayer, she let the lyrical words wash over her. They almost sounded like romantic verse the way he murmured them, with an intensity in his eyes that seemed to have nothing to do with devotion to the Blessed Virgin. She became conscious once more of the bed behind him and it occurred to her that it was quite wicked to have such thoughts with the Hail Mary echoing in her ears.

Silence bloomed between them after he finished the prayer.

Unwillingly, she said, 'Emily and I really ought to leave now.'

He pressed his lips together in resignation. 'Just one more game then.' He strode to the door and disappeared through it, calling, 'Ready or not, here I come!'

## Chapter 26

During the weeks that followed, Cormac continued to meet Emily in the guise of Oliver Davenport and the bond between them took root and strengthened as he gave her the attention and affection of a loving father which had been conspicuously absent in her life until now. With the arrival of February, the first traces of spring emerged and they went for more walks in the gardens, where he taught her the names of the birds starting to nest there and the flowers expected to blossom first. She introduced him to her favourite doll and presented him with countless painted pictures for his 'art collection' which he accepted with solemn gratitude. She and Bridget made several more visits to Raynesworth House, where the unsuspecting Lord and Lady Bewley were only too delighted to receive them, and all and sundry were pressed into playing games of hide-and-seek around the house and conducting tea parties with imaginary friends on the hearth rug. Once, Cormac took Emily into the library and had her read to him from her storybooks. Bridget's heart nearly overflowed with emotion as she observed their two fair heads bent together.

At home, it was impossible to prevent Emily from speaking about kind Mr Davenport in front of Garrett but the occasions were few; 'card games' had kept him away for many more nights.

It was these prolonged absences which gave Bridget the confidence to acquiesce when Cormac asked one day in late February if they could arrange a meeting at Wyndham House. He had something very special to give to Emily.

He arrived that afternoon with a mysterious package tucked under his arm. Emily jumped up and down when he told her it was for her but he said she could not have it until she sang a song for him. As musically deficient as she was artistically talented, she nevertheless sang an out-of-tune lullaby to which he applauded with enthusiasm. He then handed her the coveted package and she ripped off the paper to discover a gift like no other. It was a rectangular wooden box which, when she lifted its lid, revealed a sequence of compartments for storing watercolour cakes, two porcelain pans for mixing colours, and a drawer to hold brushes.

She let out a rapturous gasp. 'Oh, thank you, thank you, thank you! It's wonderful!'

'Let me see you paint something right away,' he urged, and she thrust the box into her mother's hands before running to fetch her paints and paper.

'Don't forget your smock,' Bridget called and heard Emily's groan of compliance. To Cormac she said, 'Let us go into the breakfast room. She can paint at the table there.'

In the breakfast room, she examined the interior of the box with admiration. The craftsmanship was immaculate. 'Did you make this?'

'Yes, apart from the porcelain pans. I am glad Emily likes it. I wanted her to have something from me.'

'She adores it,' she assured him. 'It is exquisite.'

'It might be somewhat sophisticated for her current abilities,' he said, taking it from her and touching one of the pans meditatively. 'But she will progress as she grows older.'

He closed the lid and her breath caught in her throat. She had not noticed when Emily had first unwrapped it, but now she could see an engraving on the top of the box. It was a stylised depiction of an oak tree. Her pulse quickened. There could be no mistaking its import; the oak tree in the centre of the orchard at Oakleigh had been a place of significance for her and Cormac throughout their relationship. It was where they had first met, where they had played as children, where they had kissed as lovers. What did he mean to imply by it?

She gathered the courage to look up at him, but his face was averted like he was listening for Emily's returning steps. Did she dare ask him about it? Before she could determine what to say, Emily dashed into the room, carrying her painting things and wearing a smock down to her knees.

'I've asked Lizzie to bring me a jar of water,' she announced, breathless. 'I'm going to paint a dog first.'

She spent a happy hour mixing colours from every watercolour cake she possessed and enjoying the praise from her admiring companions. After she completed a picture of a brown dog with a wagging tail, and another of two winged horses flying over rooftops, she painted a blurry woman in a blue dress holding an umbrella.

'This is Mama,' she said, lifting it up for Cormac to see. 'Isn't she pretty?'

He looked over her shoulder at Bridget. 'Beautiful,' he said before his gaze returned to the little girl.

Bridget's heart skipped at least two beats before resuming its normal tempo.

When Emily finished the next painting – one of two vague figures who were meant to be Lizzie and Peter – Bridget decided that the servants would get suspicious if Cormac was to stay any longer, and said, 'Gooseberry, I do believe Mr Davenport has to go now. What do you say to him before he leaves?'

Cormac's disappointment changed to astonishment and delight as Emily threw her arms around him. 'Thank you for my present. I love it!'

'Emily!' Bridget scolded when the girl drew back to reveal a blue smudge on his sleeve.

'It's no trouble,' he said, looking like he would gladly have had paint smeared on every item of clothing he owned in exchange for the hug he had just received from his daughter. 'You are very welcome, *a stór*. I hope you will get many years of enjoyment out of it.'

Bridget instructed Emily to pack up her paints into the watercolour box and bring her pictures to the nursery. Arms full, she bounced out of the room, exclaiming, 'I shall paint our birds from the gardens next time!'

Conscious that her next action ought to have been to ring the bell so that Cormac could be seen out of the house by a servant, Bridget said, 'I'll walk with you to the door.'

In the hall, he lifted his hat and coat from the stand, put them on, and grimaced theatrically.

'I must have paint on the inside of my coat now,' he said with a grin, but then his expression turned serious. 'Even though she does not know who I really am, that hug meant very much to me. *She* means very much to me.'

'I am in no doubt that the feeling is mutual,' said Bridget. 'She has become exceptionally fond of you.'

'Then I am the happiest man in the world today.'

With a smile, he turned to go.

'Wait,' she said, and put her hand over his to prevent him from pulling the door open.

He looked back at her. 'What is it?'

'I don't—' she began, and stopped. She had been about to say 'I don't know' but it wasn't true. She did know. Staring into his clear blue eyes, she recalled the taste of passion in a hay barn on a sweet September night. She remembered their declaration of love, and their physical need for each other. She could feel it bubbling inside her, heating her body to its core. She wanted him to kiss her.

She took a small step towards him so that their bodies were only inches apart. His fingers twitched beneath hers. She gazed up at him under her dark eyelashes and he inhaled sharply. Rising on her tiptoes, she tightened her grip on his hand. Their mouths were almost touching, her lips were parting...

Then they sprang apart as they heard the clatter of a door opening onto the hall, and Lizzie appeared clutching a bucket and a mop.

'Thank you very much for calling by, Mr Davenport,' Bridget said, dropping into a demure curtsey.

'Good day, Lady Wyndham,' he said with equal nonchalance. He bowed and exited through the front door.

She turned to Lizzie. How much could the maid guess from what she had just seen? Had she observed them standing as close as lovers? Furthermore, this was Mr Davenport's second visit without her master present in the house – would she find that suspect in itself?

But Lizzie betrayed no sign of what she might be privately speculating. She curtseyed and said, 'I was going to mop the hall, m'lady. If now ain't a good time, I can leave it until later?'

'Now is fine,' said Bridget. 'I shall step out of your way.'

She climbed the stairs to the nursery to check on Emily. That had been a most ill-timed end to Cormac's visit. Just one more second and her lips would have been pressed to his. With her own emotions in chaos, she wondered what he was thinking and feeling in the aftermath of their inappropriate intimacy.

## Chapter 27

Cormac prowled the streets. It was not long past daybreak; the only other people stirring at that hour were bakers and milkmen. A light mist hung above the houses and shops of London as he walked without noticing where he was going.

He had returned to Raynesworth House the previous evening but had shunned the company of Lord and Lady Bewley, retiring early to his bedchamber. Then he had been up at dawn with the servants and out of the house before the lord and lady had even woken. Unable to keep still, he had set off in no particular direction; his body just needed to be active while his brain worked so feverishly.

They had been about to kiss. If the maid had not interrupted, they would have kissed. Their lips had been so close that he had been able to feel Bridget's breath tickle his skin. Her fingers had been warm on his and her body had been very near; one more step and she would have been pushing up against him. It had been a dizzying moment, an intimate reminder of their passionate night in the hay barn so long ago.

He could not deny that he was aroused. The attraction he had felt towards her when they were younger had not diminished. Though time and heartache had taken their toll on her, he thought she was as beautiful now as she had been at nineteen, and her dark brown eyes drew him in with a magnetic force that made him yearn to lose himself in her.

So his body was being very persuasive. Still, he could not surrender to those impulses unthinkingly. Not when his brain shouted at him that it was too dangerous. The last time this had happened it had ended in disaster, and her betrayal had led him into the most dreadful period of his life.

This time it could be different, his heart whispered.

She had done a terrible thing to him but he believed she was truly remorseful about it. She could not change the past and he could not hold her tremendous error against her – it was not in his nature to keep a grudge like that. Besides, he was no saint himself; there were many people from whom he wished he could beg forgiveness, and he had no right to expect compassion if he was unwilling to bestow it.

And it was vital to remember that this was Bridget he was thinking of: his closest friend and deepest love of his youth. Could the heart ever forget an attachment as meaningful as that? Was their almost-kiss an inevitable consequence of their reunion, even though it seemed a lifetime had passed in between? In reality, could he ever be content with anyone other than her? She was also the mother of his cherished daughter; surely there could be no greater bond for two people than the creation of a child together.

In the depths of his soul, he knew what he wanted, but he was overcome with misgivings as he wondered where her own desires lay. How did she feel about the incident that had occurred in her hall yesterday afternoon? She was the one who had initiated it but perhaps she had begun to harbour doubts since it had happened. It was all too easy to get caught up in the excitement of a moment and then rethink one's actions in the sobriety of solitude and reflection.

He had to find out for certain. This was not something which he could let lie. He started to stride more purposefully as the weak springtime sun rose over the rooftops and burned off the lingering mist. The city was awake now and there were carriages rattling down the streets, men swamping the footpaths, and shops opening their front doors. He purchased a newspaper and made his way to Berkeley Square, where he lurked across the road a little way down from Wyndham House, ensuring that he had a view of its front door. He was willing to wait as long as it took.

Garrett was the first to leave the house. Cormac gave him a surreptitious glance over the top of his newspaper as he passed down the street on the opposite side. The last time he had seen this man was at Oakleigh Manor. He looked older – Cormac supposed he must be nearing his mid-thirties by now – but he had retained his good looks and he carried himself proudly as he disappeared around the corner.

Cormac resumed his waiting. His patience was rewarded when, after half an hour had passed, the front door opened again and Miss Davison emerged with Emily by her side; they made their way across the street and vanished into the gardens. This was what he had been hoping for. Now there was nobody left in the house but Bridget and her servants.

He tucked the newspaper inside his coat, crossed the street, and was approaching the building when the door opened once more and Bridget herself came out onto the top step. Anticipation mounted within him. Strangely, she was wearing a rather drab ensemble consisting of a plain bonnet, a weathered cloak and a dull-coloured dress. She pulled the door shut just as he reached the steps; looking around, she gasped to see him standing below her.

Glancing over his shoulder at a passerby, he said, 'May I come in?'

After the briefest of pauses, she nodded wordlessly.

He followed her into the hall, where he watched her remove her bonnet and cloak and drop them onto a dresser. Her back was to him but when she turned around he found it easy to read her expression. Though she was biting the end of her tongue in nervousness, her cheeks were pink with excitement.

That was all he needed to see. Perhaps he ought to have been tender but he was too exhilarated to think of such restraint. He strode across to her, pulled her to him roughly, and pressed his mouth upon hers. The kiss was fierce and almost painful with desire. She clutched at his neck, her grip ferocious, not allowing him to draw away for one second. They were starving for each other, craving the other's touch. Her back was only steps away from the dresser; he pushed her up against it, pressing the length of his body against her own. Something toppled off the dresser and made a tinkling noise as it shattered on the floor but neither of them paid any regard to it, even though they were in great danger of being discovered by one of the servants.

They remained locked in the embrace until they were forced to break apart for air. As he rubbed his face into her throat, inhaling her alluring lilac scent – how giddying it was to be able to breathe it in, breathe *her* in, at last – he heard her pant, 'Upstairs.'

They made it six steps up the staircase and then their passion overcame them again and they were kissing and clinging harder than ever, leaning against the banister for support. Compulsion made them grapple at their clothing, her fingers fumbling with the buttons on his coat, his hands groping at her skirts, but they could not carry on like this in the open spaces of the house. She grasped his wrist and tugged him up that flight of stairs and the next. They reached her bedchamber, where she ushered him in and locked the door behind them. The twist of the key and the snap of the lock into place seemed to herald their final commitment to this precarious course of action.

This time they came together more tenderly. The bruising force of their initial frenzy gentled into a slower, but no less thorough, exploration of each other's mouths. He savoured each sensation, the softness of her lips, the moist welcome of her tongue, and its insistent strokes that both gave and demanded pleasure.

She knocked off his hat to fondle his hair. They were both still wearing gloves – breaking the kiss, he loosened hers one finger at a time and plucked them off. Her hands, so often concealed, seemed almost like a private part of her body. He removed his own gloves and discarded them on the floor, then interlocked his fingers with hers in a gesture that felt as intimate as their caressing tongues. Raising their joined hands between them, he touched his lips to her knuckles. With a devilish ripple of need, he thought it might be his last gentlemanly act for quite some time.

He let go and hastened to undress her, to expose the feminine curves veiled by her plain dress. She too sought the buttons and knots of his clothing and the various layers, from his waistcoat to her petticoats, fell about their ankles. She jerked at his shirt, freeing it from the waist of his trousers, and thrust her hands up under the material, her fingertips running lightly over the planes of his back. It was a simple movement but it ignited the lower region of his body. She must have seen the fire in his eyes because she turned to lead him towards the bed, but he halted her at the bedside.

'Wait,' he said and, with a flick of his hand, indicated the fact that she still stood before him in shift and stays.

'These as well?' she said uncertainly.

'Yes,' he said firmly.

The stays would cause a delay but it had been over seven years since he had seen this woman naked and he had no intention of doing anything by halves. He turned her from him and began to unlace the back of the stays, each jerk of the cord through an eyelet like a whip against his groin. Her shoulders rose and fell as her breathing became more pronounced. He kissed her ear with the final tug and the stays dropped away from her. His anticipation climbing ever higher, he stripped off her ankle boots and the rest of her undergarments with swift movements.

He took a step back to admire the graceful line of her back and the round shape of her buttocks. He was in awe but she was self-conscious now; she crossed her arms and grasped her elbows, hunching slightly from his gaze. Alarmed at her insecurity, he moved closer again so that his shirt front pressed against her back, and enfolded his arms around hers. He clasped her wrists and coaxed her to let go of her elbows, guiding her hands to her sides. With her breasts now exposed, he could reach up and cup them both.

The air escaped her lungs in a breathy, 'Oh.'

While his previous acquaintance with them had been for just one brief night, he could tell that they had changed. Without the supportive boost of her stays, they sagged a little lower. But that by no means reduced their allure and she jumped as his body told her so.

With slow deliberation, he lowered one hand to the cluster of curls below. He stroked experimentally, shifting position and pressure until he located a spot that drew a patent physical reaction from her. She squirmed and moaned and he persevered, feeling her reserve dissolve within his embrace. Her limbs tautened as she emitted a high-pitched whimper and shuddered, then went limp. He held her, his face buried in her chestnut hair.

After a few moments, she turned and kissed him as though he were the air she needed to survive. He could feel her trembling from head to toe. She detached her lips from his to wrench off his shirt and, between them, they removed his boots and the remainder of his clothing and fell onto the bed at last. He lay over her and extended his own body along hers, their legs entwined, the hair on his chest grazing her breasts.

Her hand slipped down between them to guide him into place and he buried himself inside her as far as he could go. The idea of proceeding slowly, of any further delay, was impossible. He rushed to his release with her arms wrapped tight across his back.

Afterwards, they lay beside each other, panting with exertion. As his breathing slowed, he turned his head and found her staring at the underside of the bed's canopy, her face full of apprehension.

'What is the matter?' he asked. Considering the act they had just engaged in, there were several valid responses to his question.

'It's just—' she said, not looking at him, 'when Garrett and I...he does not...we never fully...he just pushes up my nightdress and I pull it down when he is done.'

Anger surged in him that Garrett could treat this heavenly woman so cheaply but he phrased his response with delicacy.

'I could not imagine being clothed during an experience such as this,' he said, his voice tender. 'When I was holding you, I wanted every part of my skin to touch every part of your skin. We just shared the deepest kind of intimacy there is and we had to share it completely.'

Her body was stiff; now that their fervour had subsided, she looked like she very much wanted to screen herself from him.

'I know I am not very desirable anymore,' she muttered. 'It might have been preferable to keep me covered up.'

Raising himself up on one elbow, he stared at her, speechless. She waved an impatient hand down her torso in explanation and looked away. His gaze dropped to her breasts, which did not sit so high as they had when she was nineteen, and to her abdomen, which was slightly rounded instead of flat and had silvery-white streaks across it.

'Pregnancy and breastfeeding are not without their drawbacks,' she mumbled.

'Look at me,' he said.

When she didn't respond, he tucked a finger under her chin and eased it towards him. She met his gaze reluctantly.

Summoning every ounce of earnestness, he said, 'These marks show that you brought a child into this world and nurtured her at your breast. They are nothing to be ashamed of. On the contrary, they are a badge of motherhood and you should wear them proudly.'

He caressed her shoulder, traced the line of her collar bone, and trailed a fingertip under the curve of one breast, feeling her shiver at the stimulation. His hand drifted down to her stomach where her muscles were taut with anxiety. He massaged the stretch marks on her belly over and over until at last she began to relax. Only then did he sense he had her permission to reach down to that most private place. His touch wasn't sexual but reverential.

'You are sensational,' he murmured, 'and do not ever doubt it.'

He had not taken his eyes from her face. As he watched, the tension drained from her expression, to be replaced with a breathless joy. She pulled him to her and they kissed, less frantically than before. In the calm that followed, he held her in his arms and she nestled into his side. He knew he should leave before they got caught – Miss Davison and Emily would likely be back soon – but the bedchamber door was locked and there had been no sound from the servants so he reasoned that they had a few more moments' grace to enjoy first.

Her hair, so neat when she had removed her bonnet, had come undone during their vigorous activities, and the curls now draped in disarray over his shoulder and chest. He plucked out a loose pin that was digging into him and twisted a long curl around his thumb, marvelling at the rich shade of chestnut.

'Why were you wearing such plain attire?' he said, glancing at the clothes scattered around the floor. 'It seems rather incongruous with your position.'

He felt rather than heard her chuckle. 'I was on my way to St Swithun's. Drab garments are more suitable for the workhouse. Fortunately, I have instructed the servants to neglect their usual duties as part of that routine, or else Thrussell would have been at the door to see me out. I can't imagine what he might have thought of the entrance you made.'

Cormac stroked his fingers through her tousled hair and said, 'Do you feel guilty?'

Her amusement faded. 'Yes, though I do not know why, for Garrett has done this to me many times since we married, and even before that when we were courting. But then, it is far less scandalous for a gentleman to engage in an affair than it is for a lady to do so.'

'Do you still love him?' he asked, dreading the answer he might hear.

'No, I do not,' she replied, and he let out a silent breath of relief. 'We are miserable together. He has given me a title and wealth, but neither happiness nor love. He did give me a son but sadly he left us too soon.'

Cormac started. 'What? You had another child?'

She nodded. 'Four years ago. His name was James. He was only three months old when he died.'

She sounded like she was trying very hard to keep her voice steady. He was shocked; he had had no inkling that she had borne a second child.

'I am so sorry.' He shuddered at the very notion of any harm coming to Emily and could not begin to conceive the anguish that Bridget had suffered. 'That must have been a terrible loss for you.'

Peering down at her, he saw that her eyes had lost their sparkle and one thing became much clearer to him.

'Forgive me for saying this,' he said, pressing a compassionate kiss to her temple, 'but I knew that something grievous had happened to you during our years apart. I could tell that it had changed you at a profound level. Your spirits are not the same as they once were.'

She gave him a sad smile. 'It pains me to say that there are several causes for the alteration you see in me, not least my devastation in losing you and ending up in a loveless marriage. But yes, there is very little that can compare to the desolation of losing a beloved child. He was such a dear boy.'

She was about to say something else when noises drifted up from downstairs and she jerked away from him to listen.

'Miss Davison and Emily are back. We must hurry!'

He slid off the bed and hastened to don his clothes. There was no time to undertake the intricate and time-consuming process of lacing up Bridget's stays, so she fished a dressing gown from the wardrobe and wrapped it around herself. Creeping to the door, she unlocked it and opened it a crack.

'They are climbing the stairs,' she whispered as he looped his cravat around his neck and knotted it. 'They will continue on up to the nursery and that will be your chance to slip past.'

He shrugged into his coat and came to the door. Unable to resist, he gathered her hair in one hand, drew it back to expose the nape of her neck, and bent his head to kiss the bare skin. She stifled her gasp as Emily's voice floated to them from the landing.

'I can't wait to show Mama my daffodils!'

They heard Miss Davison reply, 'She will be very pleased to see them. Let us take off our cloaks and gloves and then we shall find a jar for your flowers.'

Their footsteps grew fainter as they ascended the next flight of stairs.

Bridget turned to him. 'Quick, you should go now.'

He kissed her fully on the mouth, feeling the passion rise in him again. With great reluctance, he pulled away, checked that the landing was clear, and stole out of the bedchamber. He met no one on his way down the stairs but as he reached the bottom step he noticed that the little ornament they had smashed in their earlier tumult had been swept away and Bridget's bonnet and cloak hung tidily on the coat stand.

Discomfited that their actions had not gone unnoticed by the servants and heartily grateful for their discretion, he slipped out the front door.

## Chapter 28

Bridget's thoughts were in a whirl. She and Cormac had fallen as helplessly into her bed as they had fallen into each other's arms at Oakleigh. It was glorious but it left her with no small measure of anxiety. What did this make her? What was he thinking now? What might it mean for Emily? What would happen next?

It was fortunate that he sent her a note later that day, or she would have gone wild in her agitation. Naturally, he phrased it in the most reserved language but it conveyed an invitation to Raynesworth House the next day with the veiled suggestion that only her own presence would be necessary. If he wanted her to leave Emily behind, then that implied his intention for them to…what? Talk about what had happened? Repeat the event? Neither would be possible with Lord and Lady Bewley in attendance, that was certain.

She entered the drawing room at Raynesworth House an interminable twenty-four hours later to find Lady Bewley in a huff.

'My silly nephew,' she said, 'has mixed up the date of your visit. He told me it was Wednesday and so I arranged to call upon an acquaintance on Tuesday. But now here you are on Tuesday and it is too late for me to postpone my other engagement now.'

She bestowed a withering look upon Cormac who acted sheepish.

'I apologise once again, Aunt,' he said. 'I honestly thought I had told you Tuesday.'

'Be that as it may, I am obliged to take my leave without delay for I am already running late. You must take some refreshment before you depart, Lady Wyndham. Make sure you look after her,' she added in a stern voice to Cormac.

'Oh, I will.'

Bridget curtseyed to Lady Bewley. 'I am very sorry that we have missed each other. I look forward to the next time we meet.'

From the drawing room window, they watched the lady waddle out of the house and into her waiting carriage, which lurched away down the street.

'Where is Lord Bewley?' Bridget asked.

'Occupying his seat at a parliamentary session,' Cormac answered in a relaxed manner. 'The House of Lords doesn't often meet on a Wednesday but Tuesday is a reliable day to find him there.'

He winked. His untroubled expression made her a little easier. She trusted him. And she felt a flicker of heat stir down below.

For the benefit of Lord and Lady Bewley's servants, they sat in the drawing room for a time and drank tea in grave decorum. When the housekeeper came in to check that their comforts were being met, Cormac said to the woman, 'Do you remember that object I found in the storage room? I am going to bring Lady Wyndham there next, for she studied it in the past and might be in a position to let us know whether it can be salvaged.'

This statement baffled Bridget but the housekeeper accepted it without demur. Offering his hand but no explanation, Cormac led Bridget up through the house until they reached the top floor, which consisted of a long, deserted corridor flanked by several closed doors. Opening the last one, he gestured her inside.

'Oh, my goodness,' she said as she walked in.

The room was packed to the ceiling with every kind of domestic detritus imaginable: a wardrobe with its doors falling off its hinges, several chairs and a sofa with their stuffing spilling out, cracked mirrors, faded cushions, even an upright piano missing some of its keys. There was an air of utter abandonment about the room; it was easy to tell that nobody came in here except to deposit another item no longer regarded as having any value.

Cormac shut the door as Bridget crossed the room with difficulty, navigating her way around the clutter in order to examine the broken piano.

'How very sad,' she said, playing some of the keys which were still attached. It was woefully out of tune. 'Somebody used to love this instrument.'

'At least today it can serve a purpose again,' he said. 'When we go back downstairs, you must appraise its worth, or lack thereof, very loudly in the housekeeper's hearing.'

A thrill ran down her spine. Keeping her gaze on the keys, she said, 'You do not expect us to be disturbed here then?'

'The other rooms on this floor are sleeping quarters for the servants, who are all about their daily duties right now.' He came up behind her and slipped his arms around her waist. 'Do you still play?'

'Not very often. Music somehow lost its charm for me over the years. I think I should like Emily to learn though.'

He squeezed her at the mention of their daughter's name. 'If you can get her to put down her paints for more than two minutes.'

'Very true.'

She played a soft, two-note chord on the piano and let the sound die away. Then she turned within his arms. After just the barest hesitation, he eased her lips apart and their tongues met in a sensual dance, weaving and caressing. His body was warm, his hands light on her back. She touched his chest and felt the rapid beating of his heart beneath her fingers.

When they broke apart, it was as gently as they had come together. He kissed the tip of her nose.

'Did you ever imagine that we would be together again?' he said.

She shook her head. 'The idea was so fantastic that I never dreamed it to be possible. I think part of me doubts even now that you are here.'

He tightened his embrace so that she was flush against his body, able to feel every part of him.

'Do you still doubt?' he said with a mischievous smile.

She blushed. 'Not anymore.'

The playfulness faded from his face as he regarded her. 'We are treading a dangerous path. We ought to ask ourselves if we are prepared to continue down it, taking into account the significant risks involved. I know what my answer is, but what is yours?'

As she considered his words, her whirling thoughts over the past day coalesced into one unshakeable conviction. Taking a deep breath, she said, 'For many years, I treasured our night in the hay barn as the pinnacle of my earthly happiness. Reuniting our bodies and souls once more has made me realise that my memory of the experience did not do it justice. I am willing to accept any risk to feel such completion. With you, I am whole again.'

She supposed she ought to be embarrassed; it was unseemly for a woman to speak of such matters. But his look was full of appreciation.

'I would like to think that this is abundantly obvious by now,' he said, 'but I want to declare it in unmistakable terms: I am still very much in love with you.'

To hear those words was to soar high above the clouds. 'And I with you,' she said with a giddy joy.

Their lips joined in a chaste kiss, so sweet and pure that it was almost as if their tragic separation at Oakleigh had never transpired.

'I cannot believe this is really happening,' she breathed.

'Believe it,' he said and kissed her again, harder than before.

She realised she did not feel so apprehensive this time. Yesterday, she had been mortified when he had stripped her to her bare skin – how could a man find such physical flaws attractive? But he had made her feel perfect, despite her imperfections. Now, as he drew her down to the sofa, its insides bursting from its seams, his face and body language told her she was all he desired. He pulled her to him and she embraced him eagerly, recognising the hunger in his eyes as her own.

They sprawled awkwardly on the narrow sofa; it was not long enough to lie lengthways. Feeling wanton, she encouraged him into a sitting position and hauled at her skirts to straddle him with her knees on either side of his hips. A strange shadow passed over his expression but it was gone so fast that she wondered if it had been only a trick of the light. He stroked her legs from ankle to thigh and fingered the tops of her stockings with a hint of regret.

'God, I wish I could look at you naked again,' he said. 'But neither time nor circumstances will allow me to undress you fully this time.'

She caressed the outline of his strong jaw. 'In that case, we shall have to rely more on our other senses.'

Her lips hovered over his in invitation. He tasted her with exquisite attention to detail, addressing not only her mouth, but also her throat and the soft curves of her breasts above the neckline of her dress. She inhaled, relishing the smell of his skin. The faint trace of cologne was quite in opposition to the tang of horses that had clung to him in the past, and yet underneath it was a scent that remained unchanged, something familiar and masculine and indescribably *him*. Intoxicated by his nearness, she pressed closer, aching for the physical bond they had forged yesterday but unsure how to ask for it.

He understood nevertheless. He reached down to unbutton his fall front and adjusted her masses of skirts around them, bunching them high at her waist.

'Let's see,' he murmured. 'Which senses have we not tried yet?'

Her wits were growing muddled with yearning. 'S-sound?' she tried.

He smiled; evidently he had not expected her to offer a rational answer. 'Hmm,' he said. 'Shall I whisper sweet nothings in your ear?'

Suddenly more alert, she said, 'Anything but "darling".' He cocked an eyebrow and she cringed. 'I'm sorry, I shouldn't have said that. It's just…'

'It's what Garrett says?' he said perceptively.

'What he used to say. He hasn't for a long time.' She squirmed, appalled that she had mentioned her husband in her current position, but felt she ought to finish now. 'To me, it is an endearment empty of any true feeling.'

He didn't look offended. 'Duly noted,' he said with a solemn nod.

He took her hand and kissed the inside of her wrist, his lips locating her pulse. Its rapid throb echoed in her sensitive place below which strained against his open fall front. She rose up and settled herself upon him, sliding down with a torturous slowness that dragged groans from them both. He held her there, his face pressed to her breast, and murmured something inaudible.

'What?' she said, her breath coming shorter.

He lifted his head, his blue eyes hazy with devotion. 'I said I love you, *a rún mo chroí.*'

Clasping her hips, he urged her to take charge. She obeyed, cautious at first and then, finding a rhythm, moving with more abandon.

Panting, she asked, 'What does it mean?'

He didn't reply, leaving her to focus only on the sense of touch: the gliding friction, their sweat-drenched skin, the clench and stroke of muscles. She gasped as he spilled himself inside her at last with a ragged sound of repletion.

'Secret of my heart,' he said and sighed.

## Chapter 29

'We have excellent news to impart, dearest!'

Lucy and Alice had come to call upon Bridget at Wyndham House and Lucy was brimming with enthusiasm. 'As you know, Cassandra is hosting a ball on the fifth of March. Having speculated at length on the subject, we can finally confirm that the delightful Mr Davenport is to be in attendance!'

Apart from the ice skating incident at Regent's Park – of which Cassandra had never claimed orchestration, though she always adopted a secretive smile whenever they referred to it – Bridget's companions had encountered Cormac on just two other occasions since the first party. Both had been dull gatherings with no music or dancing and therefore little opportunity to ignite a stronger attraction. However, a ball meant that dancing would be the main agenda of the evening.

'We must therefore get Alice partnered with Mr Davenport as often as we can,' said Lucy. 'For he is bound to fall in love with her by the third dance.'

Alice coloured. 'Oh, Lucy, you know it is improper to partake in three dances with the same gentleman. How I do wish you would not say such things.'

'Why so? Do you not desire him to fall in love with you? Can you deny that you feel a particular regard for him?'

Alice's protesting squeak was reply enough.

Bridget experienced a dart of discomfort. Though reuniting with Cormac in such a meaningful way gave her the greatest joy, she now suffered the deepest guilt that she was depriving her dear friend of a romantic association. Alice did not deserve to be a spinster; she would make a good wife for any gentleman. But the very idea of Cormac being with another woman tore at Bridget's heart. And she could not dictate how he felt; it was Alice's grievous misfortune that the recipient of her affections had given himself to another.

The rest of the conversation consisted of Lucy determining ways to keep Miss Norwell as far away from Mr Davenport as possible. When she and Alice rose to leave, Bridget stood with them as she would be departing for St Swithun's shortly in the company of Lady Bewley. The lady had visited the workhouse three times already over the past few weeks and she and

Frances had connected so well that they intended to keep up a correspondence even when she returned to Bedfordshire. Whether her nephew would be returning with her was something Bridget decided not to contemplate.

The three of them went out to the hall where Thrussell appeared to open the front door, just as Emily came bounding down the stairs, Miss Davison trying to keep up behind her.

Alice beamed at her. 'How lovely to see you, Emily. Good gracious, you have grown so much!'

Emily dropped into a little curtsey and then turned to her mother. 'Mama, will we be going to see Mr Davenport today? I have a new painting for him of the bird's nest we found in the gardens!'

'Mr Davenport?' said Lucy, looking at Bridget in puzzlement. 'He has met Emily?'

Bridget endeavoured to keep her countenance calm. 'Quite by chance. I have become acquainted with his aunt, Lady Bewley, as she too takes an interest in charitable activities. She is very fond of children so Emily has accompanied me on some of my visits to Raynesworth House.'

'How nice,' said Alice with a smile.

'Indeed,' said Lucy. 'We shall take our leave of you. Let us begin counting down the days to Cassandra's ball!'

As Thrussell saw Lucy and Alice out the door, Bridget gave silent thanks that Emily had not blurted anything else. She considered the growing number of people who could reveal the extent of her and Cormac's connection – Lord and Lady Bewley, Lizzie, Miss Davison through Emily's endless chatter, and now the butler and Bridget's closest friends – and realised that they would need to exercise more vigilance.

On the night of the ball, Bridget entered Radcliffe House with a mixture of apprehension and anticipation. The merriment was in full swing and the ballroom was crowded with people dancing, mingling and gossiping. She searched for Cormac and spotted him in a set, partnered with Alice. Almost as if he sensed her presence, he glanced around and made eye contact with her. His shining gaze was enough to set her nerves tingling everywhere. She stood to the side of the dancing floor and hoped no one would notice her flaming cheeks.

At the end of the dance, it became apparent that Alice had promised the next one to Lord Newby and Cormac was swift to take Bridget for his own partner. He led her into the group of dancers and they took their places in the formation.

There was a pause before the dance started and, wondering whether he and Alice had just engaged in their crucial third dance, she said casually, 'Are you having an enjoyable evening so far?'

He chuckled. In a low voice that nobody else could hear, he said,

'Passable, with a substantial improvement upon your arrival. Alice is very amiable but she does not compare to the incredible woman next to me right now.'

She found herself reddening again. How could she do anything but melt when he spoke to her like that? The dance began and, despite the modest nature of the steps, it became extraordinarily sensual between them. Every touch, every look, was loaded with heat, reminding them of their recent clandestine encounters...

It was an effort to drag her concentration back to a more lucid train of thought. She had to tell him about Emily's injudicious comment in front of Lucy and Alice.

'We need to talk in private,' she said, peeking over his shoulder at Alice who was having difficulty maintaining rhythm with Lucy's uncoordinated husband. 'Will you meet me after this dance?'

'I am at your service,' he replied, though the mischief in his eyes rather negated the formal address.

They could not retreat to the terrace for it was a far more welcoming place in early March than it had been in the heart of January and, through the open French doors, she could see that it was teeming with guests seeking a breath of air.

'There is a door at the back of the room,' she said, familiar with the layout of Radcliffe House from so many visits over the years. 'It is not the main access to the ballroom so, with any luck, there will be nobody lingering out there. I shall go first. Delay a little while and then follow.'

He nodded with detached civility for the dance was ending and Cassandra was approaching. As usual, her attire was unforgettable; tonight her gown was lavish with lace and she wore an elaborate display of feathers in her hair.

'Mr Davenport!' she exclaimed. 'I wonder if you could assist Alice and me? We are trying to determine whether the punch has been soured by too much lemon.'

Bridget slipped away from them. She stepped out into the hallway; it was indeed deserted, lit only by a lamp mounted on a bracket by the ballroom door and a stream of moonlight which fell through an uncurtained window at the end of the corridor. There was an alcove halfway down towards the window – it may have been intended as an exhibition space for a piece of sculpture but it was vacant at present. She hid in its shadows and waited.

Several minutes passed before Cormac made his appearance. When he shut the door of the ballroom behind him, she emerged from the alcove and called his name softly. He glimpsed her hovering at the edge of the patch of moonlight and strode towards her.

'I'm sorry you had to wait so long,' he said as he approached. 'Lady

Radcliffe is the most persistent woman I have ever met.'

She meant to tell him what Emily had said in Lucy and Alice's presence. But when he reached her, she discerned the undisguised lust burning in his eyes. He pulled her into the alcove and crushed his mouth upon hers. Urgency and desire overwhelmed them, so powerful that it compelled them to abandon the caution of which she had intended to warn him – a mere wall separated them from discovery. His hands roamed all over her, caressing the tops of her breasts and stroking her waist and hips, while hers roved over him in turn, skimming across his solid chest and gripping his backside in shameless gratification. He scrabbled at her skirts.

'Why do there have to be so many layers?' he complained, his voice muffled against her lips.

She began to laugh but stifled herself when the ballroom door opened, and light, music and chatter spilled out into the hallway. The door closed again, leaving the hall dim and quiet once more, but they knew they were no longer alone.

'Where is he?' came Cassandra's ringing tones. 'I'm certain I saw him slip out here.'

'I thought I saw him too,' said another female voice which Bridget recognised as Lucy's.

Cormac released her from his embrace and they stood motionless.

'Perhaps he went this way,' Lucy suggested and, horror-struck, Bridget heard her footsteps coming down the corridor in the direction of their alcove. There was nothing whatsoever to hide behind; if she came near, she would not fail to discover them.

'No,' said Cassandra dismissively. 'There is nothing down there but a door to the servants' staircase.'

Lucy's footsteps retreated but they did not dare breathe a sigh of relief just yet. As long as Cassandra and Lucy remained in the corridor, they were trapped. If the ladies chose to wait for Cormac to reappear, they would be obliged to stay concealed and suspicion would mount ever higher with regard to Mr Davenport's mysterious absence.

But then Cassandra said, 'He could be gone to the smoking room. Henry escaped there a while ago so it is likely he will embroil Mr Davenport in a conversation about some kind of sport. The man thinks of nothing else,' she added, disgruntled.

'It may be a while before he returns then. Shall we go back in?'

'I suppose so. I do wish he would not waste his time with my husband though. I promised Alice I would have her married to Mr Davenport by midsummer and I intend to follow through on that. It would be helpful if he made more of a contribution to my efforts.'

With that, the ballroom door opened and closed once more and silence descended in the hallway.

Bridget looked at Cormac. His face was strained in the pale light of the moon. He leaned his head back against the wall of the alcove and shut his eyes.

'I cannot take much more of this,' he said. 'They are vultures. They see me as a piece of meat, not a human being.'

Her tone was sympathetic as she replied, 'That is the unfortunate lot of a handsome young man who is to inherit a fortune and estate.'

The ghost of the true Oliver floated in the wake of her words.

Cormac opened his eyes and stared straight at her. 'I can't stand it anymore. When I look over my shoulder, all I see is those women dogging my heels or potential scenarios where our connection could be discovered. I want to get out of London, and out of this life. Let's run away, you and Emily and I.'

Her breath left her body in a rush.

'Think about it,' he urged. 'The prospect of going somewhere where we could be ourselves rather than pretending to be other people. Where the three of us could be a family. Where you and I could be a couple overtly in love instead of hiding behind locked doors. I hate this duplicity, I have lived with it for too long now. I want to be me again and I want to be with you, without the disgust of deceit and the constraints of high society restricting us at every turn. Don't you crave it too?'

She was forcibly reminded of their night in the hay barn and his similarly impassioned plea back then. They were older now, but were they any wiser?

Hesitant, she said, 'I crave the simplicity of what you describe. But we are not two people alone. We have Emily and she is the most important person of all. I could not bear to bring any hardship or unhappiness upon her.'

'You would not be doing that if you came with me. I would look after you both and ensure no harm came to either of you. Listen,' he said, clutching her hands. 'We could slip away, flee on a ship before anyone realised we were missing, and go home, back to my mother and sisters and nephew. If they were willing to leave Oakleigh, they could come with us and we could all be a family together somewhere else, living the life we really want to live.'

Her jaw dropped. She had taken in every glorious thing he had just said but her mind had caught on one essential flaw. His mother, sisters and nephew. He did not know what had happened to them, that they had been driven from Oakleigh too, that there was very little hope any of them had survived. How had she been so remiss as to not realise this? And how on earth could she tell him that his family was not safe at home as he believed and that – her heart constricted horribly – it was her fault?

'Cormac –' she began in a cracked voice.

'Do not give me your answer now,' he cut in. 'I want you to take the time to consider it first. Just know this: I love you and I love Emily and I want to do everything I can to make you both happy.' He glanced out into the empty corridor. 'I am going to return to the ball now. I'll tell the ladies I went to seek a quieter spot than the terrace for some air. I cannot use the smoking room as an alibi as there is no smell of smoke on me. It's best if you wait a few minutes before following.'

He kissed her forehead and left her alone in the alcove. She gazed unseeingly at the wall, her mind blank with shock. What in the world was she going to do?

Feeling shaky, she gathered her wits and returned to the ballroom. She caught Lucy's eye as she entered; Lucy glanced over to where Cormac was conversing with Alice and then looked back at Bridget with a frown.

## Chapter 30

Bridget woke with a start the following morning, wondering why she had such a sick feeling in her stomach. Then the memory of the previous night crashed over her and the nausea intensified to a severity that had her reaching for the chamber pot.

Cormac was unaware that his family had been rendered homeless just like him. She saw now how obvious this was, for he had been banished from the estate before her mother had delivered that devastating blow. So he had lived these many years believing they still dwelled safely in the cottage that had been his childhood home. And it fell to Bridget to shatter that illusion.

She had had no other private moment with him for the remainder of the ball to divulge the terrible reality to him. But a visit to Raynesworth House had been prearranged for that afternoon – Lady Bewley wished to discuss the possibility of speaking to the Ladies of Compassion Association herself – so Bridget would be obliged to face him then.

What would he say? What would he think of her? He would never be able to look at her the same way again, forevermore seeing her as the person who had allowed ruin to come upon his beloved family. He might have been able to find it in himself to forgive her for the pain she had caused him personally, but surely he could never absolve her for inflicting such agony upon a dear mother who had already suffered far too much.

Would he terminate their relationship, rescinding his offer of the wonderful future he had just proposed to her? She despaired at the thought. She had no clear concept of the practicalities of running away; she only knew that it would be unbearable if he left her now. Their separation seven and a half years ago would be nothing compared to losing him this time, when the reason would not be the cruel manipulation of her mother but the fact that he could no longer feel any regard for her. That would be desolation beyond endurance.

Nevertheless, he must be told, of that she was in no doubt. She could not let him go one day further without knowing the unfortunate fate of his beloved mother and sweet sisters and that innocent baby. He needed to learn the horrendous truth.

But it would take all the courage she had.

The wretched hours trickled away and soon she was sitting in silent misery at Raynesworth House in the company of Lord and Lady Bewley and their 'nephew'. The elderly couple were delighted to see her, though their faces fell when they found that Emily was not in attendance. Bridget's excuse was that Emily had a cold and must remain at home to rest, which was for the most part true. The little girl did indeed have the sniffles but she was not quite as poorly as Bridget described to Lord and Lady Bewley, who clucked and fussed and pressed a variety of medicinal remedies upon her to take back to her daughter and help nurse her back to health. Cormac, too, looked alarmed but she dispelled his worries with a slight shake of her head when the lord and lady were not looking. She had decided that it was simply better for their daughter not to be present today, bearing in mind the confrontation that she knew was about to take place.

Awash with anxiety, she could scarcely keep track of the cheerful conversation around her. She was tormented by her thoughts, imagining Cormac's face when she laid bare the true state of affairs, the way he would turn his back in fury and walk away from her. It was going to be the end of all the joy of her existence. Yes, she would still have Emily and she would still love her with all her heart, but how could she ever look upon her again and not see Cormac in her mind's eye? She was sure that twenty lonely years from now the image would still feel as sharp and piercing as a dagger thrust into her side.

'Lady Wyndham, my dear? Are you quite well?'

She looked up to find four pairs of eyes staring at her, for even the maid serving the tea had paused to gape. It was plain that someone in the room had posed a question to her and she had been too preoccupied to either hear or respond.

'Pardon me,' she said weakly. 'What did you say?'

'You look rather ill,' said Lady Bewley, her brows drawn together in concern. 'It is possible you have contracted the cold that is vexing poor Emily. Shall we call for your carriage to take you home? Or, indeed, ought we to send for the physician?'

'Thank you, no, it is not so serious as that. But I believe I am in need of some fresh air. Would you mind if I took a turn about your garden?'

'Of course, that may well revive you. Perhaps Oliver could accompany you, in case you become faint?'

Cormac was on his feet before she had even bowed her head in acquiescence. He led her slowly from the drawing room for she was in fact beginning to feel lightheaded. As she stepped over the threshold at the back of the house, she thought for an instant that she was going to pass out, but then a refreshing gust of wind blew across her face and rejuvenated her. The wave of dizziness receded to be replaced by her former apprehension, multiplied tenfold now that the moment she had been dreading was fast approaching. She hastened into the garden to avoid eye contact with Cormac and heard his footsteps following her.

It was a typical March day, cool and blustery with intermittent patches of sunlight breaking through the clouds. The breeze caught at her hair and whipped loose strands into her face. She brushed them away impatiently as she hurried deeper into the garden, heading for the small, walled orchard. The irony did not escape her but inside it they would be beyond the view of any prying eyes from the house. She slipped through the door and made for the stone bench as he entered the orchard behind her.

'What is the hurry?' he said, startled by her agitated manner.

She did not reply and she did not sit down on the bench, instead wringing her hands and gulping as she tried to force air into her lungs.

He came over to her and clutched her shoulders. 'Tell me what is the matter.'

She burst into tears.

He looked aghast. 'My God, what has happened?'

She shook her head as heart-rending sobs wracked her body. She couldn't do this, she couldn't. It would be like tearing herself in half.

Understanding seemed to dawn on his face. His eyes widened and filled with horror.

'Please do not do this to me again,' he choked out, his hands dropping to his sides.

Through her tears, she gazed up at him without comprehension. 'Do what?'

His voice did not sound like his own as he said, 'Please do not say you are going to stay with him.'

She stopped sobbing out of sheer surprise; his fear could not have been further from the truth. 'I'm not going to say that. I do not want to stay with Garrett. I want to go away with you.'

In a split second, his features changed from dismay to absolute elation and he laughed in relief. 'Then why are you so upset?'

'Because you will not want to go away with me,' she said and started to weep again.

He looked bewildered. 'Why on earth not?'

With a great effort, she tried to stem her flow of grief. 'I have something awful to tell you. And after you hear it you will detest me and you will never want to see me again.'

He frowned. 'I cannot imagine that there is anything in this world that would make me feel like that towards you.'

'That is because it is too horrible to imagine,' she said hollowly.

She took a deep, shuddering breath and sat on the stone bench. The moment had come. Her next words would mark the immediate end of their snatched, sunlit time together.

'There is something you do not know,' she began, staring down at her lap, 'and it was only at the ball last night that I realised you were not aware of it. You said you wanted to go back to your family on the Oakleigh Estate, back to your mother and sisters and nephew. But this is not possible for they are no longer there.'

He tried to interrupt but she talked over him; it was easier to keep going now that she had started. 'At the end of that summer at Oakleigh, my mother ordered you to leave the estate and you did so. What you do not know is that the following morning she did the same to your whole family. She had already threatened to do it but promised she would not if I let you go and married Garrett. I made an unspeakable choice, believing I was at least saving Maggie and the others. But then she threw them off the land anyway, leaving them with no home, no money, no means of obtaining help from anyone. You know firsthand the bleak reality they must have faced. I think' – her voice splintered and she swallowed – 'I think there can be no hope for any of them.'

She forced herself to look up at him. He stood unmoving, his face white and his hands balled into fists. She waited for the onslaught of his rage but he remained immobile. This mute statue was almost more frightening than the exclamations of hatred she had been anticipating and she felt compelled to fill the agonising silence.

'I am so, so sorry,' she said thickly. 'I shall never be able to forgive myself for this and I do not expect you to either. You have every right to blame me.'

This stirred him from his trance. He blinked. 'What did you say?'

'You have every right to blame me.' Heart heavy, she shut her eyes as the tears squeezed out again.

'I do not blame you!' she heard him say in an incredulous tone and her eyes snapped open.

'What?'

'I do not blame you,' he said again and went on caustically, 'I blame your conniving *bitch* of a mother. To condemn an innocent family like that, she either has a heart of stone or no heart at all. If she were in front of me right now, I would murder her with the greatest pleasure.'

He did not look at all apologetic at his coarse language but she barely registered this. She was trying to process the fact that his loathing was not directed at her.

'I d-don't understand. You do not think it was my fault?'

'Of course not. You believed she would allow them to stay, didn't you?'

'Yes…'

'Then you were as much deceived as anyone.'

'But it was because of me that she did it.' She did not know why she was arguing, only that it was important for him to fully understand the depth of her culpability. 'Because of what I did with you.'

'If that is the case, then we are both to blame. But our only crime is that we were in love. Lady Courcey is the root of this monstrous act of cruelty. I in no way hold you responsible for her unspeakable actions.'

She felt hope rise within her. 'So you — you still want to be with me?'

'More than anything else in this world.'

This was too much. Once again, she broke down in tears. Burying her face in her hands, she found herself laughing and crying at the same time. All that fear and dread had been for nothing. He still loved her and he did not see her as the person who had destroyed his family. The sun continued to shine in her life after all.

She felt a pressure along the side of her body as he sat on the bench beside her. He tugged at her hands until she let them fall away from her face.

'Did you think I was going to leave you?' he murmured.

She nodded jerkily. He leaned forwards and kissed each of her cheeks where the tracks of her tears still glistened.

'Impossible,' he whispered in her ear. 'Unthinkable. Unendurable. I am not going anywhere without you.'

She threw her arms around him and they hugged as if they had just saved each other from a sinking ship. All uncertainty was gone. Without consciously thinking about it, she had made her decision to run away with him. The prospect of parting had been so distressing that it had driven home the stark realisation that she could not live without him; it was absurd to even entertain the notion of separation when her happiness could only exist wherever he was. And he had already proved that he reciprocated those feelings without reservation. They needed no more words to confirm their wholehearted love and commitment to one another and to their treasured daughter.

When they broke apart, she was smiling with joy but his face was set in an expression of steely determination.

'We cannot delay,' he said in a fierce voice. 'You say there is no hope for my family but I do not accept that. I want to return to Ireland and find them. There is a possibility that they may have perished but there is also every chance that they survived. I won't be able to rest until I have uncovered the truth.'

She cupped his cheek tenderly. 'Emily and I shall be with you every step of the way.'

He turned his head to the side and kissed her fingers. Then he stood and began to pace back and forth, the bare branches of the apple trees waving above his head.

'We need to make a plan. I have already been thinking about this. We must depart without telling a soul, because that was our fatal mistake at

Oakleigh. And we ought to leave during the daytime. First of all, Garrett will not realise you and Emily are missing until he returns home late in the evening. If we are lucky and he stays away for the night then it might even be the next day. Second, Lord and Lady Bewley will not become suspicious of my absence until well past nightfall. And third, it will be easier to lose ourselves in a crowd if we are pursued.'

'You are expecting us to be pursued?' she said, her elation of the previous minute diluted now with a stab of uneasiness.

'The probability is only slight. I anticipate that we shall be safely away by the time our absence is noted and the alarm is raised. But we ought to prepare for every eventuality and ensure that we depart without drawing attention to ourselves.'

'How shall we do that?'

'We must use different names. We shall be Mr and Mrs Marsh and our daughter Lizzie until we are out of harm's way. That will be an easy name for Emily to remember. I'll buy three tickets on the next ship departing for Ireland and send you word with the date and time. You and Emily will need to be ready when I come for you.'

'We will be.'

He looked at her. 'We should tell Emily who I am.'

'Yes,' she agreed at once. 'I shall tell her just before we leave. Any sooner and she might let something slip to Garrett. This will be very confusing for her, poor thing.'

'She is a bright girl and she has two parents who love her very much. She will be fine.'

He held out his hand to her; she stood and they embraced beneath the trees.

'We are really doing this,' she said, full of nerves and excitement.

'We are,' he replied.

## Chapter 31

Over the next few days, Bridget made her preparations. She surreptitiously packed a valise for herself and Emily with ruthless discrimination, selecting the plainest dresses and most sensible boots and omitting elegant mantles and decorative jewellery. One bonnet and one cloak each would be sufficient. Among a small number of personal items, she packed the silver-handled hairbrush Lady Bewley had given Emily, for both its practical use and sentimental value, and left enough space for the watercolour box, which there could be no question of leaving behind. She tried to keep the valise as light as she could for she knew there would be long days of travel ahead and the last thing they wanted was to be hauling a heavy burden along with them.

A harder challenge was the letters she must write. She and Emily could not disappear without a trace; there would be the assumption that they had been abducted and a citywide search would ensue. She needed to relay a message that it was their own choice to leave. She also wanted to attempt to say goodbye in writing as she could not do so to anyone in person. She therefore wrote separate letters to Lucy, Alice and Cassandra to apologise for the abrupt ending of her acquaintance with them, to assure them that this was what she wanted, and to wish them well with their own families and futures. She tried not to imagine the outrage and upset the letters would cause and sincerely hoped that Alice's heart would not be broken by the departure of Mr Davenport.

She wrote to Frances too, with a sadness that extended both to her dear friend and to St Swithun's itself. The place was gloomy and inhospitable and had been the site of her frightening assault by a desperate man, and yet she believed she would be sorry to bid farewell to it. Her efforts there had given her a sense of purpose in some of the bleakest hours of her existence and it would be the part of her life in London she would miss most of all when she left. She wished she could make a final substantial donation but that was impossible without Garrett's signature on the cheque, so she confined herself to infusing her letter with fervent expressions of hope for Frances's good health and the advancement of St Swithun's. She would give it and the others to Lizzie before she left; the loyal maid would ensure that the notes reached the right hands at the appropriate time.

Most difficult of all was her letter to Garrett. The desertion of his wife and child would expose him to widespread scandal which he would find excruciating to bear. But he had been unfaithful to her too and, worse, he had been hardhearted towards Emily. There was nothing to salvage from such a loveless situation, and she kept this point fixed in her mind as she penned her note.

> Garrett,
>
> Emily and I are gone. We have run away with Cormac. I am sure you have not forgotten who that is. I shall give you no details as to how he has come back into my life, nor shall I tell you where we are going. It will be futile to search for us so do not waste your time.
>
> You and I must admit to ourselves that our marriage was a failure. You were never in love with me and I was always in love with somebody else. Our greatest triumph was bringing our beloved James into this world, and I thank you for that fleeting period of joyfulness. I know you will always feel his loss as keenly as I.
>
> I wish to part on amicable terms so please understand that I hold no grudge against you. I do hope that, in time, you might come to feel the same towards me, recognising that this is the best for all concerned.
>
> Farewell,
> Bridget

It was perhaps a little brief for the termination of a relationship that had lasted nine years but it was all she could manage. She intended to return her engagement ring with the letter too but that could not be done until the last moment.

And so she waited.

On Thursday, she, Garrett and Emily were seated at the breakfast table when the morning messages arrived and with them Cormac's letter of deliverance.

> Friday morning. I will come for you.
>
> C.

He had initialled it with his true name which must mean he was convinced of their escape. She could hardly conceal her excitement and almost knocked the milk jug out of Peter's hand as the footman leaned in to place it on the table. She glanced up to find Garrett staring at her.

'Good news, my darling?' he enquired with raised eyebrows and a rather twisted smile.

'Another gathering at Cassandra's,' she said, hastily doubling over the note. She strove to keep her gaze from alighting upon Emily, fearing that her expression would reveal too much of her elation. 'I did so enjoy the last one. I am certain this next occasion will be just as entertaining.'

He folded the letter in his own hand.

'Perhaps I shall attend this time,' he said, draining his coffee cup. 'I am long overdue a visit to Radcliffe House.'

'Cassandra will be delighted,' she said with a mechanical smile.

That evening, she unpacked and repacked the secret valise three times, anxious that she was either forgetting something essential or including something that ought to be left out. When at last she was satisfied that all was in order, she wandered around her bedchamber, touching her possessions for the final time. She stroked the fur trim of her favourite mantle, trailed her fingers through the glittering pieces in her jewellery box, and said a wistful goodbye to the embroidered pillowcase that had belonged to James. The pouch containing his dark lock of hair was the only memory of her baby boy she had allowed herself to tuck into the valise.

After that, there was nothing to do but wait for the evening to end. She had eaten her last solitary dinner at the enormous dining table. She had sent Emily to bed with a special hug and kiss, knowing the upheaval that was in store for her tomorrow. She had tried reading but found it impossible to concentrate. Every minute crawled by. She wondered how Cormac was whiling away this final night alone and longed for him with a physical ache. If only Friday would come more quickly.

She had expected that she would not see Garrett again until the next morning at breakfast, but she was not long in bed when she heard him enter the hall below, quite a bit earlier than usual. His footsteps came directly up the stairs to her door and his knock was firm.

Instinct made her wary. She wished she had blown out her candle so that he would have noted the absence of light under the door and believed she was already asleep. Her teeth fastened on the tip of her tongue.

'Come in,' she said unenthusiastically.

He entered the bedchamber and closed the door behind him. His hair was tousled and his hazel eyes held a wild gleam. He stared at her for a long time without saying anything.

She grew impatient under his silent appraisal and, with all the politeness she could muster, said, 'Is there something I can do for you?'

He shrugged and his gaze roamed restlessly around the chamber before landing on her again.

'Are you with child?' he asked without warning.

Her mouth fell open in mute shock. For one panicked moment, she thought he had somehow learned of her love affair with Cormac, but then she came to her senses. The last time she and Garrett had shared a bed, the night of James's birthday in January, he had demanded a son of her. He wanted to know if there had been a product of that union.

'I—no,' she said faintly.

'We will have to try again then,' he said and approached the bed. He smelled of smoke and brandy.

She blanched. He must have tired of whichever young mistress had been diverting him these past weeks and now here he was, intending to bed his wife on the very eve of her running away from him. The timing could not be worse. She felt nauseated at the idea of betraying Cormac at this eleventh hour – her body belonged to him now, not to the man in front of her. She had to prevent this act of unfaithfulness or she would not be able to face Cormac in the morning.

He was already pulling back the bedcovers; he had not even tried to kiss her. She pressed down on the skirt of her nightdress, blocking his access.

'No, we cannot.'

His gaze whipped up to hers. 'You shall not deny your husband.'

She shivered at the frost in his tone but tried to keep the tremble from her voice as she lied, 'I have my courses. It is not possible tonight.'

He glared at her with such mistrust that she feared he might rip off her clothing to check. Then his shoulders sagged. He smoothed the bedcovers back over her and placed a detached kiss on her cheek.

'A pity,' he said and stalked from the room.

## Chapter 32

Friday morning dawned with Bridget standing at her bedchamber window, watching as the dark gardens of Berkeley Square became visible with the rising sun. Though she had tried, she had not shut her eyes all night; sleep had been unattainable with such a momentous and perilous day ahead of her. In just a few short hours she would be unshackled from the charade she had perpetuated for so long, and she, Cormac and Emily would be at liberty to live as a true family at long last. Her whole body was taut with anticipation.

One more duty remained and that was to endure the final breakfast that she and Garrett would share in this house. It was an almost silent meal. He was out of sorts, no doubt injured by her rebuff the previous night. He frowned at the bacon on his plate as though it offended him and did not even open his newspaper, something which he had never failed to do in seven and a half years.

Judging this to be a rather disproportional reaction – her excuse had been a reasonable one, after all – she said tentatively, 'Is something troubling you, Garrett?'

He looked up with a glower. 'I am just mulling over some business dealings I must see to this morning,' he said and relapsed into silence.

She said nothing further. So long as his business dealings took him out of the house, that was all that mattered. She was taken aback, however, when he rose from the table soon afterwards and left the room without even a glance in her direction. He must be even more vexed than she had realised to snub her in such a way. It was the last time she would ever see her husband and the moment felt very unfinished, but there was nothing she could do about it now. He was gone.

Once he had left the house, she was able to complete her preparations for departure. She summoned Lizzie, gave her the letters addressed to her friends, and instructed her to make sure they were not delivered until the following day; the maid took the sealed notes without question. Then she sent a request down to Monsieur Lévêque in the kitchens to put together a parcel of food as she and Emily wished to have a picnic in the gardens. After that, she informed Miss Davison that she desired Emily's company for the day and the governess was therefore free to spend it as she pleased. She found it difficult to mask the guilt she felt; their flight would have many ramifications, and one of them was that this young woman would be without employment on the morrow.

Suppressing her conscience as well as she could, she made her way to Garrett's bedchamber and slipped inside. She could smell his cologne in the air, a scent which she had never been able to separate from that of charred wood since the day he had burned the wooden bird. Going over to the bedside, she slid the engagement ring off her finger and placed it on the pillow along with her farewell letter. All at once she felt lighter, as though the ring had been exerting a heavy pressure on her hand. The tie between her and Garrett was cut; he was no longer her keeper.

Next, she went to the chest of drawers. It took only a minute or two of searching to locate her dear father's pocket watch among Garrett's clothing and possessions. She retrieved the precious item and left the room without looking back.

Her last and most vital duty was to tell Emily the truth. Heart beating in her mouth, she brought her daughter into the drawing room and closed the door. This was the decisive act that would make it all undeniably real.

'Gooseberry, come sit beside me,' she said, sitting on the sofa and drawing Emily to her. 'I have something very important I need to tell you.'

Emily looked up at her with wide blue eyes, exact replicas of Cormac's own. Bridget took a steadying breath.

'Mr Davenport is coming to visit us this morning,' she began and Emily's face lit up. 'There is something I have not told you about him. Oliver Davenport is not his real name. He is actually called Cormac McGovern.'

Emily frowned. 'Why does he need two names?'

'That is hard to explain. He used to be Cormac and then he had to be Oliver for a little while, but now he wants to be Cormac again.'

'Can everybody have two names if they want to?'

'No, it is unusual for a person to change their name. But that is not the important thing I have to tell you. The important thing is that he is your real papa.'

She scrutinised the girl's face for her reaction. Emily stared back unblinkingly.

'Do you understand? The man you know as your papa is not your father. Your father is the man you have known as Mr Davenport but who I have just told you is really called Cormac McGovern.'

She cringed. The poor thing, how on earth could she comprehend it? It was far too confusing.

But Emily, brow furrowed, was trying to repeat what her mother had said. 'Papa is not my papa. Mr Davenport is my papa. Mr Davenport is Cormac McGovern. So Cormac McGovern is my papa.'

She cast an enquiring look at her mother for confirmation.

'Yes, that is correct. Does it make sense to you? Cormac is a friend of mine from a long time ago. We knew each other before you were born. I cannot explain it fully to you now but you will understand when you are older. All you need to know at present is that he is your true father.'

'So is Mr Davenport coming to live here with us?' asked Emily with interest.

'His name is Cormac,' Bridget reminded her gently. 'He is not coming to live here. We are going to go away with him. It is essential that you listen to this part, Emily. We are leaving this house today and we are not coming back. We are going to take a ship to Ireland, the country where your father and I grew up.'

'A ship! I've never been on a ship before. Will my first papa be going on the ship too?'

'No, he will be staying here. I am afraid you won't be able to say goodbye to him for he has left the house for the day and will not be home again until after we are gone. But I have written him a note that says farewell from both of us.'

Emily nodded, betraying no sign of distress at the prospect of never again being in the presence of the man she had believed her whole life to be her father. 'Will Lizzie and Peter be coming with us?'

'No,' Bridget said again and was saddened to perceive that this was a much greater disappointment for the little girl. How significant it was that she had built a stronger emotional connection with the servants than with Garrett. He had utterly failed her as a father figure.

'We won't be taking any servants with us,' Bridget went on. 'And very few possessions. I have already packed a valise with all of the necessary things. However, I shall allow you to bring one plaything with you. Bear in mind you will have to leave the rest behind, so choose wisely.'

'My watercolour box,' said Emily straight away.

Bridget smiled. 'I thought as much.'

She was about to suggest that Emily go and fetch it when there was a quiet knock on the door and Thrussell entered.

'You have a visitor, my lady. Mr Davenport. Shall I tell him you are not at home?'

Her heart leapt. 'You may send him up,' she said, disregarding the fact that the usually unflappable butler looked quite perturbed. It was too early for callers, and a gentleman caller at that. But the time for concealment was past.

Keeping his reservations to himself, Thrussell bowed and exited, and a minute later Cormac appeared in the doorway. He was wearing a nondescript overcoat and he carried a flat cap in one hand and a valise in the other.

'That is the last time I use that name,' he said in a low voice once Thrussell had departed. Setting down the valise and depositing his cap on top of it, he looked across the room at Bridget and their eyes met in identical expressions of joy and hope. The day was here at last to seize their future and be happy together, as they had been prevented from doing for so long.

Of her own volition, Emily got up from the sofa, went over to Cormac and gazed up at him. After a beat of silence, she said, clear and steady, 'Good morning, Papa.'

Stunned, he glanced from Emily to Bridget and back again.

'Good morning, Emily,' he answered and continued hesitantly, 'You know who I am?'

'Yes, Mama has just told me. She said that you and her were friends before I was born and that you're my real papa and that we're all going away on a ship together.'

'And how do you feel about that?'

'I'm excited about going on the ship.' It seemed she was not going to say anything else until her face broke into a brilliant smile and she exclaimed, 'And I'm glad you are my papa!'

She flung her arms around his waist and hugged him. He was so astonished that it took him a second to respond, but then he wrapped his arms around her and bent to kiss the top of her head. It was a beautifully sweet moment. Bridget felt tears come to her eyes as she saw them come to his.

When they separated, he knelt in front of his daughter and grasped her two small hands in his own.

'We have a long journey ahead of us,' he told her seriously. 'At times you might find it hard to bear. Sometimes you might even wish you were back here in this house and had never left. Just know that when you are feeling tired or upset, I'll be there to look after you. I promise to care for you and your mother every step of the way. And after the journey is over, we are going to make a home and be very happy together. Maybe we shall get some chickens for you to look after. Would you like that?'

'I would!' She beamed at the idea of being mistress of a brood of chickens.

He kissed her forehead and stood again. 'Are you ready to go?' he asked Bridget.

'We are. Emily just needs to fetch her watercolour box. I have everything else packed.'

He looked down at Emily. 'Will you go and get the box now?'

'Yes, Papa,' she said and ran from the drawing room.

As soon as she was gone, Bridget and Cormac met in the middle of the room in an emotional embrace. The pressure of his arms around her told her more than any words could say; he was ecstatic.

'I can't believe it,' he murmured into her hair. 'I just cannot believe it.'

They broke apart and at the same time burst into giddy laughter. The distant sound of the front door opening and closing a floor below halted them, but she shook her head at his alarmed expression.

'That will have been Miss Davison,' she reassured him. 'I released her from her duties for the day. She must be gone to call upon an acquaintance.'

He let out a breath, relaxing again.

'I have everything arranged,' he said, pulling three slips of paper out of his pocket. 'These are our tickets for the ship. We shall board it at the river docks and it will take us down around the south coast of England and into the port of Cork in Ireland. From there, we shall travel to Oakleigh. It was the last place my family was seen for certain, so that is where we shall begin our search. Seven and a half years is a long time but the folk there might be able to remember something. Any tiny detail will help us.'

She noticed he made no reference to the fact that they would be within range of the manor house and Lady Courcey, but she said nothing about that for now.

Instead, she said, 'And Raynesworth House? How did you depart without suspicion?'

'At breakfast, I told Lord and Lady Bewley I would be away for the whole day and they should not expect me for dinner this evening. With any luck, it will be late tonight or even tomorrow morning before they grow worried. Once my absence becomes prolonged, they will eventually search my bedchamber and that is when they will discover the letter I have left for them in my writing desk, along with a notebook of poems composed by Oliver.' He sighed. 'I wrote the entire truth. It pains me to imagine how hurt and angry they will be. They have treated me like their own son and I have returned their kindness by robbing them of the bright future they had envisioned: a thriving estate and a new generation on the Bewley family tree. I am leaving them without an heir. My betrayal is deplorable.'

She squeezed his hand. 'But you need to make your own future,' she said. 'Try not to be too regretful. You are doing the right thing.'

He squeezed back. 'I know. But I shall miss them.'

Emily came dashing back into the room then, clutching her watercolour box. 'I'm ready to leave!'

Within minutes, Cormac had retrieved Bridget and Emily's valise from its hiding place beneath Bridget's bed, the watercolour box had been packed into it, and both mother and daughter stood with bonnets on their heads and cloaks fastened around their necks.

Cormac placed his own cap over his fair hair, picked up the two valises, and said simply, 'Let's go.'

Bridget led the way to the staircase. She had taken three steps down before she realised that the hall below was not empty. She froze, gasping in horror.

Garrett stood at the bottom of the stairs, staring up at her with his hands clasped behind his back.

## Chapter 33

A flood of dread swept over Bridget. Garrett's countenance was calm, as though it were not an uncommon occurrence for him to catch his wife in the act of running away with another man. Cormac appeared at Bridget's side and she sensed Emily's presence on the step behind them. As Cormac set down the two valises, his face was alight with unflinching determination. He would not give them up without a fight.

Bridget felt the blood pulsing in her ears, her nerves thrilling with fear. Their hope of escape had relied upon leaving without detection, on being gone before anyone realised they were missing. Now Garrett barred the way and he had every power to prevent them from getting past the door. Her shining image of a life with Cormac and Emily flickered like a candle flame in a draught. Don't blow out, she begged it. Please don't blow out.

Garrett spoke, his tone light and conversational. 'Going somewhere?'

'Yes,' said Cormac. 'And you're not going to stop us.'

'I think you will find yourself very much mistaken in that regard. It has been a long time since we were last face to face, Cormac. Or should I call you Mr Davenport now?'

Bridget grimaced. How could he possibly have found out? They had told no one of their plans. Could Lizzie have betrayed them, based on the questionable conduct she had witnessed between her mistress and Mr Davenport?

Trying to keep the shake out of her voice, Bridget asked, 'How did you learn of our secret?'

To her shock, Garrett said, 'Lady Newby. In the strictest confidence of the bedchamber, she imparted to her husband her concern that the relationship between her friend Lady Wyndham and their new acquaintance Mr Davenport might not be altogether proper. Of course, Newby disregarded his vow not to speak of it and came straight to me about the suspicion. A description of Mr Davenport removed all doubt as to who was involved. It appears my wife has not improved her vulgar tastes over the years.'

His lip curled as her heart sank. Lucy had been observing the tiniest clues all this time – if only she had not divulged her misgivings just as they were about to flee. Distressed, Bridget willed her tiny flame to stay alive.

Next to her, Cormac clenched his jaw. 'How did you know we would be leaving this morning?'

'I had Brewer tail you. He watched you purchase sailing tickets and bribed the clerk to tell him the date of departure. Then I was informed as soon as you entered the house a short while ago. That was all that was necessary to bring me to this juncture.' He looked amused. 'You did not genuinely believe you would get away with this, did you?'

'We have every intention of doing so,' said Cormac. 'We will be fleeing this city today as planned.'

'You shall not make it out of Berkeley Square, let alone out of the city. I have done my research on Oliver Davenport. By all accounts, he is the devoted nephew of the esteemed Lord and Lady Bewley, who at present reside at Raynesworth House. Knowing who you really are allows me to lay several charges at your feet: posing under a false identity, stealing the lord and lady's wealth, and now caught in the act of attempted kidnapping. Who knows, perhaps you murdered someone along the way as well. You are a criminal of the lowest degree and there is no chance that the law enforcement will let you sail away without capture. Your appointment with the hangman is inevitable.'

He seemed so steady in his conviction that Bridget too felt persuaded of that horrific outcome. She clutched Cormac's arm as though a constable were already standing below them, ready to drag her lover away from her.

But then Cormac said, 'You think you have halted our escape but you don't bring the power of the law with you. I do not consider you a threat. We'll be walking through that front door whether you stand in our way or not.'

The first sign of anger crossed Garrett's features. 'How dare you presume to thieve from me?' he hissed. 'Bridget and Emily are mine. You cannot just snatch them away.'

'I'm no thief. They are human beings and they are choosing to leave with me.'

'Oh, indeed? Has Emily made her own choice or is she just doing as she is told?'

'She wants to go too,' Cormac said and added boldly, 'She knows who her real father is.'

Garrett's eyes flashed. 'You have been filling her head with nonsense, I see. Emily,' he said in an authoritative manner. 'I am your father. Come down here to me.'

Emily looked uncertainly from Garrett to Cormac. After a long pause, she took a step down to squeeze between Bridget and Cormac on the stairs. Then she slipped her hand into Cormac's. Bridget could have sang with relief at the girl's innocent gesture; she had no inkling of how much it solidified Cormac's position and weakened Garrett's.

Garrett narrowed his gaze. 'That proves nothing except that you have hoodwinked her into believing a lie.'

'It is the truth and you know it,' said Bridget. 'You have known it ever since you first saw her. That is why you have never treated her as your own daughter, why you have always been so cold towards her. She has scarcely received a scrap of affection from you, which just made it all the easier for her to believe the truth. Cormac has been more of a father to her in a few short weeks than you have been in almost seven years of her life.'

'So you are content for her to be branded a bastard?' he said, incredulous. 'An outcast of society? She does not understand now, but in ten years she will hate you for it. Far better for her to remain here where she will grow up to be esteemed rather than shunned.'

Mystified by his persistence, she said, 'Why are you trying to cling on? You have never loved Emily and there is certainly no love between you and me. Why can't you just let us go?'

'It is not a question of love, it is a question of ownership. You and Emily are my wife and child as recognised by the law and I am exercising my rights as the head of this house.'

'Listen to yourself!' Cormac exploded. 'You speak as though they are inanimate objects under your control. They are individuals with real feelings. Why would they contemplate staying with you when you place such little value upon their own wishes?'

'Women and children are not entitled to such considerations.' Garrett dismissed the notion with an impatient jerk of his head. 'That is no argument in support of this ludicrous behaviour.'

'It is the strongest argument,' Bridget countered. 'You care nothing for us and that causes us to feel worthless. Why should we tolerate that anymore when Cormac makes us feel the exact opposite?'

'They deserve to be with someone who will treat them with love and respect,' said Cormac.

Garrett abandoned any further pretence at calmness as he retorted, 'You are just like Mary. You see yourself as equal to us but you're not. You are so far below our social status that the concept is laughable. The sooner you grasp that, the sooner we can put an end to this fiasco.'

Cormac stood as immobile as a block of ice. 'What did you say?'

Garrett fell silent.

Cormac released Emily's hand and took a step down the stairs. 'What did you say?' he repeated. 'What did you say about my sister?'

Bridget sensed the already-tense atmosphere heightening around them. She stared down at her sullen husband and her pale-faced lover. Cormac continued to descend the staircase, approaching Garrett one menacing step at a time.

'Did you know my sister Mary?'

'No, of course not,' Garrett said unconvincingly.

Bridget felt a tug at her arm.

'Mama, what is happening?' Emily whispered.

She shook her head, her gaze still trained on the two men. This confrontation had become about something else entirely but she had no notion what it was. What did Mary have to do with anything?

Cormac clutched the banister so tightly that his knuckles stood out stark white against the smooth, dark wood.

'How did I not realise it before?' he said, fury bubbling in his voice. 'She saw you the day she died. I was there when she saw you on the road. How could I have been so blind?'

'I have no idea what you are talking about,' said Garrett in an attempt at scorn.

'I am talking about *Mary McGovern*. The girl you exploited and then discarded once you lost interest in her!'

Bridget heard this accusation with astonishment and confusion. Garrett had never met Mary in all his time at Oakleigh Manor. 'Cormac, what —'

'Your husband is a hypocrite,' Cormac spat, glancing over his shoulder at her. His eyes were wild with rage. 'He slanders us for producing an illegitimate child when in actual fact he has one of his own.'

Her stomach twisted. The pieces fell sickeningly into place. 'Patrick?'

His livid expression confirmed it. He turned back to Garrett. He was almost at the foot of the stairs now. 'My nephew, Patrick,' he declared, 'is the forsaken son of Lord Wyndham.'

'I do not need to hear any more of this,' said Garrett. 'These lies are irrelevant to the matter at hand. I am going to send the footman to fetch a constable, who will come at once when he learns that I have apprehended a criminal in my own house.'

He looked like he was about to make a hasty retreat from the hall but Cormac was quicker. He launched himself from the last step of the stairs, grabbed Garrett by the front of his coat, and shoved him against the wall. Garrett tried to throw him off but he was unused to physical violence and struggled fruitlessly in Cormac's iron grip. Emily pressed into Bridget's side, frightened. She wrapped her arms around the girl's shoulders to comfort her and watched in alarm as Cormac pinned Garrett in place.

'You are vile!' he snarled. 'You took advantage of my sister, used her for your own pleasure, and then deserted her. She was in love with you but you cast her and your son aside. And when she killed herself, you were the only one on the whole estate who knew why. She died in despair, she died because of *you*.' He was shouting now, his hands twisted in Garrett's tailored clothes. 'Admit what you did! Admit you are the reason my sister is no longer alive!'

At that moment, the inner door into the hall opened and Lizzie came through, looking terrified. When she saw her master pinioned against the wall, she turned as though to run for help.

'Stay where you are, Lizzie,' Bridget said from the top of the stairs, her speech much steadier than she had expected. 'We do not want to involve anyone else in this.'

Lizzie stood still, wide-eyed at the entangled men before her. Cormac did not acknowledge her presence. Blue eyes locked upon hazel ones, scorching with condemnation.

'Admit it,' he growled.

Garrett sagged in his grasp. 'Yes, it was me.'

Cormac drew back an arm and punched Garrett in the face. Then he let go of him and Garrett slid to the floor, blood dripping from his nose down his chin.

'She did not understand,' he said thickly as Cormac stood over him, chest heaving. 'She thought we could be together but we came from conflicting backgrounds too disparate to reconcile. It didn't matter how I felt. My father would never have accepted her or the boy. I hurt her to drive her away. There was no other option. But I never dreamed she would take such drastic measures...'

Bridget endeavoured to absorb the hideous implications of Garrett's confession. His every action in this tale had been despicable. He had misled Mary and deceived Bridget by courting both women at the same time. He had fathered an illegitimate child and shirked all responsibility for the boy. He had cruelly abandoned Mary, an act which made her so desperate and wretched that in the end she took her own life. Bridget felt bile rising in her throat at the horrifying grief her husband had caused.

And yet, there was something in his voice, a waver which told her that perhaps he was not as pitiless as he seemed. Did he feel regret? Was Mary the woman he had spoken of – had he borne a sincere love for her, far stronger than anything he had ever felt for Bridget? But had he allowed himself to be ruled by society just as Bridget had been forced to do, against his own true desire?

That by no means excused his conduct. A woman was dead because of him. She had been a sister, a daughter, a mother, and now she was nothing but a corpse buried in cold ground.

Mirroring her thoughts, Cormac said, his demeanour deceptively controlled, 'Her death is on your hands. Drastic measures, you say. Were those measures suicide? Or murder?'

Garrett gaped. 'Are you asking me whether I killed her?'

'Hanging is an unusual method for a woman. Drowning is more common. Did you do it? Did you take steps to remove her as an inconvenience from your life?' His inflection rose ferociously towards the end, his restraint slipping again.

The look of horror on Garrett's face was more eloquent than any words he could have spoken, but he still stuttered, 'I would—*never*—she was—how dare you—I loved her!'

'Did you communicate with her at all on the estate?' Cormac demanded. 'Did you say anything to her that would have driven her to choose the path she did?'

'No.' Garrett's deep breath came through his mouth, his nose having become clogged with drying blood. 'Our only contact was when we passed each other on that road. At first, I was so fearful that she would reveal our connection, but after my temper cooled I found myself recollecting the strength of our feelings for each other. I did contemplate going to see her.' He slumped against the wall. 'And then that lady's maid brought the news of her death.'

Bridget could recall those incidents at Oakleigh so clearly. Garrett's anger with Brewer over a trifling rip in his glove. Ellen imparting Mary's tragic story through her tears. Bridget herself becoming distraught for Cormac at the loss of his sister while Garrett, she had thought, looked on coldly – when in actual fact he was concealing his own grief over the death of his lover.

Cormac crossed his arms. 'So you claim you were sincerely in love with her?'

'Yes, God help me, I was.'

'But you rejected her anyway.'

'It hadn't been my intention.' Garrett swiped a knuckle across his upper lip, smearing the blood. With a glance up at Bridget, he said, 'She was the reason I chose an Irish bride. I thought I could maintain our association in a limited way. My plan was to undertake an outward marriage with a lady who would tie me to Ireland, and continue to pay the baker to look the other way when I visited Mary in her room above the bakery. But the arrival of Patrick proved to be a rude awakening. I perceived that Mary would not be content to see me on the odd occasion when I happened to be in Dublin. The connection was too dangerous to sustain any longer, despite our mutual passion. I had to get far away from her, and decided to return to London for good. Of course, it was too late to back out of my engagement then.'

Bridget knew she ought not feel aggrieved. After all, she had long ago admitted to herself that she didn't love this man, and she was right now in the process of leaving him for another. And yet, his bald disclosure stung acutely. She had been selected from a throng of hopeful misses with the indifference of one picking a piece of fresh fish. Recalling her own genuine joy at the time, she felt like a fool. Injured tears sprang to her eyes.

'You goddamned swine,' said Cormac. 'Did you have no regard for anyone but yourself? You squandered the happiness of two women, not to mention two innocent children.'

'Children,' Garrett repeated. 'They have only been a blight on my existence. My first son forever out of reach because of his ignominious birth. My second son defeated by disease before he had hardly begun to live. And my "daughter"' - he could not keep the misery from his expression - 'a girl I knew was not mine but who resembled Mary so much that it pained me to even look at her. Had circumstances been different, she might have been our own child.'

Bridget's head swam. All along, she had assumed that Garrett detested Emily on account of her likeness to Cormac - whose only sibling to share his fair hair and blue eyes had been Mary. This revelation shed Garrett's attitude towards Emily in a new and unsettling light.

At the same time, another thought occurred to her. The night Garrett had bedded her in January, he had said he desired a son he could acknowledge. She had believed it to be a derogatory reference to Emily. Now she comprehended that he had meant Patrick.

'Children,' Garrett said again, 'have been my curse.'

Against her will, she felt a ripple of compassion for him. Cormac, however, succumbed to no such sentiment.

'I would beat you into a pulp if my daughter were not present,' he said with cold hostility. 'You are worse than the rats in the streets. It is you who should face the hangman's noose, not I. There is not the remotest possibility that I shall allow Bridget and Emily to remain within your sphere of influence. I am going to take them away with me today and you will never see them again. Do not even think of coming after us. If you do, I will expose you for the blackguard you are, even if it means condemning myself in the process. I know your secret and I can ruin you. Think hard about your reputation before you choose to follow us.'

He began to step away but, in the instant when his back was turning, Garrett leapt up and flailed at him. His fist connected squarely with Cormac's jaw. Incensed, Cormac retaliated with a blow to Garrett's stomach that knocked him back into the dresser. Lizzie squeaked in fright as the piece of furniture shook at the impact. Garrett wheezed for breath, winded, and yet he wore an insane smile as he steadied himself on the dresser.

'You believe you are in a position to make threats,' he panted, with the air of someone saving his trump card until last, 'but you are not. Did you think I would walk in here to confront you without a scheme in place? Have you not thought to wonder at the whereabouts of our ever-present butler? After Brewer informed me that you had entered the building, I sent both him and Thrussell to Raynesworth House. By this stage, Lord and Lady Bewley will be aware of the entire situation. I imagine they won't take too kindly to having been so deceived and will send constables to the river docks to intercept you. Perhaps they are even now giving the order.'

He looked triumphant. 'You do not have a hope of setting foot aboard that ship.'

Cormac wasted no more time with words. He swung out at Garrett with such force to the side of his head that he knocked him out cold. Garrett slumped to the floor, ending in an awkward, half-sitting position against the dresser. Cormac did not spare him another glance as he ran back up the stairs to where Bridget and Emily stood frozen.

'We need to hurry,' he said. 'If Lord and Lady Bewley truly have dispatched constables to the docks, then we are now in a race to reach the river before them. We must get there with all possible speed.'

Bridget swallowed the dozen things she wanted to say after such an encounter and said, 'The carriage will get us there the fastest. Lizzie,' she called down to the maid. 'Ask Sawyer to bring the carriage around at once. I am afraid we cannot answer any questions you may have but please know that my husband has no reason to dismiss you. His anger is only directed at us and, with any luck, we shall be gone far beyond his reach by the time he wakes up. Now, I beg you, send for the carriage.'

Obedient as ever, Lizzie glanced at the unconscious form of her master and darted from the hall.

'We have to be quick,' Cormac reiterated and stretched out his arms to Emily.

She shrank away, trying to hide behind Bridget's skirts.

'I know you must be frightened by what you just saw, *a stór*,' he said in a soothing tone. 'I did not want to do what I did but he is a bad man and my temper got the better of me. I swear you have nothing to fear now. Do you remember I promised to look after you?'

She nodded, biting the tip of her tongue in Bridget's own characteristic gesture of anxiety.

'I still hold to that promise. You have no reason to be scared. But we are in a very great hurry now and we must make haste if we want to catch our ship before it sails away. Will you come with me?'

He reached out again and this time she stepped into his embrace. He lifted her up, squeezed her and then looked at Bridget. Alarm filled his taut features.

'Let's get out of here,' he said. 'Can you carry the valises?'

'Yes,' she said, picking them up. They descended the stairs and disappeared out the front door, departing from the house where she had denounced her mother, lost a child, endured years of misery, and had just learned that her unfaithful husband had been accountable for a needless death.

She was not sorry to leave.

## Chapter 34

Cormac's knuckles ached and he could feel a bruise developing on his jaw where Garrett had hit him. He rubbed the spot tenderly, irked that he had allowed himself to be caught off guard.

They were in the carriage, clattering through the streets of London as fast as the coachman dared. Cormac sat across from Bridget and Emily, who both had their hands clasped in their laps. Neither of them looked hopeful or excited anymore. Bridget's gaze was focused out the window and Emily was staring at the floor of the carriage. They were both doing their best to avoid eye contact with him.

He experienced a piercing stab at his heart as he imagined what they must be thinking of him right now. Where had the passionate lover and doting father gone? They had caught a glimpse of his darker side, the part of him that had been compelled to come to the forefront when he had worked for Cunningham. He had hoped to keep that dangerous man forever hidden from them but in the altercation with Garrett he had let his buried aggression take over. No wonder they could not look at him.

And yet, how could he have curbed his fury when confronted with the man who had destroyed his sister's life? Mary had been a vivacious girl whose greatest failing had been to fall for someone above her station. She had believed that love could transcend social class but Garrett had crushed her, throwing away her affection and leaving her to raise their child alone. Her spirit had been broken – Cormac had seen that in her muted manner following her return to Oakleigh – but perhaps in time it would have mended if she had not come face to face with her false lover on the estate. The shock of seeing him, after never expecting to lay eyes on him again, must have been enormous. His fists clenched at the thought of his sister ending her life on account of such a villain. Even now, he wanted to go back to Wyndham House and rip Garrett limb from limb.

But the fiend was inconsequential now; there was nothing he could do or say to bring Mary back or make amends for his reprehensible actions. Cormac would gain nothing from him except the satisfaction of his violent urges, which he must suppress if he did not want to risk scaring Bridget and Emily further. He wished desperately for either of them to look in his direction. If he could only say something that would remind them of the person he really was, of why they had been willing to run away with him in the first place, then maybe they would be able to forget the frightening scene they had just witnessed.

However, when he spoke over the noise of the rattling carriage, it was in a tone of brisk efficiency. 'We must remember to go by different names until we are safely on the ship and away from the docks. I will be Mr Jack Marsh. You, Bridget, shall be my wife, Molly, and you, Emily, shall be our daughter, Lizzie, just like the maid back at the house. We must not answer to our true names until we are out of harm's way. Do you both understand?'

They nodded. Emily continued to stare at the floor but Bridget cast him a quick glance before looking away again. Was she having second thoughts? Smothering the panic inside him, he said no more and silence resumed in the carriage.

At last, they reached the docks on the River Thames. He was relieved to see hundreds of dockworkers, sailors and passengers milling about; the crowd would make it easier for them to pass through unnoticed. The carriage had barely stopped moving before he had thrown open the door and jumped out, snagging his coat sleeve in his hurry. The air was full of the smells and sounds of the busy dock: the whiff of fish and the stink of the Thames, the shouts of dockworkers and the creak of moored ships.

Peter was sitting up front with Sawyer. He tossed down the two valises and Cormac caught them deftly.

'Thank you,' he said. 'I hope you will not get into trouble for doing this.'

The coachman winked. 'From what I heard, you gave the master a right blow to the head and he ain't likely to wake up for a while. I reckon he'll never know we was gone.'

'Look after the lady and the young miss,' said Peter, saluting. 'We're heartily fond of them. Her ladyship's the kindest woman I ever met, always looked out for my ailing mother. And there's nuffin but sweetness in the little one.'

'I will take very good care of them both,' promised Cormac. 'My thanks again.'

He returned to the door of the carriage and helped Bridget and Emily step out into the sunlight. The day was breezy but dry, good conditions for travelling on the water. Together, all three of them turned to stare at their vessel. Larger than the one on which he had stowed away, it soared above them, its rigging whipping in the breeze. Two gangways extended from it to the dock, one for wealthy passengers who were ushered aboard without scrutiny or delay, the other for the noticeably less affluent. A line of these folk stretched from the end of the lower class gangway across the dock and a ticket inspector stood at the top of the queue, scrutinising each passenger before permitting them to pass by.

Cormac had not purchased upper class tickets. That level of luxury was behind them now, and it would have been presumptuous to spend an excessive amount of the Bewleys' money. In addition, he had guessed it more likely that any pursuers would seek them in the more genteel section of the ship, given Bridget and Emily's status. Now, he doubted the wisdom of his decision and wondered how attentive the ticket inspector was to his duties.

Nervous, he guided Bridget and Emily to the end of the queue. He was pleased to note that a flicker of excitement had crossed Emily's features at the sight of the big ship. Perhaps her sense of adventure would eclipse all her qualms. Bridget held Emily's hand and stared straight ahead; her face was grave but she seemed worried rather than hostile.

The queue inched its way across the dock. He kept glancing over his shoulder but the noise and activity around them seemed no greater than what could be expected. The arrival of the constabulary would surely cause a commotion that would be conspicuous above the rest of the hubbub.

Would Lord and Lady Bewley accompany the constables, to see him arrested? He quailed at the prospect of facing the elderly couple. His final transgression against them had been to take enough money to assist his search for his family after they arrived in Ireland. He loathed himself for his dishonesty. But they were his second family, and he must prioritise his first.

When there was only a handful of people ahead of them, he withdrew the tickets from his pocket. A knot of anxiety was growing in his stomach. What if the constables were already here and merely waiting for them to reveal themselves to the ticket inspector? Perhaps they had given the man a description and he would raise the alarm at the sight of them. There would be no hope of escape in such a scenario and he would be heading for the gallows or, at best, a prison cell for the rest of his life.

Swallowing hard, he stepped forwards with Bridget and Emily. There was just one group left in front of them now, a mother with three or four children swarming around her and a baby crying in her arms. The inspector skimmed their tickets and hurried them through, looking like he wanted to be rid of the screaming child. Then he beckoned to Cormac, hand outstretched. Cormac set the valises on the ground, smoothed out the tickets and handed them over.

The man had a stubbly chin which he scratched absent-mindedly as he examined the tickets. 'Name?'

'Jack Marsh,' said Cormac, letting his Irish brogue become pronounced. No one with a cultured accent would be expected in this line of passengers. 'And this here's my wife, Molly.'

Bridget fixed a pleasant smile upon her face. The man nodded once at her and then looked back at Cormac.

'That's some shiner you got there,' he remarked, nodding at Cormac's jaw.

He didn't miss a beat, jabbing his booted toe into the side of one of the valises. 'Fell on me when I was taking it down off the top of the wardrobe,' he said with the air of someone used to being accident-prone. 'That'll learn me to move more quickly next time.'

The man gave a short laugh and handed back the tickets. 'On you go,' he said and stood back to let them pass.

Cormac picked up the valises, shepherded Bridget and Emily onto the gangway, and stepped onto it himself. When he looked back, the inspector had already turned away to scrutinise the next person's ticket. He had not even glanced at Emily.

They made their way down to the steerage area below decks. Berths lined the walls, most of them already occupied by other travellers. Cormac found an empty one and stowed the valises beneath it. The berth next to them had been taken by the woman with the innumerable children. Her baby had stopped crying and was drowsing in her arms.

'We made it,' said Bridget in disbelief.

'We did,' said Cormac but the knot in his stomach did not go away. He wouldn't feel easy until the ship had pulled away from the dock and they were out on open water.

'May I go up to look out over the dock?' Emily asked eagerly.

'Not just yet,' he said. 'Let's wait until the ship is moving.'

'Oh, please—' she began, but her plea was drowned out by the sudden sound of shouting above deck.

Cormac and Bridget exchanged looks of panic.

'Oh, no,' she moaned.

He knew he only had a few seconds in which to act. He caught hold of Emily's shoulders and made her look straight into his eyes.

'Listen to me, *a stór*,' he said swiftly. 'We are going to play a game but I need you to make sure you follow all the rules. You are going to sit over there with that family and pretend that the nice lady is your mother. You cannot answer to the name of Emily. You have to make believe that you are Lizzie, just for a little while longer. Your mother and I are going to find different berths and pretend to be other people too. You must act like you do not know us. This will only be for a short time and then we can be together again. Do you understand everything I've just told you?'

Her voice was faint as she said, 'Yes, Papa.'

He looked over at the woman with all the children. She was staring at him in shock; she had overheard everything he had said.

'Please,' he entreated. 'I am begging you, help me protect my family. Please allow my daughter to sit with your children.'

'I don't think—' she faltered.

'*Please,*' he said again. He flung an arm out to indicate Bridget. 'This is her mother. I swear we are both just trying to do what's best for our daughter.'

'It's true,' said Bridget with deep sincerity.

The woman hesitated before saying, 'So long as it won't get us into any trouble.'

'It won't,' he said and hoped to God he was speaking the truth. 'Thank you very much, I am so grateful.' He urged Emily to join the family at the next berth. 'Keep your bonnet on and your hair tucked into your cloak. Remember, the most important rule is that you are called Lizzie. Your mother and I are going to move away now but we will come back to you as soon as the game is over, I promise.'

He and Bridget both kissed Emily and walked away from her.

'They will be looking for a couple with a child,' he said. 'We must split up too, act like we are single travellers. I'll join those men in the corner. Will you go to the women over by the stairs?'

She nodded, the tip of her tongue caught between her teeth. They touched hands and separated. The steerage quarters were loosely divided into sections for men, women, and families. He reached the men's area and sat on a vacant berth, just as the disturbance above deck grew louder and three men appeared in the hatch at the top of the steerage stairs. Everyone fell silent. One of the men was the stubbly-chinned ticket inspector; the other two were uniformed constables. Cormac surreptitiously wiped his hands on the dirty floor and ran them through the hair that was visible below the edges of his cap. His fair hair would be a key element of his description; dulling it would make it harder for them to recognise him. He hoped Emily would be a good girl and keep her own hair hidden too.

The two constables descended the stairs and began marching along the family berths, peering at the passengers. Every so often, they paused and asked somebody a question but Cormac was too far away to hear the murmured responses. He could just make out Emily across the crowded space – she appeared to be holding a whispered conversation with the child next to her, but she stopped as the constables approached her berth. They were now near enough for him to distinguish what they were saying.

'These all your children?' one of them addressed the woman cradling the baby.

'Yes,' she answered.

The other constable squinted at the children. 'What're your names?' he said gruffly.

'Peggy.'

'Tommy.'

'Rosie.'

'Danny.'

'Lizzie.'

Cormac held his breath. The constable examined each child for a long moment and then, with a grunt, turned away.

The two men continued to walk along the berths but they seemed to be losing interest now, only bestowing cursory glances upon the rest of the passengers. They barely looked at Cormac as they passed by. It became obvious that their aim had been to inspect all the children in the steerage area – they did not expect to find the false Oliver Davenport without the kidnapped girl at his side. Having failed to locate their quarry, they climbed back up the stairs and retreated out the hatch with the ticket inspector.

Cormac didn't move; he would not allow himself to believe they were safe yet. Thankfully, neither Bridget nor Emily came to look for him. A hum of chatter rose up as the passengers discussed what had just happened. He waited but nobody else came down into the steerage area except for a few straggling travellers.

After many long minutes which seemed like hours, he felt the ship's steam engine rumble into life somewhere in the bowels of the vessel.

He started to hope.

Quite a bit more time passed, but at last there was the unmistakable sensation of movement and he knew that the ship was pulling away from the dock.

A grin split his face from ear to ear. It was as though a hand of iron had been clenching inside his chest and now it had released him. They were free.

He went to Bridget first; she threw her arms around him with a happy laugh. They returned to Emily, who was still sitting on the berth and playing a clapping game with the boy beside her. She ceased clapping at their appearance.

'Our game is over now, *a stór*,' Cormac said. 'Well done, you played it brilliantly.'

She looked up at them. 'I can be Emily again?'

'Yes, forever and ever,' said Bridget.

Emily jumped up and they enfolded themselves in a joyful, three-way hug. It was overwhelming to register the complete absence of tension. They were safely on their way and, Cormac was relieved to note, it seemed that all past transgressions were to be forgotten.

'Now may I go up to look out?' Emily appealed, hopping up and down in excitement.

'In just one moment.' Cormac turned to the mother who had helped save them from detection. She was observing their elation with great interest. 'I cannot thank you enough for what you have done for me and my family today. We are in your debt, Mrs…?'

'Nancy McLoughlin.' She contemplated his words and then waved them away. 'I don't know what I just involved myself in, but I can see the happiness the three of you share so I'm sure it was nuffin God'll punish me for. You ain't in anyone's debt.'

Both Cormac and Bridget expressed their sincere thanks once again. Then they left the woman to her brood of children and climbed the steerage stairs with Emily.

Up on the deck, the sun dazzled them after the dimness below and the breeze was fresh on their cheeks. The busy city of London lay on both sides of the river as they sailed down the middle of the Thames towards the open sea. Emily was in raptures at the sight and ran to the gunwale to stare all around her.

'Are we safe now?' Bridget asked.

'I believe so, yes,' said Cormac, his pulse still thumping with the euphoria of liberation.

'I heard the two constables muttering to each other before they went back up the stairs. They thought we must not have boarded the ship yet and were going back out to search the dock. What do you think they will do when they cannot find us?'

He gazed out across the water. 'After they eventually conclude that we are not hiding somewhere in London, I suppose there is always the outside possibility that they will choose to follow us to Ireland.'

Her forehead creased. 'And if so, should we not expect them to apprehend us? The most obvious place for us to go is exactly where we are going. What is there to stop a troop of constables from seizing us at Oakleigh?'

'I cannot rule out that scenario with absolute certainty, but I do believe that it is unlikely. A pursuit across the sea would put a substantial strain on their resources. In all probability, Lord and Lady Bewley will find the law enforcement less than willing to cooperate and the chase will peter out. Having said that, it would be a very different state of affairs if we were ever to return to England. I am positive that we, or I at any rate, can never set foot in this country again.'

'And Garrett?' she said tentatively.

A wave of emotion washed over Cormac as he grieved afresh for the sister he had lost. His rage rose again but he pushed it back down.

'Garrett is no longer a concern for us. When he wakes up and discovers that we have indeed escaped, he'll know he has been defeated. He will want to hide from society for a few days as the news spreads that his wife and child have left him. After that humiliation, I doubt whether he will dare to risk the further embarrassment of trying and failing to bring you back from Ireland as well.'

'Is that what you truly believe?'

'It is. And should I prove to be wrong, no matter. We shall deal with him if the situation arises. Until then, I advise you not to worry.'

He put his arm around her shoulders and kissed her on the temple. He hoped he had sufficiently eased her qualms, although he was not quite so unconcerned about the danger as he had led her to believe. It was very feasible that they might be followed to Ireland. But better for her to be free from that fear for now.

Without warning, she said, 'I would like to visit my mother when we go back to Oakleigh.'

He dropped his arm.

'I am aware that she is the very last person you would wish to see,' Bridget went on steadily. 'However, ever since you decided we should go back there, I have known that this is something I must do. I cannot say that I am ready to make amends, but she is ill and I want to see her, even just once. She is still my mother, after all.'

He looked down at her. Her dark brown eyes stared back. It was so hard for him to believe that she and Lady Courcey were the same flesh and blood. How had such a hardhearted, malicious woman produced a daughter capable of so much compassion? Lady Courcey could go to hell and rot there for all he cared; he had no desire to be in her presence ever again, except perhaps to witness her demise.

But Bridget's gaze was earnest; this was important to her.

He sighed. 'Very well.'

She squeezed his arm. 'We ought not dwell on it for now. Let us enjoy the beautiful day and rejoice in our release.'

They turned their attention back to Emily who was off in her own world enacting various scenarios on her mighty vessel. Alternating between a captain, a pirate and a shipwreck survivor, she sailed the unknown lands, fighting off mermaids and sharks and searching for buried treasure. Cormac felt a rush of affection for the little girl and knew how fortunate he was to be standing here at this moment with the woman he loved and the child he adored, rather than being marched away in shackles by the constables. Less than an hour ago, that prospect had been frighteningly close to becoming a reality, but their luck had held out and they were now free to be a family together. While Garrett lived, there was no chance that they could ever be married but, other than the official ceremony, they were as much a husband and wife now as it was possible to be. It would be nice, he thought, to have something to symbolise that union.

He glanced down at his coat sleeve, which was fraying a little at the end. He dimly recollected catching it on the door frame as he jumped out of the carriage in his earlier haste at the dock. Smiling to himself, he started pulling at the threads, working them out of the sleeve. Hoping Bridget would see the humour in what he was about to offer her, he twisted and knotted the threads together. Once he had fashioned a smooth circle, he took her left hand and slid the circle onto her ring finger. She stared at it in surprise and then beamed up at him.

'It is plain I have not much to offer you,' he said, 'but will you be mine?'

'I will,' she said. 'Now and forever.'

They kissed, as though they had just been pronounced man and wife at the altar. When he pulled away, he noticed that her brow was furrowed.

'What is the matter?' he asked.

'Nothing, really,' she said, lowering her gaze to the ring. 'I just have one last secret to impart. Since the day we were reacquainted in London, I have wondered whether to share it with you. Now I have resolved to do so. After this, you will know everything in my soul.'

He did not know whether to feel eager or wary. 'What is it?'

'I have not told you before because I always feel such intense regret when I think of it and I did not want to burden you with that feeling too. It was a case of bad luck and bad timing. Ten minutes might have made a lifetime of difference. But I suppose it is of no great consequence now.' She twisted the ring around her finger. Then she looked up and said, 'I ran after you. The day you were banished from Oakleigh, I told you I was going to stay with Garrett, but as soon as I realised I had made the wrong decision I ran all the way to your mother's cottage, desperately hoping you were still there. But I was too late, you were gone and I had no way of knowing where. So I had to go back to Garrett and you never knew I had chosen you after all.'

He closed his eyes, imagining what might have been. If he had stayed at the cottage just a little longer... If she had discovered her mother's betrayal just a little sooner... They would have spent these seven and a half years together rather than apart. He would have seen Emily growing up. They might have had more children. Neither of them would have had to suffer the pain and loss they had been forced to endure. There would have been other hardships, needless to say, but they would have faced them hand in hand as partners, as a family, not alone and not in fear. It was a wonderful image but it was something he had always believed to have been impossible for them then. And yet here was Bridget telling him that they had been tantalisingly close to achieving it, that it had been mere moments from their grasp. She was right, it was a burden to bear this knowledge, to know that those long years need not have unravelled the way they had.

He opened his eyes. She was biting the tip of her tongue in her own typical way.

'Should I have told you?' she asked, searching his face for his reaction.

He gave her a sad smile. 'Of course. It is right for me to know.'

'I have debated for a long time over whether to tell you. I know it has no bearing now but...'

'But it is important all the same,' he finished for her. 'It is a hard truth to acknowledge, that what we lost was almost at our fingertips.' He took her hand and rubbed his thumb over the thread ring, an intoxicating sense of jubilation coursing through his veins. 'But we got it back in the end. And that is what matters most.'

# A Class Forsaken

A Matter of Class, Book Three

*For Mam, who has been giving me feedback on my writing since I was eleven years old, and for Dad, who helped me take a crucial step forwards when I needed it.
Love and gratitude to you both.*

## Chapter 1

'Arrah, here's the rain again.'

'I need to get my boy indoors. He's only after getting rid of a cough, the craythur.'

'Jaysus, 'tis coming down hard now. Hurry up, you in front!'

Cormac smiled, even when a fellow hastening past trod on his foot. The Irish accents flowed around him in eddies of urgency and commotion as folk scurried about the pier, intent on dodging the rain whether they were boarding or disembarking. After so many years surrounded by the refined voices of the upper class English, the recognisable brogue of his countrymen stirred within him the joy of homecoming. Granted, he was in Cove, a seaport town in Cork harbour, where the locals had a high-pitched inflection quite different to the flatter accents of the inhabitants of Carlow, but it would not be long before the soil of his native county would be beneath his feet once more.

He put a protective hand on Emily's shoulder, coaxing his daughter to his side to shield her from the heaving crowd.

'Stay close to me, *a stór*,' he said to her, his 'treasure'.

Her eyes, their shade of blue identical to his own, were wide with delight as she gazed about her, enamoured by the sights and sounds, from a donkey and cart clattering by to the scrawny head of a yapping dog poking out from inside its owner's coat.

Beside them, Bridget raised her face and let the rain trickle down her cheeks, like she was being baptised by the Irish skies. Then a large drop landed in her eye and she ducked her head, laughing beneath the rim of her bonnet.

The uncongenial weather could do nothing to dampen their spirits. After their frantic escape from law enforcement in London and a three-day voyage around the south coast of England, they had finally reached Ireland.

Home.

There were many uncertainties ahead, but most would have to wait; their first concern was finding a place to stay for the night. Fortunately, the friend they had made on the voyage had offered assistance in that matter.

Nancy McLoughlin followed behind them, endeavouring to keep control over her gaggle of children. Clutching her baby to her chest, she exclaimed,

'Peggy, hold onto your sister's hand afore she gets lost in the crowd. Put your cap back on, Danny, can't you see it's raining? Tommy, get back here!' she hollered as her eldest darted away from the straggling group.

Cormac neatly seized the boy by the elbow as he ran past. 'Heed your mother,' he chided. 'This is no place to go wandering.'

Nancy caught up to them with the rest of her offspring, the bundles in the two girls' arms their only luggage. Cormac and Bridget each carried a valise.

'Lord in heaven,' Nancy said, her working-class English accent at odds with the Irish voices around them, 'it's bedlam here.' She clipped Tommy about the ear. 'Don't you run off again or your father will hear of it.'

The boy assumed an angelic air of contrition.

'What's the name of the street we're looking for?' Cormac asked Nancy.

'Harbour Row,' she said. 'It looks out over the water so it ain't likely to be far.'

Glancing around the pier, he spotted a ticket seller booth whose occupant was staring out dismally through a sheet of water running off the roof. Skirting the deluge, he asked the ticket seller for directions and the fellow imparted them in a Cork accent so thick that Cormac had to ask him to repeat it twice. Finally grasping enough of the necessary details, he thanked the man and beckoned to the others, leading them away from the thronged pier.

They were looking for McLoughlin's Boarding House on Harbour Row. Nancy's husband was an Irishman whom she had met in London, but in the past year he had returned to his hometown to set up a boarding house with his unmarried sister. Nancy had received word that the enterprise was proving to be a success and she and the children were travelling now to join him. When she had learned on the ship that Cormac, Bridget and Emily would be seeking a night's accommodation after they disembarked, she had pressed them to come to the boarding house too. While they had only a limited amount of money, and most of it had to be saved to purchase a pair of horses for the next stage of their travels, they had decided that one night in a comfortable establishment would be very welcome after three nights spent in a less-than-snug ship's berth.

By the time they reached Harbour Row, the rain had eased to an intermittent spattering of drops. McLoughlin's Boarding House was easy to identify by the sign displayed over its front door proclaiming the name of the proprietor. The doorstep was scrubbed clean, flower boxes full of daffodils adorned the window sills, and the window panes were being wiped dry by a stumpy woman who had to stretch up on her toes with her cloth.

She turned when they approached the doorstep and dropped back to the flats of her feet, giving them a pleasant smile. 'Can I help you? We have some rooms available.'

Nancy said, 'Are you Agnes, Dan's sister?'

The woman's forehead furrowed and then cleared as she looked around at all the children.

'You must be Dan's wife! Bless the Lord, you've arrived at last!'

After they embraced, she cleaned the last few wet spots from the window with fastidious care and led them all inside. There ensued a furore as chaotic as the pier when Dan McLoughlin appeared from the depths of the house and his children swarmed around him, screaming with excitement. He hoisted his two daughters up into his arms and his two sons clung to his coat but he still managed to lean over and bestow a tender kiss upon Nancy and to touch the tiny fist of the baby he had not yet met.

'I'm so happy to see you all,' he said, his voice deep and thick with emotion.

Once the uproar of reunion had subsided, Nancy gestured to Cormac, Bridget and Emily.

'You have room for some guests? We met on the voyage and they're in need of accommodation for the night.'

Dan nodded genially. 'We've a fine room overlooking the harbour which should do nicely. We'll settle the arrangements shortly but first I must tell ye, children, that ye've arrived just in time. What d'ye think is happening just down the road this very afternoon, and will be gone tomorrow?'

Tommy and Danny offered a few wild guesses before their father declared, 'A circus!'

The children's screams renewed with a vigour even greater than that of greeting the father they had not seen in almost a year.

'I ain't never seen a circus!'

'Can we go?'

'Please, please, please!'

Dan laughed. 'I'll take ye myself!'

Emily turned shining eyes up to Cormac and Bridget. 'Oh, *please*!' she breathed. 'May I go with them?'

Cormac hesitated. While they were now in Ireland, which he considered home, Cove was an unfamiliar town to him and, after their difficulties leaving London, he felt wary of strangers. Was he being too overprotective to not want to let Emily out of his sight?

Nancy watched him waver in indecision. 'She'll be fine. No harm will come to her in Dan's care. And it's a lovely treat.'

He glanced at Bridget and she nodded.

'Very well,' he said, and Emily whooped as loudly as any of the McLoughlin children. 'But you must be on your best behaviour, Emily.'

'I will!' She thrust out her chest with pride.

'We'd better hurry,' Dan said. 'The clown passed by this way not long ago, shouting that it was starting soon. Let's go!'

He disappeared out the front door with Emily and the other children in his wake, like chicks following their mother hen. Nancy shifted her baby from the crook of one elbow to the other.

'A bit of peace will help this poor child nod off, I hope,' she said.

'I'll show you to Dan's room,' Agnes said to her. 'And then I'll book ye in for the night, Mr and Mrs…?'

'McGovern,' Cormac said and Bridget gave him a glowing look.

\*\*\*

Their room boasted a striking view of the harbour from its window, the departing rain clouds leaving hazy sunshine glimmering on the water's choppy surface. Bridget set down the two valises beneath the window sill and admired the vista while Cormac helped a young lad wedge a small mattress for Emily onto the floor next to the high bed. Agnes made up the mattress with sheets and blankets.

'There's water in the pitcher,' she said, indicating a washstand in the corner. 'And if ye need anything else, don't hesitate to ask.'

She shepherded the lad out of the room before her and pulled the door closed with a precise snap. Bridget surveyed their accommodation: the bed had plain but clean bedcovers and more daffodils stood in a vase on the washstand. She crossed the room to the pitcher; the prospect of washing was appealing after limited opportunities for ablutions aboard the ship.

'I'm a bit tired after the journey,' she said, 'but we really should wash.'

Cormac rubbed his jaw where a fading bruise was still visible, courtesy of his last encounter with Garrett. 'Good idea,' he said absently.

He stepped up to the washstand but, instead of touching the curved handle of the pitcher, his hands went to her waist.

'Do you know what I've noticed?' he murmured, bending his head to her.

She blinked. 'What?'

'We are alone in a bedchamber.'

His lips landed upon hers and he eased her mouth open in a deep kiss. She closed her eyes and leaned into his sturdy chest, disappearing into a blissful daze until he pulled gently away.

'Are you still feeling tired?' he asked.

Her gaze cut to the high bed. 'Not so much.'

He grinned.

They scrambled to remove their clothing and slid naked between the bed's fresh sheets, relishing the feel of soft linen against sensitive skin. Lying on their sides facing one another, she offered her mouth to him once more. He had not shaved since they left London and his stubble scraped her chin with a pleasant roughness. As they kissed, she let her hand rove down the long, smooth arc of his back, feeling the bumps of his spine and the strength in his muscles. She roamed lower and stroked the curve of his buttocks with a possessive triumph. This exceptional specimen of a man was now hers; the ring on her left hand attested to that. It was only a circle made out of thread, but to them it had as much significance as if he had given it to her at the altar before God. He was her husband and she his wife, body and soul. They had no need of a legal marriage contract to know that.

They explored each other's bodies beneath the bedcovers, hungry for satisfaction and too impatient to adopt a more leisurely pace. The sensations were all the more intense given their imposed abstinence on the ship, and it was through only a dim haze of awareness that Bridget heard footsteps coming up the boarding house stairs. As her heartbeat pounded faster, the steps grew louder, making their way along the corridor outside the bedchamber. She strove to smother a gasp but it burst from her just as a groan broke from Cormac's throat. Had the footsteps faltered? She could not be sure and she did not care. She floated down from the pinnacle of ecstasy, feeling as though she had disintegrated and the separated parts of her body were trying to knit themselves back together.

She nestled into Cormac and they lay there, recovering their senses.

'I think someone may have heard us,' she mumbled after a while.

'No matter,' he said, smoothing back a loose lock of her chestnut curls over her shoulder. 'We're as good as married now, are we not?'

She pressed a warm kiss to his chest. 'We are.'

The decadence of going to bed in the afternoon settled upon them, their limbs heavy and languid. Bridget felt a delicious sleepiness steal over her and she relaxed in Cormac's embrace. She slipped deeper towards sleep but an uncomfortable tug drew her back from oblivion. As the realisation came to her, she squirmed in discomfort.

He felt her move and stirred himself. 'What's the matter?' he asked, his speech slurred with tiredness.

'Nothing,' she said, but the word came out in a high pitch that belied her protestation.

He woke more fully and cocked an eyebrow at her.

'It's nothing,' she tried again, but her traitorous body writhed once more and he let out a snort of disbelief. She gave up the pretence. 'It's just — oh, dear God, I can't say it.' She threw her arm over her eyes. 'I need a moment to myself. Would you mind dressing and leaving the room?'

The tension in his body slackened as he understood. 'You don't really need me to leave, do you?' She heard the trace of laughter he was attempting to hold back.

Her cheeks flamed hotter than the sun. 'Yes.'

He settled back in the bed. 'I'm too comfortable to move.'

She flung her arm away in horror. 'You expect me to do it in your presence?'

'Why not?'

'Because —' she spluttered. 'It's private!'

This time he did laugh. 'Considering what we've just been doing, I don't think there's much need left for privacy, do you? Using the chamber pot will be no great revelation at this stage.'

She gaped. 'I can't…' she said weakly.

'You can. Would you prefer if I closed my eyes?'

'I'd rather you close your ears,' she muttered.

He chuckled. 'You'd best get around to it before you wet the sheets.'

Uttering a groan of embarrassment, she slid out of the bed, reached underneath it and pulled out the chamber pot. It was clean and decorated with a pretty willow pattern but she couldn't find it in herself to appreciate it. A folded rag rested neatly in the bottom of the pot. She took it out and, with a mortified glance back at the bed, where he had tactfully turned away on his side, she lowered herself over the pot. She cringed at the tinkle of liquid against ceramic but felt a surge of relief as the pressure on her bladder eased. She hastily wiped herself with the rag, pushed the pot back under the bed, and slithered back under the covers, drawing them completely over her head. He pulled them back down.

'Why are you so embarrassed?' he asked, grinning.

She scowled; he was taking far too much enjoyment from her discomfiture. 'I cannot think of a less romantic thing in this world than relieving myself in front of you. The passion in our relationship is irretrievable after this.'

He did not bother to credit this with a verbal answer. Instead, he pulled her beneath him, nestled himself at the apex between her thighs, and spent the next several minutes demonstrating to her that her assumption was preposterous.

Sweating and panting, she lay exhausted beside him. 'I believe you have made your point.'

Eyelids already drifting closed, he turned and placed a blind kiss on her cheek. '*A rún mo chroí,*' he whispered, '*go deo.*'

She loved when he spoke his native tongue; the Irish words flowed like honey. And there were no other words she loved to hear more than those.

'Secret of my heart, forever'.

## Chapter 2

Emily returned with the McLoughlin family later, full of excited chatter and awed descriptions of dancing dogs, entertaining clowns and two black-skinned performers who executed daredevil feats on the backs of horses.

'I thought they would fall off but honest to goodness they never did!'

She continued to talk nineteen to the dozen, her tone both animated and reverential, as she submitted to a thorough wash in a tin bath – which Cormac had requested after he and Bridget had finally risen from bed – before they all dressed to go down for their evening meal.

The boarding house had a communal dining room which hummed with chattering guests and the clinking of cutlery as Cormac, Bridget and Emily descended the stairs. When they entered the dining room, they spotted Nancy and her swarm of children seated at a long table and joined them there, Emily squeezing beside the two girls, Peggy and Rosie, and exclaiming about the circus performers again.

Cormac and Bridget had barely seated themselves opposite Nancy when Dan McLoughlin entered the dining room, carrying a tray of full glasses. After distributing the drinks among a group of talkative men in the corner, he came over to their long table but, instead of speaking to his wife or children, he dipped his head towards Cormac.

'Mr McGovern,' he said apologetically. 'Could I ask yourself and your wife to step out for a few moments?'

Puzzled, Cormac said, 'Of course.'

He and Bridget followed Dan out of the dining room and into the hallway beyond, where they found Agnes McLoughlin waiting for them. She folded her arms and glared at them with undisguised disgust.

'Ah, here are our well-respected guests,' she said snidely.

Dan hurried to his sister's side. 'We said we'd be calm and polite, Agnes,' he reminded her nervously, tucking his empty tray under his arm.

'I've no wish to be,' she said. 'These people don't deserve any such consideration.'

Cormac and Bridget exchanged gaping glances.

'Madam,' said Cormac, keeping control of his temper, 'can you explain why you have adopted this unjust attitude towards us?'

'Indeed I can,' she said, looking like she was itching for this confrontation. 'We're decent, God-fearing folk here and don't take kindly to those who'd engage in disgraceful behaviour under our roof.'

Shocked, he could only assume that the footsteps they had heard earlier outside their bedchamber had been hers.

'There has been nothing indecent about our behaviour. We are a lawfully married couple and —'

'Are ye?' she sneered. 'I doubt that, sir, given the evidence before my eyes.' She gestured towards Bridget. 'If that's supposed to be a wedding ring, then I'm a patron saint of Ireland.'

Bridget clasped her left hand inside her right, but everyone had seen the circle of thread, as far from a gold band as it was possible to be.

Cormac set his jaw. 'We have fallen on hard times and were obliged to sell her ring. Thank you for drawing attention to our unfortunate circumstances.'

Dan put a restraining hand on his sister's shoulder. 'We must've been mistaken,' he muttered. 'Let's leave them be.'

She shook him off. 'No,' she said. 'They're having an affair, I'm certain of it. No properly married husband and wife would be fornicating in the middle of the afternoon with such brazen passion as I heard, not if they'd been married long enough to have a daughter of that girl's age.'

Fury and embarrassment rose in Cormac's chest. 'You have been listening at keyholes? What sort of proprietor does that make you?'

'One concerned with the standards of her establishment,' she replied primly. 'This is a boarding house, not a brothel.'

'Miss McLoughlin,' said Bridget in a placating tone, 'I can assure you —'

'Be assured, Mrs McGovern, or whatever your real name might be, I can see the truth of the situation. Judging by the marked similarity in looks between this man and that unfortunate child, 'tis obvious that he's her true parent and you're the offending third party. I'm guessing his fading bruise was inflicted by his abandoned wife when she learned he was deserting her for a hussy with no morals. The fervour of your earlier activities tells me ye've but recently absconded together and hence the dissatisfaction of your wicked choices has yet to settle upon ye. 'Tis only a matter of time before it does though, and then ye'll heartily regret your actions. But know this: God won't hear your pleas for mercy and ye'll never enter his kingdom.'

Outraged, Cormac snapped, 'You have your facts entirely wrong, madam. Do not cast righteous judgement upon us when you are so ignorant of the truth.'

She bristled. 'D'you swear then, *sir*, that a legal marriage contract exists between yourself and this woman?'

She looked like she would not believe it unless she saw it printed in the newspaper. He glanced at Bridget, his shoulders sagging. Lying any further would get them nowhere; the woman was entrenched in her opinions on the situation and, while she had the particulars incorrect, her overall deduction was regrettably accurate.

Still fuming, he said through gritted teeth, 'No, it does not exist.'

Triumphant, she said, 'Such goings-on will not be tolerated in this house. Ye will remove yourselves at once and never darken our door again.'

Dan cleared his throat. 'Sister, we ought to show some compassion. They'll have difficulty finding another place to stay at this hour, and they've a child to think of.'

Agnes gave an indignant sniff and opened her mouth but Dan cut across her.

'We'll be Christian enough to allow them to stay until morning.' He looked at Cormac. 'But I'll have to ask ye not to return to the dining room with our other guests. We can bring a food tray to your room.'

Compelled to re-establish the upper hand, Agnes said, 'On no account may ye continue to share the same room. We insist that ye pay for another room and sleep apart.'

'Surely that won't be necessary –' Cormac began.

'Those are my terms,' she said with a steely gaze. 'Separate rooms or the front door.'

Humiliated, he gave a jerky nod of surrender.

She pointed to the dining room. 'And fetch your daughter. She mustn't remain among our guests either.'

He could no longer look at Bridget as he turned to do Agnes's bidding. Pushing open the door to the dining room, he heard the shrew snap at her brother, 'This is all thanks to your wife. She's a woeful judge of character to invite such profligates here.'

He couldn't make out Dan's response but hoped he would be kinder to Nancy than Agnes was being. Their companion on the voyage had been instrumental in assisting their escape from London and this was a shameful way to repay her.

'Come, *a stór*,' he said to Emily when he reached the long table. 'We are very lucky to be getting our dinner served upstairs this evening.'

He avoided Nancy's surprised look and guided his daughter away from the table, trying not to think about the stain of disgrace he and Bridget had inadvertently placed upon her.

***

Bridget woke to find herself wedged into one corner of the bed, Emily's arms and legs spread out like a starfish next to her. She rearranged the little girl's limbs into a narrower space and shuffled away from the edge where she herself was in danger of falling out. Thinking far ahead into the future (very, *very* far ahead if Cormac had any say in it), she imagined Emily getting married and sharing a bed with a disgruntled husband who would have to put up with her monopolising all the space.

The curve of her smile disappeared as the altercation from the previous night came flooding back to her. If it was so obvious that she and Cormac were not married, then that cast a great shadow on Emily's legitimacy and eligibility for marriage. Would she be able to find a man willing to overlook the taint of scandal arising from her parents' improper conduct? Bridget experienced a stab of guilt at having prioritised her own desires before her daughter's welfare. But how could she have turned away from Cormac? She could not have. They, and Emily, would have to deal with the consequences and the pertaining dishonour as best they could.

A sharp rap on the door brought her back to the present. She sat up, pulling the bedcovers up around her shoulders. 'Come in.'

Agnes McLoughlin stalked into the room, bearing a tray.

'Breakfast,' she said shortly.

Bridget considered returning the woman's rudeness in kind but opted for a more magnanimous course of action.

'Thank you,' she said as Agnes dropped the tray on a side table with a clatter. It was a paltry affair of porridge and burnt toast. 'Perhaps we could bring it to the other room to share it with — ?'

'No,' Agnes interrupted. 'I wouldn't allow it. In any case, he's not there.'

Startled, Bridget said, 'He's not?'

'My brother tells me that your *paramour*,' she said as though she were referring to a piece of rotten fish, 'left the house more than an hour ago. I can't say where he went.'

Next to Bridget, Emily began to stir.

'Very well,' she said, unwilling to expose her daughter to this woman's vitriol any more than necessary. 'We shall have our breakfast here and then go to the other room to pack, for that is where our valises are,' she added pointedly.

Agnes pursed her lips and left the room.

After the disappointing breakfast fare, which Emily barely nibbled at, they went back to the first room where Cormac had slept alone, and Bridget set about making their preparations for leaving the boarding house. She did not know what their next step would be but assumed that Cormac's absence was due to some purpose in that regard. They had spoken of purchasing two horses to make the journey to Oakleigh swifter and easier; perhaps that was what he was doing.

As she gathered their belongings into one of the valises, Emily pawed through the other.

'I want you to do my hair, Mama,' she said. 'Where is my brush?'

With a hiccup of misgiving, Bridget also searched through the valise in vain. The silver-handled hairbrush had been a gift from Lady Bewley, Cormac's 'aunt' when he had posed as Oliver Davenport, and it was one of the few sentimental items they had brought, along with the wooden watercolour box Cormac had made for his daughter and the little pouch containing the lock of hair belonging to baby James, Bridget's little boy who would remain three months old forever.

'It must be buried deep in the bottom, gooseberry,' she said. 'Here, you can use mine today instead.'

They completed their basic toilette and waited for Cormac to return, Bridget growing more and more anxious as time went on. She felt like a condemned prisoner, knowing that Agnes McLoughlin was somewhere downstairs, counting down the minutes until the filth had removed itself from her pristine environs. Bridget wanted to be gone.

A silent breath of relief escaped her when the bedchamber door opened and Cormac entered. He looked grim but his expression softened as Emily leapt up and ran forwards for a hug. Bridget's own body relaxed as she witnessed this strong reminder that, despite some of the unwelcome consequences of their flight from London, nothing could be more important than that Emily now had a loving father in her life. He embraced her and kissed her golden hair.

'Time for us to get going,' he announced in a bracing manner.

He and Bridget each picked up one of the valises and they headed for the door with Emily. Out in the corridor, they encountered Nancy McLoughlin crossing the landing, only two of her five children hanging off her.

'You're leaving,' she said, her expression serious.

'Farewell to you, Nancy,' said Bridget. 'We are so very sorry for any awkwardness we have caused you and your family. I cannot imagine that relations between you and Agnes are cheerful this morning.'

'They ain't,' Nancy replied, 'but that's down to her behaviour, not yours. Hush, Rosie, let me speak to these people for a few moments.' She patted her chattering daughter absently on the top of her head, then looked back at Bridget and Cormac. 'I knew from the manner of your departure from London that all ain't strictly lawful between you. But I've had enough time to form a sense of your characters. Whatever sins you've committed afore now, I can say that you have a lot more decency in you than that narrow-minded woman. I'm sorry you're being forced to leave in this way and I wish you well on your journey.'

'That is extremely kind of you,' said Cormac. 'But we know what our failings are, and one of them has been to put you in a discomfiting position with your sister-in-law. It was never our intention. Do please accept our apologies.'

She smiled. 'Don't you worry about my sister-in-law. She's shown her colours and I'll learn quickly how to deal with her.'

Thinking that Agnes McLoughlin might have met her match, Bridget followed Cormac and Emily downstairs to endure that woman's final censorious comments upon their ignominious departure from the boarding house.

Outside, Cormac did not lead them towards the boarding house's stables as Bridget had expected, but set off down the street at a brisk walk. She and Emily hastened to catch up but he did not slow his pace until they had reached the end of Harbour Row. There, he halted and turned to her.

'Give me your hand,' he said.

She offered him her right hand but he shook his head.

'Your other one.'

She raised her left hand. He removed her glove and, dipping his own hand into his pocket, slipped a ring onto her finger above the circle of thread. She let out a gasp. No ordinary band of gold, it depicted a love heart clasped within a pair of hands and topped with a crown. The detail in the metalwork was exquisite.

'The goldsmith told me this style has its origins in Galway and that it represents love, friendship and loyalty. I had always intended on getting you a proper ring at some stage but recent circumstances expedited matters. I'm sorry it is not under more romantic conditions that I give it to you. But,' he finished fiercely, 'I'm determined that you'll never have to suffer last night's humiliation again.'

She cupped his cheek. 'We knew that sort of censure was a risk. Everything became a risk when we did what we did. And I wouldn't change my mind for the world.'

The angry lines around his mouth diminished. 'I'm glad you think so. But from now on you are Bridget McGovern, my wife, and you have the ring to prove it. I won't have anyone questioning our morals again.'

She examined the gold ring. 'It must have been expensive...' she said hesitantly.

He sighed. 'We have all paid the price of this ring.' He looked down at Emily. '*A stór*, I have something to tell you. I'm afraid we no longer have your hairbrush. I had to sell it today.'

Emily's face fell. 'But Papa!' she cried. 'Can we not get it back?'

'We can't. You will have to share your mother's hairbrush from now on. She has a very pretty brush too.'

Emily's lip stuck out in a pout and she began to cry. 'I don't *want* to use Mama's hairbrush. I want my own!'

'That's not possible anymore,' he said patiently. 'I'm sorry that you have to suffer this loss. But there is no way to change it now.'

Emily pushed her weeping face into the front of Bridget's dress and wailed. Bridget gave the little girl a comforting squeeze around her shoulders. She knew Cormac had done what he had to do. He looked pained but compressed his lips in resignation.

'We cannot afford to ride to Oakleigh now,' he said over Emily's sobs. 'Even with the sale of the hairbrush, buying the ring has severely depleted our funds. Especially as we had to pay for two rooms last night.' His blue eyes darkened at the humiliating memory. 'And we must save most of what we have left should it be needed to find my family. We shall have to make our way on foot. It will be a more beggarly way of travelling.'

Faltering, she said, 'We have my father's pocket watch. We could…'

He shook his head again. 'Not yet. That has far more emotional significance than a hairbrush received a few weeks ago. We ought to hold onto it, in case we find ourselves in a more dire situation in the future.'

Extricating herself from Emily's grasp, she set her valise on the ground and rummaged through it. She found the pocket watch, slid it out of its protective navy satin cloth, and held it out to him.

'You should carry it. It once belonged to a good man. I'd like to see another good man have it. Consider it my equivalent gift to the ring.'

He accepted it solemnly and traced its circumference. Her father had been an important person to him too. He pocketed the watch with care.

'Come now, Emily, that's enough,' he said.

Emily seemed to recognise the weight of his use of her proper name rather than his usual Irish term of affection and her snuffling ebbed reluctantly.

'We have more adventures ahead of us,' he said. 'Let's face them with bravery.'

He raised Bridget's hand to his lips and kissed the gold ring.

## Chapter 3

The weather in March could be unpredictable in Ireland. Sometimes it came like an early summer, banishing the winter with days of gentle sunshine and refreshing breezes.

Not this March.

As a chilly rain whipped at her cheeks, Bridget contemplated the road ahead. A veritable lake of muddy water stretched from one ditch to the other, the biting wind rippling across its surface. The same wind buffeted her back as she took stock of just how wet her feet were about to become. Emily danced along the edge of the flood, splashing the toes of her boots in the water.

'There's no way around,' Cormac said with a resigned air. 'Up you get, *a stór.*'

He put down his valise to hoist Emily up onto his back. She whooped and, pointing up the road, cried, 'Sally forth, brave knight!'

Eyeing Emily's dry ankles with envy, Bridget took hold of both valises and followed Cormac to the verge. She eased one foot after the other into the water, wincing at the cold. The exposed hem of her dress, already damp and mud-spattered, greedily soaked up the watery muck. She shuffled along, the hidden ground beneath varying between a squelching consistency and a shifting bed of stones, and did her best to forget the fact that the going would have been so much easier had they been riding. She tried not to imagine what Madeleine, her frivolous friend from Dublin, would say if she could see her now.

She had been aware beforehand of the path she was choosing. She had known that there were not going to be any more lavish feasts, ballroom dancing or nights at the theatre, and she had been prepared for a basic, unvaried diet and a good deal of walking. But she had not taken much time to consider how challenging it would be to keep *clean*. The previous evening, she had washed her and Emily's grubby skirts in a stream; the result had been passable but a far cry from the standards she was accustomed to. Then there was the grim reality of having to relieve oneself behind a convenient bush – in retrospect, the chamber pot back at McLoughlin's Boarding House seemed utterly decadent. And they were only drawing to the end of their second full day on the road. The one positive thing to be said was that finding water to drink posed no problem for the rainfall kept the streams fresh and flowing.

She slipped on a loose stone and, with her hands full, barely recovered her balance. She felt the water slosh into her boots and groaned. Cormac turned back to her, Emily's arms tight around his neck.

'I'm fine,' Bridget said, forcing a smile. 'It's just a shame it's not summertime.'

He agreed with a sympathetic nod and faced forwards again, Emily encouraging her steed to race towards freedom. Cormac splashed to the far end of the flood and the pair of them cheered in victory.

'Come, Mama!' Emily exclaimed. 'You're nearly there.'

Fingers aching with the weight of the valises, Bridget nonetheless gained a boost from her daughter's exuberance and struggled onto dry ground with relief. Cormac set Emily down and looked skywards.

'There's no sign of it stopping,' he said. 'I hope we can get shelter again tonight.'

The first two nights, they had been lucky enough to encounter friendly farmers' wives who had permitted them to sleep in their hay barns. Emily had played a significant role in this, charming the women with her bright smile and sweet voice so that they could not refuse her a place to lay her golden head. Could their luck hold out for a third night? As the water soaked into her stockings, Bridget very much hoped so.

Even as she thought this, Cormac added, 'At this rate, we should take a room in an inn if we come upon one,' and it buoyed her up no end. While she strove for equanimity in the face of this challenge, she longed for a warm bed and a cosy hearth, no matter if it meant paying for them.

He took the valises from her and, with the light failing, they walked on through the countryside. Emily's feet started to drag so Cormac distracted her by pointing out the varieties of trees and hedges they passed – a source of continuous wonder to a small girl who had lived all her life in a busy, smoky city – and suggesting names for the hens she was going to look after in the future. She perked up at the mention of her hens and talked at length about how she was going to run the best-organised hen coop in the world.

There continued to be no sign of an inn or any other form of accommodation and, as darkness fell, Bridget worried that they would have to spend the night in the open after all, but then a building came into view in the twilight: a two-storey farmhouse with candlelight glowing from the windows on the lower level. She contained her moan of relief and quickened her pace to catch up with Cormac and Emily, the latter of whom had just announced that she intended to paint a sun on her hen coop so that her hens would always be cheerful.

'That is a very thoughtful idea, gooseberry,' Bridget said and added to Cormac, 'Shall we seek shelter at this farmhouse?'

'Please God they'll take us in,' he said. 'It'll be a miserable night otherwise.'

Before she could respond, they heard the sound of wheels and turned to see a donkey and cart coming towards them out of the gloom. The wheels made a sucking noise as they rolled through the mud and the farmer sitting at the front of the cart leaned over the side and spat, 'If ye get stuck one more time...'

Cormac called out a greeting and the farmer looked up in surprise. He squinted and pulled the cart to a stop next to them.

"'Tis bad weather for ye to be on the road at this hour,' he said, pointing a grimy, cracked fingernail at them. 'And with a child and all. I wouldn't be out so late myself only for the wretched wheels on this thing. They'll be the death of me.'

'We've been unlucky with the weather, it's true,' said Cormac. 'With no sign of it letting up, we're hoping to get inside for the night.'

The man harrumphed. 'And I suppose 'tis at my house ye'll be looking for shelter.'

'We certainly don't wish to be an inconvenience.' Cormac glanced up at the darkening sky. 'But if you had shelter to offer, we would be very grateful.'

The man let out another harrumph. He leaned over the side of his cart again, this time to get a better look at Emily.

She stared back without fear and asked, 'Do you have a hen coop?'

The farmer's gaze cut back to Cormac. 'That's an English accent,' he said sharply. 'And you don't sound too Irish yourself, if I'm being honest.'

Bridget kept her own mouth shut as Cormac responded in an even tone, 'Our daughter was raised in London, but my wife and I are as Irish as the day is long.'

The mistrust didn't leave the farmer's face but he gave a grumpy shrug. 'I've got a big family. If 'tis a roof ye want, it'll be one of the outhouses.'

Cormac inclined his head. 'That would be very generous, thank you.'

'Ye can follow me up to the yard so.'

The farmer snapped his reins and, with a great effort on the donkey's part, the wheels of the cart came unstuck from the mud and rolled on up the road. Bridget, Cormac and Emily trudged after, their boots slipping into the ruts the cart tracks had left behind. Bridget felt like pointing out that the farmer could have at least let Emily sit on the cart, given that it was empty, but she bit back the complaint. Beggars could not be choosers and they were lucky he was aiding them at all.

By the time they reached the farmyard, the farmer had already unharnessed the donkey; the abandoned cart lay to one side and the farmer was stamping out of the stables. He jerked his thumb towards a small shed at the far end of the yard.

'Ye can stay in there. Mind ye don't leave a mess behind.'

And with that, he marched up to the front door of his farmhouse, its windows shining invitingly, and disappeared inside.

Cormac led them over to the shed and pushed open the door with his shoulder. It fell back at his touch, tilting inside the shed on one rusted hinge. Peering in, Bridget could just make out a rough floor littered with unwanted farmyard detritus: a broken cart wheel, mounds of torn sacks, a bucket with a cracked base. It stank of mildew and dung.

Emily wrinkled her nose. 'What's that smell?'

Cormac set down the valises and cleared his throat. 'You know, *a stór*, I think this is the perfect time to continue your fun from the ship. Do you remember we were sailing the mighty seas?'

'Yes, we were searching for hidden treasure but the pirates caught up with us.' She swung out her arm in a slicing sword motion. '"Give up your ship," they said, "or walk the plank!"'

'To save our lives, we walked the plank, didn't we? Which is why we are so wet now.' He brushed at the sodden sleeve of his coat, scattering droplets across her face.

She ducked away, giggling. 'We jumped into the sea so the pirates wouldn't take us prisoner!'

Bridget chimed in, 'Luckily, land was in sight and we could swim to shore.'

'But the pirates followed us. They know we found the hidden treasure.' Cormac made a dramatic show of looking over his shoulder before pulling out the pocket watch. 'We must hide it from them tonight so they cannot get their hands on it. Do you think this is a good hiding spot?'

The little girl nodded enthusiastically. 'It's so smelly that they'll never want to search inside.'

'Then that makes it ideal for us. But first, I must scout it out to ensure it's not a trap. Here,' he said, handing the watch to Emily with a solemn bow. 'Take the treasure and guard it with your life.'

She tucked it in close to her chest. 'With my life,' she promised.

He turned back to the shed door. 'And now I bravely enter this unknown realm.' He strode inside.

Emily, round-eyed, gaped up at Bridget. 'Will he be safe, Mama?'

'Your father is the most courageous person I know,' she said, her heart bursting with adoration for him. 'I think he will be fine.'

They heard a shout from the shed. 'Get back, fiend!' There was some banging and another yell, this one of triumph. A few moments later, Cormac reappeared in the doorway, breathing heavily and wiping his forehead.

'The coast is clear,' he panted. 'I discovered one nefarious buccaneer but he will not bother us again. You may bring in the treasure now.'

Gravely, Emily tiptoed inside the shed, still hugging the coveted goods. Bridget followed, breathing through her mouth rather than her nose. The shed was dark and cramped, with just enough floor space for them all to lie down. Cormac bustled over to the corner, gathering some of the torn sacks into a pile and fashioning them into a kind of nest.

'Your bed awaits, *a stór*,' he said with a flourish.

So enamoured by the fantasy, Emily did not seem to care about the decrepit conditions of her surroundings. She snuggled into the mound of sacks, hiding the pocket watch carefully beneath one of them.

'I'll keep it safe, Papa, I promise,' she said as a yawn escaped her.

Bridget took off her cloak and laid it over her daughter, tucking the ends in around her elbows and feet.

'Sleep well, gooseberry,' she said, kissing her forehead and trying to suppress a shiver at the same time.

Emily's eyes fluttered closed and Bridget realised the poor child was so tired that she hadn't even noticed her hunger. Just like in the confrontation with Agnes McLoughlin, a spear of guilt went through her gut. She prayed this beggarly part of their lives would be fleeting.

Cormac pushed the cart wheel and bucket to one side and used the remaining sacks to cover the floor next to Emily's nest. Now that the game was over, Bridget could see the tautness in the line of his jaw. He retrieved the valises from the yard, opened his own, and dug out two shirts which he balled up to make pillows.

'My coat is large enough to cover us both,' he said, not looking at her as he knelt by the makeshift bed.

She didn't say anything, only put a hand on his shoulder. He took it and pressed a kiss to her fingers.

'I will make a better life for us than this, I swear it,' he said.

'I know,' she said. 'We will make it together.'

After he had shoved the shed door shut as tightly as he could, they lay down together on the sacks and he threw his coat over them both. It smelled like him and she breathed it in with pleasure. She tried to doze off, but she could not ignore the fact that her feet felt like two blocks of ice. They had not dried properly after their immersion in the muddy flood and now they were so frozen and uncomfortable that they hardly seemed like parts of her own body. How she longed for the bed warmer that had kept her sheets so cosy in London.

Although she did her best to keep silent, a tiny whimper leaked out of her. She hoped Cormac might have already fallen asleep, but he raised his head.

'What is it?'

'Oh, it's nothing,' she murmured.

He waited.

'It's just…my feet…'

He slid out from under the coat, leaving it wrapped around her, and slithered down their 'bed'. Reaching beneath the end of his coat, he removed the boot and stocking from one of her feet and touched her skin.

He clicked his tongue in sympathy. 'You should have said something sooner.'

He enveloped her foot in both of his hands and she moaned at the sensation. Though his fingers were not unaffected by the cold weather, they were still so much warmer than the temperature of her feet that they felt like a blanket. He briskly rubbed her sole and her instep and her toes until proper feeling began to return, and then he did the same with her other foot. By the time he had finished, she was whimpering again, this time with inarticulate gratitude.

He slipped back beneath the coat. She pressed her back to his front, he wrapped his arms around her, and they drifted off to sleep, undisturbed by pirates.

## Chapter 4

They woke to a drizzly dawn, light and raindrops seeping in through the cracks in the shed's walls. Bridget's neck felt stiff as she bent over the nest of sacks to wake Emily. The little girl, spread-eagled across the sacks, roused grudgingly.

'Can I have hot cocoa?' she mumbled, curling into a ball against the cold air inside the shed.

'I'm afraid there's no cocoa here, gooseberry. But instead we have those delicious wild mushrooms your papa found beside the road outside Cove. That kind farmer's wife cooked them for us, do you remember?'

Emily made a face. That was what they had had for breakfast the last two mornings as well. It took a long time to coax her to eat anything at all, and in the end she only managed a couple of bites before pressing her lips shut tight. Bridget cast a look of exasperation towards Cormac.

'Leave her be for now,' he said. 'She'll eat when she's hungry enough.'

They gathered up their belongings, left the sacks stacked in a neat pile in the corner, and emerged from the shed. The farmer was in the yard, kneeling by his cart and examining the spokes of its wheels. A shadow of guilt crossed his expression at their appearance.

'Grand day,' he called over, as the drizzle drifted down from the overcast sky.

'A soft one,' Cormac agreed.

The farmer stood. 'Caught me in a bad mood,' he muttered. 'I should've...could've let ye...'

Cormac shook his head. 'We're very grateful for your assistance last night. We were glad to get cover from that weather. Thank you.'

The farmer grumbled something unintelligible and coughed. 'Where are ye headed next?'

'We're making our way to Carlow, to the Oakleigh Estate.'

'Carlow?' the farmer barked. 'Ye've a ways to go yet.' He scratched his nose. 'Oakleigh. Why's that ringing a bell for me?'

Bridget frowned. 'Have you heard news from there?'

The man's eyes narrowed; it was the first time she had spoken in his presence. 'Mayhap 'tis nothing. Best be getting on your way now. Safe travels to ye.'

He nodded curtly and strode back to the farmhouse. Bridget and Cormac exchanged mystified looks.

'I'd hoped we might buy some bread and cheese from him,' said Cormac. 'But I think a further request on our part might be beyond his tolerance, whatever's vexing him.'

Shrugging, he took Emily's hand and led them both from the farmyard.

They had not gone far before they ascertained that Emily had not had a restful night's sleep. She started to dawdle while they were still within sight of the farmhouse, and a sulky look settled on her face and would not go away. She had either forgotten or did not care about last night's narrow escape from pirates and no amount of play-acting on Bridget and Cormac's parts could entice her back into the fantasy. She kicked at stones, walked intentionally into puddles her mother told her to avoid, and dragged her heels more and more as the morning wore on into the afternoon. Cormac tried to distract her with an elaborate story about a rabbit that had dashed across their path and must be the king of all rabbits because of the size of its ears, but she was having none of it.

'Why don't you sing us a song, *a stór*?' said Cormac.

'I don't want to.'

'Would you like to ride on my back for a while?'

'No.' She stuck out her lower lip and scuffed the toes of her boots into the mucky road. 'I'm hungry,' she whinged.

'We still have some mushrooms —'

'I don't *want* mushrooms!' She halted. 'I want to stop walking.'

'We have to keep going, *a stór*. I know it's a long journey but at the end of it we'll be able to make our new home. Remember, you'll have a hen coop to look after and you're going to be so busy.' Bridget noted that Cormac was careful not to give any specifics about when or where their journey might end; after all, there was no guarantee or even likelihood that Oakleigh would be their final destination.

Emily scowled. 'I don't want a new home anymore. I want to go back to my old home.' Putting her hands on her hips, she said, 'My first papa wouldn't make me walk this far.'

Bridget felt the accusation keenly. Cormac kept control over his expression, but she was certain it must have cut him very deep.

'I won't tolerate any more complaining, Emily,' he said. 'Sometimes we have to do things that are difficult. I am trying to make it easier for you. You can ride on my back if your feet are tired.'

With a defiant glare, she sat heavily on the ground. 'I'm not going any further,' she declared, her nose in the air.

Expelling an inward groan at the mud which must now cover the backside of Emily's cloak, Bridget said sharply, 'This is not the way you were raised, Emily. You do what you are told when you are told.'

Emily scrunched up her face. 'No!'

Bridget imagined the scene with Garrett standing there instead of Cormac and knew that Emily would never dare to behave this way in his presence. Garrett did not instil love, but he did instil fear. Perhaps Cormac's playful manner towards Emily had some drawbacks.

He stood contemplating their daughter for a few moments, one hand clasping the other wrist.

'Very well, Emily,' he said at last. 'I see we cannot persuade you to go any further. However, we have no time to spare on silly tantrums and your mother and I must continue on regardless. Do you remember the way back to the farmhouse? You can wait for us there, though I expect it will be several weeks before we can return to collect you. Or, if you'd prefer not to wait, you can ask the farmer to write to London to send you back. The choice is yours.'

He sent Bridget a meaningful look and then turned on his heel and walked away up the road, a decisive swing to the valise in his hand. Bridget stared down at Emily's appalled face.

'Mama?' she said tremulously.

Bridget gulped. 'I do love you very much, gooseberry,' she said and planted a quick kiss on Emily's upturned forehead. Then she followed Cormac with her own valise, leaving their daughter sitting in the middle of the road with her mouth agape.

When she caught up to Cormac, he didn't even turn his head. 'Don't look back,' he said. 'We must keep walking until we reach that bend ahead.'

They walked in silence as far as the bend and followed it around until they were out of Emily's sight. There, Cormac stopped, his cheeks red.

'What are we doing?' Bridget asked, hesitant to stoke the fire but anxious to understand.

'She needs to learn. We are travelling the countryside with the clothes on our backs and a few bare belongings. It's a precarious venture so we must be able to rely on her to obey us when necessary. We were lucky in London. If she hadn't played along back on the ship, we wouldn't have made it to Ireland at all. We can't run the risk that she might let us down in a moment of jeopardy.' He swallowed. 'I'm her father, not her playfellow. This will be a crucial lesson for her.'

'What if she goes back to the farmhouse and asks them to write to London?'

He didn't pause. 'She won't. Just give her some time.'

The words were barely out of his mouth when they heard running feet slapping muddy ground.

'Mama?' A sob. 'Papa?'

Emily came dashing around the bend and let out another sob when she saw them standing there. She started to run towards Bridget but Cormac said, 'Wait a moment, Emily.'

She came to a faltering stop, two big tears on her cheeks.
'Do you have something to say?' Cormac asked her.
'I'm s-sorry.'
'What are you sorry for?'
Her lip trembled. 'I'm s-sorry for n-not doing what I was t-told.'
'Do you understand that it's important to do what you're told?'
'Y-yes.'
'And will you do so in the future?'
A loud sniff. 'Yes. I promise.'
'Go give your mother a hug so.'

She ran forwards but encompassed her hug around them both, one hand on each of their waists and her head squashed between their hips. Bridget's valise knocked painfully against her knees.

'Were you really going to leave me?' Emily wept, her voice muffled.

'Of course not, *a stór*.' Cormac took off her bonnet and kissed her crown. 'We adore you.'

She wept harder, pressing her little arms tightly around them.

'I'm sorry,' she whimpered again.

'We have forgotten it already,' said Cormac.

Bridget did a very good impression of the farmer's harrumph. 'Well, I haven't. How are we going to clean that big muddy patch on your bottom?'

They all laughed, though Emily's effort was a bit quivery. Cormac replaced her bonnet, took out his handkerchief and cleaned her runny nose, while Bridget inspected Emily's backside.

'Hmm, it'll do for now, I suppose,' she said, giving the girl's rump a cursory wipe, followed by a light smack. 'Let's be on our way again, shall we?'

Cormac let Emily fold up his handkerchief and tuck it into her own pocket. She obediently stepped into line with them and they set off again, the rain still spitting down. This time when Cormac encouraged a song, Emily obliged by bellowing out *'Rain, rain, go away, come again another day!'* over and over and over until Bridget quite regretted Cormac's suggestion. After a few dozen renditions of the rhyme, the little girl thankfully switched to 'Little Robin Redbreast'. She had only recited it seven times when she interrupted herself with a sudden gasp.

'Did you see it?' she cried. 'There was a robin right there!' She ran ahead, chasing the bird as it flitted from hedge to hedge.

Bridget cast a sideways glance at Cormac.

'How are you after that?' she asked.

He blew out his breath. 'Hurt. Infuriated.' He looked away. 'Jealous of that damn bastard.'

'Don't be,' she said, infusing the words with all her sincerity. 'She might have obeyed him but she would never have hugged him afterwards. That kind of fear is not a trait to covet from one's child. A fit of disobedience is a small price to pay for an otherwise unconditional love. You are the luckier party.'

He gazed ahead to where Emily, peering out from under the wet rim of her bonnet, was beckoning them to come catch a glimpse of the robin, and Bridget saw the lines of dissatisfaction melt from his features.

'I know,' he said softly.

They caught up to Emily just as they heard an excitable neigh and, for the second time in two days, a farmer's cart came trundling up behind them. This one had a pony harnessed to the front and a covered bundle in the bed at the back. The farmer had a head of straggly hair which he pushed away from his brow as he looked upon the travellers. Bridget's instinct was to say nothing and let him carry on, but he stopped of his own accord.

'*Dia duit*,' he addressed Cormac.

'*Dia is Muire duit*,' Cormac returned the Irish greeting.

The farmer nodded his approval. 'Heard talk of some English folk wandering around this area making a nuisance of themselves. Just wanted to make sure you're the right sort.'

Cormac frowned. 'My wife and child have accents that may not be to your taste. If that will offend you, please don't let us delay you on your way.'

The farmer looked chastened. 'I meant no harm. 'Tisn't in my mind to accuse you of anything. Just that 'tis wise to be wary...of late...' He cast a fleeting, inexplicable glance over his shoulder towards the covered bundle in his cart. 'Beg pardon for getting us off on the wrong foot. Hackett's the name.'

'McGovern,' said Cormac.

'Pleased to meet you, Mr McGovern. Where are you and your family off to this fine day?'

Emily snorted at his generous description of the weather and he gave her a broad wink.

Mouth twitching, Cormac said, 'We're on our way to Carlow.'

'Ah, ye've still a good distance to go.'

Emily, who had approached the pony tentatively and was reaching up to touch its nose, looked crestfallen at this.

'Yes, we're aware of that,' said Cormac. 'But the thought of home keeps us going. I'm a Carlow man by birth.'

'Are you now?' Farmer Hackett pulled thoughtfully on one long hank of hair. 'Don't know many folk from Carlow but the wife has an uncle who's a priest over there. D'you know a Father Macken?'

Cormac laughed. 'I do indeed. He baptised me, would you believe.'

'Go away.' Farmer Hackett let out a barking laugh of his own. 'And are ye planning to walk the whole journey or could my Bess help ye along a bit of the way?'

Bridget's heart leapt.

Cormac touched his cap. 'We'd be very grateful for Bess's assistance.'

Emily whispered to the pony, 'Hello, Bess.'

Farmer Hackett grinned. 'Sure, hop in so and we'll see if we can take ye a little further on your journey.'

He jumped down and went around to the back of the cart to push the covered bundle to one side, shooting the travellers a furtive glance as the items beneath made clanking noises. Bridget and Cormac climbed into the back of the cart, stacked the two valises, and pulled Emily up to sit beside them. Farmer Hackett urged Bess forwards and they rolled on up the road. The jolt of movement caused the bundle to jerk towards Bridget's foot and the corner of the covering flapped up, exposing the pointed heads of several pikes. Disturbed by the sight, she nudged Cormac and pointed at them. He looked startled and frowned at the back of the farmer's head but said nothing. Bridget was thankful for the respite from walking, but the inexplicable presence of those weapons made her uncomfortable.

Despite that, the appearance of Farmer Hackett and Bess vastly improved a day that could otherwise have been miserable for the three travellers. Not a mile down the road, a fancy carriage passed them, rattling through the puddles so carelessly that Bridget, Cormac and Emily would have been drenched had they been walking on the verge.

'Toffs think they own the road,' Farmer Hackett muttered from the front of the cart. 'And everything else to boot. Damn thieving Protestants.'

Bridget caught Cormac's glance. The less said about their connection to Oakleigh, the better.

The finest part of the whole encounter was that, upon arriving at Farmer Hackett's farm, he insisted they stay for a meal and his wife fed them the best dinner they had eaten since leaving London: creamy mashed potatoes, succulent chicken, and a rich gravy.

'Can we live here?' Emily asked as she spooned up the last of her gravy-soaked mash.

Mrs Hackett chuckled. 'Ye'd be very welcome, pet, but I expect your ma and da have other plans. Maybe ye'd stay the one night though?'

Bridget smiled; the offer was too tempting to refuse. 'Thank you very much for your hospitality. You are too kind.'

Mrs Hackett and her husband gave them an actual room in the farmhouse (consigning their youngest two to the hearth in the kitchen) and they all had a most satisfying night's sleep, the strife from earlier in the day forgotten.

They departed from the farm the next morning with bread, cheese and scones packed in their valises. Emily called a wistful farewell to Bess and received an exuberant neigh in return. As they turned towards the road, Bridget felt a faint warmth on her face and looked skywards; the watery sun had emerged at last.

## Chapter 5

One step after another, one day after the next. Their surroundings remained unfamiliar to Bridget until at last a shadow appeared on the horizon, an indistinct smudge that gained definition as they drew closer. Finally, it clarified into the brown slopes of the Blackstairs Mountains, which lay south of Oakleigh Manor, not far from the limestone quarry where Bridget and Cormac had long ago played as children.

She thought her heart might leap out of her chest. She hadn't set foot on Oakleigh land in seven and a half years. Home. She was nearly home. A lump came to her throat as a thousand memories swarmed for her attention.

She felt Cormac's hand wrap around her own. Looking up, she saw her own emotion reflected in his face, fierce joy tempered by deep sorrow. Was he too recalling the way they had parted back then? The agony of their separation seemed somehow nearer, given their proximity to the location of its occurrence. Her betrayal. His banishment. Her mother's lies. His family's suffering.

Please, she prayed. Please, God, let us find them.

He gazed ahead to the mountains. 'We'll make for the cottage first,' he said. 'It's probably falling down after so many years unoccupied but I want to go there anyway.' His voice caught at the end.

She squeezed his hand. 'I understand,' she said.

They continued on. Later in the day, she began to recognise various landmarks, fields and woods where she had gone riding in her girlhood, sometimes with her father and more often with Cormac. It had been an age of innocence, she realised, when the world had been unsullied in her eyes and there had not yet been any death or loss or pain. She glanced over at Cormac, who was now carrying Emily on his back and bouncing her like she was in a saddle. Emily was laughing at the top of her lungs. She hoped their daughter's age of innocence lasted as long as it could.

This would be Emily's first time to see the place where her parents had grown up. At the end of that fateful summer at Oakleigh, she had been a mere speck inside Bridget, her presence not yet even known. Soon she would learn where she had truly come from.

The further they went into Oakleigh's domain, the more Bridget came to notice that the area was very quiet. There were no signs of men toiling in the fields, no herds of cattle or flocks of sheep, not even any farmers' carts lumbering along the road. Strangely, many of the fields appeared to be untilled. This all seemed unusual to her – springtime was when the countryside ought to be in full revival after the winter – and she was just about to comment upon it when Cormac spoke.

'Time to get down now, *a stór*,' he said to Emily.

They were nearly there.

He lowered Emily to the ground and took one of the valises back from Bridget. Then, with a deep breath, he led them up the lane that would bring them to his family's cottage.

Bridget imagined what they would see: a ramshackle structure with the door hanging off its hinges and its roof caved in. Birds might have set up homes for themselves in its walls and eaves. It would be full of dust and ghosts. Still, it might be habitable enough for them to establish a place to sleep while Cormac made his enquiries. It was unlikely that they would need to stay there for more than a few days.

They followed the familiar curve of the lane, bracing themselves for the sight of the dilapidated cottage. But the building that came into view at the side of the road was not what they expected. The whitewashed walls had not collapsed, nor had the thatched roof fallen in. On the contrary, it stood as solidly as it had seven and a half years ago. The door was intact with the top half of it open and the horse shoe still hung above it. There were hens pecking around in front of it and – the most telltale sign of all – smoke issued from the chimney.

They were still staring at each other in amazement and confusion when the half door opened and someone came out. For one absurd, joyous moment, Bridget thought she saw Maggie McGovern coming towards them.

Then she blinked and came to her senses, recognising the freckles and the woman for who she really was: her mother's lady's maid, Ellen Ryan.

At first, Ellen did not notice that she had visitors. She had come outside to shake a cloth out; a shower of crumbs fell to the ground and the hens waddled over to investigate. She was just turning to go back inside when she caught sight of the three figures standing by the side of the road. Letting out a frightened gasp, she dropped the cloth and her hand flew to her pocket. Then she looked at them again, let out an even louder gasp, and her hand went to cover her mouth which had fallen open in an expression of utter bewilderment.

Bridget offered an apologetic smile. 'Good day, Ellen.'

Ellen gaped, her eyes as wide as dinner plates. 'M-my lady,' she stuttered.

'You do not need to address me like that anymore. I am just Bridget now.' She looked over her shoulder as Cormac and Emily approached her side. 'You know Cormac, of course. And this is our daughter, Emily.'

Ellen looked as though one more surprise would knock her over. 'Your—your daughter?' she said, looking uncertainly at Cormac.

He nodded in confirmation.

At this point, Emily chirped, 'How do you do? May I play with your hens?'

This seemed to wake Ellen from her bemused state. She gave a cracked laugh and said, 'God above, I think I need to sit down. Let's go inside.'

She picked up her cloth and led them into the cottage, Emily glancing back longingly at the hens.

Once indoors, Bridget could see that not much had changed since Cormac's family had lived here. The table was turned a different way and there was no sign of Maggie's spinning wheel, but the rocking chair sat in the corner as it always had and the dresser still stood against the back wall next to the ladder leading up to the loft. A sod of turf burned in the fireplace, emanating the same familiar smell.

Ellen's expression became anxious as she watched Cormac look around. His own face was unreadable, making it impossible to tell how he felt about someone else residing in what had been his family's home for so many years.

'I'm so sorry!' she blurted. 'We'd never have settled here if we expected for one moment you'd return. But we—we thought...' She trailed away awkwardly.

'Who is "we"?' asked Cormac, still betraying nothing.

Ellen coloured. 'Liam Kirwan and I. We married nearly five years ago.'

'Oh, how wonderful!' said Bridget. 'Do you have a family?'

'Two boys. And a third child on the way.'

Bridget noticed the small bump beneath Ellen's dress and they exchanged a glowing look that could only be shared by those who have been expectant mothers. Then they both glanced over at Cormac, whose face broke into a smile.

'That is great news,' he said warmly. 'I am delighted for you.'

Ellen allowed a little relief to show on her freckled features. 'So you're not angry with us? For taking over the cottage?'

'Not for one second. I'm glad it hasn't become a derelict ruin. At least it has continued to be a home for somebody's family.'

The air became palpable with the distinct absence of Maggie McGovern and her daughters and grandson.

The ghosts lingered until Bridget asked, 'Where is Liam?'

'He's out in the woods with the boys, but I'm expecting them home in a short while.'

At that moment, Emily, who had been craning her neck over the half door to look out at the hens, hit her chin off the wooden frame and began

## A Class Forsaken

to cry. Cormac lifted her up into his arms to comfort her. Ellen stared at the two of them.

'The resemblance is remarkable,' she said, almost to herself.

Imagining that Ellen must be burning with questions, Bridget said, 'We have rather a long tale to tell.'

'I'd be very interested to hear it.'

And so they all sat at the table that Maggie McGovern had once presided over, Ellen and Bridget on one bench and Cormac opposite them with Emily in his lap. In turns, Bridget and Cormac related the events over the last seven and a half years that had brought them to this point, leaving out the murkier parts for the sake of Emily's ears and divulging only what was most necessary for Ellen to understand how they had come to be together again. They did not speak directly of Cormac's impersonation of Oliver Davenport, only hinted at a stroke of fortune that had enabled Cormac to make his way to London.

Ellen listened in silence all the way to the end. When they had finished, she let out a soft breath. 'Ah. That's indeed quite a story.'

'A story of sin,' Bridget said lightly, feeling that this would liberate Ellen to give her honest opinion about what she had just heard.

Ellen shook her head. 'It's not my place to comment on that. But I'm glad you're happy and I'm very pleased to see you. Your appearance is just so unexpected. What's brought you back here?'

Cormac opened his mouth to reply but just then they heard voices and footsteps outside the cottage and Liam, Cormac's old friend and fellow stable hand, appeared at the half door, carrying a small boy on his back. When he pushed open the door, an older boy was revealed by his knees. Liam checked at the sight of his wife's visitors. However, instead of uttering loud exclamations of surprise, he just came in, swung his son down from his back and, in his usual, unassuming manner, extended his hand to Cormac.

'Good to see you,' he said as they shook.

'You too.' Cormac grinned.

The two boys ran to their mother to receive hugs and show her the mushrooms they had picked in the woods. Emily, having perked up at the appearance of other children, looked like she was making her best effort not to regard the mushrooms with distaste. Ellen picked the smaller boy up into her lap.

'This is Aidan,' she said, kissing the top of the boy's head. 'He's two. And this,' she said, putting her arm around the other boy, 'is Liam Óg. He's three and a half years old.'

Bridget smiled at the two boys. They were both a copy of their mother, with freckles splashed across their cheeks and noses. Emily waved shyly at them.

'That's Emily,' Ellen told the boys. 'She really likes our hens. Will you take her outside and introduce them to her?'

Liam Óg responded with a solemn nod, just as one might expect from a 'young' version of Liam, while Aidan slipped down from Ellen's lap and grabbed Emily's hand.

'Come on!' he cried in his high baby voice.

'Stay right in front of the cottage,' Ellen warned.

The three of them ran through the still-open door. Bridget heard the boys naming all the hens and Emily laughing in delight as they ran around after them.

Liam moved to sit at the table with the other adults. He had retained his lanky form from his youth and he folded himself onto the bench next to Cormac.

'How are things up at the manor stables?' Cormac asked companionably. 'Have they made you stable master yet?'

Even as he said this, a strange thought occurred to Bridget: why was Liam at home during the daytime?

Liam's eyebrows shot up and he looked over at Ellen.

'I haven't had a chance to tell them yet,' she said quietly.

'Tell us what?' asked Cormac.

Liam's countenance was grave. 'I don't work on the estate anymore. Nobody does.'

'What?' said Bridget, confused. 'What can you mean by that?'

Liam looked directly at her. 'For me to tell ye what's happened, 'tis necessary to make some less than savoury comments about your mother. Please forgive me for that.' As Bridget struggled to grasp this, he continued, 'I think 'tis fair to say Lady Courcey's never been a popular woman among the tenants on Oakleigh land. Lord Courcey was a kind soul, and Lord Walcott did no harm, but she's always been cold and hard to please. Still, she showed a keen understanding of how to manage the estate and so we were all able to make a decent living.' He rested his forearms on the table. ''Til almost seven years ago. Without warning, she reinstated the tithes and anyone working the land was obliged to take on the burden that Oakleigh had once covered. It was galling for Catholic folk to be forced once again to pay tithes to the Church of Ireland, no church of ours. In addition to that, she started putting up the rents, raising them every single year, and made us all work longer hours in tougher conditions.' He stared down at his hands and went on in a lower voice. 'Life became very difficult for every man, woman and child within reach of her influence. Anyone who couldn't pay what the lady demanded was thrown off the estate. Old Fintan Kelly cried the day he was made to leave. I saw him bawling his eyes out in the courtyard. He'd tended the gardens of the big house for over four decades but that meant nothing to her. She was merciless.'

Bridget listened in mute horror. This could not be true.

'About four years back, several of us crossed over the county border to attend an anti-tithe meeting in Kilkenny. There were thousands at it, and we heard all the news and rumours from other estates and other counties: folk refusing to pay the tithes, clashes with the constabulary, attacks on Church of Ireland property. When we got back to Oakleigh, we held a secret gathering among the tenants, servants and farmers who came from every corner of the estate. We decided it was time to stand up for ourselves and for our families.'

Cormac looked astounded. 'You rebelled?'

Liam's expression was calm. 'We simply refused to pay the tithes and the increased rents. The Church of Ireland sent tithe proctors to collect what they believed they were owed, and Lady Courcey ordered her agent Mr Enright to accompany them to ensure the same for her rents. After many failed attempts, the tithe proctors saw the need to be escorted by members of the constabulary as well. We resisted as peacefully as we could, but some of the confrontations turned nasty.'

At the hardened look in Liam's eyes, Cormac asked, 'Has anyone been hurt?'

'Too many,' said Liam. He reached across the table to Ellen and she laced her fingers with his.

'We live in a constant state of fear,' she told Bridget and Cormac. 'Every day brings the dread of a tithe proctor or a rent collector coming to the door. That was why I got such a fright when you appeared. Before I realised who you were, I thought...' She reached once again for her pocket and withdrew a short knife, small but sharp. 'I keep myself prepared, just in case.'

Bridget stared at the knife. To think that Ellen, once a lady's maid to a baroness, had been reduced to defending herself and her family in such a way. And this was occurring on Oakleigh land, where Bridget could never have imagined anything like this being possible.

She tried to speak but only a croak came out. She cleared her throat weakly. 'And — and my mother knew what was happening?'

Ellen's gaze lowered. 'She did.'

'And she did nothing about it,' said Liam. A glower shadowed his features. 'So last autumn we decided we'd had enough. Between allowing all this to happen to her own tenants and continuing to increase the rents, she was crippling us and our families and we couldn't stand it any longer. At another secret meeting, we agreed to abandon the estate, all of us together. A few stragglers remained behind, fearing the lady too much to rebel, but the majority of us walked away from our positions. Maids, footmen, gardeners, stable hands, we all deserted the manor one morning last September. At the same time, excavation work halted at the quarry and the farmers stopped tending the land. They've continued to look after their livestock but keep moving them and concealing them so the tithe proctors won't seize them from the fields as payment.' He shrugged. 'We hoped Lady Courcey would relent once she realised there was no one left to maintain the estate. But she hasn't given in. She sold the horses from the stables and stopped receiving visitors to the manor. She'd prefer to see the house and land fall into disrepair and decay rather than admit she's been wrong.'

Cormac's brow creased. 'But you are still within the confines of the Oakleigh Estate. Why did she not evict you and everyone else who refused to work for her?'

'On occasion, Mr Enright shows up with a constable at someone's dwelling,' said Liam. 'But she doesn't have the means to carry out widespread evictions on such a scale. Too few remained to act on her command.'

'Who did remain?'

'Cathy was the only maid who stayed behind,' said Ellen. 'I left the household back when I married Liam so I was gone before all this took place. I think Cathy was too scared to leave but it's my belief she also took pity on Lady Courcey. Mr Buttimer and Mrs Walsh stayed for a while but in the end they left too. I heard they went seeking positions in Dublin. It was an impossible life when the lady was being so unreasonable. Now Cathy's the only one left.' She shook her head sadly. 'It hurts us to see the estate like this. We were always so proud to serve Oakleigh. No one is happy to watch it fall into decline.'

Cormac rubbed his jaw, where a beard had sprouted after so many days on the road. 'How have you managed to survive with no income?'

'We get by,' she said. 'We'd be lost without the potato crop, that's what we eat most days. The winter was hard but now that spring is here it's a little easier. Foraging in the woods usually yields something edible.' She pointed at the mushrooms lying on the tabletop. 'We trade our hens' eggs for cow's milk or flour. And also—please forgive us for this, we did feel so very guilty—we sold your mother's spinning wheel. Everyone's in the same position, and we're all trying to help each other as much as we can. But it's difficult, especially with the two boys.'

There was silence in the cottage as nobody drew attention to the glaring concern: in a few short months, Ellen and Liam would have a third child to feed. What would they do then?

'We're still lucky,' Ellen said into the quietness. 'We have a solid roof over our heads. That's more than some poor families have.'

'I am gladder than ever that you have made a home for yourselves here,' said Cormac. 'In these troubled times, it would have been a waste to let the cottage go uninhabited.'

At this point, Bridget could stay silent no longer. 'Oh, Ellen,' she burst out. 'Why did you not write to me in London and tell me what was happening here? I could have saved you all from this!'

Ellen gazed at her directly. 'Could you have?'

'I—yes, of course—I—' Bridget faltered at the sadness in Ellen's eyes. 'Do you doubt that I would have tried to help you?'

'What would you have done?' Ellen asked, her tone gentle.

Bridget hesitated. She had a stirring vision of herself receiving Ellen's letter of distress, sailing at once to Ireland, travelling to Oakleigh, and forcing her mother to undo all the damage she had done.

Then she re-imagined the scenario with more clarity. Garrett would have refused point-blank to let her go. If she had managed to get away, he would not have permitted her to take Emily with her. And once she had reached Oakleigh, what authority would she have had? She herself had signed the contract conferring guardianship of Oakleigh to her mother. Nothing but her husband's signature could reverse that, and he would never provide it. She only had the power of persuasion and that was tenuous at best, given that the last time she and her mother had spoken in person she had cast her out from Wyndham House in London on the night of Emily's birth and sworn that the lady would never set eyes upon her grandchild. Lady Courcey would not have responded favourably to any of Bridget's demands. In fact, her appearance might well have made matters worse, spurring Lady Courcey to greater ire.

Bridget let out a stifled sob and buried her face in her hands.

'She did this to punish me,' she said, her words muffled against her fingers. 'Because of what I did to her, what I cut from her life. She knew the things I loved most in this world. She could not reach Emily, and she had already inflicted all the harm she could upon Cormac, so she took out her revenge on Oakleigh.'

Which meant all this was Bridget's own fault.

It was too terrible to comprehend. Her mother had committed unspeakable sins in the past but she had never done anything on this scale before. The lady had condemned dozens and dozens of families to appalling hardship and she had done it out of pure spite; there could be no other incentive for such cruel treatment of her tenants. How could she have behaved so callously? Could she not see that she was hurting real human beings? Furthermore, the land had suffered as well; Bridget had seen as much on their way here. The estate to which her father had devoted his life was a mere shadow of what it had once been without its loyal workers to maintain it. It was disgraceful beyond belief.

Utter shame pressed down upon her. How on earth could she face Ellen and Liam when they had suffered so much at her mother's hands and, by extension, her own? But when she raised her gaze to meet theirs, she did not find accusations or blame staring back at her. On the contrary, their expressions were full of sympathy.

'We're sorry to be the ones telling ye this,' said Liam.

'It is I who should be sorry,' she replied. 'I cannot believe what she has done. It is reprehensible.' She turned her head to Cormac. 'To think we were going to pay a visit to her. Sit in her drawing room and drink tea! That is unimaginable after learning this awful news.'

'If that was your purpose in coming here,' said Ellen, 'then I think you should still do so.'

Cormac protested, 'We would not set one foot across that woman's threshold after discovering what she has done to you, to all the people on this estate.'

'It might not be very pleasant,' Ellen admitted, 'but it might still be advisable. I met Cathy a few weeks ago and she told me her ladyship's not well. I'm not certain how serious her condition is but, if you don't visit her while you're here now, it's possible you won't have another occasion in the future.'

Recollecting her mother's allusion to her ill health in her letter before Christmas, Bridget wondered if it was even worse than she had intimated. 'Is she — is she dying?'

'I cannot say. But Cathy said Mr Abbott's been by many times.'

In all her life, Bridget could not recall her mother suffering from any ailment so grave that she had needed frequent visits from the physician. Part of her felt sudden worry for her mother's wellbeing and another part immediately responded with nauseating self-loathing for feeling anything but revulsion for the woman. She lowered her gaze so as not to betray either emotion to the others.

'I have no idea what to do,' she mumbled. It was absurd to even think of paying a social call to Lady Courcey when she had exploited her tenants in such a dreadful way. But how could Bridget stay away when her mother's failing health meant that this might be her last opportunity to see her alive?

'You don't need to decide today,' Ellen said. 'Maybe a good sleep tonight will make things clearer for you in the morning.'

Bridget glanced at Cormac. He shrugged. 'I'll leave the decision up to you. You were the one who wanted to see her in the first place.'

She gave a morose nod.

'So that's why ye came back then?' said Liam. 'To see the lady?'

'Actually, no,' Cormac replied. 'We came back for my family.'

Ellen's jaw dropped. 'Didn't Bridget tell you…?' She was so shocked that she didn't even stumble over her first use of Bridget's name without a title.

'She did. I am aware that they are gone from here, that they were forced to leave after I was, but I want to find them wherever they are now. I know it was a long time ago and that my chances of locating them are slim to none. Be that as it may, I'm holding onto the hope that someone here on the estate will be able to give me some inkling as to where they went.'

'There was never any word of them,' said Ellen, looking wretched. 'They just disappeared.'

'Even so, I still have to try.' His bearded jaw was set with resolve. 'I'm sure you understand. If it were your family, you would do the same.'

'I would. But I don't know where you'd even begin to look for this information.'

'I do,' said Liam. Everyone looked at him in surprise. 'There's another meeting taking place tonight. It's been six months since we turned our backs on the estate, so word's gone out that it's time for the men to come together to discuss the next steps we might take. If you're looking to speak to as many people as possible, that's your chance right there.'

'Thank you,' said Cormac, his shoulders sagging with relief. 'That is more than I could have hoped for.'

'It's a good start,' said Ellen, smiling at her husband. 'We can look after the children here,' she added to Bridget. 'You're of course welcome to stay as long as you wish to.'

'That is very kind of you but I shall be going with Cormac to the meeting.'

Cormac looked at her sharply. 'Are you mad? No, you won't.'

Ellen and Liam said nothing but their expressions showed that they too disagreed with Bridget.

She straightened her back against their united opposition. 'I ought to go,' she said. 'My mother has done a great disservice to these people and this is an opportunity for me to beg their pardon for her conduct. I know that an apology does not put money in their pockets or food on their tables but it is all that is within my power to give and so I want to do it with humility and hope that they can see my good intention.'

'No,' Cormac repeated. 'They'll be an angry group of men. How do you think they'd react to your appearance? You're the daughter of the woman they hate.'

'He's right,' said Liam. 'You wouldn't get a warm welcome.'

She slumped in defeat. 'Very well,' she mumbled. She glanced from Ellen to Liam. 'My thanks to you both for not treating me that way when you saw me.'

'We know you,' said Ellen, 'and we know you're not to blame for what has happened. But you are a stranger to most of them. They wouldn't understand how much Oakleigh means to you.' She patted Bridget's arm. 'We'll wait here with the children. Emily can go to sleep up in the loft with the two boys. I'll make sure she's comf—' She broke off. 'Oh,' she said and, without any explanation, she stood up from the table, went over to the ladder, and disappeared up into the loft.

Bridget and Cormac looked at Liam for enlightenment but he seemed as mystified as they were. Ellen reappeared a few moments later carrying a bundle under her arm. Liam helped her down the ladder and she deposited what she had retrieved from the loft on the table in front of Cormac. It appeared to be a number of letters packaged together with a piece of string.

'I've only remembered them now,' she said, a little breathless. 'They started coming nearly four years ago, not long before Liam Óg was born, but I never opened them because they weren't addressed to us. Were they from you?'

Cormac's expression was bleak. 'They were.'

He untied the string and picked up the first letter. Bridget was able to make out the name 'Maggie McGovern' and the address of the cottage on the faded paper.

'I sent them without a signature. If she had received them, she would have known who they were from. I just wanted to help her and let her know that I was safe.'

He broke the seal on the folded letter, drew out a rolled strip of cloth and unfurled it. A coin fell out and rolled along the tabletop. Ellen caught it before it plunged off the edge.

'You should have opened them,' he said. 'This money would have been a great benefit to you these past few years.'

'It doesn't belong to us,' she said, her eyes round as she stared down at the coin sitting in her palm.

'It doesn't belong to us either,' he replied. 'I want you to have it.'

Liam said haltingly, 'We can't accept it...'

'Listen, every one of these has money in it,' said Cormac, pointing to the stack of letters. 'My mother never received them but I think she would knock our heads together if she saw us all in need and refusing to take what will otherwise go to waste. You have a family to support, and I have a family to find. We can each put the money to good use so let us divide it up and not be stupid about it.'

Bridget's heart swelled at his bracing words; Liam and Ellen too looked almost overcome with emotion.

'Thank you for your generosity,' said Ellen, tears brimming in her eyes. 'It'll be such an enormous help to us.'

'And we can use it to aid the other tenants too,' Liam added.

'That is an admirable thought,' said Cormac, 'only please make sure you do not leave yourselves short.'

He opened the rest of the letters and began separating the money into two piles as Emily, Liam Óg and Aidan came running in from outside.

'Papa, I fed the hens!' Emily exclaimed, looking very pleased with herself.

'Excellent work.' Cormac pulled her to his side in a one-armed hug. 'Do you like it here, *a stór*?'

'Oh, yes, very much!'

'I am glad to hear it, because we plan to stay here for a few days. I need to go somewhere this evening for a little while but you and your mother are going to remain here with Ellen. Will you be on your best behaviour for her?'

Emily raised her chin with determination; she would show Ellen just how well-behaved she could be.

'That's my girl,' said Cormac and plucked at her chin before letting her run off with the two boys again.

As he turned back to the table, he caught Bridget's eye and his face became sober. She was already uneasy about his plan for tonight. What kind of crowd would he meet, and would they be able to give him the information about his family that he so desperately needed?

## Chapter 6

'Who's there?' came the whisper from the darkness of the woods. 'Name yourselves!'

Two vague forms loomed from between the tree trunks, coalescing into a pair of sentries carrying pitchforks.

Liam stepped ahead of Cormac, moving forwards with his hands held up loosely.

''Tis Liam Kirwan,' he said in a low voice. 'And this here's Cormac McGovern. He's safe, I can vouch for him.'

One of the sentries gave Cormac an appraising look, before nodding to Liam. 'Go on, then. Nearly everyone's already inside.'

'Thanks, lads.'

Cormac followed Liam past the sentries. Liam had forewarned him of their presence – all of the meetings had to be guarded in this way to prevent any risk of ambush. What was more, no one could arrive via the road; the meeting place could only be approached by way of fields and woods to prevent detection.

They emerged from the woods to face the back end of a barn.

'McKinty Farm,' Liam murmured. 'Mick McKinty is the only farmer around with an outbuilding big enough to hold so many of us.'

Cormac recognised the farmstead; when he had worked at Oakleigh, he had been required now and then to take a horse to McKinty Farm to collect produce for the manor kitchens. And, further back in time, he and Bridget had on more than one occasion visited Farmer McKinty's wife to cajole her until she gave them chunks of delicious cheese to nourish them on their wild jaunts about the estate.

Liam went first, leading Cormac around to the front of the barn. He heaved open the door and several voices greeted him as he entered.

'John,' he said. 'I've brought a friend along – hope you don't mind. I think you'll remember him.'

Liam looked back over his shoulder and Cormac stepped up beside him. Standing in the doorway, his first impression was that of many bodies and bright candlelight. Every available space seemed to be taken up by men sitting or standing and the barn was lit with lanterns set on stools or hanging from brackets on the stone walls. There was a buzz of subdued talking but this came to an abrupt stop at his appearance. For a second or two, he could not distinguish anybody among the sea of faces, but then a familiar one near the front of the assembly swam into view: the wiry stable master at Oakleigh, John Corbett. He let out a shout of surprise and delight and pulled Cormac inside the barn.

'Where in God's name did you spring from?' he exclaimed, slapping Cormac on the back.

Several more men gathered around, their faces alight with astonishment and welcome. It felt like going back in time, to be once again surrounded by the stable hands and gardeners and servants who had formed the constant backdrop to life at Oakleigh. They bestowed further hearty smacks upon his shoulders.

'Welcome back, lad!'

'Jaysus, what a shocker!'

'Didn't think we'd ever see you 'round these parts again.'

'Nor I, but I'm delighted to be in your company once more,' he said, smiling around at them with genuine pleasure.

They looked taken aback, and he realised that he must sound very different to the stable hand they remembered. Belatedly, he wondered whether he ought to have assumed a less formal mode of speech with them, but it would appear patronising if he attempted that now after they had already heard him speak in such a proper manner. In any case, once learned, good pronunciation was difficult to throw off.

'What's your story, lad?' asked John in puzzlement. 'Where've you been all this time?'

'It's quite complicated,' said Cormac. He had no wish to drag up his questionable past in front of every fellow who had walked into the barn that evening. 'I have seen and done a lot of things. But it is good to be home.'

A mixed reaction greeted this comment. There were some murmurs of appreciation but many of the men looked darkly at each other as though to say 'He doesn't know what he's come back to'.

'I've heard,' he hastened to assure them. He hesitated for a moment, imagining what Bridget might think of his next words, then ploughed on. 'I've heard what's happened here on the estate, and I'm glad of it. It's about time we took back control. This isn't their land, it's ours, and it has been for hundreds of years.'

A cheer went up around him, spreading to all corners of the barn. One of the younger men – Denis, Cormac recalled, a footman from the manor – shook his hand with vigour.

He studiously avoided Liam's gaze. Liam was the only one in this barn who knew that Cormac had returned in Bridget's company and he intended for it to stay that way.

'I'm glad you think so,' said a voice beyond the nearest circle of men.

"Cause rumour has it you bedded the English filly that used to live up in the big house and that's why you had to clear off all those years ago.'

Over Denis's shoulder, Cormac spotted two unkempt men lounging on stools with their backs propped against the barn's stone wall. He recognised the one who had spoken as Joseph Hayes, a man he knew mainly by reputation and not much of that was good. The balding fellow next to him was Bernie Cuddihy, the proprietor of The Pikeman, the drinking house in the local village of Ballydarry. Both had once been involved in a skirmish outside The Pikeman involving Bridget; she had been rescued by a pair of constables but the incident had given her a fright. Reputations aside, that alone was reason enough for him to dislike them.

'My business is my own,' he said coolly. 'And why I left is none of yours.'

Joseph flashed a gap-toothed smirk as Cormac turned back to John Corbett.

'Liam has told me what you've been doing,' he said.

'I can't say I'm proud of how events have unfolded,' said John. 'Had things remained bearable, I would've been happy to stay as we were.' He shook his head. 'But she just pushed us too far.'

'It can't have been easy to decide to take action. Are you —'

Cormac broke off as five more people entered the barn. At the front was none other than Mrs Kavanagh, the cook from Oakleigh Manor. She gasped when she spotted Cormac.

'Am I seeing a ghost?' she exclaimed.

She came forwards and enveloped him in a vigorous hug. She had always been a big-bosomed woman and there was still ample flesh surrounding him, but there seemed to be somewhat less of her than he remembered and, when she pulled back, there were dark circles under her eyes. They glistened with emotion and it touched him that his unexpected reappearance could affect her so much.

'Stand aside, Maura, and let the rest of us have our turn,' said a female voice behind Mrs Kavanagh.

The pair behind the cook were Farmer McKinty and his wife. The farmer had a rather vacant look but Mrs McKinty strode forwards and wrapped her arms around Cormac. He felt a little uncomfortable, given that he had never known her as well as Mrs Kavanagh and her embrace felt quite a bit more intimate in the way she pressed her chest so tightly against him.

'Uh, good evening, Mrs McKinty,' he said, drawing back from her as politely as he could.

'Oh, you're all grown up now, you can call me Maisie,' she said with a wink. She had to be fifteen years older than him at least but, though her skin had a hardened quality to it, her face retained a certain prettiness.

Mrs Kavanagh muscled back in, shunting an affronted Maisie out of the way.

'Bless us and save us, it's good to see you,' the cook murmured, pressing her broad hand to Cormac's cheek. 'You were always a decent lad. I hope life has treated you well since we saw you last?'

'I've had my ups and downs,' he admitted. 'But it sounds like you've all suffered a great deal of hardship as well.'

Her expression darkened. She beckoned to the last two people behind her, a woman with a pronounced overbite and a man crumpling his cap in his hands. When they came forwards, Mrs Kavanagh said, 'This is my sister, Kitty, and her husband, Colm Brophy.'

Cormac understood the connection at once. 'You were tenants at Rathglaney?'

'Yes,' said Kitty Brophy, one clipped word with a world of anger contained within it.

Cormac recollected his last summer at Oakleigh and the letter Mrs Kavanagh had received from her sister telling her of the uprising on the Rathglaney Estate, which was just over the county border into Wexford. The riled tenants had attempted to burn down the big house and in the process had injured the landlord in residence, Lord Fitzwilliam. Kitty's son and husband had both been involved and arrested, and her son had later been executed.

'I'm sorry for what happened to you,' said Cormac. 'I can't imagine you've been able to find much peace.'

Kitty pursed her lips. 'We found revenge. Rathglaney is no more. We didn't fail a second time.'

'We had to try again,' said Colm, crushing his cap even tighter. 'For our boy's sake.'

'Ye were right too,' interposed Joseph Hayes, leaning back with his hands behind his head. 'Ashes was all that place was worth.'

'When Maura said something similar was happening at Oakleigh, we came to help,' said Kitty. 'We weren't the only ones. The two fellows on sentry duty used to be Rathglaney stable hands and friends of our Collie. We knew ye had a just cause to fight for.'

'And they aren't the only ones helping us,' said John. 'Word has spread, 'specially thanks to those anti-tithe meetings. Support's coming from tenants and farmers in other places, even other counties, and many of them have carted over supplies.'

Cormac frowned. 'Supplies?'

'Weapons,' said Denis eagerly. 'Pikes and pitchforks and even a few pistols. I held one.'

With a jolt, Cormac recalled riding in the back of Farmer Hackett's cart next to the covered bundle of pikes. This was larger than he had even realised.

'We bury them under the giant's claw,' Denis continued. 'Just like back in '98.'

Joseph let out a noise of exasperation. 'Arrah, let's spill all our secrets to the goddamn stranger, why don't we?'

'He's right, keep your trap shut,' Bernie Cuddihy barked at Denis.

'Come on, lads,' said John. 'I've known Cormac since he was barely up to my knees. And I knew his da before that. We can trust him.'

'Can we?' said Joseph. 'Has he given us even one scrap of information about where he's been all these years? Or why he's bothered to come back after so long? Or why he's talking so fancy and proper?'

'He's told me and my wife,' said Liam. 'We're satisfied he's the same man he always was.'

'And his mother was the best woman you could ever hope to meet,' said Mrs Kavanagh. 'So shut your gob, Joseph Hayes.'

'Thank you,' said Cormac to those who had come to his defence. Then he raised his voice so as to be heard throughout the barn. 'But Joseph's correct. I haven't told you yet why I'm back. I do have an agenda in coming here tonight.'

Angry muttering broke out on all sides.

'Just hear me out,' he said, even louder. 'Some of you may be aware that my family was evicted from their cottage about seven and a half years ago. My mother, Maggie McGovern, my three younger sisters and my nephew were forced to leave the estate as a result of a transgression on my part. To my deep regret, I only learned of this very recently, at which point I made the immediate decision to come back to Oakleigh to find them. I don't know where they are but I am hoping that there might be someone here on the estate who saw them leave, who could tell me which direction they went, or where they planned to go. Is there anyone here who can help me at all?'

There was a hum of chatter as the men digested this news.

'What did they look like, lad?' somebody called from the back.

'My mother and sisters all had dark hair and grey eyes. My sisters were aged fourteen, twelve and five and my nephew was only a baby, around three months old.'

He held his breath. The men looked around at each other, waiting for someone to speak up and say they had seen them. But no one called out again and, as he let his breath out in disappointment, a boulder formed in the pit of his stomach, heavy and sickening. This had been his most promising chance and already it had amounted to nothing.

'Sorry, lad,' John murmured to him with a sympathetic look, before addressing the room in general. 'Perhaps ye could all mention this to your wives and families when ye go home. Spread the word and see if anyone knows anything.'

Liam added, 'And bring any news ye get to myself or John. We'll make sure it's passed on.'

Cormac nodded his gratitude.

'While I have your undivided attention,' John went on to them all, 'I've got some grave news to impart. Ben Bracken was evicted this morning, along with his elderly mother.'

There were shouts of dismay and outrage. Bernie aimed a furious kick at a stray clump of hay and it went flying in all directions. Farmer McKinty looked vaguely anxious at the commotion and started mumbling to himself. No one paid him any mind.

'They're being accommodated over at Hogan Farm,' said John. 'Ben's ma is quite shook up and wants him by her side, which is why he isn't here himself to tell us the tale. But he told me Mr Enright showed up with three constables to do it.'

'That bugger's got it coming to him,' said Joseph. 'Still doing the bitch's bidding like a little lapdog. Deserves to be tossed in the Sruhawn, if you ask me.'

'Would you mind your language when we've women in the company?' said Denis hotly.

'It's no offence to me,' said Mrs Kavanagh stoutly, while Maisie McKinty offered a pert smile and shot Cormac another wink.

'There you go, you milksop,' said Joseph to Denis. The footman went red to the tips of his ears but Joseph carried on, 'What's going to be done about this?'

John folded his arms. 'We need to be careful how we handle it. Mr Enright's no servant. He mightn't have a title but he's a gentleman, the youngest son in a family from the landed gentry. He's got connections.'

'And haven't we got connections too?' demanded Joseph. 'What about that money? Couldn't we find out who 'tis coming from and put pressure on them to act?'

Cormac raised his eyebrows. 'Money?'

John looked ill at ease. 'We're getting financial help from an unknown source. We don't know who's sending it or why, but every now and then a fresh sum of money arrives. I'll get an anonymous note and find the funds buried under the giant's claw, just like the weapons. That's how we've been able to pay for the supplies coming from other places. And we save the rest to help those who've been evicted.'

Staggered, Cormac said, 'And you have no idea where it's coming from?'

''Tis got to be someone rich,' said Joseph. 'Like I said, 'tis a connection. Can't we get a message to whoever 'tis and say we want that Enright bugger stopped?'

Before anyone could respond, there was a scuffle outside the barn. The door banged open and the two Rathglaney sentries came marching in, grasping a struggling figure between them.

'Let me go!' Bridget exclaimed.

Cormac's heart plummeted to the soles of his feet.

# Chapter 7

Dead silence fell. Every pair of eyes in the barn became fixed upon Bridget, who went pale under their stares.

'That's Lady Courcey's daughter,' said Denis in disbelief.

'Found her in the woods,' said one of the sentries to John. 'She was trying to sneak up to the barn.'

'I was not sneaking,' she said indignantly. 'I just lost my bearings in the dark. I knew you were there and I fully intended to announce my presence.'

John cleared his throat. 'Your...presence comes as something of a surprise, m'lady.' He eyed Cormac, who read the questions and the suspicion in the stable master's gaze.

Trying his best to keep a lid on his anger, Cormac extricated himself from the surrounding men and stepped forwards.

'Let her go,' he said to the two sentries.

They looked to John for guidance and, at his nod, reluctantly released their grips on Bridget's upper arms. She straightened her skirts and kneaded one of her shoulders. Cormac went to stand beside her, turning to face the others in the room. His show of support seemed to boost her confidence and she kept her chin up as she too looked around at them all. She made eye contact with Mrs Kavanagh but the cook glanced away quickly.

A resentful hiss rose throughout the barn as the men muttered to one another. Cormac caught snatches of 'What's she doing here?' and 'Why's he with her?' and 'What've they come back for?'

'This doesn't look good, Cormac,' said John.

'No, I know it doesn't,' Cormac replied, resisting the urge to cast a nettled grimace in Bridget's direction.

John sighed. 'Can you explain what's going on here?'

'No need to,' barked Joseph, jumping up from his stool. ''Tis obvious. They're here to spy on our plans and turn us all in. I goddamn told you so!'

He spat on the ground at Bridget's feet.

Enraged, Cormac lunged towards Joseph but Liam pulled him back. John walked right up to Joseph and stared him in the eye, though he was at least half a foot shorter.

'Joseph Hayes, that's no way to treat a woman,' he said calmly. 'Be civilised or you'll be thrown out.'

Joseph glared at John, Cormac and Bridget in turn and then sat back down, scowling. John returned his attention to Bridget, who had shrunk back at Joseph's rudeness.

'Forgive us, m'lady. We haven't given you a proper greeting but you might understand why we have some misgivings. May we ask what's brought you here tonight?'

There was a faint tremor in Bridget's hands. Clasping them together, she said, 'Thank you, John. I do understand why my reception has been less than warm and you require no forgiveness for that. I came here tonight to say something to you all but before I do that I need to make one thing clear. You must not address me as 'my lady' anymore. I am not Miss Muldowney, I am not Lady Wyndham, I no longer belong to the upper classes. I belong to Cormac and therefore I am now simply Bridget.'

This caused quite a stir. A young lady of distinguished social standing had deserted her rich husband in favour of a poor – though admittedly well-spoken – stable hand. It was unheard of. Maisie McKinty looked highly disappointed.

After an awkward pause, John came forwards to shake Cormac's hand but, despite Bridget's protestations, he insisted on calling her, at the very least, 'Miss Bridget'. There were no echoes of goodwill from any of the other men. From their sceptical expressions, it was clear they thought Bridget was trying to hoodwink them by declaring that she was now 'one of them'.

Mrs Kavanagh seemed to be the only other person who softened a little at Bridget's announcement. She said to her sister in a carrying whisper, 'That pair have been smitten with each other since they were children. Bless them, I'm glad they've found love at last.'

Kitty Brophy snapped her teeth together. 'You think she's telling the truth?' she said, not attempting to keep quiet. 'Open your eyes, for heaven's sake. You can't believe a word English folk say. 'Tis all poison from their mouths.'

Visibly hurt, Bridget said, 'You don't even know me. How can you say such things?'

'I know your kind,' said Kitty, 'and that's enough. Most likely, you've paid that lad to act as your lover—far-fetched to begin with, as if you'd ever stoop to dallying with a Catholic peasant—and he's come here first to extract information on your behalf. I wouldn't trust you as far as I could throw you. *Téigh ar ais go Sasana, a bhitseach!*'

Colm Brophy laid a hand on his wife's elbow but his placating words were lost in a ragged cheer from the gathered men. Joseph and Bernie shouted loudest of all. However, John, Liam and Mrs Kavanagh didn't join in, and Farmer McKinty put his palms flat over his ears at the noise.

Cormac balled his hands into fists but kept his tone even as he said, 'That only goes to show the level of your ignorance of this whole situation, Mrs Brophy. Because Bridget understands exactly what you just said.' He knew her grasp of Irish was somewhat spotty but she couldn't fail to comprehend those words of abuse.

'I do,' said Bridget. 'And I will *not* go back to England.'

That shut them all up pretty quickly.

'You call me English,' she continued, 'but I was born in this country and I deem Ireland to be my home. You cast judgement upon me because of who my mother is, without giving me a chance to show you that I am nothing like her. Will you not offer me that opportunity before you throw me to the wolves?' She turned a beseeching gaze upon John. 'When have I ever given you reason to doubt me?'

He looked abashed. 'You're right,' he said. 'We're not being fair.' When a chorus of grumbles rose up, he put out a shushing hand and carried on, 'We'll let her speak.' He pointed to the Rathglaney sentries. 'You two, go back to your posts.'

They retreated with departing glances of distrust towards Bridget, closing the barn door behind them and shutting out the cool night-time air. Liam fetched a stool and John motioned Bridget to sit. Cormac took up a protective stance at her side, alert to the fact that everyone's gaze was trained keenly upon her and, whether she realised it or not, she was now on trial.

'So,' said John, 'you said you'd something to say to us all?'

'Yes,' she mumbled. Then she cleared her throat and raised her voice so that she could be heard throughout the barn. 'Yes, I have something to say. Cormac and I returned to the estate just today so we have only learned about your plight in the last few hours. Liam has told us how you have suffered. You have been reduced to the most terrible circumstances and my mother's behaviour is unpardonable in this regard. I want you to know how ashamed I am of the way she has treated you and how sorry I am that you have been forced to endure such hardships.'

She stopped speaking. There was a ringing silence as her words hung in the air. Then a gruff voice pierced it.

'That's it?'

Joseph was leaning forwards on his stool. He looked incredulous. 'We've been suffering for years, stretched so tight we're only ever a day away from starvation. Our children are skin and bone, our livelihoods are ruined. Your own damn mother put us in this position. And you've the *gall*,' he spat the word, 'to swan in here and say you're sorry? D'you think that'll fix everything?'

'Cool your temper,' said John in a warning tone.

'What about all the folk we've lost? Ben Bracken's brother got killed when the tithe proctor wouldn't take no for an answer. Bernie here buried both his sisters last year, wasted away to nothing, they were. Fintan Kelly died without a penny to his name or a roof above his head. 'Tis my belief he died of shame, between the humiliation of what that idiot grandson of his did and the way that woman disgraced him. She's got blood on her hands.'

Some of the others made noises of agreement.

Cormac saw a vein pulsing rapidly in Bridget's throat. 'I had no knowledge of or control over most of what you have just said,' she said. 'The one thing I did have a say in was the punishment of Mr Kelly's grandson for his attempted theft at the manor. And I in fact convinced my mother to commute Malachy's punishment from transportation to imprisonment. Only for me, he and his two accomplices would be in Australia now. As for the rest, I am devastated to hear of it. My heart goes out to every single family affected by this atrocity.'

Joseph shot to his feet. 'I don't believe a word she says. Her devil of a mother sent her here to fool us!'

Bridget stood herself, red-faced with indignation. Instead of frightening her, Joseph's fury seemed to have fired her up.

'I'll have you know that I have neither seen nor spoken to my mother in nearly seven years. I received one piece of correspondence from her during all that time in which she gave me no indication that there was a crisis on the estate. I was ignorant of your situation but I do still accept the blame for it. I apologise to you all this evening on behalf of my family name and for the fact that this estate has failed you. However, do not accuse me of siding with my mother in this. She has no inkling that I have even returned to Oakleigh.'

Joseph looked taken aback but, unwilling to acknowledge her innocence, merely muttered something caustic under his breath and sat back down again. Bridget spun around to the room at large and held out her palms in a gesture of helplessness.

'I am sorrier than I can say for what you are going through. I sympathise with every one of you, truly I do. I came here to express that sympathy and to assure you that my mother was inflicting this distress without my knowledge. I wish there were something that I could do to help you, now that I am conscious of the circumstances, but regrettably there is not.'

'Well, I don't know about that,' John said, looking pensive. 'I'm starting to believe your heart's in the right place. So maybe you *can* help us.'

Bridget's brow puckered. 'In what way?'

'Oakleigh is yours, isn't that right?'

'Technically, yes. But when I was twenty-one I signed the guardianship of it over to my mother for as long as she lives. And whenever she passes, it will belong to my husband, Lord Wyndham, because all of my property is his.'

Mrs Kavanagh made a huffing sound at this injustice.

John shrugged. 'What if you reclaim what's yours? Why not step in and take over from Lady Courcey while she still lives?'

'Are you asking me to depose my mother?' Bridget said in disbelief.

'I am.'

Joseph snorted, and Bernie spluttered, 'Are you daft? Why would we replace one English tyrant for another?'

'I don't think that's what would happen,' said John. 'She's Irish at heart, my gut tells me so. She doesn't want to see Oakleigh suffer. She wouldn't force the tithes upon her tenants and she'd be fair in her dealings with rents. She could rescue the estate from her mother and give us back our livelihoods.'

'But it is impossible,' said Bridget. 'I would have no legal grounds upon which to do so.'

'Acts of legality haven't been seen too often in these lands over the past few years,' Liam pointed out.

'Even so, I could not do it.' She looked bewildered.

'You'd manage it a damn sight better than how 'tis being managed now,' said John. 'You could restore Oakleigh to the way it was under your father.'

Her shoulders jerked at the mention of Lord Courcey. She wavered, then said, 'But I don't see how it could be done.' She bit the tip of her tongue as a contemplative look crossed her features. 'Mr Enright has a good knowledge of the law. Perhaps he would know some way around it –'

'Not him,' said Joseph. 'His downfall's coming too, same as your ma. He's just as bad as her.'

Bridget bristled. 'I do find that hard to believe. I recall very clearly when I was last at Oakleigh a discussion between Mr Enright and my mother in which he defended your position most compellingly. He advocated that the tithes should remain an expenditure of the estate and not be forced upon the tenants.'

Bernie sneered. 'Didn't take you long to forget the role you're meant to be playing. That Enright devil's not on our side. He's –'

For the second time that evening, the barn door banged open. The two sentries came sprinting in.

'Constables!' they shouted. 'Coming right now! They're nearly here!'

Every head swivelled towards Bridget.

'This is your doing!' Joseph roared at her.

'It's not!' she cried. 'It's not!'

'There's no time for that now,' said John quickly. 'We can't make it out ourselves but the women need to get away.'

Colm was already shunting Mrs Kavanagh, Kitty and Maisie towards the door.

'Go with them,' Cormac said to Bridget.

'No, I should stay—'

He gripped her wrist tightly. 'Go right now and don't argue.'

Fearful, she stumbled to the door. Mrs Kavanagh took her hand and they disappeared into the night.

'Where will they go?' Cormac asked John urgently.

'Colm knows where our bolthole is in the woods,' John replied. He turned to Farmer McKinty. 'Mick, open the trap door, there's a good lad.'

Making fretful smacking noises with his lips, Farmer McKinty hurried with a lopsided gait towards the back of the barn. The men jumped aside as he bent to brush away a layer of hay from the floor; he dug his finger into a metal ring and pulled at it with a grunt. A section of the floor lifted up, revealing a shallow space beneath. The men pushed the farmer out of the way and started hauling farm tools out of the hole. Cormac gaped at the array of shovels, spades, hammers, axes and pitchforks, all of which in this context became weapons. They were passed around and a shovel found its way into his hands. He tested its weight and balance; it was a larger implement than the slender dagger he used to carry when he was in Cunningham's employ, but it would do fine.

John was issuing orders in a low, purposeful voice, commanding them to hide in the corners, in the shadows, behind haystacks, and checking if everyone was adequately armed. He directed a couple of the men to blow out most of the lanterns, leaving the inside of the barn cloaked in gloom.

'Now, keep your silence,' he whispered and waved them into position, coaxing Farmer McKinty into the furthest corner from the barn's entrance, while he himself pressed his back up against the wall next to the door, his spade ready in his hand.

Cormac crouched behind a haystack next to Denis. The footman clutched an axe, fingers wrapped firmly around its handle. The only trace of his fear was a tiny twitch in the muscle of his jaw.

Cormac let out a long, steadying breath. Heavy footfalls sounded outside and gruff voices called to each other. The constables weren't even trying to be quiet.

Then the shout came: 'We know you're in there! Come out single file, unarmed with your hands raised!'

'Sure thing,' Denis muttered through barely moving lips. 'And let me tell ye where I hid my pot of gold as well.'

After a pause, the command was repeated, louder and more annoyed, but no one inside the barn moved an inch. There were indistinct grumbles which were immediately shushed, and all went quiet. Too quiet.

'Be ready,' Denis mouthed to Cormac.

Cormac gripped his shovel even tighter, straining his ears for any sound.

With an almighty clatter, the barn door burst open and feet thundered inside.

The men erupted from their hiding places and rushed the charging constables, who all carried rifles with bayonets fixed to the muzzles. One of them fired his rifle but the shot went wild and then the men were too close for the rifles to be of any use. As Cormac darted out from behind the haystack, he saw John step up behind the last constable and whack him across the back of the head with the flat side of his spade. The man crumpled.

A constable came hurtling towards Cormac, bayonet aimed straight at his chest. He sidestepped and the blade slid past his arm, half an inch from slicing his sleeve. The constable skidded as he tried to halt his momentum and fell face first into the haystack Cormac had hidden behind. Denis dashed over, dug the butt of his axe into the small of the man's back, and growled, 'Stay right where you are, rat.'

Cormac spun about to see another constable bearing down on him. Instead of trying to pierce him with his bayonet, the constable swung his rifle out and around. Cormac put up his shovel just in time and the rifle slammed against the shovel's handle, like two swords crossing blades. He took the brunt of the collision and felt the impact all the way up to his shoulders. The constable swung again but Cormac, arms still quivering from the previous blow, couldn't bring up the shovel quickly enough and the rifle connected with his temple. He fell sideways, dropping his shovel and landing hard on his hip. His vision went blurry for a second but it cleared as he rolled onto his back. The constable loomed over him, raising his rifle to stick the bayonet in him.

Cormac kicked out at the constable's legs to trip him, and the fellow toppled over with a muffled 'Oomph!' Booting the rifle out of the constable's grip, he scrambled to his knees and struck him a blow across the face. Spittle flew from the man's mouth. Eyes wide and desperate, he struggled to clamber backwards out of Cormac's reach. Cormac felt around blindly for his shovel but his hand landed on the rifle instead. He picked it up and aimed it at the constable's neck.

'Don't move,' he said, panting like he had just run ten miles.

All around him he heard shouts and expletives and exclamations of pain. There were clashes of metal against wood, fists against flesh, knuckles against teeth. The smell of the earlier rifle shot hung in the air.

It was all over with remarkable swiftness. The constabulary had underestimated the number of bodies inside the barn, the amount of weapons at their disposal, and their ability to act quickly. A few uniformed cowards scuttled out the barn door, but the rest were corralled into a loose clump in the centre of the barn, their own bayonets pointed at them. There were superficial injuries, grazes and bruises and cuts, but no serious wounds on either side of the fray.

John stood with a bloody nose in front of the group as they knelt in a ragged cluster of half a dozen men. Joseph and Bernie went around to each one to tie their hands behind their backs with lengths of rope.

'Make those bonds good and tight,' said John. 'We'll have to move them to another place so they can't be found by anyone who comes back looking. Then we'll bind their feet too and decide what to do with them.' He surveyed the constables. 'Of course, we'll have some questions to ask.'

The first of which had to be obvious.

How had they known where and when this meeting was to take place?

## Chapter 8

Cormac and Liam got back to the cottage just as dawn was breaking. In the grey gloom, it seemed like a drowsing creature hunched at the side of the road, exhaling a gentle breath of smoke from its chimney. A lone bird, up earlier than its companions, twittered from its perch on the thatched roof. Part of Cormac wanted to remain outside with the bird rather than confront what lay ahead.

Liam pushed open the door, and the wave of warmth from the smouldering fire was welcome on their chilled skin. Bridget and Ellen sat on opposite sides of the table, a single rushlight between them. It guttered in the draught. On the rafter above the hearth, one of the hens ruffled its feathers, unimpressed.

Bridget's face was taut with anxiety but it broke into relief at the sight of them.

'Oh, thank God,' she exclaimed.

She jumped up and ran to Cormac, throwing her arms around his neck. He gave her a perfunctory squeeze. She frowned as she drew back to look up into his face.

'You're hurt,' she said.

She touched his temple where the rifle had hit him. It was tender and he winced.

'I'm fine,' he replied. 'Where's Emily?'

'She's up in the loft, asleep with the two boys.'

He nodded, even as his stomach clenched. Better to get it over with. 'Will you take a walk with me?'

She looked taken aback. Ellen and Liam tactfully pretended not to be listening. 'Yes, of course...'

He said nothing else, only held the door open for her and followed her out into the dawn, closing the door softly behind them. She waited and he led her into the woods behind the cottage, the light just strong enough now that they could pick their way without tripping over roots. He remembered an occasion long ago when his older sister, Mary, had brought him into the woods like this; it had meant a significant conversation was imminent. Just like now.

He didn't walk very far, stopping when he came to a clearing in the trees where a brook bubbled unseen in the surrounding undergrowth. He turned as she entered the clearing behind him. A questioning crease had settled between her brows.

Clearing his throat, he tried to keep his tone neutral. 'The constables are locked up in the cellar at Hogan Farm. Farmer Hogan's a bachelor so he's not as concerned as some of the others about getting caught. Tell me what happened after you left the barn. You made it to the bolthole safely?'

'We did. Colm guided us to a cave deep in the woods outside McKinty Farm. I'm surprised you and I never came across it in all our gallivanting, but then again the entrance is well hidden by big tree roots. It was freezing inside it.' She shivered and wrapped her arms around herself; he couldn't tell if it was at the memory of the cave or because of the cold morning air. 'After a few nerve-wracking hours, Denis came to tell us it was safe to leave. He escorted Mrs Kavanagh, Kitty and Maisie back to the farm but said you wanted me to go to the cottage, so Colm accompanied me here.' She paused and the brook gurgled in the stillness. 'Why didn't you want me to go back to the farm?'

He ignored her question. 'Ellen must have been worried by your absence, was she?'

Her lips twisted, as though she had figured out the source of his hostility. 'She knew where I had gone. She didn't agree with my decision but she told me about the barn and the sentries so I could at least be prepared. Needless to say, she did not object to minding Emily.'

He stayed silent. Their breath misted in the space between them.

'Why didn't you want me to go back to the farm?' she asked again.

He gave her an exasperated look. 'Isn't it obvious?'

She narrowed her eyes. 'Not to me.'

'Christ above,' he said. 'Really?'

'Just spit it out,' she snapped. 'This kind of prevarication isn't like you.'

'That's because I'm trying with all my might to control my temper, and it's taking a lot of effort.'

They stared at each other. He felt his rage simmering; he was a pot coming to boil, and she was the open fire. He didn't know which was more perilous.

'Can you truly be so blind to the stupid thing you did last night?' he said very quietly.

She pursed her lips and in that moment he hated the way the action was so reminiscent of Lady Courcey.

'Stupid,' she repeated. 'Do you mean going to the barn to apologise to those men for the harm my mother has caused them and their families? To say on behalf of my family's name that I understand she has let down a generation of tenants by her actions?'

'I mean walking into a barn full of men who detest your mother down to their very bones and thinking that they would welcome your apology.'

'I am not my mother—'

'For God's sake, they don't see that.' He threw his hands up in the air. 'You are not two separate people in their eyes. You are one entity, both representative of a foreign country that has kept them downtrodden for centuries. There was the threat of murder in the way they looked at you.' And there were few times in his life when he had been more scared for her.

'John had convinced them—'

'He had convinced them of nothing. All it took was the arrival of the constables to rip away any trust they had begun to build in you. How you thought you would be able to win them over with a few words of contrition is beyond me.'

Her eyes flashed, her body rigid in the strengthening light. 'I thought no such thing. Do you really believe me to be so dim-witted? I understood exactly what I was walking into. I have never forgotten the warning you gave me that day in Ballydarry, after the incident at The Pikeman. You warned me then what these people can be like. I remembered and I went there anyway. I went in with my eyes wide open, and my nerves trembling because I was terrified, but it was something I knew I had to do, regardless of its futility.'

That gave him pause. He hadn't even considered that her behaviour might not have been a feat of utter foolishness but an act of utmost bravery. As she stood there breathing heavily and glowering at him, his admiration for her soared. However, the consequences of her actions remained unchanged.

Flatly, he said, 'They think you informed the constabulary about the meeting.'

'I didn't.'

'Then who did? How are you going to prove it wasn't you? They're not going to take your word for it.' He strode up to her and took hold of her shoulders, infusing his grip with urgency. 'Until we discover who the actual informant is, you are the one they'll blame. You can't go anywhere near those men now. They'll want to lynch you on the spot.'

When he looked into her eyes, he did not regret the fear he had placed there. She needed to be fearful so that she would be careful.

She gulped. 'I cannot fathom how deep their hatred goes. What Kitty Brophy said to me...'

'She has suffered more than most,' he reminded her. 'Her son was executed for rebelling.'

'But then why rebel?' she said, almost plaintively. She put a hand flat on his chest, like she could extract the answer from his heart. 'When they know the risks they are taking with their lives?'

He let go of her and stepped back. 'What a thing to ask. Because the risks are worth taking. Better to die a free Irishman than suffer decades of misery under English rule.'

'I appreciate that, and I recognise their desire to be free from external control.' She held out her hands, palms up. 'But they need to be realistic. Victory in revolt does not guarantee successful long-term autonomy. How do they plan to manage the land without an overseer of some kind?'

'So you think the current system is best? Lady Courcey should stay right where she is?'

'My mother is not a good example. But my father is. You saw how well the estate thrived under him. What would the people do without that kind of guardianship? Would they just grab what they can and end up fighting among themselves? There has to be some sort of structure in place to maintain stability. Otherwise, everyone and everything will suffer, including the beloved land they covet so much.'

'You're deceiving yourself,' he said witheringly. 'Nothing will be different if they remain under anyone else's thumb. At least if the rebels achieve independence, they will truly own their land again.'

She stamped her foot in the leaf litter; last autumn's leaves crackled like crumpled paper. 'At what cost? Look at the damage they are doing to people's lives and property. Denis told us the constables have been tied up as prisoners. They are no better than animals, on either side. The rebels' intentions are good but their methods are flawed, and you know it.'

'I know no such thing.' He kept going, as though caught by an irresistible current in a fast-flowing river, the words flooding from his tongue before they had even formed in his mind. 'Are you objecting because you might lose Oakleigh?'

Her jaw dropped. 'How dare you say that! Titles and riches have never held weight with me. If the ambitions of this uprising were in everyone's best interests, I would wholly support it. But I can perceive Oakleigh's worth. Its existence gives this land a strength and a stability which the tenants cannot provide for themselves.'

They glared at one another, both unyielding. Even as he felt sick for quarrelling with her, some innate part of him, bred from countless generations of discontent, could not bend. He may not have been alive during the 1798 rebellion but the memory of it ran in the veins of every Irishman and Irishwoman. How could she not see that their emancipation mattered more than anything else?

Her chest rose and fell with a long, deep breath, her dark brown eyes sadder than he had seen them in a long time.

'How dare you...' she said quietly and turned to walk back the way they had come.

He didn't call after her. He stood alone in the clearing for a minute or two, loathing himself and the situation in which they had found themselves. When they had decided to return to Ireland, becoming enmeshed in an uprising had not been part of their plan. But they had walked right into it and he couldn't see how they could step away from it now.

And yet all of it was a distraction from their true purpose, which itself appeared to be turning into a failure. Despair welled in him as he recalled the silence in the barn that had greeted his plea for news of his family. His mission to find them seemed more unachievable now than it had when he was still in London. In this moment, his mother felt as out of reach from him as the last star fading from the sky.

He whirled to a tree behind him, prepared to take out his frustration on it, but at the last second his curled fist changed to a flat palm and he pressed his hand lightly to the trunk. He couldn't lose hope. Regardless of what was happening between the tenants and Lady Courcey, he had to remember that his family was what he was here for. He would go into Ballydarry that afternoon and speak to the villagers. His mother had built a connection with the women there from many years of bartering hens' eggs; perhaps one of them might know something. If that yielded nothing, he could make enquiries in the next village up the road, and the one after that, to see if his family's steps could be retraced. The odds were desperately low, but not trying was an impossibility.

Heavy of foot and heart, he followed Bridget's path between the trees. It was by now full daylight and the woods were loud with birdsong. Part of him hoped she had not gone far and that they could reconcile before returning to the cottage, but there was no sign of her.

When he emerged from the woods, he found that the hens had been released outside; they loitered in front of the closed cottage door and he had to step over them to get to it. As he pushed it open, he heard an unexpected male voice. John Corbett stood next to the fireplace, while Liam crouched before it, adding turf to the fire. Ellen and Bridget occupied the same places at the table as they had earlier, but the rushlight had been blown out. The children were still not awake.

'—refusing to tell us where they got their information,' John was saying. There was a faint stain on his upper lip, a remnant of the bloody nose he had acquired in the barn. 'Not one of them has given in, despite our...persuasive efforts.'

Neither Bridget nor Ellen looked happy at the insinuation in that remark, but they didn't comment.

As Cormac shut the door behind him, he glanced at Bridget. She avoided eye contact. He sat on the bench next to Ellen.

Liam stood up from the hearth, wiping turf dust off his hands. 'John's just been filling us in,' he told Cormac. 'The constables won't reveal how they found out about the meeting.'

'Our highest priority has to be to identify the informant in our midst,' said John gravely.

'It wasn't me,' Bridget said at once. 'Please, John, you have to believe me.'

'I do believe you,' he said. 'But I may have a hard time convincing the others of the same. 'Tis easier for them to believe 'tis you than to imagine one of us is a traitor.'

'Do you have any idea who it could be?' asked Cormac.

'Not a notion.' John shook his head. 'It makes no sense why anyone would do it.'

'Maybe they took a bribe,' said Liam. 'Money's a powerful motivator.'

'Maybe. But 'tis hard to think of anyone willing to be a Judas when so much is at stake.' John stepped in front of the hearth and put his hands behind his back to warm them. 'Speaking of money, that's the other reason I came to talk to you. 'Tis been two months since our last "donation" from our anonymous benefactor. I gave what was left of it to Ben Bracken and his ma to tide them over after their eviction. But we can't sit around waiting for another payment, 'cause who knows when it'll run out. Maybe our benefactor will grow bored, or broke. So I want to discuss where we can gather more funds. We've added a nice selection of rifles to our cache, and now we'll need ammunition for them.'

Liam cast a fleeting, awkward look towards Cormac and Bridget before resting his hand on Ellen's shoulder. 'We've recently come into some unexpected money. We might be able to contribute it to the cause.'

Cormac's sick feeling intensified. He had sent that money to help his mother survive; the idea of it being used for weapons was so contrary to its original purpose that he couldn't even pretend to be comfortable with it. He rubbed the back of his neck apprehensively. Bridget too looked unhappy.

Ellen reached up to touch Liam's fingers. 'That money's for our family. How it's used is a decision to be made by both of us without an audience.'

Contrite, Liam dipped his head, and John's hopeful expression faded. Before he could persuade Ellen to reconsider, they heard squawks outside and a loud thump on the door. They all stared at each other in dismay. Ellen pressed her hand to her pocket, while Liam went silently to the dresser, extracting another knife from one of its drawers.

Then a voice called, 'John? You in there?'

John let out an exasperated breath. 'Jaysus, 'tis just young Denis.'

He strode over and swung out the top half of the door.

'Next time announce your name as soon as you knock, lad. Nearly scared us to death.'

Denis was sweating, his face pale. 'Heard you might be here. You need to come right now.'

'What's the matter? Come where?'

'Hogan Farm.'

John stiffened. 'Have the prisoners escaped?'

'No,' said Denis. "Tis something worse. Mr Enright's there.'

'What for, for Christ's sake? Does he want Ben and his ma living in a hole in the ground?'

'He's not there in his official capacity.' Denis swallowed. 'He...he's been badly hurt.'

'Hurt?' said Liam. 'How?'

Denis's pallor took on a greenish hue. 'You'd just better come see.'

John opened the bottom half of the door to leave. Liam started to put the knife back in the drawer, seemed to think better of it, and tucked it into his boot. Cormac, reminded uneasily of the days in Dublin when he had never walked anywhere without a dagger on his person, felt no inclination to arm himself as he rose to join them.

Bridget stood too, pressing her fingertips to the tabletop. 'I understand if the response to this is no, but I should like to come too, if I may. I wish to speak with Mr Enright and try to reconcile your current account of him with the man I used to know. I still find it difficult to comprehend his present indifference to the tenants' plight when he had previously been their staunch advocate. Not to mention, he might be able to provide some insight into the motives for my mother's behaviour.'

'I don't know if he'll be able for much conversation,' Denis mumbled.

Cormac caught the footman's eye. 'Who else is at Hogan Farm?'

'Paddy Hogan, Ben Bracken and his ma. And two men guarding the prisoners down in the cellar.'

He turned to John, who shrugged and said, 'She's probably safe enough. She'll be with us, which makes the numbers pretty even, given that I can't see old Mrs Bracken posing much of a threat.'

'Are you sure?' Cormac asked Bridget, their recent argument still tingling on his tongue.

She looked at him directly for the first time since he had re-entered the cottage. Her gaze was resolute. 'I'm sure. Let's go.'

## Chapter 9

No one spoke all the way to Hogan Farm. They took a circuitous route to avoid encountering any members of the constabulary scouring the main road, and approached the farm from behind up a steep incline. Cormac fought to keep exhaustion at bay; he had not slept in more than twenty-four hours and his hip was aching where he had fallen on it in the barn. He had developed a slight headache at his temple, but that had faded in the fresh March breeze.

Denis gulped as he led them towards the front door of the farmhouse. 'I don't know what to say to prepare ye. Miss Bridget, you might be better off staying out here.'

'I do appreciate your concern,' she said, 'but I'll come in.' She squared her shoulders.

Reluctantly, he ushered them inside. The first thing Cormac registered upon crossing the threshold was the stench of blood. The second was the moans of pain. And the third was the indignity of what lay before his eyes.

Farmer Hogan had a large kitchen table, even though he had no wife to preside over it. A pile of dirty cloths, a couple of spoons and an upturned bowl lay discarded on the floor beside it, looking like they had been thrust aside in a hurry to clear the surface. The farmer, wearing a big coat despite being indoors, was leaning over a trembling body laid out on top.

Bridget gagged and covered her mouth.

Mr Enright had been stripped down to his drawers. Someone had smashed his spectacles and then replaced them on the bridge of his nose, where they perched in a sad mockery of their original function. Angry bruises bloomed on almost every visible piece of his skin. And, the very worst of all, the tips of his fingers and toes were bloody stumps: every one of his nails had been wrenched off.

'Holy Mother of God,' said John.

Cormac struggled against his own gag reflex, a sour taste rising in the back of his throat. Liam put a hand out to the wall to steady himself and Denis kept his eyes averted, having already seen enough earlier. Nobody seemed to want to venture further into the room.

Farmer Hogan came over to them, sticking his hands deep in his coat pockets.

'Glad you could come, John,' he said in a glum voice. ''Tis an awful business.' He glanced back over his shoulder as Mr Enright emitted another weak groan. 'I know he's done wrong but 'tisn't fair to leave him in this shape. I caught one of the McKinty youngsters hanging around, probably hoping for a glimpse of the prisoners, so I sent him off to get his ma. She'd know better than me what to do here.'

'That was the right thing, Paddy, regardless of his sins,' said John. Appalled, he approached the table. He reached out as though to press a comforting hand to the agent's arm, but pulled back before he touched the bruised skin. 'Help's on its way, sir. Hold on as best you can.'

'Is —' Bridget's voice came out so cracked that she had to swallow and try again. 'Is there a blanket we could cover him with? H-he must be frozen.'

Farmer Hogan nodded. He crossed to a door at the other end of the room and called out through it. A distant voice responded. The farmer returned to them and said, 'Ben says he'll bring a blanket down in a minute. He's just getting his ma up. I'll give the poor sod my coat in the meantime.'

He shrugged out of his big coat and John helped him lay it over Mr Enright's brawny torso, careful not to brush against his wounded hands or feet. Cautious though they were, the agent whimpered in pain.

They stepped away from the table, rejoining the others by the door.

'Tell us what happened, Paddy,' said John.

Farmer Hogan raised his hand to scratch his forehead and Cormac spotted the slight tremor in his fingers. 'Well, we finished up down below just before dawn, as you know. Once most of the folk were gone, I went to check on my guests upstairs. Poor Mrs Bracken was shaking like a leaf after all the commotion. Ben said he'd take care of her so I headed for my bed, but I was hardly asleep when I heard this almighty banging on the front door. I came down and opened it, and there was the agent splayed out on the doorstep like a dead rat. I thought he was a goner until he groaned. There was no one else in sight so I don't know who did the banging. Ben helped me bring him in. Denis was still down in the cellar helping to guard the constables, so I sent him running for yourself.'

Before he could say anything else, a brisk knock heralded Maisie McKinty's appearance.

'I debated over whether to come, if I'm honest,' she said by way of greeting, entering with a basket covered in a cloth. 'But I'd better help the poor craythur. Sure, he's not going to be carrying out any more evictions any time soon.' She looked over at the kitchen table. 'Jesus, Mary and Joseph!' she said, putting out a hand on Cormac's arm to catch her balance. She leaned on him as she said, "Tis worse than I pictured it.'

She gave him a squeeze and a surreptitious wink before detaching herself and going over to the table, removing the cloth to reveal strips of bandages inside the basket. Cormac glanced at Bridget. Her eyebrows were raised; the wink had not been surreptitious enough.

Grimacing, he asked the others, 'Do we have any theories as to who did this?'

'Someone who was enraged enough to be this brutal,' said John. 'And they must have done it fairly quick last night. Who disappeared after the rumpus in the barn was over? Didn't come with the prisoners here?'

'A fair few,' said Denis, his complexion still pallid. 'We couldn't have all gone traipsing through the woods. But my money's on Joseph Hayes and Bernie Cuddihy. I thought it mighty strange that they, of all people, didn't go with us, and now I'm thinking maybe it was 'cause they had other plans in mind.'

John rubbed the back of his hand across his mouth. 'How could they know where to find him though?'

Maisie called over, 'Sure, didn't he just carry out an eviction yesterday? He had to still be in the area, couldn't have gone much further than the nearest inn suitable for a gentleman. Not too hard to find when there's only one of those for miles around. That Blackcastle place on the road to Tullow, y'know.'

Mr Enright let out an exclamation of pain as she lightly pressed a bandage over one of his fingertips and he began to cry in distressing, choking gasps. A tiny, strangled sound escaped from Bridget's own throat. She slipped past Cormac and tentatively approached the table, leaning close to Mr Enright's ear.

'Mr Enright,' she murmured. 'Can you hear me? It's Bridget, Lady Courcey's daughter.'

The agent squeezed his eyes shut, his broken spectacles quivering with the force of his sobs. Bridget eased them gently off his nose and set them aside. She put a soothing hand on the crown of his head and tried again.

'Mr Enright, do you know who I am? Do you recognise me?'

Eyes still closed, he managed an almost imperceptible nod.

'I can't express how sorry I am that this has happened to you,' she said. 'But I assure you I will do everything in my power to bring your assailants to justice.' She stroked his hair, like she was calming a distraught child. 'Did you know them? Can you identify them for us?'

He sluggishly turned his head to one side and back to the other in his best effort at a shake.

John said, 'I wonder does that mean he didn't recognise them, or did they threaten him not to reveal their identities?'

Bridget bent towards the agent's ear again. 'Did they keep their faces concealed?'

He nodded again, tears leaking down his temples to the tabletop. His mouth worked and he stuttered, 'T-two...'

'There were two of them?' asked Bridget. 'Two people attacked you?'

'Y-yes...'

'Were you at Blackcastle Inn? Was that where they found you?'

He shuddered and at last opened his eyes to look up at her.

Whatever she saw in his expression, it was enough for her to say, 'Just rest for now, Mr Enright. Don't worry about anything except getting better. Maisie will take good care of you.'

'I will, I suppose,' said Maisie indifferently.

Bridget shot her an accusatory glance. 'Try to remember he's a human being first, and an agent second,' she said.

Maisie looked like she was preparing a cutting rejoinder but then the door at the far end of the kitchen opened and a man with weather-beaten skin came through, clutching a blanket and supporting an elderly woman around her hunched shoulders.

'Don't look, Ma,' Ben Bracken said, but she shook him off.

'I will indeed look.' She hobbled over to the table, her back so stooped that she was nearly at Mr Enright's eye level. She regarded him for a beat. 'You got what was coming to you,' she said and turned away.

'Ma,' said Ben, flushing bright red. 'Where's your compassion?'

'He showed none to us when he forced us out of our home.'

'He did,' Ben protested. 'Don't you remember how apologetic he was? He said he would've spared us if he could.'

'Lies,' Mrs Bracken said dismissively. She scanned the room. 'Still free, John Corbett? Heard the constables nearly got ye.'

'We lived to tell the tale,' said John. 'They're tied up below our feet now.'

She snorted. 'Incompetent fools. Even with the right information, they couldn't do their jobs.'

John looked at her sharply. 'The right information?'

Ben said, 'Be quiet, Ma.'

'No good in that anymore,' she said. 'May as well own up. It came to naught in any case.' She smiled sweetly. 'And what harm would they do a little old woman like me?'

Everyone in the room went very still. Even Maisie paused in her attention to Mr Enright's wounds to gape at Mrs Bracken.

Ben pressed the heel of his hand to his forehead. When he dropped it, his leathery features were suffused with shame. 'Please forgive her, John. Yesterday was an upsetting experience. Ma thought they might let us keep our home if she gave them information about the uprising. While I was inside trying to plead with Mr Enright, she went out to the constables and told them about the meeting. But then they evicted us anyway. She made me stay with her here last night so that I wouldn't get caught up in the raid. And she didn't tell me the truth until this morning. Otherwise, I swear I would've warned ye.'

By the time he had finished, his words were barely audible. She, on the other hand, laughed loudly.

'Do what ye want with me. Sure, what have I got left now? This foolhardy rebellion's robbed me of one son's life and the other son's ability to earn wages and put food on our table. My daughter's gone for years, seeing the city as a better option than this godforsaken place. And that scoundrel there has robbed me of my final wish to die in the home where my parents and grandparents and great-grandparents on my mother's side all lived and died. The whole damned lot of ye can rot in hell.'

Her wrinkled face was a mask of bitterness and grief. Without waiting for their response, she shuffled back out the way she had come in.

Ben lowered his gaze. 'John, I'm so sorry.'

John grimaced. 'She's been hard done by so I can't say I blame her. I don't appreciate the way she handled it but that's neither here nor there now. At least we came out on the winning side of the raid.'

Shoulders slumped, Ben approached the table holding out the blanket. Bridget took it from him and, with Maisie's help, removed Farmer Hogan's big coat and replaced it with the blanket, tucking it around Mr Enright's battered torso and legs using slow, careful movements. Even so, he uttered incoherent ejaculations of pain. Maisie made soft, crooning noises that verged on mocking in tone. Cormac saw Bridget's jaw tighten.

John folded his arms. 'Well, now we've identified our informant, our next step is to establish who's responsible for this abomination. We need to track down Joseph and Bernie and find out whether it was them that did this.'

'If it was, they'll have gone to hide out somewhere,' said Liam. 'They won't go anyplace obvious like The Pikeman.'

'We'll put the word out for folk to start asking around,' said John. 'See if anyone's come across them since last night. We should send someone up to Blackcastle Inn as well.'

'If it's not too much to ask,' said Cormac, 'could you get them to mention my family as well? I intend to make my own enquiries in Ballydarry this afternoon, but the more people spreading the word, the better.'

'True,' John agreed. 'We'll do that.'

Cormac paused, then surprised himself by hurrying on, 'We might not be able to stay around to help with the uprising. I do recognise the importance of what you're doing but I have to prioritise the search for my family.'

Denis in particular looked dismayed but John gave a disappointed nod. ''Tis the reason ye came back in the first place. Ye've got to put them first.'

'Strikes me as unpatriotic,' muttered Maisie as she finished bandaging one of Mr Enright's hands and moved on to the other.

Bridget glared at her before saying pointedly, 'Thank you for understanding, John.' She betrayed no hint that her and Cormac's most recent private conversation had constituted a blazing argument about their involvement in the uprising.

Next to her, Ben said, 'I don't follow.'

'I'm looking for my family,' Cormac told him. 'They disappeared from the estate about seven and a half years ago and I'm desperately trying to locate them now.'

'I'm sorry to hear that,' said Ben. 'Who went missing?'

'My mother,' said Cormac, his heart cracking a little bit more every time he gave this description, 'and my three sisters, who all had dark hair, and —'

'Did they have a baby with them?' Ben interrupted.

Cormac stood stock-still. 'They did. My nephew. He would have been about three months old.'

Incredibly, Ben said, 'I think I remember them.'

Into the stunned silence, Cormac said, 'You do?' His pulse raced.

'If I recall rightly, there was a woman, two or three girls and a small baby, I couldn't tell if it was a girl or boy.'

'When was this? Where did you see them? Please tell me everything you know,' Cormac begged.

Everyone in the room was now gawking at Ben, who took a few reluctant steps forwards. Self-conscious, he fidgeted with the sleeve of his shirt, pinching the material as he spoke.

'As Ma mentioned, I've a sister who lives in Dublin. She went there years ago looking for work and got a maid's position in one of them fancy townhouses. We were fierce close as children so I've always tried to visit her as often as I can, about every ten months or so. Until he died, my brother looked after our ma and my work here while I was gone. But 'tis harder to get away now that 'tis just me and Ma. When I do go, I travel up to the city with my donkey and cart so's I can bring bits and pieces to Annie and sometimes I make room in my cart for other travellers who cross my path, 'specially if the folk are going a long way.'

'And you made room for my family?' asked Cormac, daring to hope.

'"Tis very likely. It was a long time ago and there've been many different faces over the years. But those ones stood out for me.'

'Why?'

'They were all so sad,' was Ben's simple answer. 'I was already several miles away from Oakleigh when I passed them. They were just sitting at the side of the road. It looked like they'd given up, like they couldn't go a single step further. But I don't think it was out of exhaustion. I think it was out of hopelessness.'

Cormac's chest constricted painfully. He knew what that feeling was like and he would not wish it upon anyone, least of all his poor, innocent family.

'I took pity on them,' Ben continued. He had created a stiff peak on his sleeve with all the pinching and he flattened it back down. 'They weren't heading anywhere in particular so I convinced them to get on the cart and come to Dublin with me. At least they'd have a chance in the city as opposed to staying where they were.'

'And they went with you?' pressed Cormac. 'All the way to Dublin? Where did you bring them to?'

Ben shifted from one foot to the other. 'I brought them as far into the city as I could and set them down on a street with lodgings on it. My memory's a bit shaky but the name of the lodgings was O'Meara's or O'Hara's, something like that. That was the last I saw of them 'cause I had to leave them then and go to my sister. It was the best I could do.'

'It was far more than you were obligated to do,' said Cormac, relief flooding through him. It had been so unlikely but here was a solid lead on his family's whereabouts. He wanted to kiss the man's boots with gratitude. 'Thank you very much for your kindness to them and for your help to me. I am indebted to you.'

He went over to shake Ben's hand, wringing it with vigour.

'Good luck with your search,' said Ben. 'I hope you find them.'

Behind him, Maisie shook out another strip of bandage from her basket. 'I guess this means you'll be running out on us as fast as your legs can carry you,' she said sourly.

'That's no concern of yours, Maisie,' Liam said in quiet admonishment. 'And you can't make him feel guilty for it.'

She huffed, cast a resentful glance in Cormac's direction, and returned her attention to Mr Enright's supine form.

Bridget stepped away from the table to come to Cormac's side. 'We may not go immediately. We have some things we need to discuss first.'

When he caught her eye, her gaze said 'not here'.

'As do we,' said John. ''Tis time we begin our own search to see if we can root out that slippery pair.'

He, Liam and Denis held a quick discussion and decided that John would make his way to Blackcastle Inn as he was the only one who owned a horse, while Liam and Denis would start spreading the word among the tenants about seeking out Joseph Hayes and Bernie Cuddihy, or anyone else liable to have carried out the vicious beating on Mr Enright.

John turned to Farmer Hogan. 'Can we leave him here with you, Paddy?'

The farmer bobbed his head. 'Myself and Ben will try to get him upstairs into a bed as soon as he's able for it.'

'Best pick a room with a lock so Ma can't get in and finish him off,' said Ben, seemingly in jest, though no one laughed.

With a final word of heartfelt thanks to Ben, Cormac and Bridget followed John, Liam and Denis to the door. Outside, they all took deep breaths to clear the reek of Mr Enright's blood from their noses.

'I've never seen anything like it,' said Denis weakly.

'I hope you never will again,' said John, squeezing the younger man's shoulder. He looked at Cormac and Bridget. 'Will we see ye again before ye leave?'

'You will,' promised Bridget.

They parted, setting off in various directions from the farmhouse. Cormac and Bridget followed the route they had taken to get there, descending the slope at the back of the farmhouse. It fell away towards a wide meadow, with a stretch of woodland on the horizon. As they entered the meadow, the tall grass nearly up to their knees, Bridget slid her left hand into Cormac's right.

'Can you believe it?' she said, her eyes shining with hopefulness. 'What good fortune that Ben was here.'

'It was an extraordinary stroke of luck,' he said. 'Now we know they made it all the way to Dublin and there will be no need to search every village, town and country lane between here and there. And we even have a place to begin our search in the city, if we can find those lodgings. We've been tremendously fortunate, which is a far cry from where I thought we were when the sun rose this morning.'

A loaded silence fell as their altercation at dawn billowed up again between them. He was the one to break it.

'I'm sorry for our quarrel.' He rubbed his thumb over her knuckles, grazing the circles of thread and gold on her ring finger.

'I'm sorry too,' she replied at once.

'I must especially apologise for accusing you of not wanting to lose Oakleigh.' He hung his head. 'I know your concerns were based on more selfless motivations than that.'

She waved her free hand as though banishing his apology among the blades of grass. 'I understand you meant no ill intent. But what you said in the farmhouse…about not staying to help with the uprising after all…'

He sighed. 'I feel so torn about it,' he admitted. 'On the one hand, I want the tenants to prevail. The land is theirs and they have every right to try to take it back. But on the other hand, I have to concede the point you made earlier: their methods are misguided. Could they be depended upon to rule themselves with good judgement? It is a matter of profound concern that some of them would deem this attack on Mr Enright a suitable path to take.' He swallowed. 'Dear God, that poor man's injuries. You wouldn't do it to a dog, let alone a human being.'

'It was truly appalling,' she said with a shudder.

'Perhaps we should rethink our level of involvement here, particularly now that we have a promising lead on the whereabouts of my family. All things considered, we are probably better off departing as soon as possible.'

She hesitated. 'Might I suggest one last contribution to the cause ahead of our departure? I believe it is imperative that I visit my mother before we leave.'

She waited nervously for his reaction but he didn't make any protestation.

Encouraged, she went on, 'It would not be a social call but an intercession on behalf of the people she has crushed. I cannot stand idly by when I am the only one in a position to reason with her. If she will receive me at the manor, I might be able to communicate the harm that she is causing and convince her to stop her destructive behaviour. There is no one else here who would have any hope of achieving this and so I must try, for their sakes. Surely, you see that I must.'

'I do see,' he said, knowing she was absolutely right. 'I agree with you and I think we should pay her a visit without delay.'

'You don't have to come,' she said, looking surprised. 'I do not expect you to—'

'I wouldn't dream of leaving you to face her alone,' he interrupted. 'I will be there to support you in this duty.'

She offered him a small smile but her expression was troubled. He comprehended that his presence could very well do more harm than good but there wasn't even the slightest possibility that he was going to let her call upon Lady Courcey without him by her side. The lady might say anything to get Bridget in her clutches again and, if she attempted to do it, he had to be there to prevent it. He did not want to offend Bridget by articulating out loud that she did not have the power to resist Lady Courcey by herself, but she knew as well as he did that the lady's best skill was manipulating others to suit her own ends and Bridget had proven herself all too susceptible in the past.

'Ought we to invite Ellen to come too?' she asked. 'My mother once exhibited a fondness towards her in her own limited way.'

'We can certainly ask her,' he said, 'although she may feel obliged to refuse out of loyalty to Liam.' He glanced up at the sky. 'There's time today. We should visit Lady Courcey this afternoon. And tomorrow we can continue our journey to Dublin.'

They reached the woodland at the far end of the meadow. As they slipped in among the trees, Cormac became pensive, contemplating the knowledge that Ben had given him. His family had managed to reach Dublin following their eviction from the estate. That meant they had been in the city at the same time as him; it was a wonder and a shame that their paths had never crossed. Were they still there now? He allowed himself the tiniest measure of optimism. Their mission was not as desperate as it had seemed an hour ago.

But coupled with that optimism was a quiver of worry. Following his family's tracks to Dublin meant returning to Cunningham's territory. He had thieved from the money lender the last time he had set foot in the city; he thoroughly hoped he would not encounter him this time.

Bridget squeezed his hand, rousing him from his thoughts.

'I feel I must broach the issue of Maisie McKinty,' she said. 'Does she have an attraction towards you?'

'I think she does,' he said, wincing. 'Borne out of boredom, I would hazard. From what I can gather, her husband is a bit simple.'

'She seems to have become rather embittered since the days she used to give us hunks of cheese. I find her to be quite an unlikeable woman now.'

'As do I.'

'Good,' said Bridget. After a beat, she added, 'But her behaviour did get me wondering. Did you…that is, have you ever…been with anyone else besides me?'

She peeked up at him sideways through her eyelashes and then looked away into the trees.

He baulked. He hadn't anticipated the question and didn't know how best to respond. Thomasina swam into his mind: long, black hair and bulging breasts, brazen and sultry and disinclined to take no for an answer. He couldn't imagine Bridget would take too kindly to the idea of him sharing a bed with a whore.

So, to preserve their newly restored peace, he lied.

'No,' he said. 'There was no one else.'

She didn't look back at him but he saw the corner of her mouth turn up.

They walked on through the woods, choosing an alternative meandering route to the one they had taken to get to Hogan Farm, just to err on the side of caution.

He yawned. 'I'm worn out. Can I suggest some food and a nap at the cottage before we go to the manor?'

'Oh, yes, please. I could nearly sleep standing up.'

As they navigated a dense thicket of trees further on, he misjudged the distance to one trunk and bumped his hip against it. A hiss escaped his teeth.

'What is it?' she asked as he let go of her hand and touched the sore spot.

'Just my damn hip. I fell on it last night during the raid. Feels like I've got a big bruise there.' Remembering the extent of Mr Enright's contusions, he said guiltily, 'It's nothing to complain about.'

'Are you sure? Do you want me to take a look at it?'

He faltered. When he peered at her, her expression was innocent apart from the mischievous glint in her eye.

'I don't know. Do you think it requires an examination?'

'Possibly. To make certain you haven't acquired a serious injury, of course.'

'Well, in that case...'

He stood still and opened his arms wide to invite her appraisal. When she stepped into his embrace, however, her concentration focused not on his hip but on a sensitive area of skin on his throat which appeared very receptive to the caress of her lips.

'I thought you were tired,' he murmured.

'I thought you were too.'

He tilted up her chin so that her lips landed on his own and they kissed deeply. He slid his hands into her hair; since they had left London, she could no longer style it in the latest fashion and now her loose curls tumbled untamed down her neck, as they used to when she had been a free-spirited girl roaming around Oakleigh with a wild boy at her side. He dug deep into the chestnut-coloured mane, feeling the shape of her skull beneath his fingers. Some things about her were still unknown to him. He craved the day when every contour of her, even the curve of her skull, was as familiar to him as the lips he was kissing now.

Those lips continued to revere his mouth, accompanied by a tongue that was equally assiduous in its attentions. Even as she kissed him with such ardour, her hands acted separately, opening the buttons of his coat and gliding inside. Her nimble fingers found the buttons of his waistcoat and unfastened them one by one. Pushing the waistcoat aside, she tugged at his shirt until she had liberated the front of it from his trousers. She reached up inside it, fondling his abdomen and chest. Then, very deliberately, she touched a fingertip to one of his nipples.

He gasped into her mouth. She didn't release him, only pressed her lips harder against his and caressed his nipple with unrelenting, excruciating single-mindedness. It grew more and more sensitive, while the other ached for similar consideration. Her tongue and her finger moved in unison, stroking until he was nearly undone on the spot.

Shuddering with need, he grappled for her skirts, jerking them up past her knees and thighs. The woods surrounding them were deserted but a battalion could have been congregated there watching them and he wouldn't have cared. Lips still joined, he shifted their positions so her back was to the tree he had collided with. With her skirts bundled about her waist, he lifted her up against the trunk, and she slung her unoccupied arm about his neck and locked her legs around his hips. If it hurt, he didn't notice. All he could focus on was that merciless fingertip. He skimmed his own fingers inside her drawers over her inner thighs and higher, and it became her turn to breathe her pleasure into his mouth. Her legs tightened their grip and, at last, her hand moved to address his other nipple.

He sensed her urgency and desire for forgiveness, for they were the same as his own. It had felt unnatural to fight with her the way they had; not even in their childhood had they quarrelled often, having seen eye to eye on most matters. This, then, was their act of contrition.

Bless me, Father, for I have sinned, he thought. And then for several minutes all capacity for rational thought escaped him.

## Chapter 10

Bridget rubbed her eyes and suppressed a yawn, before climbing down the ladder from the loft to the ground floor of the cottage. Cormac had already risen from their much-needed nap and was seated at the table, scrubbing at the hem of his coat with a bristly brush. His shaving things were laid out on the tabletop and his cheeks and chin were already smooth. She felt a small pang of regret; she had been partial to his rough stubble and the arousing sensation of it upon her skin.

She sat on the bench next to him and leaned in to rub her jaw against his. As her skin glided over the silky smoothness, she revised her opinion: both variations were highly pleasing.

His cheek moved as he smiled briefly but he didn't stop scouring his coat hem, brushing away the mud that had crusted there after so many days on the road.

'I ought to do my own too,' she said.

'Already done,' he said and jerked his chin towards the other side of the table where her cloak was spread out on the opposite bench, hem spotless.

He bent his head back to his task and she watched him work, making sharp strokes with the brush. His mouth was a thin line. She could only guess at the strain that was mounting in him right now – he was about to face the woman who had scattered and devastated his family. She hoped he would be able to control his temper. If he got very angry with Lady Courcey, she would take offence and be far less willing to engage with them.

A gust of air swirled into the room as Ellen came through the door with Liam Óg, Aidan and Emily in tow. All four of them looked windswept while Emily, beaming, carried a bucket full of water.

'We went to the well,' she announced to her parents, 'and I pulled up the bucket!'

'Well done,' Bridget said, and she and Ellen laughed at her unintended pun.

Cormac said nothing, only cast the bucket a dark glance as Emily handed it to Ellen along with its coiled rope. Bridget thought it likely that the bucket was the same one the McGoverns had used when they lived in the cottage, but the rope had to be newer, given that the original one lay rotting in the woods beneath the tree branch where Cormac's sister Mary had taken her own life. Bridget touched his shoulder in silent acknowledgement of that tragedy, then drew Emily towards her to neaten her hair and present the hem of her cloak for her father's eagle-eyed inspection.

Ellen had offered to take care of Emily while Bridget and Cormac went to visit Lady Courcey but Bridget had declined for two reasons. In the first place, she was eager to show Emily around the home in which she had grown up, while Emily was excited at the prospect of seeing her mother's bedchamber and the orchard and the stables. Bridget's second motive was the slim possibility that the sight of her grandchild might soften Lady Courcey more than any logical argument her daughter could present to her. It meant breaking the vow she had made on the night of Emily's birth that Lady Courcey would never set eyes on the child, but Bridget was prepared to maximise any advantage that would help make her mother see sense.

Cormac set the brush on the table and stood, shrugging into his coat. He held his body awkwardly as though his hip was paining him. Guiltily, Bridget recalled their exertions in the woods; if truth be told, her own back was rather sore. Still, she felt no urge to repent.

'We should go now,' said Cormac, with the air of one preparing for battle.

'I'm sorry I can't go with you,' said Ellen with true sincerity. She had refused their offer to come; as Cormac had suspected, her past service to the lady did not outweigh her lifetime commitment to honour her husband.

'We understand,' said Bridget. 'I do hope we'll return with positive news.'

'I hope so too,' Ellen replied, her expression nonetheless troubled.

Bridget swung on her cloak and she, Cormac and Emily departed from the cottage.

They embarked upon the route that Bridget and Cormac had trodden hundreds of times in their youth, up the lane and across the fields towards the manor house. The wind had picked up by a considerable degree since that morning; the tops of the trees bent sideways under fierce gusts and the leaves fluttered madly in the hedgerows. Emily kept laughing every time Cormac's cap threatened to blow away on him. He laughed too for her sake but otherwise he remained tight-lipped.

As they crossed Oakleigh property, they perceived further signs of the revolt that had left the land abandoned. Crop fields lay uncultivated, weeds grew unchecked, and the hedges were ragged as though they had not been trimmed in a long time. There was a distinct air of disuse about the place. In the field containing the giant's claw, they surveyed the three-pronged rock formation with unease. Were there weapons buried beneath it right now? The wind blew furious ripples across the sea of grass, as if it were the giant's laboured breathing. Bridget grasped Emily's hand and they hurried on.

They reached the last field, the Gorteen; a single crow rose up from the turf and wheeled away into the sky, cawing loudly. Shutting the gate to the Gorteen behind them, they proceeded into the manor grounds. All was eerily quiet. They passed the empty paddock and the stables to enter the cobbled courtyard, where they got their first close-up view of the house. Bridget inhaled sharply. The red-bricked manor was in a sorry state. The windows were grimy and the ivy, which had previously been an elegant adornment, had been allowed to spread uncontrolled over the walls and now encroached on every shutter and window sill.

Cormac approached the stables and pulled open the double doors. One of the doors flew out of his grip as the wind caught it and it banged sorrowfully against the wall. Inside, they gazed around in dismay. Dirty straw was strewn everywhere on the ground. A saddle had been discarded in front of one of the stalls and never picked up. The silence was deafening with the absence of stamping hooves, whinnies and snorts, men's voices calling to each other or murmuring to the horses. Cormac rested his palm on the half door of a stall, his posture slumped. With a wrench of sadness, Bridget wondered what had happened to her white mare, Bonny.

A rat scurried across the space and darted out of sight. She yelped and hauled Emily back outside. Cormac followed, closing the double doors on their memories. Heart swelling with sorrow, Bridget turned away and her glance alighted on the orchard door, its green paint peeling. She walked towards it with a sense of dread. Pushing it open, she stepped through to a wilderness that was both like and unlike the orchard she had known. The brush underfoot was a mess of rotten apples that had fallen the previous autumn and had since disintegrated into mulch. The spring daffodils had bloomed as usual but there had been no gardener to prune them back so now they hung limp and dying from their stems. However, the apple trees still stood as strong and verdant as ever and she was thankful that they at least had withstood the widespread neglect that had befallen the estate.

'Do you think our oak tree has survived?' Cormac muttered behind her.

'I would like to think that not even my mother could defeat our mighty oak tree,' she said.

Her gaze fell upon Emily peering wide-eyed around the orchard and she suddenly regretted bringing her along to witness this scene of desolation which fell so far below the high expectations she had given the little girl.

'Is this really where you grew up, Mama?' Emily asked in a small voice.

'Yes, but I am afraid it has not been looked after very well. Come, let us go visit Grandmama now. She won't be expecting us so our appearance will give her quite a surprise.'

They returned to the courtyard, staring up once again at the dismal-looking manor house.

'I think we should go in through the kitchens,' said Bridget. 'I would not feel comfortable entering by the front door.'

She crossed the cobbles and tried the latch on the kitchen door, which opened with a groan. The kitchens were dark and empty but there were signs that someone had been there not too long ago: a dim glow emanated from a pile of embers in the hearth, some dirty dishes were stacked on a bench, and a meagre amount of white flour lay abandoned on the tabletop. Bridget conjured up an image in her mind of Mrs Kavanagh presiding over this space, giving orders left, right and centre to the kitchen maids, and beaming with satisfaction when everything ran smoothly in her domain. She felt her throat tighten and hastened to get through the kitchens. There were two inner doors, one opening onto the servants' staircase and the other providing access above stairs into the back of the manor's entrance hall. She chose the latter, making for the narrow stairs beyond and leading Cormac and Emily up the steps.

They emerged into the expansive entrance hall. This looked much the same as it always had except that a thick layer of dust lay over every surface, from the handrails on the mahogany staircase to the framed paintings on the walls. They had taken no more than half a dozen steps into the hall when at last they heard sounds of movement from the floor above.

A girl came into view at the top of the grand staircase. Bridget recognised her as the scullery maid, Cathy, whom she had met on Lady Courcey's sole visit to Wyndham House at the time of Emily's birth. There were stains on her apron and straggly bits of knotted brown hair escaped from underneath her maid's cap. She was carrying a bucket and a mop and looked stressed as she descended the stairs in a hurry.

She had almost reached the bottom when she caught sight of Bridget, Cormac and Emily. Letting out a strangled shriek, she dropped her cleaning paraphernalia and clutched the banister to keep her balance. The bucket and mop clattered down the last few steps into the hall; fortunately, the bucket was almost empty and only a spatter of water wet the floor. Bridget heard a muffled call from somewhere nearby but disregarded it.

'Good afternoon, Cathy. Do you remember me? You served your mistress at my house in London several years ago. My name is Bridget and I am Lady Courcey's daughter.'

Cathy curtseyed awkwardly on the stairs but seemed unable to utter a word. Cormac stepped forwards and picked up the bucket and mop. Holding them out to the girl, he said, 'You are obviously busy at work. Are you keeping this whole house by yourself?'

She took the bucket and mop, nodding. 'I try to do the best I can but I'm not able to keep up with it all.'

'I am not surprised,' said Bridget. 'This house is designed to be kept by a staff of dozens and you are only one person. How do you even attempt to manage it?'

Cathy's face lifted a little to be receiving some pity. 'I devote my time to one main chore each day and do as much of it as possible. Today I'm mopping all the floors. Yesterday I washed all the dirty dishes but they're already piling up again.' She looked dejected. 'I can never complete a task 'cause there's just too much to do and the day is never long enough. And I have to stop whenever her ladyship calls. Sometimes 'tis hours before I can get back to my work.'

Bridget shook her head. 'You cannot keep going like this or you will wear yourself out.'

'Forgive me but my mistress says it must be done and I'm the only one left to do it.' Cathy cast her gaze down to the floor.

It was another black mark against Lady Courcey to be working this poor girl like a slave.

Frowning, Bridget said, 'We came here to see your mistress. Can you please announce our presence and ask if she is prepared to receive us now?'

'Right away, m'lady,' Cathy said, even though Bridget had purposely omitted any title when introducing herself. Scuttling down the last few steps, the maid placed the mop into the bucket and leaned it against the newel of the stairs. Then she crossed the entrance hall to the door into the drawing room, knocked softly and entered.

Bridget heard a faint voice demand, 'Did you not hear me call? What was that clatter I heard?'

'Beg pardon, m'lady,' came Cathy's reply. Her voice had become high-pitched. 'I dropped my mop and bucket. I didn't mean to disturb you. Your ladyship, you've got visitors. Your daughter's here to see you and she's with a man and a little girl. Shall I send them in?'

Total silence greeted the maid's words but Lady Courcey must have waved or nodded her acquiescence for Cathy reappeared in the hall and declared that her ladyship would see them now. Bridget and Cormac exchanged apprehensive glances as they approached the drawing room. Bridget did not fear her mother anymore but she had no expectation that this would be a pleasant encounter. How badly would the lady react to their appearance?

## Chapter 11

Bridget crossed the threshold first. The air smelled dank. The meagre light struggling through the filthy windows suffused the drawing room with a grey pallor and the lack of a fire in the hearth only added to the dreariness. Despite the gloom, Bridget's gaze was drawn at once to the figure seated in a wingback chair next to the unlit fireplace. Ellen's forewarning ought to have prepared her but she was still caught off guard. She couldn't help it; she gasped out loud.

Her mother was unrecognisable. She seemed to have aged thirty years since they had last met. She sat hunched in the chair, her thin, bony wrists poking out of the sleeves of her dress. Grey streaks snaked through her chestnut hair and the hair on her scalp seemed sparser as though some of it had fallen out, but it was pulled back from her face so that her features stood out. Her cheeks were hollow, her eyelids drooped, and her lips, which had always been a narrow line of severity, now seemed pressed together in a pale grimace of pain. She appeared shrunken, insect-like, the merest shadow of her former dominating self.

Lady Courcey raised her eyebrows sardonically at the shocked gasp Bridget had been unable to stifle. Then her expression brightened as small footsteps followed Bridget into the room and Emily appeared at her side. The poor thing looked terrified at the sight of her grandmother and once again Bridget wished that she had left Emily back at the cottage with Ellen and her two boys. Lady Courcey opened her mouth to speak but shut it with a snap as her eyes focused on the third arrival; Cormac had just materialised in the doorway. The lady began to glower.

Undeterred, Cormac took off his cap, strode into the drawing room and sat on a sofa opposite the empty hearth. He beckoned to Emily and she scampered onto the seat beside him, wriggling under his arm for safety. Lady Courcey watched without comment, her gaze upon Cormac, her lip curling in distaste. Bridget moved to a wingback chair on the other side of the fireplace and lowered herself onto it, stunned at the terrible transformation that had come upon her mother.

'Mother, are you very unwell?' she breathed.

She had expected her mother's voice to have succumbed to the change as well, to be weak and husky, scarcely audible, but it remained as sharp as ever.

'Clearly, I am in the best of health.'

Bridget bit her tongue. 'In your letter before Christmas you said you had been poorly but you gave no indication of the magnitude of your ill health. What sickness is this?'

'Mr Abbott does not know,' Lady Courcey said, looking away. 'He has performed a myriad of degrading tests and suspects it is some sort of foul internal growth, but he cannot be sure.'

'Are you in a lot of pain?'

'Constant and excruciating.'

Bridget glanced at Cormac; he was distracting Emily with a counting game on her fingers, but his head was tilted as he listened intently to the conversation.

Hesitant, she asked, 'Is it...fatal?'

Lady Courcey shrugged. 'In all likelihood.'

Bridget stared, dumbfounded. How could her mother be so blasé about her own demise?

'Why on earth did you not tell me sooner?' she said in exasperation. 'Or place a greater emphasis on the extent of your suffering? You wanted us to make amends. That is what you wrote in your letter. Do you not think that telling me you were gravely ill would have been the best motivation for reconciliation?'

'I did not seek your pity,' said Lady Courcey with a faint sneer; it looked about all she could manage with her strength so depleted. 'I merely hoped I had divulged enough to encourage you to invite me to London. All I desired was to see you one last time.'

Staggered, Bridget said, 'Surely you would not have been able to travel so far in this condition?'

'I would have done it had you asked it of me.'

'But why not invite me to Oakleigh instead?'

Baldly, Lady Courcey said, 'I did not want you to see what had happened here until after I was gone.'

Anger flared up inside Bridget. That was as good as an admission of guilt and it all but confirmed that her mother's reprehensible actions had been premeditated. Most of her compassion leaked away in an instant; perhaps this affliction was God's righteous retribution.

'Before we speak of that,' she said coolly, 'I assume you have noticed that we are not alone in the room?'

Lady Courcey narrowed her eyes at Cormac, whose shoulders tensed even as he tapped out a pattern on Emily's fingertips. Then she returned her gaze to Bridget. 'I had detected an unpleasant odour in the air, yes.'

Cormac let out a mirthless laugh.

Emily paused the counting game to whisper, 'What is funny, Papa?'

Lady Courcey's face blazed with outrage. '*Papa?*' she said with a revolted look.

'Yes,' said Bridget firmly. 'You may not wish to hear this but Cormac is—'

'I have already heard it,' Lady Courcey interrupted. 'I received a letter from your husband two days ago which detailed your unfaithfulness and lunacy.'

Nonplussed, Bridget said, 'Garrett wrote to you?' Had they travelled to Oakleigh on horseback, they might have arrived before this letter.

'He did. He suspected you might come here and he wished for me to be informed of certain recent events in advance of your arrival.'

Bridget folded her arms. 'Does he believe you can persuade me to return to him? Because that will never happen.'

Lady Courcey laughed as humourlessly as Cormac had done. 'He has no desire for that to happen. Do you think he wants you back after your humiliating conduct? His language in reference to you was quite explicit — he despises you. As he should, given the way you have mistreated him.'

'I am sure he presented himself very well as the innocent victim,' said Bridget.

'He *is* the innocent victim. You are the one who committed adultery and ran away with a miscreant, leaving him wifeless and childless.'

'He conveniently omitted the truth then,' Cormac remarked.

It was the first time he had spoken since entering the drawing room. Lady Courcey's brows drew together in surprise at his refined accent but she refused to look at him, choosing instead to address Bridget.

'Please inform the swine present in the room that I have no wish to converse with it directly.'

'Mother!' Bridget rebuked, disgusted by the lady's blatant rudeness.

'It's fine,' said Cormac, though his eyes burned with resentment. 'That kind of response is nothing more than what I have come to expect from you, Lady Courcey, although it brings into question how you think you can merit the title of "lady".' Before she could react to this insult, he went on, 'I shall continue speaking anyway. You cannot avoid listening, unless you leave the room. Your precious son-in-law was selective with the information he provided to you. He failed to mention his personal transgressions, such as his own acts of adultery and the fact that he fathered an illegitimate son ever before he and Bridget were married. These things do not cast him in as favourable a light as the role of abandoned husband so I can see why he left them out in his correspondence to you. But perhaps, in view of such facts, you might be obliged to revise your assertion of him as an "innocent victim".'

Lady Courcey stared up at the ceiling as she said to no one in particular, 'How lies may be construed as facts is beyond me.'

'I speak no lies,' said Cormac in a low voice. 'I would not make this up for sport. The illegitimate child was my own nephew and Garrett's actions drove my older sister to suicide.'

There was utter silence, apart from the sound of the wind whistling down the chimney. Emily's eyes were wide as she tried in vain to follow the grown-ups' conversation.

'So you see he is in truth a blackguard,' said Bridget into the quietness. 'When his horrendous secret came to light, there was no possible way I could have remained with him.'

'Do not fool yourself,' snapped Lady Courcey. 'You would have deserted him even if he were an angel from on high. All you ever wanted was that good-for-nothing boy and all you have done is dragged yourself into the mud. I hope you are satisfied.'

'I am satisfied,' Bridget said softly. 'I have found love, which is a difficult thing to achieve in our world. Very few are fortunate enough to experience the joy that comes from sharing true love with another. Cormac and I are two of the lucky ones. And I believe you and my father were also blessed in this regard.'

Lady Courcey's expression darkened further. 'I have no inclination to discuss your father.'

'Well, maybe you should. You have pushed him out of your thoughts for far too long. Don't you remember how he used to make you feel? I was in awe of him because he was the only person who could get you to laugh or smile or sing. You were so different in his presence.'

'I do not want to hear this,' said Lady Courcey, her voice shaking.

'You must have been a decent person once,' Bridget persisted, ignoring her mother's protest. 'How else could he have fallen in love with you? And you loved him. You weren't a perfect human being when I was a child but you would never have been capable then of what you have done since. What changed? What caused you to degenerate to such a degree?'

'He *died*,' her mother hissed. 'You have no conception of what it is like to lose someone so vital to you.'

'I *do!*' Bridget hurled back. She pointed at Cormac. 'I lost him! For years, I feared him to be dead. Not to mention, the death of your husband was the death of my father. How dare you intimate that my grief was so much less than yours? He left us both!' She sprang to her feet, driven by rage and sorrow as she recalled the pouch of fine, dark hair tucked away in her valise. 'What is more, my baby boy perished when he had only begun to live. So don't you dare say that I do not understand grief. I know what it is like to feel as though my very heart has been ripped out of me.' Her voice splintered and her chest heaved with emotion.

Lady Courcey flinched and a look of genuine compassion rippled across her haggard features. 'James was a tragic loss. Lord Wyndham wrote to me several months after it happened. I shed many tears for your little son.'

Bridget wanted to believe her but she could not reconcile the idea of her mother weeping over the death of one child while inflicting suffering upon the lives of so many. Shaking her head, she sat back down, her breath slowing as she regained control of herself. Ruefully, she realised her earlier worries had been misplaced as she had been the one to lose her temper in front of Lady Courcey, and not Cormac. He looked like he was yearning to embrace her but he stayed beside Emily, stroking their daughter's hair. She looked alarmed at her mother's sudden outburst.

Bridget faced Lady Courcey again. 'I understand that Papa's death was a devastating blow to you,' she said earnestly. 'You had a sincere connection with him, one you both knew was true right down to your very souls. Can you not see that that is what I have with Cormac? We felt it even when we were children but we were forced down separate paths. We were unlucky because, unlike you and my father, we came from different social classes and it was not acceptable for us to pursue a life together. But look at all the obstacles that were placed in our way and yet we still managed to come back to each other. Our connection could not be broken. Please tell me that you follow what I am saying, that you have a glimmer of comprehension as to why I have behaved so wildly. I could not resist the connection, just like you and Papa could not resist it.'

Lady Courcey contemplated her daughter as though she were seeing her for the very first time. Then she fixed her gaze upon Cormac, searching his face, perhaps seeking what it was that Bridget saw. Cormac remained silent and unmoving under her stare. At last, she lifted up her thin arm, pressed her fingertips to her forehead, and sighed.

'I am sorry,' she muttered. 'I know what you are begging of me and I cannot do it. You have wilfully lowered yourself to a level of abject poverty and no amount of love can excuse that.'

'Perhaps someday you will be able to understand,' said Bridget, deflated.

'Doubtful, given that my days are numbered,' said Lady Courcey.

Bridget gave her a slit-eyed look. 'Is that what has prompted your appalling behaviour? Aside from your desire to take revenge on me, you knew you were dying so why not demolish it all before you go? After all, you would never have to face the consequences.'

Lady Courcey glanced shiftily to the side and did not respond.

'Come, Mother. We have skirted around this but now we really must address it. Our purpose in coming here today was to speak about the estate.'

Lady Courcey nodded. 'How very astute of Lord Wyndham,' she said, more to herself than to her daughter.

'What do you mean by that?' asked Bridget, frowning.

'Did you not wonder what his letter was about, given that it was not a plea for you to be sent back to him?' Lady Courcey smoothed out her skirts with her cadaverous hands. 'He anticipated that you and the scrounger would try to seize the estate for your own.'

'He's mistaken—' Bridget began hotly but her mother cut her off.

'He wished for me to communicate a number of things to you but I shall summarise for it was quite a lengthy letter. First and foremost, he wanted me to remind you that Oakleigh is legally his, as stated in the papers held by Webb & Brereton in Dublin. He is still your husband in the eyes of the law and everything you once owned belongs to him. On no account may a stable hand ever believe he has a claim to this property. However, having established that, he has no immediate inclination to visit and is happy for me to continue my guardianship here.'

Bridget curled her fingers into fists. 'And is he as ignorant as I was of the deplorable state of affairs on the estate?'

'He is.'

At least it was one small point in Garrett's favour that he had not been complicit in Lady Courcey's crimes. But Bridget had few other reasons to think favourably towards him as her mother carried on.

'Your marriage will stand. You will find it impossible to sue for divorce as he has kept his extra-marital conduct discreet and you have no evidence of extreme cruelty or desertion on his part. While he is entitled to seek a divorce from you and could achieve it by the passage of a private act through Parliament, he has decided not to pursue this. He refuses to allow you the expediency of remarrying which means you and that reprobate will have to face the censure and degradation of living in sin. Should he find a suitable match for himself in the future, then and only then might he consider it.' Lady Courcey bared her teeth like a snake. 'And he would like you to remember that he could appeal for the restitution of his conjugal rights any time he pleases and force you to return to him. You may never rest easy in your adultery.'

Bridget imagined being commanded by a court to take up residence in Wyndham House again. Hearing Garrett's heavy footsteps on the stairs, permitting him access to her bedchamber, her bed, her body. Her skin crawled. She was in a separate country from him but now she wondered if it was far enough.

Lady Courcey said serenely, 'I must applaud Lord Wyndham on his perceptiveness and his management of this disgraceful situation. While it severs my daughter from her birthright, better that than to risk a common stable hand getting its dirty paws on such a prize.'

'I sure as hell don't want it,' said Cormac.

A small whisper came from his side. 'Papa, you said a bad word.'

'I know, *a stór*, I'm sorry. I won't say it again.' He looked straight at Lady Courcey, bristling with anger. 'I do not want Oakleigh. Garrett was wrong about our reason for coming back. Putting that aside, we are here today to confront you about your mishandling of the estate. You are running it into the ground and destroying your tenants' livelihoods in the process. We have seen firsthand the effects of your actions. You need to stop this folly before you ruin these people and the land entirely.'

Lady Courcey looked like she was about to retort directly to Cormac but she caught herself in time.

'What is the meaning of this?' she demanded to Bridget, her nostrils flaring. A faint spot of colour appeared high on her gaunt cheeks. 'What makes him think he is entitled to speak to me in such a way? He cannot come in here and tell me how to manage the estate!'

'At the rate you are going, there will soon be nothing left to manage,' Cormac interjected.

Bridget added her voice to his. 'He speaks the truth, Mother. You reinstated the tithes and raised the rents and treated the tenants so cruelly that they all deserted their positions last autumn. You cannot deny this for there is not a sinner to be seen working anywhere around the estate and the land is desolate.'

'I make no attempt to deny it.'

'But why do it? The estate had been thriving under your care. Why did you allow it to deteriorate and drive everyone away?' Bridget swallowed. 'Was it in retaliation for the way I spurned you? Were you taking your revenge on me?'

Lady Courcey did not reply but she cast a look of longing towards Emily and then glanced away, her eyes hardening.

Bridget felt the burden of her guilt more than ever, but she pressed on. 'Do you not see the pain that you have caused? You forced the people into this situation and now they are struggling to survive. They were dependent upon you. Are you going to pretend that you have not failed them?'

'Tenants must follow the commands of their superiors. If they do not, then they deserve to suffer.'

Baffled, Bridget said, 'Could no one else talk any sense into you? Mr Enright, or even Uncle Stuart?'

'Mr Enright endeavoured many times to convince me to see the error of my ways, and he threatened to write to Lord Wyndham about what was happening. But he capitulated quickly when I threatened him with exposure. I knew of his secret proclivities and they would not have been well received by his genteel family.' She offered no further elucidation on this but Bridget thought the accusation must have been very serious to induce Mr Enright to preside unwillingly over all those tithe collections and evictions. 'As for my brother, he visited two years ago and, when he saw the state of affairs, he beseeched me to revise my attitude. I told him to keep his nose out. I have not heard from him since. But then, for all I know,

*A Class Forsaken*

he may be dead or, if not, close to it. The last time I saw him, he was the size of an ox and he said his heart was failing.' She smirked. 'Incurable illness or no, I am still certain to outlive him.'

Bridget grimaced. 'I wish one of them had been able to make you see reason. The tenants are human beings, and you are responsible for their welfare. How can you treat them so unjustly? Think of Ellen Ryan, or Ellen Kirwan as she is now. She was a faithful servant to you for many years. Are you happy for her to be trodden into the ground just like everyone else?'

Lady Courcey looked startled. 'Ellen chose to leave my employment a long time ago. She has nothing to do with this.'

'On the contrary, she married a stable hand from the estate and he was compelled to leave his position along with everyone else. She is as deeply involved in this as any other tenant's wife. Ellen and Liam have two small boys under the age of four and she is pregnant with a third child. Her greatest worry is how to feed them all and her greatest fear is that her children will not survive to adulthood. You put those trials upon her. That is how you chose to repay her for her years of constant loyalty.'

There was another long silence; the tension in the drawing room was palpable. Bridget studied her mother. Was there the faintest indication of a conscience behind the lady's sunken eyes?

'It changes everything when you can put a familiar face upon what you have done,' said Bridget softly.

Still Lady Courcey did not respond. She avoided Bridget's gaze and seemed intent upon straightening out a stubborn crease in her dress. When at last she raised her face again, Bridget could see that it was etched with pain.

'I am tired,' she muttered. 'I need to rest now.'

Disappointed, Bridget got to her feet. 'I beg you to consider the things we have said, to see the truth in them. Will you promise to do that?'

'And what do you wish me to do with the truth?' Lady Courcey bit out, though her voice was becoming weaker.

'I think that should be very obvious. Relax your iron grip on the rents, remove the yoke of the tithes from the tenants, and let Oakleigh flourish once more. The people will come back, I know they will. They love this land; most of the families have worked on the estate for generations. If you treat them fairly, then I am in no doubt that they will all return: the stable hands, the gardeners, the maids, even Mr Buttimer, Mrs Walsh and Mrs Kavanagh. Don't you miss them?'

Lady Courcey contemplated for a moment and then confessed, 'Cathy *is* a terrible cook.'

'She has been kinder to you than you deserve,' Bridget said, but her tone was not harsh.

She moved towards the door; Cormac and Emily stood and followed her, Cormac donning his cap once more. Lady Courcey spoke behind them.

'I shall summon Cathy and get her to prepare your bedchamber for you and the girl.' Of course the invitation did not extend to Cormac.

Bridget turned back, her jaw set in irritation. 'We shall not stay at the manor. We are going to return to the cottage where we are welcome as a family.'

Lady Courcey scowled, then sighed. 'Will you call again tomorrow?'

Before Bridget could reply, Cormac said, 'We are leaving tomorrow. You will not see us again.'

Lady Courcey looked shocked. 'You are leaving the estate already?' she asked Bridget over Cormac's shoulder. 'But you have only just returned. We require more time to get reacquainted. Did you think you would resolve all the problems in one visit?'

Again, Cormac answered before Bridget could speak. 'We did not come back to the estate for the purpose of getting reacquainted with you, nor even to petition you on behalf of the tenants. Our true purpose was to search for my family. We have obtained some enlightening information as to their possible whereabouts and hence we journey on towards Dublin tomorrow morning. We cannot delay.'

'Your — your family?' faltered Lady Courcey, finally speaking to Cormac himself.

'Yes, my family. Do you remember them? You might recall that you dismissed my sisters from their employment and evicted my mother from her cottage, when they had done nothing wrong and had nowhere else to go. It was seven and a half years ago but I am confident you have not forgotten.'

Lady Courcey opened her mouth but no words came out. Cormac clenched his fists.

'If you were a decent human being, you would be feeling remorse right now. But I know that is too much to hope for. You punished my family because punishing me was not enough to satisfy you. And you waited until after I was gone so they would have no one to defend their right to remain. I only became aware of what happened to them in the last few weeks. It is the reason why we returned to Ireland, why we came back to Oakleigh, and why we leave for Dublin tomorrow. We are going to try to find the broken pieces of my family and put them back together again.'

Lady Courcey's expression was indiscernible. Then she said, 'If I begged for your forgiveness, would you give it, I wonder?'

'No,' he said without hesitation. 'Your crime is too great. How could I ever forgive an act that was committed so maliciously on a basis that was so unjustified?'

'You loathe me,' Lady Courcey observed. It was impossible to tell whether her mouth was twisted in regret or irony.

'I do. I see no reason to lie about it, for you have never hidden your abhorrence of me. And your hatred seems to know no bounds. Your granddaughter has been in your presence for the past half an hour and you have made no effort to greet or even acknowledge her, because you know that she is my offspring and not Garrett's. It speaks volumes that you are willing to forego an opportunity to meet this wonderful little girl solely on account of her blood connection to me. She also has a blood connection to you, if you cared enough to recognise that.'

Bridget winced. Lady Courcey's gaze travelled down from Cormac's disdainful countenance to the diminutive figure half hidden behind his back. She stretched out a shaky arm.

'Come here, child.'

Emily's response was to conceal herself totally from view. Bridget went to her side and bent down.

'Will you go to her, gooseberry?'

Emily nibbled her lip, looking dubious at the notion of approaching the terrifying creature that was supposed to be her grandmother.

'Do not be afraid. I will go with you.'

She drew Emily out from Cormac's protective shadow and, with a reassuring glance at his doubtful face, led her over to her mother's wingback chair. Lady Courcey reached out again and took one of Emily's hands; the girl's other hand remained clutched in Bridget's. They regarded each other for a moment or two.

'Do you know who I am?' Lady Courcey asked.

Emily nodded. 'You're my grandmama.'

'That is correct. How old are you?'

'I will be seven in May.'

'My goodness, such a big girl. Did you have a governess in London?'

'Yes, Miss Davison.'

'And what did she teach you?'

'She taught me how to read and write and count. She knows so many things about history and geography. She can even speak French. But she is not very good at art.'

'Indeed. And are you good at art?'

'I am. I like to draw and paint and I love mixing colours.'

'Do you have a favourite colour?'

'Yes, pink. I can make pink by mixing red and white. But I like how mixing blue and yellow makes green too.'

What happened next made Bridget gape with amazement. Lady Courcey smiled and pulled Emily into a hug. Emily did not let go of her mother's hand but neither did she resist her grandmother's gesture. When Lady Courcey released Emily, there was a wetness glistening in her eyes.

'You are a pet,' she said. Then she looked up at Bridget. 'Please come back tomorrow so that I may see my granddaughter again.'

'Well...perhaps we can delay our departure for one more day,' Bridget said and looked over her shoulder at Cormac. He gave a jerk of his head which she took to indicate his reluctant acquiescence.

Lady Courcey looked pleased. 'Until tomorrow, then.'

And with that, Bridget, Cormac and Emily left the drawing room. They went back across the entrance hall and descended the narrow stairs to the kitchens. There they found a harassed Cathy in the middle of preparing an inelegant-looking dish for Lady Courcey's dinner.

'Let us help you,' said Bridget compassionately. 'Three pairs of hands are better than one.'

Cormac assisted by stoking up the fire, while Bridget unearthed a plate and some cutlery and wiped them with a cloth. Even as Cathy vigorously stirred a pot over the hearth, a chime came from the row of servant bells. Shooting the others a resigned look, she set down her wooden spoon.

'I'd best go see to her ladyship,' she said. 'Thanks to ye both for helping.'

They said goodbye to the careworn maid as she departed from the kitchens. Cormac moved the pot so that it wouldn't burn while she was gone and then he, Bridget and Emily went back outside. The wind still blew fiercely, whipping at their hair and clothes as soon as they stepped into the courtyard.

On a whim, Bridget led the others back into the orchard, following the winding path until they reached the clearing at the centre where the mighty oak tree still stood, proud and tall. She let out a soundless breath of relief. The initials that she and Cormac had scratched into the trunk when they were twelve were worn but still legible. He took her hand and they gazed together at the place they had always called theirs.

'This is where your father and I met for the very first time,' Bridget said to Emily.

Emily's eyes lit up. 'How did it happen?'

Cormac grinned. 'I was hiding in this tree when your mother appeared below me, so I dropped an acorn on her head.'

'Were you angry with him, Mama?'

'A little, but not for long. He was a very interesting boy. He showed me how to climb this tree.'

Emily turned her shining face to Cormac. 'Will you show me, Papa? Please?'

He lifted her and swung her up into the tree, settling her securely in a fork between two branches.

'There you are, your highness,' he said, bowing. 'Would you care for some company?' he added and climbed lithely onto the branch next to her.

She giggled. 'You should come up too, Mama!'

Despite her skirts, Bridget did not hesitate. Within a few moments, she was nestled on the other side of Emily.

'I have not forgotten what you taught me,' she said with a grin at Cormac.

He smiled back and then they fell silent for a minute or two. They were sheltered from the wind here but they could hear it gusting through the crown of the tree. Emily started humming tunelessly to herself, her gaze following the track of a ladybird as it crawled along her branch.

At last, Bridget said, 'What did you think of her?'

Cormac removed his cap and ran his hand through his hair. 'I saw what I expected to see. She is the exact same as she ever was.'

Bridget's teeth trapped the tip of her tongue. 'I thought so too but towards the end she seemed...different. Did you detect the barest hint of a possibility that she might be able to change?'

'She might be able to change, but she is not willing to. Not even her sickness and impending demise can provide her with enough incentive to make peace and bury her prejudices before she dies.'

Bridget felt her eyes prick with tears.

'I'm sorry,' he said at once. 'I didn't mean to be flippant about her death.'

A teardrop slipped down her cheek and she dashed it away. 'It's dreadful that I should even feel this way. She is nothing short of monstrous. But I still hope that she will try to amend her ways. You don't think it's conceivable?'

'I just think she is too set in her ways at this stage,' he said, his tone gentle. 'Sometimes a person gets to a point where they cannot comprehend any alternatives.'

She sighed. 'I understand your reasoning. But I do believe we made an impact on her today, despite the horrible, insulting things she said. She was visibly shaken when I told her how Ellen and her family are suffering. She always liked Ellen and would never have intended to hurt her this way.'

'And yet she was already aware of the suffering she had inflicted upon hundreds of others and it had caused her no unease up to now. The pain for each person is the same whether or not she knows the individual.'

'I know but she would not see it like that. She cannot relate to a nameless face but she can relate to the loyal girl who helped her dress every day for so many years.'

He shrugged. 'Maybe so. Is it enough to sway her? I don't know.'

'But what about when she spoke to...' Bridget glanced down at their daughter perched between them. 'Her whole demeanour altered. That was unmistakable.' She shifted position on the branch to face Cormac more fully. 'I think I may have done great damage the day I told her she would never know her grandchild. She would have been unsullied in the baby's eyes and perhaps it would have been a way for us to start anew and for her to redeem herself. I denied her that opportunity and cast her out to nurse her grievances alone and in bitterness.' Bridget gulped. 'I wonder might circumstances have transpired differently at Oakleigh had I permitted their acquaintance? Her longing just now was quite palpable.'

'It was a softer side to her than we are accustomed to seeing,' he admitted. 'Do you think she will let her guard down like that again?'

'I would like to believe so. It was brief but it was a sign that she is not beyond redemption. I am hopeful that tomorrow we shall have a warmer reception and better luck with our appeal. After all, who can resist our sweet Emily's charms for very long?'

Emily looked up and the ladybird, which she had managed to coax onto her finger, flew away.

'Are you talking about me?' she said, wide-eyed.

'Only about how wonderful you are.' Bridget kissed the top of her head. 'We are going to visit Grandmama again tomorrow, if that is acceptable to your royal highness?'

Emily thought about it and nodded. 'Her hug was strange,' she commented and said nothing more.

They stayed a little longer where they were, savouring the nostalgia, and then they climbed down from the oak tree and made their way back to the cottage. Bridget did not know what the next day's meeting would bring but she hoped that the situation would be resolved, one way or another.

# Chapter 12

'Cormac! Cormac, wake up!'
Cormac jerked awake as someone violently shook his shoulders. He tried to get his bearings; it was pitch black but he knew that he was lying in the loft beneath the eaves of his family's cottage. There were other warm bodies near him in the darkness: Bridget and Emily. In another corner of the loft, Ellen and her two boys were nestled together like a set of three spoons. It was Liam who had woken him.

'What's the matter?' Cormac demanded as everyone in the loft began to stir. Liam was making no attempt to keep quiet.

'You've got to get up now,' he said with such authority that Cormac scrambled to rise at once. 'Bridget needs to come too.'

'Come where?'

'Outside, right away. Ellen, *a ghrá*, take care of the children.' With no further explanation, Liam disappeared down the ladder to the lower floor of the cottage.

Cormac turned to Bridget. She was only an indistinct form in the dark but he could tell she was already alert.

'What's happening?' she asked.

'I have no idea,' he said, pulling on his boots and coat and shoving his cap in his coat pocket. 'Come down below when you're ready and be quick. It sounds urgent.'

He clambered down the ladder, ignoring Ellen's own sleepy enquiry. Liam was not in the dim room below, where the embers in the fireplace had smouldered into a heap of cold ash; it had to be the very heart of night. Cormac hurried out the open door and found Liam standing in front of the cottage, looking intently at the distant sky. He followed his gaze and saw an orange glow on the horizon. It illuminated what appeared to be a thick bank of clouds hanging low in the air.

'Myself and Denis met up with John after he got back from Blackcastle Inn,' Liam said without turning his head. 'We were about to go our separate ways when we saw it.'

Cormac squinted to better focus on the unusual glow. He realised with sudden clarity that what he had mistaken for clouds was in fact a wide column of smoke. With a jolt, he understood what he was seeing just as Bridget appeared behind them.

'Why did you wake us up?' she said as she swung her cloak around her shoulders. She had not brought her bonnet. Her gaze travelled past them to the strangely-lit sky. 'What is that?'

Liam made eye contact with Cormac. 'There's only one structure in that direction that could burn with so much smoke.'

Bridget stared. 'What does he mean?' she asked Cormac.

He hesitated. 'He means that the manor is on fire.'

Her eyes widened. Without a word, she picked up her skirts and tore up the lane. Cormac and Liam hastened to follow her, leaving Ellen uttering an exclamation of alarm in the doorway behind them.

The three of them raced towards the manor house, not speaking, only running as fast as they could. For most of the way they did not have a clear line of sight to what lay ahead, but once they reached the Gorteen they had the same uninterrupted view that Cormac had had when he was only five and got his very first glimpse of the big house.

Bridget gasped and Cormac swore. Liam said nothing but his face was full of shock. The manor, which should have been impossible to see in the dark night, was lit by angry orange flames engulfing one half of the building. The wind that had been gusting so strongly earlier that day had not abated and was only adding to the conflagration, fanning the flames and blowing the thick smoke skywards. The fire was immense; already it looked like it was out of control. Bridget's childhood home was burning to the ground.

They had stopped out of sheer amazement and horror, but now they hurtled forwards again across the length of the Gorteen. Cormac heard Bridget's laboured breathing; she was clutching her side in pain but she did not slow her pace, pushing onwards towards the fiery structure. They were close enough now to hear the roar of the flames which billowed out the windows and licked hungrily at the roof.

At last, they reached the manor grounds. Panting for breath, they sprinted into the courtyard to find nearly a dozen men congregated there – Cormac recognised most of them from the meeting in Farmer McKinty's barn, along with Ben Bracken as well. A lone horse stood tethered to the door of the stables, its eyes rolling in fear. The men were staring up at the raging fire with an air of futility; empty buckets and pails lay scattered at their feet. All their heads turned as Cormac, Bridget and Liam dashed up behind them. John Corbett, face ashen, darted out from the middle of the group, Denis on his heels.

'We tried to quench it,' John exclaimed over the howl of the blaze, 'but it'd already spread too far by the time we came upon it. The whole east wing's on fire—'tis becoming an inferno. There's no way of stopping it now.'

'How the hell did it start?' Cormac demanded.

'We've no clue,' said Denis, and the other men shook their heads behind him. Ben was rubbing his brow in bewilderment. A suspicious part of Cormac wondered fleetingly whether any of them might have set it deliberately, but he perceived the genuine dismay in their features.

Bridget looked around the courtyard. 'Where is my mother? Is she safe?'

John lowered his gaze. 'Her ladyship hasn't come out of the house.'

In that moment, Cormac saw fury on his lover's face as he had never seen it before.

'Do you mean no one went inside to save her?' she screamed.

Not one of the men could bring himself to look at her.

'The fire grew at a fierce rate,' John tried, staring at his boots. 'It was too dangerous...'

Bridget had turned away from him before he had finished speaking. 'Cormac!' she cried. 'My mother!'

He quailed. There was a desperate plea in her eyes that he did not want to acknowledge. Her hands reached out impulsively to him. He glanced at the flames surging out of the windows above them. Was she really asking him to do this? Enter a burning house to save the life of a woman who had caused him and his family so much harm? He did not know if he had it in him to be so selfless. Bridget knew how much he despised Lady Courcey.

But when had he ever been able to refuse Bridget anything?

He dug his cap out of his coat pocket and jammed it on his head.

'Cormac, you can't,' said John, aghast. ''Tis suicide.'

'The fire seems to be concentrated in one half of the house so far,' Cormac said levelly. 'Lady Courcey may well be alive in the other half which means there might still be a chance to rescue her before it is too late.' He turned to Bridget. 'Where is your mother's bedchamber? If she has made no attempt to escape from the house, then it could be that she is still asleep and unaware that the building is ablaze.'

The expression on Bridget's face was a tortured mixture of extreme guilt and utter gratefulness. 'It is past my own bedchamber on the first floor, the second last room on the west wing corridor. What a mercy the fire started in the east wing!'

Lucky for him.

'I'll be back as soon as I can,' he said and gave her a brief kiss, hoping it would not be their last.

'Be safe,' she choked and added as a frantic afterthought, 'Cathy is in there too!'

He nodded and turned away. Paying no heed to the other men who called to him to come back, he entered the burning manor house by the door to the kitchens. Fear mounted in him with every step.

Wisps of smoke wafted about the kitchen space but there were no flames in sight. He took a breath and the smoky air scratched at his throat. He picked up a discarded cloth from the kitchen table – it looked like the one Bridget had used mere hours ago – and soaked it in a basin of dirty water sitting next to it. Disregarding the foul odour from the old water, he tied the cloth around his nose and mouth and left the kitchens via the inner door leading above stairs.

When he reached the entrance hall, he got a further glimpse of the terrifying extent of the fire. The east wing of the manor was destroyed. The doors to the library and dining room hung off their hinges and both rooms were consumed by flames. He could only presume that the bedchambers above were in a similar state. The west wing, which included the drawing room and the ballroom, did appear to be as yet unscathed but it would not be long before the fire devoured its way in that direction, as it was already rippling into the entrance hall from the ruined library. He ran for the mahogany staircase, taking the steps three at a time.

At the top of the staircase, he paused and looked left and right. The east wing corridor was lit up with flames bursting from the upstairs rooms; the blistering heat of the blaze gusted up the hallway towards him. Sweating, he started making his way down the west wing corridor which was darker but still clogged with suffocating smoke. The cloth he had tied around his face was already drying out and, as its effectiveness decreased, so the harmfulness of the smoke increased. He began coughing so hard that he had to crouch down for a few moments to breathe in the clearer air close to the floor. Eyes watering and still bending low, he scuttled on to the second last door in the corridor. It was ajar. He gave a loud knock – why was he bothering with manners at a time like this? – and pushed it open.

The bedchamber was empty. The bed looked as though it had been slept in that night but Lady Courcey was nowhere to be seen. His heart sank; how was he supposed to find her now? For one second, he considered ending his search right there and simply telling Bridget that he had been too late. But then her pleading eyes swam into his mind and he knew he would never again be able to face her with honesty if he did not make every effort to save her mother now.

Exhaling in exasperation, he was about to leave the bedchamber when his gaze landed on a little table by the bedside. A pitcher and basin sat on top of it. He hurried over and found that the pitcher was blessedly full of water. Ripping the cloth from his face, he once again saturated it before tying it back on. The effect was immediate and it became easier to breathe. Thankful for this small relief, he exited the room with renewed vigour.

Back in the corridor, he stared down its length and instantly dismissed the rooms at the far end in the east wing; if Lady Courcey was in any of those, she was already dead. The fire had crept further along the corridor almost to the top of the staircase. Soon his escape route would be cut off. Panic rising in him, he dashed to the door nearest to the staircase and opened it. He found himself in Bridget's old bedchamber, recognising the burgundy curtains on the bed and the sheepskin rug at its foot; this room too was empty. He spared half a glance for the dressing table where a number of girlish items – a hairbrush, a jewellery box, a brooch in the shape of a flower – lay scattered on its surface, before he hastened back into the hallway.

Tongues of flame were blackening the newel of the staircase. The fire had raced up the wallpapered walls and now stretched greedily along the ceiling towards the west wing. He ran for the furthest door on the corridor and at last found what he was looking for. In this room, which turned out to be yet another bedchamber, he discovered Lady Courcey seated in a state of serenity on the bed, wearing only her nightdress and clutching a small object in her hands. It appeared to be a smoking pipe. Other things were strewn on the bedcover beside her: a man's hat, a long coat, and a riding whip.

He checked in the doorway, startled to come upon such a calm scene in the midst of the tumult. He looked around; were they in what might once have been Lord Courcey's bedchamber?

Then he came to his senses, darted forwards, pulled the cloth down from his nose and mouth, and panted, 'Lady Courcey! It's time to go!'

She looked up in mild surprise. She blinked at him but made no move to rise. Instead, she looked down at the pipe again.

'He never went anywhere without his pipe,' she murmured to herself. 'He was not a smoker but it belonged to his father and to his father before him. He just always kept it close.'

Cormac stared at the lady. Had she gone mad? He glanced over his shoulder and saw the bright glow through the doorway. They did not have much time before the fire reached it and blocked their way out.

Heart hammering, he approached the bed and said very clearly, 'The manor is on fire. We need to get out at once.'

She picked up the riding whip and cradled it in her emaciated arms. 'He loved that horse so much. It was almost as dear to him as his daughter. I should never have had it killed.'

Cormac shifted uneasily. He had no desire to watch this decaying woman take inventory of her dead husband's belongings, especially when it would not please her to know that the man's pocket watch was now in his own possession.

She reached out and stroked the collar of the long coat. 'He was wearing this the very first day I met him—'

Cormac lost patience. 'Constance!' he bellowed.

This at last provoked a reaction. Her face snapped upwards and she looked affronted by his familiar use of her name.

'What?' she said, the single word loaded with resentment.

## A Class Forsaken

'Has it escaped your notice that there is a fire burning outside your door?' He flung out an arm behind him. 'You cannot stay here any longer. It is time to leave. Right now!' he added loudly as the lady still did not get to her feet.

She regarded him with vague curiosity. 'Why are you here?'

'Isn't it obvious?' he spluttered. 'I'm here to get you out!'

'Why?' she persisted. 'You do not care if I die.'

He looked at her and she looked back. They both knew that what she said was true.

'But Bridget does,' he finally answered.

'So you are willing to risk your own life in order to save mine, even though you loathe me down to the very marrow of my bones? And all because Bridget wishes it?'

'"Willing" is a strong word but that is what I am doing, yes.'

He heard crackling and looked around to see that the fire was licking the door jamb. Smoke glided into the room with it and he coughed.

'Please—' he said hoarsely.

'That was an exceedingly stupid thing to do.'

He glared at her. Her predilection to disparage him could not be restrained even when they were both in mortal danger.

Then she said, 'But it is also a mark of such loyalty and love that I cannot comprehend its vastness. What you have done tonight proves that you would do anything for my daughter. I cannot say that you are a better man than Lord Wyndham but I am certain he would never walk into a burning house to rescue his mother-in-law. I have misjudged you.'

Cormac's jaw dropped. He was so taken aback that he could not say a word.

'Having said that,' she went on wryly, 'you have wasted your efforts. I am not leaving this room.'

He shook his head to clear the fog from his brain. 'What do you mean? There's still time.'

Even as he said it, he sensed a rising heat at his back and doubted the truth of his words.

'Not for me.' Her tone was matter-of-fact. 'The sand in my hourglass has trickled away to nothing. And if my alternative is to shrivel into a diseased corpse in a matter of weeks or months, then dying tonight is by far the better option.'

'But Bridget wants you to live,' he said in desperation. A line of flame whispered along the ceiling, while fear thrummed in his veins.

'Thankfully, she has no choice in the matter. I do not know how this conflagration has come about but I am going to seize the opportunity with both hands. I am tired of waiting to die.'

He sagged in defeat. 'What will I tell her?'

'Tell her whatever you want. You can paint my name as blackly as you wish. I shall not be there to defend myself. Say that I went to my death cursing her name. Or say that I dropped to my knees and begged for forgiveness. The possibilities are endless; you have the power to shape my daughter's thoughts with as much or as little bias as you desire.'

She glanced above her where the flame was beginning to flicker at the canopy of the four-poster bed.

'I suggest you leave now,' she said, 'unless you wish to share a fiery grave with me.'

He most certainly did not wish that.

'Goodbye, then,' he said awkwardly and turned away from her.

'Cormac,' she said. Was it the first time she had ever spoken his name? He looked back and saw that her cheeks had become red from the overpowering heat in the room; she appeared more human now at the moment of her death than the pale, insect-like creature they had visited only that afternoon.

'Yes?' he said.

She stared him straight in the eye. 'That little girl is a treasure. I was careless with my own. Make sure you look after yours.'

'I will,' he replied.

Turning back to the door again, he found that it was now encircled with flames. He pulled the cloth up over his face even though it was as dry as paper once more. Shrugging out of his coat, he swung it over his head and back. He did not look at Lady Courcey as he ran forwards and leapt through the doorway.

As soon as he landed in the corridor, he knew he was in trouble. The fire now blazed in every direction, consuming the west wing as viciously as it had the east wing. It was crucial that he get out of the house right now. He looked towards the staircase and saw that the fire had reached the steps; he had to assume that the way down to the entrance hall below was not a safe course of escape. He needed to find another way out.

That was when he remembered the servants' staircase – it wound up through the house from the kitchens and could provide him with an alternative route back to the ground. He had climbed that narrow stairs up to the second floor many years ago when he had visited Bridget on her sickbed after she had been caught out in the thunderstorm. Recalling the heavy rain that had fallen during that storm and longing for a single drop of it now to soothe his dry, parched throat, he scanned the opposite wall of the corridor in search of the first floor servants' door. He spotted it set discreetly into the wall and, relieved, he rushed to it.

The stairwell beyond was congested with smoke but there were no flames in sight. He shut the door behind him and checked his coat to make sure it had not caught fire. Wheezing, he struggled down the stairs, his thoughts growing hazy. All he could concentrate on was taking one step at a time and breathing as shallowly as possible. He got to the bottom of the stairs and blearily reached for the latch on the door to the kitchens.

Instant and searing pain made him withdraw his hand at once and snapped his mind back to attention. Eyes smarting, he examined his fingers and found them raw and blistered. The latch on the door was red-hot and, with his senses back in focus, he could hear the snarl of the fire burning on the other side of it. With despairing clarity, he realised the blaze had spread to the kitchens, cutting off his passage to outside. The courtyard, where fresh air and Bridget waited, was a mere thirty feet away from him but it might as well have been in Cove for all he could do to reach it.

In that moment, his fear escalated into blind terror. Dropping his coat, he crouched down and put his arms over his head. He did not want to die, not yet, not like this. He imagined the excruciating agony of burning to death – probably what he was feeling in his fingers but on every inch of his skin and a hundred times worse. Lady Courcey may have chosen it as her form of departure from this world but he emphatically did not want to follow suit. His instinct was to shout for help, even though the gesture would be futile.

And then, bizarrely, he heard someone scream, 'Help! Help me!'

It was not Lady Courcey. It sounded like the voice was coming from further up the servants' stairwell. With a jolt of guilt, he remembered Cathy.

He sprang to his feet, seized his coat and ran up the stairs, shouting, 'Cathy, I'm coming!'

He met the maid halfway up; she was descending from the servants' quarters at the top of the house. She wore boots and had put on a cloak over her nightdress. She looked scared out of her wits and her face was streaked with tears but she appeared to be unharmed.

'What're we going to do?' she wept.

He made an instantaneous decision. 'This stairs is a dead end,' he said. 'We're going to go down the main staircase instead.'

He prayed that it wouldn't be completely blocked or they would perish inside this house. Tearing the cloth from his face, he tied it across Cathy's nose and mouth.

'Come with me,' he said and grabbed her hand with his unhurt one.

He pulled her to the servants' door leading back into the first floor corridor. He wrapped his coat around his other hand and gingerly eased open the door. A cloud of smoke billowed into the stairwell and he put his elbow up to his mouth. The fire raged along the corridor but he judged that there was enough space to get through. There would have to be.

'Take off your cloak and do this,' he called to Cathy over the clamour of the fire and demonstrated swinging his coat over his head and shoulders. She copied him, her face peeking out nervously from the folds of the cloak.

'Now we're going to run as fast as we can to the stairs.'

She shrank away but he dragged her mercilessly through the gap in the door. As he did so, he thought he heard a fit of coughing coming from the last bedchamber in the corridor. He didn't stop; it was too late for the lady now.

The heat seemed to have doubled in its intensity and the smoke was so irritating on his eyes that he had to narrow them to slits. He dashed along the corridor, coming to a halt when he reached the top of the mahogany staircase. The banisters were ablaze but between them the fire surged only in pockets down the flight of steps. If they could avoid the worst sections and make it down to the entrance hall, they might be safe. He squinted around to make sure Cathy had followed him; she was at his side but her terrified eyes above the strip of cloth were focused on something behind him. He spun about to see most of the floor in the east wing disintegrating and disappearing into the rooms below. The thunder of the collapsing floor was deafening.

'Hurry!' he hollered at Cathy, tucking his coat more securely around him. It wasn't much protection but it was better than nothing. 'Down the staircase now. Don't stop for any reason!'

They hastened down the stairs as swiftly as they dared. He led the way, sweating and fighting to catch his breath. He sidestepped the pockets of fire, picking out the safest path to the bottom. But the last few steps blazed across from edge to edge.

'We have to jump!' he yelled to Cathy. 'I'll go first and then I'll catch you.'

He didn't give her a chance to argue. He leapt over the flaming steps and crashed onto the floor of the entrance hall, his knees buckling. Regaining his balance, he turned and held out his arms. Eyes wide and fearful, Cathy bent her knees and jumped, but not far enough. Her booted feet landed on the bottom step and, stumbling, she let out a high-pitched screech of pain. He wrenched her out of the fire but the damage was done; the hem of her nightdress was alight. He threw his coat around her legs and rolled with her across the floor of the hall, his cap falling off as he did so. The flames were quenched but she still shrieked. When he pulled the coat away, the burns showed up on her legs in angry, red blisters.

He winced but there was no time to lose; his priority was to establish their escape route. He leapt to his feet and hurtled to the front door. It was locked and Cathy was in no condition to tell him where the key might be. He whirled around and sprinted over to the drawing room. Rather than risk burning his hand again, he rushed at the drawing room door and heaved his whole body weight against it. Weakened by the fire, it gave way more easily than he had expected and he fell into the room.

More fire. Every object in the room was ablaze, including Bridget's magnificent grand piano. He did not stop to think. He lifted the piano stool into the air and threw it at one of the windows. It smashed through the glass and a huge gust of air came blasting into the drawing room, sending the flames into flurries. He ran back out to the entrance hall where Cathy was curled up in agony on the floor. He hauled her to her feet, ignoring her screams, and lifted her up into his arms, leaving his coat and her cloak behind. Carrying her into the drawing room and over to the window, he hoisted her through the jagged gap and she fell to the ground on the other side. He climbed out himself, scraping his skin on broken glass in the process, and landed with a thud on the gravel below. Knowing that they still needed to put some distance between themselves and the burning house, he forced Cathy to crawl with him across the ground until they were a good forty feet from the building. It was only then that he judged they were safe and he collapsed in exhaustion.

He breathed in a deep lungful of cool air and started coughing and spluttering. He heard Cathy choking too and glanced over to see her on her hands and knees, retching onto the gravel. Her legs looked swollen and raw. That kind of injury would take weeks to heal. He was lucky that his blistered hand was the worst thing that had happened to him.

He rolled over onto his back and lay there, his body still wracked by hacking coughs. Through a haze of pain and fatigue, he perceived shouts and running footsteps on the gravel.

'They're here! I told ye I heard breaking glass!'

In the next instant, he heard Bridget's voice screaming his name and felt her hands clutching at his face. For a moment he couldn't place the contrasting sensations of rough and smooth against his cheek; then he blurrily realised it was the two rings he had given her. That day in Cove when he had slid the gold ring into place above the thread ring on her finger seemed a lifetime ago.

'Oh, Cormac!' she sobbed. 'I am so, so sorry! As soon as you walked into the house, I regretted letting you go. I never should have asked you to do such a thing. I was terrified I was going to lose you forever. But you're alive, thank goodness you're alive!'

She wrapped her arms around him and held him tight. But something was strange; she seemed far away from him and his vision was going dim. As he slipped into unconsciousness, he heard her calling to him but he couldn't answer.

# Chapter 13

Bridget's heart seized as Cormac's head lolled away from her.

'Cormac!' she cried. 'Dear God, *no!*'

She became vaguely aware of the sound of hooves and wheels crunching gravel behind her but she had no thought in her mind other than her lover lying lifeless in her arms. She screamed his name again and violently shook his shoulders. He remained slack and unresponsive. She cradled him and wailed, unable to accept it as true.

Several pairs of boots came into her line of sight and a gruff voice said, 'Let him go, madam. We are taking him into custody.'

She gazed up to see four members of the constabulary, uniformed, armed and steely-eyed, staring down at her.

'P-pardon?' she stammered.

'Release him at once. He's our prisoner. And so is that girl there.'

She gaped. The only thing she understood was that they wanted to take Cormac away from her, so she pulled him closer to her chest. Footsteps came stamping up beside her.

'What's the meaning of this?' John Corbett demanded.

A younger constable answered him. 'This fellow here is a criminal. We saw him escaping from the house, and the girl too. Arson's a hanging offence.'

The enthusiasm with which he announced this stirred a memory in Bridget's mind. She considered the constable more closely. He was a man in his twenties now but she remembered him when he had still been a novice and had threatened the men who'd intimidated her outside The Pikeman with a slight waver in his voice. Almost eight years later, Constable Tierney showed no signs of trepidation as he held his rifle and bayonet at ease, poised to use them at the merest hint of resistance.

She glanced at the first constable who had spoken and recognised Constable Quirke. Even eight years ago, he had seemed weary of his role – now he looked downright surfeited. He turned his jaded gaze towards John as the stable master clicked his tongue in protestation.

'Arrah, you've got it all wrong,' he said. 'The chap went into the house to save the lives of the inhabitants. He had nothing to do with starting the fire.'

Constable Tierney shrugged. 'We'll leave that for the magistrate to decide. Get him to the wagon, boys.'

The third and fourth constables swung their rifles over their shoulders so their hands were free to seize Cormac. Beyond them, a horse-drawn wagon stood waiting.

'No!' Bridget snapped. 'You're not taking him anywhere.'

'You have no say in the matter, madam,' said Constable Quirke, though his eyes looked confused, as though he was struggling to place her. Of course, it would be difficult for him to match the well-dressed Miss Muldowney he had met long ago with the woman now before him, when she was not clothed in the fashions of the upper classes and clutched a criminal so fiercely to her.

'I think—' She gulped and sobbed, 'I think he's dead!' Tears spilled down her cheeks as she voiced the greatest fear she had ever known.

'What?' John exclaimed. He dropped to his knees beside her and felt Cormac's neck for a pulse. After a tense moment or two, his shoulders visibly relaxed and he let out a breath. 'You craythur, don't you worry. He's not dead, just passed out. He must've taken in a fierce amount of smoke.'

The air escaped her lungs in a shuddering gasp and she wept all the harder. 'Thank heaven,' she whimpered and kissed Cormac's sooty forehead.

John frowned. 'He doesn't look good though. The sooner Liam gets back, the better.'

She wiped the back of her hand across her face, nodding. As soon as Cormac had entered the burning house to search for Lady Courcey, Liam had jumped on John's horse and ridden to seek out the nearest physician, anticipating with good sense that medical help would be needed on the scene. She prayed he would get back to them with all possible speed.

Constable Tierney huffed. 'If he's alive, he's coming with us.'

John stood and folded his arms. 'I'm telling ye, ye've got the wrong man. There are near a dozen men over there who'll confirm he was one of the last to arrive here tonight.'

The other men from the courtyard were hovering at a distance, their postures wary; they looked ready to bolt at a second's notice. After all, barely twenty-four hours ago they had been complicit in an illegal meeting of rebels and the incarceration of some of these constables' comrades-in-arms. Denis was the only one who had come near – he was kneeling over Cathy and looked as white as a ghost, even with the glow cast from the burning building.

Constable Quirke scratched his nose tiredly. 'If not him, then who? A fire this big doesn't start by accident. There's foul play behind this.'

'We don't know how it happened,' said John. 'But you're welcome to stay and search the grounds if you think the perpetrators might still be nearby admiring their handiwork.'

Constable Quirke narrowed his eyes. 'And who might you be to be offering a welcome such as that? You're acting like a person in charge around here and that strikes me as mighty suspect, given what's been happening at Oakleigh this past while.' He stepped closer to John, staring at him intently.

To John's credit, he did not recoil at the constable's approach. Coolly, he said, 'I'm only a concerned parishioner who came running when I thought I could be of service. Like right now, I'm going to help this young lady bring her man to a place where he can recover from his injuries.'

He gestured to Denis, who shuffled over, his expression guarded.

'Give me a hand, lad,' John said, and he put a gentle palm on Bridget's shoulder. Sniffing, she released her grip on Cormac and allowed John and Denis to lift him between them.

'Where to?' asked the footman.

'The stables,' said John. 'They're not joined to the house so there's no danger of them catching fire too.' He whistled to the men clustered nearby. 'Will one of ye bring the girl?'

Ben Bracken detached himself from the group and jogged over to Cathy. He bent down and murmured, 'I've got you, pet.'

She moaned when he moved her and he took care not to jostle her as he straightened up with her securely in his grasp.

Paying no heed to the four constables, who watched them with blatant distrust, John, Denis and Ben carried the two invalids around the corner of the house and back to the courtyard. Great billows of smoke poured off the building and swirled around them in the night air. Numbly, Bridget realised that her mother had not made it out of the house.

One of the other men opened the double doors of the stables to let them through, and there ensued a flurry of activity as old mounds of straw were fashioned into makeshift beds for the patients. They laid Cormac out in one stall and Cathy in another and rooted around in the loft above for any discarded rushlights or blankets they could find. Ben discovered the abandoned saddle Bridget and Cormac had seen the previous day and used it to prop up Cathy's thighs so her blistered legs would not touch the straw.

Bridget lingered by Cormac's side, subtly but undeniably ignored by the men. John was the only one who continued to acknowledge her; the rest acted like she was a shadow in the corner of the stable stall. She understood why and did not blame them. There was no question but that she deserved their censure.

She knelt next to Cormac, her skirts and cloak spreading out around her. As her gaze roved over his body for signs of injury, she noticed the burns on his fingers. She squeezed her eyes shut, sick with shame.

What she had done had been inexcusable to the point of insanity. What on earth could she have been thinking to ask him to put his life in such danger? In a moment of the most extreme selfishness, she had begged for his help and thus placed him in an impossible situation: if he acquiesced, his own life would hang in the balance, but if he refused, she would hold him responsible for her mother's death. He could only have given her one answer to her request, and that answer had almost cost him his life and might have left Emily without a father.

Had he perished, she was sure the men's attitude towards her would have been far more vocal. But by providence or his own innate luck he still lived and so they confined their reproach to a discreet disregard for her presence. However, any respect they might have held for her was lost – she had shown herself willing to risk the life of a good man for the sake of an evil woman. She was hardly any better than her ruthless mother. She hung her head in disgrace. There was just one good thing that could be said about the whole debacle: at least Cathy had been saved, which meant only one soul had died inside the house, and not two.

Bridget clutched the folds of her cloak as hard as she could, her knuckles protesting against the strain. Her mother was gone. The burning house was her tomb and she was now beyond all redemption. Only Bridget and Cormac knew there had been the faintest hope that the lady might be open to change. To everyone else, she remained a hardhearted tyrant and that was the final memory they would retain of her forever. They were probably glad she was dead.

Bridget did not cry. Yes, there was sadness but above all there was emptiness. Now she had lost both her father and her mother and she had been unable to say a proper goodbye to either one. She felt unfinished, like she could never be quite whole again.

Someone gave an almighty shout outside the stables and her eyes flew open. Had the physician arrived? She struggled to her feet, hampered by her skirts, and dashed out of the stall, but in the courtyard she found only Denis. His arms were outstretched, his face tilted up to the sky.

'Rain!' he cried. "Tis raining!'

A few more men joined them, cheering. John Corbett clapped his hands in relief and Ben Bracken flung his cap into the air. Bridget looked upwards. Thick clouds had gathered above the plumes of smoke and drops spattered her forehead. If it strengthened and lasted long enough, it would douse the raging fire in the manor.

Too late.

Shoulders leaden, she turned to go back into the stables, but a movement by the orchard wall caught her eye. Three male figures were gathered before the peeling door – had they come through it or had they just congregated near it? They crossed the cobbles, two of the figures pushing the third in front of them. When the light of the fire fell upon their features, she recognised them as Joseph Hayes and Bernie Cuddihy, shoving Farmer McKinty ahead of them. The farmer was crying.

'John!' Joseph called out, his posture full of swagger. 'We've got him.'

John stalked forwards, scowling. 'We've been looking for the pair of ye. Where've ye been this past day?'

'Never mind that,' said Bernie. 'Wait 'til we tell ye what we saw.' He smacked Farmer McKinty on the back. ''Tis better to own up now, Mick. They might go easier on you if you do.'

The farmer blubbered but didn't say anything. Joseph shook his head in exaggerated disappointment.

'Ah, Mick. We're trying to help you here.' He held out his hands, palms up, to the other men who had crowded close. 'I'm sorry to be the one telling ye this but we caught him in the act. It was too late to stop him but we're both witnesses to the truth.'

'What're you on about?' John said impatiently.

Joseph elbowed the farmer. 'Tell them. Tell them it was you started the fire.'

Bridget felt something unpleasant sprout in the pit of her stomach as the rain began to come down more heavily. She didn't like leaving Cormac unattended for so long, but she couldn't turn her back on what was happening.

Farmer McKinty snivelled, his nose running. 'I d-did it,' he managed to get out, rubbing at his eyes like a child.

Denis stared, mouth open. 'Mick started it?' he said disbelievingly to the other two.

'Saw him with my own eyes,' said Bernie. He motioned to John with a loud sigh. 'I guess you'll be wanting to send for the constabulary.'

John's jaw tautened. Then, to Bridget's surprise, he swivelled in her direction and said to her in a confidential tone, 'M'lady? What's your opinion on this?'

She blinked. Why had he relapsed to that formal address again? She had been happy to tolerate 'Miss Bridget'.

When she said nothing, he prompted, 'What d'you want to do, m'lady?'

'What do *I* want?' she said. 'Surely I have no say?'

'They're your tenants. They're under your orders.'

'My —' she began and stopped. She goggled at John as realisation dawned. 'You mean…?'

His countenance softened at her sheer astonishment. 'You're the lady of the big house now.'

She stood frozen. He was correct. With Lady Courcey's death, her contracted guardianship of the estate had come to an end, and thus responsibility for it had reverted back to the title-holder. Her daughter.

## A Class Forsaken

Garrett could lay claim to Oakleigh in legal terms, but he was in London, while Bridget was standing right here on the land that her father had always intended to be hers.

A wave of powerful emotion surged up inside her as the restraints her mother and Garrett had long imposed upon her fell away. She had a duty here, and she intended to carry it out to the best of her ability.

She cast a cold eye towards Farmer McKinty. His cheeks were soaked with tears and raindrops. Then she looked past him to Joseph and Bernie.

'You claim you saw this man set the fire?' she said.

They both nodded confidently.

'Then where have you been all this time while others were making efforts to quench it?'

Bernie's answer came at once. 'He ran away from us. We had to catch him and bring him back.'

'And what were you doing on the manor grounds in the first place, and at such a late hour?'

'Hunting rabbits,' Joseph chimed in. 'We saw one run under the gate at the Gorteen, so we followed it. Caught Mick red-handed.' His expression was smug, like he knew their story was watertight.

'I see,' said Bridget. 'And where were you last night?'

'At the barn, with everyone else,' said Joseph, his eyes wide and innocent. 'You saw us there.'

'Yes, but you were not present later at Hogan Farm. Where did you go after the meeting?'

'Hunting.' He crossed his arms. ''Tis how we spend many nights. We've got families to feed and that's no easy task these days, thanks to your damn mother.'

'Indeed. And did you go hunting before or after you paid a visit to Blackcastle Inn?'

He narrowed his gaze. 'We were nowhere near Blackcastle Inn.'

She feigned surprise. 'Oh, how very strange. Because Mr Enright can identify both of you as having been there before dawn.'

'He can't have,' said Bernie, indignant. 'Sure, we were wearing –'

Joseph jabbed Bernie in the ribs and he snapped his mouth shut, going red in the face.

Bridget drew herself up. 'As of this moment, I refuse to believe a single word that comes out of your mouths. And I hold you accountable for the destruction that has occurred here tonight.'

Joseph sneered. 'You've got no proof! You can't –'

The rest of his words were swallowed in a clatter of hooves on cobbles. Bridget's heart leapt as Liam, angel that he was, came riding into the courtyard accompanied by a bearded man on another horse; she recognised him as Mr Abbott, her mother's physician who had tended

Bridget herself when she contracted a fever after the thunderstorm. Behind them came a third male rider whose face was not familiar to her.

Liam slid from his horse, panting. 'We got back as quick as we could. Thank God 'tis raining now. Is everyone safe?' He looked around, taking in the hostile stance of the assembled group and the still-weeping farmer at the centre. 'What's going on here?'

Bridget decided that she had no time for the criminals right now. 'Ben, could you and some of the others escort these men into the harness room in the stables and stand guard over them? I shall deal with them presently. Please be sure to treat Farmer McKinty with kindness. And perhaps, John, you could find the constables on the grounds and alert them to this new development in the situation.'

'I can do that,' said John, his expression grim but approving.

Joseph's jaw fell open, while Bernie said weakly, 'There are constables already here? We thought we'd be long gone before...'

Bridget did not deign to respond. Ben and the others didn't look very happy about taking her orders but they led Joseph, Bernie and Farmer McKinty away, disregarding the protests from the first two and gently steering the stumbling farmer through the stable doors. John left the courtyard at a trot to seek out the constables, while Bridget returned her attention to Liam and the physician, who had also dismounted from his horse.

'Thank you for coming at this late hour, Mr Abbott, I am so grateful.'

The physician detached a black medical case from his saddle. 'Lady Courcey has been a regular patient of mine for several years. This is not my first night-time visit to her. Her waning health has been a sad sight to behold, but I shall do what I can to help.'

Bridget bowed her head. 'I'm afraid my mother is beyond your help, sir. She did not escape the conflagration.'

Liam inhaled sharply. 'What about—'

She gave him a reassuring nod, even though she felt far from reassured herself now that she had spent several minutes absent from Cormac's side. What if his condition had worsened in the meantime? She addressed Mr Abbott with a rising sense of urgency. 'While my mother cannot be saved, there are two other victims of the fire who would gladly receive your attention.'

He knit his brows. 'Who? Lady Courcey was the only upper class resident in the house.'

It maddened her that this could be an impediment but she kept a tight rein on her temper. 'That is true,' she said, 'but would you deny your assistance to two lower class individuals just because of the circumstances of their birth?'

He let out a huff. 'This is highly irregular. I do not tend servants and suchlike.'

'I appeal to your Christian goodness, sir,' she said, ignoring the rain that was growing into a downpour and drenching her bare head. 'Please, only you can provide the care they desperately need.'

Touchily, he said, 'Oh, very well. Direct me to them.' He snapped his fingers at Denis, who still lingered nearby. 'You there, look after my horse.'

Despite being a footman and not a stable hand, Denis took hold of the reins.

'Speaking of Christian goodness, this is Father Macken,' Liam interjected, waving over the third man who had descended from his horse with the difficulty of a person suffering from stiff joints. 'I thought it best to seek him out too…in case the last rites might be needed…'

Bridget swallowed. 'I sincerely hope that will not be the case, but thank you, Father, for coming. Perhaps you could bless them with a swift recovery?'

'I shall appeal to the Lord Jesus and the Blessed Virgin Mary to watch over them,' Father Macken said in a wavering voice.

He was advanced in years, with sagging jowls and wrinkles around his eyes and mouth. By his name, Bridget knew him to be the priest at St Mary's Catholic Church in Ballydarry. She had never attended Mass there but Cormac had brought her inside the empty church on a number of occasions. She was glad Liam had thought to summon the priest, but she made no mention of the soul lost within the manor house; Lady Courcey had not been a Roman Catholic.

She led Mr Abbott and Father Macken into the stables and pointed out the two stalls where Cormac and Cathy lay. Though she knew Cathy's legs were badly burnt, she directed the physician to Cormac's stall first because at least the maid was awake, while Cormac's lapse into unconsciousness was an increasing source of worry. When she tried to follow Mr Abbott into the stall, he made an irritable gesture at her.

'Don't crowd me,' he said. 'I need time and space to examine him. Leave me be for now.'

Anxious, she said, 'Will you tell me if he awakens?'

He let the half door of the stall swing shut without answering her.

As she turned away in frustration, she remembered the trembling, disfigured form of Mr Enright lying on Farmer Hogan's kitchen table. She resolved that, after the physician had finished examining Cormac and Cathy, she would attempt to persuade him to visit Hogan Farm. He would have less grounds for objection, given that Mr Enright was a member of the landed gentry.

Because Mr Abbott clearly had no desire for company, she guided Father Macken to Cathy's stall instead. She did not follow him in, but she heard the maid's soft whimpers and the old priest's comforting murmurs.

The clip-clop of hooves drew her attention back to the stable doors, where Liam and Denis were bringing the three horses in out of the rain. Denis averted his gaze from her, blushing but determined to follow the lead of the majority in shunning her. Too ashamed to keep her head up, she trained her eyes on the compacted earth beneath her feet until they had passed her by, leading the animals into stalls at the further end of the stables, away from the improvised hospital wing.

When she looked up again, her gaze fell upon the closed door of the harness room. Ben and two others stood outside it. Steeling herself, she crossed the central aisle of the stables.

'Ben, could I please ask you to accompany me inside?' she asked, forcing her voice not to quiver. She had to maintain a facade of composure in order to confront this next challenge.

His expression was grim but he took off his cap and stepped aside to let her through.

The harness room was bare of any articles that might have marked its original function; the pegs, hooks and racks along the walls were empty of halters, reins and saddles. All the room contained was three men clustered in the far corner, two of them leaning in an intimidating fashion over the third.

'You heard me, Mick,' said Joseph in a growl. 'You've got to convince them it was you.'

Farmer McKinty was on his hunkers, his hands close to his head like he was afraid they might hit him. Joseph and Bernie jumped back as Bridget entered, followed by Ben who stood near the door, ready to intervene if the two men proved difficult.

'Mick's got something to say—' Joseph began at once but Bridget silenced him with a glare. She strode over to the farmer and squatted next to him. He had scrunched his eyes shut and mucus coated his lip and chin. She fished inside her pocket, praying for a handkerchief, and found one.

'Shall we clean you up?' she said gently.

When he opened his eyes, he made weak smacking noises with his lips and moaned fretfully. She doubted his ability to understand her intention, so she wiped his face for him, then folded the handkerchief and tucked it into his fist.

'You just rest there for a little while,' she said and patted him on the shoulder before rising again.

She faced Joseph and Bernie with her shoulders back; at least here she was not the most contemptible person present.

'You have committed a terrible crime,' she said.

'It wasn't us,' Bernie insisted.

She bestowed a withering look upon him. 'Please dispense with the denials. Not for one second can I believe that Farmer McKinty acted of his own free will. You may have set the fire yourselves or you may have coerced him into doing it, but either way you are the culpable ones.'

Bernie threw a glower of resentment in Joseph's direction. Mutinous, Joseph shrugged and scoffed, 'Arrah, there's worse in this world than what we did.'

'Indeed?' said Bridget. 'Worse than murder?'

He blinked, and Bernie repeated, 'Murder?'

'Yes.'

'We didn't kill anybody,' said Joseph, his forehead creased in confusion.

'And yet my mother is dead,' she said with surprising calmness.

His eyes bulged. 'The lady's dead?' He shot an accusing look over at Ben. 'You didn't tell us that!'

Ben scratched his nose and stared ahead, saying nothing.

Joseph whirled back to Bridget, his expression more panicky. 'We didn't know she'd died. We didn't mean for that to happen.'

She gave a contemptuous snort. 'You expect me to believe that?'

"Tis the truth!' he said, his voice rising in pitch as he realised the enormity of the charge being laid against them. 'I swear 'tis the truth!'

'Honest to God, 'tis!' said Bernie earnestly.

Bridget folded her arms. 'So you are saying that you set fire to the manor with the belief that you were not putting anyone's lives in danger?'

Joseph wiped his sweaty hands on his unkempt clothes. 'We wanted to scare her. The big house is a symbol of her wealth and power. We wanted to damage it so she'd realise she wasn't untouchable. But there should've been plenty of time for her to escape. Why didn't she get out of the house?'

Bridget wanted to know the answer to that question too. But that was a conversation she must have with Cormac, not with Joseph Hayes.

'My mother still had one maid working for her. The servants' sleeping quarters were on the topmost floor. Do you think the girl had a decent chance of escape?'

'Did she die too?' Bernie asked hollowly.

'She was saved. No thanks to you.'

They both stared at the floor. In the silence, Farmer McKinty's whimpers became audible; he was rocking on his haunches in the corner and sucking on the edge of Bridget's handkerchief. She hoped it was a clean edge.

Regarding Joseph and Bernie with revulsion, she carried on, 'And now to your other crime. The appalling attack on the land agent, Mr Enright.'

She waited for them to protest but neither of them said anything. Her stomach turned. Their silence may as well have been a confession. Knowing with certainty that the two men before her had instigated that vile atrocity made her want to flee from the room, as though their very presence was poisonous, but she stood her ground and, when she spoke, her voice was quiet and controlled.

'I cannot fathom the depraved mind that could do that to another human being. No man, no matter how despicable you deem him to be, deserves such disfigurement, indignity or pain.' She let her hands drop to her sides. 'Answer me this: did you go directly to Blackcastle Inn after the raid on the barn?'

Joseph gave a tiny jerk of his head.

'And where did you conceal yourselves afterwards? Men went searching for you but you were nowhere to be found.'

'We got Mick to hide us in his barn,' muttered Bernie. 'Figured it was the last place anyone would think to look.'

She pursed her lips. 'The way you have abused that poor man is deplorable. Your wickedness knows no bounds.'

Her blood was boiling but she strained to preserve her cool exterior. She clasped her hands before her. 'The assault on Mr Enright alone would be enough to condemn you. But coupling that with what has transpired here tonight…' She took a breath. 'I have no choice but to exact punishment with a severity proportional to the offences you have committed. And I believe nothing less than transportation will be appropriate.'

Joseph's gaze snapped up, his eyes full of scorn. 'You? What power do *you* have here?'

'Have you so soon forgotten my mother's passing? With her death, the responsibility for Oakleigh has come into my keeping. It is my duty to pass judgement upon you, or at least to communicate it to those who will carry it out.' She bared her teeth. 'Did you know that, as the land agent, Mr Enright serves as the local magistrate on behalf of the Courcey title? He would have the authority to reason with me to have your sentence commuted. But I don't think he is likely to plead for leniency in this case, do you?'

Joseph's lip curled. She saw in his face the exact moment when he realised the ghastly future which now lay before him. Without warning, he lunged for her, his hands stretching for her throat. Ben leapt forwards but he was not quick enough. Bridget felt Joseph's fingers close around her neck.

In the next instant, they were ripped away and Joseph was lying flat on his back, grunting as the wind was knocked out of him. Farmer McKinty stood over him, breathing heavily, the handkerchief still in his grasp. Ben hauled Joseph to his feet and shoved him into the furthest corner of the room from Bridget. He dragged Bernie away from her too, but the fellow showed no resistance, cowering away from Ben's threatening fist.

Before Bridget could recover her breath, footfalls pounded outside the harness room and John appeared at the door, flanked by Constables Quirke and Tierney.

'That's them,' John said, pointing at Joseph and Bernie.

The constables aimed their rifles in the direction of the pair of men. Joseph and Bernie exchanged glances of misery and defeat. In the absence of their bravado, they appeared small and weak, as insignificant as mice.

Bridget stepped forwards and addressed them for the last time. 'You are no longer welcome on Oakleigh land. However, your families may remain and I will ensure that that they are looked after.'

Joseph opened his mouth but she turned on her heel and left without another word.

She felt a potent energy thrumming in her veins as she strode through the stables and out into the rain, desiring solitude. She sucked in the cool, damp air. The feeling of power was intoxicating.

And that scared her.

## Chapter 14

It was an hour or two past dawn and the rain had stopped falling. The light was grey, the air was cold, and the manor house was a smoking ruin. The skeleton of the outer red-bricked walls still stood forlornly in the weak daylight, but the building's elegant innards had been demolished. There was no hope of salvage. Oakleigh Manor was no more.

Ash floated in the air, settling on the cobbles of the courtyard and in Bridget's hair. She lingered next to the gaping frame where the kitchen door had once hung and touched her palm to the blackened bricks, the carcass of a great creature with its entrails mangled.

Mrs Kavanagh and her sister stood nearby. The cook was weeping copiously, her hands pressed to her face.

'I don't know why you're so upset,' Kitty Brophy said, her tone snide. 'This is a *good thing.*'

The woman did not understand. She couldn't see that Mrs Kavanagh was not grieving for a pile of charred debris, but for the loss of a place called home. No matter the terrible developments of recent years, Oakleigh had for so long held them all in its bosom. It had been the seat of the Courcey title but more importantly the seat of their affections. It had been a cherished refuge and the beating heart of this land. And now it was gone.

'M'lady?' said a man's voice.

Bridget looked around, wiping her cheeks. John was crossing the cobbles towards her, his expression neither friendly nor unfriendly as he approached.

'Yes?' she said.

'He's awake.'

Her stomach flipped sickeningly. She of course wanted Cormac to be awake but she dreaded facing him after what she had put him through. She took in a trembling breath.

'Will he see me now?'

'He asked for you,' said John, betraying no hint of what Cormac's disposition had been when he had made the request.

She followed John back to the stables where a couple of men loitered inside by the doors. Their features hardened at the sight of her; she suffered their silent condemnation without complaint. John held open the half door of Cormac's stall for her and she edged inside.

Fresh rushlights had been lit and placed on a bench along one wall. By their light, she discerned Mr Abbott leaning over Cormac on the makeshift straw bed. Her heart jumped into her mouth. He was lying on his back with his eyes closed but they fluttered open when she came in. His burnt hand was wrapped in a loose bandage and there were jagged cuts on his other hand – apart from that he appeared to be physically sound. However, it was a shock to hear him speak.

'Bridget,' he said in a scratchy whisper. He winced but forced out, 'You're safe? John told me about the constables...'

His voice was unrecognisable as his own, a husky croak far removed from his usual, smooth tones. He must have inhaled a great deal of smoke to bring about such a stark alteration. She felt even worse than she had before entering the stall.

'Never mind me,' she said wretchedly. 'How are you feeling?'

His answer was lost in a fit of coughing. Mr Abbott gave him a mechanical pat on the shoulder and moved aside to make room for Bridget in the tight space.

'Don't let him talk for long,' he warned her. He put a roll of bandages into his medical case, closed it with a snap, and exited the stall. John let the half door swing shut and Bridget and Cormac were left alone.

She knelt beside the straw bed and gazed at her injured lover. His hair was caked with soot and his eyelids looked heavy, as if it were an effort for him to keep them open. Guilt gnawed at her insides but she could not bring herself to speak. If she opened her mouth to ask for forgiveness, she was liable to dissolve into floods of tears. So she just rested her hand on his unbound one and did not say anything.

He, too, was silent for a long time. Then he said hoarsely, 'Is Cathy in a bad way?'

'She's sleeping,' said Bridget. 'Mr Abbott gave her laudanum for the pain. Her burns are severe but he said she will heal.'

'That's good to hear.' He took his hand away to rub his eyes. When he dropped it again, he did not place it back with hers but instead let it fall to his lap. She felt a hiccup of unease.

There was a rap on the half door and they looked up to see Father Macken there. He raised his arm in an apologetic wave.

'I've been by already,' he said. 'But I heard you'd woken.'

Cormac struggled to sit up. 'Come in, Father,' he rasped.

The priest entered the stall. The disturbance in the night had taken its toll on the elderly man and his posture was stooped with tiredness.

'Liam Kirwan feared the last rites might be needed,' he said, 'but I'm glad that wasn't the case.'

'You and me both,' said Cormac. A shadow crossed his face and, in a brief moment of uncharacteristic antagonism, he added in a mutter, 'Pity my sister never got them.'

Bridget comprehended what he meant and, had their hands still been clasped, she would have squeezed his now. It had been Father Macken himself who had denied Mary the sacrament of the last rites because she had intentionally ended her own life.

The priest did not appear to have heard Cormac's bitter words. 'By all accounts you acted bravely last night,' he said. 'God bless you for your efforts to save the maid.'

Cormac let out a sigh, the exertion of ill will too great to sustain. 'Thank you, Father.'

Father Macken looked in Bridget's direction. 'My condolences on the loss of your mother,' he said, somewhat stiffly. 'Have you sent word to St Canice's?'

She shook her head. St Canice's was the Church of Ireland establishment in Ballydarry and her father was interred in the graveyard there. Of course her mother would wish to be buried alongside him. But no one had yet gone into the rubble to retrieve her body...or what remained of it.

'I can go by there on my way back to the village,' said Father Macken. 'I'll let them know their services are needed.'

'I would greatly appreciate that,' she said.

Cormac cleared his throat, the sound as rough as nails. 'Father, I've just remembered. We met your niece and her husband on our journey here and they told us to send you their regards.'

He glanced at Bridget and she took over in the telling of how they had encountered Farmer Hackett and been so well received by him and his wife at their farm.

Father Macken beamed. 'Well now, isn't that lovely to hear? I know we're not meant to have favourites, be they children or nieces and nephews, but she was always mine.' The end of his sentence was nearly swallowed in the yawn he tried, and failed, to suppress.

The corner of Cormac's mouth lifted. 'Go away home to your bed, Father. Thank you again for coming and for your prayers.'

The priest made the sign of the cross and backed out of the stall, yawning even more widely.

After he was gone, Bridget realised she had been grateful for his interruption. Now she and Cormac were by themselves again and a dense cloud of tension rose in the air between them.

He looked down at his bandage, picking at it with his fingernails. 'Do you want me to tell you what happened with your mother?'

She stiffened. After a beat, she said, 'Yes.'

'She said that I could lie,' he muttered, almost to himself. 'She said that I could give you whatever version of events I wanted. But I think the truth is best in the long run.' He looked up at Bridget with red-rimmed eyes irritated by the smoke. 'Your mother chose to die last night. She had an opportunity to escape but she did not take it. It was her wish to depart this life and she fulfilled that wish.'

Bridget was unable to respond for several seconds. 'I d-don't understand.'

'I found her. She was upstairs in your father's bedchamber and she had his things about her. She knew the house was on fire but made no move to flee. I tried to convince her to come with me but she refused.' He rubbed the back of his hand across his forehead, smearing the soot there. 'In the end I had to leave her. There was no way of changing her mind.'

Bridget tried to swallow but her throat was too dry. Could it be true? Had her mother's demise in the fire been a deliberate act?

'I know this must be hard for you to hear,' he said, his voice little more than a croak, 'but she was aware that she was not going to live for much longer and she decided that sooner was better than later.'

Bridget felt dazed. Yesterday her mother had seemed intent upon seeing her granddaughter again; there had been a sense of purpose in her manner. But mere hours later she had given up on life altogether.

'Did she—did she say anything to you? Did she have any message for me?'

He was about to speak when he was overcome by another bout of coughing. She looked around anxiously for a cup of water but there was none. The fit passed and, wheezing and eyes watering, he was able to reply, 'There was no message. She just told me to look after Emily better than she had looked after you.' He paused. 'She also said that she had misjudged me.'

Bridget's heart lifted. Was that a sign that her mother had repented? Had she at last, in her dying moments, accepted Cormac for who he was? Perhaps she had even begged his forgiveness for what she had done to his family.

'I would not give too much weight to that,' he rasped, as if he had read her mind. 'It was not a scene of lamentation and reconciliation. She was still your mother through and through, unremorseful to the end.'

Bridget was disappointed. He could have let her hold on to that tiny shred of consolation. But then she remembered that she did not deserve any such solace to her conscience.

It was time to make her apology, insufficient though it would be.

'Cormac, I am so awfully sorry.' Tentatively, she reached out and laid a gentle hand on his arm. He did not react to her touch. 'What I did to you was unpardonable. I had no right to ask you to put your life at such risk but I was frightened for my mother and I knew you would not say no. I took advantage of you and abused our bond of love and trust.' Self-loathing clawed at her throat. Tears filled her eyes but she tried to hold them back. 'I cannot ask for your forgiveness because I know I am not worthy of it, but I swear in my disgrace that I will endeavour to earn it over time by any means within my grasp.' A single tear escaped, making its lonely way down her cheek. 'I realise that this is poor comfort for how much you have suffered but please let me know if there is anything I can do to begin making things right again between us.'

For several long moments, he stared into his lap. When he looked up, his countenance told her that he agreed with everything she had said, but his words were not harsh.

'Just please do not ask me to do something like that again,' he murmured.

'I promise,' she said, eyes lowered.

Neither of them said anything else. There was no need for him to reproach her further for she knew full well the magnitude of her wrongdoing. She considered asking him about how he had saved Cathy and escaped from the fire, but then she remembered the physician's caution to avoid letting him talk too much. She swallowed her questions and the silence stretched between them until they heard another light knock. This time it was Liam standing beyond the half door of the stall.

'I brought a visitor,' he said and held open the door to reveal Emily in front of him.

Her fretful expression cleared at the sight of her parents. Bridget stood up and stepped away as Cormac lay back and held out his arms. Emily slipped into them, laying herself on the straw next to her father and hugging him like she had not seen him in a year. No words were necessary. Bridget felt sad and a little bit excluded; she and Cormac had not shared a similar exchange of affection. She reminded herself that she could not expect that yet – he would let her know when he was ready for such intimacy again.

Liam started to leave the stall but she caught his eye and motioned for him to stay. He stepped inside and she joined him near the door.

'How is Ellen?' she asked, keeping her voice quiet.

'She's fine now, but she was sick with worry while we were gone. I wasn't able to return to the cottage 'til dawn so she spent all that time not knowing what was happening and imagining the worst. She's very relieved that Cormac and Cathy are safe but she passes on her sympathies to you regarding your mother.'

'That is very kind of her,' said Bridget automatically.

'She said she'll come up here as soon as she can get someone from the village to mind the boys. She doesn't want to have that rowdy pair running around in the middle of all the commotion.'

Bridget nodded. She hoped Ellen would come before too long. She felt suddenly desperate for her companionship and counsel.

'I hear you decided on a sentence of transportation,' said Liam, his face grave.

She sighed. 'I did. Do you believe it was the right course of action?'

"Tisn't my place to say. But I do think your mother would've been less lenient.'

'I know. She would probably have had them hanged on the spot for the irreparable damage they have done to the manor.'

'Such a reckless thing to do,' he said, shaking his head. 'And wicked how they dragged Mick McKinty into it. I met Maisie on the road and she's fit to tear strips off them. Least they're off your hands now. You're far better off without tenants like them.'

Bridget became aware of Cormac's gaze upon her and turned to see him leaning up on one elbow. He glanced sharply from her to Liam.

'What are you two talking about?' he asked in his hoarse voice.

She shifted uncomfortably. Her gut told her that this was going to make matters even worse. 'Joseph Hayes and Bernie Cuddihy. They are going to be transported to Australia.'

'On whose orders?' said Cormac, but he looked like he already knew the answer.

'Mine,' she said unwillingly. Then she added in desperation, as though to justify the act, 'I hold the Courcey title. There was nobody else to give the command.'

His face darkened. He said nothing aloud but a current of communication flowed from him to Bridget through his expression. She understood at once that the last thing he wanted was for her to assume the management of the Oakleigh Estate. That would tie them to a level of society from which he wished to escape. They would not be free to lead a simple life with such a burden of responsibility on her shoulders. In the short term, they might even be forced to separate if she chose to remain on her estate while he continued to look for his family. Her new status created a web of complications which would only exacerbate the strain that had mounted between them after the events of the previous night.

A fresh flood of guilt washed over her.

'I need to get some air,' she blurted and hurried out of the stall, brushing past Liam who, oblivious to the silent message Cormac had just conveyed, looked confused by her abrupt departure.

She hastened out of the stables and across the cobbled courtyard, avoiding the startled stares of Mrs Kavanagh and Kitty Brophy. Rounding the corner of the ruined manor, she made for the tree-lined gravelled avenue. The constables' horse-drawn wagon was gone; the two criminals had been whisked away in it after the altercation in the harness room. She pounded the loose stones beneath her feet, putting distance between herself and Cormac with every step.

What did he expect her to do? Should she abandon Oakleigh and leave it to decay the way her mother had done? It was her duty to take care of the tenants' concerns; they had been neglected for far too long. Whether Cormac liked it or not, undertaking that task was her birthright. Perhaps it was not a position she desired to hold but she could not shirk it for that reason alone.

Still, she abhorred the other consequences of that decision. If she stayed to manage the estate and he left to seek his family in Dublin, they might be parted for weeks, maybe longer. Who would keep Emily? Their little family would be broken up after it had only just been formed.

Then there was the question of whether the tenants would even welcome her. What was to stop them from rising up against her as they had her mother? It could likely be quite a dangerous course of action and that made her fearful.

Through the mire of her thoughts, she heard the braying of a donkey and looked up in surprise. The animal was labouring into view further down the avenue, pulling a cart. She recognised the driver at the front as Farmer Hogan and, to her relief, Ellen was perched next to him.

She kept walking to meet them. When they reached her, the farmer pulled on the reins and the donkey came to a halt, letting out another 'Hee-haw!' as it strained its head towards Bridget to greet her. Ellen climbed down to the ground with a protective hand over her pregnant bump and, in an atypical move for a former lady's maid whose old habits were hard to break, hugged Bridget tightly. She took a great deal of comfort from the embrace.

When they pulled apart, Ellen said, 'We brought someone with us.'

She led Bridget around to the back of the cart where a figure sat propped up in its bed. Stuffed sacks had been positioned on all sides to keep him upright and secure in spite of the jerky movements of the cart. He was fully clothed but he wore no spectacles or boots, and bandages bound his hands and feet.

'Mr Enright!' Bridget exclaimed. 'What are you doing here? Ought you not to be resting in bed?'

The land agent gave her a wan smile. 'Perhaps, but I insisted on coming.'

'Wouldn't take no for an answer,' said Farmer Hogan, twisting around in his seat. 'Said I had to figure out a way to get him here. This was the best I could come up with.'

'And then they passed me in the lane so I hopped on too,' said Ellen. 'A grand way to save my boots from the mud after the heavy rain.'

Bridget rested her hand on the side panel of the cart. 'Mr Enright, I'm pleased to say that Mr Abbott, my mother's physician, is still on the grounds. I had intended to ask him to call upon you at Hogan Farm, but now he can examine your wounds while you're here.'

He shrugged. The clothes Farmer Hogan had given him didn't fit well across his muscular shoulders and the action looked awkward. 'That can wait. Firstly, I would beg you for a word in private.'

Farmer Hogan and Ellen exchanged glances.

'Looks like a mighty fine spot for a quick stroll, don't you think?' the farmer said.

'It does,' she agreed. 'I spotted a fine clump of daffodils back along the avenue which I should like to go back and admire, if you'll accompany me?'

Before they departed, Farmer Hogan helped Bridget into the cart so she could sit opposite Mr Enright for their conversation. Then he and Ellen disappeared down the avenue, chattering blithely about spring flowers.

Mr Enright waited until they had vanished from view before saying, 'You'll forgive me but a significant degree of discretion is required for some of the things I'm about to say.'

Bridget shifted her weight to avoid one of the sacks digging into her knee. 'I shall exercise prudence in all that we discuss. You have my word.'

'Thank you, my lady.'

'Oh, you don't need to address me — '

'Yes, I do,' he interrupted. 'That is one of the first lessons you must learn. You held a title in London so you understand how it works but I suspect you might not regard it the same way here, where you once lived as a child. However, you are the Lady Courcey and others must accord you that respect.'

She viewed the issue somewhat differently but did not argue the point, given that he had already begun to grow paler with the effort of talking.

He continued, 'As well as my respect, I must offer you my thanks. You treated me with great compassion at the farm when I was struggling to come to terms with my ordeal. Thank you for your kindness and for encouraging others to act likewise.'

'It was the least I could do,' she murmured. 'I cannot describe how sorry I am for what you have suffered.'

'There are many on this estate who will believe I got my just reward.' His hands twitched, like he wanted to clench them but couldn't. 'I tell you plainly, I have hated the role I've been forced to play these past years. I could see the estate falling to ruin around me but could do nothing to stop it. Your mother sat in her privileged seclusion and would not entertain any of my pleas to show leniency to the tenants. It was truly devastating both to witness it and to be an unwilling participant.'

He paused and she waited, sensing he had more to say and was steeling himself to say it. By now, all colour had drained from his face.

'I...' he said slowly. 'I tried to reason with her. I said I would inform Lord Wyndham. I threatened to resign from my role as land agent. But she—she had incriminating information about me which she promised to use against me if I hindered her in any way.' He ground his teeth. 'By a foolish oversight on my part, I left a document of a...personal nature in among the accounts which I had brought to the manor for her perusal. She discovered it, read its contents and comprehended that she had the means to keep me under her thumb for the rest of my life.' He looked Bridget directly in the eye. 'My lady, would you consider yourself to be of a similar character to your mother?'

Barely a heartbeat passed before she said, 'No, not in the slightest. I have long believed that almost all of who I am was given to me by my father. I have my failings,' she added, once more recalling with regret the events of the previous night, 'but they are not the same as my mother's.'

'I suspected as much,' he said, 'having witnessed your spirited disposition as a child and your solicitous conduct at Hogan Farm. I hope and believe that I can trust you.' He lowered his gaze. 'I will not go so far as to describe the subject matter of the letter, but you may well guess its substance. I received it from a gentleman with whom I have been...acquainted for many years. Our connection is not known in upper class circles.'

Bridget kept her expression composed but she could fully see why her mother had identified the letter as an instrument of power.

'My acquaintance's rank in society is much higher than my own. For his sake, I could not risk our connection becoming exposed. So I did as your mother bade me. I ensured the forced collection of rents, liaised with the tithe proctors, carried out the evictions. I had no other choice. And I am reviled the length and breadth of the estate for it.'

Bridget pressed her fingertips to her lips, shocked at what the agent had been compelled to endure. 'I am appalled that she coerced you in this way. At least you are now free from her control.'

He glanced up. 'Yes, and I believe you can put her mistakes to rights.'

Bridget gulped. 'There are many aspects of the situation to consider, not to mention some complications which may prove challenging to overcome.'

'I can perceive some of them myself already,' he said, nodding. 'Chief among them is that the tenants have developed a thirst for independence. You may find it difficult at first for them to accept you in this role, given the damage your mother has done to it.'

'There may be other impediments that you have not foreseen,' she said weakly.

'I understand that your husband is the legal owner of the property,' he went on, 'but he has never expressed an interest in running it himself. Now that your mother's guardianship has ended, a new arrangement could be reached whereby you are contracted to be the overseer of the estate in your husband's name. Such a contract could easily be drawn up by Webb & Brereton in Dublin.'

'Mr Enright,' she said. 'I do appreciate your thoughts on this and I acknowledge that your contribution is highly valuable. However, there are particular circumstances of which I must make you aware before any decisions can be made.'

'I'm certain whatever they are they can be overcome,' he said with a confidence she did not share. 'My lady, you know you must do this. It is your obligation. You alone can restore Oakleigh to what it once was.'

Some colour had returned to his features. In his animation, he accidentally knocked one bandaged hand against the other and he let out a hiss of pain at the contact. As she offered him a sympathetic look, she noticed Ellen and Farmer Hogan strolling back up the avenue. Ellen clutched a small bunch of daffodils; they appeared to be past their best but she raised them towards Bridget with a smile.

'Perhaps we can continue this discussion at a later stage,' she said to Mr Enright. 'But please know that I will treat everything you have disclosed to me with absolute discretion.'

He dipped his head in gratitude.

The ambling pair reached the cart and Farmer Hogan called out a greeting. His donkey, upon hearing its master's voice, brayed enthusiastically in return. The farmer helped Bridget back down to the gravel and, after thanking him, she turned to Ellen.

'May we talk?' she asked. 'I am in need of your advice.' She peeked back hastily at Mr Enright. 'On a separate matter to what you and I have just discussed, needless to say.' Well, the two conversations were related but she would not be delving into the agent's private affairs.

He waved one bandaged hand in acknowledgement as Ellen said, 'Yes, of course.'

'You go on ahead,' Bridget said to Farmer Hogan. 'Please take Mr Enright up to the stables to be examined by Mr Abbott. We shall follow on foot.'

Farmer Hogan climbed back into his seat and clicked his tongue at the waiting donkey. The animal trotted forwards and the cart moved on, carrying Mr Enright in the direction of the house. Bridget hoped the men there would keep their resentment towards him to a minimum; he had already suffered enough.

As they receded from sight, Ellen said, 'What happened last night was just dreadful. How is Cormac faring?'

Bridget looked away.

'What's the matter?' asked Ellen. 'He hasn't taken a turn for the worse, has he?'

Bridget shook her head and, in a brief summary, related the

circumstances of the previous night and that morning which had led to her current dilemma, culminating in Mr Enright's insistence that she was now obligated to run the Oakleigh Estate and Cormac's unmistakable opposition to that role.

'I don't know what I should do,' she finished. 'I feel like my head and my heart are at war with each other.'

Ellen chewed her lip. 'And you'd like my opinion?'

'Very much so.'

'Well, I think it's quite plain what you must do.'

'It is?' said Bridget, startled.

'Of course. You must go with Cormac, no question about it.'

'But Oakleigh—'

'You shouldn't be concerned about Oakleigh. You've spent enough of your life doing your duty. Now you should satisfy your own heart.'

'But all the tenants—'

'Sell the estate. Or appoint a steward to manage it on your behalf if you wish to keep it in your family. But whatever you do, pass the responsibility on to someone else. You don't want to be parted from Cormac again, not even for a short time, knowing how much it's cost you both to get to this point. You should follow him wherever he wants to go because where he is lies your happiness.'

Bridget stared at Ellen as the murkiness cleared from her brain. It was so glaring in its simplicity. Ellen was right. Bridget belonged with Cormac but there was still a way to ensure that the estate was managed as it ought to be. Her mind toiled feverishly as she pictured how it might come together. Yes, it could work.

'Oh, Ellen, bless you for such excellent enlightenment,' she said, giving her a fervent hug.

She slipped her arm through Ellen's and they walked back up the avenue towards the house. Ellen gasped when the blackened and crumbling building came into sight.

'What a crying shame,' she murmured.

They made their way around the corner of the manor house back to the cobbled courtyard. Farmer Hogan had stopped his cart in the middle of the courtyard and Mr Abbott was perched in the back of it next to Mr Enright, removing the bandages from one of his hands and examining the fingertips. Denis, Ben and a few of the other men milled around, some averting their eyes, others watching in morbid fascination and not a little antipathy. To Bridget's surprise, Cormac was standing at the front of the cart and speaking to the farmer. What was he doing up and about already? He glanced past the farmer's shoulder, saw Bridget and Ellen coming and hastened towards them. Bridget was taken aback to perceive that he had a slight limp.

'What is wrong with your leg?' she asked before he could say anything.

'It's fine. I think I just twisted my ankle when I fell out of the drawing room window.' His voice was still husky but his eyes did not seem quite so heavy. 'Why did you leave? I followed you outside but I could not find you anywhere.'

'I just needed some space to think,' she said. 'I did not go far.'

Looking troubled, he said, 'I'm sorry about the way I reacted before. It wasn't fair of me to be like that.'

'Never fear,' she said. 'I believe I have a solution to our quandary.'

He tilted his head, wary. 'You do?'

In response, she went up to the group of men gathered near the cart and asked, 'Could one of you please fetch John Corbett to me?'

They stared sullenly back at her until Denis dropped his gaze and disappeared into the stables. She returned to Cormac and Ellen.

'Why are they all looking so surly?' Cormac asked, his brow furrowed.

She focused on the cobbles, remorse flooding her insides once more. 'They bear a rather strong dislike towards me for what I did to you last night.'

His eyes narrowed. 'That is a matter between you and me and nobody else.'

He limped over to the men. One of them called out, 'Good to see you on your feet, lad.'

'Thank you for your concern,' he said shortly. 'Now it seems I have to remind you that, regardless of your opinions on the events of last night, that lady over there is a *lady*. You need to treat her with the proper courtesy. Please ensure you do so from now on.'

An array of burning cheeks received his rebuke. Then each man tipped his cap at Bridget and mumbled, 'M'lady.'

Astonished, she nodded back in acknowledgement. Cormac returned to her side and put a protective arm around her shoulders just as John and Denis emerged from the stables. John was beaming.

'Your little girl is a pure gem,' he said to Bridget and Cormac. 'Mrs Kavanagh's in there now learning all about the importance of washing paintbrushes right after use.'

They laughed. 'That sounds like our Emily,' said Cormac.

Turning serious, Bridget extricated herself from his grasp. 'John, could I ask you to approach the cart with me, please?'

Curious, he followed her to the back of the cart where she looked up at the physician. 'Mr Abbott, might I beg you to pause your ministrations for just a few minutes? There are some matters I need to discuss with Mr Enright and Mr Corbett.'

The physician huffed but lowered himself down from the cart. 'As you wish.'

Bridget said to Mr Enright, 'Please do accept my apologies for the fact that you are not in a more dignified position for this. I hope you will forgive me but I would rather not delay.'

Baffled, he said, 'It's fine.'

She continued on, addressing both the agent and the stable master, but allowing her words to carry to Cormac, Ellen and the other surrounding men. 'As you are aware, the responsibility for Oakleigh passed to me at the moment of my mother's death in the early hours of this morning and I am expected to take on the management of the estate. However, this is a position that I do not wish to fill for I have family obligations to which I must adhere first and foremost.' Mr Enright's mouth opened to object but she raised her voice to forestall him. 'This means that I shall need someone else to run the estate on my behalf. I therefore propose that, in my absence, I appoint you as joint stewards of the Oakleigh Estate.'

A shocked silence greeted her speech. She glanced over at Cormac to see that he was as astounded as the others. She looked back at John and Mr Enright.

'What say you?' she said when they still did not speak.

'M'lady,' John spluttered. 'I can't speak for Mr Enright but I'm telling the truth when I say I'm in no way qualified for a role of such magnitude.'

'I am also not worthy of it, after the part I have played in Oakleigh's downfall,' said Mr Enright, so flummoxed that he swung his arm out in a gesture of bemusement and hit one of the stuffed sacks. He grimaced.

Bridget lifted her chin, dismissing their arguments. 'On the contrary. Mr Enright, for many years you supervised the running of Oakleigh under my father's direction to the point where it was once one of the finest estates in the country. I am fully aware that its recent deterioration was not of your voluntary doing and I bear witness to the fact that you have always had the people's best interests at heart.' She turned to John. 'And you, Mr Corbett, used to run the most efficient stables I have ever seen. You have a thorough understanding of this land and, more importantly, you know the men, women and children who have lived and worked here for so long. You have been their leader in the uprising and only you can convince them to desist or carry on with their rebellion. But I am confident they will come back to Oakleigh in an instant if it is to be under your management.' She pushed her shoulders back, unshakable in her conviction. 'I believe both of you will be fair and you will restore the estate to its former splendour and dignity.'

Further silence. The jaws of all the surrounding men gaped open. Some of them didn't seem to grasp yet exactly what was happening, but Denis's face was shining and he was gazing at Bridget with something close to reverence as she threw away decades of tradition. Ellen, too, looked very pleased.

Bridget took a slow, steadying breath. Once again, she felt the intoxicating sense of power she had experienced upon meting out punishment to Joseph and Bernie – it surged beneath her skin like fire. Only this time she was no longer scared of it. Her mother had abused such power but Bridget would not let it consume her.

'I envision a very different future for Oakleigh,' she declared. 'It shall not be a dictatorship in the Courcey name. I shall leave it almost entirely in your hands and I encourage you to take your guidance from the people. But I have just three stipulations. Firstly, I desire you to release the constables imprisoned at Hogan Farm. Secondly, Oakleigh must undertake the payment of the tithes on behalf of the tenants again. And thirdly, I should like to see the manor rebuilt.' She registered their dumbfounded reactions. 'It will be years in the making, I appreciate that. But it will provide a significant source of employment for those who might otherwise have served within its walls or on its grounds.' She could have said more but she suspected any further revelations might cause them all to faint. She offered John and Mr Enright a gentle smile of encouragement. 'I can think of no two better men for the job. Will you accept this honourable task?'

After a pause, John said, 'Thank you, m'lady, I will.'

Mr Enright added, 'Good gracious, yes.'

'That is wonderful.' She clasped her hands together in delight. 'We shall need to go through a formal process with the solicitors in Dublin in order to make the appointment official, but at least it is agreed upon now. I am very glad.'

Her sentiment was not shared by all around her. Several of the watching men looked distrustful and some muttered under their breath to each other.

Cormac came to her side, looking dazed. 'Are you certain this is what you want to do?'

'Yes. I could not be more certain.' She dropped her voice to a murmur so only he could hear. 'The alternative would have been for us to part, at least for a time, and I could not abide that thought. I love you and I will go with you to the ends of the earth if that is where you need to go. We belong together, always and everywhere.'

His face filled with the utmost relief. He wrapped his arms around her and kissed her warmly on the lips.

They heard little footsteps pattering on the cobbles and then a scandalised voice rang out, 'Papa, you're kissing Mama in front of all these people!'

Bridget and Cormac smiled at each other and kissed again.

## Chapter 15

'Get your fresh fish!' bellowed a woman as she pushed her laden wheelbarrow across the street.

'Get out of the road!' a coachman roared back at her.

She made an obscene gesture at him and continued to holler about the freshness of her produce. He flung a curse in her direction and drove on, avoiding a collision with her barrow by mere inches.

Ben Bracken manoeuvred his donkey and cart carefully around the fishwife and carried on along the Dublin street. Cormac, sitting in the back of the cart with Bridget and Emily, hoped his daughter hadn't caught the coachman's swear word.

He tugged at his cap, pulling it more securely over his head. Liam had given it to him for his own had been lost in the fire, but it was looser and didn't fit quite as well. He was also wearing a long coat that had belonged to Denis – of all the men, the footman was closest in height and stature to Cormac and the coat was actually a decent match in size. Despite their protestations, he had paid them both for their contributions.

He gazed around, absorbing their environs: the footpaths thronged with jostling men, the orphans begging on street corners, the cacophony of shouts and clattering wheels and hoof beats, the stench of the gutters. It was all so familiar and not one bit of it brought back a welcome memory.

In the midst of the smoky city, he longed for the green fields they had left behind. He felt the sting of regret deep inside him; their time at Oakleigh had been all too brief.

'We will be back,' he and Bridget had promised Ellen and Liam on their departure, but who knew how much time would pass before they could keep that promise?

Leaving his family's cottage yet again had been a difficult parting, made easier only by the fact that he knew good people lived there and would look after it. Without the threat of tithe proctors or eviction notices, the Kirwans could now keep a happier home and Liam would get employment in the rebuilding of the manor house, so the arrival of their third child could be an impending event of joy rather than concern.

Next to Cormac in the cart, Bridget directed Emily's attention to a cluster of four pigeons perched on the roof of a nearby building. They were eyeing the fishwife's wheelbarrow with avid interest. Emily waved enthusiastically at the birds and encouraged her mother to join in; Bridget did so, but her smile was forced.

The loss of her own mother weighed upon her, Cormac knew, because she could not grieve openly. She had no mourning clothes to wear but, more than that, she was alone in her sorrow; no other person of her acquaintance suffered any distress over Lady Courcey's death. Cormac could offer support but not sympathy, and Bridget's closest surviving family was her uncle, Lord Walcott, with whom Lady Courcey herself had said she had become estranged. Bridget had written to her uncle's estate at Lockhurst Park in England and informed him of his sister's death but they had not stayed at Oakleigh long enough to receive his reply.

Very few people had attended the burial of the lady's scant remains recovered from the rubble of the house. Ellen and Liam had come out of respect for Bridget, while Mr Enright, John Corbett and Mrs Kavanagh, who could recall a time when Lord Courcey had been alive and Lady Courcey had not been quite so tyrannical, had also made an appearance. Cormac and Bridget had told no one that the lady's death had been an intentional act instead of an accident, thus allowing her to be buried in consecrated ground. Cormac felt it was more than Lady Courcey deserved but he had not objected for Bridget's sake.

After Lady Courcey's burial in the graveyard at St Canice's, he had visited the graves of his father and brother at St Mary's and, beyond the graveyard's wall, his sister. He had knelt before the mossy earth concealing their bones and made an earnest vow that he would not rest until he had located the remainder of their family.

'Help me, Da,' he had implored. 'Help me find Ma and the others. Let you and Patrick and Mary guide me to them.'

They would be his spiritual guides, but his actual guide came in the form of Ben Bracken. He had very kindly arranged an unscheduled trip to visit his sister in Dublin in order to take Cormac, Bridget and Emily all the way to the street where he had brought Cormac's mother, sisters and nephew seven and a half years previously. Mrs Bracken, being too frail to make the journey, had remained behind in the hospitality of Farmer Hogan, a source of relief for all concerned, except perhaps the farmer.

Ben sat at the front of the cart, driving his donkey on through streets that grew more crowded the closer they got to the centre of the city. He turned his head from one side to the other and Cormac caught a sidelong glimpse of the man's frown. He experienced a ripple of worry; had Ben forgotten the route he had taken with Cormac's family? But then his weather-beaten countenance cleared and he directed the donkey onto another street lined with a variety of establishments, from pawnbrokers and grocers to wine and spirit merchants. The strong smell of hops from a local brewery drifted on the air, causing Emily to screw up her nose.

Ben called over his shoulder, 'This area's the Liberties and we're heading along Meath Street. I'm sure it was up here on the left...' A few seconds later, he let out an exclamation of satisfaction. 'I was right, there 'tis.'

He brought the cart to a stop in front of a narrow, three-storey building. Many of the premises along the street were in a ramshackle state and this one was no exception. Its windows were grimy, their frames were warped and peeling, and bird droppings plastered the sills. Two signs hung crookedly in the window on the ground floor: one read 'Tobacconist' and the other read 'Lodgings' and both included crude illustrations of those services. Flaking letters above the front door spelled 'O'Hara's'.

Ben turned around in his seat, looking pleased. 'I'm right glad I could remember the way.'

'You have my deepest gratitude,' said Cormac. His voice was still a little rough, though the hoarseness was not as pronounced as it had been in the immediate aftermath of the fire; he sounded mostly like himself again. 'I can never thank you enough for bringing us here or for the assistance you gave my family so long ago.'

Ben shrugged away the compliment. 'Happy to help. Only wish there was more I could do. You sure ye'll be able to manage from here?'

'Yes,' said Cormac firmly. They could trespass upon the man's generosity no further. 'We'll be fine. You must go visit your sister now.'

Ben nodded, his face serious. ''Tis been longer than I'd like since I've seen her. The last time I got to Dublin was before we lost our brother. And she's got an anxious nature, does Annie.' He brightened. 'Mayhap my good news will cheer her up. Jaysus, she might even come home with me to work behind the counter. Now wouldn't that be a tonic for my ma?'

When Ben returned to Oakleigh, he intended to take over the proprietorship of The Pikeman, left vacant by Bernie Cuddihy. Cormac thought it was a splendid idea; an upstanding fellow like Ben would transform the place from a seedy drinking hole to a more respectable establishment. Mrs Bracken, impossible to please, had not shown any approval of the notion but perhaps the return of her long-absent daughter might soften her.

Cormac jumped out of the cart, helped Bridget and Emily down to the footpath, and retrieved their valises from the cart's bed next to a small parcel of clothes and food for Annie. Handing one of the valises to Bridget, he went to the front of the cart to bid farewell to Ben. His limp had all but disappeared but he still wore a light bandage over his burnt fingers. He offered his unhurt hand to grasp Ben's.

'Thank you very much again,' he said.

'I wish ye the best,' Ben replied. 'And I hope you find your family, lad.'

He took his leave; they watched him and his donkey and cart merge into the flow of other carts and wagons along the street until he had disappeared from sight. Then they turned and stared up at O'Hara's.

Cormac was filled with apprehension. This was the last known location of his family. Had they stayed here for long? Could they in fact still be here now? Perhaps that was the shadow of his mother beyond that upstairs window or the voice of his sister Margaret floating out through it. There was only one way to find out.

He led Bridget and Emily up to the building's entrance. The door, scratched and stained, was partly open, possibly to entice passersby to make a purchase or to stay the night – there was nothing else about the place to encourage them to stop. He pushed the door open further and they entered.

The front hall of the building was unwelcoming, cold and poorly lit. A couple of threadbare chairs stood against one wall and opposite them was a high counter behind which an old woman was half obscured. Above her head were a few dusty shelves piled with pipes, pipe cleaners and snuff boxes. When she saw that she had three potential customers, she hurried around the counter to greet them. She was short and stooped with wiry, grey hair and more than a few bristles sticking out of her chin. She grinned, revealing several gaps among her teeth. Cormac felt Emily shrink closer to his side.

'Good day to yous,' she leered. 'Looking for a new snuff box, sir? Take a look at my fine range here where I guarantee you'll find something to suit your tastes. Or mayhap yous are in need of accommodation? I've got a cosy family room available on the first floor, very comfortable.'

Cormac shook his head. 'We are not looking for snuff boxes or lodgings.'

The woman's grin disappeared. 'What d'yous want then?'

'Are you Mrs O'Hara?' he enquired, ignoring her abrupt change in attitude.

'I am. Who's asking?'

'Mr McGovern,' he said with a slight bow. 'I am looking for some members of my family and I heard a rumour that they are staying here or at least stayed here once. Can you confirm whether that is the case?'

Mrs O'Hara eyed him. 'Would their name be McGovern too?'

'Yes.'

'I've no one by that name on the books right now.'

His heart sank. 'Are you sure? Perhaps you could check —'

'I'm sure.'

'Or did anyone by that name reside here in the past? They may have moved on since.'

'No one by that name's ever been a guest here,' she said stubbornly.

'Maybe they used a different name,' he said in desperation. 'If I could just describe them to you —'

'Stop wasting my time,' the old lady cut in and went back behind the counter. 'D'yous think I can remember the face of every person who's walked through that door?'

He persevered anyway. 'It would have been about seven and a half years ago, if you were the proprietor back then. A woman, three girls and a baby boy, all with dark hair. They would not have had many belongings with them.'

Mrs O'Hara opened her mouth to make another angry retort but then she shut it again. She peered at Cormac more closely and squinted at Bridget and Emily too.

'I do remember them,' she admitted.

Hope leapt inside Cormac. 'Please tell me what you know. How long did they stay here for?'

'They didn't stay here,' she said with a scornful look.

'But you just said you remembered them,' said Bridget.

'Just 'cause they came in the door doesn't mean they got a room, lovie. They couldn't afford to stay.'

Cormac looked around the dingy hall, wondering what kind of extortionate prices the old woman was charging. 'How is it that you remember them then?'

Mrs O'Hara pursed her lips. 'They were so desperate to get a room. They'd only a few coins on them but they were willing for all five of them to share a room the size of a broom closet and they offered to do work for me to make up the difference.'

'And you didn't help them?' Cormac said in a terse voice.

'This here's a business, not a charity,' she said indifferently. 'No money, no room. I just wanted them to leave. The baby wouldn't stop bawling.' She scowled at the memory.

Anguished by the fact that their promising lead was turning into a dead end, Cormac entreated, 'Do you have any idea where they might have gone next?'

She shrugged. 'None whatsoever.'

Deflated, his shoulders slumped. 'Thank you for your time,' he said flatly and steered Bridget and Emily back towards the door. He could sense Mrs O'Hara's gaze upon him all the way. Outside, he walked a few paces and halted.

Bridget placed a consoling hand on his arm. 'What do you want to do now?'

He sighed. 'Let's go to the solicitors' office and get that out of the way. Then we can figure out where to continue our search next.'

Mr Enright had given them the address of Webb & Brereton Solicitors on Baggot Street. They asked for directions in one of the pawnbroker establishments further up the street from O'Hara's and set off towards the solicitors' office. It was in a more prosperous part of the city so, as they neared it, they began to see cleaner streets, smarter shop fronts, and pedestrians and carriages of a more affluent sort.

They found Webb & Brereton Solicitors nestled between an apothecary and a dressmaker's. Cormac took a breath and gently tugged Emily's bonnet to make her look up at him.

'Do you remember the game we played on the ship where we pretended to be different people, *a stór*?'

She nodded.

'I'm going to play that game again today, for a little fun. You don't need to be anyone else, just Emily. Let your mama and me do all the talking here.'

She nodded again, a slight crease between her fair eyebrows, and he hated himself for having to be a liar in front of her.

But this was his area of expertise.

Looking to Bridget for one final glance of reassurance, he stepped up to the building's front door and rapped the brass knocker twice. After a pause, they heard footsteps beyond the door and it opened. A neat young man peered out.

'Yes?'

'Viscount Wyndham,' Cormac announced, his voice cultivated and confident. 'I seek an immediate interview with Messrs Webb and Brereton. Extenuating circumstances, which I shall divulge presently, prevented me from writing in advance.'

The young man gaped. 'S-sir?' At Cormac's outraged glare, he amended hastily, 'I mean, m-my lord. I—your presence is…unanticipated…'

His gaze travelled downwards, taking in the valises in Cormac and Bridget's hands and their very ordinary clothing.

Tone clipped, Cormac said, 'I reiterate, extenuating circumstances have brought me here today. For that same reason I do not have a calling card to show you. Do please let us continue this discourse on the doorstep.'

The man leapt back, pulled the door wide and admitted them inside. They entered a long hallway with a parquet floor.

'I'm Mr Croft,' said the man. 'Apprentice to Mr Brereton. P-please allow me to notify him of your arrival, Lord Wyndham.'

'Indeed, and shall I wait in the hallway until such time as he is ready to receive me?'

Blushing, Mr Croft ushered them into a chamber off the hall with plain furnishings and a single sofa. Bridget and Emily sat down but Cormac remained standing.

Looking around at them disconcertedly, Mr Croft said, 'You—you travel without a servant, my lord?'

'My valet has gone ahead to arrange our accommodation. I do admire your talent for procrastination, Mr Croft.'

Cowed, the apprentice disappeared for several minutes. When he returned, he was still red-faced.

'Please accept my deepest regrets for keeping you waiting, my lord. Mr Webb is poorly and not here today but Mr Brereton would be honoured to receive you.'

'My wife's attendance is also pertinent to the proceedings,' said Cormac, and Bridget stood to join them.

'May we prevail upon you to keep an eye on our daughter for a brief time?' she asked Mr Croft with a smile full of apology and charm. 'She will not give you any trouble.'

Speechless, the apprentice bobbed his head. Leaving Emily and the valises behind with a murmured 'Be good' from Bridget and no acknowledgement at all from Cormac, they re-entered the hallway with Mr Croft and he directed them to another door further along it. He knocked, announced them, conducted them inside, and bowed out of the room again.

The furnishings in this office were more luxuriant than in the previous chamber, with wood panelling on the walls, comfortable chairs, and a broad desk. A large portrait hung above the desk portraying a man with a bulbous nose, a clean-shaven chin, and an impressive set of whiskers on both cheeks. Its subject sat beneath it, identical in every way, save that the artist had generously given the nose a more proportional shape to the rest of the face.

Mr Brereton stood when they entered and greeted them with a bow. 'It is an honour, Lord Wyndham, Lady Wyndham. We have communicated in writing but never had the personal pleasure.'

This was what Bridget had suspected but until this moment they had not been certain. The tension inside Cormac uncoiled the tiniest bit.

'Please sit.' The solicitor motioned them to two chairs opposite his desk and continued, 'I do lament the fact that you were kept waiting. Mr Croft still has much to learn. He was rendered quite confused by your appearance.'

All three of them sat and Mr Brereton said no more, evidently viewing this as an opportunity for the unexpected arrivals to explain themselves.

Cormac took time to settle himself in his seat before replying, 'We have been through quite an ordeal, so you will have to forgive our lack of forewarning. The first thing I must tell you, and it grieves me to say it, is that my mother-in-law, Lady Courcey, has passed away.'

He resolutely avoided eye contact with Bridget at his blatant lie.

Mr Brereton rocked back in his chair, shocked. 'Good gracious. My sincere condolences. How did this happen?'

'Unfortunately, the Oakleigh Estate has fallen foul of tenant unrest. In a most barbaric act of rebellion, two disgruntled tenants set fire to Oakleigh

Manor. I'm afraid the manor succumbed to the blaze and Lady Courcey perished inside it.'

Mr Brereton's eyes bulged. 'Mr Webb and I had heard vague reports of some dissatisfaction on the estate, but Lady Courcey had assured us in her correspondence that it was but a trifling matter. I am most sorry to hear that it grew to such a scale and that her life was the deplorable cost.'

Cormac lowered his gaze in a moment of respectful silence. When he looked up again, he said, 'My wife and child and I had reached Carlow only the day before to commence our sojourn with the lady. We too were caught in the conflagration—a most traumatic experience—but we managed to escape the house with our lives.' He raised his bandaged hand and then waved his other one to indicate the clothes he and Bridget wore. 'You must excuse our modest travelling attire. All of the possessions we had brought on our journey were lost in the fire. We have just arrived in the city but our next call will be to a tailor's and a dressmaker's. I trust this explanation will allay Mr Croft's concerns about our humble appearance.'

Mr Brereton's hands fluttered and his protuberant nose went crimson. 'Of course, of course, and I do beg your pardon if he caused you any offence—'

'It is fine,' said Cormac levelly.

For a few awkward seconds, no one spoke. Then Mr Brereton said cautiously, 'And you are here today…'

'To address the legal ramifications of Lady Courcey's death,' answered Cormac.

'I see. Yes, her guardianship has ended with her passing. Do you wish to appoint another guardian in her place?'

'I do. My wife.'

Mr Brereton blinked and looked at Bridget. 'Your wife?'

'That is correct,' said Cormac, affecting an inflection of impatience. 'She holds the Courcey title and bears an inexplicable concern for the fate of the estate and its tenants. I have no wish to be bothered by it so long as it becomes a profitable asset again. Therefore the arrangement will be thus: Lady Wyndham will be named the new guardian of the Oakleigh Estate in perpetuity, and she in turn has identified two individuals, Mr Laurence Enright and Mr John Corbett, to act as joint stewards on her behalf. There is a great deal to be done to revive the property. All monies earned from the collection of rents shall be funnelled directly back into its restoration and shall not be channelled towards any other purpose. I desire you to draw up a contract to reflect this arrangement.'

He made a show of taking out his pocket watch and checking the time in order to achieve two objectives: the first was to put pressure on Mr Brereton to hurry along with the proceedings, and the second was to place the watch on display for the solicitor's discreet observation. Lord

Courcey's pocket watch would be noted in their records as being in Lord Wyndham's possession. It was irrefutable proof that the gentleman in question sat right now in this office.

Mr Brereton did indeed take notice of the watch and, without making any reference to it, said, 'Very good, my lord. It will be done as you have requested. We shall need some time to prepare the document. Can we make an appointment for you and Lady Wyndham to return to our office next Tuesday to provide your signatures? We shall require the signatures of the stewards as well.'

Cormac had expected this delay so he did not object. 'Tuesday is acceptable,' he said. 'However, the stewards must remain in Carlow to oversee the beginning of the reconstruction of Oakleigh Manor. You will have to send the document to the estate with instructions for it to be signed in the presence of witnesses and they will return it to you. In addition, any future correspondence may be sent directly to Oakleigh for the attention of Mr Enright and Mr Corbett. I do not wish to be troubled by it in London. I trust this will all be satisfactory?'

'Yes, my lord,' said Mr Brereton.

One potential impediment to this plan was that Cormac might not be able to forge Garrett's signature accurately when the time came to sign the document. But he had flaunted his injured hand; if he kept the bandage on next Tuesday, he could blame it for any defect in his penmanship.

The greater concern of course was that Garrett would get wind of their machinations and expose the fraud. He would be bound to hear about it sooner or later, especially if he made enquiries into the running of the estate once the news of Lady Courcey's death reached him. But overturning their decision would require him to take on the management of the estate himself, or else place it back in the hands of a steward, with Mr Enright being the most likely candidate. Perhaps he would see that Oakleigh would prosper and eventually bring him revenue with no effort at all needed on his part.

Mr Brereton and Cormac spoke back and forth about the particulars of the contract, seeking no input from Bridget. She sat by meekly and neither of them acknowledged her again until the end of the discussion when, as they all stood, Mr Brereton said to her, 'Have you informed Lord Walcott of Lady Courcey's death?'

'Yes,' she said, 'I wrote to Lockhurst Park before we left Oakleigh.'

He scratched his whiskers, looking surprised. 'Your uncle is not in England. He currently resides in Dublin, on Rutland Square.'

She too was startled. 'He does? How do you know this?'

'He has written to us on a number of occasions enquiring after his sister's affairs at Oakleigh. I gather they have not been on speaking terms for some time which prevented him from corresponding with her directly.

Naturally, we could not divulge anything to him due to the agreement of confidentiality that exists between us and our clients. But he does persist in asking.' Mr Brereton's lips pressed together in a prim line of displeasure.

Cormac exchanged a glance with Bridget. Why would Lord Walcott take that level of interest in Oakleigh?

Frowning, Bridget said, 'Could you direct us to Rutland Square, sir? As his niece and closest kin, it should be my duty to deliver the news of my mother's death to him in person, given that we are both in the same city.'

The solicitor described the route and then said, 'It would be quite a distance to walk. Allow me to arrange a conveyance for your service.'

'Thank you, no,' said Cormac. 'We shall be paying a visit to the adjacent dressmaker's next so we shall make our transport arrangements from there.'

They began to turn for the door but Mr Brereton asked, his brows knitted together, 'And where will you be staying while in Dublin?' He added hurriedly, 'If we need to alter the date of the appointment, that is?'

'Courcey House on Merrion Square,' Cormac said with cool composure, though he had no desire for anyone to be able to trace their whereabouts. 'And do kindly adhere to the Tuesday appointment. We wish to return to London as soon as possible.'

'Indeed, my lord.'

Mr Brereton darted around his desk to hold the door open for them and they took their leave. In the other chamber, they found Mr Croft staring nonplussed at Emily as she chattered about how she would soon be mistress of a fine hen coop. Cormac hastened to extract her from the conversation, ordering her to his side. Downcast, she scurried to obey. He bent and grasped the two valises, dismissing the pinch of pain in his burnt fingers.

'I hope you had a productive meeting, s—my lord?' said Mr Croft. Cormac didn't like the crease of doubt on the apprentice's forehead.

'It was satisfactory,' he replied curtly. 'We now have other places to be.'

Mr Croft scuttled to escort them to the front door. He bowed them out and they turned aside in the direction of the dressmaker's as he lingered, shutting the door. They eventually heard it close and, instead of entering that establishment, they continued to walk along Baggot Street.

Bridget exhaled. 'My nerves are overwrought. I can't imagine how you had the mettle to keep up such a performance for nearly five years.'

He didn't want to think about that time. Assuming the persona of Oliver Davenport and dwelling in England as the nephew of Lord and Lady Bewley had released him from the shackles of poverty and iniquity that had plagued him in Dublin, but it had been another kind of imprisonment. What was worse, the Bewleys had been truly honourable people which had made his deception all the more reprehensible. It was not a talent in which he was proud to claim proficiency.

Shutting out those thoughts, he said, 'Do you really want to visit your uncle?'

'I think so, yes,' she said. 'It would be the decent thing to do.'

'How will you explain my presence?'

Her eyes twinkled. 'I happen to have an idea for that.'

## Chapter 16

They chose to walk to Rutland Square, following Mr Brereton's prescribed route which took them over the River Liffey via Carlisle Bridge. The bridge was busy with pedestrians and carriage traffic; Bridget kept a firm hold on Emily's hand and a wary eye on the strangers rushing by. A jumble of noise filled the air, along with the pervading stink of the river. Undeterred by the smell, Emily tugged on Bridget's iron grip.

'Can I look over the edge? Please?' She swivelled to Cormac on her other side. 'Please, Papa? I can see a boat coming!'

He smiled at her exuberance. 'Why not?'

Whooping, she dragged them over to the parapet and Cormac relinquished the two valises to Bridget so he could lift Emily up. They watched as the vessel neared the bridge, glided under the arch below them, and vanished out of sight. Though it was only a barge and much smaller than the ship that had brought them down the Thames in London, it reminded Bridget of their escape that day. To her, the expanse of flowing water signified a flight to freedom. If one held one's nose.

Cormac let a beaming Emily back down to the ground. He plucked at her chin. 'Now, don't forget, you're not to call me Papa at the next place we're going to visit.'

Her bright expression dimmed. 'I won't.' Then she asked the question Bridget had dreaded to hear. 'Why?'

This was not exactly the ideal place but Cormac straightened his shoulders and Bridget steeled herself for the truths their daughter needed to learn.

'I'm afraid we can't explain some of the reasons properly to you until you're older, *a stór*. But there are a lot of people in this world who think your mother and I should not be friends. She was born in a fancy house like you, while I was born in that cottage where we stayed with Auntie Ellen. Many people believe this means we are not equal and that we can never associate with each other. So sometimes we need to pretend we are not friends when we go to certain places.'

A man hurrying past brushed roughly against Bridget's shoulder and she heard him mutter that the bridge wasn't a place for idle chat. Disregarding him, she crouched in front of Emily and held her solemn blue gaze.

'What your papa said is true. People make judgements based on social status and not on whether we are kind to others. You must remember, Emily, the most important thing is not how much wealth or property you own but that you're a good person. And if you find love, seize it with both hands, no matter what way it comes to you.'

The little girl rocked forwards on her toes. 'I shall, Mama,' she promised.

Bridget pressed a kiss to Emily's forehead. 'Let's keep going, gooseberry. Your feet must be getting tired but we're nearly there.'

When she rose, Cormac gave her a look full of tenderness and she felt the conviction deep in her heart that they were wholly right to lead Emily down a different path to the one imposed upon them by the established social order. He took back the valises and they carried on across the bridge.

They reached Rutland Square just as a chilly rain began to spit down. Seeking out the number of the house where Lord Walcott was residing, they located it along the north side of the square; a broad flight of steps climbed to its front door. Cormac rapped the knocker, then stepped back to the footpath, leaving Bridget and Emily alone on the top step. A tall footman answered the door.

'Good afternoon,' said Bridget. 'Could you please inform Lord Walcott that his niece and grandniece are here to see him?'

The footman acknowledged the request with more aplomb than Mr Croft. 'Certainly, my lady. I shall have to check if his lordship is disposed to receive callers. Would you care to step in from the rain?' He sent a quizzical glance in the direction of Cormac who was hovering in the background.

Bridget waved a dismissive hand behind her. 'My manservant. He will escort us, if that is agreeable to you.'

The footman bowed and permitted the three of them to cross the threshold into the entrance hall of the house, which had a staircase of shallow steps leading up to the next level. For the second time that day, they were ushered into a room to wait and, after taking Bridget and Emily's cloaks and bonnets, the footman withdrew to announce their arrival to his master.

Cormac peered out the window at the increasing rainfall. 'Perhaps we should take a hackney back to Merrion Square afterwards.'

'I think that's a good idea,' said Bridget. Emily didn't look like she could walk much further; her head was sagging like a wilting flower.

When the footman returned, his expression was sombre. 'His lordship will receive you but he respectfully requests that your visit be kept short as he is not feeling very well at present.'

'Oh,' said Bridget. 'Yes, of course. In light of that, may my manservant accompany us? I should like Lord Walcott to meet his grandniece but she has a boisterous nature. If she grows unruly or fatigues him overmuch, this fellow can take charge of her.'

If the footman thought it strange that Bridget would have a man instead of a maid for such a task, or that Emily's weary demeanour appeared the exact opposite of boisterous, he did not comment upon it. Inviting Cormac to leave the valises behind, he led them out of the room and up the stairs.

They waited outside a door as he announced Bridget and Emily and then he directed them inside. They found themselves in the library: richly furnished and well stocked, it was a welcoming space with a roaring fire in the hearth. Lord Walcott reclined on a chaise longue to one side of the fireplace. Bridget could not believe her eyes – her portly uncle had grown even larger since the last time she had seen him. Any trace of his neck had become lost in folds of fat that started at his chin and disappeared beneath his loosely tied cravat. His belly spilled out before him, stretching his enormous waistcoat almost to the point of bursting, and each of his thighs had to be the size of her waist. One of his legs was propped up on the chaise longue and a cloth lay over that foot.

A small dog was curled up next to his outstretched leg. It raised its head at the new arrivals, let out a weak yap, and rested its snout back on its paws.

'The maid will bring refreshments shortly,' the footman said and departed.

Cormac assumed a discreet position in the corner of the room, while Bridget and Emily approached the chaise longue. Lord Walcott's breath came in short, shallow pants and his face was mottled and sweaty.

'Greetings to you, Uncle Stuart,' said Bridget. 'This is my daughter, Emily. I hope we find you in good health.' She felt absurd even saying it.

He emitted a wheezy chuckle. 'I regret you do not. Forgive me for not rising to welcome you.' He gestured towards his covered foot. 'Gout. I am recovering from a recent attack and am still in a great deal of discomfort.' He shifted a little and winced. 'Confounded affliction. I wouldn't wish it on my worst enemy.'

'I am very sorry to hear it.' Bridget eyed her uncle uneasily, recalling how her mother had said his heart was failing. He looked like he might expire in front of them at any moment.

'Thank you for saying so. You were always my favourite niece.' He laughed at his own joke – Bridget was his *only* niece – and gestured to the chaise longue on the other side of the hearth.

Bridget and Emily sat with their backs to Cormac. Lord Walcott twinkled at Emily.

'And this delightful lamb is your daughter? Can you give me a curtsey, little girl?'

She obediently got up and dropped into a neat curtsey. 'Greetings to you, Granduncle.'

As she took her seat again, he grinned. 'What a pretty young thing. If she keeps those looks, she'll be snapped up once she comes out. I wager she'll have ten proposals before the end of her first season.' He pointed a pudgy finger at Bridget. 'You and Wyndham better keep a close eye on her. Some of those libertines might not have the patience to wait for her answer.'

Bridget could practically hear Cormac grinding his teeth behind her.

'Thank you for your advice, Uncle,' she said, feeling an odd twinge of regret that Emily would never experience the thrill of her first season. 'I shall take it into due consideration.'

He fished a handkerchief out of his pocket with some difficulty and mopped his damp brow. 'So what brings you to Ireland, my girl, and to my own doorstep?'

'My original purpose was to sojourn in Carlow for a little while but, alas, I come bearing ill news. I must inform you that my mother has died.'

Given the rift that had existed between him and his sister, she had not expected a great outpouring of emotion, but neither had she anticipated the veritable gleam that came into his eyes. He leaned forwards, insofar as his great bulk allowed him to.

'Is that so?' he said, looking intrigued. He made a poor attempt to veil it by passing a hand over his face in an attitude of distress. 'What a very sad loss. Can you tell me how it happened?'

She nipped the tip of her tongue with her teeth. 'I believe you are aware that my mother made some rather drastic changes to the way Oakleigh was managed over the past few years?'

'It had...come to my attention.'

'As it turned out, she pushed the tenants too far. They rose in rebellion against her, a conflict that culminated in two of the tenants setting fire to the manor. My mother did not escape the conflagration.'

Lord Walcott's skin grew even more patchy as he absorbed this. 'Indeed?' he murmured. 'So the insurgence was a direct cause of her death.' He sat back. 'And what will happen to the estate now?'

'I have taken responsibility for it,' she said.

His eyes flashed with anger. 'You have?'

Perplexed by his reaction, she said, 'So to speak. My role will be nominal for the most part. I have established an arrangement whereby the management of the estate has been placed in the custody of the land agent, Mr Enright, and the stable master, Mr Corbett. Mr Enright provides experience while Mr Corbett holds a strong link to the tenants. Between them, they will work in the best interests of the people. I hope in time that the tenants will gain greater autonomy over the land.'

'Oho!' cried Lord Walcott. He smacked a fist on his meaty thigh. 'I am very pleased to hear it. Well done, my girl, I highly approve. You'll do a far better job than your mother ever did if you can already see that the power of Oakleigh should rest in the hands of the people. That's where it belongs for it exists on their land.'

She stared at him. She had the strong impression that she was missing a vital component of their conversation.

Behind her, she heard Cormac mutter, 'The money,' but his words went unnoticed by Lord Walcott as the library door opened and a maid came in carrying a tray. While she bustled about setting out the teapot, milk jug, sugar bowl and cups on a table next to Lord Walcott, Bridget's mind worked furiously. The money...the anonymous benefactor...could it be possible? She accepted a cup of tea with an absent-minded thanks. The maid also handed a cup of milk to Emily, who took it with a wide yawn.

After the maid had left the room, Bridget studied her uncle with a fresh perspective. He was contemplating his own tea with faint disdain while darting a glance of longing at a decanter of whiskey standing on the mantelpiece.

'Remember the physician's advice,' he grumbled to himself and took a small sip from his teacup.

'Uncle,' Bridget began slowly.

He swallowed the tea like it was a particularly nasty tonic. 'Hmm?'

'Has your interest in Oakleigh been...more than academic?'

His expression turned cagey. 'I don't know what you mean.'

She raised her eyebrows. 'I think perhaps you do.'

He set his cup down on the table beside him and clicked his tongue softly at his dog. The creature stirred itself, crept sluggishly up the chaise longue, and crawled onto its master's vast lap. Lord Walcott scratched the dog's ears as it settled and shut its eyes. He looked back at Bridget.

'What is it that you suspect?' he asked.

She clutched the delicate handle of her teacup so hard she thought she might crack it. 'It was you, wasn't it? You sent the money to the rebels.'

He shrugged one large shoulder. 'Yes.'

It took all her willpower not to turn around to Cormac. 'I am dumbfounded, Uncle. When did you become a revolutionary?'

He laughed. 'What, does it surprise you that I fell in love with the Irish land as much as you did?' He daubed his handkerchief once more across his forehead. 'Before I first visited Oakleigh, I was merely curious. The rebellion in 1798, the Act of Union in 1801. Who was this savage race who spilled so much blood for the sake of their homeland and whose overbearing neighbour felt the need to crush their independence in every conceivable way?' Stroking the dog's back, he focused his gaze on the blazing fire. 'But once I came to Ireland to assume the guardianship of Oakleigh and I beheld the beauty of this country, I understood why they fought so hard. And I came to sympathise with their cause.'

At a loss for words, Bridget took a gulp of her tea. Next to her, Emily had finished her milk and now slouched forwards, looking listlessly at her toes.

'The Irish are justified in coveting sovereign control over their own land. I did what I could to assist one small faction of them in that aspiration.' He grunted. 'Though I suppose, given the consequences of their uprising, I now have my sister's blood on my hands.'

Bridget flinched. Even if her uncle felt remorse for his actions, he could not change what he had done. That chapter in the life of their family was now closed.

But another chapter was only just beginning.

'Uncle Stuart,' she said, hoping she was taking the right gamble, 'if you are sympathetic to the Irish people, does that mean you believe they are not inferior?'

His answer was interrupted by the reappearance of the footman. 'My lord, you desired me to intervene if the visit became prolonged —'

'Go away, Simon, go away,' said Lord Walcott, flapping his hands. 'We are having a far more interesting conversation than I had anticipated. Leave us be.'

Rebuffed, the footman exited again, red all the way to the tips of his ears.

Lord Walcott regarded Bridget with squinting eyes. 'That is quite the fascinating question, my girl. If our countrymen are to be believed, the Irish are an uncouth, dim-witted race ruled by Rome. But I conjecture you and I are cut from a different cloth to our compatriots and view them with greater perception.'

She didn't consider the English her compatriots but that was beside the point. 'Without a doubt, Uncle.' She turned around deliberately to Cormac. 'Shall we tell him?'

He rubbed his chin with the knuckles of his bandaged hand. 'If you think so.'

She nodded and, guarded, he came forwards to stand at the end of the chaise longue she and Emily sat upon. Lord Walcott peered at them, puzzled.

'I must reveal something to you, Uncle,' said Bridget, enunciating her words so he could not pretend he had misheard. 'When it comes to the Irish, I am more broad-minded than you might ever have believed. This is Cormac McGovern, once a stable hand on the Oakleigh Estate. In the past month, I have deserted my husband and run away from London to be with him.'

'What the devil —' Lord Walcott spluttered.

She barrelled on. 'I fell in love with him that summer my mother and I returned to Oakleigh. Well, I do believe I always loved him but that was when I first realised it.'

She reached out to grasp Cormac's hand. His gaze was warm when he looked down at her but his jaw tightened as he glanced back at Lord

Walcott. Her uncle's eyes were bulging out of their sockets.

'Are you being serious?' he said, his complexion almost purple.

'Quite,' she responded. 'Come sit with us,' she added to Cormac and, after a slight hesitation, he joined them on the chaise longue.

Emily slithered into his lap. As he wrapped his arms around her, she said sleepily, 'I thought you weren't supposed to be my papa in this house.'

A second exclamation of 'What the devil!' erupted from the other chaise longue.

Calmly, Bridget said, 'Take a closer look, Uncle. And recall what I said about that summer at Oakleigh...and how long ago that was.'

She watched her uncle compare the two fair heads, the two pairs of clear blue eyes, the way Emily nestled into Cormac's paternal embrace. His mouth opened and closed like a fish.

At last, he said, 'Does Wyndham know?'

'He has known since her birth. And he has punished me time and again for it. Ours was not a happy marriage.'

He twisted his lips. 'And you view that as justification for taking leave of your senses? Good Lord, the mind boggles!'

She tried to quell the disappointment welling inside her. 'I thought you believed the Irish were not inferior to us.'

'Race is a different matter to class. He's still a stable hand.'

'And proud of it, my lord,' said Cormac, his voice controlled. 'I feel no shame at my humble beginnings. I know what it is to be a man who possesses nothing but his name and that has proved a far more valuable education than that which any gentleman's tutor can provide.'

Lord Walcott gaped. His fingers convulsed in the hair on his dog's back and the animal gave a faint bark of disgruntlement. He patted it distractedly while he contemplated the improbable family in front of him.

At length, he said gruffly, 'While I don't pretend to approve, I am too old and ill to concern myself with it. Do what you will, if it makes you happy. Though in truth I ought not to be surprised, given that your mother's blood runs in your veins.'

Startled, Bridget said, 'What on earth can you mean by that? My mother opposed any hint of a connection between us, even an innocent childhood friendship.'

The corner of her uncle's mouth turned up. 'Ah, the hypocrisy of it. How amusing.' At Bridget's obvious confusion, he went on, 'Must I remind you that Lockhurst Park is the seat of an earldom? Your mother was an earl's daughter. Lady Constance married down when she wed a mere baron.'

'But my father was a member of the peerage,' she protested.

'And two ranks below your mother. Our parents had it in mind to match her with a marquess so to see her sink to the lowest possible level of the aristocracy was deeply displeasing to them. Nevertheless, she was intractable and would have no one else. Their love match was the talk of London.'

It was Bridget's turn to gape. No one had ever told her that her parents' union had been viewed in a negative light. But her astonishment quickly transformed into indignation. Hypocrisy indeed – how dared her mother censure her for favouring Cormac over Garrett when she herself had flouted the expectations of society? But then, perhaps her objection had risen from the bitterness of experience.

Faltering, she said, 'Did my mother regret it?'

'Not when Angus was alive,' he said. 'But I'm sure acutely so once he was deceased.'

For a single second, Bridget allowed herself to envision a future where Cormac was dead and she and Emily were left utterly alone. The horror from the night of the fire swept over her and she shied away from the frightening picture she had conjured up. She pressed a surreptitious hand to his thigh to reassure herself of his solid presence. He offered her a comforting wink; he could not otherwise move to respond to her touch for Emily had fallen asleep in his arms.

Bridget scrutinised her uncle. 'Were *you* against my mother's choice?'

He fidgeted with a button on his waistcoat. 'At first, yes. Not only was he at the lower end of the peerage, but he was also Anglo-Irish and that made me mistrustful. Of course, once we became acquainted, I comprehended that he was the best of gentlemen.' He picked up his cup of tea, regarded it dubiously and placed it back down. 'He was the one who stirred my curiosity about Ireland. He encouraged me many times to visit Oakleigh but, alas, I did not make it there until after his death. I do believe he and I would have seen eye to eye on the plight of the Irish people.'

Cormac cleared his throat. 'On that matter, my lord, I would ask you a question. You have involved yourself in the rebel cause, but what of the lawful route? Would you speak for the Irish in Parliament?'

'I'm afraid it's too late for that,' said Lord Walcott, sweeping one thick arm out to indicate his giant frame. 'I shall never sit in Parliament again. In fact, it is likely I shall never leave this house again, save for in a wooden box.'

'Oh, Uncle,' said Bridget, 'is your health truly that precarious?'

'It is,' he said without dramatics as he touched his chest. 'The pain has become my frequent companion. It is only a matter of time before my heart gives out entirely.' He smiled sadly at the dog in his lap. 'My other companions have left me one by one. Brutus is the last fellow still by my side and not for long, I fear. This is a house of creatures waiting to die.'

'I don't wish to be indelicate,' said Bridget, 'but what will happen to Lockhurst Park? You are a bachelor.'

'Yes indeed, and I suppose it is not too late to marry, is it? Some women might still consider me a tempting catch—those of the money-grabbing sort, at least—but it wouldn't be worth the effort. At any rate, I doubt my ability to produce an heir at this stage.' He grimaced. 'There is a second cousin gleefully anticipating the day I go to meet my maker. He will inherit the title and Lockhurst Park, and I believe he has had the audacity to spawn two sons already so his own line is secure. I'm confident that when I encounter my father in the afterlife he will box me soundly for allowing the estate to slip away down a different branch of the family tree, but there you have it. I'll hold out as long as I can anyway, just to spite my cousin.'

By the end of this speech, he was taking a short breath after every three or four words. Alarmed, Bridget said, 'We should leave you to rest. This has been quite enough agitation for one afternoon. Might we call on you again while we are in Dublin?'

'Eh?' he said. 'You'll stay here, of course.'

'That is very kind of you but we intend to stay at Courcey House.'

'Do they know you are coming?'

'Not yet but—'

He lifted his hand in a feeble motion; he might have been aiming for a dismissive wave but it flopped back into his lap after rising only an inch or two. 'The house won't be ready. It'll be cold and they won't have a good joint of beef in. Stay here. I can assure you, a fine roast beef will be served this evening.'

Bridget glanced at Cormac and then down at the slumbering Emily. From the little girl's perspective, staying in Rutland Square was the more appealing option. Moreover, it would mean not having to go back out into the rain, and there might even be enough time before dinner to bathe properly, a true indulgence in their current way of life.

'Perhaps just the one night then,' said Bridget. 'If you're certain we shall not be a nuisance to your staff.'

'They'll have the rooms ready in no time,' said Lord Walcott. He arched one eyebrow. 'How many rooms?'

She tried not to blush. 'Two. Cormac and I shall share.'

'Hmm,' muttered Lord Walcott, but he said nothing more.

## Chapter 17

Waking up in a large bed was a luxury to which they were not accustomed. Eyes still closed, Cormac stretched out, relishing the feel of the comfortable mattress under his back. Turning on his side, he reached out blindly for Bridget and found her drowsily reaching out for him too. His forehead bumped against hers and, with a soft laugh, he opened his eyes.

She looked up at him from beneath her eyelashes. 'Good morning,' she murmured, her voice husky with sleep.

He answered her with a kiss. He meant it to be chaste, a simple morning greeting between two lovers, but their love was still so new – and the bed was such a novelty – that the purity of the kiss degenerated into something altogether more hot-blooded.

They took full advantage of the rare occasion of privacy and, amid the rumpled sheets, made a more intimate acquaintance with the secret parts of each other's bodies. He inhaled the aroma of her skin and his senses ignited. She had abandoned her lilac perfume back in London and without it her own innate scent had come to the fore – it was even more arousing than the lilac fragrance and he could not get enough of it.

As he slid her nightdress up, he discovered a trio of freckles clustered on her right hip in the pattern of a triangle; he pressed his lips to them before removing her nightdress entirely. When it was her turn to disrobe him, she stripped him from behind and, with a hushed exclamation of surprise and delight, informed him that a faint blemish sat at the base of his spine, which he himself had not even been aware of.

'It looks rather like the shape of a leaf,' she said. 'How unusual. Let me examine it in more detail.' But, strangely, her attention became fixed on the area just below it instead.

Their tumble was swift and joyful and satisfying. They kept their sounds of pleasure as quiet as possible, conscious that the other inhabitants in the house would be waking too, and afterwards, when she still held him inside her, she whispered 'I love you' and he thought he might melt with devotion.

It would have been so easy to fall back into slumber, but the day ahead beckoned. They rose and dressed and Bridget went to waken Emily in another bedchamber down the corridor, while Cormac sought out Lord

Walcott. He found him in the library, where they had dined the previous evening at a table the servants had carried in. Had they not later heard the footman assisting his master to bed, Cormac would have believed the man had not moved from this very spot. He supposed that with a bulk so great climbing the stairs had to be a daunting prospect and one to be entertained only in necessity.

Lord Walcott was reading a newspaper on his chaise longue, his leg propped up as it had been the day before. As Cormac entered, he gave a snort and folded the paper over in disgust.

'Good morning, my lord,' said Cormac. 'How does your foot fare today?'

'Hurts like blazes,' Lord Walcott replied, but at least his shortness of breath seemed to have abated. 'Where is my niece?'

'Rousing our daughter. They will be down shortly.' Cormac took a seat on the other chaise longue, avoiding Brutus who lay asleep at one end, legs extended.

Lord Walcott gave him a menacing look. 'You will do right by them?'

'I guarantee you I will. Nothing matters to me more than their safety and happiness.'

Lord Walcott cocked his head. 'Does my niece truly comprehend all that she's forsaken? Her behaviour has been so very reckless, and there will be consequences for the girl too.'

Cormac kept his voice level. 'She understands.'

'And what do you plan to do next? Where will you build your life together? In what capacity can you provide for them? Have you given a single thought to those considerations or are you still too drunk on love to recognise the uncertainty of your situation?'

Gritting his teeth at being lectured like a schoolboy, Cormac said, 'Thank you, my lord, for your concern. I assure you, I am fully conscious of the nature of our situation and have deliberated at length over the many precarious aspects of it. I have a happy and secure future in mind for us, but there is another pressing matter which I must address first.'

He went on to describe the particulars relating to their ongoing search for the missing members of his family, beginning with the eviction that took place seven and a half years ago and concluding with their unsuccessful visit to O'Hara's yesterday.

When he had finished, Lord Walcott scowled. 'Good Lord, my sister must have been made of ice to do such a thing and not feel any compunction about it.'

Cormac could have added a litany of other colourful adjectives to describe Lady Courcey but decided there was nothing to be gained from it. 'We intend to continue our search, even though we are currently without any promising leads. But I wonder, my lord, would you be in a position to also make enquiries about my family? Could you use your connections to gain access to certain records? I'm thinking we should seek out the names of mission society converts or' – he swallowed – 'death notices and the like. Would you be willing to assist us?'

'Hmm,' said Lord Walcott. 'You do realise, my boy, that if their circumstances deteriorated to the worst degree and they strayed into the most destitute areas of this city, their activities or deaths might not have entered any records?'

'I do realise that,' said Cormac, willing his voice not to crack. 'But I at least have to try. Will you help?'

Lord Walcott did not reply at first. He smoothed out the creases on the folded newspaper in his lap, fastidiously lining up the edges. At last, he said, 'You strike me as quite the singular man. You were born to nothing and yet you speak as well as any gentleman. You defy the conventions of society and yet your moral compass is evidently strong. Your fervour does you credit. I can see why my niece is so drawn to you.' He sighed. 'Yes, I shall help.'

Bridget and Emily entered the library just then and the business of breakfast commenced, the servants bustling in to accommodate the meal in the most convenient manner for their corpulent master. While they ate, Lord Walcott interrogated them on their next steps.

'I would like to begin today by going back to Meath Street,' said Cormac. 'It was the last known whereabouts of my family. Perhaps we can trace their movements to somewhere else in that locality.'

'And you will return here this evening?' Lord Walcott urged.

'Thank you for your generosity, Uncle,' said Bridget, 'but we shall stay in Merrion Square tonight. We gave that address to the solicitor so we must at least make an appearance, lest he try to contact us there.'

Her uncle looked disappointed. 'Very well. But you will come visit me again soon?'

Bridget gave him a fond smile. 'We shall.'

They took their valises with them when they departed from Rutland Square. The day was dull but dry. As they crossed the picturesque Wellington Bridge over the River Liffey, having paid a ha'penny each for the service, Cormac pondered the Grace of God Mission Society. Could his family have happened across it, or another like it? He hoped they would not have been as bull-headed as himself and that they would have taken the soup. If seeking them in the vicinity of Meath Street proved fruitless, he decided they would try the mission society next.

They had no difficulty relocating the Liberties district – the smell of hops guided their way. Standing at the top of Meath Street, they gazed down its length.

Refusing to be daunted, Cormac said to Bridget, 'We'll commence our search here and then explore the surrounding streets. My family's chief priority would have been finding somewhere to stay so we must be on the alert for any lodgings or shelters.'

They started down the street, peering at names painted above doorways and signs placed in windows. Emily trotted between them, holding Bridget's hand. As they passed the dilapidated front of O'Hara's, Cormac gave it and its surly proprietor within a surreptitious glower. They were nearly gone past the building when the door opened wide and a figure appeared in the doorway. Looking back in alarm, he wondered if the old lady had caught his dirty look and come out to upbraid him. But it wasn't Mrs O'Hara.

The main difference to how he remembered her was her clothing. Stepping out onto the footpath, she wore full petticoats and had wrapped a shawl over her bodice, which covered a great deal more of her than she had customarily displayed. But her long curtain of black hair was the same, as were her round lips – and the provocative smile that curved them upwards.

His stomach turned over.

'Good day, Mr McGovern,' Thomasina called.

At the mention of his surname, Bridget stopped and looked back too.

'Let's keep going,' he muttered to her, but Thomasina was approaching them with quick steps and it was too late to ignore her.

She grinned. 'Oh, I was so hoping you'd return to Meath Street. What a happy reunion this is.'

Stiffly, he said, 'I'm afraid we have an urgent matter to attend to and really can't delay.' He tried to encourage Bridget and Emily on down the street but Bridget stood her ground.

'Won't you introduce us?' she said with a frown.

He cringed. How could he introduce Thomasina when he did not even know her last name?

Her grin practically split her face as she comprehended his predicament. Altering her expression to one of pure innocence, she parroted, 'Yes, won't you introduce us?'

His face burned with mortification and anger. 'What are you doing here?' he said through clenched teeth.

She gestured behind her. 'Biddy O'Hara is my auntie. Sometimes she lets me take clients here if she's got a room free.'

Bridget shot a sharp glance at Cormac. He sensed the situation slipping out of his control, the pieces of it crumbling through his fingers. Unable to look at her, he asked Thomasina, 'Why in God's name were you hoping I'd return to Meath Street? How did you find out I'd even been here?'

'Auntie sent a message to me. She recognised your name and knew you and I had been…on familiar terms.' She adopted a look of angelic sorrow. 'I had told her how important you were to me and how much I missed you.'

Next to him, Bridget went rigid. 'Cormac,' she said. 'What is going on?'

Thomasina beamed. 'Cormac,' she said with an air of satisfaction. 'I never knew your name.'

Seething, he said to Bridget, 'Nothing's going on. This conversation is over.'

Before he could turn away, Thomasina grabbed his arm, the smile wiped from her features.

'Just you wait a second,' she hissed. 'Aren't you forgetting something?'

He shrugged her off. 'Leave me be, Thomasina. We haven't got anything to say to each other.'

'Fine,' she said, putting her hands on her hips. 'But don't you remember where I work? I can go back to the lodgings right now and tell them I've seen McGovern here in the city. How d'you reckon Cunningham will react to that?'

His blood went cold. He scanned the busy street, half expecting the money lender or his chief lackey, Munroe, to sidle out from the crowd with murder in their eyes. That kind of danger hanging over them was the last thing they needed.

He levelled her with an icy gaze. 'What do you want?'

'Money,' she replied promptly. 'Enough to get out of Dublin and away from those brutes.'

She tucked her black hair behind one ear and he saw it: the faint trace of a healing bruise on her cheek.

He exhaled slowly. 'Very well. I'll get you some money.' Bridget twitched but he continued to avoid her eye.

'You better,' Thomasina said. 'It'll go badly for your daughter if you don't.'

He took a protective step in front of Emily. 'Don't you *dare* threaten my daughter,' he growled.

'Oh, is she your daughter too?' Thomasina bared her teeth. 'No, I mean your *other* daughter.'

He was certain he had misheard. Two wagons were passing each other on the street just then and the drivers were shouting greetings and good-natured obscenities to one another. They were so loud that he could convince himself he had not heard Thomasina properly.

But one glance at Bridget's frozen countenance told him he had.

He shook his head. 'You're lying,' he said to Thomasina.

She looked genuinely hurt. 'Why, because all whores lie?'

'No, because it's not possible,' Bridget bit out, addressing Thomasina for the first time. Her voice shook on the last word.

Thomasina winked at Cormac. 'Been keeping me a secret, have you?' She crossed her arms and jutted out her chin. 'Sorry to disappoint, lovie. The brat's yours. Born on Valentine's Day after the summer you ran off without a trace.'

He closed his eyes briefly. He had bedded Thomasina a month before he boarded the ship to England. A birth the following February added up and meant the child was four years old now. His insides churned. Could it really be true? When he opened his eyes, both Bridget and Thomasina were staring at him expectantly.

Despising himself, he mumbled to Bridget, 'It's possible.'

A tiny gasp escaped her, while Thomasina looked smug.

Wanting to quash that infuriating satisfaction, he retorted, 'But it's not beyond all doubt. How many other men did you service around that time? What proof is there that the child is definitely mine?'

Her face fell and he was dismayed to see tears welling in her eyes. 'There's no need to be so vulgar, 'specially with little ears listening.' She motioned to Emily, who had tucked herself under Bridget's arm. 'As a matter of fact, I was...less active 'round that time. I took ill, but you never noticed 'cause you were acting like I didn't exist after what had happened between us. And then by the time I knew for sure, you were already gone.'

He felt rotten, for the way he had treated her then and the way he was treating her now. Holy God, what was he supposed to do?

Bridget looked like she was biting the tip of her tongue hard enough to draw blood. But when she spoke, her tone was surprisingly gentle. 'Do you want him to acknowledge her? To give your daughter his name? Tell us what you seek from him.'

Thomasina appeared taken aback at her unexpected ally. 'Just the money. I want to take Henny away and live in the country, far from the misery and violence and dirty dealings that go on in that place. That's all I want.'

'Henny?' said Cormac. 'That's her name?'

'Henrietta.' Thomasina's lip twisted wryly. 'I called her that so both of us would be reminded that our mas wanted boys instead.'

They were all silent after that, a cluster of mute figures in the midst of the street's hectic activity.

Thomasina gnawed on her full bottom lip. Hesitantly, like the thought had never occurred to her, she said to Cormac, 'D'you...d'you want to meet her?'

Bridget answered for him. 'Yes,' she said. 'Could you bring her here tomorrow? We can give you the money then as well.'

Thomasina squinted at her. Cormac couldn't blame her if she was doubting Bridget's motives, because he was wondering about them too. 'You mean it?' she said.

Bridget nodded, her face an impassive mask.

Thomasina tugged her shawl a little tighter around herself. 'We'll be here tomorrow afternoon so. Come at five. If yous don't show up, I'll go straight to Cunningham.'

She spun on her heel and went back to O'Hara's, slipping through the door with one final backward glance.

Cormac dredged up the courage to look at Bridget and was unsurprised to see her mask fracturing, shafts of fury glinting in the cracks.

'Feel free to slap me,' he said. 'It might make us both feel better.'

'I certainly don't want to do anything to make *you* feel better,' she said, her voice brittle. 'Nor do I wish to strike you in front of Emily. Perhaps I'll save it for later.'

He fiddled with the handle on his valise. 'I won't try to stop it when it comes. You must consider me an awful cad.'

'I don't think you grasp why I'm so furious,' she snapped. 'It's not because you lay with another woman.' She jabbed her finger in the centre of his chest. 'It's the fact that you *lied* to me about it.'

He rubbed the back of his clammy neck. 'I do see now that it was a colossal mistake to do that. But my encounter with Thomasina was not something I was proud of. I preferred to forget it had ever happened.'

'Well, you can't forget about it anymore,' she said with a short, grim laugh. 'There were consequences to what you did.' She added, almost plaintively, 'Do you think she's telling the truth?'

He blew out his cheeks. 'God, I don't know. I'd rather not believe her, but I'm so afraid it's true.'

'We may have a clearer idea tomorrow. That's why I agreed that we should meet Henrietta. If she takes after her mother, we shall be no better informed. But if she has Emily's colouring...'

They both looked down at Emily who peeked up at them with interest. 'Colouring? Can I take out my watercolour box?'

'Not right now, *a stór*,' said Cormac. 'Let's keep walking for the time being.'

He urged Bridget and Emily onwards and they moved down the street until O'Hara's was no longer in view.

It felt like a nest of snakes had taken up residence in the pit of his stomach, writhing and trying to slither up his throat. He was disgusted with himself. How could he have let this happen – twice?

The revelation about Emily had been a wonderful discovery, an unforeseen marvel that had taken his breath away with joy. Henrietta was a shock of quite a different kind. If she was truly his, she had been conceived in an act between virtual strangers that had been without love or even tenderness, only lust and a dull rage.

He heard Bridget gulp in a lungful of air. Pale-faced, she said, 'If she is your child, you cannot forgo your responsibilities to her.'

'I know,' he said at once. Now that he was aware of the situation, he could not shy away from it. But he didn't have a notion how Thomasina or Henrietta might fit into the future he planned to share with Bridget and Emily, and the rest of his family if they were ever found.

'For now, let's return to our original purpose, shall we?' he said and was relieved to receive a nod of acquiescence in response. He supposed he wouldn't see the full extent of her anger until they were alone.

They continued along Meath Street, on the lookout for signs displaying any type of accommodation. Cormac got his hopes up when they found two more sets of lodgings, both in better condition than O'Hara's, but neither of the proprietors recognised the description of his family at all.

They came to a corner where another narrower street met Meath Street. At first glance, the buildings appeared to be more residential than mercantile. On impulse, Cormac led Bridget and Emily down it. This was not an area he had ever wandered into during his period of poverty in Dublin. As he gazed around, he realised that, despite the fact that the inhabitants could boast of a roof over their heads, they were not much better off than he had ever been. The dwellings squatted in a long, sullen line on either side of the street and made O'Hara's look like a palace. Many of them had no doors, and most of their windows were cracked, broken or altogether missing. Rubbish littered the ground and the smell of hops could not quite conceal the odour of human waste. There were some people walking along the footpaths here too but they lacked the purpose of those hurrying up and down Meath Street and were far more bedraggled.

Cormac sensed Bridget's unease as two men across the way gave them a hard stare.

'We won't linger here long,' he assured her.

He halted at the next open doorway and decided to make an enquiry within. The way these rundown houses practically sat on top of each other, it was reasonable to assume that the occupants would be familiar with their neighbours and, judging from the attitude of the two men who were still watching them closely, suspicious of strangers. If a family of five had roamed into their midst, someone would have noticed.

Taking the glares of mistrust into account, he debated whether it was wise to bring Bridget and Emily inside.

'I'll just take a brief look myself,' he said. 'If it seems unsafe, we won't go any further.'

As he stepped across the threshold straight into the front room, he glimpsed six or seven scrawny figures crouched in the shadows. Low voices told him there were more people in another room beyond, and sporadic footsteps tapped on the ceiling above. He put out his hand to make sure Bridget and Emily did not follow him in. It was a tenement building, with numerous inhabitants occupying a space designed for far fewer. These poor souls were only a hair's breadth away from destitution

*A Class Forsaken*

and he knew from past experience that such people were dangerous when their territory was threatened.

Proving his point, one of the figures in the front room leapt up, a youth with a scarred face and a hostile expression.

'There's no more space,' he said roughly.

'I'm not looking to stay,' Cormac said in a clear, calm voice. 'I'm just searching for some people.'

'You won't find any of *your* people here.' The youth narrowed his eyes at Cormac's clothes which, while plain and unassuming, were still finer than anything worn by the ragged occupants of this tenement.

'If I could just—'

'Get out!' the fellow yelled, raising two clenched fists.

Bridget and Emily both jumped in fright behind Cormac. It was time to retreat – he did not want to risk putting them in danger and there was no telling what the youth might do to force him out.

Then he heard another voice say, 'What's going on?' and the frail form of an old man emerged from the back room. He looked weak with hunger and clung to the door frame for support.

'Intruders,' growled the youth.

Cormac lifted his free hand in a non-threatening gesture. 'I only wish to ask about some family relatives and then I'll be on my way.'

'You can be on your way right—'

'Shut up, Marty,' the old man said wearily. He offered Cormac an apologetic shrug. 'He don't like strangers. You're best off leaving.'

'I understand,' said Cormac. 'But could I just take one moment of your time to ask if you know of a family named McGovern? Or if you remember a woman, three girls and a baby who might have been in this vicinity seven or eight years ago?'

The old man shrugged again. 'I wasn't here then.'

Cormac started to turn away.

'But Tess was,' the old man added. 'You could ask her. She knows everyone 'round these parts.'

'Tess?' Cormac repeated. 'Where is she?'

A third shrug. 'She's not here right now. Can't say when she'll be back.'

'Might she be here tomorrow?' Cormac pressed.

'She might. She might not. Tess makes her own rules.'

Cormac nodded. 'Very well. I'll call again and hope our paths will cross. Thank you for the information.'

The old man said nothing. Marty was still simmering with hostility, so Cormac backed out and rejoined Bridget and Emily beyond the doorstep.

'You heard all that?' he asked.

'Yes,' said Bridget. 'It's better than another dead end. Perhaps this Tess will know something.'

'I hope so.' He shot her a guilty look. 'And I suppose this means we have two reasons to return to this area tomorrow.'

She pursed her lips. 'I suppose it does.'

## Chapter 18

They took a hackney to Merrion Square that evening and Bridget was glad of it, not caring one jot about its shabby appearance and grubby interior. It felt positively regal after their long day walking the Dublin streets. Her fingers ached from carrying the valise and she suspected she had a blister on her left foot. Emily, the little angel, had lasted as well as she could but she had grown more and more fractious as time wore on until Cormac had agreed it was best to call a halt to their search for the day. They had left the Liberties with no better lead than the absent Tess and a great deal of unpleasantness to process.

Bridget avoided Cormac's gaze as they were jolted about inside the hackney. She was still trying to come to terms with what she had learned today. He had lied to her, and so successfully that she had not had an inkling of the deceit. She knew he had been a practised liar in his guise of Oliver Davenport, but she had made the arrogant and erroneous assumption that she was immune to his abilities. Now her trust in him had taken a blow and she wondered what else he might still be keeping concealed. If she asked him outright, would she recognise the truth?

But then, she had lied to him too. She had said her wrath wasn't attributable to the fact that he had lain with another woman...except that it was. His admission of it had stung bitterly. He had led her to believe that she was and would forever be the only woman to know him in that intimate way. But now there was Thomasina with her sultry smiles and full lips and Bridget could not stop herself from picturing the two of them together, their bodies entangled and those luscious lips pressed to places they had no business being.

Her heart ached. He had given something so precious to someone he clearly held no regard for – a physical transaction, nothing more. She herself had been obliged to carry out such emotionless transactions in her marriage bed but she couldn't conceive of the idea of doing so voluntarily. A sense of dismal disillusionment filled her.

Emily tugged on her arm. 'I'm hungry,' she whined.

They had eaten a swift meal at a tavern earlier – in a snug away from the disgruntled men who frowned upon the presence of a woman and a child in their domain – but that had been hours ago.

'We'll have supper very soon,' Bridget promised. She did not know what kind of supper the cook at Courcey House might be able to prepare for them at such short notice but it would do fine, despite her uncle's opinions on the matter.

Part of her wished they were returning to Rutland Square for the night. Her affection for her uncle had grown immensely in consequence of his revelations the previous day and, besides, she would have liked to check that he had not keeled over since they had departed after breakfast.

But another part of her acknowledged the sense in making the staff at Courcey House aware of their presence in Dublin. They needed to ensure no suspicion would be aroused should Mr Brereton find the need to send a message there.

Cormac cleared his throat and she glanced at him; he looked uncomfortable and she got the impression that more unwelcome news was on its way.

'I think we should only stay in Merrion Square for one night,' he said.

'Why?' They had been on the move for so long now that it was an attractive prospect to reside in one place for a few days and not have to carry those accursed valises everywhere.

'I believe it would be wise not to settle for long in any single location while we're in the city.'

'Why?' she said again, sounding like Emily when she was in a particularly inquisitive mood.

He took off his cap and fidgeted with it in his lap. 'I would harbour some concern that we may soon be at risk of being followed.'

Alarmed, she said, 'What do you mean?'

He cringed. 'Thomasina,' he said, muttering her name like it was an expletive. 'After she disappears from Cunningham's lodgings, they will likely come looking for her. Not out of any worry for her personal welfare, but because they would consider her a piece of their property with no right to walk out of there whenever she pleased. If they trace her steps to Meath Street, they'll question Mrs O'Hara and she will be able to inform them that she's seen me.' He rubbed at the peak of his cap and then abruptly fixed his eyes on Bridget's. 'There's no doubt that they will attempt to hunt me down. We shall need to be vigilant. The best way to elude detection is to cover our tracks and never stay in any place for more than one night.'

Her resentment at hearing Thomasina's name on his tongue (which triggered an unpalatable image of their tongues converging in a heated kiss) was supplanted by fear. His apprehension was palpable: Cunningham and his men were to be avoided at all costs.

'Very well,' she mumbled as the hackney lurched to a halt.

'Merrion Square,' the driver called out.

They stepped down onto the footpath with their valises. Dusk was falling and the street lamps were being lit. As Cormac paid the driver,

Bridget took Emily's hand and scanned the square, trying to get her bearings to identify Courcey House. In the next pool of light on the footpath, a well-dressed lady was approaching, accompanied by her maid.

'Good gracious,' Bridget heard her say. 'Who would have the indecency to show up to this square in a tatty contraption such as that?'

Startled, she thought she recognised the voice – and when the lady drew nearer and her auburn ringlets became discernible, she was left in no uncertainty. She turned towards the hackney, hoping to go unnoticed, but the lady came to a sudden standstill a few feet away.

'Bridget?' she exclaimed.

As Cormac froze next to her, Bridget turned back reluctantly, plastering a smile onto her face. 'Oh, my goodness, Madeleine!'

Her old friend stared at her, stunned. 'Good grief, what on earth brings you here?' She let out a happy laugh. 'I haven't seen you in so many years. I am speechless with delight!'

She stepped forwards as though to embrace Bridget but faltered. Her gaze focused upon the hackney she had derided so vocally, and then roved over Bridget's plain clothing and the minimal baggage she carried. It came to rest upon Cormac, who had finished paying the driver and had adopted a subservient attitude behind Bridget with his head lowered. As the hackney rolled away from them, Madeleine's bewildered expression returned to Bridget.

'What is going on here?' she asked, her brow furrowed.

Bridget kept her smile fixed in place. 'I made arrangements to sojourn in Dublin for a time. I have long been overdue a visit home to Ireland and I yearned to show my daughter the place where I spent my formative years.'

Madeleine looked down at Emily but, instead of gushing over her as most women were wont to do, she squinted back at Bridget.

'But where is Lord Wyndham? And why do you dress like that, and travel in such a conveyance? And this man –' She gestured towards Cormac. 'Why is *he* with you?'

'He is my manservant and escorted us on our journey.'

Madeleine shook her head, her ringlets bounding emphatically. 'That cannot be correct.' She peered at him. 'I recognise him by his hair. The shade of it is so distinctive.'

It was only then that Bridget realised Cormac had forgotten to replace his cap; it was clutched in his hand along with the valise he carried.

'Yes, you would have encountered him at Oakleigh when you came to visit that summer –'

'That is true,' Madeleine cut across her, 'but I have seen him more recently than that.' She glared. 'Although his hair and clothes were much dirtier at the time, I am certain it was him. I came upon him here, in this very square. *Begging.*'

Bridget cast a quick glance at Cormac and he gave her an infinitesimal nod. She scrabbled to amend her story.

'I admit he has had to cope with many struggles in the past. He travelled to London a few years ago to make a new life for himself. My husband and I agreed to offer him a position and he has given us no cause to regret it. He is very hard-working.'

'Forgive my impertinence,' said Madeleine, her voice hard, 'but I do believe you are lying to me.' All of a sudden, her jaw dropped and she said in a horrified whisper, 'Has he *abducted* you?'

Bridget clicked her tongue. 'Come now, you are letting your imagination run away with you.'

'Well then, tell me the truth and I won't have to imagine!'

Behind Madeleine, her maid was standing agog. There was no one else walking along the footpath on this side of the square but Bridget saw a curtain twitch in the window of the nearest house.

'I confess all is not what it seems,' she said, 'but we cannot discuss it out here in the open. Let us go inside and I can explain everything.'

Peeking about furtively, Madeleine scowled and said, 'Very well. Do you intend to stay at Courcey House?'

'We have yet to make our presence known,' said Bridget. 'And I expect the commotion that will ensue upon our arrival would not be conducive to a serious discussion between ourselves.'

Looking as though it pained her, Madeleine said, 'We shall go to my own residence then. I live here on the square now,' she added proudly.

She led the way along the footpath, chin in the air and her maid scuttling close behind her. Bridget, Cormac and Emily followed at a discreet distance.

'Miss Wallace, is that her name?' Cormac muttered.

'Mrs Matthew Parnell since her marriage,' Bridget replied in a low voice. 'She wed an acquaintance of Garrett's. They first met during his birthday celebrations at Oakleigh.'

'Are you going to tell her the truth?'

'I think I may have no choice.'

They trailed Madeleine down the next side of the square where she paused halfway along it. When they caught up to her, she said frankly, 'I cannot receive you in the drawing room. It would be inconceivable.'

Bridget concealed her sigh. 'Then receive us in whichever room you deem the most appropriate. The kitchens, perhaps?'

She meant it half in jest but Madeleine gave a grave nod. 'Yes, that ought to do.'

However, once inside the grand townhouse, Madeleine absurdly had to ask the surprised footman where to locate the kitchens and, once they got there, they found it in an uproar preparing for dinner because the master had sent a message to say that he would be late.

The housekeeper goggled to see her mistress below stairs but offered her own room for them to speak in private and even procured some biscuits for Emily. They shut the door on the noise from the kitchens and Madeleine took the most comfortable chair, while Bridget and Emily sat at the housekeeper's small table. Cormac remained standing by the door, his posture tense.

'This is most unseemly,' said Madeleine with a sniff. 'Matthew may not have inherited his title yet but I shall be a viscountess one day and this subterfuge is really quite beneath me.'

'We can leave whenever you wish,' said Bridget tightly.

'Not until I hear it all.' Madeleine's eyes gleamed and it struck Bridget that she could very well be the topic of discussion in every drawing room in Dublin before the week was out.

'I suspect you have already guessed what is afoot,' she said. 'Do you need me to say it out loud?'

Madeleine's gaze flitted to Cormac and back to Bridget. 'Yes.'

Wondering if their past friendship would count for nothing after this, Bridget said, 'I shall not meander around the issue then. I am guilty of infidelity. Cormac is my lover and we have run away to be together.' She decided not to mention anything about Emily's parentage. Madeleine could draw her own conclusions if she was perceptive enough to see it.

Madeleine let out an abrupt breath. 'That is an even more fantastic tale than an abduction.'

Bridget splayed her hands out on the table. 'It's the truth.'

Incredulous, Madeleine said, 'What could have possessed you to do such a thing? Have you lost your mind?'

'I have not.'

'Pray, be rational,' Madeleine implored. 'You were a well-respected lady of London society. You had wealth, position, servants, a life of leisure. What would prompt you to discard all that for a miserable existence with a beggar? He can offer you nothing that Lord Wyndham does not already give you.'

'He offers me love.'

'You ought to know your place and keep to it rather than reaching for the ridiculous notion of love. It does not exist.'

'It does, and it transcends all else. I am far happier with Cormac than I ever was with Garrett. Our marriage was a failure.'

Madeleine's gaze darkened. 'That does not give you the right to abandon your vows whenever you choose. What woman is truly happy with her lot? The rest of us have learned to tolerate our circumstances. Why not you?'

Bridget read the jealousy in her old friend's eyes. She thought back to the letters she had received over the years in London, pages filled with reports of married bliss and family blessings. Had Madeleine been lying through her teeth every time she put pen to paper? That would have been Bridget's fate too, had she stayed with Garrett – decades of pretence for the sake of appearances.

'I know I have made the right decision,' she said quietly. Even the reality of Cormac's indiscretion with Thomasina could not change that.

Madeleine appeared not to hear her. Countenance brightening, she said, 'Perhaps there is still time for you to rectify your mistake and save your reputation. You could go back to London and beg Lord Wyndham's forgiveness. His anger might be great but I'm certain his gratitude would be greater.'

'There is no inducement in this whole world that would compel me to return to Garrett.'

'But your standing in society will be forever ruined,' Madeleine lamented. 'And your daughter! Good gracious, have you considered for one moment the damage you are inflicting upon her? She will be a social pariah for the rest of her life.'

They all looked at Emily who was munching contentedly on her biscuits. Cormac winced at the accusation but Bridget remained composed.

'We do not rank social status as a measure of happiness,' she said.

Madeleine threw her hands up in the air. 'What a luxury for you. And what a pity we cannot all afford to adopt such ideals. Might I point out, your misdeeds will be a detriment to those who must claim to have associated with you. I cannot fathom your selfishness.' She crossed her arms, sulky and reproachful.

Bridget set her jaw. 'Please accept my apologies for any inconvenience this may cause you.'

She wished they had never come here. She had been hopeful that Madeleine would relent as Lord Walcott had done, but there was no hint of understanding in the other woman's attitude.

Rising from the table, she said, 'I think we should leave now.'

'You are not going to Courcey House, are you?' Madeleine asked. At Bridget's nod, she touched her fingers to her lips, her expression shocked. 'How can you have the audacity? You will bring shame to the square.'

Before Bridget could reply, Cormac interjected, 'I believe we have had quite enough of your censure, Mrs Parnell. Our activities need be of no concern to you or the other inhabitants of this square.'

Madeleine displayed the usual surprise that came from those who did not expect any level of eloquence in Cormac's speech, but then her eyes blazed with anger. 'This cannot be permitted to happen. As soon as Matthew comes home, I shall tell him what has transpired here and he will do all that is within his power to run you out of the square.' She raised her voice as Cormac opened the door and the sound of bedlam from the kitchens came rushing into the housekeeper's room. 'Furthermore, I shall press him to write at once to Lord Wyndham to inform him where you are. It will only be a matter of time before you are traced and this farce is brought to an end.'

Appalled, Bridget urged Emily to her feet. 'Come, gooseberry, we must go.' As Emily snatched up the last biscuit, Bridget said to Madeleine, 'I beg you to recall the friendship we once shared. Please do not act against us. We have no intention to cause harm to anyone else.'

'I am acting in your own best interests,' said Madeleine primly. 'You will comprehend that in due course.'

She tailed them back to the entrance of the house, clucking her disapproval. Just as they reached the front door, the footman opened it and Matthew Parnell came striding through. He checked at the sight of strangers in his home but Cormac, leading the way, did not stop. He brushed past Mr Parnell, beckoning Bridget and Emily to do the same.

As they hurried down the steps, they heard Madeleine say shrilly, 'Oh, Matthew, there is such a scandal. I beseech you to write to Lord Wyndham directly…'

Fleeing down the street, Bridget knew she would never see Madeleine again.

\*\*\*

There was no question of them staying at Courcey House now, not even for one night; the necessity of disappearing into the city without a trace had become a more immediate consideration. Instead, Cormac posed once again as Bridget's manservant and left a message with the butler at Courcey House that his mistress and her husband were in Dublin but that they were residing with her uncle for a few days. Any letters addressed to her or Lord Wyndham could be forwarded to Rutland Square. They could trust Lord Walcott, he felt sure of that.

He didn't think it would be wise to avail of the gentleman's hospitality for a second night in a row, however, and neither he nor Bridget felt inclined to traipse all the way back across the Liffey again anyway, so they sought out a room in a nearby inn instead. Thanks to the anonymous letters he had been sending his mother for years, and even though he had given a portion to Liam and Ellen, money was not a significant problem for them at present – although their funds would take a blow after their meeting with Thomasina tomorrow.

As he closed the curtains across the narrow window of their room, he shot a guilt-ridden glance towards Bridget. She had finished tucking Emily into the low truckle bed – the little girl was already fast asleep – and was opening her valise to extract her nightdress.

'Do you want me to sleep on the floor?' he asked.

Her shoulders tightened and she did not look at him as she shook out the garment.

He shrugged out of his coat and draped it over the back of the single chair in the room. 'I'm ready for that slap too, if now is convenient for you.'

The corner of her mouth twitched but she covered it up by pursing her lips, tugging at a loose thread on one of the nightdress's cuffs.

He crossed over to her and turned his head, presenting his cheek. Her hand came up, but only to pat it lightly.

'I'm too tired to put the effort in,' she said.

'But you are still angry?' he said cautiously.

She returned her attention to the loose thread, plucking at it until it came free. 'I don't have any right to be. After all, neither of us believed we would ever meet again. You were entitled to engage in a relationship with whomever you chose.' She looked up at him. 'Though between Maisie McKinty and Thomasina, I am feeling like quite the jealous woman.'

'Don't be,' he said. '*Táim i ngrá leatsa amháin.*'

'You love only me,' she repeated in a murmur. 'I am very glad to hear it.'

He touched a gentle kiss to her forehead, but that was all.

She did not make him sleep on the floor.

## Chapter 19

Cormac kept looking over his shoulder after they left the inn the next morning, valises in hand. It was too soon for Cunningham and his men to harbour suspicions about Thomasina's whereabouts for she would not flee the lodgings until that afternoon, and of course Matthew Parnell's letter would have to travel across the sea before Garrett would receive the information he needed to pursue them, but that did not prevent Cormac's nerves from jangling at every shout or striding step behind them. The Dublin streets seemed ominous, with unseen threats lying in wait around each corner.

The first place they visited was the premises of the Grace of God Mission Society. His mouth soured when he saw the bronze plaque and recalled the fleeting hope he had felt when he had lurched through those open double doors. The cruelty of this institution was unfathomable – how could they be in such an influential position to help the needy and yet only offer aid to those of their own Protestant religion?

Next to him, Bridget said, 'I received a letter from here once, in response to my futile attempts to locate you. The deacon said you refused to take their soup.'

He stared up at the deceptively welcoming facade. 'I couldn't conceive of renouncing the faith in which my parents had raised me. I could no more stop being a Catholic than I could stop being an Irishman. It's in my blood.' He sighed. 'And I suspect my mother would have been too devout to capitulate either.'

Nonetheless, they made their enquiries within. It was not Deacon Haybury but a different deacon who greeted them. He was very pleasant and checked their register of converts but, as expected, he came across no one by the name of McGovern. He advised them where they could find other mission societies situated nearby and, with no better leads, they decided to visit them one by one.

Later in the morning, emerging from yet another of these institutions without success, Cormac spotted an establishment further along the street selling a variety of goods, including children's toys. On impulse, he went inside and purchased a doll to give to Henrietta. Bridget didn't comment but he wondered if she was thinking the same as him – would the gift be tantamount to an acknowledgement of fatherhood? Still, it would be unkind to meet the child empty-handed.

He could not neglect Emily so he bought a doll for her too and she gasped with delight upon receiving it.

'Oh, Papa,' she breathed, hugging it to her chest. 'She is just beautiful.'

As he gazed down at her happy face, so easy to please, he speculated on what Henrietta's reaction might be. Did she have any playthings of her own? What had her four years of life been like so far, growing up in that cesspit that was barely one step away from a brothel?

The day progressed with one negative response after another to all enquiries about his family. By the time they reached O'Hara's at ten minutes to five, Cormac's spirits were very low. After this, they would go back to the tenement, where he hoped the mysterious Tess would be present and able to impart some scrap of helpful information. But first, he had to brace himself for a meeting with Thomasina and her daughter.

When they entered the dingy front hall, Mrs O'Hara peered at them from behind her high counter with a gap-toothed sneer.

'Oh, it's yourself, is it? Come to take responsibility for your recklessness?'

He ground his teeth. 'Is Thomasina here?'

She jerked her head towards a door at the rear of the hall. 'They're in the back room. Thought yous would want a bit of privacy. Straight down to the end.'

He strode past her with a clipped word of thanks and pushed open the door she had indicated. Bridget and Emily followed him into a narrow, shadowy corridor. There was one door off to the side and another down at the end, both closed. He proceeded down the corridor, his stomach in knots at the coming encounter.

At the last possible second, it occurred to him that this might be a trap. What if Thomasina's plan was actually to hand him over to Cunningham via this ruse? Could Munroe and the other men be lurking behind the door?

'I've suddenly got a bad feeling,' he muttered to Bridget. 'If this turns out to be some sort of ambush, grab Emily and run out of here as fast as you can. I'll be right behind you.'

Eyes wide with alarm, she gave a shaky nod.

Taking a deep breath, he nudged open the door with his elbow, ready to forestall a blow if it came his way. Nothing happened. He stepped across the threshold and scanned the room swiftly. There were only two people in it and he loosened his held breath in relief – only for it to hitch again in his throat.

Thomasina was perched on a chair against the opposite wall, and next to her on a low stool sat her daughter. The girl was her offspring without a doubt for she was the image of her mother, with an identical head of black hair and the same shaped mouth in miniature form. Her simple frock, threadbare and stained, fell to her shins and beneath its hem she was barefoot. Cormac wished he had bought her shoes instead of a doll. He set his valise down on the floor as Bridget and Emily came in behind him. Bridget shut the door and stood awkwardly in front of it, looking like she didn't know whether she should partake in the conversation or not. Emily stared curiously, her new doll cradled in her arm.

Thomasina prodded Henrietta's shoulder. 'Go on, get up. Here he is.'

The girl got to her feet. She was small for her four years, a mere slip of a thing. She stuck a finger in her mouth and started biting the skin around the nail.

Thomasina stood too. 'Let me get this right,' she said. 'May I present Miss Henrietta Brennan?' She dipped into a mocking curtsey, wobbled and caught her balance with a laugh.

Cormac knelt in front of the little girl. 'Good afternoon, Henrietta,' he said.

She said nothing back, only kept gnawing on her finger. Her nails were caked with dirt. Flinching, he took a gentle hold of her wrist and coaxed the finger out of her mouth.

'It is nice to meet you,' he tried but she still did not speak.

He looked into her eyes, which were not his shade of vivid blue but a warm light brown. He had never taken much notice of Thomasina's eyes before but now he stole a glimpse to compare them to the girl's. They were also light brown – the only difference appeared to be some lighter golden flecks in Henrietta's irises. She took after her mother in practically every respect.

Her lack of fair hair and blue eyes alleviated some of his fears, though only marginally so. There was no solid evidence to say that she was his daughter, but equally there was nothing conclusive to say that she wasn't.

'Come on, Henny,' said Thomasina. 'Say "It's nice to meet you too after all these years". Tell him your favourite colour and the songs you like to sing. Y'know, things he'd already know if he'd been around.' She gave Cormac a wicked grin.

He did not credit her with a response. Instead, he reached behind him and pulled over his valise.

'I have a present for you,' he said and, withdrawing the doll from the valise, held it out to Henrietta.

She gazed at it and then peeked up at her mother. Thomasina's brow was puckered in surprise but she said, 'Go ahead, you can take it.'

Hesitant, Henrietta accepted the doll, clutching one arm gingerly.

'Do you know what to say when someone gives you a present?' Cormac asked her.

Thomasina glowered. 'She never gets presents, so no.' She prodded

Henrietta's shoulder again. 'Say "Thank you", Henny.'

So quiet that she was scarcely audible, the girl whispered, 'Thank you.'

'You're very welcome.' Cormac rose and motioned to the stool. 'Do you want to sit again?'

She did as he suggested and he took the chair Thomasina had vacated.

'You'll have to come up with a name for her,' he said. 'What do you think you will call her?'

She didn't answer. Her grimy fingers were tracing the painted hair on the doll's head (black like her own), the closed mouth with its sombre expression, the wooden limbs, and the pretty cream dress with lace cuffs. She was wholly captivated by this new creature that now belonged to her.

Then she touched the doll's head to her cheek and, with a subtle splintering of his heart, it became clear to Cormac: all little girls just want someone to hug them.

Without thinking, he lifted her onto his knee and put his arm around her. She did not resist and leaned back against his chest, although her attention remained fixated on the doll.

He glanced at Bridget but her expression was unreadable. Thomasina was staring with open-mouthed astonishment. Emily walked past them both and came right up to Henrietta.

'I have one too,' she said, holding out her own doll. 'Do you want to play?'

Henrietta considered for a moment before sliding down off Cormac's knee. Emily led her over to the corner of the room and they hunkered there, Emily doing most of the chattering while the two dolls and the two girls – could they be half sisters? – met for the first time.

Cormac got up again, his legs somewhat unsteady. Thomasina threw him a baffled look.

'You must have a way with children,' she said. 'The brat usually runs and hides when she sees a man coming.'

He didn't like to think what kind of mistreatment Henrietta might have been subjected to by the men in the lodgings – they were liable to kick a child out of the way as easily as a dog.

'She's very small for her age,' he said reprovingly.

Thomasina arched an eyebrow. 'She's underfed. What did you expect?' She put her hands on her hips. 'We need to be going soon. Where's my money?'

He withdrew a pouch from the pocket of his coat; it jangled as he held it out to her. She snatched it from him and opened it to examine its contents.

'Make sure you use a portion of it to buy her some shoes and better clothes.'

She closed the bag, satisfied. 'I will.'

'Ow!' The cry came from the corner of the room. Emily swivelled to them

*A Class Forsaken*

with an injured expression, holding up her hand. 'She pinched me!'

Henrietta looked innocent, stroking her doll's head and balancing its feet on her bare toes.

Thomasina tutted at Emily. 'Or are you telling a fib, little miss tattler?'

Cormac frowned. 'You don't get to talk to her that way.'

'Well, we know who'll always be the favourite, won't we?' Thomasina said with a huff. Tucking the pouch of money inside her bodice, she snapped, 'Get up, Henny. We're leaving.'

Cormac felt a shard of unhappiness lodge inside his gut. Was that all the time they would have? It seemed far too short.

He caught Thomasina's elbow. 'Where are you going next?' he asked.

'Smithfield Market,' she said. 'I've made arrangements to meet a fellow there. He's going to take us north out of the city.'

He didn't ask who the fellow was and she didn't offer any further information, but he hoped he was a decent man who would treat her and Henrietta well. There had been a distinct shortage of decent men in their lives up to now, that was for sure.

As she shrugged out of his grip, he asked, 'Do you need anything else? Is there any other way I can help you both?'

She shook her head. 'I promise you'll never see us again.'

Bridget stepped aside as Thomasina stalked to the door. She hurried into the corridor beyond and Henrietta followed on her heels. The little girl didn't look back but she still grasped the doll tightly.

Cormac released a slow exhalation, while Bridget checked the red pinch mark on the back of Emily's hand and kissed it better. His mind was in a whirl. Surely he hadn't done enough. He ought to go after them and offer to do more – but then what exactly could he offer? He had no fixed abode right now and any sort of settled existence was impossible until he had found his family. Perhaps they were far better off without him.

Dispirited, he stooped over Emily and gave her a kiss too. She snuffled but shed no tears. Then, lacking the energy to discuss what had just happened, he said, 'Shall we go?'

Bridget nodded wordlessly. They picked up their valises and returned to the front hall. Mrs O'Hara flung a few more choice accusations at him but he didn't register what she said. Emerging onto the street, he swept his gaze in both directions but Thomasina and Henrietta had already vanished. With a sigh, he led Bridget and Emily along Meath Street until they came to the corner where it crossed with the street of tenement buildings. They turned onto it and walked along until they found the one they had entered the previous day.

Marty was once again ready to disabuse them of any notion that their presence might be welcome. The scars on his face stood out vividly as he hollered, 'Get out of here!'

Cormac raised his voice to be heard over him. 'Don't you remember us from yesterday? We're looking for Tess, that's all. Is she here?'

'Go away!'

Exasperated, Cormac tried to see past Marty into the back room, wondering where the frail old man was. The silhouette of a figure appeared in the doorway – a womanly shape, shorter and curvier than the old man. She stepped through into the front room and Cormac got such a shock that he nearly fell over.

She was several years older and she had a harsher countenance but he would have recognised that distinctive shade of red hair anywhere. Although the only time he had ever met this girl was nearly five years ago, it was not an encounter easily forgotten: it had been his last night in Dublin before he had got on a ship out of the country and it had been her first night attempting to sell herself for money.

Her hair was still the same but her demeanour was quite different. In that warehouse on the docks she had seemed self-conscious, timid, hunched over with the shame of what she had tried and failed to do. Now she stood with her shoulders back and her chin thrust out, her manner self-assured and her gaze unsympathetic. Her rouged cheeks and painted lips, together with her low-cut bodice and the raised hem of her skirt which exposed an unseemly amount of ankle and stocking, led Cormac to the regrettable conclusion that he had not succeeded in turning her away from that objectionable profession.

She regarded them with suspicion. 'What d'yous want?'

He did not know what to say. 'Do you – do you remember me?'

Her eyes narrowed and then opened wide. She took a step back in amazement. It had been a long time ago but he supposed she would not easily forget the face of a stranger who had handed her a lot of money without expecting something in return.

'You!' she blurted. 'What're you doing here?'

'I'm looking for my family. I had no inkling that I might come across you.'

She started to say something else but Marty interrupted her. 'They've got to leave. There's no space for them.'

'I have already told you that we don't want to stay,' Cormac said stridently.

Marty's eyes flashed and he took several menacing paces forwards. Cormac felt Bridget tugging at the back of his coat to pull him out of harm's way, but Tess put a firm hand on the youth's shoulder.

'Marty, we've talked about this. If your behaviour gets too out of hand, we'll throw you out. Calm down. These people aren't going to harm you.'

He still looked mutinous, growling low in his throat. She shook her head and turned to Cormac.

'Maybe we should speak outside. I was getting ready to leave anyway.'

Her day's work was only about to start, he inferred, but he just nodded.

'I've got to fetch my shawl. I'll meet yous out there in a moment.' She disappeared into the back room.

He felt the heat of Marty's glare and ushered Bridget and Emily back out to the footpath where they waited for Tess to emerge. The same two men from yesterday were once again scrutinising them from across the street.

'Who is she?' Bridget demanded, and it was plain she was beginning to fear he had bedded all the scarlet women in Dublin.

'I was never a customer of hers,' he hastened to assure her. 'She was barely more than a child when we met. Do you recall, when I told you about my past, I mentioned saving a girl from a thug and giving her some money? She's that girl.' He blinked. 'That incident was actually what prompted me to board the same ship as Oliver Davenport. I suppose we have a great deal to thank her for, when you think about it.'

The distrust faded from Bridget's expression and she looked relieved. 'Perhaps we do.'

He felt sad for Tess. She had seemed so young back then but now she appeared old beyond her years. Life on the streets had toughened her, and she had been compelled to assume the most unspeakable occupation for a woman. Of course, he could not condemn her when he recollected the path he had been forced to take himself, but he was sorry that the money had not helped her enough to avoid it.

She materialised in the doorway a minute later with a frayed shawl wrapped around her shoulders, concealing her low-cut attire. She joined them on the footpath and the two men opposite turned away, satisfied.

Cormac offered her a smile. 'So your name is Tess?'

'Teresa,' she said. 'Tess to my friends,' she added, one corner of her mouth upturned. 'Sorry about Marty. He gets awful fretful 'round strangers.' She stared at him in wonderment. 'I never thought I'd see you again.'

'Nor I you. This is quite the chance encounter, just like that night was.'

She gave a wistful smile. 'I used to think of you as my guardian angel. I longed so much for you to reappear so's I could thank you right.'

Bridget cleared her throat; from Tess's ardent gaze, it was not hard to guess in what manner she would have liked to thank him. He hastily introduced Bridget and Emily so that the relationship boundaries could be made quite clear. Tess looked Bridget up and down, disappointment registering on her face. This was palpably not how she had imagined the scene playing out.

Discomfited, Cormac said, 'I hope the money was a help to you?'

'Oh,' she said, focusing on him again. 'Yes, it helped us a lot.'

'Us?'

'I shared it with my friends.'

'That was generous of you,' he said, surprised. 'Alone, that money could have lasted you for months.'

She shrugged. 'Their ma was sick. She needed it more than I did.'

'I take it that it was not long then before you had to...' He trailed off.

Her eyes hardened. 'That's none of your business. I did what I had to do. Now, if you'll 'scuse me.'

She swung her red hair over her shoulder and brushed past them.

'Wait,' he called after her. 'I did not mean to offend you. But I just have one question to ask you before you go. Please.'

He was not sure why she stopped and turned around, but maybe she felt she owed him for the good deed he had done for her so long ago.

'What is it?' she said irritably.

He set down his valise, holding out his hands in a conciliatory way. 'We are looking for some members of my family who have been missing for many years. Their last known whereabouts is only around the corner from here so there is a high possibility that they may have wandered into this area. We were led to believe that you know the local inhabitants better than anyone. All I am asking is if you can tell me whether they ever came to this street or even whether they might still be here now.'

She folded her arms. 'Not likely. Most of the people 'round here are new enough. We'd a disease that wiped out a lot of us a couple of winters ago.'

He flinched.

'Sorry,' she said, softening a little. 'Maybe your family was lucky. What do they look like?'

He repeated the familiar description. 'A woman, three girls — two in their adolescence and the third a good deal younger — and a newborn baby boy, although he must be nearly eight years old by this stage. They all have dark hair and their surname is McGovern.'

She stumbled backwards, total disbelief written all over her features. She seemed too stunned to speak.

Hope rose in Cormac. He took an urgent step towards her. 'Do you know them?'

She stared open-mouthed at him. At last, she whispered, 'Are you Maggie's boy?'

He felt a burst of emotion inside him. 'I am!' Was she about to tell him that his mother was inside that very tenement building? Was he on the verge of being reunited with his sisters? 'Are they here? How do you know my family?'

She hesitated for the longest time before answering. 'They were my friends.'

He heard her use of the past tense but he did not want to acknowledge it. 'Where are they?' he demanded. 'Where is my mother?'

She was unwilling to meet his gaze. 'Your mother's dead,' she said softly.

Something seemed to have happened to Cormac's senses. Tess continued to speak but her voice had grown distorted and distant, and everything around him had gone foggy. The boulder in the pit of his stomach, his constant companion throughout his search for his missing family, felt like a ton weight. He became vaguely conscious of a pair of arms encircling him but he could not move, either to lean into the embrace or shake it off. It was only when he felt a pressure on his right knee that he regained a proper sense of awareness and glanced down. Emily was hugging his leg and staring up at him with huge eyes.

She should not have to hear any of this.

'Let's go somewhere,' he muttered. 'I need to hear it all from the start.'

Tess shook her head. 'I can't. Time's passing. I've got places to be.'

'Forget about that tonight.'

'That's easy for you to say,' she said, her tone rising. 'You won't be the one with no money for food in the morning.'

'I will give you money,' he said, digging his hand into his pocket and pulling out some coins.

She eyed the money but did not take it. 'I'm not going to be in your debt again.'

'There will be no debt.' His voice was laced with desperation. 'You know what happened to my family and I am offering payment for that information. It will be a fair exchange. Please, I am begging you.'

She twisted her lips as she weighed up his proposal. Then she relented. 'Fine so.'

He looked at Bridget, whose arms were still around him. 'We should put Emily to bed. This is not for her ears.'

She nodded in agreement, pain and compassion in her eyes.

## Chapter 20

They had to walk the length of several streets before they located an inn in the vicinity that seemed reputable enough. They paid for two rooms beside each other and, after cajoling Emily into eating a bowl of watery stew from the inn's available fare, put her to bed in one of the rooms. It was early in the evening but she was so exhausted from their day's walking that she did not gripe. Bridget hummed a lullaby to her and Cormac silently stroked her hair, while Tess observed without comment, her brows drawn together with something like envy.

Once Emily had fallen asleep, they went into the other room so that they could talk freely. The only furniture in the room was a bed and two worn chairs with arms by the window. Cormac offered Tess a chair but she sat on the edge of the bed so he and Bridget claimed the chairs. The light outside was still bright, although the timbre of it implied that twilight was not far away.

'Would you care for something to eat too?' Bridget said to Tess. 'We can ask the innkeeper to bring it up.' She did not suggest food for herself or Cormac and he was glad; he didn't think he would be able to stomach it.

'No, thanks,' said Tess. 'Best be getting on with it.' She dropped her shawl onto the bedcover and pulled her mane of red hair over one shoulder; it was long enough to reach the top of her bodice and covered the swell of one breast, though the other remained exposed. 'So what d'yous want to know?'

'Everything,' said Cormac, both dreading and aching to hear the truth. 'Don't omit a single detail. Where did you first encounter my family?'

'Right in that shelter where yous met me this evening. It was their first winter in the city. They always said afterwards if I hadn't found them they'd all have been dead by New Year's. And they were right—that winter was cruel. But I'd been on the streets for three years at that stage and I knew how to survive.' She crossed one leg over the other, showing even more of her stockings. 'I had different hideouts but I often went to that place because there was a black boy who would trade blankets and things. I stumbled upon your family in one of the rooms upstairs. They were starving. It was a miracle the poor baby was still alive. At first, I was just going to ignore them—I wasn't too keen on trying to help others when I could hardly feed myself—but I took pity on them. The mother, Maggie,

588

reminded me of my own ma before she died. She had kind eyes.'

Cormac twitched but said nothing.

'The building was in better shape then than it is now. If you were lucky enough to have a blanket, it was possible to warm up a little. Maggie used to stay there with Orlaith and the baby while I took Margaret and Bronagh out and showed them the best places to find food.'

At the sound of his sisters' names, Cormac gripped the arms of his chair. Bridget reached out and placed her hand over his.

'We survived that winter, every single one of us. Another girl in the shelter had recently lost her own newborn baby so she wet-nursed Patrick. I was sure he wouldn't make it but he was a strong boy. Then we'd a fine summer and it was much easier to find food. We all became very close and Maggie said I was like another daughter to her.' Tess bowed her head and fingered the unravelling hem of her shawl, hiding whatever emotion her face might have revealed. 'The next winter was mild but the following winter was much worse. Your ma took ill and she didn't get better when the spring came. We didn't know what sickness it was but she had fever and chills and coughed all the time. I tried to steal some medicine from an apothecary but I was caught and whipped before I could get away. We wondered if we should take her to the workhouse but she wouldn't hear of being parted from her girls. Our last resort was to pay for the medicine and we knew there was only one way to get the money. The night I met you' – Tess nodded at Cormac – 'was the first time Margaret and I went walking the streets.'

'But you were just girls,' said Bridget in a hushed tone. 'You were just two young girls.'

Tess's mouth contorted into a hard smile. 'For some men, it's the younger the better. But I didn't have to go through with it 'cause my guardian angel appeared with more money than I'd ever seen in my life. Poor Margaret wasn't so lucky though. She had to see it through and her customer was quite brutal with her. She was in pain for days afterwards.'

Cormac shut his eyes. That was his sweet sister she was talking about. Gentle, kind Margaret, reduced to a whore. If only it had been her and not Tess whom he had come across that night in the warehouse, he could have put an end to all this.

He heard Tess continue: 'Between the two of us, we'd gathered enough money to buy some decent food and the medicine for Maggie. The apothecary said it would work if she took it for long enough. But it got used up quick so we went out again. I hoped my guardian angel would appear to me a second time but no such luck. It came to be a regular thing for us. Maggie didn't know what we were doing. Margaret told her we were making money by selling flowers on the street and Maggie believed her.'

Tess paused. When she spoke again, her voice was fainter. 'What happened next was unexpected. Maggie was the one who was sick and we concentrated all our efforts on trying to make her better. But what I didn't know, and what your other sisters didn't know, was that Margaret had also fallen ill. It wasn't the same disease your ma had. I reckon it was something she picked up on the streets. She hid it as long as she could but it got so bad she couldn't keep it from us anymore. She'd a fever too so we tried to give her some of Maggie's medicine but she wouldn't take it. By the end she couldn't breathe proper and she got awful confused. It was unbearable to watch. She faded very fast and died one night in July. I'd known her less than three years.'

Cormac felt angry tears pricking his closed eyelids. While Margaret had been dying, he had been studying mathematics and philosophy at Bewley Hall. While his mother and sisters had been struggling to keep their family together, he had adopted a new aunt and uncle for himself. It was appalling.

Sighing, Tess said, 'After that, your ma gave up. There's no other way to describe it. She'd suffered too much and it was agony for her to try to bear the loss of yet another child. Even though she'd two daughters and a grandson yet alive, she just let go. I did all I could to convince a medical man to come see her but it was too late. She died only four days after Margaret.'

Cormac's hands whipped up to his head. He grabbed fistfuls of his hair and pulled as hard as he could. He needed to feel pain, he needed to punish himself, he needed to suffer. His mother had endured so much beyond what any person should have to tolerate in one life. He was consumed by immeasurable guilt; the night of sweet innocence he and Bridget had shared in the hay barn had set off the chain of events that had led to this unutterable horror. If he could turn back the clock and find his mother and transfer all of her pain onto himself, he would do it in an instant and he would be full of gladness that her torment was now his – it was no more than he deserved.

'Cormac, stop,' he heard Bridget whisper and felt her tugging at his hands.

Dispirited, he let them drop to the arms of his chair again. Opening his eyes, he saw the tears on Tess's cheeks. She must have been very devoted to his family to go to such extreme lengths to try to save his mother.

'What about the others?' he said lifelessly. 'Bronagh, Orlaith and Patrick. How did they die?'

'They're not dead,' said Tess. 'Or at least, I don't think so anyway.'

He leapt from his chair, shock blazing through his veins.

'What?' he cried. 'I thought they were all dead! Why did you not take me to them at once when you found out who I was?'

"Cause I don't know where they are!' she responded with equal heat. 'It's been years since I've seen them.'

He tried to calm himself but remained on his feet. 'When was your last contact with them?' he asked, keeping his voice as steady as he could.

Still looking insulted, she said, 'A couple of months after Margaret and Maggie died. Bronagh was the first to disappear. We woke up one morning and she was gone. I think she ran away and my guess is she went to America. She used to talk about it a lot, even when her ma and sister were still alive. She wanted us all to go, thought we'd have a better chance of survival there. But by that stage Maggie was already too weak to walk, let alone travel on a ship, and where would we've gotten the money for six tickets anyway? After Maggie's death, Bronagh became so withdrawn. I figured it was her own way of dealing with her grief but now I think she was distancing herself to make it easier to leave. Selfish maybe, but it would've been the right thing for her own sake.'

That sounded like Bronagh, fierce and fearless. Only she would contemplate crossing the ocean to a new continent all by herself.

'So she might still be alive,' Cormac said with a measure of relief.

'She might,' Tess acknowledged.

'And Orlaith and Patrick? Do you know what happened to them?'

Tess's shoulders drooped. 'Poor little Orlaith. She'd to grow up so fast. She was laden with adult concerns at the age of only eight. I was willing to look after her and Patrick but she said I'd done enough for her family and she didn't want to burden me any longer. She began leaving the shelter every morning with Patrick and coming back very late at night. She'd never tell me where they'd been. This went on for weeks. Then one day they returned and she said it was the last time I'd see them. They came back just to say goodbye. I begged her to tell me where they were going but she refused. She claimed she was too ashamed of what she'd done.'

Cormac blanched. 'Not Orlaith too...'

'No. She swore to me she hadn't resorted to that. But it was still something so disgraceful she wouldn't speak of it. We hugged and they left. I haven't laid eyes on them from that day to this.'

He sank back into his chair. 'So they may still be alive but we have no idea where. They could be gone to America too, for all we know.'

Tess hesitated. 'I don't think so. I've a feeling they're still in Dublin.'

He looked up sharply. 'Why do you say that?'

'That black boy in our shelter, Eli. He came and went as he pleased and he'd an awful temper but he always had a soft spot for little Orlaith. Used to give her spare bits of food and the like. He buggered off to some other hideout a while back but I bumped into him about a year ago in an alley behind a grocer's shop and he told me he thought he'd seen Orlaith the previous week.'

Cormac's breath snagged in his throat. 'Where?'

'On a square of fine houses in the centre of the city. He goes scavenging there every now and then 'cause rich people throw out so much good food. I've always stayed away. There are more constables on watch and I don't want to risk getting caught. But I went there after what Eli told me. He said the girl had looked like Orlaith from a distance and she'd been wearing maid's clothes so I wondered if she'd managed to get employment in one of the houses. I searched 'round for her but I never saw her walking on the street and I couldn't exactly go knocking on doors. So I left and I didn't go back again. It's possible Eli was mistaken.'

'It is also possible that he was correct,' said Cormac, getting fired up again. It was the slimmest of leads but he was going to cling to it with all he had. 'In the morning, I want you to come with us to this square. We will keep looking for Orlaith and Patrick until we find them.'

Bridget bobbed her head fervently beside him. Tess nodded too and wiped her eyes on the corner of her shawl.

A sudden thought occurred to Cormac. 'This Eli. He had black skin? Did he have a milky eye too, by any chance?'

Tess gaped. 'He did. How did you know?'

Cormac rubbed his hand over his mouth. 'I believe we bumped into each other once. He tried to steal from me.'

Tess gave a cracked chuckle. 'That sounds like Eli.'

Cormac remembered how the black youth had attempted to wrest his blanket from him – the only thing he had possessed at the time apart from the clothes on his back. Now he wondered whether Eli had been thieving the blanket for further trade or to give as a gift to Orlaith. Anguish welled in him. How could his path have been so close to his family's and yet never actually crossed? If only he had known…could he have saved them?

He swallowed. 'Ma and Margaret. What happened to their bodies?'

Tess winced. 'I was hoping you wouldn't ask that.' Embarrassment coloured her cheeks and her gaze flicked away from him. 'Dublin's known for its medical men but they need to practise their skills to improve their knowledge. Their lackeys are on the lookout everywhere. If they're not grave robbing, they're hunting for corpses in the poorer parts of the city and they'll usually give a few coins. Two fellows came looking that July and I—I let them t-take—' She stuttered to a stop. Then, very formally, she said, 'Please forgive me. It was a hideous thing to do.'

'There is nothing to forgive,' said Cormac, even though it distressed him to imagine what had happened next. 'On the contrary, I am so very grateful to you. Thank you for everything you did for my family. They were lucky to have you as their friend.'

'I don't think luck was something they had much of.' She sniffed. 'I was happy to do anything I could to help them. They were such kind people and they never harmed anyone but this city just kept battering them 'til they couldn't get back up.' Her chin trembled. 'They meant a great deal to me. They were the closest thing I had to a real family after my own ma was gone.'

It had grown darker in the room as the daylight faded outside but no one moved to light a lamp.

Tess fingered a lock of her red hair. 'They used to talk about you all the time.'

Cormac felt deeply sad at this. 'Did they?'

'Maggie said you were an exact copy of your da in both looks and talents. There was nothing you couldn't do with a piece of wood. And Margaret always talked about how good you were with animals, 'specially horses. They never knew what happened to you but they hoped and prayed you were alive and well, wherever you were. Except—' All of a sudden, she fell silent.

'Except what?' he said, startled.

She pressed her lips together and her forehead creased. 'They were troubled,' she said in a low voice. 'We heard rumours of a vicious thug on the streets. He worked for that bastard money lender, Cunningham, and he went by the name of McGovern. He was ruthless. He terrorised the people who owed Cunningham money and even threatened their small children to make them pay up. Your family feared this man might be you 'cause of the name, but they hoped it was just a coincidence. Maggie couldn't believe her son would be capable of doing such things.'

The atmosphere in the room became tense. Cormac felt an icy chill run down his back. His family had heard about the despicable things he had done. They had not been certain it was him but they had harboured some suspicions. Wretched shame coursed through him. His throat tightened and he could not speak.

Tess stared at him with dawning horror as the silence lengthened between them. She swallowed audibly. Then, grabbing her shawl, she bounded to her feet and ran for the door.

Cormac got there just as she wrenched the door open with her two hands. He slammed it shut and stood in her way so she could not get past. She backed into a corner of the room, a mixture of terror and revulsion on her face. Her gaze flipped from Cormac to Bridget, who had also jumped up from her chair, and back to Cormac.

'Please understand—' he started but she cut him off.

'I don't want to hear what you've got to say,' she hissed. 'For the first time, I'm glad your family's no longer here. At least they never had to learn the horrible truth. They would've been heartbroken.'

'I know that.' The thought of it made his gut twist. 'I hate myself for what I did. It is a period of my life that I utterly regret. But I was desperate.

I was as poverty-stricken as the rest of you when I came to Dublin and it was the only way I could stay alive. You know what that feels like. You have been forced to resort to an abject level of conduct as well.'

'My actions have harmed no one but myself,' she countered. 'We heard such terrible stories of cruelty. You laughed in the faces of mothers who begged for their children's lives. You took more than what borrowers owed just to line your own pockets. You tortured people for fun.'

He listened to these accusations with deep shock. 'The rumours you heard were grossly exaggerated. I never did any of those things.'

'You're a liar.' Her expression was full of loathing. 'I should've realised who you were. Back in the warehouse when you pulled a knife on that first disgusting customer of mine, you said you worked for Cunningham. But he'd a lot of toughs working for him. You could've been any one of them. And then I found out your name today but I still didn't make the connection. I'm such a fool.'

'Listen to me,' he said in exasperation. 'Yes, I worked for Cunningham but that was a long time ago and I am not that person anymore. You have spent this evening in my company. You can see that I have a child with me. Have I given any reason, by my behaviour or my language, for you to be afraid? I am not a threat to you or to anyone else.'

'You're a piece of slime. And slime just gets slimier over the years.'

He was astounded by the vitriol coming from the girl's mouth. She despised the person she believed him to be. But her opinion was based on hearsay which was wildly inaccurate – he could never have stooped so low as to torture someone for enjoyment. He was unable to fathom how such lies had spread.

'I gave you all that money,' he pointed out. 'That was an unselfish act which does not correspond very well with your image of the fiend known as McGovern.'

In the waning light, he could make out the obstinate expression on her face. She said nothing.

He exhaled. 'I am no danger to you but plainly you are not willing to accept that. Are you going to flee as soon as I step away from this door?'

'Yes,' she said without hesitation.

'Will you not come with us in the morning to find Orlaith and Patrick?'

'I'm not going anywhere with you tomorrow. I won't lead you within a mile of them if I can help it. They're far better off without you.'

Cormac looked at Bridget helplessly. She had been watching the heated exchange between him and Tess with increasing apprehension. Now, at his unspoken plea, she stepped forwards to intervene.

'Are you certain about that?' she said.

'What?' Tess snapped, glancing at her before returning her angry gaze to Cormac.

'Are you certain that Orlaith is better off without her brother? That Patrick is better off without his uncle? Would they not be grateful to piece some of their family back together?'

'Not when they realise who he is and what he's done,' Tess said through clenched teeth.

'You have a fallacious view of Cormac McGovern,' Bridget told her. 'You have heard these untrue reports about him and credited them as fact without verifying their validity. Yes, he did work for that money lender. He made a mistake. Who in this room has not? But I have known Cormac for most of his life and I know that he is a good man and that he loves his family. You told us how fondly they used to speak of him. Do you not think that the remnants of this family deserve to be reunited?'

Tess finally looked straight at Bridget. She appeared less sure of herself in the face of this unswerving loyalty from such a well-spoken lady. But she was stubborn.

'You know one version of McGovern,' she said, 'and I know another. Orlaith and Patrick shouldn't run the risk of encountering the worse of the two.'

'Is that not a decision they ought to make for themselves?'

Bridget's words hung in the air. Tess huddled in the corner, chewing on her lip.

'But they're still so young,' she said at last. 'Orlaith must be barely thirteen and Patrick can't yet be eight.'

'All the more reason for them to have an older family member to take care of them. Their own flesh and blood. That has to be better than whatever lives they are leading now. They could be children again.'

Cormac watched Tess anxiously. She vacillated for a few moments longer and then she gave a grudging nod.

'I suppose I don't have the right to decide for them,' she muttered. 'Maybe it's only fair they're allowed to make up their own minds. But I won't go out of my way to help yous. I'll tell yous where to go and then I want to leave. Understood?'

'Very well,' said Cormac. 'We cannot ask for more than that.'

Looking as though it was against her better judgement, she said, 'Stephen's Green. That's where Eli thought he saw Orlaith. But of course there's no certainty that it was her.'

Cormac pressed his nails into his palms with relief. He was very glad she had not said Merrion Square for he didn't know how they would have been able to show their faces there again. 'We will maintain hope that it was, and trust that we will find her there tomorrow.'

They stared at each other, a wary truce between them. Then she glanced at the door and he stepped away from it.

'Thank you again,' he said. 'I appreciate all of your help and hope you might come to realise in time that I am not the evil beast you deem me to be. Will you accept the money I offered you earlier?'

'No,' she said. She bolted for the door and they watched her red hair whisk out of sight.

With a shaky breath, he sank down onto the edge of the bed. Bridget sat next to him.

'It is difficult to come to terms with the fact that someone can hate me with such intensity,' he said weakly, looking down into his lap. 'I'm thankful you were able to convince her to help us.'

'Do you think she told us the truth?' Bridget cast a worried look at the still-open door.

'We have no way of knowing for certain, but I think she did. She would not want to be the person who got in the way of the McGoverns finding a degree of happiness at last. Her affection for them all was genuine. It was apparent how much it cost her to speak of their deaths.'

His voice fractured on the last word. He turned to Bridget and saw the tears glistening in her eyes.

'Poor Maggie and Margaret,' she whispered.

The truth of it crashed over him, and some part of him deep in his very core compressed under the weight of it and shattered. A mangled sound, laced with agony and loss and remorse, slipped from his throat. He fumbled for Bridget's embrace, needing her to anchor him before it crushed him entirely. She held him in the darkness and together they mourned the passing of two gentle souls.

## Chapter 21

There was no sleep to be had. Cormac felt as though someone were sticking pins into him throughout the night, jerking him back to wakefulness whenever he was about to drop off. Nightmarish images of his mother and sister's final excruciating days swam before his eyelids and guilt gouged out his insides, leaving him in shreds by the dawn.

He rose with sluggish limbs and his mind in a stupor. Bridget's bleary gaze told him she had spent the night in a similar fashion. While he made a weary effort to shave, she folded her nightdress and eyed their valises sitting side by side at the end of the bed.

'Perhaps we could leave them in the charge of the innkeeper?' she said hopefully. 'It would be a relief not to lug them about all day and we could return in the evening to retrieve them and seek out alternative accommodation.'

Exhausted, he made no objection. They arranged it with the innkeeper and also procured a parcel of black pudding and hard-boiled eggs to eat during the day, although he himself still didn't feel remotely hungry. It wasn't until they got outside, when the fresh air, damp with an early morning mist, struck his face, that some semblance of energy returned to his body. As Emily skipped ahead of them clutching her new doll, which she refused to leave behind, he reminded himself of their purpose and discovered that a tiny scrap of optimism still remained.

They made their way through the Dublin streets to the square of St Stephen's Green. Bridget knew it from her youth for it was one of the most respectable addresses in the city. Terraces of elegant, red-bricked townhouses lined the square on all sides, and in the centre was the green itself, a park enclosed by railings and accessible only to the square's inhabitants. The houses exuded affluence and had wide steps leading up to entrances topped with semicircular fanlights. Iron railings surrounded open wells at the fronts of the houses, with flights of steps allowing direct access down to the cellars.

The enormity of their task was quite plain to them. There had to be more than sixty residences on the square and Orlaith and Patrick could be in any one of them or none at all.

With a grimace at Bridget, Cormac said, 'I regret to say it but I think the best way to approach the matter is to be methodical and visit every house in turn.'

It would be immensely time-consuming but, if nothing else, they would be able to rule out each one with absolute certainty. It would also be more thorough than Tess's aimless wandering, but then she had been correct – there could have been no possibility of her going to knock on doors. Cormac and Bridget looked respectable enough that they would not be turned away at first glance and ought to at least get the opportunity to state their case.

The mist persisted and threatened to develop into rain as they approached the first house. Cormac opened the gate in the front railings and led Bridget and Emily down the steps to the cellar as that was where they were most likely to find luck, if there was any to be found. Perhaps Orlaith would be working in the kitchens or the scullery; maybe Patrick would be cleaning knives or shoes. He could also very well be shovelling manure in the mews at the rear of the houses, so that was another avenue they could pursue later if their enquiries via the front access proved to be in vain.

Cormac rapped on the cellar door. A cook answered it, her face and apron covered in flour. Her manner was civil as it was clear that Cormac was no mere milkman.

'Can I help yous?'

'I hope that you can,' said Cormac. 'I am looking for my sister. It is possible that she is a maid in one of these houses. She is thirteen with dark hair and there should be a little boy with her around the age of seven. Does this description sound familiar to you?'

The cook scowled when she realised that the callers were not there to serve any purpose for her master or mistress.

'They're not at this address,' she said and closed the door with a snap.

The day wore on in much the same manner. They visited house after house and met with varying levels of curiosity, suspicion and downright rudeness. They spoke mainly to cooks and maids and, once or twice, a housekeeper. From each one the answer was almost always the same: nobody on the staff fitted the description of either the girl or the boy. A number of times there was a dark-haired housemaid but it was never Orlaith.

They stopped to eat the black pudding and eggs in the early afternoon before embarking along the third side of the square. The rain had held off for the most part but now scattered drops were starting to fall in earnest. At the first house on this side, a maid stood at the top of the cellar steps, watching a coalman shovel a delivery down the coal hole in the footpath. She had dark hair but she looked like she was in her early twenties, too old to be Orlaith.

'Who're yous?' she said as they approached her.

'This is Mabel,' Emily said, holding up her doll, and the maid gave her an indulgent smile.

For what seemed like the thousandth time in his life, Cormac explained why they were there and who they were looking for. 'Are they here or have you ever seen them on the square?'

He was braced for the usual negative response but the girl did not answer right away. Her brow furrowed in contemplation.

'I'm not sure,' she said slowly. 'Maybe...'

He felt his spirits lift. 'Do you know them?'

She shook her head. 'Not the boy, anyway. There are no young lads employed in any of the houses 'round here. But the girl... There's a dark-haired girl working for a household two doors down from here. She's been there for a few years. I remember when she started 'cause I noticed how young she was, no more than eight or so, and I wondered how poor her family must've been to let her go out working at such an age. I don't know if maybe she could be your sister?'

There was a yell from the open cellar door below. 'Stop your dawdling, for pity's sake, can't you see it's raining!'

Alarmed, the girl thanked the coalman and scurried down the steps.

'My sincerest gratitude for your help,' Cormac called after her.

'You're welcome!' she exclaimed over her shoulder and was gone.

He looked at Bridget and Emily, feeling nervous. 'Well, let's follow her suggestion,' he said and led them past the next house on the street and on to the one after it.

He tugged his cap down against the raindrops as they descended the steps to the cellar door. A housekeeper answered his knock, a set of keys jangling at her waist. Beyond her was a storage room with a flagstone floor.

'Yes?' she said, her manner just shy of impatient.

He told her their purpose. She frowned in puzzlement as she listened but at the mention of Patrick her face changed. Shock and then fear filled her expression.

'Don't waste my time,' she said brusquely and tried to slam the door on them.

He put out a firm arm to hold it open. 'Do you know something? Tell me! Are they in this house?'

At that moment, an inner door into the storage room opened and a girl appeared, carrying a coal bucket. She was young and her dark hair was pinned back beneath her maid's cap. It had been seven and a half years since Cormac had last seen her but he recognised her at once; she was almost identical to their sister Margaret except that her grey eyes were larger and rounder. Her eyes had always been her most prominent feature.

'Orlaith!'

She dropped the bucket and it toppled over; fragments of coal spilled across the floor and a cloud of black dust flew up into the air.

The housekeeper clicked her tongue. 'Stupid girl! Clean that up this instant!'

With a startled glance at Cormac, Orlaith fell to her knees on the flagstones and began picking up the pieces of coal.

'Can't that wait a minute?' he said indignantly to the housekeeper. 'I'm her brother. We haven't seen each other in years.'

'She was stupid enough to drop it so it's her responsibility to clear away the mess.'

'Stop calling her that,' he said, his temper rising with every word out of the woman's mouth. 'Orlaith, come here.'

She peeped up, frightened, as she tipped the coal lumps back into the bucket.

'You have no authority in this household,' the housekeeper barked and tried to force the door shut again.

To her outrage, he pushed it open and darted into the storage room. He seized Orlaith's wrist and pulled her to her feet.

'You're not staying here any longer. Where's Patrick? Let's find him and leave.'

At the mention of their nephew's name, her eyes grew even bigger and she shook her head.

'Is he not here?'

'No,' she said in a tremulous voice. 'Patrick's not here.'

'Then let's go.' He towed her towards the outer door, leaving sooty footprints on the flagstone floor.

'Where do you think you're going?' The angry housekeeper barred their way, one hand on her keys as though she intended to lock them in. 'The girl works here. She can't just up and leave whenever she fancies. That coal dust needs to be cleaned up. It's everywhere.'

'Do it yourself then,' Cormac said curtly, sidestepping the woman and hastening outside with Orlaith. Bridget and Emily both gaped at the sudden development in events. The four of them hurried up the steps while the housekeeper stood in the doorway and shouted at Orlaith to come back at once. They emerged onto the street just as the rain became heavier.

'We need to find shelter,' Cormac said to the others.

'There's a church over on Whitefriar Street,' said Orlaith. "Tis this way.'

She led them off the square and along one street and then another, circumnavigating other pedestrians who were dashing to escape the worsening weather. She said nothing, shoulders hunched as she pounded the footpath ahead of them. They reached the church just as the shower became a deluge and ran for cover inside its doors.

The vestibule was vacant of people but a few congregants knelt in pews further up the nave. Even though the rain drummed a loud and rhythmic beat on the doors, a hushed silence reigned within. Cormac felt a lump come to his throat. It had been so long since he had attended a Catholic Mass. In England he had been obliged to go to Protestant services with Lord and Lady Bewley, and since returning to Ireland there had barely been time for a quick, mumbled prayer at St Mary's in Ballydarry. He dipped his fingers in the holy water font and blessed himself. He thought of showing Emily how to bless herself too but she was bemoaning Mabel's wet face. While Bridget dug out a handkerchief to dry the doll, he turned to look at his sister.

She was filthy. There was coal dust all over her and the rain had mixed with it to leave streaky black stains across the front of her apron and on her arms and hands. But she was Orlaith. Those eyes were unmistakable. And yet they were different…they seemed empty somehow.

She stared at him. 'Are you really Cormac?' She had a thick Dublin accent and no wonder; she had spent more of her life in the city than she had in Carlow.

'I am. Do you remember me, chicken?'

She twitched at the endearment. 'I don't remember much of our old life,' she said. 'But your face is familiar. What're you doing here?'

'I came back to seek out all of our family but it seems that you are the only one left. I am sorry that I could not find you sooner. You have had an appalling ordeal here in Dublin.'

Instead of replying, she looked back outside to the pouring rain. He did not understand. There was no joy, no relief – just blankness. In fact, the only emotion he had seen her express since her appearance in the storage room was fear. It was almost as if she had not wanted to be found.

He took a tentative step towards her. She backed away from him. Then it struck him – she had said that Patrick was not there at the house. Had something bad happened to him for which she felt responsible? Perhaps that was why she was putting distance between herself and those who had known him.

'Orlaith, is Patrick dead?' he murmured, at pains to keep any trace of reproach from his tone.

She swallowed. 'No, he's not. Our nephew's alive and well.'

'Then where is he?'

'He's in the house you've just taken me from.'

Cormac was mystified. 'But you said –'

'I said *Patrick* wasn't there. And that was the truth. He goes by the name of Edward now.'

Cormac didn't know what to say. He glanced at Bridget; her brows were drawn together in confusion.

'Can you please tell us what happened?' she asked.

Orlaith clenched her jaw and turned her back to them. She was tall for thirteen but her posture was stooped. When she spoke again, Cormac had to strain to hear her over the hammering rain.

'I hoped I'd never have to explain this to anyone.'

Without looking at them, she plodded into the nave, genuflected and took a seat in the last pew. After a hesitant moment, Cormac removed his cap and joined her. Bridget and Emily followed and slid into the pew in front of them.

'We must be very quiet in here, gooseberry,' said Bridget.

Emily nodded and whispered the same to Mabel. While she rocked the doll like a baby, Bridget half pivoted towards the back pew. Cormac faced forwards, not wanting Orlaith to feel like she was under interrogation, but he tilted his head slightly in her direction. She sat staring at her knees as the rain pelted the church's windows.

'Y'know, I wasn't even nine years old when I knew what it was like to be desperate,' she said, her voice pitched low. 'By then, most of my family were either dead or gone. Only myself and my nephew were left—two homeless, penniless children. What chance did we have? The easiest thing would've been to lie down and wait for death to take us too.'

Cormac listened with a horrible heaviness in his bones. There was such dejection in her words. That depth of hopelessness led one to commit the kinds of unspeakable acts to which Mary and Oliver had both resorted.

'But I wasn't like Mary,' said Orlaith, echoing what he was thinking. 'I didn't give up. I tried to find a way out. There was a girl, Tess, who said she'd look after us but she was living rough too which meant she couldn't do anything to help us really. We'd stay stuck where we were for the rest of our lives. And I didn't want that, not for me and not for Patrick who was only three years old and had lived practically his whole life in poverty. So I went out walking with him every day, not in places we knew, but in areas where rich people lived. I knocked on cellar doors and offered my services as a housemaid, a scullery girl, anything at all. But I'd no luck. Nobody was willing to take me on when I'd a little boy in tow. Still, I kept trying.'

She wiped her fingers on her apron, only succeeding in making the sooty smears worse.

'Then I knocked on yet another cellar door and came face to face with the nasty housekeeper yous just met. Mrs Twomey's her name. For the first time, I wasn't turned away as soon as I said I'd my nephew with me. She stared at Patrick in a very cold, calculating way. I remember it gave me the shivers. She told me to wait, disappeared inside and returned with the mistress of the house herself, Lady Anner. The lady said she wanted to help me and the best way she could do that was to take Patrick from me 'cause I was far too young to be looking after him but she and her husband could give him a happy home at Anner House. At first, I didn't understand what she was saying but then I realised she was offering to take Patrick in as her own son. I found out afterwards Lord and Lady Anner's five-year-old boy had died only two or three months before that and Lady Anner was unable to have any more children. Their one and only child was gone forever and Patrick was an unexpected chance to replace him, probably the only chance they'd ever have.'

Cormac resisted the urge to interrupt, though his tongue tingled with questions.

Orlaith's features were expressionless as she continued to speak. 'I suppose I should've said no. But it was an opportunity for me to shift the burden to someone else and for Patrick to grow up in a proper home. So I agreed on two conditions: that we could go back to say goodbye to Tess and that I could stay in the household too and still be allowed to see Patrick. Lady Anner said she was already doing me a great kindness and I shouldn't expect anything more, but she considered herself a generous woman so she offered me a position as a scullery maid. I was to work for free 'til my debt to her had been repaid. I took her at her word. After we came back from the shelter, Patrick was brought above stairs and I was set to work in the kitchens.'

For a few moments, Orlaith was quiet. An elderly man trudged from the vestibule up the nave, his hat and coat soaking and tiny puddles pooling on the floor in his wake. Her gaze followed him as he entered a pew halfway up towards the altar and knelt down. She shrugged.

'It took me several days to realise I'd been lied to. Lady Anner renamed Patrick as Edward and gave him his own bedchamber, a governess, rich food and fine clothes. I was never allowed to see him. She went out of her way to make sure we were always kept apart. It was more than a year later when I laid eyes on him again and by that stage he'd forgotten me. He recognised me only as a maid and had no memory of his first family. Lady Anner had succeeded in creating a new son and heir for herself. But it seems my debt hasn't yet been repaid 'cause I still work without pay, four and a half years later.' She bowed her head. 'So now you know the wicked thing I did. I as good as sold my nephew in exchange for regular meals and a proper roof over my head. I doubt if God or Ma will ever forgive me.'

'Don't be so hard on yourself,' Cormac murmured, his heart full of pity. 'Mrs Twomey and Lady Anner were the ones at fault for exploiting you. You were just a child and you only did what you believed was best in order to improve the quality of life for yourself and Patrick.'

Shaking her head, she rooted in her pocket, drew out a string of rosary beads, and pressed her lips to the cross that hung from them. At the sight of them, the air drained from Cormac's lungs.

'Are those—' he croaked. 'Are those Ma's?'

He reached out but she slid a few inches down the bench away from him, tucking the beads inside her closed fist.

'You don't get to touch them,' she snapped, loudly enough that the elderly man further up the pews half turned his head in disapproval. Bridget gave him a small wave of apology while Orlaith lowered her voice to a hiss. 'What right have you to lay your hands on anything that belonged to Ma? Where were *you* when the last members of your family were struggling to stay alive?'

Cormac sagged. 'You are quite right to accuse me. It is my fault your circumstances were so grim that you were driven to such wretched measures. I am to blame for all the troubles that have befallen our family.'

'We both are,' said Bridget, her knuckles white as she gripped the back of the pew.

'What d'yous mean?' Orlaith looked astonished that they were prepared to assume responsibility for every awful thing that had happened to the McGoverns.

Given that she was too young to remember much of their former lives in Carlow, Cormac went back to the start and provided her with a brief account of the most pertinent details of the past eight years, from his liaison with Bridget that last summer at Oakleigh right through to their encounter with Tess the previous evening. Orlaith reacted to nothing, not when he confessed that he had indeed been that McGovern of whom they had heard such shocking rumours, nor even when, hoping to redeem himself somewhat, he told her he had also been the mysterious stranger who had given Tess all the money that had been used to pay for their mother's medicine. He wondered if his questionable interactions with Oliver Davenport and Lord and Lady Bewley might elicit a response but, arms folded, she remained taciturn throughout.

'And, thanks to Tess, you are the one member of our family whom I have managed to locate,' he finished. 'Although it is possible that Bronagh is alive somewhere in America.'

When he stopped talking, he noticed the silence in the church had deepened even further and realised the torrent outside had finally eased.

Orlaith's gaze narrowed. 'And what d'you plan to do with me now you've found me?'

He sensed her resistance and chose his language with care. 'What I hope is that you, and possibly Patrick, will come with me, Bridget and Emily to begin a new life as a family somewhere else, far away from this miserable city. But that is only if you wish it. I shall not force you into something you do not want to do.'

While it pained him to give her the option of rejecting them, he knew it was the correct thing to say. She was young but she was mature beyond her years, and she had both the entitlement and the capacity to make this decision for herself.

She mulled over his words. 'I thought what I'd done was wicked, but what you've done is worse. We heard dreadful stories about Cunningham's man McGovern. Were those things really carried out by my brother's hand?'

'Some of them, yes,' he admitted, 'but most of the nastier stories are untrue. Lies were spread which bolstered my reputation far beyond its due. However, for the terrible acts I did commit I have no excuse other than that I was in a hideously dark place and I thought I had no way out. I had believed I was alone in that regard, but now I am aware that my whole family shared the same nightmare.'

'And yet,' she said, glaring at Bridget, 'none of us would've had to experience that hell at all if your mother had been less vengeful.'

Bridget raised her chin against the girl's incriminating tone. 'I am conscious of my mother's failings and I make no attempt to absolve her. But she has since paid the price with her death and can no longer hurt anybody.'

'The damage has already been done,' Orlaith muttered. She looked back at Cormac. 'If I was to leave with yous, where would we go?'

He hesitated. He had been contemplating that question ever since they had met Tess and she had told them of his family's fate, but he had not yet discussed it with Bridget.

Taking the plunge, he said, 'I think perhaps America. I propose that we follow Bronagh across the ocean and search for her over there. If we find her, we can then settle down and make a new home for ourselves, either there or back here in Ireland.'

He glanced at Bridget. They would need to consider many aspects of his proposition before they could act upon it, and of course her responsibility to Oakleigh would be at the forefront of her mind. But a slow smile spread across her face and she laid a gentle palm on Emily's head, as though communicating a blessing from both of them.

Orlaith's countenance, on the other hand, was far more guarded. She stared down at Maggie's rosary beads, rolling one of the spheres between her thumb and forefinger. Cormac ached to hold them, the only physical thing he could remember his mother by – her nimble fingers had counted those beads hundreds of times.

Orlaith touched the cross, tracing her fingertip down the length of it. At last, she nodded. 'Yes. I'll go with yous.'

'Good,' he said, and the boulder inside him disintegrated into tiny pieces and melted away. 'I am glad.'

He hoped their mother and father were looking down on them.

Although he could never repair his whole family, at least he and Orlaith had been reunited. He recalled with fondness the little girl who had taken such attentive care of her hens, but she was not the young woman before him. Thirteen-year-old Orlaith was cold and tough and, from her doubtful expression, she still harboured misgivings towards him. She was willing to come with them but it might take months or years for him to earn her trust again and even longer for any kind of sibling love to grow between them.

Bridget cleared her throat. 'What about Patrick? Are we going to attempt to make contact with him?'

'Yes,' said Cormac. 'We shall go back to Anner House and explain how this unusual situation arose. Patrick ought to be with his true family now.'

The corners of Orlaith's mouth tightened. 'Yous can try, but I don't think yous'll succeed.'

On this pessimistic note, they left the church pews and Cormac led his lover, his child and his sister back along the wet streets the way they had come. It was time to retrieve the last remaining member of his family in this city which had treated them all so cruelly.

## Chapter 22

The rain had ceased but the trees in the park in the centre of St Stephen's Green still dripped with moisture. When they reached Anner House, Orlaith opened the gate in the railings to go down the cellar stairs but Cormac stopped her with a shake of his head.

'None of us are servants anymore,' he said. 'We shall announce our presence at the front entrance.'

She raised her eyebrows and followed him, Bridget and Emily up the steps to the broad space before the front door. He used the gleaming brass knocker to give two sharp taps. A footman in livery answered almost at once.

'We are here to see Lady Anner,' Cormac declared.

The footman gave him an appraising look. 'Who may I say is calling?'

'Mr Cormac McGovern. I wish to speak with the lady on a family matter of some importance.'

His tone was so sincere and urgent that the footman began to open the door wider to admit them. Then his gaze fell upon Orlaith at the back of the group.

'What are you doing?' he shot at her. 'You shouldn't be here. Get back to the scullery.'

Cormac stepped sideways to block her from the footman's line of sight and reproachful words. 'She is meant to be here. She is my sister and a vital part of the family matter I need to discuss with Lady Anner.'

The footman's countenance grew perplexed; it was plain he was ignorant of the arrangement that had brought Orlaith into this house. Cormac supposed very few of the servants were privy to the information – it was not a secret that the Anners would wish to be widely known.

Without warning, the door was jerked out of the footman's grasp and Mrs Twomey appeared in the entry, livid.

'It's time for you to leave,' she said.

'We are not going anywhere until we have spoken to Lady Anner,' said Cormac. 'She can receive us in her drawing room or she can meet us here on her front steps, but either way she *shall* see us. I know you are aware of the situation involving my sister and nephew and I am certain you are wise enough to concede that it would be best for every party concerned to resolve it as soon as possible.'

She ground her teeth, glowering at him like he was a nasty insect she wanted to squash beneath her heel. Then she pulled on the footman's elbow and they both vanished inside the house, shutting the door firmly behind them. Cormac glanced at the others – Bridget was biting the tip of her tongue, Orlaith was scowling, and Emily was fastidiously straightening Mabel's dress. He looked back at the brass knocker and waited.

It was several minutes before he heard muted speech on the other side of the door. It swung open and a lady materialised in the gap. She was tall with flaxen curls twisted up into an elaborate hairstyle. Her face was beautiful but not youthful.

'What is this about?' she said in a surprisingly soft voice.

'Lady Anner, my name is Cormac McGovern and I am here to discuss two issues of great consequence relating to my family. One is with regard to my youngest sister, Orlaith, and the other pertains to our nephew, Patrick.'

Lady Anner looked beyond him to where Orlaith stood. 'Your sister is shirking her duties and ought to return below stairs at once. As for your nephew, there is no one by the name of Patrick living under this roof.'

'As I understand it, our nephew goes by the name of Edward now.'

'There is a boy called Edward, but he is not your nephew.'

'We are all cognisant of the true state of affairs,' said Cormac levelly. 'There is no need to tell falsehoods.'

The lady's nostrils flared but when she spoke her voice was still silky smooth. 'What is it you wish to say to me, Mr McGovern?'

He sensed her anger beneath her calm exterior and it sparked his own; how could she stand there without any compunction for what she had done?

Unclenching his jaw with effort, he said, 'Four and a half years ago, my sister and nephew showed up at your cellar door and you seized the opportunity to acquire a son and a slave. You separated them until the boy no longer recognised his aunt and you worked her to the bone under the pretence that she was paying you back an enormous debt. Such cruelty and abuse is unpardonable. I was not there to stop it then but I am here to stop it now. I intend to take Orlaith and Patrick away with me today.'

Lady Anner's expression was derisive. 'And what makes you think that I shall give them up to you?'

'You have no right to keep them. Patrick is not your blood relation and Orlaith is not employed here by legitimate means. You took advantage of two small children who had no protector, but that power is no longer yours.'

Her lip curled. 'On the contrary, that power is still very much mine. Any number of servants and neighbours will attest to the fact that my husband

and I took a small boy into our home four and a half years ago and that, in an unrelated circumstance, a young girl has worked in our kitchens for a similar length of time. If you take them away you will be branded an abductor and incarcerated.'

Baffled, Cormac said, 'But what lies have you fed those servants and neighbours? You hardly made it known that you had plucked a homeless boy off the streets.'

'Indeed I did not, for that is not what happened. It is common knowledge that Edward is my husband's nephew.'

Cormac stared at her. 'I beg your pardon?'

With angelic serenity, she said, 'My husband's brother, Mr George Whitmore, was always a sickly fellow so he resided in the countryside for the sake of his health. When we lost our own dear son, George became heir presumptive to the Anner title. If he produced no issue, the title would go to a more distant, and shall I say less suitable, relative.' She smiled. 'Imagine our delight, therefore, when we heard that George had fallen in love and married a young lady of irreproachable birth. Sadly, their happy time together was all too brief. His wife did not survive childbirth and George's health worsened over the ensuing years so my husband and I agreed to take their young child into our own loving home. It was the least we could do to ease George's burden.'

Cormac blinked rapidly, unable to believe what he was hearing.

Lady Anner carried on, 'Edward knows we are his aunt and uncle but he has come to look upon us as his parents and he even calls us Mother and Father now. We are all he has left since poor George passed away not two years ago. Naturally, we shall continue to take care of him like a son. He is now next in line to inherit the barony of Anner.'

Cormac could barely speak. 'This is outrageous!' he spluttered. 'You have fabricated this story to serve your own ends.'

'That is a despicable accusation,' she said, unruffled. 'And one that nobody will believe.'

He was at a loss for words. Next to him, Bridget looked stunned but she found her tongue and said to Lady Anner, 'Do you genuinely claim this as fact to your acquaintances? Patrick is not your flesh and blood. And Orlaith is nothing more than a skivvy to you. Cormac is all that remains of their true family.'

'But you have no proof. You cannot even argue that they look much alike.'

'Have you no *conscience*?' Cormac demanded. 'You know that you are at fault, that you have lied and used these children. Do you not have any scruples about what you have done?'

'How dare you speak to me in such a way?' she said, as soft-spoken as ever. 'Get off my property at once.'

'I want to see Patrick,' he insisted.
'That is preposterous. You will not set one foot across this threshold. My staff will make sure of that. And you, girl,' she added to Orlaith, 'you have been idle for long enough. Go back to the scullery right away. You will work as late tonight as is necessary to catch up on all your tasks.'
Orlaith folded her arms. 'I'm leaving with my brother. I don't work for yous anymore.'
For the first time, Lady Anner looked properly furious. Then her face changed. She twisted to look at someone out of Cormac's sight.
'Take him back upstairs,' she ordered. 'He is not allowed to go outside.'
'But I want to go splashing in the puddles!' a boy's voice whined.
'I said go back upstairs at once.' Her voice was now tinged with apprehension. 'Do you hear me? No, Edward!'
She stretched out her arms as a young boy came pelting through the doorway. He dodged her grasp and ran out onto the broad top step where he stopped short in his bid for freedom at the sight of all the strangers. Cormac seized this sudden chance.
'Greetings, Patrick,' he said, stooping to shake the boy's hand. 'My name is Cormac and I am your uncle.'
Lady Anner tried to drag the boy back into the house but he danced out of her reach again. He stared up at Cormac. He was a handsome child with thick, black hair, hazel eyes and a proud stance. He looked very much like Garrett but Cormac could detect a little of Mary around his nose and mouth.
'But I don't have any uncles apart from Father,' he said. 'And why did you call me Patrick? My name is Edward.'
'Come inside this instant,' Lady Anner commanded but he ignored her.
'Who are you really?' he asked Cormac.
Despite the wet steps, Cormac knelt on one knee to look the boy in the eye. 'I told you the truth. I am your uncle and you are my nephew. When you were born, you were named Patrick by your mother who is now dead. You spent the first three years of your life with your grandmother and aunties until this lady took you into her home. She told you your name was Edward but that was a lie. While we are grateful that she looked after you, we have come to take you away with us for we are your true family.'
The boy's features were alight with excitement; this was an adventure far beyond what he had expected when he had run outside. 'And who are the rest of these people?'
'This is my wife, Bridget,' said Cormac. 'And this is our daughter, Emily. She is your cousin.'
Emily beamed and waved Mabel's arm.
'And this is Orlaith.' Cormac indicated his sister at the back. 'She is your aunt.'

The boy frowned at her. 'But she is a servant.'

'She used to be,' Cormac acknowledged.

'Then it cannot be real.' The boy's face fell in disappointment. 'I thought it would be a lark to run away for a little while but you are not telling me the truth. I know I am not related to any servants.'

'In fact, you are. I was once a servant too, a stable hand. But it doesn't make a difference. We are still your family.'

'No, you are not,' the boy said rudely. 'Look at her. She's dirty. She is not part of my family and neither are you. I am only related to people of noble blood.'

'Patrick—'

'You will address me as Master Whitmore, I'll thank you to remember that,' the boy said, drawing himself up to his full small height.

Cormac stared at him incredulously and then looked up at Lady Anner's smug expression. He got to his feet, incensed.

'You have indoctrinated him with notions of nobility,' he said, the disgust of it making his blood boil. 'Notions which will only breed arrogance and conceit. You have ruined him.'

'Edward merely takes pride in his class and his heritage,' she said with satisfaction.

He shook his head in disbelief. She knew as well as he did that this boy had lived on the streets for three years. Just because he couldn't remember it did not mean it hadn't happened. She and her husband were fooling him and fooling themselves.

He glanced over his shoulder. Orlaith's face was easy to read; she was unsurprised, for the scene had played out just as she had predicted it would. She did not look sad – he supposed she had given up on their nephew a long time ago.

Was there any prospect of convincing him of the truth? Discouraged, Cormac surveyed the boy's contemptuous countenance. His nephew was entrenched in his new persona. On the one hand, he appeared to be content, and they could be guaranteed that his physical and financial needs would be met. But what about his character? It had already taken a great deal of damage – if Lady Anner continued to rear him on such supercilious principles, the boy would end up even vainer than his father. Patrick was his sister's son; Cormac did not want to fail Mary by abandoning her child to this contemptible woman.

With one last effort, he bent again to the boy's level and said, 'We are planning to travel to America. How would you like to come with us and visit a whole new continent? We can tell you all about your real parents. We are your true flesh and blood and we promise to look after you.'

The boy took a step backwards to Lady Anner's side. 'Please leave our home now.'

*A Class Forsaken*

The lady placed her hand on his shoulder and smiled sweetly.

Cormac shrugged and rose. 'Very well. I am sorry to leave you behind, but I hope that you have a happy life.'

He turned to head down the steps. Bridget, Emily and Orlaith made to follow.

'Where are you going, girl?' Lady Anner said, raising her voice the tiniest bit. 'You are still our scullery maid.'

Orlaith looked back at her with open disdain. 'You might be able to control the boy but you've no more power over me. I'm no longer your slave. Good riddance to you and Mrs Twomey.'

Lady Anner and her 'son' watched in shock as Orlaith marched down the steps and away from the house. Cormac, Bridget and Emily hurried to catch up with her.

'Did you leave anything behind that you wanted?' Bridget asked. 'Any possessions or keepsakes?'

'No,' said Orlaith, pressing her hand to her pocket where Maggie's rosary beads were stowed. 'Everything I want is in America. Let's go there.'

## Chapter 23

As they walked back in the direction of the Liberties to fetch their valises from the inn, Cormac and Bridget apprised Orlaith of some more things that had occurred during their years of separation, including the uprising and the burning of Oakleigh Manor, and – though it pained Cormac to admit it – their contact with Thomasina and Henrietta. He felt ashamed to reveal such an appalling indiscretion, but it was best to be honest about everything family-related; if Thomasina had been telling the truth, then Henrietta was Orlaith's niece.

Orlaith showed no signs of condemnation. While they waited for a fine carriage to pass by so they could cross the street, she said thoughtfully, 'We used to have a hen called Henrietta, didn't we?'

'We did,' he said with a smile. It made him glad to see her remembering their old life.

The carriage rattled past and they crossed over to the other side; the inn was located just a little further down the street. It was growing late in the evening, but the sun had emerged before dusk and a slanting shaft of light struck the inn's windows. The streets were still wet from the earlier rainfall and they too glimmered in the rays of the setting sun.

As they approached the inn, they passed an alleyway where three men loitered at its mouth sharing a smoking pipe between them. Cormac and the others had almost gone by when one of the men spoke.

'Oliver Davenport?'

Cormac's head whipped around in recognition of the name – too late he realised his mistake. Two of the men leapt forwards and seized his arms. Bridget screamed and Emily cried 'Papa!' as the men dragged him into the alley and shoved him up against the wall, nearly wrenching his shoulder out of its socket.

'Shut your traps afore I shut them for you,' the third man in the group snarled and he herded Bridget, Emily and Orlaith into the alleyway too.

There was no direct sunlight in the narrow passage and it took a few moments for Cormac's vision to adjust to the gloom. He did not recognise the faces of any of the men. The two pinning him to the wall were both clean-shaven and one of them had pockmarked cheeks. The third had a rust-coloured beard and had taken up a menacing stance in front of Bridget, Emily and Orlaith, who cowered against the opposite wall. He still held the pipe and brandished it at them, forcing them into a tighter huddle. From the little the men had said, Cormac could tell by their accents that they were English.

'What do you want from us?' he demanded. The mention of Oliver Davenport's name was ominous; this was no ordinary robbery.

'There's someone who fancies a word with you,' growled the man with the pockmarks.

Pinioned in place, Cormac could only twist his head towards the entrance of the alleyway. The fine carriage they had glimpsed hardly a minute earlier had returned, coming to a stop out on the street. It occurred to him belatedly that a conveyance of that elegance was incongruous in such a working class part of the city; the sight of it ought to have rung a warning bell straight away. A footman came around and opened the door to allow its passenger to alight.

An older gentleman emerged, white-haired beneath his hat and carrying a beechwood cane. He stepped down to the footpath without any sign of frailty and strode forwards, stopping just inside the mouth of the alley.

There was silence until Emily burst out with joy, 'Uncle Bewley, are you here to save us?'

Lord Bewley had spent more than one entertaining afternoon kneeling on the hearth rug at Raynesworth House in London attending tea parties with Emily's imaginary friends, but he did not even respond to the little girl now. He leaned on his cane and his gaze swept over them all, leaving Cormac until last.

'Good evening, Oliver,' he said. It was a mocking greeting; every single person in the alleyway knew that Cormac was not Oliver Davenport.

Cormac did not know what to say so he just replied, 'Good evening, Lord Bewley.'

The earl's mouth curved wryly – he was 'Uncle' no more. He gestured to the two men who held Cormac in their grip. 'Release him.'

They let go and stood back from him, but remained poised for action. Massaging his shoulder, he cast a fleeting look towards Bridget. She was trembling with panic and held Emily's small hand tightly. The little girl clutched Mabel just as hard. Next to them, Orlaith surveyed the scene with her fists furled.

Lord Bewley regarded him coolly. 'Your true name is Cormac McGovern?'

Cormac nodded, recalling the letter he had left for the Bewleys before fleeing from London. Little had he known then that he would be facing the consequences of its contents in person.

'We have had some difficulty in tracking you down,' said Lord Bewley. 'It took us several days after you absconded to realise that you were not still in London and that you must have escaped on that ship after all. It was a cunning feat, but then all the evidence suggests you are quite the sly creature.'

Cormac did not protest. Lord Bewley deserved the opportunity to castigate him.

'How did you find us?' he asked.

'The law enforcement informed me that you were gone beyond their interest but if I was able to return you to England they would exact the proper punishment upon you. I therefore began my own investigation and approached this young lady's husband for information.' Lord Bewley waved his cane in Bridget's direction. 'He was happy to oblige and told us that the most likely place you would go would be Oakleigh Manor. A series of inopportune delays meant that by the time we landed in Ireland and reached the estate you had already departed from it. However, we learned you were not gone long and that you were bound for Dublin so we followed you here. My men asked for you in both savoury and unsavoury circles and struck lucky today when they met a girl who could say with absolute certainty that you had stayed at this inn last night.'

Tess. No doubt she had been all too pleased to assist.

'We did not think we would be so fortunate that you would return for a second night, until the innkeeper informed us that he was holding your luggage for you. So we placed ourselves in the vicinity and here you are.'

Cormac cursed himself for not insisting upon taking their valises with them that morning. They could have stayed at any other inn in the city tonight and Lord Bewley would have been none the wiser.

'I am afraid this is the end for you, Mr McGovern,' said Lord Bewley.

Heart sinking, Cormac believed him. The earl was a powerful man. 'What do you plan to do with me?'

'I will have you sent to prison for the rest of your life, though even that is too lenient. I can only hope there is a magistrate willing to bestow a greater punishment.'

'No!' gasped Bridget. 'Please, no!'

Lord Bewley turned to her, distaste written on his face. 'Lady Wyndham, my esteem for you has fallen to less than nothing. You may be considered party to Mr McGovern's crimes for you were aware of his duplicity and informed no one. In my opinion, you are just as guilty and ought to stand before a magistrate as well. However, your husband has bargained for your freedom. So you and your daughter shall both come with me. As for this other girl, I do not know who she is but she is of no concern to me. She may leave whenever she pleases.'

'I'll stay, thanks,' Orlaith said tartly at the same time as Bridget said, 'Emily and I are not going back to Garrett!'

'You misunderstand,' said Lord Bewley. 'He has not requested that I return you to him, only that I make arrangements to ensure your safety.

He directed me to deliver you and the child into the protection of your uncle in England, your closest relative apart from your estranged mother. I confess that Lord Wyndham's resentment was palpable but his underlying regard for your wellbeing was unmistakable.'

It seemed that Garrett, too, had been unaware that Lord Walcott was residing in Dublin and not in England, but now was not the time to correct the mistake. Bridget was looking perplexed. 'Regard for our wellbeing? Well, even so, we shall still refuse to go with you.'

Lord Bewley stared at her. 'Why would you stay? There is nothing left for you here. This man's life is over, I will make sure of that.'

Bridget's eyes met Cormac's across the narrow space. Their future was disappearing like a wisp of smoke dispersing into the sky.

'Please,' she begged, reaching out imploring hands towards Lord Bewley. 'Have mercy.'

'*Mercy*? There can be no mercy for the wrongs that have been perpetrated. My wife and I have been robbed of our nephew, the only family we had left. Mr McGovern claims in his despicable letter that Oliver left this world by his own hand but we shall never have any proof of that. His passing may very well have been expedited by the imposter himself.'

'I didn't kill him!' Cormac exclaimed. He took a step forwards and the pockmarked man immediately shoved him backwards. He lost his balance and fell back against the wall. 'I did not kill Oliver. Everything I wrote in my letter to you was the truth.'

'Then you cannot deny your other transgressions,' said Lord Bewley, his eyes bulging. 'That you stole Oliver's clothing and possessions, that you presented yourself to us as our nephew, that you made us believe for nearly five years that you were of Bewley flesh and blood. We gave you an education. We intended for you to inherit the family estate. But you were a stranger and a thief in our home. It was all a pretence. You betrayed us.'

There was a shake in his voice that told Cormac just how immense that betrayal was. The Bewleys had felt genuine affection for their 'nephew', had even begun to view him as a son, and to find out that those feelings of attachment had been based on a lie must have been a very painful discovery. Lord and Lady Bewley were grieving.

Cormac's words were quiet but heartfelt as he said, 'I am deeply sorry for the distress I have caused you both. It was never my intention to hurt either of you.'

Lord Bewley gave a sceptical grunt. 'Well, you did. My wife wept for two solid days after you ran off. She is distraught over what has happened. She had become exceedingly fond of you.'

'And I of her,' said Cormac, saddened to think of Lady Bewley crying over the sins he had committed. 'She had become like a second mother to me.' He pressed his palms to the wall behind him, his skin scraping the rough surface. 'Please understand, my actions were not driven by malice when I entered your lives. And equally there was no evil intended when I left. My departure was compelled by a profound love for that exceptional woman standing there and by a fear for the uncertain welfare of my first mother. My whole family was in crisis and I had to try my best to save them.'

Lord Bewley's grip tightened so much on his cane that his knuckles looked ready to pop. 'I don't see how you can profess to uphold values of any sort,' he muttered. 'And particularly not when it comes to the sacred bond of family.'

'I do value the bond of family, I swear it,' said Cormac. 'I have travelled miles in search of my lost family members. To my despair, I was too late to save my mother and one of my sisters. But I have located another sister' – he gestured towards Orlaith – 'and am determined to find the third, even if it means crossing an ocean to do it. And I stood on a doorstep in St Stephen's Green this afternoon and did all I could to reclaim a nephew who has been taken in by a family there, despite the futility of it.'

Lord Bewley had appeared to be wavering but at this he drew himself up in indignation. 'Are you serious? You have a lowborn nephew living in the care of an upper class family?'

Cormac admitted, 'I do.'

The earl seethed. 'It seems being an impostor is an abominable family trait.'

Cormac lowered his gaze. 'I can only say again how remorseful I am for the way I deceived you. I was desperate and I made an irresponsible decision.'

'And you will pay for that decision now,' Lord Bewley said grimly, signalling with his cane for his men to take Cormac away.

'You'll pay for more than that,' came a voice from behind Lord Bewley before the men could even move.

All heads turned towards the mouth of the alley. Cormac's limbs went weak. The last rays of the dying sun framed none other than the money lender, Cunningham, flanked by four of his men, the thickset build of Munroe discernible among them.

An overwhelming sense of hopelessness invaded Cormac. Lord Bewley was a decent man and might have been persuaded to show leniency; Cunningham could never be swayed to be anything less than ruthless.

'Take them,' Cormac said urgently to Lord Bewley, motioning towards Bridget, Emily and Orlaith. 'Take them with you and leave right now.'

The earl did not heed him. 'Who are you?' he asked as Cunningham strolled forwards, his men following in his wake. Cormac spotted a thin-lipped sneer on one man's face and recognised him as Lawlor, the fellow who had thrown a stick of firewood at him the day he had first encountered this gang. How he wished he'd never retaliated and just walked away.

'The name's Cunningham,' said the money lender. 'I'd like a word with our man McGovern here.'

He casually let his coat fall open to reveal a pistol nestled at his side.

Lord Bewley looked at Cormac in horror. 'What sort of shady dealings have you been involved in?'

'The shadiest,' Cunningham said with a grin. 'Now, sir, you look like a gentleman of honour and I have no bone to pick with you. So why don't you and your men just walk away and we'll take over from here.'

Lord Bewley shook his head. 'Mr McGovern has committed acts of an unlawful nature. I came here to apprehend him and ensure that justice is served.'

'Mr McGovern will not be making it out of this alley alive,' said Cunningham, his tone mocking at the formal address. 'Is that justice enough for you?'

Aghast, Lord Bewley said, 'You are going to murder him? What has he done to merit such a violent end?'

'Acts of an unlawful nature. Against *me*, and in that case there's only one method of redress.'

'I cannot...' Lord Bewley swallowed. 'I do not think I can permit this to happen.'

Cunningham raised his eyebrows. 'It's going to happen whether you permit it or not. And the longer you stay here, the likelier it is you'll join him. I recommend that you and your men go back to your fancy carriage and head home in the happy knowledge that your goal has been achieved.'

A shadow of fear crossed Lord Bewley's face. Cunningham was not giving him an empty threat. He glanced at Cormac – was that regret in his eyes? Perhaps some vestige of affection yet remained. But Cunningham was serious and Lord Bewley's own life mattered more to him than the life of a lawbreaker whom he still wanted to see imprisoned. He nodded at his three men and they came to his side.

'We shall leave now,' said Lord Bewley. 'We do not wish to interfere. May we take the females with us too?'

'No, you may not,' said Cunningham. 'They will not be making it out of this alley alive either.'

Abject terror made Cormac's insides turn to ice. 'For the love of God, no!' he cried.

'Now, wait just a moment,' objected Lord Bewley.

Bridget scooped Emily up into her arms to shield her from harm. Both of them had tears on their cheeks. Orlaith was not crying but she looked like she very much wished Cormac had never knocked on Mrs Twomey's door that day.

'What is the matter?' said Cunningham with a look of innocent enquiry.

'You are talking about slaughtering a woman and two girls,' said Lord Bewley, white-faced. 'You have no reason to do so.'

'My reason is that they are connected to McGovern, and I want to obliterate him in every respect.'

Cormac started towards Cunningham and found himself in the vice-like grip of Munroe with a dagger at his throat.

'Where d'you think you're going?' Munroe snarled.

'Please,' Cormac said in a strangled voice. 'I am begging you. They have done nothing to hurt you. Just let them go.'

Cunningham laughed and clapped his hands together. 'Isn't this ironic? That is just what our borrowers always used to say to you. And how did you respond?'

'I never killed anyone! They always gave me what I wanted before it got that far. But you already have what you want. You've got me, you don't need them.'

Cunningham cocked his head to one side. 'True. But perhaps I would like to kill them for my own amusement.'

'For heaven's sake, man,' entreated Lord Bewley. 'The little one is only six years old. You do not want her on your conscience.'

'You'd be surprised what my conscience can tolerate.'

Lord Bewley went red with outrage. 'That is quite enough, sir. I imagine Mr McGovern's presence in this alley is non-negotiable, but I shall not leave the other three behind. You said your name is Cunningham. If you refuse to release them, I shall do everything within my power to find out who you are in this city and, make no mistake, I shall ruin you and whatever dastardly dealings you are involved in.'

Even as Cormac experienced the deepest gratitude towards Lord Bewley, he wondered if the earl could in fact exert that much influence in Dublin circles. Whether he was bluffing or not, he puffed out his chest like he could take over as Lord Lieutenant of Ireland if it suited him.

Cunningham looked bored. 'Very well, very well,' he said, flapping his hand. 'The females can go too. That just leaves us with McGovern which means we shall have to make him last an awfully long time.'

Cormac baulked as Munroe pressed the dagger harder into his neck.

'Rotten brutes!'

Orlaith's cry resounded off the alley walls. She ran at Munroe and pummelled his torso with her fists. He fell back in surprise, letting go of Cormac. He raised his hand to strike her but Lord Bewley's pockmarked lackey intervened, catching Munroe by the wrist. Lawlor darted forwards to assist his comrade and, in the chaos of the ensuing struggle, Bridget rushed to Cormac with Emily still in her arms. He embraced them both, burying his face in Bridget's hair, breathing in her familiar smell. He was terrified but he couldn't allow it to show.

'It will be fine,' he whispered. 'Go with Lord Bewley. I'll escape and meet you at Tess's shelter. I love you.'

She shook her head and began to sob. Emily grew hysterical and clutched the collar of his coat. In the crook of her elbow, Mabel's solemn eyes stared up at him.

He dropped a quick kiss on his daughter's wet cheek and choked out, 'Take good care of your mother, *a stór.*'

Over the noise of the skirmish, Lord Bewley barked, 'It's time to leave!'

The man with the rust-coloured beard tossed aside the pipe he still held and seized Bridget; she tried to cling to Cormac but the man pulled her and Emily away. His pockmarked associate ducked beneath Munroe's swinging arm and dragged Orlaith with him to the top of the alleyway where Lord Bewley's other man stood protectively in front of the earl. They all retreated to the carriage out on the street; Cormac heard Bridget scream his name before she, Emily and Orlaith were bundled inside it. Lord Bewley followed them and his men climbed up front with the coachman or onto the back with the footman. The coachman whipped the horses and the carriage rattled away out of sight.

Once it was gone, the alley became very quiet. Twilight had fallen and the gloom had thickened even further but Cormac could still make out the figures and hostile countenances surrounding him. Munroe spat blood on the ground and touched a knuckle to his split lip, his dagger hanging slackly from his other hand. Lawlor and the other two men looked to Cunningham for their next move. The money lender's expression was dispassionate.

'What possessed you to return?' he said to Cormac, tutting in mock disappointment. 'You should have known you were a dead man as soon as you set foot in this city again.'

Cormac attempted to quell his fear as he recalled the promise he had just made to Bridget. Had it been wrong of him to give her what could very well be false hope? What prospect did he have of breaking free from this gang's clutches? He could try to run for it but he would have to get past five men first. He could fight them but they were armed and he had no weapons whatsoever. He couldn't conceive of any other route of escape.

God, he wished he could hold Bridget in his arms again. What would she do if he didn't come back? Would she still go to America with the girls? He and Orlaith had been reunited mere hours ago – now he might never get to know the young woman his sister had become. And Emily, his beloved baby girl. He could not bear the thought of never seeing her again.

He pushed down his burgeoning despair. He had to maintain hope.

Folding his arms across his chest, he said, 'How did you find me?'

'Thomasina Brennan,' said Cunningham with a grin. Cormac's stomach dropped. Had Thomasina taken the money and informed on him as well? But then Cunningham continued, 'Lawlor spotted her by chance at Smithfield Market, hopping onto a cart to flee the city. He brought her back to the lodgings and she eventually admitted that you had shown up at her auntie's place. We spoke to Mrs O'Hara and after that managed to trace you to the inn on this street. You know, with a reputation like yours, you shouldn't be throwing your name around so much.'

Cormac nodded. 'I've been hearing a lot about my reputation in the last day or two. It seems I was quite the animal in my heyday and yet I cannot recollect doing many of the things of which I have been accused. Can you explain that to me?'

Munroe gave a nasty chuckle. 'We might've embellished the stories a little. Fear's a powerful motivator when it comes to producing money.'

'And money is all I care about,' said Cunningham. He was not grinning anymore. 'What made you think you could steal from me and get away with it?'

'I didn't take it for myself,' Cormac said, recalling the wine merchant's profits he had bestowed upon Tess. 'I gave it to someone else who desperately needed it.'

'That doesn't make a blind bit of difference,' snarled Cunningham. 'It didn't end up in my coffers. But if you didn't use it yourself, then clearly you found some other way to make your fortune, given the generous sum we found in Thomasina's possession.'

'I suppose it's too much to hope that you'll let her leave with it,' Cormac said bleakly.

This time Lawlor laughed and the other two beside him joined in. 'She don't need it anymore.'

A chill ran down Cormac's back and his arms dropped to his sides. 'What do you mean?'

'Got what was coming to her, didn't she?' Lawlor gestured respectfully towards Munroe. 'All credit to himself.'

Cormac thought he was going to be sick. Swallowing bile, he struggled to speak. 'She's...dead?'

Munroe shrugged. 'Bitch couldn't take a beating.'

The wrath that rose up in Cormac threatened to strangle him. 'You goddamned monster,' he hurled at Munroe. 'Why couldn't you let her be? She just wanted to make a better life for herself and her child.'

'She knew you were back and didn't tell us. That kind of disloyalty doesn't go unpunished.'

A tremendous wave of anguish tore through Cormac. 'The little girl — Henrietta — is she —'

'She's still alive.'

'But you've left her without a mother!'

Unconcerned, Munroe said, 'The other wenches will make sure she remembers to eat. Probably.'

'I'm going to take her away from that place,' Cormac growled, even though he had no feasible plan for even getting out of the alleyway.

'She's not yours to take.' Munroe paused, then sniggered. 'Or is that what Thomasina told you? To get the money off you?'

Cormac hesitated as the others sneered. Even Cunningham's lips curved into a smirk.

Munroe flipped his dagger and caught it neatly by the hilt. 'The brat could belong to any one of a dozen men. But Thomasina picked me for the honour. Came to me on Christmas morning with the newborn, calling her a Christmas gift. As if any fellow would be pleased to see a girl instead of a boy.'

Christmas? But that was all wrong. If it had been the first Christmas after Cormac had fled Dublin, then the child would have been born at only seven months and surely wouldn't have survived. If it had been the second Christmas, then that would put Henrietta's age at not even three and a half years old and would mean he had left the country months before she had even been conceived.

'I chose not to believe it,' said Munroe, 'but Thomasina has stuck to the same tune all along. Even named the chit after me.' He made a mocking bow. 'First name's Henry.'

Cormac could only gape.

Cunningham clicked his tongue and said, 'You know, it strikes me as strange that you would be concerned about a whore and her spawn when you have far more pressing things to be worrying about, *Mr* McGovern.'

Munroe strode forwards and dug his fist into Cormac's stomach, making him double up in pain. Winded, he was unable to block the next punch to his face but he recovered enough to dodge the third shot and swing out at Munroe; his knuckles connected with the other man's chin. A stinging pain coursed through his fingers – he had used his burnt hand and, though the wound had nearly healed, the skin was still tender. Gritting his teeth, he drove his heel into Munroe's shin, causing him to stumble backwards. Munroe slipped on the dropped pipe and landed heavily on his backside.

Cormac might have seized that moment to make a dash for it, but the peak of the loose cap he had acquired from Liam fell into his eyes and he didn't see the blow coming from Lawlor. There was the fleshy sound of skin smacking skin and his head snapped sideways, the cap soaring off into the gloom. He bit the inside of his cheek and tasted the coppery tang of blood. Then the other two men stepped up to fight, leaving him with hardly an instant to breathe. One of them jabbed him in the shoulder he had twisted earlier and he let out a sharp hiss of pain. The other shoved him backwards and his skull slapped against the wall behind him. He slid down it, dazed, and they kicked at his legs and upper body until he managed to struggle to his feet again. He lashed out at them but his punches were becoming slower and fewer of them were making contact. Munroe and Lawlor joined back in too and he became progressively weaker under their concerted attack, while Cunningham observed with a look of deep satisfaction.

Cunningham was the key, he thought as the edges of his vision went momentarily blurry. These lackeys were nothing without their leader. If he could take Cunningham out, he might stand a chance. But it was impossible to get to him; four savage men stood in the way. And they were winning. He tried to duck as Munroe's fist came flying towards him once more but the blow landed on his ear and knocked him flat on his back on the dirty ground of the alley.

'Enough,' he heard Cunningham say as his head swam. 'Let us make the damage more precise.'

Cormac did not understand what he meant until Munroe knelt over him with the dagger, the smell of his sweat rippling off him.

'Where to begin?' he said, dangling the blade lazily over Cormac's face. 'Maybe your eyeballs. You're not going to need them for much longer.'

In such close proximity, Cormac had a detailed view of Munroe's own eyes. He saw the golden flecks in his irises, just like Henrietta's, and, with a surge of sadness for the little girl, recognised the truth in them.

'Or your tongue?' Munroe went on. 'You won't be in a position to kiss that strumpet of yours anymore.'

Cormac did not wait to hear more. In one swift movement, he reached out to grab the dagger and head-butted Munroe at the same time, ignoring the pain that rocked through him. Munroe fell backwards, clutching his nose, as Cormac rolled to his knees, secured his grip on the dagger and hurled it in Cunningham's direction. It sailed through the air and the point of it lodged in the centre of his stomach. Cormac had been aiming for the bastard's black heart but it had been a long time since he had wielded such a weapon. Though it was still a decent shot, he did not stop to admire it. In the short second when everyone stared in surprise at the unexpected turn of events, he was on his feet and bolting for the mouth of the alleyway.

He had just reached the street when a single shot rang out.

## Chapter 24

Lord Bewley's carriage hurtled down the street away from the violent scene in the alleyway, its occupants tossed around like marbles in the coachman's haste to get away. Bridget clung to the arm strap for support and wrapped her other arm around Emily's shoulders. The little girl was still crying. Of course, she would not understand what had just happened, but she could sense her mother's anguish and tell that they had left her father behind with some very bad men. With an enormous effort, Bridget forced herself to stop weeping in order to put on a brave face for her daughter. Orlaith sat opposite them in a daze. Beside her, Lord Bewley was twisting his cane anxiously in his hands.

Nobody spoke for several minutes. Bridget's fingers were trembling, even though she, Emily and Orlaith were now out of harm's way. But Cormac was still in danger, the worst kind of danger imaginable. Those men had at least one dagger and a pistol while he was unarmed, and there were five of them and only one of him. What hope did he have?

No, she must not despair. She curled her left fist, feeling the coarseness of the thread ring in contrast with the smooth metal of the gold ring. Drawing courage from them, she dug her fingernails into her palm and clenched her jaw. She could not allow herself to contemplate the idea that he might die. In their last embrace, he had been confident of his escape and so must she be. To believe anything else would be unbearable.

'Where are we going?' she asked, breaking the tense silence.

'To the docks,' said Lord Bewley. 'The sooner we get out of this infernal country, the better.'

'By no means shall we leave with you! We must go back.'

'Go back? Have you lost your wits?' He stopped twisting his cane to glare at her. 'It is best for everyone if we put this whole sordid affair behind us.'

'We need to turn around,' she insisted. 'He said he would meet us at the shelter.'

'My dear, he will not meet you. He is going to perish at the hands of those men. Forgive me for my brutal honesty, but it is a certainty.'

'I refuse to believe it,' she said desperately. 'You will take us to the shelter or we shall get out and walk there ourselves.'

He shook his head. 'Having seen the type of men who populate these streets, I think it would be unwise to let ladies walk them alone at night.'

'Then the gentlemanly thing to do would be to escort us where we wish to go.'

He shrugged helplessly. 'You are setting yourself up for a terrible disappointment.'

'No, I am not,' she said, digging her nails in even harder. 'I would appreciate your assistance in this regard, but we shall return on foot if we must.'

Disgruntled, he said, 'That won't be necessary. I have enough preying on my conscience tonight without adding the abandonment of three females to the list. Where do you want to go?'

'Thank you, I am grateful. The shelter is near Meath Street. If we return to the Liberties, I will recognise the correct street once I see it.'

Lord Bewley knocked on the coachman's partition with his cane and gave the instruction to turn back. It was clear from his frowning countenance that it was against his better judgement. As he settled again in his seat, he gave Bridget a curious look. She arched her eyebrows in defiant enquiry.

He angled his head as though scrutinising a rare creature in a cage. 'I am trying to fathom what motivates you, Lady Wyndham. You had a fine life in London but you relinquished it to abscond with a liar and a thief. Now you are being presented with an opportunity to return to a privileged lifestyle, and yet you still choose the inferior option. What drives you to behave in such an unusual fashion?'

'It is all a matter of opinion,' she answered. 'To me, the inferior option would be to go back to the insipid existence of a lady of leisure with wealth but no love. Cormac has brought me happiness that I scarcely knew was possible. I would not forsake him for all the riches in the world. And I do not intend to forsake him tonight. If he says that he will meet us at the shelter, then he will.'

Lord Bewley absorbed this in astonishment and lapsed into pensive silence. Bridget wondered if her words would make any impact on his attitude. The walls of upper class society were high and thick but she would continue to whittle away at them brick by brick.

Next to her, Emily's tears had quietened to intermittent snuffles. Her eyelids were beginning to droop; the poor child was exhausted. Bridget kissed the top of her head.

'It won't be long until we see Papa again,' she murmured.

She glanced at Orlaith, caught the girl's dubious expression and raised her chin, challenging her to make a contradiction. Orlaith shrugged and looked out the window. Bridget could not tell what the girl planned to do but it appeared she was going to remain with them for the time being, at least until they knew her brother's fate.

Bridget peered out of the other window; night was falling quickly but she could still make out their surroundings. The carriage had retraced its route but the coachman had avoided the street with the inn and was travelling down a different street instead. This one was unfamiliar to her but then they turned onto the next one and she recognised the ugly face of O'Hara's.

'It is just around the corner from here,' she told Lord Bewley.

He nodded and passed the information on to the coachman.

'This is it,' she said a minute later. 'Please let us out now.'

The carriage came to a stop at Lord Bewley's order. The footman opened the door and first Orlaith and then Bridget and Emily stepped down. The little girl was whimpering from sheer fatigue; Mabel dangled limply from her hand.

'Lady Wyndham.'

Bridget turned back; Lord Bewley was leaning forwards in his seat. 'Yes?'

'Would you care for me to wait here until such time as you know for certain whether…?' He trailed off.

She pictured the mistrustful eyes of the local inhabitants. 'I regret to tell you that I do not think your prolonged presence in this vicinity would be appreciated.'

His gaze darted up the street. 'Then let me say this. I do not intend to linger in this country any longer than I have to. But I am going to delay my departure for another day. If your hopes are not realised, please know that you and your daughter, and the other girl if she wishes it, may have safe passage with me back to England.'

'That is very generous. However, we shall not be going with you. If we leave Ireland, we will travel west, not east. But thank you for your kind offer. And please give my regards to Lady Bewley.'

She curtseyed. He looked startled but not disapproving of their proposed destination. He lifted his hat.

'Be safe,' he said.

The footman closed the door and resumed his position, and the carriage rolled away. Bridget looked around; the last vestiges of daylight had almost subsided and there were no lamps lit on this street. It would be best to get inside quickly. She surveyed the tenement building with its vacant windows and shabby exterior. What had prompted Cormac to suggest it as their rendezvous point? They could not expect a warm welcome from Tess. But this was the place he had chosen and she was going to ensure that she would be there for him if – *when* – he arrived. Part of her wondered if he might have even reached the shelter before them.

She knew as soon as they stepped through the doorway that he had not. Marty had been sleeping and gave them a horrible reception when he woke to find strangers in his territory. Fortunately, Tess appeared from the back room and calmed him down. He retreated into a corner, muttering about 'nuisances' and 'peace and quiet'.

Tess turned with her hands on her hips, ready to deliver a cutting retort, but then her gaze travelled past Bridget to Orlaith. Her jaw dropped.

'O-Orlaith?'

For the first time since they had discovered her at Anner House – it had only been earlier that day but it seemed like a century ago – Orlaith smiled.

'Tess,' she said with warmth.

They embraced each other like long-lost sisters, and Bridget belatedly recognised Cormac's astuteness in sending them here. Tess drew back and regarded Orlaith in amazement.

'I can't believe they found you.' She looked over at Bridget and Emily and frowned. 'Where's—'

'There has been some trouble,' Bridget broke in. 'We need to stay here for a little while, but I hope not for long. Would that be acceptable?'

'What trouble?' said Tess with both confusion and suspicion.

Keeping it brief, Bridget described their predicament and explained how Cormac had promised to meet them here as soon as he was able to break free from his captors.

'And you believed him?' said Tess.

'*Yes.* May we wait here until he comes?'

With a fleeting glance at Orlaith, Tess nodded. 'But, y'know, Cunningham isn't known for his mercy or his carelessness. You should start preparing yourself for the worst.'

Bridget closed her ears to the warning. 'Is there someplace where Emily could lie down? We have been walking for most of the day and she is all but asleep on her feet.'

Tess squinted at Marty, still grumbling in the corner, and said, 'Come upstairs.'

She led them through to the back room of the shelter and up a rickety staircase to the next floor. They glimpsed other ragged figures who shied away from them, slipping out of sight into the shadows. Orlaith appeared to be struggling to conceal her feelings and Bridget imagined how difficult it must be for her to return to the place where her mother and sister had died.

Tess showed Bridget a small pile of blankets in one of the upstairs rooms.

'This is my own place for sleeping. Your little girl can rest here.'

'Thank you very much,' said Bridget. She looked down at Emily, who was sagging with weariness. 'Time for bed, gooseberry.'

Emily stared around the room and then up at Bridget. 'I don't want to sleep alone.'

'I am going to be right here beside you,' Bridget replied, attempting to smile. She knelt on the floorboards next to the blankets and beckoned Emily to her. Emily lay down and Bridget arranged the blankets around her, tucking Mabel in too.

'Is Papa all right?' Emily asked in a tiny voice.

'Of course. He is going to be here when you wake up.' She prayed that Cormac would make that statement true. 'Go to sleep. You have nothing to be afraid of.'

She stroked Emily's golden curls and before long the little girl's eyelids fluttered and closed.

Orlaith and Tess were deep in conversation over by a broken window but Bridget, loath to intrude on their reunion, did not join them. She sat alone with her sleeping daughter and her own thoughts.

And what frightening thoughts they were. She could feel the grip of despair threatening to take hold of her again. The longer Cormac took to appear, the less likely it was that he would. It was so hard to keep up hope when all the evidence suggested that such expectation was folly. Cunningham and the men he led were diabolical thugs. It would take an extraordinary amount of luck for Cormac to survive an encounter with them. Was he that lucky? Or was the danger just too much this time?

She pressed her hands to her mouth to prevent her emotions from spilling over. She could not imagine how she would even breathe without Cormac. It was agony not knowing whether he was alive or dead, whether their fate had already been decided. She was in the dark – mind, body and soul.

She could not say how much time had passed – it might have been five minutes, or it might have been five hours – but gradually she became aware of a commotion downstairs. Marty was shouting in the room below and he was making no effort to be quiet.

'—tired of people walking in here!' she heard him bellow. 'Get out, I'm trying to sleep!'

Her mind was sluggish but she managed to process the fact that someone had disturbed his slumber.

There was somebody at the door.

She jumped to her feet and dashed for the staircase. Orlaith and Tess came running behind her. She took the stairs two at a time, slipped four steps from the bottom and fell to the floor on her hands and knees. Picking herself up, she tore into the front room and stopped dead.

The old man who had first told them about Tess stood in the centre of the room holding up a rushlight and pleading to Marty for some peace; the rushlight's dim glow illuminated the youth, who had taken up a hostile stance in the doorway, blocking the entrance to a figure beyond him.

'Go on, get out of here!' he roared.

'Marty, move out of the way!' Tess snapped behind Bridget.

She seemed to be the only person to whom he listened. He swore and stood back.

And there was Cormac. Bridget uttered a passionate cry of relief and rushed towards him. He leaned against the door jamb and smiled at her.

'There you are,' he rasped.

Then he fell through the doorway and onto the dusty floorboards in front of her. She gasped and dropped to her knees beside him. That was when she saw the blood soaking the sleeve of his coat and the small hole in his upper arm.

'He's been shot!'

To her surprise, Tess knelt down next to her.

'Turn him over,' she said urgently.

They rolled Cormac onto his back and Tess beckoned the old man closer with the rushlight so she could scrutinise the front of Cormac's arm.

'There's another hole here,' she said, pointing. 'That's good, means the ball came out the other side. But he's lost a lot of blood. We'll need to work fast.'

Bridget stared in shock as Tess took charge, ordering Marty to fetch a bowl and fill it from the water fountain at the end of the street. He obeyed with only a minimal amount of grousing. She began pulling Cormac's coat off him, answering Bridget's look of astonishment with a grimace.

'This isn't the first time I've seen a man shot. When you've lived on the streets as long as I have, you get to learn a thing or two about survival. Perhaps in another life I could've been a nurse.'

'And you are willing to help him?' Bridget stuttered. 'Despite what you believe about him?'

'If Cunningham tried to kill him,' said Tess, now ripping Cormac's shirt sleeve away to expose the gash in his flesh, 'then maybe he's a good man after all.'

Before Bridget could respond, Cormac murmured her name. She leaned in close to him and grasped his hand, disregarding his bloody knuckles.

'I'm here.'

'Emily? Orlaith?'

'They're safe too.'

'I ran,' he mumbled. 'They...didn't follow...knew they had got me. Dizzy...lost my bearings...but I found you.'

Even in the dimness, she could make out the marks and swelling on his face that showed how viciously the men had beaten him. She gulped.

'Yes, you did. You found me. And you must stay with me now. Don't leave me again. Do you promise?'

His eyelids flickered shut. When he opened them again, he had difficulty focusing on her.

'Some promises...hard to keep.'

She heard Tess calling to Orlaith to find some rags to bind the wound but blocked it all out, concentrating only on those disorientated blue irises.

'This one you have to keep,' she said firmly. 'Do you hear me? Promise me that you will stay with me.'

His breathing was shallow and erratic. She kissed his lips.

'Promise me.'

'I...'

His voice was so weak that she could scarcely hear him. Crouching next to his battered body while Tess staunched the bleeding from his arm and bandaged the wound, she prayed to God that he would not lose his grip on life.

'Orlaith,' she croaked and the girl bent down beside her. 'I need you to take a message to Rutland Square.'

It was the only possible source of aid left to her. She gave Orlaith directions for locating the square and Lord Walcott's residence.

'Please go there as quick as you can,' she entreated. 'Tell my uncle we need his help.'

Orlaith glanced down at her brother and, without another second's delay, vanished out the doorway.

Bridget stroked Cormac's hair. 'Speak to me,' she coaxed. 'Explain what happened in the alley.'

So fearful of his slurred speech and unfocused gaze, she encouraged and bullied him to keep talking. She was terrified that if she let him fall asleep, he might never wake up. The minutes stretched, distorted beyond any resemblance to the normal passage of time, and she began to feel that this was the longest day of her life.

At last, Orlaith reappeared and her look of optimism gave Bridget a shred of hope. Despite the lateness of the hour, her uncle had responded to her plea for help and had sent a carriage to the tenement to bear Cormac back to Rutland Square where Lord Walcott's own physician would treat him. Bridget, Emily, Orlaith and Tess all piled into the carriage too, Tess still applying pressure to the dressing on Cormac's arm, and they clattered towards Lord Walcott's house through the quiet city streets, where a faint gleam in the sky foretold that the dawn was about to break.

# Chapter 25

Cormac winced as he stirred awake, reluctant to open his eyes lest the action add to his list of aches. He could tell he was lying on a soft surface of some sort, probably a bed, but that provided little comfort to the blinding pain in his temples or the dull throbbing in his arm or the tenderness in his jaw and limbs. His stomach roiled with nausea and he focused for several moments on not being sick. Once he was reasonably confident that the worst of it had passed, he risked opening his eyelids.

A figure sat by the bed; he blinked and Bridget swam into focus. She was gazing down into her lap.

'Bridget?'

Her head snapped up. Anxiety and hope filled her features. She stood and leaned over him. 'Yes, it's me. You know it's me?'

'Of course,' he said.

She covered her mouth and started to weep.

Mystified, he added, 'How could I not?'

She cried harder, heaving unashamed, shuddering sobs of relief. He squinted against the light and waited until her tears had subsided enough to respond.

'Yesterday you were confused,' she said with a sniff. 'And the day before was worse. Do you recall much of the past few days?'

He concentrated, even though it hurt to do so. 'I can remember sporadic headaches.' He grimaced. 'And a bout of severe vomiting, if I'm not mistaken. The rest is a bit of a blur.'

She nodded. 'Your sense of awareness was erratic at best. We've been so worried but my uncle's physician said to give it some time. Dear God, you have no idea how happy I am to see such clarity in your eyes.'

She cupped his cheek and kissed his lips. When she sat back in her chair, he pushed aside the bedcovers.

'What are you doing?' she objected, jumping to her feet again.

'Getting up?' he tried.

'You shall do no such thing.' She pulled the bedcovers firmly back into place. 'You'll lie there until the physician says otherwise.'

This was wise advice, for the thumping in his head had intensified. He lay back against the pillows. 'Where's Emily?'

Bridget sat on the edge of the bed, perhaps to prevent further attempts at escape. 'Off shadowing her new aunties with adoration.'

'Aunties?' he repeated, worried that his confusion had returned.

'She's decided that Tess is as good as an aunt to her. Orlaith and Tess have been inseparable since they reunited.'

He was very glad to hear that for his sister's sake, even if his own standing in Tess's eyes was uncertain.

'What about Cunningham?'

Bridget's face darkened at the name. 'My uncle prevailed upon his footman, Simon, to make some cautious enquiries. It seems by all accounts that Cunningham has vanished and his men have scattered.'

She went on to tell him that the footman had heard rumours of rejoicing in the back alleys of Dublin at the disappearance of Cunningham. It would surely not be long before one of his thugs decided to take up his mantle but for now the money lender's business was in tatters. However, Simon had confirmed that Thomasina's associates remained in the lodgings that had been occupied by Cunningham's men, and perhaps it would be only a matter of time before the building turned into a brothel.

This news once more spurred a desire in Cormac to leave his bed but Bridget was unyielding on the matter. He was obliged to wait for the arrival of the physician, who chose not to make an appearance until the following morning. Upon the man's examination of him, Cormac made light of any residual aches and pains to achieve his release. In spite of Bridget's protestations that he still needed to rest, the first thing he did once he was finally permitted to rise was to go straight to Cunningham's lodgings.

When he strode into the place, the women goggled at him.

'Here, where d'you think you're going?' one of them demanded.

'Rest assured, I don't intend to stay long,' he said, his skin crawling at being under that roof again.

He hunted high and low and eventually found Henrietta hiding in a cupboard with her doll tucked under her arm. She looked dirtier than ever and ravenous with hunger. He picked her up, ignoring the pain in his injured arm, and cast an admonishing glare at the women who had followed on his heels as he searched.

'Did you forget she was here?' he accused them.

'We was looking after her, we swear!'

He carried Henrietta and the doll out of there without a backward glance.

Though it was against his better judgement, he brought her to O'Hara's on Meath Street. Mrs O'Hara's gap-toothed mouth fell open when he entered her shabby establishment and set the child down in front of her.

'She's your grandniece and you're the only family she has left,' he declared.

She didn't reproach him for neglecting his paternal obligations, so he could only assume she had been wise to Thomasina's lies. She peered down at Henrietta, who was chewing on the skin around one of her fingernails.

'Are you going to do the right thing?' Cormac asked.

Mrs O'Hara faltered for only a moment before nodding and, to his shock, a tear rolled down one of her withered cheeks.

'My dear Thomasina, bless her soul. She's gone to God too soon. Yes, I'll take care of her little girl.'

Cormac crouched on his hunkers to say goodbye to Henrietta. She didn't speak, only clasped the doll to her like she would never let it go. He felt a tug of regret behind his ribs as he walked out the door.

Afterwards, he told Bridget what had happened in a despondent voice, while she replaced the bandage on the wound in his arm which had started leaking blood again.

'I hope I've made the right decision,' he said, passing a hand over his aching forehead in doubt. 'Part of me wanted to bring Henrietta with us but Mrs O'Hara is her flesh and blood. I couldn't take her away while she still has family in Ireland.'

'Moreover, the responsibility for her doesn't fall to you,' Bridget reminded him gently, for he had imparted the details of Henry Munroe's startling revelation. 'She isn't your child.'

He let out a sigh. 'But the point is she could have been.'

Bearing that in mind, he resolved to correspond with Mrs O'Hara in the future to see how Henrietta was faring. He hoped that, notwithstanding the loss of her mother, she would lead a happier existence away from the dreadful place where her life had begun.

Bridget finished binding the wound on his arm and rolled up the used bandage. Casting a critical eye over his battered appearance, she said, 'You are going to create quite a stir at the solicitors' office.'

They had been obliged to postpone the Tuesday appointment at Webb & Brereton Solicitors until Cormac had recovered his full faculties and the swelling on his face had diminished somewhat. Even so, his lingering bruises caused Mr Croft's eyebrows to nearly vanish into his hairline upon their arrival at Baggot Street. They invented a story about an assault by a brigand on the street and succeeded in signing the contract drawn up by Mr Brereton, but they were all too aware that the circumstances of their two visits had come across as highly irregular. Any subsequent correspondence the solicitors might choose to send to Wyndham House in London, despite Cormac's instruction to write directly to the stewards at Oakleigh, would alert Garrett to their deception.

Taking that into account, Bridget opted to write to Garrett herself and explain what had transpired at Oakleigh, from Lady Courcey's despicable actions which had triggered the uprising to Bridget's decision to appoint Laurence Enright and John Corbett as joint stewards. She placed a great emphasis on the fact that the new arrangement would bring Garrett income without the slightest need for his involvement.

'I hope he will react in a reasonable way and see that it is for the best,' she said to Cormac as she sealed the letter.

He offered a one-armed shrug, avoiding any jerky movement with his injured arm – his rescue of Henrietta had impeded the healing process somewhat. 'If he chooses to make trouble and insists upon taking control of the estate, then perhaps we can encourage the tenants to revolt again.'

She laughed but he hadn't spoken entirely in jest.

Their lives became ruled by letters as they awaited responses to the enquiries Lord Walcott had sent out. When he learned of Tess's speculation that Bronagh may have travelled to America, he dispatched messages to the authorities managing the various ports around Ireland, seeking information as to whether her name had appeared on any passenger lists over the past five years. He used the power of his title to encourage the officials to adopt the utmost speed in their replies.

Cormac and Bridget were taking breakfast with him one morning in the library when Simon carried in a tray bearing a letter.

'Oho!' he exclaimed and Brutus emitted a feeble yap at the loud noise. Lord Walcott hushed the dog as he opened the letter. 'It is from the Cork Harbour Commissioners.' He scanned it quickly and repeated, 'Oho,' with a deep pitch of satisfaction.

Burning with the desire to know its contents, Cormac said calmly, 'What does it say, my lord?'

Lord Walcott beamed. 'They have a record of a Bronagh McGovern on one of their passenger lists.' He skimmed down the letter again. 'It was two years ago. The ship in question stopped at Cove on its way from Liverpool to Boston.'

Cormac's heart almost burst with exhilaration. 'That is such welcome news.'

'Do you believe it's her?' Bridget said breathlessly.

'It could very well be. She doesn't have a common name, after all.' He frowned. 'Only two years ago though. If it's our Bronagh, that means three years passed between her running away from Dublin and getting on the ship in Cork. What could she have been doing during all that time?'

'Perhaps she was earning the money to pay for her ticket?' Bridget suggested.

'Speaking of tickets,' Lord Walcott said, 'it says here that her ticket was purchased as part of a pair, according to their records, but the ink on the second name was smeared and regrettably illegible.'

This was surprising but pleasing to hear. Whomever she had travelled with, Cormac was glad she had found a companion and had not made the journey alone. While the letter was not irrefutable evidence that the Bronagh McGovern on the passenger list was his own sister, it was the closest to proof they could expect to obtain. This Bronagh had crossed the Atlantic Ocean and so they would follow through on their decision to do the same.

# Chapter 26

The breeze was cool on Bridget's cheeks. Seagulls wheeled and screeched in the air above and merry waves lapped the hull of the ship. The ocean spread out in every direction around her. It was blue and calm beneath the cloudless sky, a day of perfect weather on this lengthy sea crossing. She breathed in deeply, her palms resting on the gunwale and loose tendrils of hair tickling her face.

The sound of laughter came to her – Emily playing with Orlaith and Tess further up the deck of the ship. Waving her imaginary sword, Emily loudly proclaimed that she was already seven and a quarter years old, therefore she would be the one in charge of the treasure they would seize from the next pirate ship that came sailing by. Six had been a turbulent year for her but seven was going to be better. Much, much better. Even Orlaith and Tess had been convinced to hope for greater things across the water.

Bridget smiled as a hand drew her hair away from her neck and a pair of lips pressed a kiss to her exposed nape. She glanced back at Cormac, who gave her a boyish grin. After all the perils he had faced, he was alive and well, and she thanked God every day for it.

So much had happened since they had landed in Ireland and yet, with all their travels around the country, they had ended up back in Cove. Naturally, they had not looked for accommodation at McLoughlin's Boarding House but, while they had arranged passage on the next ship heading for Boston, they had sought out Nancy McLoughlin, who had been delighted to see them. Her children were growing like weeds and she had intimated that she had the bigoted Agnes firmly under her thumb.

When they had finally boarded the ship bound for America, it had been with no small amount of sadness for they did not know when they would return to Irish shores. But family came first – even though, by crossing the ocean to seek one family member, they had left another behind. Still, they had not left Patrick in an unhappy situation, from his own perspective at least. He was spoiled but he was neither hungry nor cold, and he would grow up with the best of everything. While the encounter on the doorstep of Anner House had ostensibly achieved nothing, it was still possible that they had sown seeds of doubt in his young mind. Perhaps when he got older he would become more curious about the family who had first raised him. All they could do was wait and see.

'I can see land!' The cry came from Emily who jumped up and down on the deck and pointed excitedly.

Everyone stared at the horizon. There was a faint smudge far out in the distance where the water met the sky – could it be land? Was America in sight? Emily came running towards Bridget and Cormac, leaping into Cormac's arms with a squeal. His injury was now fully healed and he swung Emily around, causing her to shriek with glee. Bridget was glad to see her enthusiasm. The poor child had struggled with seasickness early in the voyage so it was cheering to see her in high spirits once again.

'We're nearly there!' Emily said happily.

'Thanks be to God,' Cormac replied.

Emily responded by blessing herself. She had taken to doing this at any mention of God since Cormac had shown her how to do it. He had also been teaching her Catholic prayers for he and Bridget had decided that they would baptise Emily in the Catholic faith once they reached America. Bridget intended to convert as well, and the prospect of it brought her joy.

Emily looked out across the water again. 'Do I have time to make a painting of it?' she begged. 'I still have two sheets of paper left.'

Once she had recovered from her seasickness, her painting had kept her entertained during the long, monotonous days at sea. Her watercolour box remained safe in her possession, for Simon had gone to the inn to retrieve their valises from the innkeeper when Bridget had been too anxious to stir from Cormac's side.

'I don't see why not,' Cormac said to Emily. 'It will be quite a while yet before we get to dock.'

Beaming, she slid down out of his grasp and called, 'Come on, Auntie Orlaith, Auntie Tess! Let's go painting.'

Orlaith followed her niece at once, accompanying her in the direction of their cabin. Throughout the voyage, Bridget had continually felt gratitude towards her uncle who had both insisted upon them travelling as cabin passengers and provided them with enough funds to do so. Having witnessed the deplorable conditions that the steerage passengers had been forced to endure these past weeks at sea, Bridget could only shudder at the thought of their suffering. She had made a habit of slipping biscuits into her pocket so that if any of the young children from steerage came near her on deck she could give them a bite to eat to fill their constantly rumbling stomachs.

Tess trailed after Orlaith and Emily but came to a stop in front of Bridget and Cormac. She glanced out at the distant smudge, her red hair fluttering in the breeze.

'Who would've thought Teresa O'Leary would ever clap eyes on the coastline of America?' She shook her head. 'If only my ma could see me now.'

When she looked at them again, her gaze focused solely on Cormac, freezing Bridget out of the conversation.

'I want to apologise,' Tess said. 'I was wrong about you. I made some nasty accusations that evening at the inn and I'd like to take them back because it's plain as day the person you are doesn't match the reputation of the brute McGovern. Maybe you did some bad things in your time, but sure haven't we all?' She peered down at the deck. 'And I'm sorry for telling those men where to find you. You didn't deserve that, 'specially not with all the trouble it brought.'

'You don't need to say any of this,' Cormac interjected. 'Honestly, I don't hold it against you.'

'I *do* need to say it.' Her tone was almost angry. 'You're the reason I'm about to set foot on American soil instead of heading out onto the streets in search of another man who'll pay me if I satisfy him.' Her cheeks had gone as red as her hair. 'I have a whole new life ahead of me. You're my guardian angel all over again.'

When she peeked up at him once more, there was an unmistakable glow in her eyes. She reached out with both of her hands and he automatically took them.

'Thank you,' she said fervently, 'for saving me.'

She dropped his hands and hurried away after Orlaith and Emily. He turned to Bridget, looking embarrassed at Tess's praise.

'That was more demonstrative than we are used to seeing from her,' he said, for Tess had kept to herself or Orlaith's company for most of the voyage. 'I'm glad we've been able to make her life better. She is as much a part of the McGovern family now as any of us.'

Bridget didn't think Tess viewed him as a brother but she kept her observations to herself. 'Here's hoping we can add another sister in due course.'

His expression grew sombre. Would they find Bronagh? What lay ahead of them in this unknown country?

'Here's hoping,' he echoed.

Moving to stand behind her, he encircled his arms around her waist. He kissed her temple and together they looked out to the horizon again. His chest expanded against her back in a deep breath. Then his hands tightened on her belly, feeling the roundness that had not been there before.

She smiled. 'Yes,' she said in answer to his unspoken question. 'Another impending addition to the McGovern family. Are you happy?'

'I don't think I have the words to express how I feel,' he said, but the strength of his embrace told her enough.

# What's Next

Thank you for reading! Would you like to spend more time in Bridget and Cormac's world? Join the **Susie Murphy Readers' Club** on www.susiemurphywrites.com, where you will receive a collection of five free short stories which are prequels to the whole series. You will see exactly how Bridget and Cormac became friends, how they were first torn asunder, and the tumultuous events that brought about their transition from childhood to adulthood.

In addition, you will get a sixth story which is a companion story to A Class Entwined. Do you remember the scene in A Class Entwined where Bridget was stunned to see Cormac appear at the party at Radcliffe House? The companion story tells that scene from Cormac's point of view! By joining the Susie Murphy Readers' Club, you will also be the first to get updates about A Matter of Class, including book release details and other bonus content.

Did you enjoy these books? If you did, please help other readers discover Bridget and Cormac's story by leaving an honest review about A Matter of Class on Amazon and/or Goodreads. A short review will make a huge difference in spreading the word about this series.

The next novel in the series is A Class Coveted, available now.

# Acknowledgements
# A Class Apart

Thanks first of all must go to Averill Buchanan for her excellent editorial advice and Andrew Brown for designing such a beautiful cover. They helped shape this book inside and out, and I am so grateful for their expertise.

Next I wish to thank all the people who helped me at various stages along my publishing journey: Mary Arrigan, Sr Cecilia O'Dwyer, Eoin Purcell, Catherine Ryan Howard, Robert Doran, Vanessa O'Loughlin, and Corinne DeMaagd. Most of these people won't even know why they are on this list, but believe me when I say their generosity did not go unappreciated.

Huge hugs go to my early readers and cheerleaders: Miriam Lanigan, Claire Moloney, Grace Noon, Noreen Shanahan, and Laura Mason. They read my unpolished manuscript, offered invaluable feedback (especially that important piece of advice, Miriam!), and never wavered in their belief that I would make it someday. Thanks so much also to Petra Hanlon, TL Harty, and all those who have engaged with me about my book online or in person.

I want to say a massive thank you to my amazing parents and to the rest of my family who have been so supportive of my dream to become a published author. Words cannot express how much it has meant to me.

Lastly, my unending gratitude goes to my husband, Bob, who has had to endure countless discussions about grammar rules and the 19th century over the past few years. He has continued to encourage me when at times I might otherwise have stumbled. All my love.

# Acknowledgements
## A Class Entwined

My sincere thanks to Averill Buchanan for her terrific editorial feedback, and to Andrew Brown at Design for Writers for producing another gorgeous cover. Between them both, I knew my book was in very safe hands.

One of the most special things about writing and publishing is joining a community of people who are so kind and generous when it comes to everything about books. I can't say thank you enough to each and every person who has spread the word about A Class Apart or A Class Entwined, be it in big or little ways. I am especially grateful to the following for helping to give my novels a push out into the world: Hazel Gaynor, Pam Lecky, Ashley O'Melia, John Butler, Deirdre O'Toole, Eoin Hoctor, Fran Curry, Anne O'Grady, Shane Cahill, Yvette Poufong, Laura Whitmore, Vanessa O'Loughlin, Mary Tod, Heather Webb, The Book Trail, Anne Mendez, Linda Green, Claire Bridle, Valerie Whitford, Lisa Redmond, Stacie Tyson, Suzanne Leopold, Kathleen Kelly, Jenny Q, Diana G. Tierney, Lauralee Jacks, Margaret Cook. You are all legends.

My deepest gratitude goes to my husband, family and friends for their enthusiastic encouragement. I am incredibly lucky to be surrounded by such wonderful support.

Lastly, thank YOU for reading. It's such an amazing feeling to have actual readers, and I appreciate every single response, whether it's writing a review, interacting online, or sending me a message. I'm so happy that you are following Bridget and Cormac's journey and I already can't wait to show you what happens next...!

# Acknowledgements
# A Class Forsaken

My heartfelt thanks to Averill Buchanan for her keen editorial eye and to Andrew Brown at Design for Writers for creating such a stunning cover for this book.

My husband, Bob, deserves high billing for his unending patience. I can recall the night I came to bed at 2am after working on a particular scene and proceeded to discuss the intricacies of 19th century inheritance law with him. Happily, I teased out the plot line that was giving me trouble, but I'm sure Bob would have much preferred to be asleep.

I owe a debt of gratitude to my first readers of this book: Bob Murphy, Miriam Bourke, Grace Noon, Miriam Lanigan, Noreen Uí Ghríofa, and Claire Moloney. They offered feedback on the manuscript with a tremendous generosity of both time and thought.

Huge thanks next to my advance reader team who agreed to read this book before it was released. Their passion for Bridget and Cormac's story has been an absolute joy to behold.

A very special mention goes to Michele Quirke who has done so much to spread the word about this series that I need to start paying her a commission. She is a superstar in the Twitter writing community.

Elizabeth Bell also merits particular recognition for her timely advice, astute observations and empathetic support.

Words cannot express how grateful I am to the authors, bloggers and book reviewers who have been so willing to shine a light on my little corner of the book world. Thank you especially to Claire Bridle, Lisa Redmond, Trish Hannon, Valerie Whitford, Ashley O'Melia, Anne Mendez, Stacie Tyson, Tony Riches, Kelsey Gietl, Nicola Cassidy, and Niamh Boyce.

I greatly appreciate the kindness of Anne O'Grady at the Tipperary Star and Fran Curry at Tipp FM.

Thanks, as always, to my fantastic family and friends for their enthusiasm and support.

Finally, I acknowledge YOU, my wonderful readers. Thank you so much for reading and for continuing to follow Bridget and Cormac's journey. Your lovely messages, reviews and comments mean more to me than I could ever say.

## Get in Touch

www.susiemurphywrites.com
www.facebook.com/susiemurphywrites
www.twitter.com/susiemwrites
www.instagram.com/susiemurphywrites

Printed in Great Britain
by Amazon